CITY & ISLINGTON COLLEGE
SA005844

The Oxford Book Of Sixteenth Century Verse

The Oxford Book Of Sixteenth Century Verse

Chosen by

E. K. Chambers

London
Oxford University Press
New York Toronto

Oxford University Press, Ely House, London W. 1

LONDON OXFORD GLASGOW NEW YORK
TORONTO MELBOURNE WELLINGTON CAPE TOWN
IBADAN NAIROBI DAR ES SALAAM LUSAKA ADDIS ABABA
KUALA LUMPUR SINGAPORE JAKARTA HONG KONG TOKYO
DELHI BOMBAY CALCUTTA MADRAS KARACHI

ISBN 0 19 812126 1

First edition 1932
Reprinted 1939, 1945, 1950, 1955
1961 (with corrections), 1966, 1970, and 1976

Printed in Great Britain
at the University Press, Oxford
by Vivian Ridler
Printer to the University

PREFACE

THE long tradition of medieval poetry ends with a burst of sweetness in the religious carols. On the threshold between old and new stands the remarkable achievement of *The Nutbrown Maid*, in which a theme of balladry is brought to the purpose of a conscious and fully ordered craftsmanship. The rapid improvisation of Skelton has its links both with the past and with the future. It is easy to undervalue Skelton. His is the only authentic voice which comes to us from the first quarter of the sixteenth century. But musical composition had long been cultivated in England, and from the art of the lutenist the art of poetry made a fresh beginning in the literate and light-of-love court of Henry the Eighth. A rather irritating kind of scholarship insists that Sir Thomas Wyatt was chiefly notable for the acclimatization of the Italian sonnet, and the Earl of Surrey for the invention of blank verse. Such a method of approach to poetry is of little value, except perhaps for the uses of classroom discipline. It is the pageant of genius which makes the history of literature, not the procession of influences. The source of a poem, in form or in substance, is surely the least important thing about it. Wyatt's hesitating and perhaps unfinished translations from Petrarch are comparatively negligible. But in lyric, sung or based on the models of song, he is a master of the first order, with an accomplished touch on a wide range of rhythms, and a spiritual temper which subdues the old conventions of the amorous duel to the expression of an unfettered personality. Surrey, up to his untimely end, had proved himself a worthy successor. A third was Thomas Sackville, who after the splendid onset of his boyhood fell silent, and died, still in silence, as a Jacobean. And with him the first impulse of Tudor poetry came to an abrupt close. That the hectic days of Edward the Sixth and of Mary did not prove favourable to letters is intelligible. But it is not easy to see why the first half of Elizabeth's reign, when the furies of religious controversy were lulled, and a settled and prosperous national life was shaping itself, should have proved so barren. Perhaps the simplest explanation is that no new genius happened to be born. Much verse, indeed, was written, and the habit of publication grew up among court hangers-on in search of patronage. But the Turbervilles, Gascoignes, Churchyards, and their like, rarely rise for a moment above mediocrity, and most of the men concealed behind the attractive title-pages of the *Paradise of Dainty Devices* and the *Gorgeous Gallery of Gallant Inventions* move us no more than the dullards who bring up the tail of Tottel's *Songs and Sonnets*. The most hopeful of them was Edward de Vere, Earl of Oxford, a real courtier, but an ill-conditioned youth, who also became mute in later life. The revival begins with Edmund Spenser's *Shepherd's Calendar* in 1579. And thereafter, of course, there is God's plenty.

As a result, the anthologist, when he has taken his account of Skelton and Wyatt, Surrey and Sackville, finds himself with little more than twenty years from which to gather the rest of his garland. This has its advantage and its disadvantage. On the one hand he is able to allow himself a somewhat intensive treatment of the greater writers, without exceeding the reasonable scope of a single volume; on the other, he loses the aesthetic pleasure of setting forth only the very best. In the present case an attempt has been made to apply a standard of absolute poetry, rather than one of merely historic interest, and it is hoped that little has been included which has not some positive merit, even if it is only that of a single perfect phrase. A decent tenderness has been shown to the beginners, and here and there a concession is made to the glamour of a famous name. It may be doubted whether Henry the Eighth or Queen Elizabeth really deserve their places, but it would be hard altogether to deny them access to a presence-chamber so full of the subjects who once thronged their own.

Elizabethan poetry is characteristically a light-hearted poetry, in the manner of the Renaissance throughout Europe. It plays upon the coloured surface of things, rather than draws from the wells. Its inspiration is in the lust of the eyes and the pride of life. It hymns the splendours of a palace, and passes in like spirit to dwell on the simpler felicities of the spring. It lays its emphasis on beauty and desire, roses and the moon. All is, as Sidney put it, to make the too much loved earth more lovely. If a note of regret creeps in, it is only that desire is hard of fruition and that beauty wanes as the roses fade. And so—

Vivamus, mea Lesbia, atque amemus.

The theme is too familiar to need elaboration here. It finds abundant example throughout the pages that follow; in the classical narratives of Spenser and Drayton and Marlowe, where the slightness of the invention is overhung with ornamental texture, like some great composition of Paolo Veronese; in the long bead-rolls of the sonneteers; in the constant pastorals, happiest in their lyrical moments, and often tending to childishness in the formal eclogues; in the wealth of pure lyric itself, which overflows into the pages of romances, and chequers the dialogue of plays. The lyric is perhaps at its very best in the song-books, where the dangerous Elizabethan exuberance is chastened into unwonted spareness and acquires a new poignancy in conformity with the musician's art.

> Beauty guards thy looks. The rose
> In them pure and eternal is.

How much of the writing of his contemporaries Campion makes lucid in those twelve words.

But there is another aspect of the sixteenth century to be considered. It is not merely that the most thorough-going zest in earthly things is subject to the changes and chances of mortality.

> Queens have died young and fair,
> Dust hath closed Helen's eye.

No doubt poets in every age have sometimes stopped to think of that. But Tudor life, in particular, even under the comparatively mild sway of Elizabeth, was far from being all a revel and a Maying. The darling buds were often shaken by rough winds. At court, behind the scenes, the struggle for existence was severe. There were overweening ambitions and shattered hopes, conflicting loyalties and revelations of intrigue. Many broken men and some dissatisfied idealists went under. The stately progress might at any moment stop for a tragedy. It is curious to reflect that at least six and possibly eight of the contributors to this volume met death on the scaffold. And poetry, never for long forgetful of her kinship to philosophy, could not but turn sometimes from the phenomenal glitter to look into the eternal verities. For such delvings, too, ample room has had to be found; for the afterthoughts of Sidney and of Spenser, for the disillusionment of Greville and the quietism of Dyer, for the sombre regrets of Ralegh, for the renunciations of Southwell, for the deep reaches of Shakespeare's sonnets, for the moral essays of Daniel and Davies. All are needed, to give the Elizabethan vision in its true perspective. The later verse of Daniel has often been unduly neglected. The easy-going amorist, who so lightly changed the hair of Delia from golden to sable in the process of revising a sonnet, was at heart a philosopher. The sober texture of his *Musophilus* and *Epistles* may seem a little drab against the brilliant harmonies of his fellows. But it has a delicate beauty of its own, and his fervid apprehension of spiritual truths too often flouted around him brings us much of the riper wisdom of the century.

The anthologist has some special troubles of scholarship to face in this period. Much verse circulated in manuscript before it came, if it ever did come, to the printer. A good deal seems to be irretrievably lost, including some which we would gladly recover. Where are the ten original cantos of Ralegh's *Cynthia*, the music of the summer's nightingale? Where are what Gabriel Harvey called 'the preserved dainties' of Robert Cecil? There must have been much more of Dyer, to judge by his contemporary reputation, than has come down to us. Davies, at the end of his *Orchestra*, apostrophizes a group of fellow-poets, and at several of them we can only dimly guess. Whom did he mean by

> the bay, the marigold's darling,
> Whose sudden verse Love covers with his wing?

It is pretty praise. Time is, perhaps, not likely now to give up these secrets. And even among what remains to us there is much masterless poetry, gathered without a name into such collections as the *Phoenix Nest* or the *Poetical Rhapsody*, where 'Anomos' or 'A.W.' is still an unsolved riddle, or scattered through private 'commonplace-books', often with conflicting or unreliable ascriptions. It has been thought desirable to add to this volume a few notes, indicating briefly, for those who care to know, the more doubtful questions of authorship. Dates are of course even more vague. But in any case, when a large number of authors are writing concurrently, it is only possible to arrange them in an approximate chronological order, which may reasonably be made subject to a little grouping, through which contrasts and affinities may emerge. A more difficult problem has been that of where to stop. It was comparatively simple to disentangle the beginning of the sixteenth century from the fifteenth, but even if the end of it is extended to cover the reign of Elizabeth, it still finds a continuous flood of literature in mid-career; and although a difference between the sixteenth and the seventeenth-century temper is recognizable, it was slow to establish itself. Only hand-to-mouth solutions have proved feasible. Thus Shakespeare, Daniel, Ralegh, and Campion are dealt with exhaustively in this volume. Ben Jonson and Donne are left entirely to its successor. Only for chronology, indeed, can Donne be an Elizabethan. Drayton and Chapman, who hopelessly overlap the dividing line, must be cut asunder.

A few points of technical handling should be made clear. The source cited at the end of each poem is normally the earliest print in which it is found, or alternatively what appears to be on the whole the best manuscript. But the actual texts given often contain readings from other versions, and a few emendations, by others or even of my own, have been admitted. Spelling, capitalization, and punctuation have been systematically modernized. These are matters in which less scruple is called for than in dealing with the more carefully produced work of later centuries. Elizabethan punctuation, even in print and still more in manuscript, is often chaotic. But, where an intention of the author has been apparent, some regard has been paid to it. The titles given to poems are generally editorial and have been reduced to a minimum by the grouping of songs and sonnets.

It need hardly be said that the editor is abundantly conscious of the deep debt which he owes to the taste and research of earlier anthologists. He comes late into a field from which many harvests have been gathered in bygone years. And he desires to express his more immediate gratitude to Professors Oliver Elton and F. P. Wilson and to Mr. Kenneth Sisam for much invaluable help, both in selection and in the handling of textual points.

E. K. C.

ANONYMOUS

1 *The Nutbrown Maid*

Squire

BE it right or wrong, these men among
  On women do complain,
Affirming this, how that it is
  A labour spent in vain
To love them well, for never a dell
  They love a man again;
For let a man do what he can,
  Their favour to attain,
Yet if a new to them pursue,
  Their first true lover than
Laboureth for nought, and from her thought
  He is a banished man.

Puella

I say not nay, but that all day
  It is both writ and said
That woman's faith is, as who saith,
  All utterly decayed;
But nevertheless, right good witness
  In this case might be laid,
That they love true, and continue.
  Record the Nutbrown Maid,
Which from her love, when, her to prove,
  He came to make his moan,
Would not depart, for in her heart
  She loved but him alone.

among] at times   dell] bit

Squire

Then between us let us discuss,
  What was all the manner
Between them two; we will also
  Tell all the pain, in fere,
That she was in. Now I begin,
  So that ye me answer.
Wherefore all ye that present be
  I pray you give an ear.
I am the knight; I come by night,
  As secret as I can,
Saying, 'Alas! thus standeth the case,
  I am a banished man.'

Puella

And I your will for to fulfil
  In this will not refuse,
Trusting to shew, in wordės few,
  That men have an ill use
To their own shame women to blame,
  And causeless them accuse.
Therefore to yow I answer now,
  All women to excuse,
'Mine own heart dear, with you what cheer?
  I pray you, tell anon,
For in my mind of all mankind
  I love but you alone.'

Squire

'It standeth so; a deed is do,
  Wherefore much harm shall grow.

in fere] together, in dialogue   do] done

My destiny is for to die
  A shameful death, I trow,
Or else to flee; the one must be.
  None other way I know,
But to withdraw as an outlaw,
  And take me to my bow.
Wherefore adieu, my own heart true!
  None other rede I can,
For I must to the greenwood go
  Alone a banished man.'

Puella

'O Lord, what is this worldės bliss,
  That changeth as the moon?
My summer's day in lusty May
  Is darked before the noon.
I hear you say farewell. Nay, nay,
  We depart not so soon.
Why say ye so? Whither will ye go?
  Alas! what have ye done?
All my welfare to sorrow and care
  Should change, if ye were gone,
For in my mind of all mankind
  I love but you alone.'

Squire

'I can believe, it shall you grieve,
  And somewhat you distrain;
But afterward your painės hard
  Within a day or twain

rede] counsel distrain] distress

Shall soon aslake, and ye shall take
  Comfort to you again.
Why should ye nought? for to take thought,
  Your labour were in vain.
And thus I do; and pray you to,
  As heartily as I can,
For I must to the greenwood go
  Alone a banished man.'

Puella

'Now sith that ye have shewed to me
  The secret of your mind,
I shall be plain to you again,
  Like as ye shall me find.
Sith it is so, that ye will go,
  I will not leave behind;
Shall never be said the Nutbrown Maid
  Was to her love unkind.
Make you ready, for so am I,
  Although it were anon,
For in my mind of all mankind
  I love but you alone.'

Squire

'Yet I you rede to take good heed
  What men will think and say;
Of young and old it shall be told
  That ye be gone away
Your wanton will for to fulfil,
  In greenwood you to play,
And that ye might from your delight
  No longer make delay.

nought] not   take thought] grieve   sith] since   leave] remain

Rather than ye should thus for me
   Be called an ill woman,
Yet would I to the greenwood go
   Alone a banished man.'

Puella

'Though it be sung of old and young
   That I should be to blame,
Theirs be the charge that speak so large
   In hurting of my name;
For I will prove that faithful love
   It is devoid of shame,
In your distress and heaviness
   To part with you the same.
And sure all tho that do not so
   True lovers are they none;
But in my mind of all mankind
   I love but you alone.'

Squire

'I counsel you, remember how
   It is no maiden's lore,
Nothing to doubt, but to run out
   To wood with an outlaw;
For ye must there in your hand bear
   A bow, ready to draw,
And as a thief thus must ye live,
   Ever in dread and awe,
By which to you great harm might grow.
   Yet had I liefer than,
That I had to the greenwood go
   Alone a banished man.'

part] share   tho] those

Puella

'I think not nay, but as ye say,
It is no maiden's lore;
But love may make me for your sake,
As I have said before,
To come on foot, to hunt and shoot,
To get us meat in store.
For so that I your company
May have, I ask no more;
From which to part it maketh mine heart
As cold as any stone,
For in my mind of all mankind
I love but you alone.'

Squire

'For an outlaw, this is the law,
That men him take and bind,
Without pity hanged to be,
And waver with the wind.
If I had need, as God forbid!
What rescous could ye find?
Forsooth, I trow, ye and your bow
For fear would draw behind;
And no marvail, for little avail
Were in your counsel than;
Wherefore I to the wood will go
Alone a banished man.'

Puella

'Right well know ye that women be
Full feeble for to fight;

rescous] rescue

No womanhead is it indeed
  To be bold as a knight.
Yet in such fear if that ye were,
  With enemies day and night
I would withstand, with bow in hand,
  To grieve them as I might,
And you to save, as women have
  From death men many one;
For in my mind of all mankind
  I love but you alone.'

Squire

'Yet take good heed, for ever I dread
  That ye could not sustain
The thorny ways, the deep valleys,
  The snow, the frost, the rain,
The cold, the heat, for, dry or wet,
  We must lodge on the plain,
And, us above, none other roof
  But a brake bush or twain;
Which soon should grieve you, I believe,
  And ye would gladly than
That I had to the greenwood go
  Alone a banished man.'

Puella

'Sith I have here been partener
  With you of joy and bliss,
I must also part of your woe
  Endure, as reason is.

Yet am I sure of one pleasure;
  And, shortly, it is this,
That where ye be, me seemeth, perdy,
  I could not fare amiss.
Without more speech, I you beseech
  That we were soon agone,
For in my mind of all mankind
  I love but you alone.'

Squire

'If ye go thider, ye must consider,
  When ye have lust to dine,
There shall no meat be for to get,
  Nor drink, beer, ale, ne wine;
Ne sheetės clean to lie between,
  Made of thread and twine;
None other house but leaves and boughs
  To cover your head and mine.
Lo, mine heart sweet, this ill diet
  Should make you pale and wan;
Wherefore I to the wood will go
  Alone a banished man.'

Puella

'Among the wild deer, such an archer,
  As men say that ye be,
Ne may not fail of good vitail,
  Where is so great plenty;
And water clear of the river
  Shall be full sweet to me,
With which in heal I shall right well
  Endure, as ye shall see.

perdy] by God   ne] nor   vitail] victual   heal] health

And, or we go, a bed or two
  I can provide anon,
For in my mind of all mankind
  I love but you alone.'

Squire

'Lo, yet before ye must do more,
  If ye will go with me,
As cut your hair up by your ear,
  Your kirtle by your knee,
With bow in hand, for to withstand
  Your enemies, if need be;
And this same night before daylight,
  To woodward will I flee.
If that ye will all this fulfil
  Do it shortly as ye can;
Else will I to the greenwood go
  Alone a banished man.'

Puella

'I shall as now do more for you
  Than longeth to womanhead,
To short my hair, a bow to bear,
  To shoot in time of need.
O my sweet mother, before all other
  For you I have most dread;
But now, adieu! I must ensue
  Where fortune doth me lead.
All this make ye. Now let us flee,
  The day cometh fast upon;
For in my mind of all mankind
  I love but you alone.'

Squire

'Nay, nay, not so! ye shall not go,
  And I shall tell you why.
Your appetite is to be light
  Of love, I well espy;
For, right as ye have said to me,
  In like wise, hardily,
Ye would answer whosoever it were
  In way of company.
It is said of old, soon hot, soon cold;
  And so is a woman.
Wherefore I to the wood will go
  Alone a banished man.'

Puella

'If ye take heed, yet is no need
  Such words to say by me;
For oft ye prayed, and long assayed,
  Or I you loved, perdy.
And though that I of ancestry
  A baron's daughter be,
Yet have ye proved how I you loved,
  A squire of low degree;
And ever shall, what so befall,
  To die therefore anon,
For in my mind of all mankind
  I love but you alone.'

Squire

'A baron's child to be beguiled,
  It were a cursed deed;
To be fellow with an outlaw,
  Almighty God forbid!

Yet better were the poor squier
  Alone to forest yede,
Than ye shall say another day
  That by my wicked rede
Ye were betrayed. Wherefore, good maid,
  The best rede that I can,
Is that I to the greenwood go
  Alone a banished man.'

Puella

'Whatever befall, I never shall
  Of this thing you upbraid;
But if ye go, and leave me so,
  Then have ye me betrayed.
Remember you well how that ye deal;
  For if ye, as ye said,
Be so unkind to leave behind
  Your love, the Nutbrown Maid,
Trust me truly, that I shall die
  Soon after ye be gone,
For in my mind of all mankind
  I love but you alone.'

Squire

'If that ye went, ye should repent;
  For in the forest now
I have purveyed me of a maid,
  Whom I love more than you.
Another fairer than ever ye were,
  I dare it well avow;
And of you both each should be wroth
  With other, as I trow.

yede] went

It were mine ease to live in peace,
   So will I, if I can;
Wherefore I to the wood will go
   Alone a banished man.'

Puella

'Though in the wood I understood
   Ye had a paramour,
All this may nought remove my thought,
   But that I will be your;
And she shall find me soft and kind
   And courteous every hour,
Glad to fulfil all that she will
   Command me to my power.
For had ye, lo! an hundred mo,
   Yet would I be that one,
For in my mind of all mankind
   I love but you alone.'

Squire

'Mine own dear love, I see thee prove
   That ye be kind and true,
Of maid and wife, in all my life,
   The best that ever I knew.
Be merry and glad, be no more sad!
   The case is changed new,
For it were ruth that for your truth
   Ye should have cause to rue.
Be not dismayed! Whatsoever I said
   To you, when I began,
I will not to the greenwood go;
   I am no banished man.'

Puella

'These tidings be more glad to me
  Than to be made a queen,
If I were sure they should endure;
  But it is often seen,
When men will break promise, they speak
  The wordės on the spleen.
Ye shape some wile me to beguile
  And steal fro me, I ween.
Then were the case worse than it was,
  And I more woebegone;
For in my mind of all mankind
  I love but you alone.'

Squire

'Ye shall not need further to dread.
  I will not disparage
You, God defend! sith you descend
  Of so great a lineage.
Now understand! To Westmorland,
  Which is my heritage,
I will you bring, and with a ring
  By way of marriage
I will you take, and lady make
  As shortly as I can.
Thus have ye won an earlės son,
  And not a banished man.'

Ambo

Here may ye see that women be
  In love, meek, kind, and stable.

on the spleen] lightly

Let never man reprove them than,
Or call them variable;
But rather pray God that we may
To them be comfortable,
Which sometime proveth such as he loveth,
If they be charitable.
For sith men would that women should
Be meek to them each one,
Much more ought they to God obey,
And serve but him alone.

Richard Arnold, *Customs of London*, 1503 ?; *Balliol MS.* 354

STEPHEN HAWES

1475 ?–1523 ?

2 ### *The Epitaph of Graunde Amoure*

O MORTAL folk! you may behold and see
How I lie here, sometime a mighty knight;
The end of joy and all prosperity
Is death at last, thorough his course and might;
After the day there cometh the dark night;
For though the day be never so long,
At last the bells ringeth to evensong.

And my self called La Graunde Amoure,
Seeking adventure in the worldly glory,
For to attain the riches and honour,
Did think full little that I should here lie,
Till death did mate me full right privily.
Lo what I am! and whereto you must!
Like as I am so shall you be all dust.

if] whether

Then in your mind inwardly despise
The brittle world, so full of doubleness,
With the vile flesh, and right soon arise
Out of your sleep of mortal heaviness;
Subdue the devil with grace and meekness,
That after your life frail and transitory
You may then live in joy perdurably.

Written 1505–6; *Pastime of Pleasure*, xlii, 1509

SIR THOMAS MORE

1478–1535

3 *A Rueful Lamentation on the Death of Queen Elizabeth*

O YE that put your trust and confidence
In worldly joy and frail prosperity,
That so live here as ye should never hence,
Remember death and look here upon me.
Ensample I think there may no better be.
Your self wot well that in this realm was I
Your queen but late, and lo now here I lie.

Was I not born of old worthy lineage?
Was not my mother queen, my father king?
Was I not a king's fere in marriage?
Had I not plenty of every pleasant thing?
Merciful God, this is a strange reckoning:
Riches, honour, wealth and ancestry
Hath me forsaken, and lo now here I lie.

fere] consort

SIR THOMAS MORE

If worship might have kept me, I had not gone.
  If wit might have me saved, I needed not fear.
If money might have holp, I lacked none.
  But O good God what vaileth all this gear?
  When death is come, thy mighty messenger,
    Obey we must, there is no remedy;
    Me hath he summoned, and lo now here I lie.

Yet was I late promised otherwise,
  This year to live in wealth and delice.
Lo whereto cometh thy blandishing promise,
  O false astrology and divinatrice,
  Of God's secrets making thy self so wise?
    How true is for this year thy prophecy!
    The year yet lasteth, and lo now here I lie.

O brittle wealth, aye full of bitterness,
  Thy single pleasure doubled is with pain.
Account my sorrow first and my distress,
  In sundry wise, and reckon there again
  The joy that I have had, and I dare sayn,
    For all my honour, endured yet have I
    More woe than wealth, and lo now here I lie.

Where are our castles now, where are our towers?
  Goodly Richmond, soon art thou gone from me;
At Westminster that costly work of yours,
  Mine own dear lord, now shall I never see.
  Almighty God vouchsafe to grant that ye
    For you and your children well may edify.
    My palace builded is, and lo now here I lie.

Written in 1503; stt. i–vi, *Workes in the Englysh tonge*, 1557.

delice] delight

SIR THOMAS MORE

4 ### *Lewis, the Lost Lover*

FIE! flattering Fortune, look thou never so fair,
Or never so pleasantly begin to smile,
As though thou wouldst my ruin all repair;
During my life, thou shalt not me beguile.
Trust shall I God, to enter, in a while,
His haven of Heaven sure and uniform.
Ever after thy calm, look I for a storm.

Written c. 1535; *Ib.* 2.

JOHN SKELTON

c. 1460–1529

5 ### *The Sparrow's Dirge*

Placebo,
Who is there? Who?
Dilexi.
Dame Margery!
Fa, re, my, my,
Wherefore and why, why?
For the soul of Philip Sparrow,
That was late slain at Carrow
Among the Nunnės Black,
For that sweet soulės sake
And for all sparrows' souls
Set in our bead-rolls,
Pater noster qui
With an *Ave Mari,*
And with the corner of a creed,
The more shall be your meed.

When I remember again
How my Philip was slain,
Never half the pain
Was between you twain,
Pyramus and Thesbe,
As then befell to me.
I wept and I wailed,
The tearės down hailed,
But nothing it availed
To call Philip again,
Whom Gib, our cat, hath slain.
Gib, I say, our cat
Worried her on that
Which I loved best.
It cannot be expressed,
My sorrowful heaviness,
But all without redress;
For within that stound,
Half slumbering in a sound,
I fell down to the ground.
Unneth I cast mine eyes
Toward the cloudy skies,
But when I did behold
My sparrow dead and cold,
No creature but that would
Have rued upon me,
To behold and see
What heaviness did me pang,
Wherewith my hands I wrang,
That my sinews cracked
As though I had been racked,

stound] moment   sound] swoon   unneth] hardly

So pained and so strained
That no life well nigh remained.
  I sighed and I sobbed
For that I was robbed
Of my sparrow's life.
O maiden, widow, and wife,
Of what estate ye be,
Of high or low degree,
Great sorrow then ye might see,
And learn to weep at me.
Such painès did me fret
That mine heart did beat,
My visage pale and dead,
Wan and blue as lead;
The pangs of hateful death
Well nigh had stopped my breath.
  Heu, heu, me,
That I am woe for thee!
Ad Dominum cum tribularer clamavi.
Of God nothing else crave I
But Philip's soul to keep
From the marish deep
Of Acherontes' well,
That is a flood of hell;
And from the great Pluto,
The prince of endless woe;
And from foul Alecto
With visage black and blo;
And from Medusa, that mare,
That like a fiend doth stare;
And from Megera's edders,

marish] marsh   blo] livid   mare] hag   edders] adders

For ruffling of Philip's feders,
And from her fiery sparklings
For burning of his wings;
And from the smokės sour
Of Proserpina's bower;
And from the dennės dark
Where Cerberus doth bark,
Whom Theseus did affray,
Whom Hercules did outray,
As famous poets say;
From that hell-hound
That lieth in chainės bound
With ghastly headės three,
To Jupiter pray we
That Philip preserved may be!
Amen, say ye with me!
Dominus,
Help now, sweet Jesus!
Levavi oculos meos in montes.
Would God I had Zenophontes,
Or Socrates the wise,
To show me their devise
Moderately to take
This sorrow that I make
For Philip Sparrow's sake!
So fervently I shake,
I feel my body quake;
So urgently I am brought
Into careful thought.
Like Andromach, Hector's wife,

feders] feathers outray] vanquish Zenophontes] Xenophon devise] device

Was weary of her life,
When she had lost her joy,
Noble Hector of Troy;
In like manner also
Increaseth my deadly woe,
For my sparrow is go.
   It was so pretty a fool;
It would sit on a stool
And learned after my school
For to keep his cut,
With, 'Philip, keep your cut!'
   It had a velvet cap,
And would sit upon my lap
And seek after small worms
And sometime white bread crumbs;
And many times and oft
Between my brestės soft
It would lie and rest;
It was proper and prest.
   Sometime he would gasp
When he saw a wasp;
A fly or a gnat,
He would fly at that;
And prettily he would pan
When he saw an ant;
Lord, how he would pry
After the butterfly!
Lord, how he would hop
After the gressop!
And when I said, 'Phip! Phip!'
Then he would leap and skip,

go] gone   keep cut] behave   prest] alert   gressop] grasshopper

And take me by the lip.
Alas, it will me slo
That Philip is gone me fro!
Si iniquitates.
Alas, I was evil at ease!
De profundis clamavi,
When I saw my sparrow die!

Written c. 1504; *The Boke of Phyllyp Sparowe*, c. 1545

6 *The Commendations of Mistress Jane Scrope*

HOW shall I report
All the goodly sort
Of her features clear,
That hath none earthly peer?
Her favour of her face,
Ennewed with all grace,
Comfort, pleasure, and solace,
Mine heart doth so embrace,
And so hath ravished me,
Her to behold and see,
That, in wordės plain,
I cannot me refrain
To look on her again.
Alas, what should I feign?
It were a pleasant pain
With her aye to remain.
Her eyėn gray and steep
Causeth mine heart to leap.
With her browės bent,
She may well represent

slo] slay   Ennewed] tinted   what] why   steep] bright

JOHN SKELTON

Fair Lucres, as I ween,
Or else fair Polexene,
Or else Caliope,
Or else Penolope;
For this most goodly flower,
This blossom of fresh colour,
So Jupiter me succour,
She flourisheth new and new
In beauty and virtue.
Hac claritate gemina
O gloriosa femina,
Memor esto verbi tui servo tuo!
Servus tuus sum ego.
  The Indy sapphire blue
Her veinės doth ennew,
The orient pearl so clear
The whiteness of her leer;
The lusty ruby ruds
Resemble the rose-buds;
Her lipės soft and merry
Embloomed like the cherry,
It were an heavenly bliss
Her sugared mouth to kiss.
  Her beauty to augment,
Dame Nature hath her lent
A wart upon her cheek,
Who so list to seek,
In her visage a scar,
That seemeth from afar
Like to the radiant star,

leer] complexion
ruds] cheeks

All with favour fret,
So properly it is set.
She is the violet,
The daisy delectable,
The columbine commendable,
The jelofer amiable;
For this most goodly flower,
This blossom of fresh colour,
So Jupiter me succour,
She flourisheth new and new
In beauty and virtue.
Hac claritate gemina
O gloriosa femina,
Bonitatem fecisti cum servo tuo, domina,
Et ex praecordiis sonant praeconia.
  And when I perceived
Her wart, and conceived,
It cannot be denayed
But it was well conveyed,
And set so womanly,
And nothing wantonly,
But right conveniently,
And full congruently,
As Nature could devise,
In most goodly wise.
Who so list behold,
It maketh lovers bold
To her to sue for grace,
Her favour to purchase.
The scar upon her chin,

with favour fret] graciously patterned
jelofer] gillyflower

Enhached on her fair skin,
Whiter than the swan,
It would make any man
To forget deadly sin,
Her favour to win;
For this most goodly flower,
This blossom of fresh colour,
So Jupiter me succour,
She flourisheth new and new
In beauty and virtue.
Hac claritate gemina
O gloriosa femina,
Defecit in salutare tuum anima mea.
Quid petis filio, mater dulcissima? ba ba,
Soft, and make no din,
For now I will begin
To have in remembrance
Her goodly dalliance
And her goodly pastance.
So sad and so demure,
Behaving her so sure,
With wordės of pleasure
She would make to the lure,
And any man convert
To give her his whole heart.
She made me sore amazed,
Upon her when I gazed,
Me thought mine heart was crazed,
My eyėn were so dazed;
For this most goodly flower,
This blossom of fresh colour,

Enhached] inlaid pastance] pastime sad] serious

So Jupiter me succour,
She flourisheth new and new
In beauty and virtue.
Hac claritate gemina,
O gloriosa femina,
Quomodo dilexi legem tuam, domina!
Recedant vetera, nova sint omnia.
  And to amend her tale,
When she list to avale,
And with her fingers small
And handės soft as silk,
Whiter than the milk,
That are so quickly veined,
Wherewith my hand she strained,
Lord, how I was pained!
Unneth I me refrained,
How she me had reclaimed
And me to her retained,
Embracing therewithal
Her goodly middle small
With sidės long and straight.
To tell you what conceit
I had then in a trice,
The matter were too nice,
And yet there was no vice,
Nor yet no villainy,
But only fantasy;
For this most goodly flower,
This blossom of fresh colour,

avale] condescend   unneth] hardly
how] to such an extent
reclaimed] subdued

So Jupiter me succour,
She flourisheth new and new
In beauty and virtue.
Hac claritate gemina
O gloriosa femina,
Iniquos odio habui.
Non calumnientur me superbi.
  But whereto should I note
How often did I tote
Upon her pretty foot?
It raised mine heart root
To see her tread the ground
With heelės short and round.
She is plainly express
Egeria, the goddess,
And like to her image
Importuned with courage,
A lovers' pilgrimage.
There is no beast savage,
Nor no tiger so wood,
But she would change his mood,
Such relucent grace
Is formed in her face;
For this most goodly flower,
This blossom of fresh colour,
So Jupiter me succour,
She flourisheth new and new
In beauty and virtue.
Hac claritate gemina
O gloriosa femina,
Mirabilia testimonia tua!

tote] gaze wood] mad

Sicut novellae plantationes in juventute sua.
So goodly as she dresses,
So properly she presses
The bright golden tresses
Of her hair so fine,
Like Phebus' beamės' shine.
Whereto should I disclose
The gartering of her hose?
It is for to suppose
How that she can wear
Gorgeously her gear,
Her fresh habiliments,
With other implements
To serve for all intents,
Like Dame Flora, queen
Of lusty summer green;
For this most goodly flower,
This blossom of fresh colour,
So Jupiter me succour,
She flourisheth new and new
In beauty and virtue.
Hac claritate gemina
O gloriosa femina,
Clamavi in toto corde, exaudi me!
Misericordia tua magna est super me.
Her kirtle so goodly laced,
And under that is braced
Such pleasures that I may
Neither write nor say;
Yet, though I write not with ink,
No man can let me think,

let] hinder

For thought hath liberty,
Thought is frank and free;
To think a merry thought,
It cost me little nor nought.
Would God mine homely style
Were polished with the file
Of Cicero's eloquence,
To praise her excellence;
For this most goodly flower,
This blossom of fresh colour,
So Jupiter me succour,
She flourisheth new and new
In beauty and virtue.
Hac claritate gemina,
O gloriosa femina,
Principes persecuti sunt me gratis.
Omnibus consideratis,
Paradisus voluptatis
Haec virgo est dulcissima.
My pen it is unable,
My hand it is unstable,
My reason rude and dull,
To praise her at the full,
Goodly mistress Jane,
Sober, demure Diane.
Jane this mistress hight,
The lodestar of delight,
Dame Venus of all pleasure,
The well of worldly treasure.
She doth exceed and pass
In prudence dame Pallas;
For this most goodly flower,

This blossom of fresh colour,
So Jupiter me succour,
She flourisheth new and new
In beauty and virtue.
Hac claritate gemina
O gloriosa femina!
Requiem aeternam dona eis, Domine!
With this psalm, *Domine probasti me*,
Shall I sail over the sea,
With *Tibi, Domine, commendamus*,
On pilgrimage to saint Jamės,
For shrimpės and for pranės,
And for stalking cranės;
And where my pen hath offended,
I pray you it may be amended
By discreet consideration
Of your wise reformation.
I have not offended, I trust,
If it be sadly discussed.
It were no gentle guise
This treatise to despise,
Because I have written and said
Honour of this fair maid.
Wherefore should I be blamed,
That I Jane have named,
And famously proclaimed?
She is worthy to be enrolled
With letters of gold.
Car elle vault.

Written c. 1504; *The Boke of Phyllyp Sparowe*, c. 1545

pranės] prawns

7 *To Mistress Margery Wentworth*

WITH margeran gentle,
  The flower of goodlihood,
Embroidered the mantle
  Is of your maidenhood.

Plainly, I cannot glose
  Ye be, as I divine,
The pretty primèrose,
  The goodly columbine.

With margeran gentle,
  The flower of goodlihood,
Embroidered the mantle
  Is of your maidenhood.

Benign, courteous, and meek,
  With wordės well devised,
In you, who list to seek,
  Be virtues well comprised.

With margeran gentle,
  The flower of goodlihood,
Embroidered the mantle
  Is of your maidenhood.

Garlande of Laurell, 1523; *Cotton MS. Vitellius* E x

margeran] marjoram   glose] flatter

8 *To Mistress Isabel Pennell*

BY Saint Mary, my lady,
Your mammy and your daddy
Brought forth a goodly baby.

My maiden Isabel,
Reflaring rosabel,
The flagrant camomel,

The ruddy rosary,
The sovereign rosemary,
The pretty strawberry,

The columbine, the nept,
The jelofer well set,
The proper violet;

Ennewed your colour
Is like the daisy flower
After the April shower.

Star of the morrow gray,
The blossom on the spray,
The freshest flower of May,

Maidenly demure,
Of womanhood the lure;
Wherefore I you assure,

reflaring] redolent   flagrant] fragrant   nept] mint
jelofer] gillyflower   ennewed] tinted

It were an heavenly health,
It were an endless wealth,
A life for God himself,

To hear this nightingale
Among the birdės small
Warbling in the vale,

'Dug, dug,
Jug, jug!
Good year and good luck!'
With 'Chuck, chuck, chuck, chuck!'

Garlande of Laurell, 1523; *Cotton MS. Vitellius* E x

To Mistress Margaret Hussey

MERRY Margaret, as midsummer flower,
Gentle as falcon or hawk of the tower,
With solace and gladness,
Much mirth and no madness,
All good and no badness;
So joyously,
So maidenly,
So womanly,
Her demeaning;
In every thing
Far far passing
That I can indite
Or suffice to write
Of merry Margaret, as midsummer flower,
Gentle as falcon or hawk of the tower.

As patient and as still,
And as full of good will,
As the fair Isyphill,
Coliander,
Sweet pomander,
Good Cassander;
Steadfast of thought,
Well made, well wrought.
Far may be sought
Erst than ye can find
So courteous, so kind,
As merry Margaret, the midsummer flower,
Gentle as falcon or hawk of the tower.

Garlande of Laurell, 1523; *Cotton MS. Vitellius* E x

KING HENRY THE EIGHTH

1491–1547

10

The Holly

Green groweth the holly; so doth the ivy.
Though winter blastės blow never so high,
Green groweth the holly.

As the holly groweth green,
And never changeth hue,
So I am, ever hath been
Unto my lady true;

As the holly groweth green
With ivy all alone,
When flowerės cannot be seen
And green wood leaves be gone.

Isyphill] Hypsipyle coliander] coriander
pomander] ball of perfume Cassander] Cassandra

Now unto my lady
  Promise to her I make,
From all other only
  To her I me betake.

Adieu, mine own lady,
  Adieu, my special,
Who hath my heart truly,
  Be sure, and ever shall!

Additional MS. 31922

11 *To His Lady*

WHERETO should I express
  My inward heaviness?
No mirth can make me fain,
  Till that we meet again.

Do way, dear heart! Not so!
  Let no thought you dismay.
Though ye now part me fro,
  We shall meet when we may.

When I remember me
  Of your most gentle mind,
It may in no wise agree
  That I should be unkind.

The daisy delectable,
  The violet wan and blo,
Ye are not variable.
  I love you and no mo.

betake] give   do way] have done   blo] pale

I make you fast and sure.
   It is to me great pain
Thus long to endure
   Till that we meet again.

Addl. MS. 31922

12 *Pastime*

PASTIME with good company
   I love and shall, until I die.
Grudge who list, but none deny!
So God be pleased, thus live will I.
   For my pastance,
   Hunt, sing and dance,
   My heart is set.
      All goodly sport
      For my comfort
   Who shall me let?

Youth must have some dalliance,
Of good or ill some pastance.
Company me thinks the best,
All thoughts and fancies to digest;
   For idleness
   Is chief mistress
   Of vices all.
      Then who can say
      But mirth and play
   Is best of all?

pastance] pastime

Company with honesty
Is virtue, vices to flee;
Company is good and ill,
But every man has his free will.
  The best ensue,
  The worst eschew!
  My mind shall be,
    Virtue to use,
    Vice to refuse;
  Thus shall I use me.

Ibid.

WILLIAM CORNISH

14 ? –1523

13

Desire

You and I and Amyas,
Amyas and you and I,
To the green wood must we go, alas!
You and I, my life, and Amyas.

THE knight knocked at the castle gate;
The lady marvelled who was thereat.

To call the porter he would not blin;
The lady said he should not come in.

The portress was a lady bright;
Strangêness that lady hight.

She asked him what was his name;
He said 'Desire, your man, Madame.'

blin] cease

She said 'Desire, what do ye here?'
He said 'Madame, as your prisoner.'

He was counselled to brief a bill,
And show my lady his own will.

'Kindness,' said she, 'would it bear,'
'And Pity,' said she, 'would be there.'

Thus how they did we cannot say;
We left them there and went our way.

Addl. MS. 31922

14 *Gratitude*

PLEASURE it is
  To hear, iwis,
 The birdės sing.
The deer in the dale,
The sheep in the vale,
 The corn springing.
God's purveyance
For sustenance
 It is for man.
Then we always
To him give praise,
 And thank him than,
 And thank him than.

Bassus, 1530

brief a bill] draw up a petition iwis] truly

HEATH

temp. Hen. VIII

15

Women

THESE women all
Both great and small
Are wavering to and fro,
Now here, now there,
Now everywhere;
But I will not say so.

So they love to range,
Their minds doth change
And make their friend their foe;
As lovers true
Each day they choose new;
But I will not say so.

They laugh, they smile,
They do beguile,
As dice that men doth throw.
Who useth them much
Shall never be rich;
But I will not say so.

Some hot, some cold,
There is no hold
But as the wind doth blow;
When all is done,
They change like the moon;
But I will not say so.

HEATH

So thus one and other
Taketh after their mother,
  As cock by kind doth crow.
My song is ended,
The best may be amended;
  But I will not say so.

Harleian MS. 7578

ANONYMOUS

16 *Absence*

WESTERN wind, when will thou blow,
  The small rain down can rain?
Christ, if my love were in my arms
  And I in my bed again!

Royal MSS., Appendix 58

17 *Dawn*

BY a bank as I lay,
  Musing myself alone, hey ho!
A birdės voice
Did me rejoice,
Singing before the day;
And methought in her lay
She said, winter was past, hey ho!
Then dyry come dawn, dyry come dyry, come dyry!
Come dyry, come dyry, come dawn, hey ho!

The master of music,
The lusty nightingale, hey ho!
Full merrily
And secretly
She singeth in the thick;
And under her breast a prick,
To keep her fro sleep, hey ho!
Then dyry come dawn, dyry come dyry, come dyry!
Come dyry, come dyry, come dawn, hey ho!

Awake therefore, young men,
All ye that lovers be, hey ho!
This month of May,
So fresh, so gay,
So fair be fields on fen;
Hath flourish ilka den.
Great joy it is to see, hey ho!
Then dyry come dawn, dyry come dyry, come dyry!
Come dyry, come dyry, come dawn, hey ho!

Ibid.

18 *A Secret*

IF I had wit for to indite
Of my lady both fair and free,
Of her goodness then would I write.
Shall no man know her name for me,
Shall no man know her name for me.

I love her well with heart and mind;
She is right true, I do it see;
My heart to have she doth me bind.
Shall no man know her name for me.

ilka den] every slope

She doth not waver as the wind;
  Nor for no new me change doth she;
But alway true I do her find.
  Shall no man know her name for me.

If I to her then were unkind,
  Pity it were, that I should thee;
For she to me is alway kind.
  Shall no man know her name for me.

Learning it were for women all
  Unto their lovers true to be.
Promise I make that know none shall,
  Whiles that I live, her name for me.

My heart she hath, and ever shall,
  Till by death departed we be.
Hap what will hap, fall what shall fall,
  Shall no man know her name for me.

Royal MSS., Appendix 58; *Addl. MS.* 31922

19 *Youth*

LET not us that youngmen be
  From Venus' ways banished to be.
Though that age with great disdain
Would have youth love to refrain,
In their minds consider you must
How they did in their most lust.

thee] thrive

For if they were in like case,
And would then have gotten grace,
They may not now then gainsay
That which then was most their joy.
Wherefore indeed, the truth to say,
It is for youth the meetest play.

Addl. MS. 31922

20 *Pastourelle*

'HEY, troly loly lo, maid, whither go you?'
'I go to the meadow to milk my cow.'
'Then at the meadow I will you meet,
To gather the flowers both fair and sweet.'
'Nay, God forbid, that may not be!
I wis my mother then shall us see.'

'Now in this meadow fair and green
We may us sport and not be seen;
And if ye will, I shall consent.
How say ye, maid? be ye content?'
'Nay, in good faith, I'll not mell with you!
I pray you, sir, let me go milk my cow.'

'Why will ye not give me no comfort,
That now in these fields we may us sport?'
'Nay, God forbid, that may not be!
I wis my mother then shall us see.'

'Ye be so nice and so meet of age,
That ye greatly move my courage.
Sith I love you, love me again;
Let us make one, though we be twain.'
'I pray you, sir, let me go milk my cow.'

mell] meddle

'Ye have my heart, say what ye will;
Wherefore ye must my mind fulfil,
And grant me here your maidenhead,
Or ellės I shall for you be dead.'
'I pray you, sir, let me go milk my cow.'

'Then for this once I shall you spare;
But the next time ye must beware,
How in the meadow ye milk your cow.
Adieu, farewell, and kiss me now!'
'I pray you, sir, let me go milk my cow.'

Addl. MS. 31922

21 *A Dream*

BENEDICITE, what dreamed I this night?
  Methought the world was turned up so down;
The sun, the moon, had lost their force and light;
  The sea also drowned both tower and town.
  Yet more marvel how that I heard the sound
    Of onės voice saying 'Bear in thy mind,
    Thy lady hath forgotten to be kind.'

To complain me, alas, why should I so,
  For my complaint it did me never good?
But by constraint now must I shew my woe
  To her only which is mine eyės food,
  Trusting sometime that she will change her mood,
    And let me not alway be guerdonless,
    Sith for my truth she needeth no witness.

Addl. MS. 5465

up so down] upside down

JOHN HEYWOOD

c. 1497–c. 1580

22 *On the Princess Mary*

GIVE place, you ladies, and be gone,
  Boast not yourselves at all,
For here at hand approacheth one,
  Whose face will stain you all.

The virtue of her lively looks
  Excels the precious stone;
I wish to have none other books
  To read or look upon.

In each of her two crystal eyes
  Smileth a naked boy;
It would you all in heart suffice
  To see that lamp of joy.

I think nature hath lost the mould
  Where she her shape did take,
Or else I doubt if nature could
  So fair a creature make.

She may be very well compared
  Unto the phoenix kind,
Whose like was never seen nor heard,
  That any man can find.

In life she is Diana chaste,
  In truth, Penelope;
In word and eke in deed steadfast.
  What will you more we say?

JOHN HEYWOOD

If all the world were sought so far,
  Who could find such a wight?
Her beauty twinkleth like a star
  Within the frosty night.

Her rosial colour comes and goes
  With such a comely grace,
More readier too than doth the rose
  Within her lively face.

At Bacchus' feast none shall her meet,
  Ne at no wanton play;
Nor gazing in an open street,
  Nor gadding as a stray.

The modest mirth that she doth use
  Is mixed with shamefastness.
All vice she doth wholly refuse,
  And hateth idleness.

O Lord, it is a world to see
  How virtue can repair
And deck her in such honesty,
  Whom nature made so fair.

Truly, she doth as far exceed
  Our women nowadays,
As doth the gillyflower a weed,
  And more, a thousand ways.

How might we do to have a graff
  Of this unspotted tree,
For all the rest are plain but chaff,
  Which seem good corn to be.

graff] graft

JOHN HEYWOOD

This gift alone I shall her give,
  When death doth what he can;
Her honest fame shall ever live
  Within the mouth of man.

Written 1534; *Songes and Sonettes*, Tottel, 1557

SIR THOMAS WYATT

c. 1503–1542

23 ### *Rondeau*

WHAT, no perdy! ye may be sure.
  Think not to make me to your lure,
  With words and cheer so contrarying,
  Sweet and sour counterweighing.
Too much it were still to endure;
Truth is tried where craft is in ure;
But though ye have had my heartès cure
  Trow ye I dote without ending?
                    What, no perdy!

Though that with pain I do procure
For to forget that once was pure,
  Within my heart shall still that thing
  Unstable, unsure, and wavering,
Be in my mind without recure?
                    What, no perdy!

Egerton MS. 2711

perdy] by God   ure] use   recure] remedy

24 *The Hind*

WHOSO list to hunt, I know where is an hind,
But as for me, *helas!* I may no more.
The vain travail hath wearied me so sore,
I am of them that furthest come behind.
Yet may I, by no means, my wearied mind
Draw from the deer; but as she fleeth afore
Fainting I follow. I leave off therefore,
Since in a net I seek to hold the wind.
Who list her hunt, I put him out of doubt,
As well as I, may spend his time in vain;
And graven with diamonds in letters plain
There is written, her fair neck round about,
'*Noli me tangere*, for Caesar's I am,
And wild for to hold, though I seem tame.'

Egerton MS. 2711

25 *The Galley*

MY galley, charged with forgetfulness,
Thorough sharp seas in winter nights doth pass
'Tween rock and rock; and eke mine enemy, alas!
That is my Lord, steereth with cruelness;
And every oar a thought in readiness,
As though that death were light in such a case.
An endless wind doth tear the sail apace
Of forced sights, and trusty fearfulness;
A rain of tears, a cloud of dark disdain,
Hath done the wered cords great hinderance,
Wreathed with error and eke with ignorance.
The stars be hid that led me to this pain.
Drowned is reason that should me consort,
And I remain despairing of the port.

Ibid.

sights] sighs wered] worn *or* wearied

26

May Time

YOU that in love find luck and abundance,
And live in lust and joyful jollity,
Arise, for shame, do away your sluggardy;
Arise, I say, do May some observance!
Let me in bed lie dreaming in mischance;
Let me remember the haps most unhappy,
That me betide in May most commonly,
As one whom love list little to advance.
Sepham said true that my nativity
Mischanced was with the ruler of the May;
He guessed, I prove, of that the verity;
In May my wealth, and eke my life I say
Have stonde so oft in such perplexity.
Rejoice! let me dream of your felicity.

Ibid.

27

In Spain

TAGUS, farewell, that westward with thy streams
Turns up the grains of gold already tried;
With spur and sail for I go seek the Thames,
Gainward the sun that showeth her wealthy pride,
And to the town that Brutus sought by dreams,
Like bended moon, doth lean her lusty side.
My king, my country, alone for whom I live,
Of mighty love the wings for this me give.

Written 1539; *Ibid.*

stonde] stood   gainward] flowing against

28

Epigram

A FACE that should content me wonders well,
Should not be fair but lovely to behold,
With gladsome cheer all grief for to expel;
With sober looks so would I that it should
Speak without words such words as none can tell;
The tress also should be of crisped gold.
With wit and these, might chance I might be tied
And knit again the knot that should not slide.

Egerton MS. 2711

29

To His Lady

MADAM, withouten many words,
Once, I am sure, ye will or no.
And if ye will, then leave your bourds
And use your wit and show it so,

And with a beck ye shall me call;
And if of one, that burneth alway,
Ye have any pity at all,
Answer him fair with yea, or nay.

If it be yea, I shall be fain;
If it be nay, friends as before;
Ye shall another man obtain,
And I mine own and yours no more.

Ibid.

wonders] wondrous bourds] jests

30

Remembrance

THEY flee from me, that sometime did me seek
With naked foot, stalking in my chamber.
I have seen them gentle, tame, and meek,
That now are wild, and do not remember
That sometime they put themselves in danger
To take bread at my hand; and now they range
Busily seeking with a continual change.

Thanked be fortune it hath been otherwise
Twenty times better; but once, in special,
In thin array, after a pleasant guise,
When her loose gown from her shoulders did fall,
And she me caught in her arms long and small,
Therewith all sweetly did me kiss
And softly said, 'Dear heart how like you this?'

It was no dream; I lay broad waking:
But all is turned, thorough my gentleness,
Into a strange fashion of forsaking;
And I have leave to go of her goodness,
And she also to use newfangleness.
But since that I so kindly am served,
I would fain know what she hath deserved.

Ibid.

danger] subjection small] slim

31

Patience

PATIENCE, though I have not
The thing that I require,
I must, of force, God wot,
Forbear my most desire;
For no ways can I find
To sail against the wind.

Patience, do what they will
To work me woe or spite,
I shall content me still
To think both day and night;
To think and hold my peace,
Since there is no redress.

Patience, withouten blame,
For I offended nought;
I know they know the same,
Though they have changed their thought.
Was ever thought so moved
To hate that it hath loved?

Patience of all my harm,
For fortune is my foe;
Patience must be the charm
To heal me of my woe.
Patience without offence
Is a painful patience.

Egerton MS. 2711

SIR THOMAS WYATT

32

Fortune

MARVEL no more although
  The songs I sing do moan,
For other life than woe
  I never proved none.

And in my heart also
  Is graven with letters deep
A thousand sighs and mo,
  A flood of tears to weep.

How may a man in smart
  Find matter to rejoice?
How may a mourning heart
  Set forth a pleasant voice?

Play who that can that part:
  Needs must in me appear
How fortune, overthwart,
  Doth cause my mourning cheer.

Perdy! there is no man
  If he never saw sight,
That perfectly tell can
  The nature of the light.

Alas! how should I than,
  That never tast but sour,
But do as I began
  Continually to lour.

But yet perchance some chance
  May chance to change my tune;
And when such chance doth chance
  Then shall I thank fortune.

And if such chance do chance,
  Perchance, ere it be long,
For such a pleasant chance
  To sing some pleasant song.

Egerton MS. 2711

33 *A Promise*

ONCE as methought Fortune me kissed,
  And bade me ask what I thought best,
And I should have it as me list,
  Therewith to set my heart in rest.

I asked nought but my dear heart
  To have for evermore mine own;
Then at an end were all my smart,
  Then should I need no more to moan.

Yet, for all that, a stormy blast
  Had overturned this goodly day,
And Fortune seemed at the last
  That to her promise she said nay.

But, like as one out of despair,
  To sudden hope revived I;
Now Fortune sheweth herself so fair
  That I content me wonderly.

My most desire my hand may reach,
  My will is alway at my hand;
Me need not long for to beseech
  Her that hath power me to command.

What earthly thing more can I crave?
  What would I wish more at my will?
Nothing on earth more would I have,
  Save that I have, to have it still.

For Fortune hath kept her promise,
  In granting me my most desire;
Of my sufferance I have redress,
  And I content me with my hire.

Ibid.

34

To His Lute

MY lute, awake! perform the last
Labour that thou and I shall waste,
  And end that I have now begun;
For when this song is sung and past,
  My lute, be still, for I have done.

As to be heard where ear is none,
As lead to grave in marble stone,
  My song may pierce her heart as soon.
Should we then sigh, or sing, or moan?
  No, no, my lute, for I have done.

The rocks do not so cruelly
Repulse the waves continually,
  As she my suit and affection;
So that I am past remedy,
  Whereby my lute and I have done.

grave] engrave

SIR THOMAS WYATT

Proud of the spoil that thou hast got
Of simple hearts thorough love's shot,
By whom, unkind, thou hast them won,
Think not he hath his bow forgot,
Although my lute and I have done.

Vengeance shall fall on thy disdain,
That makest but game on earnest pain;
Think not alone under the sun
Unquit to cause thy lovers plain,
Although my lute and I have done.

Perchance thee lie withered and old,
The winter nights that are so cold,
Plaining in vain unto the moon;
Thy wishes then dare not be told.
Care then who list, for I have done.

And then may chance thee to repent
The time that thou hast lost and spent
To cause thy lovers sigh and swoon;
Then shalt thou know beauty but lent,
And wish and want as I have done.

Now cease, my lute! this is the last
Labour that thou and I shall waste,
And ended is that we begun;
Now is this song both sung and past.
My lute, be still, for I have done.

Egerton MS. 2711

unquit] unrequited

35

A Protest

HEAVEN and earth, and all that hear me plain,
  Do well perceive what care doth cause me cry,
Save you alone, to whom I cry in vain,
  'Mercy! Madame, alas! I die, I die!'

If that you sleep, I humbly you require
  Forbear a while, and let your rigour slake;
Since that by you I burn thus in this fire,
  To hear my plaint, dear heart, awake! awake!

Since that so oft ye have made me to wake
  In plaint and tears, and in right piteous case,
Displease you not, if force do now me make
  To break your sleep, crying 'Alas! alas!'

It is the last trouble that you shall have
  Of me, Madame, to hear my last complaint;
Pity at last your poor unhappy slave,
  For in despair, alas! I faint, I faint.

It is not now, but long and long ago,
  I have you served, as to my power and might,
As faithfully as any man might do,
  Claiming of you nothing of right, of right;

Save of your grace only to stay my life
  That fleeth as fast as cloud afore the wind,
For, since that first I entered in this strife,
  An inward death hath fret my mind, my mind.

If I had suffered this, to you unware,
  Mine were the fault and you nothing to blame,
But since you know my woe and all my care,
  Why do I die? Alas! for shame, for shame.

I know right well my face, my look, my tears,
  Mine eyes, my words, and eke my dreary cheer
Have cried my death full oft unto your ears.
  Hard of belief, it doth appear, appear.

A better proof I see that ye would have,
  How I am dead; therefore, when ye hear tell,
Believe it not, although ye see my grave.
  Cruel, unkind! I say farewell! farewell!

Egerton MS. 2711

36 *His Lady's Hand*

O GOODLY hand
  Wherein doth stand
My heart distract in pain!
  Fair hand, alas!
  In little space
My life that doth restrain.

  O fingers slight
  Departed right,
So long, so small, so round;
  Goodly begone,
  And yet alone
Most cruel in my wound!

  With lilies white
  And roses bright
Doth strive thy colour fair;
  Nature did lend
  Each finger's end
A pearl for to repair.

departed] separated   begone] conditioned   repair] adorn

Consent at last,
Since that thou hast
My heart in thy demesne,
For service true
On me to rue
And reach me love again.

And if not so,
Then with more woe
Enforce thyself to strain
This simple heart
That suffereth smart,
And rid it out of pain.

Ibid.

37 *Treizaine*

IF in the world there be more woe
Than I have in my heart,
Whereso it is, it doth come fro,
And in my breast there doth it grow,
For to increase my smart.
Alas! I am receipt of every care,
And of my life each sorrow claims his part.
Who list to live in quietness
By me let him beware,
For I by high disdain
Am made without redress,
And unkindness, alas! hath slain
My poor true heart, all comfortless.

Ibid.

38 *To His Pen*

MY pen, take pain a little space
To follow that which doth me chase,
And hath in hold my heart so sore;
But when thou hast this brought to pass,
My pen, I prithee, write no more.

Remember, oft thou hast me eased,
And all my pain full well appeased;
But now I know, unknown before,
For where I trust I am deceived;
And yet, my pen, thou canst no more.

A time thou hadst, as others have,
To write which way my hope to crave;
That time is past, withdraw therefore.
Since we do lose that others save,
As good leave off and write no more.

In worth to use another way,
Not as we would, but as we may;
For once my loss is past restore,
And my desire is my decay,
My pen, yet write a little more.

To love in vain who ever shall,
Of worldly pain it passeth all,
As in like case I find. Wherefore
To hold so fast and yet to fall!
Alas! my pen, now write no more.

Since thou hast taken pain this space
To follow that which doth me chase,
  And hath in hold my heart so sore,
Now hast thou brought my mind to pass.
  My pen, I prithee write no more.

Addl. MS. 17492

39

Varium et Mutabile

IS it possible
  That so high debate,
  So sharp, so sore, and of such rate,
  Should end so soon and was begun so late?
Is it possible?

Is it possible
  So cruel intent,
  So hasty heat and so soon spent,
  From love to hate, and thence for to relent?
Is it possible?

Is it possible
  That any may find
  Within one heart so diverse mind,
  To change or turn as weather and wind?
Is it possible?

Is it possible
  To spy it in an eye
  That turns as oft as chance on die,
  The truth whereof can any try?
Is it possible?

It is possible
  For to turn so oft,
  To bring that lowest that was most aloft,
  And to fall highest, yet to light soft.
It is possible.

All is possible,
  Who so list believe;
  Trust therefore first, and after preve,
  As men wed ladies by licence and leave,
All is possible.

Addl. MS. 17492

40 *An Appeal*

AND wilt thou leave me thus?
  Say nay, say nay, for shame!
  To save thee from the blame
  Of all my grief and grame.
And wilt thou leave me thus?
    Say nay! say nay!

And wilt thou leave me thus,
  That hath loved thee so long
  In wealth and woe among?
  And is thy heart so strong
As for to leave me thus?
    Say nay! say nay!

And wilt thou leave me thus,
  That hath given thee my heart,
  Never for to depart
  Neither for pain nor smart;
And wilt thou leave me thus?
    Say nay! say nay!

preve] prove grame] vexation

And wilt thou leave me thus,
 And have no more pity
 Of him that loveth thee?
 Helas! thy cruelty!
 And wilt thou leave me thus?
  Say nay! say nay!

Ibid.

41

Resignation

IN faith methinks it is no right
 To hate me thus for loving ye.
So fair a face, so full of spite!
 Who would have thought such cruelty?
 But since there is no remedy,
  That by no means ye can me love,
  I shall you leave and other prove.

For if I have for my good will
 No reward else but cruelty,
In faith, thereof I can no skill,
 Since that I loved ye honestly;
 But take heed I will till I die,
  Or that I love so well again,
  Since women use so much to feign.

Ibid.

42

Betrayal

HOW should I
 Be so pleasant
 In my semblant,
As my fellows be?

skill] understand   or] before   semblant] appearance

SIR THOMAS WYATT

Not long ago
It chanced so,
   As I did walk alone,
I heard a man
That now and than
   Himself did thus bemoan:

'Alas!' he said,
'I am betrayed
   And utterly undone;
Whom I did trust
And think so just
   Another man hath won.

'Love did assign
Her to be mine,
   And not to love none new;
But who can bind
Their fickle kind,
   That never will be true?

'My service due
And heart so true
   On her I did bestow;
I never meant
For to repent
   In wealth nor yet in woe.

'Each western wind
Hath turned her mind
   And blown it clean away:
Thereby my wealth,
My mirth and health,
   Are driven to great decay.

'Fortune did smile
A right short while
  And never said me nay,
With pleasant plays
And joyful days
  My time to pass away.

'Alas! alas!
The time so was;
  So never shall it be,
Since she is gone
And I alone
  Am left as ye may see.

'Where is the oath,
Where is the troth,
  That she to me did give?
Such feigned words
With silly bourds
  Let no wise man believe.

'For even as I
Thus woefully
  Unto myself complain,
If ye then trust,
Needs learn ye must
  To sing my song in vain.'

How should I
  Be so pleasant
  In my semblant,
As my fellows be?

Addl. MS. 17492

bourds] jests

43

Steadfastness

FORGET not yet the tried intent
Of such a truth as I have meant;
My great travail so gladly spent
Forget not yet!

Forget not yet when first began
The weary life ye know, since whan
The suit, the service, none tell can;
Forget not yet!

Forget not yet the great assays,
The cruel wrong, the scornful ways,
The painful patience in denays,
Forget not yet!

Forget not yet, forget not this,
How long ago hath been, and is,
The mind that never meant amiss
Forget not yet!

Forget not then thine own approved,
The which so long hath thee so loved,
Whose steadfast faith yet never moved;
Forget not this!

Addl. MS. 17492

denays] denials

44

The Lute Obeys

BLAME not my lute! for he must sound
Of these or that as liketh me;
For lack of wit the lute is bound
To give such tunes as pleaseth me.
Though my songs be somewhat strange,
And speaks such words as touch thy change,
Blame not my lute!

My lute, alas! doth not offend,
Though that perforce he must agree
To sound such tunes as I intend
To sing to them that heareth me;
Then though my songs be somewhat plain,
And toucheth some that use to feign,
Blame not my lute!

My lute and strings may not deny,
But as I strike they must obey;
Break not them then so wrongfully,
But wreak thyself some wiser way;
And though the songs which I indite
Do quit thy change with rightful spite,
Blame not my lute!

Spite asketh spite, and changing change,
And falsed faith must needs be known;
The fault so great, the case so strange,
Of right it must abroad be blown;
Then since that by thine own desert
My songs do tell how true thou art,
Blame not my lute!

Blame but thy self that hast misdone
  And well deserved to have blame;
Change thou thy way, so evil begone,
  And then my lute shall sound that same;
But if till then my fingers play
By thy desert their wonted way,
          Blame not my lute!

Farewell, unknown! for though thou break
  My strings in spite with great disdain,
Yet have I found out, for thy sake,
  Strings for to string my lute again.
And if, perchance, this foolish rhyme
Do make thee blush at any time,
          Blame not my lute!

Addl. MS. 17492

45

Farewell

WHAT should I say,
  Since faith is dead,
And truth away
  From you is fled?
  Should I be led
    With doubleness?
    Nay, nay, mistress!

I promised you,
  And you promised me,
To be as true,
  As I would be.
  But since I see
    Your double heart,
    Farewell my part!

begone] conditioned   by] about

Though for to take
  It is not my mind,
But to forsake
  One so unkind,
  And as I find
    So will I trust,
    Farewell, unjust!

Can ye say nay,
  But that you said
That I alway
  Should be obeyed?
  And thus betrayed,
    Or that I wist,
    Farewell, unkissed!

Ibid.

46

To his Heart

AH! my heart, ah! what aileth thee
  To set so light by liberty,
Making me bond when I was free?
  Ah! my heart, ah! what aileth thee?

When thou were rid from all distress,
Void of all pain and pensiveness,
To choose again a new mistress,
  Ah! my heart, ah! what aileth thee?

When thou were well, thou could not hold;
To turn again, that were too bold.
Thus to renew my sorrows old,
  Ah! my heart, ah! what aileth thee?

or] before wist] knew

Thou knowest full well that but of late
I was turned out of Lovės gate,
And now to guide me to this mate!
  Ah! my heart, ah! what aileth thee?

I hoped full well all had been done,
But now my hope is ta'en and won,
To my torment to yield so soon,
  Ah! my heart, ah! what aileth thee?

Addl. MS. 17492

47

His Reward

WITH serving still
  This have I won,
For my goodwill
  To be undone.

And for redress
  Of all my pain,
Disdainfulness
  I have again.

And for reward
  Of all my smart,
Lo, thus unheard
  I must depart!

Wherefore all ye
  That after shall
By fortune be
  As I am, thrall,

Example take
  What I have won;
Thus for her sake
  To be undone!

Ibid.

48

Constancy

PERDY! I said it not,
  Nor never thought to do;
As well as I, ye wot,
  I have no power thereto;
And if I did, the lot
  That first did me enchain
Do never slack the knot,
  But strait it to my pain.

And if I did, each thing,
  That may do harm or woe,
Continually may wring
  My heart whereso I go.
Report may always ring
  Of shame of me for aye,
If in my heart did spring
  The word that ye do say.

If I said so, each star,
  That is in heaven above,
May frown on me to mar
  The hope I have in love;
And if I did, such war,
  As they brought out of Troy,
Bring all my life afar
  From all this lust and joy.

And if I did so say,
  The beauty that me bound
Increase from day to day
  More cruel to my wound,

strait] tighten

With all the moan that may,
  To plaint may turn my song;
My life may soon decay,
  Without redress, by wrong.

If I be clear fro thought,
  Why do ye then complain?
Then is this thing but sought
  To turn me to more pain.
Then that that ye have wrought,
  Ye must it now redress;
Of right therefore ye ought
  Such rigour to repress.

And as I have deserved,
  So grant me now my hire;
Ye know I never swerved,
  Ye never found me liar.
For Rachel have I served,
  (For Leah cared I never)
And her I have reserved
  Within my heart for ever.

Addl. MS. 17492

49 *Liberty*

TANGLED I was in lovės snare,
  Oppressed with pain, torment with care,
Of grief right sure, of joy full bare,
Clean in despair by cruelty.
But ha! ha! ha! full well is me,
For I am now at liberty.

The woeful day so full of pain,
The weary night all spent in vain,
The labour lost for so small gain;
To write them all it will not be.
But ha! ha! ha! full well is me,
For I am now at liberty.

Everything that fair doth show,
When proof is made it proveth not so,
But turneth mirth to bitter woe,
Which in this case full well I see.
But ha! ha! ha! full well is me,
For I am now at liberty.

Too great desire was my guide,
And wanton will went by my side;
Hope ruled still, and made me bide
Of lovės craft th' extremity.
But ha! ha! ha! full well is me,
For I am now at liberty.

With feigned words which were but wind,
To long delays I was assigned;
Her wily looks my wits did blind;
Thus as she would I did agree.
But ha! ha! ha! full well is me,
For I am now at liberty.

Was never bird tangled in lime,
That brake away in better time,
Than I, that rotten boughs did climb,
And had no hurt but 'scaped free.
Now ha! ha! ha! full well is me,
For I am now at liberty.

Ibid.

50 *Honesty*

THROUGHOUT the world if it were sought,
Fair words enough a man shall find;
They be good cheap, they cost right nought,
Their substance is but only wind.
But well to say, and so to mean,
That sweet accord is seldom seen.

Songes and Sonettes, Tottel, 1557

51 *Epitaph of Sir Thomas Gravener*

UNDER this stone there lieth at rest
A friendly man, a worthy knight,
Whose heart and mind was ever prest
To favour truth, to farther right.

The poor's defence, his neighbour's aid,
Most kind always unto his kin,
That stint all strife that might be stayed,
Whose gentle grace great love did win.

A man that was full earnest set
To serve his prince at all assays;
No sickness could him from that let,
Which was the shortening of his days.

His life was good, he died full well,
The body here, the soul in bliss.
With length of words why should I tell
Or farther show that well known is?
Since that the tears of more and less
Right well declare his worthiness.

Harleian MS. 78

cheap] merchandize prest] ready stint] spared let] hinder

52

Of the Courtier's Life

MINE own John Poins, since ye delight to know
  The cause why that homeward I me draw,
And fly the press of courts whereso they go,

Rather than to live thrall, under the awe
  Of lordly looks, wrapped within my cloak,
To will and lust learning to set a law;

It is not for because I scorn and mock
  The power of them, to whom fortune hath lent
Charge over us, of right, to strike the stroke.

But true it is that I have always meant
  Less to esteem them than the common sort,
Of outward things that judge in their intent,

Without regard what doth inward resort.
  I grant some time that of glory the fire
Doth touch my heart; me list not to report

Blame by honour, and honour to desire.
  But how may I this honour now attain,
That cannot dye the colour black a liar?

My Poins, I cannot frame my tune to feign,
  To cloak the truth for praise without desert
Of them that list all vice for to retain.

I cannot honour them that sets their part
  With Venus and Bacchus all their life long,
Nor hold my peace of them although I smart.

by honour] about honour

I cannot crouch nor kneel to do so great a wrong,
  To worship them, like God on earth alone,
That are as wolves these silly lambs among.

I cannot with wordės complain and moan,
  Nor suffer nought, nor smart without complaint,
Nor turn the word that from my mouth is gone.

I cannot speak and look like as a saint;
  Use wiles for wit, or make deceit a pleasure;
And call craft counsel, for profit still to paint.

I cannot wrest the law to fill the coffer
  With innocent blood to feed myself fat,
And do most hurt where that most help I offer.

I am not he that can allow the state
  Of high Caesar, and damn Cato to die,
That with his death did 'scape out of the gate

From Caesar's hands (if Livy do not lie),
  And would not live when liberty was lost;
So did his heart the common weal apply.

I am not he such eloquence to boast
  To make the crow in singing as the swan;
Nor call the lion of coward beasts the most,

That cannot take a mouse as the cat can;
  And he that dieth for hunger of the gold
Call him Alexander; and say that Pan

Passeth Apollo in music manifold;
  Praise Sir Topias for a noble tale,
And scorn the story that the knightė told;

Praise him for counsel that is drunk of ale,
  Grin when he laugheth that beareth all the sway,
Frown when he frowneth and groan when he is pale;

On others' lust to hang both night and day.
  None of these points would ever frame in me,
My wit is nought, I cannot learn the way.

And much the less of things that greater be,
  That asken help of colours of device
To join the mean with each extremity,

With the nearest virtue to cloak alway the vice.
  And as to purpose, likewise it shall fall
To press the virtue that it may not rise;

As drunkenness good fellowship to call;
  The friendly foe with his fair double face,
Say he is gentle, and courteous therewithal;

And say that favell hath a goodly grace
  In eloquence; and cruelty to name
Zeal of justice; and change in time and place;

And he that suffereth offence without blame
  Call him pitiful; and him true and plain
That raileth reckless to every man's shame;

Say he is rude that cannot lie and feign;
  The lecher a lover; and tyranny
To be the right of a prince's reign.

I cannot, I, no, no, it will not be!
  This is the cause that I could never yet
Hang on their sleeves that way, as thou mayst see.

purpose] conversation   favell] duplicity

A chip of chance more than a pound of wit;
  This maketh me at home to hunt and to hawk,
And in foul weather at my book to sit;

In frost and snow then with my bow to stalk.
  No man doth mark where so I ride or go;
In lusty leas at liberty I walk;

And of these news I feel nor weal nor woe,
  Save that a clog doth hang yet at my heel.
No force for that; for it is ordered so,

That I may leap both hedge and dyke full well.
  I am not now in France to judge the wine,
With savoury sauce the delicates to feel;

Nor yet in Spain where one must him incline,
  Rather than to be, outwardly to seem;
I meddle not with wits that be so fine.

Nor Flanders' cheer letteth not my sight to deem
  Of black and white, nor taketh my wit away
With beastliness; they beasts do so esteem.

Nor I am not where Christ is given in prey
  For money, poison and treason at Rome,
A common practice used night and day.

But here I am in Kent and Christendom,
  Among the Muses where I read and rhyme.
Where if thou list, my Poins, for to come,
  Thou shalt be judge how I do spend my time.

C.C.C.C. MS. 168

no force] it matters not

HENRY HOWARD, EARL OF SURREY

1517?–1547

53 *In Windsor Castle*

SO cruel prison how could betide, alas,
As proud Windsor, where I in lust and joy
With a king's son my childish years did pass
In greater feast than Priam's sons of Troy?
Where each sweet place returns a taste full sour;
The large green courts where we were wont to hove
With eyes cast up unto the maidens' tower,
And easy sighs, such as folk draw in love;
The stately sails, the ladies bright of hue,
The dances short, long tales of great delight,
With words and looks that tigers could but rue,
Where each of us did plead the other's right;
The palm-play where, despoiled for the game,
With dazed eyes oft we by gleams of love
Have missed the ball and got sight of our dame,
To bait her eyes, which kept the leads above;
The gravelled ground, with sleeves tied on the helm,
On foaming horse, with swords and friendly hearts,
With cheer, as though the one should overwhelm,
Where we have fought and chased oft with darts;
With silver drops the meads yet spread for ruth,
In active games of nimbleness and strength,
Where we did strain, trailed by swarms of youth,
Our tender limbs that yet shot up in length;
The secret groves which oft we made resound
Of pleasant plaint and of our ladies' praise,
Recording soft what grace each one had found,

What hope of speed, what dread of long delays;
The wild forest, the clothed holts with green,
With reins avaled, and swift ybreathed horse,
With cry of hounds and merry blasts between,
Where we did chase the fearful hart a force;
The void walls eke that harboured us each night,
Wherewith, alas! revive within my breast
The sweet accord, such sleeps as yet delight,
The pleasant dreams, the quiet bed of rest,
The secret thoughts imparted with such trust,
The wanton talk, the divers change of play,
The friendship sworn, each promise kept so just,
Wherewith we passed the winter nights away.
And with this thought the blood forsakes my face,
The tears berain my cheeks of deadly hue,
The which as soon as sobbing sighs, alas!
Upsupped have, thus I my plaint renew:
'O place of bliss, renewer of my woes,
Give me account where is my noble fere,
Whom in thy walls thou didst each night enclose,
To other lief, but unto me most dear.'
Echo, alas! that doth my sorrow rue,
Returns thereto a hollow sound of plaint.
Thus I alone, where all my freedom grew,
In prison pine with bondage and restraint;
And with remembrance of the greater grief
To banish the less, I find my chief relief.

Written 1542; *Addl. MS.* 36529

avaled] lowered a force] vigorous fere] comrades lief] beloved

54
The Cornet

I NEVER saw you, madam, lay apart
Your cornet black, in cold nor yet in heat,
Sith first ye knew of my desire so great,
Which other fancies chased clean from my heart.
Whiles to my self I did the thought reserve,
That so unware did wound my woeful breast,
Pity I saw within your heart did rest.
But since ye knew I did you love and serve,
Your golden tress was clad alway in black,
Your smiling looks were hid thus evermore,
All that withdrawn that I did crave so sore.
So doth this cornet govern me, alack!
In summer's sun, in winter breath of frost,
Of your fair eyes whereby the light is lost.

Ibid.

55
To His Lady

SET me whereas the sun doth parch the green,
Or where his beams may not dissolve the ice,
In temperate heat, where he is felt and seen,
With proud people, in presence sad and wise;
Set me in base, or yet in high degree,
In the long night, or in the shortest day,
In clear weather, or where mists thickest be,
In lofty youth, or when my hairs be gray;
Set me in earth, in heaven, or yet in hell,
In hill, in dale, or in the foaming flood,
Thrall, or at large, alive whereso I dwell,
Sick, or in health, in ill fame, or in good;
Yours will I be, and with that only thought
Comfort myself when that my hap is nought. *Ibid.*

cornet] horn-shaped head-dress sith] since

56

Spring

THE soote season, that bud and bloom forth brings,
With green hath clad the hill and eke the vale.
The nightingale with feathers new she sings;
The turtle to her make hath told her tale.
Summer is come, for every spray now springs.
The hart hath hung his old head on the pale;
The buck in brake his winter coat he flings;
The fishes float with new repaired scale;
The adder all her slough away she slings;
The swift swallow pursueth the flies small;
The busy bee her honey now she mings;
Winter is worn that was the flowers' bale.
And thus I see among these pleasant things
Each care decays; and yet my sorrow springs.

Songes and Sonettes, Tottel, 1557

57

Night

ALAS! so all things now do hold their peace,
Heaven and earth disturbed in no thing.
The beasts, the air, the birds their song do cease;
The nightės chare the stars about doth bring;
Calm is the sea; the waves work less and less.
So am not I, whom love, alas! doth wring,
Bringing before my face the great increase
Of my desires, whereat I weep and sing,
In joy and woe, as in a doubtful ease:
For my sweet thoughts sometime do pleasure bring;
But by and by, the cause of my disease
Gives me a pang, that inwardly doth sting,
When that I think what grief it is again,
To live and lack the thing should rid my pain. *Ibid.*

soote] sweet make] mate mings] remembers chare] chariot

58

Consolation

WHEN raging love with extreme pain
Most cruelly distrains my heart,
When that my tears, as floods of rain,
Bear witness of my woeful smart;
When sighs have wasted so my breath
That I lie at the point of death,

I call to mind the navy great
That the Greeks brought to Troyė town,
And how the boistous winds did beat
Their ships, and rent their sails adown;
Till Agamemnon's daughter's blood
Appeased the gods that them withstood.

And how that in those ten years' war
Full many a bloody deed was done,
And many a lord that came full far
There caught his bane, alas! too soon;
And many a good knight overrun,
Before the Greeks had Helen won.

Then think I thus: sith such repair,
So long time war of valiant men,
Was all to win a lady fair,
Shall I not learn to suffer then,
And think my life well spent to be,
Serving a worthier wight than she?

boistous] boisterous sith] since repair] coming

Therefore I never will repent,
But pains contented still endure;
For like as when, rough winter spent,
The pleasant spring straight draweth in ure,
So, after raging storms of care,
Joyful at length may be my fare.

Songes and Sonettes, Tottel, 1557

59 *Love's Rebel*

WHEN summer took in hand the winter to assail,
With force of might and virtue great his stormy blasts to quail,
And when he clothed fair the earth about with green,
And every tree new garmented, that pleasure was to seen,
Mine heart 'gan new revive, and changed blood did stur
Me to withdraw my winter woe, that kept within the door.
'Abroad!' quod my desire; 'assay to set thy foot,
Where thou shalt find the savour sweet; for sprung is every root.
And to thy health, if thou were sick in any case,
Nothing more good, than in the spring the air to feel a space.
There shalt thou hear and see all kinds of birds ywrought
Well tune their voice with warble small, as nature hath them taught.'
Thus pricked me my lust the sluggish house to leave,
And for my health I thought it best such counsel to receive.
So on a morrow forth, unwist of any wight,
I went to prove how well it would my heavy burden light.
And when I felt the air so pleasant round about,
Lord! to my self how glad I was that I had gotten out.
There might I see how Ver had every blossom hent,

ure] use   stur] stir   quod] quoth   unwist] unknown
hent] opened

And eke the new betrothed birds ycoupled how they went.
And in their songs methought they thanked nature much,
That by her licence all that year to love their hap was such,
Right as they could devise to choose them feres throughout.
With much rejoicing to their Lord thus flew they all about.
Which when I 'gan resolve, and in my head conceive
What pleasant life, what heaps of joy, these little birds receive,
And saw in what estate I, weary man, was brought,
By want of that they had at will, and I reject at nought,
Lord! how I 'gan in wrath unwisely me demean.
I cursed Love, and him defied; I thought to turn the stream.
But when I well beheld he had me under awe,
I asked mercy for my fault, that so transgressed his law.
'Thou blinded god,' (quod I) 'forgive me this offence;
Unwittingly I went about to malice thy pretence.'
Wherewith he gave a beck, and thus me thought he swore,
'Thy sorrow ought suffice to purge thy fault, if it were more.'
The virtue of which sound mine heart did so revive,
That I, methought, was made as whole as any man alive.
But here ye may perceive mine error, all and some,
For that I thought that so it was; yet was it still undone;
And all that was no more but mine impressed mind,
That fain would have some good relief of Cupid well assigned.
I turned home forthwith, and might perceive it well,
That he aggrieved was right sore with me for my rebel.
My harms have ever since increased more and more,
And I remain, without his help, undone for ever more.
A mirror let me be unto ye lovers all.
Strive not with Love; for if ye do, it will ye thus befall.

Ibid.

feres] mates   reject] rejected   demean] behave
malice] slight   rebel] rebellion

60 *The Seafarer*

O HAPPY dames, that may embrace
  The fruit of your delight,
Help to bewail the woeful case
  And eke the heavy plight
Of me, that wonted to rejoice
The fortune of my pleasant choice;
Good ladies, help to fill my mourning voice.

In ship, freight with rememberance
  Of thoughts and pleasures past,
He sails that hath in governance
  My life while it will last;
With scalding sighs, for lack of gale,
Furthering his hope, that is his sail,
Toward me, the sweet port of his avail.

Alas! how oft in dreams I see
  Those eyes that were my food;
Which sometime so delighted me,
  That yet they do me good;
Wherewith I wake with his return,
Whose absent flame did make me burn:
But when I find the lack, Lord, how I mourn!

When other lovers in arms across
  Rejoice their chief delight,
Drowned in tears, to mourn my loss
  I stand the bitter night
In my window, where I may see
Before the winds how the clouds flee.
Lo! what a mariner love hath made me!

avail] disembarking

And in green waves when the salt flood
   Doth rise by rage of wind,
A thousand fancies in that mood
   Assail my restless mind.
Alas! now drencheth my sweet foe,
That with the spoil of my heart did go,
And left me; but, alas! why did he so?

And when the seas wax calm again
   To chase fro me annoy,
My doubtful hope doth cause me plain;
   So dread cuts off my joy.
Thus is my wealth mingled with woe,
And of each thought a doubt doth grow;
'Now he comes! Will he come? Alas, no, no!'

Songes and Sonettes, Tottel, 1557

61 *His Incomparable Lady*

GIVE place, ye lovers, here before
   That spent your boasts and brags in vain;
My lady's beauty passeth more
   The best of yours, I dare well sayn,
Than doth the sun the candle-light,
Or brightest day the darkest night.

And thereto hath a troth as just
   As had Penelope the fair;
For what she saith, ye may it trust,
   As it by writing sealed were;
And virtues hath she many mo,
Than I with pen have skill to show.

drencheth] drowns   plain] to lament

I could rehearse, if that I would,
  The whole effect of Nature's plaint,
When she had lost the perfect mould,
  The like to whom she could not paint.
With wringing hands how she did cry,
And what she said, I know it, I.

I know she swore with raging mind,
  Her kingdom only set apart,
There was no loss, by law of kind,
  That could have gone so near her heart;
And this was chiefly all her pain,
She could not make the like again.

Sith Nature thus gave her the praise,
  To be the chiefest work she wrought;
In faith, methink, some better ways
  On your behalf might well be sought,
Than to compare, as ye have done,
To match the candle with the sun.

Songes and Sonettes, Tottel, 1557

62 *Martial's Quiet Life*

MY friend, the things that do attain
  The happy life be these, I find:
The riches left, not got with pain;
  The fruitful ground, the quiet mind;

The equal friend; no grudge, no strife;
  No charge of rule, nor governance;
Without disease the healthy life;
  The household of continuance;

sith] since

The mean diet, no dainty fare;
  Wisdom joined with simpleness;
The night discharged of all care,
  Where wine the wit may not oppress;

The faithful wife, without debate;
  Such sleeps as may beguile the night
Content thyself with thine estate;
  Neither wish death, nor fear his might.

W. Baldwin, *Treatise of Moral Philosophy*, 1547

63 *Dido's Hunting*

THEN from the sea the dawning 'gan arise.
The sun hoist up, the chosen youth 'gan throng
Unto the gates; the hayes so rarely knit,
The hunting-staves with their broad heads of iron,
And of Massile the horsemen, forth they break;
Of scenting hounds a kennel huge likewise.
And at the threshold of her chamber door
The Carthage lords did on their queen await;
The trampling steed, with gold and purple decked,
Fiercely stood chawing on the foaming bit.
Then issued she, awaited with a train,
Clad in a cloak of Tyre bordered full rich.
Her quiver hung behind her back, her tress
Knotted in gold, her purple vesture eke
Buttoned with gold. The Trojans of her train
Before her go, with gladsome Iulus.
Aeneas eke, the goodliest of the rout,
Makes one of them and joineth close the throngs.

hayes] nets   rout] troop

Like when Apollo leaveth Lycia,
His wintering place, and Xanthus' floods likewise,
To see Delos, his mother's mansion,
For to repair and furnish new her choir,
The Cretians and folk of Driopes
And painted Agathirth do howl and cry,
Environing the altars round about,
When that he walks upon Mount Cynthus' top,
His sparkled tress repressed with garlands soft
Of tender boughs, and tressed up in gold,
His quiver darts clattering behind his back:
So fresh and lusty did Aeneas seem;
Such loudly port in countenance doth show.
But to the hills and wild holts when they came,
From the rock's top the wild savage roës
Avail the hill, and on the other side,
Over the launds, they 'gan to take their course.
The harts likewise, in troops taking their flight,
Raising the dust, the mountains fast forsook.
The child Iulus, blithe of his swoft steed,
Amids the plain now pricks by them, now these,
And to encounter wisheth oft in mind
The foaming boar, instead of fearful beasts,
Or lion brown might from the hill descend.
In the meanwhile the heavens 'gan rumble sore;
In tail whereof a mingled shower with hail.
The Tyrian folk and scattered Trojan youth
And Venus' nephew the cottages for fear
Sought round about; the floods fell from the hills.
Queen Dido, with the Trojan prince alone,

sparkled] flowing avail] descend launds] lawns, open spaces swoft] swift

Chanced on a den. Our mother then, the earth,
And Juno, that hath charge of marriage,
First tokens gave with burning gledes of flame,
And, privy to the wedlock, lightning skies;
And the nymphs wailed from the mountain's top.
  Ay me! this was the foremost day of mirth,
And of mischief the first occasion eke.
Respect of fame no longer her withholds,
Ne museth she to frame her love by stealth.
Wedlock she calls it; under the pretence
Of which fair name she cloaketh now her fault.

Virgil, Aeneid, iv. 165–223; *Hargrave MS.* 205

ANONYMOUS

64 *Death*

O DEATH, rock me asleep,
  Bring me to quiet rest,
Let pass my weary guiltless ghost
  Out of my careful breast.
Toll on, thou passing bell;
Ring out my doleful knell;
Let thy sound my death tell.
  Death doth draw nigh;
  There is no remedy.

My pains who can express?
  Alas, they are so strong;
My dolour will not suffer strength
  My life for to prolong.

gledes] flashes

ANONYMOUS

Toll on, thou passing bell;
Ring out my doleful knell;
Let thy sound my death tell.
    Death doth draw nigh;
    There is no remedy.

Alone in prison strong
    I wait my destiny.
Woe worth this cruel hap that I
    Should taste this misery!
Toll on, thou passing bell;
Ring out my doleful knell;
Let thy sound my death tell.
    Death doth draw nigh;
    There is no remedy.

Farewell, my pleasures past,
    Welcome, my present pain!
I feel my torments so increase
    That life cannot remain.
Cease now, thou passing bell;
Rung is my doleful knell;
For the sound my death doth tell.
    Death doth draw nigh;
    There is no remedy.

Rimbault MS.

WILLIAM BALDWIN

15 ?–c. 1569

65 *The Beloved to the Spouse*

LO, thou, my Love, art fair!
Myself have made thee so;
Yea, thou art fair indeed,
Wherefore thou shalt not need
In beauty to despair;
For I accept thee so,
For fair.

For fair, because thine eyes
Are like the culvers white,
Whose simpleness in deed
All others do exceed:
Thy judgement wholly lies
In true sense of spright
Most wise.

Canticles of Solomon, 1549

66 *The Spouse to the Beloved*

CHRIST, my Beloved, which still doth feed
Among the flowers, having delight
Among his faithful lilies,
Doth take great care for me indeed,
And I again with all my might
Will do what so his will is.

culvers] doves

WILLIAM BALDWIN

My Love in me and I in him,
  Conjoined by love, will still abide
    Among the faithful lilies,
Till day do break, and truth do dim
  All shadows dark and cause them slide,
    According as his will is.

Canticles of Solomon, 1549

ANONYMOUS

67 *A Song of Ale*

Back and side go bare, go bare,
  Both hand and foot go cold,
But belly, God send thee good ale enough
  Whether it be new or old!

BUT if that I may have truly
  Good ale my belly full,
I shall look like one, by sweet Saint John,
  Were shorn against the wool.
Though I go bare, take you no care,
  I am nothing a-cold,
I stuff my skin so full within
  Of jolly good ale and old.

I cannot eat but little meat,
  My stomach is not good;
But sure I think that I could drink
  With him that weareth an hood.
Drink is my life; although my wife
  Some time do chide and scold,
Yet spare I not to ply the pot
  Of jolly good ale and old.

ANONYMOUS

I love no roast but a brown toast,
  Or a crab in the fire;
A little bread shall do me stead;
  Much bread I never desire.
Nor frost, nor snow, nor wind I trow,
  Can hurt me if it would,
I am so wrapped within and lapped
  With jolly good ale and old.

I care right nought, I take no thought
  For clothes to keep me warm;
Have I good drink, I surely think
  Nothing can do me harm:
For truly than I fear no man,
  Be he never so bold,
When I am armed and throughly warmed
  With jolly good ale and old.

But now and than I curse and ban,
  They make their ale so small;
God give them care and evil to fare!
  They stry the malt and all.
Such peevish pew, I tell you true,
  Not for a crown of gold,
There cometh one sip within my lip,
  Whether it be new or old.

Good ale and strong maketh me among
  Full jocund and full light,
That oft I sleep and take no keep
  From morning until night.

stry] destroy peevish pew] thin stuff among] at times

Then start I up and flee to the cup;
  The right way on I hold;
My thirst to staunch, I fill my paunch
  With jolly good ale and old.

And Kit my wife, that as her life
  Loveth well good ale to seek,
Full oft drinketh she, that ye may see
  The tears run down her cheek.
Then doth she troll to me the bowl,
  As a good malt-worm should,
And say 'Sweet-heart, I have take my part
  Of jolly good ale and old.'

They that do drink till they nod and wink,
  Even as good fellows should do,
They shall not miss to have the bliss,
  That good ale hath brought them to.
And all poor souls that scour black bowls,
  And them hath lustily trolled,
God save the lives of them and their wives,
  Whether they be young or old!

Dyce MS.

R. WEVER

temp. Edward VI

68 *Youth*

IN a herber green, asleep where I lay,
The birds sang sweet in the mids of the day;
I dreamed fast of mirth and play.
    In youth is pleasure, in youth is pleasure.

herber] arbour   mids] midst

Methought I walked still to and fro,
And from her company could not go;
But when I waked it was not so.
In youth is pleasure, in youth is pleasure.

Therefore my heart is surely pight
Of her alone to have a sight,
Which is my joy and heart's delight.
In youth is pleasure, in youth is pleasure.

Lusty Juventus, c. 1560

JOHN HARINGTON

c. 1554

69 *A Sonnet made on Isabella Markham, when I First Thought her Fair, as she Stood at the Princess's Window in Goodly Attire and Talked to Divers in the Court-Yard.*

WHENCE comes my love? O heart, disclose!
'Twas from cheeks that shame the rose,
From lips that spoil the ruby's praise,
From eyes that mock the diamond's blaze.
Whence comes my woe? As freely own,
Ah, me! 'twas from a heart like stone.

The blushing cheek speaks modest mind,
The lips befitting words most kind.
The eye does tempt to love's desire,
And seems to say 'tis Cupid's fire.
Yet all so fair but speak my moan,
Since nought doth say the heart of stone.

pight] fixed

JOHN HARINGTON

Why thus, my love, so kind bespeak
Sweet lip, sweet eye, sweet blushing cheek,
Yet not a heart to save my pain?
O Venus! take thy gifts again;
Make not so fair to cause our moan,
Or make a heart that 's like our own!

Nugae Antiquae, 1769

THOMAS, LORD VAUX

1510–1556

70 ### *The Image of Death*

I LOATHE that I did love,
  In youth that I thought sweet;
As time requires, for my behove,
  Methinks they are not meet.

My lusts they do me leave,
  My fancies all be fled,
And tract of time begins to weave
  Grey hairs upon my head.

For age with stealing steps
  Hath clawed me with his crutch,
And lusty life away she leaps,
  As there had been none such.

My Muse doth not delight
  Me as she did before;
My hand and pen are not in plight,
  As they have been of yore.

plight] condition

THOMAS, LORD VAUX

For reason me denies
  This youthly idle rhyme;
And day by day to me she cries,
  'Leave off these toys in time.'

The wrinkles in my brow,
  The furrows in my face,
Say, limping age will lodge him now
  Where youth must give him place.

The harbinger of death,
  To me I see him ride;
The cough, the cold, the gasping breath
  Doth bid me to provide

A pickaxe and a spade,
  And eke a shrouding sheet,
A house of clay for to be made
  For such a guest most meet.

Methinks I hear the clerk
  That knolls the careful knell,
And bids me leave my woeful work,
  Ere nature me compel.

My keepers knit the knot
  That youth did laugh to scorn,
Of me that clean shall be forgot,
  As I had not been born.

Thus must I youth give up,
  Whose badge I long did wear;
To them I yield the wanton cup,
  That better may it bear.

THOMAS, LORD VAUX

Lo, here the bared skull,
By whose bald sign I know
That stooping age away shall pull
That youthful years did sow.

For beauty with her band
These crooked cares hath wrought,
And shipped me into the land
From whence I first was brought.

And ye that bide behind,
Have ye none other trust;
As ye of clay were cast by kind,
So shall ye waste to dust.

Songes and Sonettes, Tottel, 1557

71 *Death in Life*

HOW can the tree but waste and wither away
That hath not sometime comfort of the sun?
How can that flower but fade and soon decay
That always is with dark clouds over-run?
Is this a life? Nay, death you may it call,
That feels each pain and knows no joy at all.

What foodless beast can live long in good plight?
Or is it life where senses there be none?
Or what availeth eyes without their light?
Or else a tongue to him that is alone?
Is this a life? Nay, death you may it call,
That feels each pain and knows no joy at all.

Whereto serve ears if that there be no sound?
  Or such a head where no device doth grow
But all of plaints, since sorrow is the ground
  Whereby the heart doth pine in deadly woe?
Is this a life? Nay, death you may it call,
That feels each pain and knows no joy at all.

Paradise of Dainty Devices, 1576

72

Content

WHEN all is done and said, in the end thus shall you find,
He most of all doth bathe in bliss that hath a quiet mind;
And, clear from worldly cares, to deem can be content
The sweetest time in all his life in thinking to be spent.

The body subject is to fickle Fortune's power,
And to a million of mishaps is casual every hour;
And death in time doth change it to a clod of clay;
Whenas the mind, which is divine, runs never to decay.

Companion none is like unto the mind alone,
For many have been harmed by speech; through thinking, few or none.
Fear oftentimes restraineth words, but makes not thoughts to cease;
And he speaks best that hath the skill when for to hold his peace.

Our wealth leaves us at death, our kinsmen at the grave;
But virtues of the mind unto the heavens with us we have.
Wherefore, for virtue's sake, I can be well content
The sweetest time of all my life to deem in thinking spent.

Ibid.

casual] liable

NICHOLAS GRIMALD

1519?–1562?

73

A Truelove

WHAT sweet relief the showers to thirsty plants we see,
What dear delight the blooms to bees, my truelove is to me.
As fresh and lusty Ver foul winter doth exceed,
As morning bright, with scarlet sky, doth pass the evening's weed,
As mellow pears above the crabs esteemed be,
So doth my love surmount them all, whom yet I hap to see.
The oak shall olives bear, the lamb the lion fray,
The owl shall match the nightingale in tuning of her lay,
Or I my love let slip out of mine entire heart,
So deep reposed in my breast is she, for her desert.
For many blessed gifts, O happy, happy land,
Where Mars and Pallas strive to make their glory most to stand,
Yet, land, more is thy bliss that in this cruel age
A Venus' imp thou hast brought forth, so steadfast and so sage.
Among the Muses nine, a tenth if Jove would make,
And to the Graces three a fourth, her would Apollo take.
Let some for honour hunt, and hoard the massy gold;
With her so I may live and die, my weal cannot be told.

Songes and Sonettes, Tottel, 1557

weed] raiment   fray] frighten   or] before   imp] child

74 *Virtue*

WHAT one art thou, thus in torn weed yclad?
'Virtue, in price whom ancient sages had.'
Why poorly 'rayed? 'For fading goods past care.'
Why double-faced? 'I mark each fortune's fare.'
This bridle, what? 'Mind's rages to restrain.'
Tools why bear you? 'I love to take great pain.'
Why wings? 'I teach above the stars to fly.'
Why tread you death? 'I only cannot die.'

Ibid.

ANONYMOUS

75 *Harpalus' Complaint of Phillida's Love*

PHILLIDA was a fair maid
And fresh as any flower,
Whom Harpalus, the herdman, prayed
To be his paramour.

Harpalus and eke Corin
Were herdmen both yfere;
And Phillida could twist and spin,
And thereto sing full clear.

But Phillida was all too coy
For Harpalus to win;
For Corin was her only joy,
Who forced her not a pin.

yfere] in company forced] cared for

How often would she flowers twine,
   How often garlands make
Of cowslips and of columbine,
   And all for Corin's sake!

But Corin he had hawks to lure,
   And forced more the field;
Of lovers' law he took no cure,
   For once he was beguiled.

Harpalus prevailed nought,
   His labour all was lost;
For he was farthest from her thought,
   And yet he loved her most.

Therefore waxed he both pale and lean,
   And dry as clot of clay;
His flesh it was consumed clean,
   His colour gone away.

His beard it had not long be shave,
   His hair hung all unkempt;
A man most fit even for the grave,
   Whom spiteful love had spent.

His eyes were red and all forwatched,
   His face besprent with tears;
It seemed unhap had him long hatched
   In mids of his despairs.

His clothes were black and also bare,
   As one forlorn was he;
Upon his head always he ware
   A wreath of willow tree.

forwatched] worn with watching   mids] midst

His beasts he kept upon the hill,
And he sate in the dale;
And thus, with sighs and sorrows shrill,
He gan to tell his tale:

'O Harpalus,' thus would he say,
'Unhappiest under sun,
The cause of thine unhappy day
By love was first begun;

'For thou went'st first by suit to seek
A tiger to make tame,
That sets not by thy love a leek,
But makes thy grief her game.

'As easy it were for to convert
The frost into the flame,
As for to turn a froward heart
Whom thou so fain wouldst frame.

'Corin he liveth carėless,
He leaps among the leaves;
He eats the fruits of thy redress;
Thou reaps, he takes the sheaves.

'My beasts, awhile your food refrain,
And hark your herdman's sound,
Whom spiteful love, alas, hath slain,
Throughgirt with many a wound.

'Oh, happy be ye, beastės wild,
That here your pasture takes;
I see that ye be not beguiled
Of these, your faithful makes.

makes] mates

'The hart he feedeth by the hind,
 The buck hard by the doe;
The turtle-dove is not unkind
 To him that loves her so;

'The ewe she hath by her the ram,
 The young cow hath the bull;
The calf, with many a lusty lamb,
 Do feed their hunger full.

'But, wellaway! that nature wrought
 Thee, Phillida, so fair;
For I may say that I have bought
 Thy beauty all too dear.

'What reason is it that cruelty
 With beauty should have part?
Or else that such great tyranny
 Should dwell in woman's heart?

'I see therefore to shape my death
 She cruelly is prest,
To th' end that I may want my breath;
 My days been at the best.

'O Cupid, grant this my request
 And do not stop thine ears,
That she may feel within her breast
 The pains of my despairs;

'Of Corin that is carêless
 That she may crave her fee,
As I have done, in great distress,
 That loved her faithfully.

prest] ready

'But since that I shall die her slave,
Her slave and eke her thrall,
Write you, my friends, upon my grave
This chance that is befall:

'Here lieth unhappy Harpalus
Whom cruel love hath slain,
By Phillida unjustly thus
Murdered with false disdain.'

Songes and Sonettes, Tottel, 1557

76 *The Seafarer*

SHALL I thus ever long, and be no whit the near?
And shall I still complain to thee, the which me will not hear?
Alas! say nay! say nay! and be no more so dumb,
But open thou thy manly mouth, and say that thou wilt come;
Whereby my heart may think, although I see not thee,
That thou wilt come (thy word so sware) if thou a live man be.
The roaring hugy waves they threaten my poor ghost,
And toss thee up and down the seas, in danger to be lost;
Shall they not make me fear that they have swallowed thee?
But as thou art most sure alive, so wilt thou come to me;
Whereby I shall go see thy ship ride on the strand,
And think and say 'Lo where he comes', and 'Sure here will he land';
And then I shall lift up to thee my little hand,
And thou shalt think thine heart in ease, in health to see me stand.
And if thou come indeed (as Christ thee send to do!)
Those arms which miss thee now, shall then embrace thee too;

Each vein to every joint the lively blood shall spread,
Which now, for want of thy glad sight, doth show full pale
and dead.
But if thou slip thy troth, and do not come at all,
As minutes in the clock do strike, so call for death I shall,
To please both thy false heart, and rid myself from woe,
That rather had to die in troth than live forsaken so.

Songes and Sonettes, Tottel, 1557

77 *On the Death of Phillips*

BEWAIL with me, all ye that have professed
Of music th' art by touch of cord or wind;
Lay down your lutes and let your gitterns rest,
Phillips is dead, whose like you can not find,
Of music much exceeding all the rest.
Muses, therefore of force now must you wrest
Your pleasant notes into an other sound;
The string is broke, the lute is dispossessed,
The hand is cold, the body in the ground.
The lowering lute lamenteth now therefore
Phillips her friend that can her touch no more.

Ibid.

78 *On Edward Seymour, Duke of Somerset*

EXPERIENCE now doth show what God us taught
before,
Desired pomp is vain and seldom doth it last;
Who climbs to reign with kings may rue his fate full sore;
Alas, the woeful end that comes with care full fast!
Reject him doth renown; his pomp full low is cast;
Deceived is the bird by sweetness of the call;
Expel that pleasant taste wherein is bitter gall.

Such as with oaten cakes in poor estate abides,
Of care have they no cure; the crab with mirth they roast.
More ease feel they than those that from their height down
 slides;
Excess doth breed their woe, they sail in Scylla's coast,
Remaining in the storms till ship and all be lost.
Serve God, therefore, thou poor, for lo! thou lives in rest;
Eschew the golden hall, thy thatched house is besT.

Ibid.

79 *On the Vanity of Man's Life*

VAIN is the fleeting wealth
 Whereon the world stays,
Sith stalking time by privy stealth
 Encroacheth on our days;

And eld, which creepeth fast
 To taint us with her wound,
Will turn each bliss unto a blast,
 Which lasteth but a stound.

Of youth the lusty flower,
 Which whilom stood in price,
Shall vanish quite within an hour,
 As fire consumes the ice.

Where is become that wight
 For whose sake Troyė town
Withstood the Greeks till ten years' fight
 Had razed their walls adown?

sith] since stound] moment

Did not the worms consume
  Her carrion to the dust?
Did dreadful death forbear his fume
  For beauty, pride, or lust?

Songes and Sonettes, Tottel, 1557

THOMAS SACKVILLE, EARL OF DORSET

1536–1608

80 *The Induction to the Mirror for Magistrates*

THE wrathful winter, 'proaching on apace,
  With blustering blasts had all ybared the treen,
And old Saturnus, with his frosty face,
  With chilling cold had pierced the tender green;
  The mantles rent, wherein enwrapped been
    The gladsome groves that now lay overthrown,
    The tapets torn, and every bloom down blown.

The soil, that erst so seemly was to seen,
  Was all despoiled of her beauty's hue;
And soote fresh flowers, wherewith the summer's queen
  Had clad the earth, now Boreas' blasts down blew;
  And small fowls flocking in their song did rue
    The winter's wrath, wherewith each thing defaced
    In woeful wise bewailed the summer past.

Hawthorn had lost his motley livery,
  The naked twigs were shivering all for cold,
And dropping down the tears abundantly;
  Each thing, methought, with weeping eye me told
  The cruel season, bidding me withhold
    Myself within; for I was gotten out
    Into the fields, whereas I walked about.

tapets] tapestries　　　soote] sweet

When lo! the night with misty mantles spread
  'Gan dark the day and dim the azure skies;
And Venus in her message Hermes sped
  To bloody Mars, to will him not to rise,
  While she herself approached in speedy wise;
    And Virgo, hiding her disdainful breast,
    With Thetis now had laid her down to rest.

Whiles Scorpio, dreading Sagittarius' dart,
  Whose bow prest bent in fight the string had slipped,
Down slid into the ocean flood apart,
  The Bear, that in the Irish seas had dipped
  His grisly feet, with speed from thence he whipped;
    For Thetis, hasting from the Virgin's bed,
    Pursued the Bear, that ere she came was fled.

And Phaethon now, near reaching to his race
  With glistering beams, gold streaming where they bent,
Was prest to enter in his resting place.
  Erythius, that in the cart first went,
  Had even now attained his journey's stent;
    And, fast declining, hid away his head,
    While Titan couched him in his purple bed.

And pale Cynthia, with her borrowed light,
  Beginning to supply her brother's place,
Was past the noonstead six degrees in sight,
  When sparkling stars amid the heaven's face
  With twinkling light shone on the earth apace,
    That, while they brought about the nightės chare,
    The dark had dimmed the day ere I was ware.

prest] ready stent] close chare] chariot

And sorrowing I to see the summer flowers,
The lively green, the lusty leas, forlorn,
The sturdy trees so shattered with the showers,
The fields so fade that flourished so beforn,
It taught me well all earthly things be born
To die the death, for nought long time may last;
The summer's beauty yields to winter's blast.

Then looking upward to the heaven's leams,
With nightės stars thick powdered everywhere,
Which erst so glistened with the golden streams
That cheerful Phoebus spread down from his sphere,
Beholding dark oppressing day so near;
The sudden sight reduced to my mind
The sundry changes that in earth we find:

That musing on this worldly wealth in thought,
Which comes and goes more faster than we see
The flickering flame that with the fire is wrought,
My busy mind presented unto me
Such fall of peers as in this realm had be,
That oft I wished some would their woes descrive,
To warn the rest whom fortune left alive.

And straight forth stalking with redoubled pace,
For that I saw the night drew on so fast,
In black all clad there fell before my face
A piteous wight, whom woe had all forwaste;
Forth from her eyne the crystal tears outbrast,
And sighing sore, her hands she wrung and fold,
Tare all her hair, that ruth was to behold.

leams] lights descrive] describe outbrast] outburst

Her body small, forwithered and forspent,
  As is the stalk that summer's drought oppressed;
Her welked face with woeful tears besprent,
  Her colour pale, and, as it seemed her best,
  In woe and plaint reposed was her rest;
    And as the stone that drops of water wears,
    So dented were her cheeks with fall of tears:

Her eyes swollen with flowing streams afloat;
  Wherewith, her looks thrown up full piteously,
Her forceless hands together oft she smote,
  With doleful shrieks that echoed in the sky;
  Whose plaint such sighs did straight accompany,
    That, in my doom, was never man did see
    A wight but half so woebegone as she.

I stood aghast, beholding all her plight,
  'Tween dread and dolour so distrained in heart
That, while my hairs upstarted with the sight,
  The tears outstreamed for sorrow of her smart;
  But when I saw no end that could apart
    The deadly dule which she so sore did make,
    With doleful voice then thus to her I spake:

'Unwrap thy woes, whatever wight thou be,
  And stint betime to spill thyself with plaint;
Tell what thou art, and whence, for well I see
  Thou canst not dure, with sorrow thus attaint.'
  And with that word of sorrow, all forfaint
    She looked up, and prostrate as she lay,
    With piteous sound, lo, thus she 'gan to say:

welked] wrinkled   doom] opinion   dule] woe   stint] cease
spill] destroy

'Alas! I wretch whom thus thou seest distrained
With wasting woes that never shall aslake,
Sorrow I am, in endless torments pained
Among the Furies in the infernal lake,
Where Pluto, god of Hell, so grisly black,
Doth hold his throne, and Lethe's deadly taste
Doth reave remembrance of each thing forepast.

'Whence come I am, the dreary destiny
And luckless lot for to bemoan of those
Whom Fortune, in this maze of misery,
Of wretched chance most woeful mirrors chose;
That when thou seest how lightly they did lose
Their pomp, their power, and that they thought most sure,
Thou mayst soon deem no earthly joy may dure.'

Whose rueful voice no sooner had out brayed
Those woeful words wherewith she sorrowed so,
But out, alas, she shright and never stayed,
Fell down, and all to-dashed herself for woe:
The cold pale dread my limbs 'gan overgo,
And I so sorrowed at her sorrows eft
That, what with grief and fear, my wits were reft.

I stretched myself and straight my heart revives,
That dread and dolour erst did so appale;
Like him that with the fervent fever strives,
When sickness seeks his castle health to scale,
With gathered spirits so forced I fear to avale;
And rearing her with anguish all fordone,
My spirits returned and then I thus begun:

reave] rob brayed] ejaculated shright] shrieked
eft] again avale] sink

THOMAS SACKVILLE, EARL OF DORSET

'O Sorrow, alas! sith Sorrow is thy name,
And that to thee this drear doth well pertain,
In vain it were to seek to cease the same;
But as a man himself with sorrow slain,
So I, alas, do comfort thee in pain,
That here in sorrow art forsunk so deep
That at thy sight I can but sigh and weep.'

I had no sooner spoken of a sike,
But that the storm so rumbled in her breast,
As Aeolus could never roar the like;
And showers down rained from her eyne so fast
That all bedrent the place, till at the last
Well eased they the dolour of her mind,
As rage of rain doth swage the stormy wind.

For forth she paced in her fearful tale:
'Come, come,' quod she, 'and see what I shall show;
Come hear the plaining and the bitter bale
Of worthy men by Fortune's overthrow;
Come thou and see them rueing all in row.
They were but shades that erst in mind thou rolled;
Come, come with me, thine eyes shall them behold.'

What could these words but make me more aghast,
To hear her tell whereon I mused while ere?
So was I mazed therewith, till at the last,
Musing upon her words, and what they were,
All suddenly well lessoned was my fear;
For to my mind returned how she telled
Both what she was and where her wone she held.

sike] sigh bedrent] drenched swage] assuage wone] abode

Whereby I knew that she a goddess was,
And therewithal resorted to my mind
My thought, that late presented me the glass
Of brittle state, of cares that here we find,
Of thousand woes to silly men assigned;
And how she now bid me come and behold,
To see with eye that erst in thought I rolled.

Flat down I fell, and with all reverence
Adored her, perceiving now that she,
A goddess sent by godly providence,
In earthly shape thus showed herself to me,
To wail and rue this world's uncertainty;
And while I honoured thus her godhead's might,
With plaining voice these words to me she shright:

'I shall thee guide first to the grisly lake
And thence unto the blissful place of rest,
Where thou shalt see and hear the plaint they make
That whilom here bare swing among the best;
This shalt thou see, but great is the unrest
That thou must bide before thou canst attain
Unto the dreadful place where these remain.'

And with these words, as I upraised stood,
And 'gan to follow her that straight forth paced,
Ere I was ware, into a desert wood
We now were come, where, hand in hand embraced,
She led the way and through the thick so traced
As, but I had been guided by her might,
It was no way for any mortal wight.

swing] sway

THOMAS SACKVILLE, EARL OF DORSET

But lo, while thus amid the desert dark
  We passed on with steps and pace unmeet,
A rumbling roar, confused with howl and bark
  Of dogs, shook all the ground under our feet,
  And struck the din within our ears so deep
    As, half distraught, unto the ground I fell,
    Besought return, and not to visit hell.

But she, forthwith uplifting me apace,
  Removed my dread, and with a steadfast mind
Bade me come on, for here was now the place,
  The place where we our travail end should find;
  Wherewith I arose, and to the place assigned
    Astoined I stalk, when straight we approached near
    The dreadful place that you will dread to hear.

An hideous hole all vast, withouten shape,
  Of endless depth, o'erwhelmed with ragged stone,
With ugly mouth and grisly jaws doth gape,
  And to our sight confounds itself in one.
  Here entered we, and yeding forth, anon
    An horrible loathly lake we might discern,
    As black as pitch, that cleped is Averne:

A deadly gulf where nought but rubbish grows,
  With foul black swelth in thickened lumps that lies,
Which up in the air such stinking vapours throws
  That over there may fly no fowl but dies,
  Choked with the pestilent savours that arise;
    Hither we come, whence forth we still did pace,
    In dreadful fear amid the dreadful place.

astoined] astonished yeding] going cleped] called swelth] filth

And first, within the porch and jaws of hell,
  Sat deep Remorse of Conscience, all besprent
With tears, and to herself oft would she tell
  Her wretchedness, and cursing never stent
  To sob and sigh, but ever thus lament
    With thoughtful care as she that, all in vain,
    Would wear and waste continually in pain.

Her eyes unsteadfast, rolling here and there,
  Whirled on each place, as place that vengeance brought,
So was her mind continually in fear,
  Tossed and tormented with the tedious thought
  Of those detested crimes which she had wrought;
    With dreadful cheer and looks thrown to the sky,
    Wishing for death, and yet she could not die.

Next saw we Dread, all trembling how he shook,
  With foot uncertain proffered here and there,
Benumbed of speech, and with a ghastly look
  Searched every place, all pale and dead for fear,
  His cap borne up with staring of his hair,
    'Stoined and amazed at his own shade for dread,
    And fearing greater dangers than was need.

And next, within the entry of this lake,
  Sat fell Revenge, gnashing her teeth for ire,
Devising means how she may vengeance take,
  Never in rest till she have her desire;
  But frets within so far forth with the fire
    Of wreaking flames, that now determines she
    To die by death, or venged by death to be.

besprent] sprinkled

THOMAS SACKVILLE, EARL OF DORSET

When fell Revenge, with bloody foul pretence,
  Had showed herself as next in order set,
With trembling limbs we softly parted thence,
  Till in our eyes another sight we met,
  When from my heart a sigh forthwith I fet,
    Rueing, alas, upon the woeful plight
    Of Misery, that next appeared in sight.

His face was lean and somedeal pined away,
  And eke his hands consumed to the bone,
But what his body was I cannot say,
  For on his carcass raiment had he none,
  Save clouts and patches, pieced one by one;
    With staff in hand and scrip on shoulders cast,
    His chief defence against the winter's blast.

His food, for most, was wild fruits of the tree,
  Unless sometimes some crumbs fell to his share,
Which in his wallet long, God wot, kept he,
  As on the which full daintily would he fare;
  His drink, the running stream; his cup, the bare
    Of his palm closed; his bed, the hard cold ground;
    To this poor life was Misery ybound.

Whose wretched state when we had well beheld,
  With tender ruth on him and on his fears,
In thoughtful cares forth then our pace we held;
  And by and by another shape appears,
  Of greedy Care, still brushing up the breres,
    His knuckles knobbed, his flesh deep dented in,
    With tawed hands and hard ytanned skin.

fet] fetched   somedeal] somewhat   tawed] hardened

THOMAS SACKVILLE, EARL OF DORSET

The morrow gray no sooner hath begun
 To spread his light, even peeping in our eyes,
When he is up and to his work yrun;
 But let the night's black misty mantles rise,
 And with foul dark never so much disguise
  The fair bright day, yet ceaseth he no while,
  But hath his candles to prolong his toil.

By him lay heavy Sleep, the cousin of Death,
 Flat on the ground and still as any stone,
A very corpse, save yielding forth a breath.
 Small keep took he whom Fortune frowned on
 Or whom she lifted up into the throne
  Of high renown; but as a living death,
  So, dead alive, of life he drew the breath.

The body's rest, the quiet of the heart,
 The travail's ease, the still night's fere was he,
And of our life in earth the better part;
 Reaver of sight, and yet in whom we see
 Things oft that tide, and oft that never be;
  Without respect esteeming equally
  King Croesus' pomp and Irus' poverty.

And next in order sad Old Age we found,
 His beard all hoar, his eyes hollow and blind,
With drooping cheer still poring on the ground,
 As on the place where nature him assigned
 To rest, when that the sisters had untwined
  His vital thread and ended with their knife
  The fleeting course of fast declining life.

fere] companion

There heard we him with broken and hollow plaint
  Rue with himself his end approaching fast,
And all for nought his wretched mind torment
  With sweet remembrance of his pleasures past,
  And fresh delights of lusty youth forewaste;
    Recounting which, how would he sob and shriek,
    And to be young again of Jove beseek!

But, and the cruel fates so fixed be
  That time forepast cannot return again,
This one request of Jove yet prayed he,
  That in such withered plight and wretched pain
  As eld, accompanied with his loathsome train,
    Had brought on him, all were it woe and grief,
    He might a while yet linger forth his life:

And not so soon descend into the pit
  Where Death, when he the mortal corpse hath slain,
With reckless hand in grave doth cover it,
  Thereafter never to enjoy again
  The gladsome light, but in the ground ylain,
    In depth of darkness waste and wear to nought,
    As he had never into the world been brought.

But who had seen him sobbing, how he stood
  Unto himself and how he would bemoan
His youth forepast, as though it wrought him good
  To talk of youth, all were his youth foregone,
  He would have mused and marvelled much, whereon
    This wretched Age should life desire so fain,
    And knows full well life doth but length his pain.

beseek] beseech   but, and] but, if

Crookbacked he was, tooth-shaken, and blear-eyed,
  Went on three feet, and sometime crept on four,
With old lame bones that rattled by his side,
  His scalp all pilled and he with eld forlore;
  His withered fist still knocking at Death's door,
    Fumbling and drivelling as he draws his breath;
    For brief, the shape and messenger of Death.

And fast by him pale Malady was placed,
  Sore sick in bed, her colour all foregone,
Bereft of stomach, savour, and of taste,
  Ne could she brook no meat, but broths alone;
  Her breath corrupt, her keepers every one
    Abhorring her, her sickness past recure,
    Detesting physic and all physic's cure.

But oh, the doleful sight that then we see!
  We turned our look and on the other side
A grisly shape of Famine mought we see,
  With greedy looks and gaping mouth that cried
  And roared for meat, as she should there have died;
    Her body thin and bare as any bone,
    Whereto was left nought but the case alone.

And that, alas, was gnawn on everywhere,
  All full of holes, that I ne mought refrain
From tears to see how she her arms could tear,
  And with her teeth gnash on the bones in vain,
  When all for nought she fain would so sustain
    Her starven corpse, that rather seemed a shade
    Than any substance of a creature made.

pilled] bald   recure] remedy   mought] might

Great was her force, whom stone wall could not stay,
  Her tearing nails snatching at all she saw;
With gaping jaws that by no means ymay
  Be satisfied from hunger of her maw,
  But eats herself as she that hath no law;
    Gnawing, alas, her carcass all in vain,
    Where you may count each sinew, bone, and vein.

On her while we thus firmly fixed our eyes,
  That bled for ruth of such a dreary sight,
Lo, suddenly she shright in so huge wise,
  As made hell gates to shiver with the might;
  Wherewith a dart we saw, how it did light
    Right on her breast, and therewithal pale Death
    Enthrilling it, to reave her of her breath.

And by and by a dumb dead corpse we saw,
  Heavy and cold, the shape of Death aright,
That daunts all earthly creatures to his law;
  Against whose force in vain it is to fight;
  Ne peers, ne princes, nor no mortal wight,
    No towns, ne realms, cities, ne strongest tower,
    But all, perforce, must yield unto his power.

His dart, anon, out of the corpse he took,
  And in his hand, a dreadful sight to see,
With great triumph eftsoons the same he shook,
  That most of all my fears affrayed me;
  His body dight with nought but bones, perdy,
    The naked shape of man there saw I plain,
    All save the flesh, the sinew, and the vein.

enthrilling] piercing

THOMAS SACKVILLE, EARL OF DORSET

Lastly, stood War, in glittering arms yclad,
  With visage grim, stern looks, and blackly hued;
In his right hand a naked sword he had,
  That to the hilts was all with blood imbrued;
  And in his left, that kings and kingdoms rued,
    Famine and fire he held, and therewithal
    He razed towns and threw down towers and all.

Cities he sacked and realms, that whilom flowered
  In honour, glory, and rule above the best,
He overwhelmed and all their fame devoured,
  Consumed, destroyed, wasted, and never ceased,
  Till he their wealth, their name, and all oppressed;
    His face forhewed with wounds, and by his side
    There hung his targe, with gashes deep and wide.

In midst of which, depainted there, we found
  Deadly Debate, all full of snaky hair,
That with a bloody fillet was ybound,
  Out-breathing nought but discord everywhere.
  And round about were portrayed, here and there,
    The hugy hosts, Darius and his power,
    His kings, princes, his peers, and all his flower:

Whom great Macedo vanquished there in fight
  With deep slaughter, despoiling all his pride,
Pierced through his realms and daunted all his might.
  Duke Hannibal beheld I there beside,
  In Canna's field victor how he did ride,
    And woeful Romans that in vain withstood,
    And consul Paulus covered all in blood.

THOMAS SACKVILLE, EARL OF DORSET

Yet saw I more: the fight at Thrasimene,
  And Trebery field, and eke when Hannibal
And worthy Scipio last in arms were seen
  Before Carthago gate, to try for all
  The world's empire, to whom it should befall;
    There saw I Pompey and Caesar clad in arms,
    Their hosts allied and all their civil harms:

With conquerors' hands, forbathed in their own blood,
  And Caesar weeping over Pompey's head.
Yet saw I Sulla and Marius where they stood,
  Their great cruelty and the deep bloodshed
  Of friends; Cyrus I saw and his host dead,
    And how the queen with great despite hath flung
    His head in blood of them she overcome.

Xerxes, the Persian king, yet saw I there
  With his huge host that drank the rivers dry,
Dismounted hills, and made the vales uprear,
  His host and all yet saw I plain, perdy!
  Thebês I saw, all razed how it did lie
    In heaps of stones, and Tyrus put to spoil,
    With walls and towers flat evened with the soil.

But Troy, alas! methought, above them all,
  It made mine eyes in very tears consume,
When I beheld the woeful weird befall,
  That by the wrathful will of gods was come;
  And Jove's unmoved sentence and foredoom
    On Priam king and on his town so bent,
    I could not lin, but I must there lament.

lin] cease

And that the more, sith destiny was so stern
  As, force perforce, there might no force avail,
But she must fall, and by her fall we learn
  That cities, towers, wealth, world, and all shall quail.
  No manhood, might, nor nothing mought prevail;
    All were there prest full many a prince and peer,
    And many a knight that sold his death full dear:

Not worthy Hector, worthiest of them all,
  Her hope, her joy; his force is now for nought.
O Troy, Troy, Troy, there is no boot but bale;
  The hugy horse within thy walls is brought;
  Thy turrets fall, thy knights, that whilom fought
    In arms amid the field, are slain in bed,
    Thy gods defiled and all thy honour dead.

The flames upspring and cruelly they creep
  From wall to roof till all to cinders waste;
Some fire the houses where the wretches sleep,
  Some rush in here, some run in there as fast;
  In every where or sword or fire they taste;
    The walls are torn, the towers whirled to the ground;
    There is no mischief but may there be found.

Cassandra yet there saw I how they haled
  From Pallas' house, with spercled tress undone,
Her wrists fast bound, and with Greeks' rout empaled;
  And Priam eke, in vain how did he run
  To arms, whom Pyrrhus with despite hath done
    To cruel death, and bathed him in the baign
    Of his son's blood, before the altar slain.

prest] ready   spercled] flowing   rout] troop
empaled] hemmed in   baign] bath

But how can I describe the doleful sight
  That in the shield so livelike fair did shine?
Sith in this world I think was never wight
  Could have set forth the half, not half so fine.
  I can no more but tell how there is seen
    Fair Ilium fall in burning red gledes down,
    And from the soil great Troy, Neptunus' town.

Herefrom when scarce I could mine eyes withdraw,
  That filled with tears as doth the springing well,
We passed on so far forth till we saw
  Rude Acheron, a loathsome lake to tell,
  That boils and bubs up swelth as black as hell;
    Where grisly Charon, at their fixed tide,
    Still ferries ghosts unto the farther side.

The aged god no sooner Sorrow spied,
  But hasting straight unto the bank apace,
With hollow call unto the rout he cried
  To swerve apart and give the goddess place.
  Straight it was done, when to the shore we pace,
    Where, hand in hand as we then linked fast,
    Within the boat we are together placed.

And forth we launch full fraughted to the brink,
  When with the unwonted weight the rusty keel
Began to crack as if the same should sink.
  We hoise up mast and sail, that in a while
  We fet the shore, where scarcely we had while
    For to arrive, but that we heard anon
    A three-sound bark confounded all in one.

gledes] glowing ashes   bubs] bubbles

We had not long forth passed but that we saw
  Black Cerberus, the hideous hound of hell,
With bristles reared and with a three-mouthed jaw
  Fordinning the air with his horrible yell,
  Out of the deep dark cave where he did dwell.
    The goddess straight he knew, and by and by,
    He 'peased and couched while that we passed by.

Thence come we to the horror and the hell,
  The large great kingdoms and the dreadful reign
Of Pluto in his throne where he did dwell,
  The wide waste places and the hugy plain,
  The wailings, shrieks, and sundry sorts of pain,
    The sighs, the sobs, the deep and deadly groan,
    Earth, air, and all, resounding plaint and moan.

Here puled the babes, and here the maids unwed
  With folded hands their sorry chance bewailed,
Here wept the guiltless slain, and lovers dead,
  That slew themselves when nothing else availed;
  A thousand sorts of sorrow here, that wailed
    With sighs and tears, sobs, shrieks, and all yfere,
    That oh, alas, it was a hell to hear.

We stayed us straight, and with a rueful fear
  Beheld this heavy sight, while from mine eyes
The vapoured tears downstilled here and there,
  And Sorrow eke, in far more woeful wise,
  Took on with plaint, upheaving to the skies
    Her wretched hands, that with her cry the rout
    'Gan all in heaps to swarm us round about.

yfere] together

THOMAS SACKVILLE, EARL OF DORSET

Lo here, quod Sorrow, princes of renown,
  That whilom sat on top of Fortune's wheel,
Now laid full low, like wretches whirled down,
  Even with one frown, that stayed but with a smile;
  And now behold the thing that thou, erewhile,
    Saw only in thought, and what thou now shalt hear,
    Recount the same to kesar, king, and peer.

A Mirror for Magistrates, Induction, 1563

RICHARD EDWARDES

c. 1523–1566

81 *Amantium Irae Amoris Redintegratio*

IN going to my naked bed as one that would have slept,
I heard a wife sing to her child, that long before had wept.
She sighed sore and sang full sweet to bring the babe to rest,
That would not rest, but cried still, in sucking at her breast.
She was full weary of her watch and grieved with her child,
She rocked it and rated it until on her it smiled.
Then did she say, 'Now have I found the proverb true to prove,
The falling out of faithful friends is the renewing of love.'

Then took I paper, pen, and ink, this proverb for to write,
In register for to remain of such a worthy wight.
As she proceeded thus in song unto her little brat,
Much matter uttered she of weight, in place whereas she sat;
And proved plain there was no beast, nor creature bearing life,
Could well be known to live in love without discord and strife.
Then kissed she her little babe and sware by God above,
'The falling out of faithful friends is the renewing of love.'

She said that neither king, ne prince, ne lord could live aright,
Until their puissance they did prove, their manhood, and
their might;
When manhood shall be matched so that fear can take no
place,
Then weary works makes warriors each other to embrace,
And leave their force that failed them, which did consume the
rout,
That might before have lived their time and nature out.
Then did she sing as one that thought no man could her
reprove,
'The falling out of faithful friends is the renewing of love.'

She said she saw no fish, ne fowl, nor beast within her haunt
That met a stranger in their kind, but could give it a taunt.
Since flesh might not endure, but rest must wrath succeed,
And force the fight to fall to play in pasture where they feed,
So noble nature can well end the works she hath begun,
And bridle well that will not cease, her tragedy in some.
Thus in her song she oft rehearsed, as did her well behove,
'The falling out of faithful friends is the renewing of love.'

'I marvel much, perdy!' (quoth she), 'for to behold the rout,
To see man, woman, boy, and beast, to toss the world about.
Some kneel, some crouch, some beck, some check, and some
can smoothly smile,
And some embrace others in arms, and there think many a
wile.
Some stand aloof at cap and knee, some humble and some stout,
Yet are they never friends indeed until they once fall out.'
Thus ended she her song, and said, before she did remove,
'The falling out of faithful friends is the renewing of love.'

Paradise of Dainty Devices, 1576

82 *May*

WHEN May is in his prime, then may each heart rejoice;
When May bedecks each branch with green, each bird strains forth his voice.
The lively sap creeps up into the blooming thorn;
The flowers, which cold in prison kept, now laughs the frost to scorn.
All nature's imps triumphs whiles joyful May doth last;
When May is gone, of all the year the pleasant time is past.

May makes the cheerful hue, May breeds and brings new blood;
May marcheth through every limb, May makes the merry mood.
May pricketh tender hearts their warbling notes to tune;
Full strange it is, yet some we see do make their May in June.
Thus things are strangely wrought whiles joyful May doth last;
Take May in time, when May is gone the pleasant time is past.

All ye that live on earth, and have your May at will,
Rejoice in May, as I do now, and use your May with skill.
Use May while that you may, for May hath but his time,
When all the fruit is gone, it is too late the tree to climb.
Your liking and your lust is fresh whiles May doth last;
When May is gone, of all the year the pleasant time is past.

Ibid.

ARTHUR GOLDING

c. 1536–c. 1605

83 *Philemon and Baucis*

UPON the hills of Phrygie near a teyle there stands a tree
Of oak enclosed with a wall. Myself the place did see.
For Pithey unto Pelops' fields did send me where his father
Did sometime reign. Not far fro thence there is a pool which
rather
Had been dry ground inhabited. But now it is a mere,
And moorcocks, coots, and cormorants do breed and nestle
there.
The mighty Jove and Mercury his son in shape of men
Resorted thither on a time. A thousand houses when
For room to lodge in they had sought, a thousand houses
barred
Their doors against them. Ne'ertheless one cottage afterward
Received them, and that was but a pelting one indeed.
The roof thereof was thatched all with straw and fennish reed.
Howbeit two honest ancient folk (of whom she Baucis hight
And he Philemon) in that cote their faith in youth had plight;
And in that cote had spent their age. And for they patiently
Did bear their simple poverty, they made it light thereby,
And showed it no thing to be repined at at all.
It skills not whether there for hinds or master you do call,
For all the household were but two; and both of them obeyed,
And both commanded. When the gods at this same cottage
stayed,
And ducking down their heads, within the low made wicket
came,
Philemon, bringing each a stool, bade rest upon the same

teyle] lime-tree   rather] formerly   pelting] petty

Their limbs; and busy Baucis brought them cushions, homely gear.
Which done, the embers on the hearth she 'gan abroad to stir,
And laid the coals together that were raked up overnight,
And with the brands and dried leaves did make them gather might,
And with the blowing of her mouth did make them kindle bright.
Then from an inner house she fetched sere sticks and clifted brands,
And put them broken underneath a skillet with her hands.
Her husband from their garden plot fetched coleworts. Of the which
She shredded small the leaves, and with a fork took down a flitch
Of resty bacon from the balk made black with smoke, and cut
A piece thereof, and in the pan to boiling did it put.
And while this meat a-seething was, the time in talk they spent,
By means whereof away without much tediousness it went.
There hung a bowl of beech upon a spirget by a ring.
The same with warmed water filled the two old folk did bring
To bathe their guests' foul feet therein. Amid the house there stood
A couch, whose bottom, sides, and feet were all of sallow wood,
And on the same a mat of sedge. They cast upon this bed
A covering which was never wont upon it to be spread,
Except it were at solemn feasts; and yet the same was old
And of the coarsest, with a bed of sallow meet to hold.
The gods sat down. The aged wife, right chare and busy as
A bee, set out a table, of the which the third foot was

skillet] pan resty] rancid balk] beam
spirget] peg chare] careful

A little shorter than the rest. A tilesherd made it even
And took away the shoringness; and when they had it driven
To stand up level, with green mints they by and by it wiped.
Then set they on it Pallas' fruit with double colour striped,
And cornels kept in pickle moist, and endive, and a root
Of radish, and a jolly lump of butter fresh and soote,
And eggs rare roasted. All these cates in earthen dishes came.
Then set they down a graven cup made also of the same
Self kind of plate, and mazers made of beech, whose inner side
Was rubbed with yellow wax. And when they paused had a tide,
Hot meat came piping from the fire. And shortly thereupon
A cup of green hedge wine was brought. This ta'en away, anon
Came in the latter course, which was of nuts, dates, dried figs,
Sweet-smelling apples in a maund made flat of osier twigs,
And prunes and plums and purple grapes cut newly from the tree,
And in the mids a honeycomb new taken from the bee.
Besides all this there did ensue good countenance overmore,
With will not poor nor niggardly. Now all the while before,
As often as Philemon and Dame Baucis did perceive
The empty cup to fill alone, and wine to still receive,
Amazed at the strangeness of the thing, they 'gan straightway
With fearful hearts and hands held up to frame themselves to pray,
Desiring for their slender cheer and fare to pardoned be.
They had but one poor goose, which kept their little tenantry,
And this to offer to the gods their guests they did intend.
The gander wight of wing did make the slow old folk to spend

shoringness] slant   cornels] wild berries   rare] lightly
mazers] cups   maund] basket   wight] quick

Their pains in vain, and mocked them long. At length he
seemed to fly
For succour to the gods themselves, who bade he should not die.
'For we be gods' (quoth they) 'and all this wicked township shall
Aby their guilt. On you alone this mischief shall not fall.
No more, but give you up your house, and follow up this hill
Together, and upon the top thereof abide our will.'
They both obeyed. And as the gods did lead the way before,
They lagged slowly after with their staves, and laboured sore
Against the rising of the hill. They were not mickle more
Than full a flightshot from the top, when looking back they
saw
How all the town was drowned save their little shed of straw.
And as they wondered at the thing and did bewail the case
Of those that had their neighbours been, the old poor cote so
base,
Whereof they had been owners erst, became a church. The
props
Were turned into pillars huge; the straw upon the tops
Was yellow, so that all the roof did seem of burnished gold;
The floor with marble paved was; the doors on either fold
Were graven. At the sight hereof Philemon and his make
Began to pray in fear. Then Jove thus gently them bespake:
'Declare thou righteous man, and thou O woman meet to have
A righteous husband, what ye would most chiefly wish or
crave.'
Philemon, taking conference a little with his wife,
Declared both their meanings thus: 'We covet during life,
Your chaplains for to be, to keep your temple. And because
Our years in concord we have spent, I pray, when death near
draws,

aby] abide, pay for make] mate

Let both of us together leave our lives; that neither I
Behold my wife's decease, nor she see mine when I do die.'
Their wish had sequel to their will. As long as life did last,
They kept the church. And being spent with age of years forepast,
By chance as standing on a time without the temple door
They told the fortune of the place, Philemon old and poor
Saw Baucis flourish green with leaves, and Baucis saw likewise
Philemon branching out in boughs and twigs before her eyes.
And as the bark did overgrow the heads of both, each spake
To other while they might. At last they each of them did take
Their leave of other both at once, and therewithal the bark
Did hide their faces both at once. The Phrygians in that park
Do at this present day still show the trees that shaped were
Of their two bodies, growing yet together jointly there.
These things did ancient men report, of credit very good;
For why there was no cause why they should lie. As I there stood,
I saw the garlands hanging on the boughs, and adding new
I said, 'Let them, whom God doth love, be gods, and honour due
Be given to such as honour him with fear and reverence true.'

Ovid's Metamorphosis, viii. 795–909, 1567

JOHN PIKERYNG

c. 1567

84 *Haltersick's Song*

FAREWELL, adieu, that courtly life,
  To war we tend to go;
It is good sport to see the strife
  Of soldiers on a row.
    How merrily they forward march,
      These enemies to slay;
    With 'Hey, trim' and 'Trixy' too
      Their banners they display.

Now shall we have the golden cheats,
  When others want the same;
And soldiers have full many feats,
  Their enemies to tame.
    With cucking here and booming there,
      They break their foe's array;
    And lusty lads amid the fields
      Their ensigns do display.

The drum and flute play lustily,
  The trumpet blows amain,
And venturous knights courageously
  Do march before their train.
    With spear in rest so lively dressed,
      In armour bright and gay,
    With 'Hey, trim' and 'Trixy' too
      Their banners they display.

The History of Horestes, 1567

cucking] shouting like cuckoos

WILLIAM CECIL, LORD BURGHLEY

1520–1598

85 *To Mistress Anne Cecil, upon Making her a New Year's Gift*

AS years do grow, so cares increase;
 And time will move to look to thrift:
Though years in me work nothing less,
 Yet, for your years, and New Year's gift,
 This housewife's toy is now my shift!
  To set you on work, some thrift to feel,
  I send you now a spinning wheel.

But one thing first, I wish and pray,
 Lest thirst of thrift might soon you tire,
Only to spin one pound a day,
 And play the rest, as time require:
 Sweat not! (oh fie!) fling rock in fire!
  God send, who send'th all thrift and wealth,
  You, long years; and your father, health!

Written 1568; *Lansdowne MS.* 104

rock] distaff

THOMAS HOWELL

c. 1568

86 *The Rose*

WHENAS the mildest month
Of jolly June doth spring,
And gardens green with happy hue
Their famous fruits do bring;
When eke the lustiest time
Reviveth youthly blood,
Then springs the finest featured flower
In border fair that stood.
Which moveth me to say,
In time of pleasant year,
Of all the pleasant flowers in June
The red rose hath no peer.

Arbor of Amitie, 1568

GEORGE TURBERVILLE

c. 1540–c. 1598

87 *The Lover to his Lady*

MY girl, thou gazest much
Upon the golden skies:
Would I were heaven! I would behold
Thee then with all mine eyes.

Epitaphs, Epigrams, Songs and Sonnets, 1567

88 *The Lover to the Thames of London, to Favour his Lady Passing thereon*

THOU stately stream that with the swelling tide
'Gainst London walls incessantly dost beat,
Thou Thames, I say, where barge and boat doth ride,
And snow-white swans do fish for needful meat!

When so my Love, of force or pleasure, shall
Flit on thy flood as custom is to do,
Seek not with dread her courage to appal,
But calm thy tide, and smoothly let it go,
As she may joy, arrived to siker shore,
To pass the pleasant stream she did before.

To welter up and surge in wrathful wise,
As did the flood where Helle drenched was
Would but procure defame of thee to rise.
Wherefore let all such ruthless rigour pass,
So wish I that thou mayst with bending side
Have power for aye in wonted gulf to glide.

Epitaphs, Epigrams, Songs and Sonnets, 1567

89 *To his Friend, Promising that though her Beauty Fade, yet his Love shall Last*

I WOT full well that beauty cannot last;
No rose that springs but lightly doth decay,
And feature like a lily leaf doth waste,
Or as the cowslip in the midst of May;
I know that tract of time doth conquer all,
And beauty's buds like fading flowers do fall.

siker] secure

GEORGE TURBERVILLE

That famous dame, fair Helen, lost her hue
When withered age with wrinkles changed her cheeks,
Her lovely looks did loathsomeness ensue,
That was the *A per se* of all the Greeks.
And sundry mo that were as fair as she,
Yet Helen was as fresh as fresh might be.

No force for that, I price your beauty light,
If so I find you steadfast in good will.
Though few there are that do in age delight,
I was your friend, and so do purpose still;
No change of looks shall breed my change of love,
Nor beauty's want my first good will remove.

Tragical Tales, 1587

GEORGE GASCOIGNE

c. 1542–1577

90 *Inscription in a Garden*

IF any flower that here is grown,
Or any herb, may ease your pain,
Take and accompt it as your own,
But recompense the like again;
For some and some is honest play,
And so my wife taught me to say.

If here to walk you take delight,
Why, come and welcome, when you will;
If I bid you sup here this night,
Bid me another time, and still
Think some and some is honest play,
For so my wife taught me to say.

force] matter

Thus if you sup or dine with me,
If you walk here or sit at ease,
If you desire the thing you see,
And have the same your mind to please,
Think some and some is honest play,
And so my wife taught me to say.

A Hundreth Sundrie Flowres, 1573

91

A Farewell

'AND if I did, what then?
Are you aggrieved therefore?
The sea hath fish for every man,
And what would you have more?'

Thus did my mistress once
Amaze my mind with doubt;
And popped a question for the nonce,
To beat my brains about.

Whereto I thus replied:
'Each fisherman can wish,
That all the seas at every tide
Were his alone to fish.

'And so did I, in vain,
But since it may not be,
Let such fish there as find the gain,
And leave the loss for me.

'And with such luck and loss
I will content myself,
Till tides of turning time may toss
Such fishers on the shelf.

'And when they stick on sands,
That every man may see,
Then will I laugh and clap my hands,
As they do now at me.'

The Adventures of Master F.I.;
Ibid.

THOMAS CHURCHYARD

1520 ?–1604

92

Old-Time Service

WITH merry lark this maiden rose,
And straight about the house she goes,
With swapping besom in her hand;
And at her girdle in a band
A jolly bunch of keys she wore;
Her petticoat fine laced before,
Her tail tucked up in trimmest guise,
A napkin hanging o'er her eyes,
To keep off dust and dross of walls,
That often from the windows falls.
Though she was smug, she took small ease,
For thrifty girls are glad to please;
She won the love of all the house,
And pranked it like a pretty mouse,
And sure at every word she spake,
A goodly curtsy could she make;
A stirring housewife every where,
That bent both back and bones to bear.
She never sleeped much by night,
But rose sometimes by candle-light

smug] trim

To card and spin, or sew her smock;
There could no sooner crow a cock,
But she was up, to sleek her clothes,
And would be sweet as any rose.
Full cleanly still the girl would go
And handsome in a house also,
As ever saw I country wench.
She sweeped under every bench,
And shaked the cushions in their kind;
When out of order she did find
A rush, a straw or little stick,
She could it mend, she was so quick
About her business every hour.
This maid was called her mistress' flower.
She bare the keys of ale and beer,
And had the rule of better cheer.
She was not nice, nor yet too kind,
Too proud, nor of too humble mind,
Too fine, nor yet too brave, I trow.
She had, as far as I do know,
Two fair new kirtles to her back;
The one was blue, the other black.
For holy days she had a gown,
And every yard did cost a crown,
And more by eighteen pence, I guess;
She had three smocks, she had no less,
Four rails and eke five kerchers fair.
Of hose and shoes she had a pair;
She needed not no more to have;
She would go barefoot for to save
Her shoes and hose, for they were dear.

rails] nightgowns

She went to town but once a year,
At Easter or some other day,
When she had licence for to play.
I had forgotten for to tell,
She had a purse she loved well,
That hanged at a ribbon green,
With tassels fair, and well beseen;
And as for gloves and knives full bright
She lacked not, nor trifles light,
As pins and laces of small cost.
I have to you rehearsed most
Of all her goods. Now to the form
And making of this creeping worm.
Her port was low, her face was fair;
It came no sooner in the air,
But it would peel, her cheeks were thin.
God knows she had a tender skin.
The worst mis-shape this minion had,
Her legs were swollen very bad;
Some heavy humour down did fall.
Her foot was narrow, short and small,
Her body slender as a snig;
But sure her buttocks were full big;
That came, I think, from sitting mich;
And in her side she had a stitch,
That made her oft short-winded, sure.
But her complexion was full pure.
She was well made from top to tail;
Yea, all her limbs, withouten fail,
Were fine and feat. She had a hand,

beseen] arranged minion] darling snig] eel
mich] much feat] well made

THOMAS CHURCHYARD

There was no fairer in the land,
Save that with toil it changed hue.
Her fingers small, her veins full blue;
Her nails a little largely grown;
Her hair much like the sun it shone;
Her eyes as black as jet did seem;
She did herself full well esteem.
Her lips were red, but somewhat chapped.
Her tongue was still and seldom clapped.
She spake as she were in a cloud,
Neither too soft nor yet too loud,
And tripped upon the floor as trim,
Ye would have thought that she did swim
As she did go, such was her pace.
She minced fine, like Mistress Grace,
That at the Dagger dwelled once,
Who made good pies of marrow-bones.
I dare depose upon a book,
She was as good a maiden cook,
As ever dressed a piece of meat;
And for a banquet, small or great,
And raising paste, she passed still.
As soon as flour came from the mill,
She made the goodliest cakes thereof,
And baked as fair a household loaf,
As e'er was seen or set on board.
What needs more talk? At one bare word,
The greatest lady in a shire
She might have served seven year.

A Fayned Fancye betweene the Spider and the Gowte, 43–152; *The Firste Parte of Churchyardes Chippes*, 1575

WILLIAM HUNNIS

? –1597

93 *The Shipmen*

WHAT watch, what woe, what want, what wrack,
  Is due to those that toil the seas.
Life led with loss, of pains no lack,
  In storms to win much restless ease;
    A bedless board in sea's unrest
    May hap to him that chanceth best.

How sundry sounds with lead and line
  Unto the deep the shipman throws;
'No foot to spare!' he cries oft times,
  'No near!' when 'How?' the master blows.
    If Neptune frown, all be undone;
    Straightway the ship the wrack hath won.

These dangers great do oft befall
  On those that sheer upon the sand;
Judge of their lives, the best who shall?
  How vile it is, few understand.
    Alack, who then may judge their game?
    Not they which have not felt the same.

But they that fall in storms and wind,
  And days and years have spent therein,
Such well may judge, since proof they find,
  In rage no rest till calm begin.
    No more than those, that love do feign,
    Give judgement of true lovers' pain.

Paradise of Dainty Devices, 1576

BEWE

c. 1576

94 *Actaeon*

I WOULD I were Actaeon, whom Diana did disguise,
To walk the woods unknown whereas my lady lies;
A hart of pleasant hue I wish that I were so,
So that my lady knew alone me and no mo;

To follow thick and plain, by hill and dale alow,
To drink the water fain, and feed me with the sloe.
I would not fear the frost, to lie upon the ground,
Delight should quite the cost, what pain so that I found.

The shaling nuts and mast that falleth from the tree
Should serve for my repast, might I my lady see;
Sometime that I might say when I saw her alone,
'Behold thy slave, all day that walks these woods unknown!'

Gorgeous Gallery of Gallant Inventions, 1578

THOMAS PROCTOR

c. 1578

95 *Respice Finem*

LO, here the state of every mortal wight,
See here the fine of all their gallant joys;
Behold their pomp, their beauty, and delight,
Whereof they vaunt as safe from all annoys.

To earth the stout, the proud, the rich shall yield,
The weak, the meek, the poor shall shrouded lie
In dampish mould; the stout with spear and shield
Cannot defend himself when he shall die.

thick] thicket   quite] requite   shaling] falling from the husk

The proudest wight, for all his lively shows,
  Shall leave his pomp, cut off by dreadful death;
The rich, whose hutch with golden ruddocks flows,
  At length shall rest uncoined in dampish earth.

By Nature's law we all are born to die,
  But where or when, the best uncertain be;
No time prefixed, no goods our life shall buy,
  Of dreadful death no friends shall set us free.

We subject be a thousand ways to death;
  Small sickness moves the valiant's heart to fear;
A little push bereaves your breathing breath
  Of brave delights, whereto you subject are.

Your world is vain; no trust in earth you find;
  Your valiant'st prime is but a brittle glass;
Your pleasures vade, your thoughts a puff of wind;
  Your ancient years are but a withered grass.

Ibid.

96 *A Proper Sonnet, how Time Consumeth All Things*

AY me, ay me! I sigh to see the scythe afield;
  Down goeth the grass, soon wrought to withered hay.
Ay me, alas! ay me, alas! that beauty needs must yield,
  And princes pass, as grass doth fade away.

Ay me, ay me! that life cannot have lasting leave,
  Nor gold take hold of everlasting joy.
Ay me, alas! ay me, alas! that time hath talents to receive,
  And yet no time can make a sure stay.

hutch] chest   ruddocks] red coins

Ay me, ay me! that wit cannot have wished choice,
  Nor wish can win that will desires to see.
Ay me, alas! ay me, alas! that mirth can promise no rejoice,
  Nor study tell what afterward shall be.

Ay me, ay me! that no sure staff is given to age,
  Nor age can give sure wit that youth will take.
Ay me, alas! ay me, alas! that no counsel wise and sage
  Will shun the show that all doth mar and make.

Ay me, ay me! come Time, shear on and shake thy hay;
  It is no boot to balk thy bitter blows.
Ay me, alas! ay me, alas! come Time, take every thing away,
  For all is thine, be it good or bad that grows.

Gorgeous Gallery of Gallant Inventions, 1578

ANONYMOUS

97 *The Lover Exhorteth his Lady to be Constant*

NOT light of love, lady!
  Though fancy do prick thee,
Let constancy possess thy heart.
  Well worthy of blaming
  They be, and defaming,
From plighted troth which back do start.
    Dear dame,
  Then fickleness banish
  And folly extinguish,
  Be skilful in guiding
    And stay thee from sliding.

  The constant are praised,
  Their fame high is raised,
Their worthiness doth pierce the sky.

ANONYMOUS

The fickle are blamed,
Their lightilove shamed,
Their foolishness doth make them die.
As well
Can Cressid bear witness,
Forge of her own distress,
Whom leprosy painted
And penury tainted.

Still Muses are busy
To tell us of Thisbe,
Whom steadfastness doth much commend.
And Camma is placed
To blame the defaced,
That light of love do send.
Phedra
Is checked most duly
Because that untruly,
Forced thereto by love light,
She slayeth Hippolite.

A spring of annoyance
And well of disturbance
Newfangleness in love hath been;
It killeth the master,
It poisons the taster,
No worldly wight by it doth win.
Therefore,
Good lady, be constant,
So shall you not be shent
But worthily praised,
As you have deserved.

Ibid.

shent] disgraced

98 *A New Courtly Sonnet of the Lady Greensleeves*

GREENSLEEVES was all my joy,
  Greensleeves was my delight;
Greensleeves was my heart of gold,
  And who but Lady Greensleeves.

Alas, my Love! ye do me wrong
  To cast me off discourteously;
And I have loved you so long,
  Delighting in your company.
    Greensleeves was all my joy, &c.

I have been ready at your hand,
  To grant whatever you would crave;
I have both waged life and land,
  Your love and goodwill for to have.
    Greensleeves was all my joy, &c.

I bought thee kerchers to thy head,
  That were wrought fine and gallantly;
I kept thee both at board and bed,
  Which cost my purse well favouredly.
    Greensleeves was all my joy, &c.

I bought thee petticoats of the best,
  The cloth so fine as fine might be;
I gave thee jewels for thy chest,
  And all this cost I spent on thee.
    Greensleeves was all my joy, &c.

waged] risked

Thy smock of silk, both fair and white,
  With gold embroidered gorgeously;
Thy petticoat of sendal right;
  And thus I bought thee gladly.
    Greensleeves was all my joy, &c.

Thy girdle of gold so red,
  With pearls bedecked sumptuously;
The like no other lasses had,
  And yet thou wouldst not love me.
    Greensleeves was all my joy, &c.

Thy purse and eke thy gay gilt knives,
  Thy pincase gallant to the eye;
No better wore the burgess wives,
  And yet thou wouldst not love me.
    Greensleeves was all my joy, &c.

Thy crimson stockings all of silk,
  With gold all wrought above the knee;
Thy pumps as white as was the milk,
  And yet thou wouldst not love me.
    Greensleeves was all my joy, &c.

Thy gown was of the grassy green,
  Thy sleeves of satin hanging by,
Which made thee be our harvest queen,
  And yet thou wouldst not love me.
    Greensleeves was all my joy, &c.

Thy garters fringed with the gold,
  And silver aglets hanging by,
Which made thee blithe for to behold,
  And yet thou wouldst not love me.
    Greensleeves was all my joy, &c.

sendal] fine silk

My gayest gelding I thee gave,
  To ride wherever liked thee;
No lady ever was so brave,
  And yet thou wouldst not love me.
    Greensleeves was all my joy, &c.

My men were clothed all in green,
  And they did ever wait on thee;
All this was gallant to be seen,
  And yet thou wouldst not love me.
    Greensleeves was all my joy, &c.

They set thee up, they took thee down,
  They served thee with humility;
Thy foot might not once touch the ground,
  And yet thou wouldst not love me.
    Greensleeves was all my joy, &c.

For every morning when thou rose,
  I sent thee dainties orderly,
To cheer thy stomach from all woes,
  And yet thou wouldst not love me.
    Greensleeves was all my joy, &c.

Thou couldst desire no earthly thing
  But still thou hadst it readily;
Thy music still to play and sing,
  And yet thou wouldst not love me.
    Greensleeves was all my joy, &c.

And who did pay for all this gear
  That thou didst spend when pleased thee?
Even I that am rejected here,
  And thou disdain'st to love me.
    Greensleeves was all my joy, &c.

Well, I will pray to God on high,
  That thou my constancy mayst see,
And that yet once before I die,
  Thou wilt vouchsafe to love me.
    Greensleeves was all my joy, &c.

Greensleeves, now farewell! adieu!
  God I pray to prosper thee;
For I am still thy lover true.
  Come once again and love me.
    Greensleeves was all my joy,
      Greensleeves was my delight;
    Greensleeves was my heart of gold,
      And who but Lady Greensleeves.

Handful of Pleasant Delights, 1584

99 *The Old Cloak*

THIS winter's weather it waxeth cold,
  And frost it freezeth on every hill,
And Boreas blows his blasts so bold
  That all our cattle are like to spill.
Bell, my wife, she loves no strife;
  She said unto me quietly,
Rise up, and save cow Crumbock's life!
  Man, put thine old cloak about thee!

He. O Bell my wife, why dost thou flyte?
  Thou kens my cloak is very thin;
It is so sore and over wore,
  A crickė thereon cannot rin.

spill] perish   flyte] scold   crickė] cricket, insect   rin] run

Then I'll no longer borrow nor lend;
  For once I'll new apparelled be;
To-morrow I'll to town and spend;
  For I'll have a new cloak about me.

She. Cow Crumbock is a very good cow;
  She has been always good to the pail;
She has helped us to butter and cheese, I trow,
  And other things she will not fail.
I would be loth to see her pine.
  Good husband, counsel take of me;
It is not for us to go so fine.
  Man, take thine old cloak about thee!

He. My cloak it was a very good cloak,
  It hath been always good to the wear;
It hath cost me many a groat;
  I have had it this four and forty year.
Sometime it was of the cloth in grain;
  It is now but a sigh clout, as you may see;
It will neither hold out wind nor rain;
  And I'll have a new cloak about me.

She. It is four and forty years ago
  Sine the one of us the other did ken;
And we have had, betwixt us two,
  Children either nine or ten;
We have brought them up to women and men;
  In the fear of God I trow they be.
And why wilt thou thyself misken?
  Man, take thine old cloak about thee!

cloth in grain] scarlet cloth   sigh clout] a rag for straining

ANONYMOUS

He. O Bell my wife, why dost thou flyte?
Now is now, and then was then.
Seek all the world now throughout,
Thou kens not clowns from gentlemen;
They are clad in black, green, yellow, and blue,
So far above their own degree.
Once in my life I'll take a view;
For I'll have a new cloak about me.

She. King Stephen was a worthy peer;
His breeches cost him but a crown;
He held them sixpence all too dear,
Therefore he called the tailor lown.
He was a wight of high renown,
And thou's but of a low degree.
It 's pride that puts this country down:
Man, put thy old cloak about thee!

He. O Bell my wife, why dost thou flyte?
Now is now, and then was then.
We will now live obedient life,
Thou the woman and I the man.
It 's not for a man with a woman to threap,
Unless he first give o'er the play.
As we began, so will we keep;
And I'll have mine old cloak about me.

Percy Folio MS.

threap] argue

QUEEN ELIZABETH

1533–1603

100 *Youth and Cupid*

WHEN I was fair and young, and favour graced me,
Of many was I sought, their mistress for to be;
But I did scorn them all, and answered them therefore,
'Go, go, go, seek some otherwhere,
Importune me no more!'

How many weeping eyes I made to pine with woe,
How many sighing hearts, I have no skill to show;
Yet I the prouder grew, and answered them therefore,
'Go, go, go, seek some otherwhere,
Importune me no more!'

Then spake fair Venus' son, that proud victorious boy,
And said: 'Fine dame, since that you be so coy,
I will so pluck your plumes that you shall say no more,
Go, go, go, seek some otherwhere,
Importune me no more!'

When he had spake these words, such change grew in my breast
That neither night nor day since that, I could take any rest.
Then lo! I did repent that I had said before,
'Go, go, go, seek some otherwhere,
Importune me no more!'

Rawlinson Poet. MS. 85

QUEEN ELIZABETH

101 *The Daughter of Debate*

THE doubt of future foes exiles my present joy,
And wit me warns to shun such snares as threaten mine annoy.
For falsehood now doth flow and subject faith doth ebb,
Which would not be, if reason ruled or wisdom weaved the web.
But clouds of toys untried do cloak aspiring minds,
Which turn to rain of late repent by course of changed winds.
The top of hope supposed the root of ruth will be,
And fruitless all their graffed guiles, as shortly ye shall see.
The dazzled eyes with pride, which great ambition blinds,
Shall be unseeled by worthy wights, whose foresight falsehood finds.
The daughter of debate, that eke discord doth sow,
Shall reap no gain where former rule hath taught still peace to grow.
No foreign banished wight shall anchor in this port;
Our realm it brooks no stranger's force, let them elsewhere resort.
Our rusty sword with rest shall first his edge employ
To poll their tops that seek such change and gape for joy.

The Arte of English Poesie, 1589

unseeled] opened

EDWARD DE VERE, EARL OF OXFORD

1550–1604

102 *A Choice*

WERE I a king, I could command content;
  Were I obscure, hidden should be my cares;
Or were I dead, no cares should me torment,
  Nor hopes, nor hates, nor loves, nor griefs, nor fears.
    A doubtful choice, of these three which to crave,
    A kingdom, or a cottage, or a grave.

Chetham MS. 8012

103 *Of the Birth and Bringing up of Desire*

WHEN wert thou born, Desire?
  In pride and pomp of May.
By whom, sweet boy, wert thou begot?
  By Self Conceit, men say.
Tell me, who was thy nurse?
  Fresh Youth, in sugared joy.
What was thy meat and daily food?
  Sad sighs and great annoy.
What haddest thou to drink?
  Unfeigned lovers' tears.
What cradle wert thou rocked in?
  In hope devoid of fears.
What brought thee to thy sleep?
  Sweet thoughts, which liked me best.
And where is now thy dwelling-place?
  In gentle hearts I rest.

Doth company displease?
  It doth, in many one.
Where would Desire then choose to be?
  He loves to muse alone.
What feedeth most thy sight?
  To gaze on favour still.
Whom finds thou most thy foe?
  Disdain of my good will.
Will ever age or death
  Bring thee unto decay?
No, no! Desire both lives and dies
  A thousand times a day.

Rawlinson Poet. MS. 85

104 *White and Red*

WHAT cunning can express
  The favour of her face,
To whom in this distress
  I do appeal for grace?
    A thousand Cupids fly
    About her gentle eye:

From whence each throws a dart
  That kindleth soft sweet fire
Within my sighing heart,
  Possessed by desire.
    No sweeter life I try
    Than in her love to die.

EDWARD DE VERE, EARL OF OXFORD

The lily in the field,
  That glories in his white,
For pureness now must yield
  And render up his right.
    Heaven pictured in her face
    Doth promise joy and grace.

Fair Cynthia's silver light,
  That beats on running streams,
Compares not with her white,
  Whose hairs are all sunbeams.
    Her virtues so do shine,
    As day unto mine eyne.

With this there is a red
  Exceeds the damask rose,
Which in her cheeks is spread,
  Whence every favour grows.
    In sky there is no star,
    That she surmounts not far.

When Phoebus from the bed
  Of Thetis doth arise,
The morning blushing red
  In fair carnation wise,
    He shows it in her face,
    As queen of every grace.

This pleasant lily white,
  This taint of roseate red,
This Cynthia's silver light,
  This sweet fair Dea spread,
    These sunbeams in mine eye;
    These beauties make me die.

Phoenix Nest, 1593

SIR PHILIP SIDNEY

1554–1586

105 *Sonnets of Astrophel*

(i)

LOVING in truth, and fain in verse my love to show,
 That she, dear she, might take some pleasure of my pain,
Pleasure might cause her read, reading might make her know,
 Knowledge might pity win, and pity grace obtain,
I sought fit words to paint the blackest face of woe;
 Studying inventions fine, her wits to entertain,
Oft turning others' leaves to see if thence would flow
 Some fresh and fruitful showers upon my sun-burned brain.
But words came halting forth, wanting Invention's stay;
 Invention, Nature's child, fled step-dame Study's blows,
And others' feet still seemed but strangers in my way.
 Thus, great with child to speak, and helpless in my throes,
  Biting my truant pen, beating myself for spite,
  'Fool,' said my Muse to me, 'look in thy heart and write.'

(ii)

LET dainty wits cry on the Sisters nine,
 That, bravely masked, their fancies may be told;
Or Pindar's apes flaunt they in phrases fine,
 Enamelling with pied flowers their thoughts of gold;
Or else let them in statelier glory shine,
 Ennobling new-found tropes with problems old;
Or with strange similes enrich each line,
 Of herbs or beasts which Ind or Afric hold.
For me, in sooth, no Muse but one I know;
Phrases and problems from my reach do grow,
 And strange things cost too dear for my poor sprites.
How then? even thus—in Stella's face I read
What love and beauty be; then all my deed
 But copying is, what in her Nature writes.

(iii)

IT is most true that eyes are formed to serve
The inward light, and that the heavenly part
Ought to be king, from whose rules who do swerve,
Rebels to Nature, strive for their own smart.
It is most true what we call Cupid's dart
An image is which for ourselves we carve,
And, fools, adore in temple of our heart,
Till that good god make church and churchman starve.
True, that true beauty virtue is indeed,
Whereof this beauty can be but a shade,
Which elements with mortal mixture breed.
True, that on earth we are but pilgrims made,
And should in soul up to our country move;
True, and yet true that I must Stella love.

(iv)

YOU that do search for every purling spring
Which from the ribs of old Parnassus flows,
And every flower, not sweet perhaps, which grows
Near thereabouts into your poesy wring;
You that do dictionary's method bring
Into your rhymes, running in rattling rows;
You that poor Petrarch's long-deceased woes
With new-born sighs and denizened wit do sing;
You take wrong ways; those far-fet helps be such
As do bewray a want of inward touch,
And sure at length stolen goods do come to light.
But if, both for your love and skill, your name
You seek to nurse at fullest breasts of Fame,
Stella behold, and then begin to indite.

(*v*)

IN highest way of heaven the Sun did ride,
Progressing then from fair Twins' golden place,
Having no scarf of clouds before his face,
But shining forth of heat in his chief pride;
When some fair ladies, by hard promise tied,
On horseback met him in his furious race;
Yet each prepared with fan's well-shading grace
From that foe's wounds their tender skins to hide.
Stella alone with face unarmed marched,
Either to do like him which open shone,
Or careless of the wealth, because her own.
Yet were the hid and meaner beauties parched;
Her daintiest bare went free; the cause was this,
The Sun, which others burned, did her but kiss.

(*vi*)

WITH how sad steps, O Moon, thou climb'st the skies!
How silently, and with how wan a face!
What! may it be that even in heavenly place
That busy archer his sharp arrows tries?
Sure, if that long-with-love-acquainted eyes
Can judge of love, thou feel'st a lover's case;
I read it in thy looks; thy languished grace
To me, that feel the like, thy state descries.
Then, even of fellowship, O Moon, tell me,
Is constant love deemed there but want of wit?
Are beauties there as proud as here they be?
Do they above love to be loved, and yet
Those lovers scorn whom that love doth possess?
Do they call virtue there ungratefulness?

(vii)

I MIGHT—unhappy word!—oh me, I might,
  And then would not, or could not, see my bliss;
Till now, wrapped in a most infernal night,
  I find how heavenly day, wretch, I did miss.
Heart, rent thyself, thou dost thyself but right;
  No lovely Paris made thy Helen his,
No force, no fraud, robbed thee of thy delight,
  Nor Fortune of thy fortune author is;
But to myself myself did give the blow,
  While too much wit, forsooth, so troubled me
That I respects for both our sakes must show,
  And yet could not by rising morn foresee
    How fair a day was near; oh, punished eyes,
    That I had been more foolish, or more wise!

(viii)

COME, sleep, O sleep, the certain knot of peace,
  The baiting place of wit, the balm of woe,
The poor man's wealth, the prisoner's release,
  Th' indifferent judge between the high and low;
With shield of proof shield me from out the prease
  Of those fierce darts despair at me doth throw;
O make me in those civil wars to cease;
  I will good tribute pay, if thou do so.
Take thou of me smooth pillows, sweetest bed,
  A chamber deaf to noise and blind to light,
A rosy garland and a weary head;
  And if these things, as being thine by right,
    Move not thy heavy grace, thou shalt in me,
    Livelier than elsewhere, Stella's image see.

prease] crowd

(*ix*)

HAVING this day my horse, my hand, my lance
Guided so well that I obtained the prize,
Both by the judgement of the English eyes
And of some sent from that sweet enemy, France;
Horsemen my skill in horsemanship advance,
Town-folks my strength; a daintier judge applies
His praise to sleight which from good use doth rise;
Some lucky wits impute it but to chance;
Others, because of both sides I do take
My blood from them who did excel in this,
Think Nature me a man of arms did make.
How far they shot awry! The true cause is,
Stella looked on, and from her heavenly face
Sent forth the beams which made so fair my race.

(*x*)

BECAUSE I breathe not love to every one,
Nor do not use set colours for to wear,
Nor nourish special locks of vowed hair,
Nor give each speech a full point of a groan,
The courtly nymphs, acquainted with the moan
Of them who in their lips Love's standard bear,
'What, he!' say they of me, 'Now I dare swear
He cannot love; no, no, let him alone.'
And think so still, so Stella know my mind.
Profess indeed I do not Cupid's art;
But you, fair maids, at length this true shall find,
That his right badge is but worn in the heart;
Dumb swans, not chattering pies, do lovers prove;
They love indeed who quake to say they love.

(*xi*)

NO more, my dear, no more these counsels try;
Oh, give my passions leave to run their race;
  Let Fortune lay on me her worst disgrace;
Let folk o'ercharged with brain against me cry;
Let clouds bedim my face, break in mine eye;
  Let me no steps but of lost labour trace;
  Let all the earth with scorn recount my case;
But do not will me from my love to fly.
I do not envy Aristotle's wit,
  Nor do aspire to Caesar's bleeding fame;
Nor aught do care though some above me sit;
  Nor hope nor wish another course to frame,
    But that which once may win thy cruel heart;
    Thou art my wit, and thou my virtue art.

(*xii*)

STELLA, the only planet of my light,
Light of my life, and life of my desire,
  Chief good whereto my hope doth only aspire,
World of my wealth, and heaven of my delight,
Why dost thou spend the treasures of thy spright,
  With voice more fit to wed Amphion's lyre,
  Seeking to quench in me the noble fire
Fed by thy worth, and kindled by thy sight?
And all in vain; for while thy breath most sweet
  With choicest words, thy words with reasons rare,
Thy reasons firmly set on Virtue's feet,
  Labour to kill in me this killing care,
    O think I then, what paradise of joy
    It is, so fair a virtue to enjoy!

(*xiii*)

I NEVER drank of Aganippe well,
  Nor ever did in shade of Tempe sit,
And Muses scorn with vulgar brains to dwell;
  Poor layman I, for sacred rites unfit.
Some do I hear of poets' fury tell,
  But, God wot, wot not what they mean by it;
And this I swear by blackest brook of hell,
  I am no pick-purse of another's wit.
How falls it then, that with so smooth an ease
  My thoughts I speak, and what I speak doth flow
In verse, and that my verse best wits doth please?
  Guess we the cause? What, is it thus? Fie, no.
    Or so? Much less. How then? Sure thus it is;
    My lips are sweet, inspired with Stella's kiss.

(*xiv*)

HIGHWAY, since you my chief Parnassus be,
  And that my Muse, to some ears not unsweet,
  Tempers her words to trampling horses' feet
More oft than to a chamber-melody,
Now, blessed you, bear onward blessed me
  To her, where I my heart, safe left, shall meet;
  My Muse and I must you of duty greet
With thanks and wishes, wishing thankfully.
Be you still fair, honoured by public heed;
  By no encroachment wronged, nor time forgot;
Nor blamed for blood, nor shamed for sinful deed;
  And, that you know I envy you no lot
    Of highest wish, I wish you so much bliss,
    Hundreds of years you Stella's feet may kiss!

(*xv*)

STELLA, think not that I by verse seek fame,
Who seek, who hope, who love, who live but thee;
Thine eyes my pride, thy lips mine history;
If thou praise not, all other praise is shame.
Nor so ambitious am I as to frame
A nest for my young praise in laurel tree;
In truth I swear, I wish not there should be
Graved in mine epitaph a poet's name.
Ne, if I would, I could just title make,
That any laud to me thereof should grow,
Without my plumes from others' wings I take;
For nothing from my wit or will doth flow,
Since all my words thy beauty doth indite,
And love doth hold my hand and makes me write.

(*xvi*)

WHEN far-spent night persuades each mortal eye,
To whom nor art nor nature granteth light,
To lay his then mark-wanting shafts of sight,
Closed with their quivers, in sleep's armoury,
With windows ope then most my mind doth lie,
Viewing the shape of darkness, and delight
Takes in that sad hue, which with th' inward night
Of his mazed powers keeps perfit harmony.
But when birds charm, and that sweet air which is
Morn's messenger, with rose-enamelled skies,
Calls each wight to salute the flower of bliss;
In tomb of lids then buried are mine eyes,
Forced by their lord, who is ashamed to find
Such light in sense, with such a darkened mind.

Written c. 1580–1; *The Countess of Pembroke's Arcadia*, 1598

perfit] perfect

106 *Songs of Astrophel*

(*i*)

DOUBT you to whom my Muse these notes intendeth,
Which now my breast o'ercharged to music lendeth?
To you, to you, all song of praise is due;
Only in you my song begins and endeth.

Who hath the eyes which marry state with pleasure?
Who keeps the key of Nature's chiefest treasure?
To you, to you, all song of praise is due;
Only for you the heaven forgat all measure.

Who hath the lips where wit in fairness reigneth?
Who womankind at once both decks and staineth?
To you, to you, all song of praise is due;
Only by you Cupid his crown maintaineth.

Who hath the feet whose step of sweetness planteth?
Who else, for whom Fame worthy trumpets wanteth?
To you, to you, all song of praise is due;
Only to you her sceptre Venus granteth.

Who hath the breast whose milk doth passions nourish?
Whose grace is such that when it chides doth cherish?
To you, to you, all song of praise is due;
Only through you the tree of life doth flourish.

Who hath the hand which without stroke subdueth?
Who long dead beauty with increase reneweth?
To you, to you, all song of praise is due;
Only at you all envy hopeless rueth.

Who hath the hair which loosest, fastest, tieth?
Who makes a man live then glad, when he dieth?
  To you, to you, all song of praise is due;
Only of you the flatterer never lieth.

Who hath the voice which soul from senses sunders?
Whose force but yours the bolts of beauty thunders?
  To you, to you, all song of praise is due;
Only with you not miracles are wonders.

Doubt you to whom my Muse these notes intendeth,
Which now my breast o'ercharged to music lendeth?
  To you, to you, all song of praise is due;
Only in you my song begins and endeth.

(ii)

ONLY joy, now here you are,
Fit to hear and ease my care;
Let my whispering voice obtain
Sweet reward for sharpest pain;
Take me to thee, and thee to me.
'No, no, no, no, my dear, let be.'

Night hath closed all in her cloak,
Twinkling stars love-thoughts provoke,
Danger hence good care doth keep,
Jealousy itself doth sleep;
Take me to thee, and thee to me.
'No, no, no, no, my dear, let be.'

Better place no wit can find,
Cupid's yoke to loose or bind;
These sweet flowers on fine bed too
Us in their best language woo;
Take me to thee, and thee to me.
'No, no, no, no, my dear, let be.'

This small light the moon bestows
Serves thy beams but to disclose;
So to raise my hap more high,
Fear not, else none can us spy;
Take me to thee, and thee to me.
'No, no, no, no, my dear, let be.'

That you heard was but a mouse,
Dumb sleep holdeth all the house;
Yet asleep, methinks, they say,
Young folks, take time while you may;
Take me to thee, and thee to me.
'No, no, no, no, my dear, let be.'

Niggard Time threats, if we miss
This large offer of our bliss,
Long stay ere he grant the same;
Sweet, then, while each thing doth frame,
Take me to thee, and thee to me.
'No, no, no, no, my dear, let be.'

Your fair mother is a-bed,
Candles out and curtains spread;
She thinks you do letters write;
Write, but let me first indite;
Take me to thee, and thee to me.
'No, no, no, no, my dear, let be.'

Sweet, alas, why strive you thus?
Concord better fitteth us;
Leave to Mars the force of hands,
Your power in your beauty stands;
Take thee to me, and me to thee.
'No, no, no, no, my dear, let be.'

Woe to me, and do you swear
Me to hate? but I forbear;
Cursed be my destines all,
That brought me so high to fall;
Soon with my death I will please thee.
'No, no, no, no, my dear, let be.'

(iii)

O YOU that hear this voice,
  O you that see this face,
Say whether of the choice
  Deserves the former place.
Fear not to judge this bate,
For it is void of hate.

This side doth Beauty take,
  For that doth Music speak,
Fit orators to make
  The strongest judgements weak.
The bar to plead their right
Is only true delight.

bate] debate

Thus doth the voice and face,
  These gentle lawyers, wage,
Like loving brothers, case
  For father's heritage,
That each, while each contends,
Itself to other lends.

For Beauty beautifies,
  With heavenly hue and grace,
The heavenly harmonies;
  And in that faultless face
The perfect beauties be
A perfect harmony.

Music more lofty swells
  In phrases nobly placed.
Beauty as far excels
  In action aptly graced.
A friend each party draws
To countenance his cause.

Love more affected seems
  To Beauty's lovely light,
And Wonder more esteems
  Of Music wondrous might.
But both to both so bent
As both in both are spent.

Music doth witness call
  The ear his truth to try.
Beauty brings to the hall
  Eye judgement of the eye.
Both in their objects such,
As no exceptions touch.

The Common Sense, which might
  Be arbiter of this,
To be forsooth upright,
  To both sides partial is.
He lays on this chief praise,
Chief praise on that he lays.

Then Reason, princess high,
  Whose throne is in the mind,
Which music can in sky
  And hidden beauties find,
Say whether thou wilt crown
With limitless renown.

(iv)

IN a grove most rich of shade,
When birds wanton music made,
May, then young, his pied weeds showing,
New-perfumed with flowers fresh growing,

Astrophel with Stella sweet
Did for mutual comfort meet,
Both within themselves oppressed,
But each in the other blessed.

Him great harms had taught much care;
Her fair neck a foul yoke bare:
But her sight his cares did banish;
In his sight her yoke did vanish.

Wept they had, alas the while!
But now tears themselves did smile,
While their eyes, by love directed,
Interchangeably reflected.

Sigh they did; but now betwixt
Sighs of love were glad sighs mixed;
With arms crossed, yet testifying
Restless rest and living dying.

Their ears hungry of each word,
Which the dear tongue would afford;
But their tongues restrained from walking,
Till their hearts had ended talking.

But, when their tongues could not speak,
Love itself did silence break;
Love did set his lips asunder,
Thus to speak in love and wonder:

'Stella, sovereign of my joy,
Fair triumpher of annoy,
Stella, star of heavenly fire,
Stella, lodestar of desire;

'Stella, in whose shining eyes
Are the lights of Cupid's skies,
Whose beams, where they once are darted,
Love therewith is straight imparted;

'Stella, whose voice, when it speaks,
Senses all asunder breaks;
Stella, whose voice, when it singeth,
Angels to acquaintance bringeth;

'Stella, in whose body is
Writ each character of bliss;
Whose face all, all beauty passeth,
Save thy mind, which yet surpasseth:

'Grant, O grant; but speech, alas!
Fails me, fearing on to pass:
Grant; O me! what am I saying?
But no fault there is in praying.

'Grant, O dear, on knees I pray',
(Knees on ground he then did stay)
'That, not I, but, since I love you,
Time and place for me may move you.

'Never season was more fit,
Never room more apt for it;
Smiling air allows my reason;
These birds sing, "Now use the season".

'This small wind, which so sweet is,
See how it the leaves doth kiss;
Each tree in his best attiring
Sense of love to love inspiring.

'Love makes earth the water drink,
Love to earth makes water sink;
And, if dumb things be so witty,
Shall a heavenly grace want pity?'

There his hands, in their speech, fain
Would have made tongue's language plain;
But her hands, his hands repelling,
Gave repulse all grace excelling.

Then she spake; her speech was such,
As not ears but heart did touch;
While such wise she love denied,
As yet love she signified.

'Astrophel', said she, 'my love,
Cease in these effects to prove;
Now be still, yet still believe me,
Thy grief more than death would grieve me.

'If that any thought in me
Can taste comfort but of thee,
Let me, fed with hellish anguish,
Joyless, hopeless, endless languish.

'If those eyes you praised be
Half so dear as you to me,
Let me home return, stark blinded
Of those eyes, and blinder minded.

'If to secret of my heart
I do any wish impart,
Where thou art not foremost placed,
Be both wish and I defaced.

'If more may be said, I say
All my bliss in thee I lay;
If thou love, my love content thee,
For all love, all faith, is meant thee.

'Trust me, while I thee deny,
In myself the smart I try;
Tyrant honour doth thus use thee;
Stella's self might not refuse thee.

'Therefore, dear, this no more move,
Lest, though I leave not thy love,
Which too deep in me is framed,
I should blush when thou art named.'

Therewithal away she went,
Leaving him to passion, rent
With what she had done and spoken,
That therewith my song is broken.

(*v*)

'WHO is it that this dark night
  Underneath my window plaineth?'
It is one who from thy sight
  Being, ah! exiled, disdaineth
Every other vulgar light.

'Why, alas! and are you he?
  Be not yet those fancies changed?'
Dear, when you find change in me,
  Though from me you be estranged,
Let my change to ruin be.

'Well, in absence this will die;
  Leave to see and leave to wonder.'
Absence sure will help, if I
  Can learn how myself to sunder
From what in my heart doth lie.

'But time will these thoughts remove;
  Time doth work what no man knoweth.'
Time doth as the subject prove;
  With time still the affection groweth
In the faithful turtle dove.

SIR PHILIP SIDNEY

'What if you new beauties see,
  Will not they stir new affection?'
I will think they pictures be,
  Image like of saint's perfection,
Poorly counterfeiting thee.

'But your reason's purest light
  Bids you leave such minds to nourish.'
Dear, do reason no such spite;
  Never doth thy beauty flourish
More than in my reason's sight.

'But the wrongs love bears will make
  Love at length leave undertaking.'
No, the more fools it do shake,
  In a ground of so firm making
Deeper still they drive the stake.

'Peace, I think that some give ear;
  Come no more lest I get anger.'
Bliss, I will my bliss forbear,
  Fearing, sweet, you to endanger;
But my soul shall harbour there.

'Well, begone, begone, I say,
  Lest that Argus' eyes perceive you.'
Oh, unjust Fortunės sway,
  Which can make me thus to leave you,
And from louts to run away.

Written c. 1580–1581; *The Countess of Pembroke's Arcadia*, 1598

107 *The Nightingale*

THE nightingale, as soon as April bringeth
  Unto her rested sense a perfect waking,
While late bare earth, proud of new clothing, springeth,
  Sings out her woes, a thorn her song-book making;
  And mournfully bewailing,
Her throat in tunes expresseth
What grief her breast oppresseth
  For Tereus' force on her chaste will prevailing.
O Philomela fair, O take some gladness,
That here is juster cause of plaintful sadness.
    Thine earth now springs, mine fadeth;
    Thy thorn without, my thorn my heart invadeth.

Alas, she hath no other cause of anguish
  But Tereus' love, on her by strong hand wroken,
Wherein she suffering, all her spirits languish:
  Full womanlike complains her will was broken.
  But I, who daily craving,
Cannot have to content me,
Have more cause to lament me,
  Since wanting is more woe than too much having.
O Philomela fair, O take some gladness,
That here is juster cause of plaintful sadness.
    Thine earth now springs, mine fadeth;
    Thy thorn without, my thorn my heart invadeth.

Certain Sonnets; Arcadia, 1598

wroken] imposed

108 *A Litany*

RING out your bells, let mourning shows be spread;
For Love is dead.
All Love is dead, infected
With plague of deep disdain;
Worth, as nought worth, rejected,
And Faith fair scorn doth gain.
From so ungrateful fancy,
From such a female franzy,
From them that use men thus,
Good Lord, deliver us!

Weep, neighbours, weep! do you not hear it said
That Love is dead?
His death-bed, peacock's folly;
His winding-sheet is shame;
His will, false-seeming holy;
His sole executor, blame.
From so ungrateful fancy,
From such a female franzy,
From them that use men thus,
Good Lord, deliver us!

Let dirge be sung and trentals rightly read,
For Love is dead.
Sir Wrong his tomb ordaineth
My mistress Marble-heart,
Which epitaph containeth,
'Her eyes were once his dart.'

trentals] masses for the dead

From so ungrateful fancy,
From such a female franzy,
From them that use men thus,
Good Lord, deliver us!

Alas! I lie, rage hath this error bred;
Love is not dead.
Love is not dead, but sleepeth
In her unmatched mind,
Where she his counsel keepeth,
Till due desert she find.
Therefore from so vile fancy,
To call such wit a franzy,
Who Love can temper thus,
Good Lord, deliver us!

Certain Sonnets; Arcadia, 1598

109 *Immortality*

WHO hath his fancy pleased
With fruits of happy sight,
Let here his eyes be raised
On Nature's sweetest light;
A light which doth dissever
And yet unite the eyes;
A light which, dying never,
Is cause the looker dies.

She never dies, but lasteth
In life of lover's heart;
He ever dies that wasteth
In love his chiefest part.

Thus is her life still guarded
  In never-dying faith;
Thus is his death rewarded,
  Since she lives in his death.

Look, then, and die; the pleasure
  Doth answer well the pain;
Small loss of mortal treasure
  Who may immortal gain.
Immortal be her graces,
  Immortal is her mind;
They, fit for heavenly places;
  This, heaven in it doth bind.

But eyes these beauties see not,
  Nor sense that grace descries;
Yet eyes deprived be not
  From sight of her fair eyes;
Which as of inward glory
  They are the outward seal,
So may they live still sorry,
  Which die not in that weal.

But who hath fancies pleased
  With fruits of happy sight,
Let here his eyes be raised
  On Nature's sweetest light!

Ibid.

110

A Farewell

OFT have I mused, but now at length I find,
Why those that die, men say they do depart.
'Depart!'—a word so gentle, to my mind,
Weakly did seem to paint death's ugly dart.
But now the stars, with their strange course, do bind
Me one to leave, with whom I leave my heart;
I hear a cry of spirits faint and blind,
That, parting thus, my chiefest part I part.
Part of my life, the loathed part to me,
Lives to impart my weary clay some breath;
But that good part, wherein all comforts be,
Now dead, doth show departure is a death—
Yea, worse than death; death parts both woe and joy.
From joy I part, still living in annoy.

Certain Sonnets; Arcadia, 1598

111

Desire

THOU blind man's mark, thou fool's self-chosen snare,
Fond fancy's scum, and dregs of scattered thought;
Band of all evils, cradle of causeless care;
Thou web of will, whose end is never wrought;
Desire, desire! I have too dearly bought,
With price of mangled mind, thy worthless ware;
Too long, too long, asleep thou hast me brought,
Who should my mind to higher things prepare.
But yet in vain thou hast my ruin sought;
In vain thou madest me to vain things aspire;
In vain thou kindlest all thy smoky fire;
For virtue hath this better lesson taught,
Within myself to seek my only hire,
Desiring nought but how to kill desire.

Ibid.

112 *Splendidis Longum Valedico Nugis*

LEAVE me, O Love, which reachest but to dust;
  And thou, my mind, aspire to higher things;
Grow rich in that which never taketh rust;
  Whatever fades but fading pleasure brings.
Draw in thy beams, and humble all thy might
  To that sweet yoke where lasting freedoms be;
Which breaks the clouds and opens forth the light,
  That doth both shine and give us sight to see.
O take fast hold; let that light be thy guide
  In this small course which birth draws out to death,
And think how evil becometh him to slide,
  Who seeketh heaven, and comes of heavenly breath.
    Then farewell, world; thy uttermost I see;
    Eternal Love, maintain thy life in me.

Ibid.

113 *True Love*

MY true love hath my heart and I have his,
  By just exchange one for another given;
I hold his dear, and mine he cannot miss,
  There never was a better bargain driven.
    My true love hath my heart and I have his.

His heart in me keeps him and me in one,
  My heart in him his thoughts and senses guides;
He loves my heart, for once it was his own,
  I cherish his, because in me it bides.
    My true love hath my heart and I have his.

Arte of English Poesie, 1589

114 *A Country Song*

THE lad Philisides
Lay by a river side,
In flowery field a gladder eye to please;
His pipe was at his foot,
His lambs were him beside;
A widow turtle near on bared root
Sat wailing without boot.
Each thing both sweet and sad
Did draw his boiling brain
To think and think with pain
Of Mira's beams, eclipsed by absence bad.
And thus, with eyes made dim
With tears, he said, or sorrow said for him:
'O earth, once answer give;
So may thy stately grace
By north or south still rich adorned live;
So Mira long may be
On thy then blessed face,
Whose foot doth set a heaven on cursed thee;
I ask, now answer me,
If th' author of thy bliss,
Phoebus, that shepherd high,
Do turn from thee his eye,
Doth not thy self, when he long absent is,
Like rogue, all ragged go,
And pine away with daily wasting woe?
Tell me, you wanton brook;
So may your sliding race
Shun loathed-loving banks with cunning crook;

So in you ever new
Mira may look her face,
And make you fair with shadow of her hue;
So when to pay your due
To mother sea you come,
She chide you not for stay,
Nor beat you for your play;
Tell me, if your diverted springs become
Absented quite from you,
Are you not dried? Can you yourselves renew?
Tell me, you flowers fair,
Cowslip and columbine;
So may your make this wholesome spring time air
With you embraced lie,
And lately thence untwine,
But with dew drops engender children high;
So may you never die,
But, pulled by Mira's hand,
Dress bosom hers, or head,
Or scatter on her bed;
Tell me, if husband spring time leave your land
When he from you is sent,
Wither not you, languished with discontent?
Tell me, my siily pipe;
So may thee still betide
A cleanly cloth thy moistness for to wipe;
So may the cherries red
Of Mira's lips divide
Their sugared selves to kiss thy happy head;
So may her ears be led,
Her ears where music lives,

make] mate

To hear and not despise
Thy liribliring cries;
Tell if that breath, which thee thy sounding gives,
Be absent far from thee,
Absent alone canst thou, then, piping be?
Tell me, my lamb of gold;
So mayst thou long abide
The day well fed, the night in faithful fold;
So grow thy wool of note
In time, that, richly dyed,
It may be part of Mira's petticoat;
Tell me, if wolves the throat
Have caught of thy dear dam,
Or she from thee be stayed,
Or thou from her be strayed,
Canst thou, poor lamb, become another's lamb,
Or rather, till thou die,
Still for thy dam with baa-waymenting cry?
Tell me, O turtle true;
So may no fortune breed
To make thee nor thy better-loved rue;
So may thy blessings swarm,
That Mira may thee feed
With hand and mouth, with lap and breast keep warm;
Tell me if greedy arm
Do fondly take away,
With traitor lime, the one,
The other left alone;
Tell me, poor wretch, parted from wretched prey,
Disdain not you the green,

liribliring] warbling
baa-waymenting] lamenting with bleats

Wailing till death shun you not to be seen?
Earth, brook, flowers, pipe, lamb, dove
Say all, and I with them,
Absence is death, or worse, to them that love.
So I, unlucky lad,
Whom hills from her do hem,
What fits me now but tears and sighings sad!
O Fortune, too too bad!
I rather would my sheep
Th 'adst killed with a stroke,
Burnt cabin, lost my cloak,
Than want one hour those eyes which my joys keep
O, what doth wailing win?
Speech without end were better not begin.
My song, climb thou the wind,
Which Holland sweet now gently sendeth in,
That on his wings the level thou mayst find
To hit, but kissing hit
Her ears, the weights of wit.
If thou know not for whom thy master dies,
These marks shall make thee wise.
She is the herdress fair that shines in dark,
And gives her kids no food, but willow's bark.'
This said, at length he ended
His oft sigh-broken ditty;
Then rose, but rose on legs which faintness bended,
With skin in sorrow dyed,
With face the plot of pity,
With thoughts, which thoughts, their own tormentors, tried;
He rose, and straight espied
His ram, who to recover
The ewe another loved,

With him proud battle proved.
He envied such a death in sight of lover,
And always westward eying,
More envied Phoebus for his western flying.

Written 1580–3; *Arcadia*, 1598

115 *Solitariness*

OH SWEET woods, the delight of solitariness!
Oh, how much I do like your solitariness!
Where man's mind hath a freed consideration,
Of goodness to receive lovely direction;
Where senses do behold th' order of heavenly host,
And wise thoughts do behold what the Creator is.
Contemplation here holdeth his only seat,
Bounded with no limits, borne with a wing of hope,
Climbs even unto the stars; Nature is under it.
Nought disturbs thy quiet, all to thy service yields;
Each sight draws on a thought (thought, mother of science);
Sweet birds kindly do grant harmony unto thee;
Fair trees' shade is enough fortification,
Nor danger to thyself if be not in thyself.

O sweet woods, the delight of solitariness!
Oh, how much I do like your solitariness!
Here nor treason is hid, veiled in innocence;
Nor envy's snaky eye finds any harbour here;
Nor flatterers' venomous insinuations,
Nor cunning humourists' puddled opinions,
Nor courteous ruin of proffered usury,
Nor time prattled away, cradle of ignorance,
Nor causeless duty, nor cumber of arrogance,
Nor trifling title of vanity dazzleth us,
Nor golden manacles stand for a paradise.
Here wrong's name is unheard, slander a monster is.
Keep thy spright from abuse; here no abuse doth haunt.
What man grafts in a tree dissimulation?

O sweet woods, the delight of solitariness!
Oh, how well I do like your solitariness!
Yet, dear soil, if a soul closed in a mansion
As sweet as violets, fair as lily is,
Straight as cedar, a voice stains the canary bird's,
Whose shade safely doth hold, danger avoideth her;
Such wisdom that in her lives speculation;
Such goodness that in her simplicity triumphs;
Where envy's snaky eye winketh or else dieth;
Slander wants a pretext, flattery gone beyond;
Oh! if such a one have bent to a lonely life,
Her steps glad we receive, glad we receive her eyes,
And think not she doth hurt our solitariness,
For such company decks such solitariness.

Ibid.

116 *Sleep*

LOCK up, fair lids, the treasure of my heart;
  Preserve those beams, this age's only light;
To her sweet sense, sweet sleep, some ease impart,
  Her sense too weak to bear her spirit's might.
  And while, O sleep, thou closest up her sight,
Her sight where Love did forge his fairest dart,
  Oh, harbour all her parts in easeful plight;
Let no strange dream make her fair body start.
But yet, O dream, if thou wilt not depart
  In this rare subject from thy common right,
  But wilt thyself in such a seat delight,
Then take my shape, and play a lover's part.
    Kiss her from me, and say unto her spright,
    Till her eyes shine I live in darkest night. *Arcadia*, 1598

117 *Madrigal*

WHY dost thou haste away,
  O Titan fair, the giver of the day?
Is it to carry news
To western wights what stars in east appear?
Or dost thou think that here
Is left a sun, whose beams thy place may use?
Yet stay, and well peruse
What be her gifts, that make her equal thee;
Bend all thy light to see
In earthly clothes enclosed a heavenly spark;
Thy running course cannot such beauties mark.
No, no; thy motions be
Hastened from us, with bar of shadow dark,
Because that thou, the author of our sight,
Disdain'st we see thee stained with other's light. *Ibid.*

SIR EDWARD DYER

?–1607

118

Kingdom

MY mind to me a kingdom is,
  Such present joys therein I find,
That it excels all other bliss
  That world affords or grows by kind.
Though much I want which most would have,
Yet still my mind forbids to crave.

No princely pomp, no wealthy store,
  No force to win the victory,
No wily wit to salve a sore,
  No shape to feed a loving eye;
To none of these I yield as thrall,
For why my mind doth serve for all.

I see how plenty suffers oft,
  And hasty climbers soon do fall;
I see that those which are aloft
  Mishap doth threaten most of all;
They get with toil, they keep with fear:
Such cares my mind could never bear.

Content I live, this is my stay,
  I seek no more than may suffice;
I press to bear no haughty sway;
  Look, what I lack my mind supplies.
Lo! thus I triumph like a king,
Content with that my mind doth bring.

For why] Because

SIR EDWARD DYER

Some have too much, yet still do crave;
  I little have, and seek no more.
They are but poor, though much they have,
  And I am rich with little store.
They poor, I rich; they beg, I give;
They lack, I leave; they pine, I live.

I laugh not at another's loss;
  I grudge not at another's gain;
No worldly waves my mind can toss:
  My state at one doth still remain.
I fear no foe, I fawn no friend;
I loathe not life, nor dread my end.

Some weigh their pleasure by their lust,
  Their wisdom by their rage of will;
Their treasure is their only trust,
  A cloaked craft their store of skill:
But all the pleasure that I find
Is to maintain a quiet mind.

My wealth is health and perfect ease,
  My conscience clear my choice defence;
I neither seek by bribes to please,
  Nor by deceit to breed offence.
Thus do I live; thus will I die;
Would all did so as well as I!

Rawlinson Poet. MS. 85

119 *A Modest Love*

THE lowest trees have tops, the ant her gall,
  The fly her spleen, the little sparks their heat;
The slender hairs cast shadows, though but small,
  And bees have stings, although they be not great;
Seas have their source, and so have shallow springs;
And love is love, in beggars as in kings.

Where rivers smoothest run, deep are the fords;
  The dial stirs, yet none perceives it move;
The firmest faith is in the fewest words;
  The turtles cannot sing, and yet they love:
True hearts have eyes and ears, no tongues to speak;
They hear and see, and sigh, and then they break.

Poetical Rhapsody, 1602

120 *Cynthia*

AMIDST the fairest mountain tops,
  Where Zephyrus doth breathe
The pleasant gale, that clothes with flowers
  The valleys underneath,

A shepherd lived, that dearly loved
  (Dear love time brought to pass)
A forest nymph, who was as fair
  As ever woman was.

His thoughts were higher than the hills
  Whereof he had the keep,
But all his actions innocent,
  As humble as his sheep:

Yet had he power, but her pure thoughts
Debarred his powers to rise
Higher than kissing of her hands
Or looking in her eyes.

One day (I need not name the day
To lovers of their sorrows,
But say, as once a shepherd said,
Their moan nights have no morrows)

He from his sheep-cot led his sheep
To pasture in the lease,
And there to feed while he, the while,
Might dream of his disease.

And all alone (if he remain
Alone, that is in love)
Unto himself alone he mourned
The passions he did prove.

'O heavens! (quoth he) are these th' effects
Of faithful love's deserts?
Will Cynthia now forsake my love?
Have women faithless hearts?

'And will not wits, nor words, nor works,
Nor long-endured laments,
Bring to my plaints pity or peace,
Or to my tears contents?

lease] pasture

SIR EDWARD DYER

'I, that enchained my love desires,
From changing thoughts as free,
As ever were true thoughts to her,
Or her thoughts false to me.

'I that for her my wandering sheep
Forsook, forgot, forwent,
Nor of myself, nor them took keep,
But in her love's content.

'Shall I, like meads with winter's rain,
Be turned into tears?
Shall I, of whose true feeling pain
These greens the record bears,

'Causeless, be scorned, disdained, despised?
Then, witness this desire,
Love was in woman's weed disguised,
And not in men's attire.'

And thus he said, and down he lies,
Sighing as life would part:
'O! Cynthia, thou hast angel's eyes,
But yet a woman's heart.'

Gentleman's Magazine, lxxxii, 1812

FULKE GREVILLE, LORD BROOKE

1554–1628

121 *Caelica*

LOVE, the delight of all well-thinking minds,
  Delight, the fruit of virtue dearly loved,
Virtue, the highest good that reason finds,
  Reason, the fire wherein men's thoughts be proved,
Are from the world by Nature's power bereft,
And in one creature for her glory left.

Beauty her cover is, the eye's true pleasure;
  In honour's fame she lives, the ear's sweet music;
Excess of wonder grows from her true measure;
  Her worth is passion's wound and passion's physic;
From her true heart clear springs of wisdom flow,
Which, imaged in her words and deeds, men know.

Time fain would stay that she might never leave her,
  Place doth rejoice that she must needs contain her,
Death craves of heaven that she may not bereave her,
  The heavens know their own and do maintain her.
Delight, Love, Reason, Virtue, let it be
To set all women light but only she.

Caelica, written c. 1586; in *Certain Learned and Elegant Works*, 1633

122

To His Lady

MORE than most fair, full of that heavenly fire
  Kindled above to show the Maker's glory,
Beauty's first-born, in whom all powers conspire
  To write the Graces' life, and Muses' story,
If in my heart all saints else be defaced,
Honour the shrine where you alone are placed.

Thou window of the sky, and pride of spirits,
  True character of honour in perfection,
Thou heavenly creature, judge of earthly merits,
  And glorious prison of man's pure affection,
If in my heart all nymphs else be defaced,
Honour the shrine where you alone are placed.

Ibid.

123

His Lady's Eyes

YOU little stars that live in skies,
  And glory in Apollo's glory,
In whose aspects conjoined lies
  The Heaven's will and Nature's story,
Joy to be likened to those eyes,
  Which eyes make all eyes glad or sorry;
For when you force thoughts from above,
These overrule your force by love.

And thou, O Love, which in these eyes
  Hast married Reason with Affection,
And made them saints of Beauty's skies,
  Where joys are shadows of perfection,

Lend me thy wings that I may rise
Up not by worth but thy election;
For I have vowed, in strangest fashion,
To love, and never seek compassion.

Caelica, 1633

124 *Change*

THE world, that all contains, is ever moving;
The stars within their spheres for ever turned;
Nature, the queen of change, to change is loving,
And form to matter new is still adjourned.
Fortune, our fancy-god, to vary liketh;
Place is not bound to things within it placed;
The present time upon time passed striketh;
With Phoebus' wandering course the earth is graced.
The air still moves, and by its moving cleareth;
The fire up ascends, and planets feedeth;
The water passeth on, and all lets weareth;
The earth stands still, yet change of changes breedeth.
Her plants, which summer ripes, in winter fade;
Each creature in unconstant mother lieth;
Man made of earth, and for whom earth is made,
Still dying lives, and living ever dieth.
Only, like fate, sweet Myra never varies,
Yet in her eyes the doom of all change carries.

Ibid.

125

Love's Glory

FIE, foolish earth, think you the heaven wants glory,
  Because your shadows do yourself benight?
All 's dark unto the blind, let them be sorry;
  The heavens in themselves are ever bright.
Fie, fond desire, think you that love wants glory,
  Because your shadows do yourself benight?
The hopes and fears of lust may make men sorry,
  But love still in herself finds her delight.
Then earth, stand fast, the sky that you benight
  Will turn again, and so restore your glory;
Desire, be steady, hope is your delight,
  An orb wherein no creature can be sorry;
    Love being placed above these middle regions
    Where every passion wars itself with legions.

Ibid.

126

Myra

I, WITH whose colours Myra dressed her head,
  I, that ware posies of her own hand-making,
I, that mine own name in the chimneys read
  By Myra finely wrought ere I was waking;
    Must I look on, in hope time coming may
    With change bring back my turn again to play?

I, that on Sunday at the church-stile found
  A garland sweet, with true-love knots in flowers,
Which I to wear about mine arm was bound,
  That each of us might know that all was ours;
    Must I now lead an idle life in wishes,
    And follow Cupid for his loaves and fishes?

I, that did wear the ring her mother left,
  I, for whose love she gloried to be blamed,
I, with whose eyes her eyes committed theft,
  I, who did make her blush when I was named;
    Must I lose ring, flowers, blush, theft, and go naked,
    Watching with sighs, till dead love be awaked?

I, that, when drowsy Argus fell asleep,
  Like jealousy o'erwatched with desire,
Was ever warned modesty to keep,
  While her breath, speaking, kindled Nature's fire;
    Must I look on a-cold, while others warm them?
    Do Vulcan's brothers in such fine nets arm them?

Was it for this that I might Myra see
  Washing the water, with her beauties, white?
Yet would she never write her love to me.
  Thinks wit of change, while thoughts are in delight?
    Mad girls must safely love, as they may leave;
    No man can print a kiss; lines may deceive.

Caelica, 1633

127 *Love and Fortune*

FACTION, that ever dwells
In courts where wit excels,
    Hath set defiance;
Fortune and Love have sworn
That they were never born
    Of one alliance.

FULKE GREVILLE, LORD BROOKE

Cupid, that doth aspire
To be god of desire,
    Swears he gives laws;
That where his arrows hit,
Some joy, some sorrow it;
    Fortune no cause.

Fortune swears weakest hearts,
The books of Cupid's arts,
    Turn with her wheel;
Senses themselves shall prove
Venture hath place in love;
    Ask them that feel.

This discord it begot
Atheists that honour not.
    Nature thought good,
Fortune should ever dwell
In courts where wits excel,
    Love keep the wood.

Thus to the wood went I,
With Love to live and die;
    Fortune's forlorn.
Experience of my youth
Thus makes me think the truth
    In desert born.

My saint is dear to me,
Myra herself is she,
    She fair and true;
Myra that knows to move
Passions of love with love.
    Fortune, adieu!

Ibid.

128 *Youth and Maturity*

THE nurse-life wheat, within his green husk growing,
  Flatters our hope, and tickles our desire,
Nature's true riches in sweet beauties showing,
  Which set all hearts, with labour's love, on fire.
No less fair is the wheat when golden ear
  Shows unto hope the joys of near enjoying;
Fair and sweet is the bud, more sweet and fair
  The rose, which proves that time is not destroying.
Caelica, your youth, the morning of delight,
  Enamelled o'er with beauties white and red,
All sense and thoughts did to belief invite,
  That love and glory there are brought to bed;
    And your ripe years love none; he goes no higher,
    Turns all the spirits of man into desire.

Caelica, 1633

129 *Absence and Presence*

ABSENCE, the noble truce
  Of Cupid's war,
Where, though desires want use,
    They honoured are,
Thou art the just protection
Of prodigal affection;
    Have thou the praise.
When bankrupt Cupid braveth,
Thy mines his credit saveth
    With sweet delays.

FULKE GREVILLE, LORD BROOKE

Of wounds which presence makes
With beauty's shot
Absence the anguish slakes,
But healeth not.
Absence records the stories
Wherein desire glories;
Although she burn,
She cherisheth the spirits,
Where constancy inherits
And passions mourn.

Absence, like dainty clouds
On glorious-bright,
Nature's weak senses shrouds
From harming light.
Absence maintains the treasure
Of pleasure unto pleasure,
Sparing with praise.
Absence doth nurse the fire,
Which starves and feeds desire
With sweet delays.

Presence to every part
Of beauty ties;
Where wonder rules the heart,
There pleasure dies.
Presence plagues mind and senses
With modesty's defences;
Absence is free.
Thoughts do in absence venture
On Cupid's shadowed centre;
They wink and see.

But thoughts, be not so brave
  With absent joy;
For you with that you have
  Yourself destroy.
The absence which you glory
Is that which makes you sorry,
  And burn in vain;
For thought is not the weapon
Wherewith thought's ease men cheapen,
  Absence is pain.

Caelica, 1633

130

Cynthia

AWAY with these self-loving lads,
Whom Cupid's arrow never glads!
Away, poor souls, that sigh and weep
In love of those that lie asleep!
  For Cupid is a meadow-god,
  And forceth none to kiss the rod.

Sweet Cupid's shafts, like destiny,
Do causeless good or ill decree;
Desert is born out of his bow;
Reward upon his wing doth go.
  What fools are they that have not known
  That Love likes no laws but his own!

My songs they be of Cynthia's praise,
I wear her rings on holy days;
In every tree I write her name,
And every day I read the same.
  Where Honour Cupid's rival is,
  There miracles are seen of his.

cheapen] purchase

If Cynthia crave her ring of me,
I blot her name out of the tree.
If doubt do darken things held dear,
Then well fare nothing once a year!
    For many run, but one must win;
    Fools, only, hedge the cuckoo in.

The worth that worthiness should move
Is love, that is the bow of Love.
And love as well the foster can
As can the mighty nobleman.
    Sweet Saint, 'tis true you worthy be,
    Yet without love nought worth to me.

Ibid.

131 *Love and Honour*

IN the window of a grange,
Whence men's prospects cannot range
Over groves and flowers growing,
Nature's wealth and pleasure showing,
But on graves where shepherds lie,
That by love or sickness die;
In that window saw I sit
Caelica adorning it,
Sadly clad for sorrow's glory,
Making joy glad to be sorry,
Showing sorrow in such fashion,
As truth seemed in love with passion;
Such a sweet enamel giveth
Love restrained that constant liveth.
Absence, that bred all this pain,
Presence healed not straight again;

foster] forester

Eyes from dark to sudden light
See not straight, nor can delight.
Where the heart revives from death,
Groans do first send forth a breath
So, first looks did looks beget,
One sigh did another fet;
Hearts within their breast did quak
While thoughts to each other spake.
Philocell entranced stood,
Racked and joyed with his good;
His eyes on her eyes were fixed,
Where both true love and shame were mixed;
In her eyes he pity saw,
His love did to pity draw,
But love found, when it came there,
Pity was transformed to fear.
Then he thought that in her face
He saw love and promised grace.
Love calls his love to appear,
But, as soon as it came near,
Her love to her bosom fled,
Under honour's burdens dead.
Honour in love's stead took place
To grace shame with love's disgrace;
But, like drops thrown on the fire,
Shame's restraints enflamed desire.
Desire looks and in her eyes
The image of itself espies,
Whence he takes self-pity's motions
To be Cynthia's own devotions;
And resolves fear is a liar,
Thinking she bids speak desire.

But true love, that fears and dare
Offend itself with pleasing care,
So divers ways his heart doth move,
That his tongue cannot speak of love.
Only in himself he says,
'How fatal are blind Cupid's ways'.

Caelica, 1633

132 *Caelica and Philocell*

IN the time when herbs and flowers,
Springing out of melting powers,
Teach the earth that heat and rain
Do make Cupid live again,
Late when Sol, like great hearts, shows
Largest as he lowest goes,
Caelica with Philocell
In fellowship together fell.
Caelica, her skin was fair,
Dainty auburn was her hair;
Her hair Nature dyed brown,
To become the mourning gown
Of Hope's death, which to her eyes
Offers thoughts for sacrifice.
Philocell was true and kind,
Poor, but not of poorest mind;
Though mischance to harm affected
Hides and holdeth worth suspected.
He good shepherd loved well,
But Caelica scorned Philocell.
Through enamelled meads they went,
Quiet she, he passion-rent.

Her worths to him hope did move;
Her worths made him fear to love.
His heart sighs and fain would show
That which all the world did know;
His heart sighed the sighs of fear,
And durst not tell her love was there.
But as thoughts in troubled sleep
Dreaming fear, and fearing weep;
When for help they fain would cry,
Cannot speak, and helpless lie:
So while his heart, full of pain,
Would itself in words complain,
Pain of all pains, lover's fear,
Makes his heart to silence swear.

ll. 1–36; *Caelica*, 1633

133

Time and Eternity

YOU that seek what life is in death,
Now find it air that once was breath,
New names unknown, old names gone,
Till time end bodies, but souls none.
Reader! then make time, while you be,
But steps to your eternity.

Ibid.

134

Despair

WHO grace for zenith had,
From which no shadows grow,
Who hath seen joy of all his hopes
And end of all his woe;

Whose love beloved hath been
 The crown of his desire,
Who hath seen sorrow's glories burnt
 In sweet affection's fire;

If from this heavenly state,
 Which souls with souls unites,
He be fallen down into the dark
 Despaired war of sprights;

Let him lament with me,
 For none doth glory know,
That hath not been above himself,
 And thence fallen down to woe.

But if there be one hope
 Left in his languished heart,
If fear of worse, if wish of ease,
 If horror may depart;

He plays with his complaints,
 He is no mate for me,
Whose love is lost, whose hopes are fled,
 Whose fears for ever be.

Yet not those happy fears,
 Which show desire her death,
Teaching with use a peace in woe,
 And in despair a faith.

No, no, my fears kill not,
 But make uncured wounds,
Where joy and peace do issue out,
 And only pain abounds.

Unpossible are help,
  Reward and hope to me;
Yet, while unpossible they are,
  They easy seem to be.

Most easy seems remorse,
  Despair and death to me;
Yet, while they passing easy seem,
  Unpossible they be.

So neither can I leave
  My hopes that do deceive,
Nor can I trust my own despair,
  And nothing else receive.

Thus be unhappy men
  Blest to be more accurst;
Near to the glories of the sun,
  Clouds with most horror burst.

Like ghosts raised out of graves,
  Who live not, though they go,
Whose walking fear to others is
  And to themselves a woe;

So is my life by her,
  Whose love to me is dead,
On whose worth my despair yet walks,
  And my desire is fed.

I swallow down the bait
  Which carries down my death;
I cannot put love from my heart,
  While life draws in my breath.

FULKE GREVILLE, LORD BROOKE

My winter is within,
  Which withereth my joy,
My knowledge seat of civil war,
  Where friends and foes destroy;

And my desires are wheels,
  Whereon my heart is borne,
With endless turning of themselves,
  Still living to be torn.

My thoughts are eagles' food,
  Ordained to be a prey
To worth; and being still consumed,
  Yet never to decay.

My memory, where once
  My heart laid up the store
Of help, of joy, of spirit's wealth,
  To multiply them more,

Is now become the tomb
  Wherein all these lie slain,
My help, my joy, my spirit's wealth,
  All sacrificed to pain.

In paradise I once
  Did live and taste the tree,
Which shadowed was from all the world,
  In joy to shadow me.

The tree hath lost his fruit,
  Or I have lost my seat;
My soul both black with shadow is
  And over-burnt with heat.

Truth here for triumph serves
  To show her power is great,
Whom no desert can overcome,
  Nor no distress entreat.

Time past lays up my joy,
  And time to come my grief;
She ever must be my desire
  And never my relief.

Wrong her lieutenant is;
  My wounded thoughts are they,
Who have no power to keep the field,
  Nor will to run away.

O rueful constancy,
  And where is change so base,
As it may be compared with thee
  In scorn and in disgrace?

Like as the kings forlorn,
  Deposed from their estate,
Yet cannot choose but love the crown,
  Although new kings they hate;

If they do plead their right,
  Nay, if they only live,
Offences to the crown alike
  Their good and ill shall give;

So I would I were not,
  Because I may complain,
And cannot choose but love my wrongs,
  And joy to wish in vain.

This faith condemneth me;
  My right doth rumour move;
I may not know the cause I fell,
  Nor yet without cause love.

Then, Love, where is reward,
  At least where is the fame
Of them that, being, bear thy cross,
  And, being not, thy name?

The world's example, I,
  A fable, everywhere,
A well from whence the springs are dried,
  A tree that doth not bear.

I, like the bird in cage,
  At first with cunning caught,
And in my bondage for delight
  With greater cunning taught,

Now owner's humour dies,
  I neither loved nor fed
Nor freëd am, till in the cage
  Forgotten I be dead.

The ship of Greece, the streams,
  And she, be not the same
They were, although ship, streams, and she
  Still bear their antique name.

The wood which was is worn,
  Those waves are run away,
Yet still a ship, and still a stream,
  Still running to a sea.

FULKE GREVILLE, LORD BROOKE

She loved and still she loves,
But doth not still love me;
To all except myself yet is,
As she was wont to be.

O, my once happy thoughts,
The heaven where grace did dwell!
My saint hath turned away her face,
And made that heaven my hell;

A hell, for so is that
From whence no souls return,
Whence, while our sprights are sacrificed,
They waste not, though they burn.

Since then this is my state,
And nothing worse than this,
Behold the map of death-like life,
Exiled from lovely bliss.

Alone among the world,
Strange with my friends to be,
Showing my fall to them that scorn,
See not or will not see;

My heart a wilderness,
My studies only fear,
And, as in shadows of curst death,
A prospect of despair;

My exercise must be
My horrors to repeat,
My peace, joy, end, and sacrifice
Her dead love to entreat;

FULKE GREVILLE, LORD BROOKE

My food the time that was,
  The time to come my fast,
For drink the barren thirst I feel
  Of glories that are past;

Sighs and salt tears my bath,
  Reason my looking-glass,
To show me he most wretched is,
  That once most happy was;

Forlorn desires my clock,
  To tell me every day,
That time hath stolen love, life, and all
  But my distress away;

For music heavy signs,
  My walk an inward woe,
Which like a shadow ever shall
  Before my body go.

And I myself am he
  That doth with none compare,
Except in woes and lack of worth,
  Whose states most wretched are.

Let no man ask my name,
  Nor what else I should be;
For *Greiv-Ill*, pain, forlorn estate,
  Do best decipher me.

Caelica, 1633

135 *Farewell to Cupid*

FAREWELL, sweet boy, complain not of my truth;
Thy mother loved thee not with more devotion;
For to thy boy's play I gave all my youth;
Young master, I did hope for your promotion.
While some sought honours, prince's thoughts observing,
Many wooed fame, the child of pain and anguish,
Others judged inward good a chief deserving,
I in thy wanton visions joyed to languish.
I bowed not to thy image for succession,
Nor bound thy bow to shoot reformed kindness;
Thy plays of hope and fear were my confession,
The spectacles to my life was thy blindness.
But Cupid, now farewell, I will go play me
With thoughts that please me less, and less betray me.

Caelica, 1633

136 *Epitaph on Sir Philip Sidney*

SILENCE augmenteth grief, writing increaseth rage,
Staled are my thoughts, which loved and lost the wonder of our age:
Yet quickened now with fire, though dead with frost ere now,
Enraged I write I know not what; dead, quick, I know not how.

Hard-hearted minds relent and rigour's tears abound,
And envy strangely rues his end, in whom no fault she found.
Knowledge her light hath lost; valour hath slain her knight.
Sidney is dead; dead is my friend; dead is the world's delight.

Place, pensive, wails his fall whose presence was her pride;
Time crieth out, 'My ebb is come; his life was my spring tide.'
Fame mourns in that she lost the ground of her reports;
Each living wight laments his lack, and all in sundry sorts.

He was (woe worth that word!) to each well-thinking mind
A spotless friend, a matchless man, whose virtue ever shined,
Declaring in his thoughts, his life, and that he writ,
Highest conceits, longest foresights, and deepest works of wit.

He, only like himself, was second unto none,
Whose death (though life) we rue, and wrong, and all in vain
do moan.
Their loss, not him, wail they, that fill the world with cries,
Death slew not him, but he made death his ladder to the skies.

Now sink of sorrow I, who live, the more the wrong!
Who wishing death, whom death denies, whose thread is all
too long;
Who tied to wretched life, who looks for no relief,
Must spend my ever dying days in never ending grief.

Heart's ease and only I, like parallels, run on,
Whose equal length keep equal breadth, and never meet in one;
Yet for not wronging him, my thoughts, my sorrow's cell,
Shall not run out, though leak they will, for liking him so well.

Farewell to you, my hopes, my wonted waking dreams,
Farewell, sometimes enjoyed joy; eclipsed are thy beams.
Farewell, self-pleasing thoughts, which quietness brings forth;
And farewell, friendship's sacred league, uniting minds of
worth.

And farewell, merry heart, the gift of guiltless minds,
And all sports which for life's restore variety assigns;
Let all that sweet is void; in me no mirth may dwell.
Philip, the cause of all this woe, my life's content, farewell!

Now rhyme, the son of rage, which art no kin to skill,
And endless grief, which deads my life, yet knows not how to
    kill,
Go, seek that hapless tomb, which if ye hap to find,
Salute the stones, that keep the limbs, that held so good a mind.

The Phoenix Nest, 1593

A. W.

c. 1586

137 *Where his Lady Keeps his Heart*

SWEET Love, mine only treasure,
    For service long unfeigned,
    Wherein I nought have gained,
Vouchsafe this little pleasure,
    To tell me in what part
    My lady keeps my heart.

If in her hair so slender,
    Like golden nets entwined,
    Which fire and art have fined,
Her thrall my heart I render,
    For ever to abide
    With locks so dainty tied.

If in her eyes she bind it,
Wherein that fire was framed,
By which it is inflamed,
I dare not look to find it;
I only wish it sight,
To see that pleasant light.

But if her breast have deigned
With kindness to receive it,
I am content to leave it,
Though death thereby were gained;
Then, lady, take your own,
That lives for you alone.

Poetical Rhapsody, 1602

138 *Ladies' Eyes Serve Cupid both for Darts and Fire*

OFT have I mused the cause to find,
Why Love in ladies' eyes doth dwell.
I thought, because himself was blind,
He looked that they should guide him well.
And sure his hope but seldom fails,
And Love by ladies' eyes prevails.

But time at last hath taught me wit,
Although I bought my wit full dear;
For by her eyes my heart is hit,
Deep is the wound, though none appear.
Their glancing beams as darts he throws,
And sure he hath no shafts but those.

I mused to see their eyes so bright,
  And little thought they had been fire;
I gazed upon them with delight,
  But that delight hath bred desire.
What better place can Love require,
Than that where grow both shafts and fire?

Poetical Rhapsody, 1602

139 *Upon Visiting his Lady by Moonlight*

THE night, say all, was made for rest;
  And so say I, but not for all:
To them the darkest nights are best,
  Which give them leave asleep to fall;
    But I that seek my rest by light
    Hate sleep, and praise the clearest night.

Bright was the moon, as bright as day,
  And Venus glistered in the west,
Whose light did lead the ready way,
  That brought me to my wished rest:
    Then each of them increased their light
    While I enjoyed her heavenly sight.

Say, gentle dames, what moved your mind
  To shine so bright above your wont?
Would Phoebe fair Endymion find?
  Would Venus see Adonis hunt?
    No, no, you feared by her sight
    To lose the praise of beauty bright.

At last for shame you shrunk away,
  And thought to reave the world of light;
Then shone my dame with brighter ray,
  Than that which comes from Phoebus' sight:
    None other light but her's I praise,
    Whose nights are clearer than the days.

Ibid.

140 *Petition to Have her Leave to Die*

WHEN will the fountain of my tears be dry?
  When will my sighs be spent?
When will desire agree to let me die?
  When will thy heart relent?
It is not for my life I plead,
Since death the way to rest doth lead;
    But stay for thy consent,
    Lest thou be discontent.

For if myself without thy leave I kill,
  My ghost will never rest;
So hath it sworn to work thine only will,
  And holds that ever best;
For since it only lives by thee,
Good reason thou the ruler be.
    Then give me leave to die,
    And show thy power thereby.

Ibid.

reave] rob

A. W.

141 *Dispraise of Love and Lovers' Follies*

IF love be life, I long to die,
  Live they that list for me;
And he that gains the most thereby
  A fool at least shall be:
But he that feels the sorest fits
'Scapes with no less than loss of wits.
    Unhappy life they gain
    Which love do entertain.

In day by feigned looks they live,
  By lying dreams in night;
Each frown a deadly wound doth give,
  Each smile a false delight.
If 't hap their lady pleasant seem,
It is for other's love they deem;
    If void she seem of joy,
    Disdain doth make her coy.

Such is the peace that lovers find.
  Such is the life they lead,
Blown here and there with every wind,
  Like flowers in the mead.
Now war, now peace, then war again,
Desire, despair, delight, disdain;
    Though dead, in midst of life;
    In peace, and yet at strife.

Poetical Rhapsody, 1602

A. W.

142 *In Praise of the Sun*

THE golden sun that brings the day,
And lends men light to see withal,
In vain doth cast his beams away,
Where they are blind on whom they fall.
There is no force in all his light,
To give the mole a perfect sight.

But thou, my sun, more bright than he,
That shines at noon in summer tide,
Hast given me light and power to see,
With perfect skill my sight to guide.
Till now I lived as blind as mole,
That hides her head in earthly hole.

I heard the praise of beauty's grace,
Yet deemed it nought but poet's skill;
I gazed on many a lovely face,
Yet found I none to bind my will:
Which made me think, that beauty bright
Was nothing else but red and white.

But now thy beams have cleared my sight,
I blush to think I was so blind;
Thy flaming eyes afford me light,
That beauty's blaze each where I find:
And yet these dames, that shine so bright,
Are but the shadow of thy light.

Ibid.

143 *Hopeless Desire soon Withers and Dies*

THOUGH naked trees seem dead to sight,
  When winter wind doth keenly blow,
Yet if the root maintain her right,
  The spring their hidden life will show:
    But if the root be dead and dry,
    No marvel though the branches die.

While hope did live within my breast,
  No winter storm could kill desire;
But now disdain hath hope oppressed,
  Dead is the root, dead is the spire.
    Hope was the root, the spire was love;
    No sap beneath, no life above.

And as we see the rootless stock
  Retain some sap, and spring a while;
Yet quickly prove a lifeless block,
  Because the root doth life beguile:
    So lives desire which hope hath left,
    As twilight shines when sun is reft.

Poetical Rhapsody, 1602

144 *A Song in Praise of a Beggar's Life*

BRIGHT shines the sun; play, beggars, play!
Here 's scraps enough to serve to-day.
What noise of viols is so sweet,
  As when our merry clappers ring?
What mirth doth want where beggars meet?
  A beggar's life is for a king.

Eat, drink, and play ; sleep when we list ;
Go where we will, so stocks be missed.
    Bright shines the sun ; play, beggars, play!
    Here 's scraps enough to serve to-day.

The world is ours, and ours alone,
  For we alone have world at will ;
We purchase not, all is our own ;
  Both fields and streets we beggars fill.
Nor care to get nor fear to keep
Did ever break a beggar's sleep.
    Bright shines the sun; play, beggars, play!
    Here 's scraps enough to serve to-day.

A hundred head of black and white
  Upon our gowns securely feed;
If any dare his master bite,
  He dies therefore, as sure as creed.
Thus beggars lord it as they please;
And none but beggars live at ease.
    Bright shines the sun; play, beggars, play!
    Here 's scraps enough to serve to-day.

Ibid.

CHIDIOCK TICHBORNE

ob. 1586

145 *Elegy*

MY prime of youth is but a frost of cares,
  My feast of joy is but a dish of pain,
My crop of corn is but a field of tares,
  And all my good is but vain hope of gain;
    The day is past, and yet I saw no sun,
    And now I live, and now my life is done.

My tale was heard and yet it was not told,
  My fruit is fallen and yet my leaves are green,
My youth is spent and yet I am not old,
  I saw the world and yet I was not seen;
    My thread is cut and yet it is not spun,
    And now I live, and now my life is done.

I sought my death and found it in my womb,
  I looked for life and saw it was a shade,
I trod the earth and knew it was my tomb,
  And now I die, and now I was but made;
    My glass is full, and now my glass is run,
    And now I live, and now my life is done.

Verses of Praise and Joy, 1586

CHARLES TILNEY ob. 1586

146 *The Cobblers' Song*

Trumpart. We cobblers lead a merry life,
All. Dan, dan, dan, dan;
Strumbo. Void of all envy and of strife,
All. Dan diddle dan.
Dorothy. Our ease is great, our labour small,
All. Dan, dan, dan, dan;
Strumbo. And yet our gains be much withal,
All. Dan diddle dan.
Dorothy. With this art so fine and fair,
All. Dan, dan, dan, dan,
Trumpart. No occupation may compare,
All. Dan diddle dan.
Strumbo. For merry pastime and joyful glee,
Dan, dan, dan, dan,
Dorothy. Most happy men we cobblers be,
Dan diddle dan.

Trumpart. The can stands full of nappy ale,
Dan, dan, dan, dan ;
Strumbo. In our shop still withouten fail,
Dan diddle dan.
Dorothy. This is our meat, this is our food,
Dan, dan, dan, dan ;
Trumpart. This brings us to a merry mood,
Dan diddle dan.
Strumbo. This makes us work for company,
Dan, dan, dan, dan,
Dorothy. To pull the tankards cheerfully,
Dan diddle dan.
Trumpart. Drink to thy husband, Dorothy,
Dan, dan, dan, dan ;
Dorothy. Why, then, my Strumbo, there 's to thee,
Dan diddle dan.
Strumbo. Drink thou the rest, Trumpart, amain,
Dan, dan, dan, dan ;
Dorothy. When that is gone, we'll fill 't again,
Dan diddle dan.

Locrine, 1595

ROBERT SOUTHWELL

c. 1561–1595

147 *Times Go by Turns*

THE lopped tree in time may grow again,
Most naked plants renew both fruit and flower ;
The sorriest wight may find release of pain,
The driest soil suck in some moistening shower.
Times go by turns, and chances change by course,
From foul to fair, from better hap to worse.

The sea of Fortune doth not ever flow,
She draws her favours to the lowest ebb
Her tides hath equal times to come and go,
Her loom doth weave the fine and coarsest web.
No joy so great but runneth to an end,
No hap so hard but may in fine amend.

Not always fall of leaf, nor ever spring,
No endless night, yet not eternal day;
The saddest birds a season find to sing,
The roughest storm a calm may soon allay.
Thus, with succeeding turns, God tempereth all,
That man may hope to rise, yet fear to fall.

A chance may win that by mischance was lost;
The net, that holds no great, takes little fish;
In some things all, in all things none are crossed;
Few all they need, but none have all they wish.
Unmeddled joys here to no man befall;
Who least, hath some; who most, hath never all.

Saint Peter's Complaint, 1595

148 *Content and Rich*

I DWELL in Grace's court,
Enriched with Virtue's rights;
Faith guides my wit, Love leads my will,
Hope all my mind delights.

In lowly vales I mount
To pleasure's highest pitch;
My silly shroud true honour brings;
My poor estate is rich.

unmeddled] unmixed shroud] shelter

ROBERT SOUTHWELL

My conscience is my crown,
  Contented thoughts my rest;
My heart is happy in itself;
  My bliss is in my breast.

Enough, I reckon wealth;
  A mean the surest lot,
That lies too high for base contempt,
  Too low for envy's shot.

My wishes are but few,
  All easy to fulfil;
I make the limits of my power
  The bonds unto my will.

I have no hopes but one,
  Which is of heavenly reign;
Effects attained, or not desired,
  All lower hopes refrain.

I feel no care of coin;
  Well-doing is my wealth;
My mind to me an empire is,
  While grace affordeth health.

I clip high-climbing thoughts,
  The wings of swelling pride;
Their fall is worst, that from the height
  Of greatest honour slide.

Sith sails of largest size
  The storm doth soonest tear,
I bear so low and small a sail
  As freeth me from fear.

ROBERT SOUTHWELL

I wrestle not with rage,
  While fury's flame doth burn;
It is in vain to stop the stream
  Until the tide doth turn.

But when the flame is out,
  And ebbing wrath doth end,
I turn a late enraged foe
  Into a quiet friend.

And taught with often proof,
  A tempered calm I find
To be most solace to itself,
  Best cure for angry mind.

Spare diet is my fare,
  My clothes more fit than fine;
I know I feed and clothe a foe
  That pampered would repine.

I envy not their hap,
  Whom favour doth advance;
I take no pleasure in their pain,
  That have less happy chance.

To rise by other's fall
  I deem a losing gain;
All states with others' ruins built
  To ruin run amain.

No change of Fortune's calms
  Can cast my comforts down;
When Fortune smiles, I smile to think
  How quickly she will frown.

And when in froward mood
She proves an angry foe,
Small gain I found to let her come,
Less loss to let her go.

Saint Peter's Complaint, 1595

149

Loss in Delay

SHUN delays, they breed remorse;
Take thy time while time doth serve thee;
Creeping snails have weakest force,
Fly their fault lest thou repent thee.
Good is best when soonest wrought,
Lingered labours come to nought.

Hoist up sail while gale doth last,
Tide and wind stay no man's pleasure;
Seek not time when time is past,
Sober speed is wisdom's leisure.
After-wits are dearly bought,
Let thy fore-wit guide thy thought.

Time wears all his locks before,
Take thy hold upon his forehead;
When he flies he turns no more,
And behind his scalp is naked.
Works adjourned have many stays,
Long demurs breed new delays.

Seek thy salve while sore is green,
Festered wounds ask deeper lancing;
After-cures are seldom seen,
Often sought, scarce ever chancing.
Time and place give best advice,
Out of season, out of price.

Crush the serpent in the head,
  Break ill eggs ere they be hatched;
Kill bad chickens in the tread,
  Fligg they hardly can be catched.
In the rising stifle ill,
Lest it grow against thy will.

Drops do pierce the stubborn flint,
  Not by force but often falling;
Custom kills with feeble dint,
  More by use than strength prevailing.
Single sands have little weight,
Many make a drowning freight.

Tender twigs are bent with ease,
  Aged trees do break with bending;
Young desires make little prease,
  Growth doth make them past amending.
Happy man, that soon doth knock
Babble babes against the rock!

Saint Peter's Complaint, 1595

150 *The Burning Babe*

As I in hoary winter's night stood shivering in the snow,
  Surprised I was with sudden heat which made my heart to glow;
And lifting up a fearful eye to view what fire was near,
A pretty Babe all burning bright did in the air appear;

fligg] fledged   prease] pressure

Who, scorched with excessive heat, such floods of tears
did shed,
As though his floods should quench his flames which with his
tears were fed.
'Alas!' quoth he, 'but newly born in fiery heats I fry,
Yet none approach to warm their hearts or feel my fire but I.
My faultless breast the furnace is, the fuel wounding thorns;
Love is the fire, and sighs the smoke, the ashes shame and
scorns;
The fuel justice layeth on, and mercy blows the coals;
The metal in this furnace wrought are men's defiled souls:
For which, as now on fire I am to work them to their good,
So will I melt into a bath to wash them in my blood.'
With this he vanished out of sight and swiftly shrunk
away,
And straight I called unto mind that it was Christmas day.

Ibid., 1602

151 *New Heaven, New War*

COME to your heaven, you heavenly choirs!
Earth hath the heaven of your desires;
Remove your dwelling to your God,
A stall is now his best abode;
Sith men their homage do deny,
Come, angels, all their fault supply.

His chilling cold doth heat require,
Come, seraphins, in lieu of fire;
This little ark no cover hath,
Let cherubs' wings his body swathe;
Come, Raphael, this Babe must eat,
Provide our little Toby meat.

Let Gabriel be now his groom,
That first took up his earthly room ;
Let Michael stand in his defence,
Whom love hath linked to feeble sense ;
Let graces rock when he doth cry,
And angels sing his lullaby.

The same you saw in heavenly seat,
Is he that now sucks Mary's teat ;
Agnize your King a mortal wight,
His borrowed weed lets not your sight ;
Come, kiss the manger where he lies,
That is your bliss above the skies.

This little Babe, so few days old,
Is come to rifle Satan's fold ;
All hell doth at his presence quake,
Though he himself for cold do shake ;
For in this weak unarmed wise
The gates of hell he will surprise.

With tears he fights and wins the field,
His naked breast stands for a shield;
His battering shot are babish cries,
His arrows looks of weeping eyes,
His martial ensigns cold and need,
And feeble flesh his warrior's steed.

His camp is pitched in a stall,
His bulwark but a broken wall;
The crib his trench, hay-stalks his stakes,
Of shepherds he his muster makes ;
And thus, as sure his foe to wound,
The angels' trumps alarum sound.

My soul, with Christ join thou in fight;
Stick to the tents that he hath pight;
Within his crib is surest ward,
This little Babe will be thy guard;
If thou wilt foil thy foes with joy,
Then flit not from this heavenly boy.

Saint Peter's Complaint, 1602

152 *New Prince, New Pomp*

BEHOLD, a silly tender Babe
  In freezing winter night
In homely manger trembling lies,
  Alas, a piteous sight!

The inns are full; no man will yield
  This little pilgrim bed,
But forced he is with silly beasts
  In crib to shroud his head.

Despise him not for lying there,
  First, what he is inquire;
An orient pearl is often found
  In depth of dirty mire.

Weigh not his crib, his wooden dish,
  Nor beasts that by him feed;
Weigh not his Mother's poor attire,
  Nor Joseph's simple weed.

This stable is a Prince's court,
  This crib his chair of state;
The beasts are parcel of his pomp,
  The wooden dish his plate.

The persons in that poor attire
  His royal liveries wear;
The Prince himself is come from heaven;
  This pomp is prized there.

With joy approach, O Christian wight,
  Do homage to thy King;
And highly praise his humble pomp,
  Which he from heaven doth bring.

Saint Peter's Complaint, 1602

153 *Upon the Image of Death*

BEFORE my face the picture hangs,
  That daily should put me in mind
Of those cold qualms and bitter pangs,
  That shortly I am like to find:
    But yet, alas, full little I
    Do think hereon that I must die.

I often look upon a face
  Most ugly, grisly, bare, and thin;
I often view the hollow place,
  Where eyes and nose had sometimes been:
    I see the bones across that lie,
    Yet little think that I must die.

I read the label underneath,
  That telleth me whereto I must;
I see the sentence eke that saith
  'Remember, man, that thou art dust!'
    But yet, alas, but seldom I
    Do think indeed that I must die.

Continually at my bed's head
  A hearse doth hang, which doth me tell,
That I ere morning may be dead,
  Though now I feel myself full well:
    But yet, alas, for all this, I
    Have little mind that I must die.

The gown which I do use to wear,
  The knife wherewith I cut my meat,
And eke that old and ancient chair
  Which is my only usual seat;
    All these do tell me I must die,
    And yet my life amend not I.

My ancestors are turned to clay,
  And many of my mates are gone;
My youngers daily drop away,
  And can I think to 'scape alone?
    No, no, I know that I must die,
    And yet my life amend not I.

Not Solomon, for all his wit,
  Nor Samson, though he were so strong,
No king nor person ever yet
  Could 'scape, but death laid him along:
    Wherefore I know that I must die,
    And yet my life amend not I.

ROBERT SOUTHWELL

Though all the East did quake to hear
  Of Alexander's dreadful name,
And all the West did likewise fear
  To hear of Julius Caesar's fame,
    Yet both by death in dust now lie.
    Who then can 'scape, but he must die?

If none can 'scape death's dreadful dart,
  If rich and poor his beck obey,
If strong, if wise, if all do smart,
  Then I to 'scape shall have no way.
    Oh! grant me grace, O God, that I
    My life may mend, sith I must die.

Maeoniae, 1595

ANONYMOUS

154 *The Quiet Mind*

I JOY not in no earthly bliss;
  I force not Croesus' wealth a straw;
For care I know not what it is;
  I fear not Fortune's fatal law.
My mind is such as may not move
For beauty bright, nor force of love.

I wish but what I have at will;
  I wander not to seek for more;
I like the plain, I climb no hill;
  In greatest storms I sit on shore,
And laugh at them that toil in vain,
To get what must be lost again.

force not] care not for

I kiss not where I wish to kill;
  I feign not love where most I hate;
I break no sleep to win my will;
  I wait not at the mighty's gate.
I scorn no poor, nor fear no rich;
I feel no want, nor have too much.

The court and cart I like nor loathe;
  Extremes are counted worst of all;
The golden mean between them both
  Doth surest sit and fear no fall.
This is my choice; for why I find
No wealth is like the quiet mind.

W. Byrd, *Psalms, Sonnets and Songs*, 1588

155 *The Herdmen*

WHAT pleasure have great princes,
  More dainty to their choice,
Than herdmen wild, who careless
  In quiet life rejoice,
And Fortune's fate not fearing
Sing sweet in summer morning?

Their dealings plain and rightful
  Are void of all deceit;
They never know how spiteful
  It is to kneel and wait
On favourite presumptuous,
Whose pride is vain and sumptuous.

for why] because

All day their flocks each tendeth;
  At night they take their rest,
More quiet than who sendeth
  His ship into the East,
Where gold and pearl are plenty,
But getting very dainty.

For lawyers and their pleading
  They esteem it not a straw;
They think that honest meaning
  Is of itself a law;
Where conscience judgeth plainly,
They spend no money vainly.

O happy who thus liveth,
  Not caring much for gold,
With clothing which sufficeth
  To keep him from the cold.
Though poor and plain his diet,
Yet merry it is and quiet.

W. Byrd, *Psalms, Sonnets and Songs*, 1588

156 *Philon*

WHILE that the sun with his beams hot
  Scorched the fruits in vale and mountain,
Philon the shepherd, late forgot,
  Sitting besides a crystal fountain
In shadow of a green oak tree,
Upon his pipe this song played he:
  'Adieu love, adieu love, untrue love!
  Your mind is light, soon lost for new love.

ANONYMOUS

'So long as I was in your sight,
  I was as your heart, your soul, your treasure;
And evermore you sobbed, you sighed,
  Burning in flames beyond all measure.
Three days endured your love to me,
And it was lost in other three.
  Adieu love, adieu love, untrue love!
  Your mind is light, soon lost for new love.

'Another shepherd you did see,
  To whom your heart was soon enchained;
Full soon your love was lept from me;
  Full soon my place he had obtained.
Soon came a third your love to win,
And we were out, and he was in.
  Adieu love, adieu love, untrue love!
  Your mind is light, soon lost for new love.

'Sure you have made me passing glad,
  That you your mind so soon removed,
Before that I the leisure had,
  To choose you for my best beloved;
For all my love was past and done,
Two days before it was begun.
  Adieu love, adieu love, untrue love!
  Your mind is light, soon lost for new love.'

W. Byrd, *Songs of Sundry Natures*, 1589

157 *The Fate of Narcissus*

WHERE Cadmus, old Agenor's son, did rest and plant
his reign,
Narcissus (of his offspring) there for beauty fame did gain.
His mother was Lyriope, fair Thetis' fairer daughter,
Whom chiefest as the choicest wooed, and brave Cephisus
caught her.
Boeotia was the fertile realm, Parnassus' plain the place,
Where this admired youth was born, this lass-lad form and face.
No nymph so fair but wished him hers, howbeit all in vain;
His self-love wrought his self-loss, and his beauty proved his
bane,
Who, proud of Nature's plenty, held all others in disdain:
Till God, who had created man the fairest creature,
(Howbeit but a shadow of his proper feature,
More differing far than sunshine from the sun's self-substance
pure)
Narcissus' over-scornful pride not longer would endure,
But from his form, that pleased him most, his plague did thus
procure.
As this same fond self-pleasing youth stood at a fountain's
brim,
And proudly sees his shadow there, admiring every limb,
Echo, an amiable nymph, long amorous of him,
But loving, unbeloved, now, at least to please her eye,
Conveys herself, unseen, into a thicket joining by;
And there, as much o'er-gone with love, as he o'er-gone with
pride,
She hears, and sees, and would have pleased three senses more
beside.

And nothing more than every part, thus stealth-seen, liked her,
And nothing less, than hidden with unhidden to confer;
For well it had contented then in more than sight to err,
Although not meanly did his scorn 'gainst it her stomach stir.
Meanwhile the lad (such power hath pride men's senses to subdue)
Dotes on his shadow, now supposed to be a substance true;
And lastly woos so formally in words and gestures sweet,
That Echo found his error; and, he saying, 'Let us meet',
'Let's meet', quoth Echo, mockingly; which, hearing, he with speed
(Believing that his shadow was a nymph, and spake in deed)
Did leap into the fountain, where that gallant, drowning thus,
Hath left example how like pride may cause like plague to us.
How smooth-tongued Echo, that for him in all, save voice, did pine,
To quit his scorn, baned other fools, alike vain-glorious fine,
By smoothing them, is Naso's tale, no purpose here of mine:
But how Narcissus' shadow and this Echo's voice, though they
Have long been dead, haunt now the world, is it we mean to say.

Albion's England, 1596

EDMUND SPENSER

1552?–1599

158 *The Oak and the Brere*

THERE grew an aged tree on the green,
A goodly Oak sometime had it been,
With arms full strong and largely displayed,
But of their leaves they were disarrayed;

The body big, and mightily pight,
Throughly rooted, and of wondrous height.
Whilom had been the king of the field,
And mochel mast to the husband did yield,
And with his nuts larded many swine.
But now the gray moss marred his rine,
His bared boughs were beaten with storms,
His top was bald, and wasted with worms,
His honour decayed, his branches sere.
  Hard by his side grew a bragging Brere,
Which proudly thrust into th' element,
And seemed to threat the firmament.
It was embellished with blossoms fair,
And thereto aye wonned to repair
The shepherds' daughters, to gather flowers,
To paint their garlands with his colours.
And in his small bushes used to shroud
The sweet nightingale singing so loud;
Which made this foolish Brere wax so bold,
That on a time he cast him to scold
And sneb the good Oak, for he was old.
  'Why stand'st there (quoth he) thou brutish block?
Nor for fruit, nor for shadow serves thy stock.
Seest, how fresh my flowers been spread,
Dyed in lily white, and crimson red,
With leaves engrained in lusty green,
Colours meet to clothe a maiden Queen.
Thy waste bigness but cumbers the ground,
And dirks the beauty of my blossoms round.
The mouldy moss, which thee accloyeth,

pight] fixed   mochel] much   wonned] were wont
sneb] snub   dirks] darkens   accloyeth] encumbers

My cinnamon smell too much annoyeth.
Wherefore soon, I rede thee, hence remove,
Lest thou the price of my displeasure prove.'
So spake this bold Brere with great disdain.
Little him answered the Oak again,
But yielded, with shame and grief adawed,
That of a weed he was overcrawed.
  It chanced after upon a day,
The husbandman self to come that way,
Of custom for to surview his ground,
And his trees of state in compass round.
Him when the spiteful Brere had espied,
Causeless complained, and loudly cried
Unto his lord, stirring up stern strife:
'O my liege lord, the god of my life,
Pleaseth you ponder your suppliant's plaint,
Caused of wrong, and cruel constraint,
Which I your poor vassal daily endure;
And but your goodness the same recure,
Am like for desperate dule to die,
Through felonous force of mine enemy.'
  Greatly aghast with this piteous plea,
Him rested the goodman on the lea,
And bade the Brere in his plaint proceed.
With painted words tho 'gan this proud weed,
(As most usen ambitious folk)
His coloured crime with craft to cloak.
  'Ah, my sovereign, lord of creatures all,
Thou placer of plants both humble and tall,
Was not I planted of thine own hand,
To be the primrose of all thy land,

rede] advise   adawed] daunted   recure] remedy   dule] grief

With flowering blossoms, to furnish the prime,
And scarlet berries in summer time?
How falls it then, that this faded Oak,
Whose body is sere, whose branches broke,
Whose naked arms stretch unto the fire,
Unto such tyranny doth aspire;
Hindering with his shade my lovely light,
And robbing me of the sweet sun's sight?
So beat his old boughs my tender side,
That oft the blood springeth from wounds wide;
Untimely my flowers forced to fall,
That been the honour of your coronal.
And oft he lets his canker-worms light
Upon my branches, to work me more spite;
And oft his hoary locks down doth cast,
Wherewith my fresh flowerets been defaced.
For this, and many more such outrage,
Craving your goodlihead to assuage
The rancorous rigour of his might,
Nought ask I, but only to hold my right;
Submitting me to your good sufferance,
And praying to be guarded from grievance.'
   To this the Oak cast him to reply
Well as he couth: but his enemy
Had kindled such coals of displeasure,
That the good man nould stay his leisure,
But home him hasted with furious heat,
Increasing his wrath with many a threat.
His harmful hatchet he hent in hand,
(Alas, that it so ready should stand)
And to the field alone he speedeth.

couth] knew   hent] took

(Ay, little help to harm there needeth)
Anger nould let him speak to the tree,
Enaunter his rage mought cooled be:
But to the root bent his sturdy stroke,
And made many wounds in the waste Oak.
The axe's edge did oft turn again,
As half unwilling to cut the grain;
Seemed, the senseless iron did fear,
Or to wrong holy eld did forbear.
For it had been an ancient tree,
Sacred with many a mystery,
And often crossed with the priestès crew,
And often hallowed with holy water dew.
But sik fancies weren foolery,
And broughten this Oak to this misery.
For nought mought they quitten him from decay;
For fiercely the good man at him did lay.
The block oft groaned under the blow,
And sighed to see his near overthrow.
In fine the steel had pierced his pith,
Tho down to the earth he fell forthwith.
His wondrous weight made the ground to quake;
Th' earth shrunk under him, and seemed to shake.
There lieth the Oak, pitied of none.
  Now stands the Brere like a lord alone,
Puffed up with pride and vain pleasance:
But all this glee had no continuance.
For eftsoons Winter 'gan to approach,
The blustering Boreas did encroach,
And beat upon the solitary Brere;
For now no succour was seen him near.

enaunter] lest crew] cruse sik] such tho] then

Now 'gan he repent his pride too late:
For naked left and disconsolate,
The biting frost nipped his stalk dead,
The watery wet weighed down his head,
And heaped snow burdened him so sore,
That now upright he can stand no more;
And being down, is trod in the dirt
Of cattle, and bruised, and sorely hurt.
Such was th' end of this ambitious Brere,
For scorning eld.

The Shepheardes Calender, Februarie 102–238, 1579

159 *Elisa*

YE dainty nymphs, that in this blessed brook
Do bathe your breast,
Forsake your watery bowers, and hither look,
At my request;
And eke you virgins, that on Parnasse dwell,
Whence floweth Helicon the learned well,
Help me to blaze
Her worthy praise,
Which in her sex doth all excel.

Of fair Elisa be your silver song,
That blessed wight;
The flower of virgins, may she flourish long,
In princely plight.
For she is Syrinx' daughter without spot,
Which Pan the shepherds' God of her begot:
So sprang her grace
Of heavenly race,
No mortal blemish may her blot.

See, where she sits upon the grassy green,
    (O seemly sight)
Yclad in scarlet like a maiden Queen,
    And ermines white.
Upon her head a cremosin coronet,
With damask roses and daffodillies set:
    Bay-leaves between,
    And primroses green
Embellish the sweet violet.

Tell me, have ye seen her angelic face,
    Like Phoebe fair?
Her heavenly haviour, her princely grace,
    Can you well compare?
The red rose medled with the white yfere
In either cheek depeincten lively cheer.
    Her modest eye,
    Her majesty,
Where have you seen the like, but there?

I saw Phoebus thrust out his golden head,
    Upon her to gaze:
But when he saw, how broad her beams did spread,
    It did him amaze.
He blushed to see another sun below,
Ne durst again his fiery face outshow:
    Let him, if he dare,
    His brightness compare
With hers, to have the overthrow.

medled] mingled   yfere] together

EDMUND SPENSER

Shew thyself, Cynthia, with thy silver rays,
    And be not abashed;
When she the beams of her beauty displays,
    O how art thou dashed?
But I will not match her with Latona's seed;
Such folly great sorrow to Niobe did breed.
    Now she is a stone,
    And makes daily moan,
Warning all other to take heed.

Pan may be proud, that ever he begot
    Such a bellibone,
And Syrinx rejoice, that ever was her lot
    To bear such an one.
Soon as my younglings cryen for the dam,
To her will I offer a milkwhite lamb:
    She is my goddess plain,
    And I her shepherds' swain,
Albeit forswonk and forswat I am.

I see Calliope speed her to the place,
    Where my goddess shines;
And after her the other Muses trace,
    With their violins.
Been they not bay branches, which they do bear,
All for Elisa in her hand to wear?
    So sweetly they play,
    And sing all the way,
That it a heaven is to hear.

bellibone] goodly one   forswonk] tired   forswat] sweaty

EDMUND SPENSER

Lo, how finely the Graces can it foot
    To the instrument;
They dancen deftly, and singen soote,
    In their merriment.
Wants not a fourth Grace, to make the dance even?
Let that room to my lady be yeven:
    She shall be a Grace,
    To fill the fourth place,
And reign with the rest in heaven.

And whither runs this bevy of ladies bright,
    Ranged in a row?
They been all ladies of the lake behight,
    That unto her go.
Chloris, that is the chiefest nymph of all,
Of olive branches bears a coronal:
    Olives been for peace,
    When wars do surcease;
Such for a princess been principal.

Ye shepherds' daughters, that dwell on the green,
    Hie you there apace;
Let none come there, but that virgins been,
    To adorn her grace.
And when you come, whereas she is in place,
See, that your rudeness do not you disgrace:
    Bind your fillets fast,
    And gird in your waist,
For more fineness, with a tawdry lace.

soote] sweet   yeven] given

Bring hither the pink and purple columbine,
    With gillyflowers;
Bring coronations, and sops in wine,
    Worn of paramours.
Strew me the ground with daffodowndillies,
And cowslips, and kingcups, and loved lilies:
    The pretty paunce,
    And the chevisaunce,
Shall match with the fair flower delice.

Now rise up Elisa, decked as thou art,
    In royal array;
And now ye dainty damsels may depart
    Each one her way,
I fear, I have troubled your troops too long;
Let Dame Elisa thank you for her song.
    And if you come hither,
    When damsons I gather,
I will part them all you among.

The Shepheardes Calender, April 37–153, 1579

160 *The Contempt of Poetry*

Piers. CUDDY, for shame hold up thy heavy head,
And let us cast with what delight to chase,
    And weary this long lingering Phoebus' race.
Whilom thou wont the shepherds' lads to lead,
    In rhymes, in riddles, and in bidding base;
Now they in thee, and thou in sleep art dead.

sops in wine] pinks   paunce] pansy
chevisaunce] an unknown flower.   base] prisoners' base

Cuddy. Piers, I have piped erst so long with pain,
That all mine oaten reeds been rent and wore;
And my poor Muse hath spent her spared store,
Yet little good hath got, and much less gain.
Such pleasance makes the grasshopper so poor,
And ligg so laid, when winter doth her strain.

The dapper ditties, that I wont devise,
To feed youths fancy, and the flocking fry,
Delighten much; what I the bet for thy?
They han the pleasure, I a slender prize.
I beat the bush, the birds to them do fly.
What good thereof to Cuddy can arise?

Piers. Cuddy, the praise is better than the price,
The glory eke much greater than the gain.
O what an honour is it, to restrain
The lust of lawless youth with good advice;
Or prick them forth with pleasance of thy vein,
Whereto thou list their trained wills entice.

Soon as thou 'gin'st to set thy notes in frame,
O how the rural routs to thee do cleave.
Seemeth thou dost their soul of sense bereave,
All as the shepherd, that did fetch his dame
From Pluto's baleful bower withouten leave:
His music's might the hellish hound did tame.

Cuddy. So praisen babes the peacock's spotted train,
And wondren at bright Argus' blazing eye:
But who rewards him e'er the more for thy?
Or feeds him once the fuller by a grain?
Sike praise is smoke, that sheddeth in the sky,
Sike words been wind, and wasten soon in vain.

ligg] lie han] have routs] troops for thy] therefore sike] such

Piers. Abandon then the base and viler clown,
  Lift up thyself out of the lowly dust;
  And sing of bloody Mars, of wars, of jousts,
Turn thee to those, that wield the awful crown,
  To doubted knights, whose woundless armour rusts,
And helms unbruised waxen daily brown.

There may thy Muse display her fluttering wing,
  And stretch herself at large from east to west;
  Whether thou list in fair Elisa rest,
Or if thee please in bigger notes to sing,
  Advance the worthy whom she loveth best,
That first the white bear to the stake did bring.

And when the stubborn stroke of stronger stounds
  Has somewhat slacked the tenour of thy string,
  Of love and lustihead tho mayst thou sing,
And carol loud, and lead the Miller's round,
  All were Elisa one of thilk same ring.
So mought our Cuddy's name to heaven sound.

Cuddy. Indeed the Romish Tityrus, I hear,
  Through his Maecenas left his oaten reed,
  Whereon he erst had taught his flocks to feed,
And laboured lands to yield the timely ear,
  And eft did sing of wars and deadly dread,
So as the heavens did quake his verse to hear.

But, ah! Maecenas is yclad in clay,
  And great Augustus long ago is dead:
  And all the worthies liggen wrapped in lead,
That matter made for poets on to play;
  For ever, who in derring doe were dread,
The lofty verse of them was loved aye.

doubted] redoubted   stounds] troubles   tho] then

But after virtue 'gan for age to stoop,
And mighty manhood brought a bed of ease,
The vaunting poets found nought worth a pease,
To put in press among the learned troop.
Tho 'gan the streams of flowing wits to cease,
And sunbright honour penned in shameful coop.

And if that any buds of poesy
Yet of the old stock 'gan to shoot again;
Or it men's follies mote be forced to feign,
And roll with rest in rhymes of ribaldry;
Or as it sprung, it wither must again.
Tom Piper makes us better melody.

Piers. O peerless Poesy, where is then thy place,
If nor in prince's palace thou do sit,
(And yet is prince's palace the most fit)
Ne breast of baser birth doth thee embrace?
Then make thee wings of thine aspiring wit,
And, whence thou camest, fly back to heaven apace.

Cuddy. Ah! Percy, it is all too weak and wan,
So high to soar, and make so large a flight.
Her pieced pinions been not so in plight,
For Colin fits such famous flight to scan.
He, were he not with love so ill bedight,
Would mount as high, and sing as soote as swan.

Piers. Ah! fon, for love does teach him climb so high,
And lifts him up out of the loathsome mire.
Such immortal mirror, as he doth admire,
Would raise one's mind above the starry sky;
And cause a caitiff courage to aspire,
For lofty love doth loathe a lowly eye.

soote] sweet fon] fool

Cuddy. All otherwise the state of poet stands,
For lordly love is such a tyrant fell,
That where he rules, all power he doth expel.
The vaunted verse a vacant head demands,
Ne wont with crabbed care the Muses dwell.
Unwisely weaves, that takes two webs in hand.

Who ever casts to compass weighty prize,
And thinks to throw out thundering words of threat,
Let pour in lavish cups and thrifty bits of meat,
For Bacchus' fruit is friend to Phoebus wise.
And when with wine the brain begins to sweat,
The numbers flow as fast as spring doth rise.

Thou kenst not, Percy, how the rhyme should rage.
O, if my temples were distained with wine,
And girt in garlands of wild ivy twine,
How I could rear the Muse on stately stage,
And teach her tread aloft in buskin fine,
With quaint Bellona in her equipage.

But ah! my courage cools ere it be warm,
For thy, content us in this humble shade,
Where no such troublous tides han us assayed;
Here we our slender pipes may safely charm.
Piers. And when my goats shall han their bellies laid,
Cuddy shall have a kid to store his farm.

The Shepheardes Calender, October, 1579

161 *Beauty*

WHAT time this world's great workmaster did cast
To make all things, such as we now behold,
It seems that he before his eyes had placed
A goodly pattern, to whose perfect mould
He fashioned them as comely as he could;
That now so fair and seemly they appear,
As nought may be amended anywhere.

That wondrous pattern, wheresoe'er it be,
Whether in earth laid up in secret store,
Or else in heaven, that no man may it see
With sinful eyes, for fear it to deflower,
Is perfect Beauty which all men adore,
Whose face and feature doth so much excel
All mortal sense, that none the same may tell.

Thereof as every earthly thing partakes,
Or more or less by influence divine,
So it more fair accordingly it makes,
And the gross matter of this earthly mine,
Which closeth it, thereafter doth refine,
Doing away the dross which dims the light
Of that fair beam, which therein is empight.

For through infusion of celestial power,
The duller earth it quickeneth with delight,
And life-full spirits privily doth pour
Through all the parts, that to the lookers' sight
They seem to please. That is thy sovereign might,
O Cyprian queen, which flowing from the beam
Of thy bright star, thou into them dost stream.

empight] fixed

That is the thing which giveth pleasant grace
  To all things fair, that kindleth lively fire,
Light of thy lamp, which shining in the face,
  Thence to the soul darts amorous desire,
  And robs the hearts of those which it admire;
    Therewith thou pointest thy son's poisoned arrow,
    That wounds the life, and wastes the inmost marrow.

How vainly then do idle wits invent,
  That Beauty is nought else, but mixture made
Of colours fair, and goodly temperament
  Of pure complexions, that shall quickly fade
  And pass away, like to a summer's shade,
    Or that it is but comely composition
    Of parts well measured, with meet disposition.

Hath white and red in it such wondrous power,
  That it can pierce through th' eyes unto the heart,
And therein stir such rage and restless stour,
  As nought but death can stint his dolour's smart?
  Or can proportion of the outward part
    Move such affection in the inward mind,
    That it can rob both sense and reason blind?

Why do not then the blossoms of the field,
  Which are arrayed with much more orient hue,
And to the sense most dainty odours yield,
  Work like impression in the looker's view?
  Or why do not fair pictures like power shew,
    In which oft-times we nature see of art
    Excelled, in perfect limning every part?

stour] disturbance stint] stay

But ah! believe me, there is more than so
  That works such wonders in the minds of men.
I that have often proved, too well it know;
  And who so list the like assays to ken,
  Shall find by trial, and confess it then,
    That Beauty is not, as fond men misdeem,
    An outward show of things, that only seem.

For that same goodly hue of white and red,
  With which the cheeks are sprinkled, shall decay,
And those sweet rosy leaves, so fairly spread
  Upon the lips, shall fade and fall away
  To that they were, even to corrupted clay.
    That golden wire, those sparkling stars so bright,
    Shall turn to dust, and lose their goodly light.

But that fair lamp, from whose celestial ray
  That light proceeds, which kindleth lovers' fire,
Shall never be extinguished nor decay,
  But when the vital spirits do expire,
  Unto her native planet shall retire,
    For it is heavenly born and cannot die,
    Being a parcel of the purest sky.

For when the soul, the which derived was
  At first, out of that great immortal Spright,
By whom all live to love, whilom did pass
  Down from the top of purest heaven's height,
  To be embodied here, it then took light
    And lively spirits from that fairest star,
    Which lights the world forth from his fiery car.

Which power retaining still or more or less,
  When she in fleshly seed is eft enraced,
Through every part she doth the same impress,
  According as the heavens have her graced,
  And frames her house, in which she will be placed,
    Fit for herself, adorning it with spoil
    Of th' heavenly riches, which she robbed erewhile.

Thereof it comes, that these fair souls, which have
  The most resemblance of that heavenly light,
Frame to themselves most beautiful and brave
  Their fleshly bower, most fit for their delight,
  And the gross matter by a sovereign might
    Tempers so trim, that it may well be seen
    A palace fit for such a virgin queen.

So every spirit, as it is most pure,
  And hath in it the more of heavenly light,
So it the fairer body doth procure
  To habit in, and it more fairly dight
  With cheerful grace and amiable sight.
    For of the soul the body form doth take;
    For soul is form, and doth the body make.

Written in youth; *Fowre Hymnes*, ii. 29–133, 1596

eft] afterwards   enraced] implanted

162 *Prince Arthur*

SHE heard with patience all unto the end,
And strove to master sorrowful assay,
Which greater grew, the more she did contend,
And almost rent her tender heart in tway;
And love fresh coals unto her fire did lay;
For greater love, the greater is the loss.
Was never lady loved dearer day,
Than she did love the knight of the Red Cross;
For whose dear sake so many troubles her did toss.

At last when fervent sorrow slaked was.
She up arose, resolving him to find
Alive or dead; and forward forth doth pass,
All as the dwarf the way to her assigned:
And evermore in constant careful mind
She fed her wound with fresh renewed bale;
Long tossed with storms, and beat with bitter wind,
High over hills, and low adown the dale,
She wandered many a wood, and measured many a vale.

At last she chanced by good hap to meet
A goodly knight, fair marching by the way
Together with his squire, arrayed meet.
His glitterand armour shined far away,
Like glancing light of Phoebus' brightest ray;
From top to toe no place appeared bare,
That deadly dint of steel endanger may:
Athwart his breast a baldrick brave he ware,
That shined, like twinkling stars, with stones most precious rare.

baldrick] belt

And in the midst thereof one precious stone
  Of wondrous worth, and eke of wondrous mights,
Shaped like a lady's head, exceeding shone,
  Like Hesperus amongst the lesser lights,
  And strove for to amaze the weaker sights;
Thereby his mortal blade full comely hung
  In ivory sheath, ycarved with curious sleights;
Whose hilts were burnished gold, and handle strong
Of mother pearl, and buckled with a golden tongue.

His haughty helmet, horrid all with gold,
  Both glorious brightness and great terror bred;
For all the crest a dragon did enfold
  With greedy paws, and over all did spread
  His golden wings; his dreadful hideous head,
Close couched on the beaver, seemed to throw
  From flaming mouth bright sparkles fiery red,
That sudden horror to faint hearts did show;
And scaly tail was stretched adown his back full low.

Upon the top of all his lofty crest,
  A bunch of hairs discoloured diversely,
With sprinkled pearl and gold full richly dressed,
  Did shake, and seemed to dance for jollity,
  Like to an almond tree ymounted high
On top of green Selinis all alone,
  With blossoms brave bedecked daintily;
Whose tender locks do tremble every one
At every little breath, that under heaven is blown.

His warlike shield all closely covered was,
Ne might of mortal eye be ever seen;
Not made of steel, nor of enduring brass,
Such earthly metals soon consumed been:
But all of diamond perfect, pure, and clean,
It framed was, one massy entire mould,
Hewn out of adamant rock with engines keen,
That point of spear it never percen could,
Ne dint of direful sword divide the substance would.

The same to wight he never wont disclose,
But when as monsters huge he would dismay,
Or daunt unequal armies of his foes,
Or when the flying heavens he would affray;
For so exceeding shone his glistering ray,
That Phoebus' golden face it did attaint,
As when a cloud his beams doth overlay;
And silver Cynthia waxed pale and faint,
As when her face is stained with magic arts' constraint.

No magic arts hereof had any might,
Nor bloody words of bold enchanter's call,
But all, that was not such as seemed in sight,
Before that shield did fade, and sudden fall:
And when him list the rascal routs appal,
Men into stones therewith he could transmew,
And stones to dust, and dust to nought at all;
And when him list the prouder looks subdue,
He would them gazing blind, or turn to other hue.

transmew] transmute

Ne let it seem, that credence this exceeds,
  For he that made the same was known right well
To have done much more admirable deeds.
  It Merlin was, which whilom did excel
  All living wights in might of magic spell:
Both shield, and sword, and armour all he wrought
  For this young Prince, when first to arms he fell;
But when he died, the Fairy Queen it brought
To Fairy Land, where yet it may be seen, if sought.

The Faerie Queene, I. vii. 27–36, 1590

163 *Cymochles and Phaedria*

A HARDER lesson, to learn continence
  In joyous pleasure, than in grievous pain;
For sweetness doth allure the weaker sense
  So strongly, that uneathes it can refrain
  From that, which feeble nature covets fain:
But grief and wrath, that be her enemies,
  And foes of life, she better can restrain;
Yet virtue vaunts in both their victories,
And Guyon in them all shews goodly masteries.

Whom bold Cymochles travelling to find,
  With cruel purpose bent to wreak on him
The wrath, which Atin kindled in his mind,
  Came to a river, by whose utmost brim
  Waiting to pass, he saw whereas did swim
Along the shore, as swift as glance of eye,
  A little gondelay, bedecked trim
With boughs and arbours woven cunningly,
That like a little forest seemed outwardly.

uneathes] hardly   gondelay] gondola

And therein sat a lady fresh and fair,
  Making sweet solace to herself alone;
Sometimes she sang, as loud as lark in air,
  Sometimes she laughed, as merry as Pope Joan,
  Yet was there not with her else any one,
That might to her move cause of merriment:
  Matter of mirth enough, though there were none,
She could devise, and thousand ways invent,
To feed her foolish humour, and vain jolliment.

Which when far off Cymochles heard, and saw,
  He loudly called to such as were aboard,
The little bark unto the shore to draw,
  And him to ferry over that deep ford.
  The merry mariner unto his word
Soon hearkened, and her painted boat straightway
  Turned to the shore, where that same warlike lord
She in received; but Atin by no way
She would admit, all be the knight her much did pray.

Eftsoons her shallow ship away did slide,
  More swift, than swallow shears the liquid sky,
Withouten oar or pilot it to guide,
  Or winged canvas with the wind to fly;
  Only she turned a pin, and by and by
It cut a way upon the yielding wave.
  Ne cared she her course for to apply;
For it was taught the way, which she would have,
And both from rocks and flats itself could wisely save.

And all the way, the wanton damsel found
  New mirth, her passenger to entertain;
For she in pleasant purpose did abound,
  And greatly joyed merry tales to feign,
  Of which a storehouse did with her remain,
Yet seemed, nothing well they her became;
  For all her words she drowned with laughter vain,
And wanted grace in uttering of the same,
That turned all her pleasance to a scoffing game.

And other whiles vain toys she would devise
  As her fantastic wit did most delight;
Sometimes her head she fondly would aguise
  With gaudy garlands, or fresh flowrets dight
  About her neck, or rings of rushes plight;
Sometimes to do him laugh, she would assay
  To laugh at shaking of the leavės light,
Or to behold the water work, and play
About her little frigate, therein making way.

Her light behaviour and loose dalliance
  Gave wondrous great contentment to the knight,
That of his way he had no sovenance,
  Nor care of vowed revenge, and cruel fight,
  But to weak wench did yield his martial might.
So easy was to quench his flamed mind
  With one sweet drop of sensual delight,
So easy is, t'appease the stormy wind
Of malice in the calm of pleasant womankind.

aguise] deck   sovenance] remembrance

Diverse discourses in their way they spent,
'Mongst which Cymochles of her questioned
Both what she was, and what that usage meant,
Which in her cot she daily practised.
'Vain man' (said she) 'that wouldst be reckoned
A stranger in thy home, and ignorant
Of Phaedria (for so my name is read)
Of Phaedria, thine own fellow servant;
For thou to serve Acrasia thyself dost vaunt.

'In this wide inland sea, that hight by name
The Idle Lake, my wandering ship I row,
That knows her port, and thither sails by aim,
Ne care, ne fear I, how the wind do blow,
Or whether swift I wend, or whether slow:
Both slow and swift alike do serve my turn,
Ne swelling Neptune, ne loud thundering Jove
Can change my cheer, or make me ever mourn;
My little boat can safely pass this perilous bourne.'

Whiles thus she talked, and whiles thus she toyed,
They were far past the passage, which he spake,
And come unto an island, waste and void,
That floated in the midst of that great lake.
There her small gondelay her port did make,
And that gay pair issuing on the shore
Disburdened her. Their way they forward take
Into the land, that lay them fair before,
Whose pleasance she him shewed, and plentiful great store.

It was a chosen plot of fertile land,
  Amongst wide waves set, like a little nest,
As if it had by Nature's cunning hand
  Been choicely picked out from all the rest,
  And laid forth for ensample of the best.
No dainty flower or herb, that grows on ground,
  No arboret with painted blossoms drest,
And smelling sweet, but there it might be found
To bud out fair, and her sweet smells throw all around.

No tree, whose branches did not bravely spring;
  No branch, whereon a fine bird did not sit;
No bird, but did her shrill notes sweetly sing;
  No song but did contain a lovely dit:
  Trees, branches, birds, and songs were framed fit,
For to allure frail mind to careless ease.
  Careless the man soon wox, and his weak wit
Was overcome of thing that did him please;
So pleased, did his wrathful purpose fair appease.

Thus when she had his eyes and senses fed
  With false delights, and filled with pleasures vain,
Into a shady dale she soft him led,
  And laid him down upon a grassy plain;
  And her sweet self without dread, or disdain,
She set beside, laying his head disarmed
  In her loose lap, it softly to sustain,
Where soon he slumbered, fearing not be harmed,
The whiles with a loud lay she thus him sweetly charmed.

wox] waxed

'Behold, O man, that toilsome pains dost take,
The flowers, the fields, and all that pleasant grows,
How they themselves do thine ensample make,
Whiles nothing envious Nature them forth throws
Out of her fruitful lap; how, no man knows,
They spring, they bud, they blossom fresh and fair,
And deck the world with their rich pompous shows;
Yet no man for them taketh pains or care,
Yet no man to them can his careful pains compare.

'The lily, lady of the flowering field,
The flower-deluce, her lovely paramour,
Bid thee to them thy fruitless labours yield,
And soon leave off this toilsome weary stour;
Lo, lo! how brave she decks her bounteous bower,
With silken curtains and gold coverlets,
Therein to shroud her sumptuous belamour,
Yet neither spins nor cards, ne cares nor frets,
But to her mother Nature all her care she lets.

'Why then dost thou, O man, that of them all
Art lord, and eke of nature sovereign,
Wilfully make thyself a wretched thrall,
And waste thy joyous hours in needless pain,
Seeking for danger and adventures vain?
What boots it all to have, and nothing use?
Who shall him rue, that swimming in the main,
Will die for thirst, and water doth refuse?
Refuse such fruitless toil, and present pleasures choose.'

stour] trouble belamour] lover

By this she had him lulled fast asleep,
  That of no worldly thing he care did take;
Then she with liquors strong his eyes did steep,
  That nothing should him hastily awake:
  So she him left, and did herself betake
Unto her boat again, with which she cleft
  The slothful wave of that great grisly lake;
Soon she that island far behind her left,
And now is come to that same place, where first she weft.

The Faerie Queene, II. vi. 1–18, 1590

164 *Guardian Angels*

AND is there care in heaven? and is there love
  In heavenly spirits to these creatures base,
That may compassion of their evils move?
  There is: else much more wretched were the case
  Of men, than beasts. But, O! th' exceeding grace
Of highest God, that loves his creatures so,
  And all his works with mercy doth embrace,
That blessed angels he sends to and fro,
To serve to wicked man, to serve his wicked foe.

How oft do they their silver bowers leave,
  To come to succour us, that succour want?
How oft do they with golden pinions cleave
  The flitting skies, like flying pursuivant,
  Against foul fiends to aid us militant?
They for us fight, they watch and duly ward,
  And their bright squadrons round about us plant,
And all for love, and nothing for reward:
O! why should heavenly God to men have such regard?

The Faerie Queene, II. viii. 1, 2, 1590

weft] wafted

165 *The Bower of Bliss*

EFTSOONS they heard a most melodious sound,
  Of all that mote delight a dainty ear,
Such as at once might not on living ground,
  Save in this paradise, be heard elsewhere:
  Right hard it was, for wight, which did it hear,
To read, what manner music that mote be;
  For all that pleasing is to living ear,
Was there consorted in one harmony,
Birds, voices, instruments, winds, waters, all agree.

The joyous birds, shrouded in cheerful shade,
  Their notes unto the voice attempered sweet;
Th' angelical soft trembling voices made
  To th' instruments divine respondence meet;
  The silver sounding instruments did meet
With the bass murmur of the waters' fall;
  The waters' fall with difference discreet,
Now soft, now loud, unto the wind did call;
The gentle warbling wind low answered to all.

There, whence that music seemed heard to be,
  Was the fair witch herself now solacing,
With a new lover, whom through sorcery
  And witchcraft she from far did thither bring:
  There she had him now laid a-slumbering,
In secret shade, after long wanton joys;
  Whilst round about them pleasantly did sing
Many fair ladies, and lascivious boys,
That ever mixed their song with light licentious toys.

mote] might

And all that while, right over him she hung,
With her false eyes fast fixed in his sight,
As seeking medicine, whence she was stung,
Or greedily depasturing delight:
And oft inclining down with kisses light,
For fear of waking him, his lips bedewed,
And through his humid eyes did suck his spright,
Quite molten into lust and pleasure lewd;
Wherewith she sighed soft, as if his case she rued.

The whiles some one did chant this lovely lay:
'Ah see, whoso fair thing dost fain to see,
In springing flower the image of thy day;
Ah see the virgin rose, how sweetly she
Doth first peep forth with bashful modesty,
That fairer seems, the less ye see her may;
Lo see soon after, how more bold and free
Her bared bosom she doth broad display;
Lo see soon after, how she fades, and falls away.

'So passeth, in the passing of a day,
Of mortal life the leaf, the bud, the flower,
Ne more doth flourish after first decay,
That erst was sought to deck both bed and bower,
Of many a lady, and many a paramour:
Gather therefore the rose, whilst yet is prime,
For soon comes age, that will her pride deflower;
Gather the rose of love, whilst yet is time,
Whilst loving thou mayst loved be with equal crime.'

He ceased, and then 'gan all the quire of birds
  Their diverse notes t' attune unto his lay,
As in approvance of his pleasing words.
  The constant pair heard all, that he did say,
  Yet swerved not, but kept their forward way,
Through many covert groves, and thickets close,
  In which they creeping did at last display
That wanton lady, with her lover loose,
Whose sleepy head she in her lap did soft dispose.

Upon a bed of roses she was laid,
  As faint through heat, or dight to pleasant sin,
And was arrayed, or rather disarrayed,
  All in a veil of silk and silver thin,
  That hid no whit her alabaster skin,
But rather shewed more white, if more might be:
  More subtle web Arachne cannot spin,
Nor the fine nets, which oft we woven see
Of scorched dew, do not in th' air more lightly flee.

Her snowy breast was bare to ready spoil
  Of hungry eyes, which n'ote therewith be filled,
And yet through languor of her late sweet toil,
  Few drops, more clear then nectar, forth distilled,
  That like pure orient pearls adown it trilled,
And her fair eyes, sweet smiling in delight,
  Moistened their fiery beams, with which she thrilled
Frail hearts, yet quenched not; like starry light,
Which, sparkling on the silent waves, does seem more bright.

n'ote] could not

The young man sleeping by her seemed to be
  Some goodly swain of honourable place,
That certès it great pity was to see
  Him his nobility so foul deface:
  A sweet regard, and amiable grace,
Mixed with manly sternness did appear,
  Yet sleeping, in his well proportioned face,
And on his tender lips the downy hair
Did now but freshly spring, and silken blossoms bear.

His warlike arms, the idle instruments
  Of sleeping praise, were hung upon a tree,
And his brave shield, full of old monuments,
  Was foully razed, that none the signs might see;
  Ne for them, ne for honour cared he,
Ne ought, that did to his advancement tend,
  But in lewd loves, and wasteful luxury,
His days, his goods, his body he did spend:
O horrible enchantment, that him so did blend!

The Faerie Queene, II. xii. 70–80, 1590

166 *The Mask of Cupid*

ALL suddenly a stormy whirlwind blew
Throughout the house, that clapped every door,
With which that iron wicket open flew,
  As it with mighty levers had been tore;
  And forth issued, as on the ready floor
Of some theatre, a grave personage,
  That in his hand a branch of laurel bore,
With comely haviour and countenance sage,
Yclad in costly garments, fit for tragic stage.

Proceeding to the midst, he still did stand,
  As if in mind he somewhat had to say,
And to the vulgar beckoning with his hand,
  In sign of silence, as to hear a play,
  By lively actions he 'gan bewray
Some argument of matter passioned;
  Which done, he back retired soft away,
And passing by, his name discovered,
Ease, on his robe in golden letters ciphered.

The noble maid, still standing, all this viewed,
  And marvelled at his strange intendiment;
With that a joyous fellowship issued
  Of minstrels, making goodly merriment,
  With wanton bards, and rhymers impudent,
All which together sung full cheerfully
  A lay of love's delight, with sweet concent;
After whom marched a jolly company,
In manner of a mask, enranged orderly.

The whiles a most delicious harmony
  In full strange notes was sweetly heard to sound,
That the rare sweetness of the melody
  The feeble senses wholly did confound,
  And the frail soul in deep delight nigh drowned:
And when it ceased, shrill trumpets loud did bray,
  That their report did far away rebound,
And when they ceased, it 'gan again to play,
The whiles the maskers marched forth in trim array.

The first was Fancy, like a lovely boy,
  Of rare aspect, and beauty without peer;
Matchable either to that imp of Troy,
  Whom Jove did love, and chose his cup to bear,
  Or that same dainty lad, which was so dear
To great Alcides, that when as he died,
  He wailed womanlike with many a tear,
And every wood, and every valley wide
He filled with Hylas' name; the nymphs eke Hylas cried.

His garment neither was of silk nor say,
  But painted plumes, in goodly order dight,
Like as the sunburnt Indians do array
  Their tawny bodies, in their proudest plight:
  As those same plumes, so seemed he vain and light,
That by his gait might easily appear;
  For still he fared as dancing in delight,
And in his hand a windy fan did bear,
That in the idle air he moved still here and there.

And him beside marched amorous Desire,
  Who seemed of riper years, than th'other swain,
Yet was that other swain this elder's sire,
  And gave him being, common to them twain:
  His garment was disguised very vain,
And his embroidered bonnet sat awry;
  'Twixt both his hands few sparks he close did strain,
Which still he blew, and kindled busily,
That soon they life conceived, and forth in flames did fly.

Next after him went Doubt, who was yclad
  In a discoloured coat, of strange disguise,
That at his back a broad capuccio had,
  And sleeves dependent Albanese-wise:
  He looked askew with his mistrustful eyes,
And nicely trod, as thorns lay in his way,
  Or that the floor to shrink he did advise,
And on a broken reed he still did stay
His feeble steps, which shrunk, when hard thereon he lay.

With him went Danger, clothed in ragged weed,
  Made of bear's skin, that him more dreadful made,
Yet his own face was dreadful, ne did need
  Strange horror, to deform his grisly shade;
  A net in th'one hand, and a rusty blade
In th'other was, this Mischief, that Mishap;
  With th'one his foes he threatened to invade,
With th'other he his friends meant to enwrap:
For whom he could not kill, he practised to entrap.

Next him was Fear, all armed from top to toe,
  Yet thought himself not safe enough thereby,
But feared each shadow moving to and fro,
  And his own arms when glittering he did spy,
  Or clashing heard, he fast away did fly,
As ashes pale of hue, and wingy-heeled;
  And evermore on Danger fixed his eye,
'Gainst whom he always bent a brazen shield,
Which his right hand unarmed fearfully did wield.

capuccio] hood

With him went Hope in rank, a handsome maid,
  Of cheerful look and lovely to behold;
In silken samite she was light arrayed,
  And her fair locks were woven up in gold;
  She alway smiled, and in her hand did hold
An holy water sprinkle, dipped in dew,
  With which she sprinkled favours manifold,
On whom she list, and did great liking show,
Great liking unto many, but true love to few.

And after them Dissemblance, and Suspect,
  Marched in one rank, yet an unequal pair:
For she was gentle, and of mild aspect,
  Courteous to all, and seeming debonair,
  Goodly adorned, and exceeding fair:
Yet was that all but painted, and purloined,
  And her bright brows were decked with borrowed hair;
Her deeds were forged, and her words false coined,
And always in her hand two clews of silk she twined.

But he was foul, ill favoured, and grim,
  Under his eyebrows looking still askance;
And ever as Dissemblance laughed on him,
  He loured on her with dangerous eye-glance,
  Shewing his nature in his countenance;
His rolling eyes did never rest in place,
  But walked each where, for fear of hid mischance,
Holding a lattice still before his face,
Through which he still did peep, as forward he did pace.

clews] skeins

Next him went Grief, and Fury matched yfere;
  Grief all in sable sorrowfully clad,
Down hanging his dull head, with heavy cheer,
  Yet inly being more, than seeming sad:
  A pair of pincers in his hand he had,
With which he pinched people to the heart,
  That from thenceforth a wretched life they lad,
In wilful languor and consuming smart,
Dying each day with inward wounds of dolour's dart.

But Fury was full ill apparelled
  In rags, that naked nigh she did appear,
With ghastly looks and dreadful dreary head;
  For from her back her garments she did tear,
  And from her head oft rent her snarled hair:
In her right hand a firebrand she did toss
  About her head, still roaming here and there;
As a dismayed deer in chase embossed,
Forgetful of his safety, hath his right way lost.

After them went Displeasure and Pleasance,
  He looking lumpish and full sullen sad,
And hanging down his heavy countenance;
  She cheerful fresh and full of joyance glad,
  As if no sorrow she ne felt ne drad;
That evil matched pair they seemed to be:
  An angry wasp th'one in a phial had
Th'other in hers an honey-lady bee.
Thus marched these six couples forth in fair degree.

snarled] tangled   embossed] hard pressed

After all these there marched a most fair dame,
  Led of two grisly villains, th'one Despight,
The other cleped Cruelty by name:
  She, doleful lady, like a dreary spright,
  Called by strong charms out of eternal night,
Had death's own image figured in her face,
  Full of sad signs, fearful to living sight;
Yet in that horror shewed a seemly grace,
And with her feeble feet did move a comely pace.

Her breast all naked, as net ivory,
  Without adorn of gold or silver bright,
Wherewith the craftsman wonts it beautify,
  Of her due honour was despoiled quite,
  And a wide wound therein (O rueful sight)
Entrenched deep with knife accursed keen,
  Yet freshly bleeding forth her fainting spright,
(The work of cruel hand) was to be seen,
That dyed in sanguine red her skin all snowy clean.

At that wide orifice her trembling heart
  Was drawn forth, and in silver basin laid,
Quite through transfixed with a deadly dart,
  And in her blood yet steaming fresh embayed:
  And those two villains, which her steps upstayed,
When her weak feet could scarcely her sustain,
  And fading vital powers 'gan to fade,
Her forward still with torture did constrain,
And evermore increased her consuming pain.

net] pure   embayed] balked

Next after her the winged God himself
  Came riding on a lion ravenous,
Taught to obey the manage of that elf,
  That man and beast with power imperious
  Subdueth to his kingdom tyrannous:
His blindfold eyes he bade a while unbind,
  That his proud spoil of that same dolorous
Fair dame he might behold in perfect kind;
Which seen, he much rejoiced in his cruel mind.

Of which full proud, himself uprearing high,
  He looked round about with stern disdain;
And did survey his goodly company:
  And marshalling the evil ordered train,
  With that the darts, which his right hand did strain,
Full dreadfully he shook that all did quake,
  And clapped on high his coloured wings twain,
That all his many it afraid did make:
Tho blinding him again, his way he forth did take.

Behind him was Reproach, Repentance, Shame;
  Reproach the first, Shame next, Repent behind;
Repentance feeble, sorrowful, and lame,
  Reproach despiteful, careless, and unkind,
  Shame most ill favoured, bestial, and blind:
Shame loured, Repentance sighed, Reproach did scold;
  Reproach sharp stings, Repentance whips entwined,
Shame burning brand-irons in her hand did hold:
All three to each unlike, yet all made in one mould.

many] train   tho] then

And after them a rude confused rout
  Of persons flocked, whose names is hard to read:
Amongst them was stern Strife, and Anger stout,
  Unquiet Care, and fond Unthriftyhead,
  Lewd Loss of Time, and Sorrow seeming dead,
Inconstant Change, and false Disloyalty,
  Consuming Riotise, and guilty Dread
Of heavenly vengeance, faint Infirmity,
Vile Poverty, and lastly Death with infamy.

There were full many mo like maladies,
  Whose names and natures I note readen well;
So many mo, as there be fantasies
  In wavering women's wit, that none can tell,
  Or pains in love, or punishments in hell;
All which disguised marched in masking wise,
  About the chamber with that damosel,
And then returned, having marched thrice,
Into the inner room, from whence they first did rise.

The Faerie Queene, III. xii. 3–26, 1590

167 *Love*

THE rugged forehead that with grave foresight
  Wields kingdoms' causes, and affairs of state,
My looser rimes (I wot) doth sharply wite,
  For praising love, as I have done of late,
  And magnifying lovers' dear debate;
By which frail youth is oft to folly led,
  Through false allurement of that pleasing bait,
That better were in virtues discipled,
Than with vain poems' weeds to have their fancies fed.

note] cannot   wite] blame

Such ones ill judge of love, that cannot love,
  Ne in their frozen hearts feel kindly flame:
For thy they ought not thing unknown reprove,
  Ne natural affection faultless blame,
  For fault of few that have abused the same.
For it of honour and all virtue is
  The root, and brings forth glorious flowers of fame,
That crown true lovers with immortal bliss,
The meed of them that love, and do not live amiss.

Which whoso list look back to former ages,
  And call to count the things that then were done,
Shall find, that all the works of those wise sages,
  And brave exploits which great heroës won,
  In love were either ended or begun:
Witness the father of philosophy,
  Which to his Critias, shaded oft from sun,
Of love full many lessons did apply,
The which these stoic censors cannot well deny.

To such therefore I do not sing at all,
  But to that sacred Saint my sovereign Queen,
In whose chaste breast all bounty natural
  And treasures of true love enlocked been,
  'Bove all her sex that ever yet was seen:
To her I sing of love, that loveth best,
  And best is loved of all alive I ween;
To her this song most fitly is addressed,
The Queen of love, and Prince of peace from heaven blest.

for thy] therefore

Which that she may the better deign to hear,
  Do thou, dread infant, Venus' darling dove,
From her high spirit chase imperious fear,
  And use of awful majesty remove:
  Instead thereof with drops of melting love,
Dewed with ambrosial kisses, by thee gotten
  From thy sweet smiling mother from above,
Sprinkle her heart, and haughty courage soften,
That she may hark to love, and read this lesson often.

The Faerie Queene, IV. *intr.*, 1596

168 *The House of Ate*

HER name was Ate, mother of debate,
  And all dissension, which doth daily grow
Amongst frail men, that many a public state
  And many a private oft doth overthrow.
  Her false Duessa who full well did know,
To be most fit to trouble noble knights,
  Which hunt for honour, raised from below,
Out of the dwellings of the damned sprights,
Where she in darkness wastes her cursed days and nights.

Hard by the gates of hell her dwelling is,
  There whereas all the plagues and harms abound,
Which punish wicked men, that walk amiss:
  It is a darksome delve far under ground,
  With thorns and barren brakes environed round,
That none the same may easily out win:
  Yet many ways to enter may be found,
But none to issue forth when one is in;
For discord harder is to end than to begin.

And all within the riven walls were hung
With ragged monuments of times forepast,
All which the sad effects of discord sung:
There were rent robes and broken sceptres placed,
Altars defiled, and holy things defaced,
Disshivered spears, and shields ytorn in twain,
Great cities ransacked, and strong castles razed,
Nations captived, and huge armies slain;
Of all which ruins there some relics did remain.

There was the sign of antique Babylon,
Of fatal Thebes, of Rome that reigned long,
Of sacred Salem, and sad Ilion,
For memory of which on high there hung
The golden apple, cause of all their wrong,
For which the three fair goddesses did strive:
There also was the name of Nimrod strong,
Of Alexander, and his Princes five,
Which shared to them the spoils that he had got alive.

And there the relics of the drunken fray,
The which amongst the Lapithes befell,
And of the bloody feast, which sent away
So many Centaurs' drunken souls to hell,
That under great Alcides' fury fell;
And of the dreadful discord, which did drive
The noble Argonauts to outrage fell,
That each of life sought others to deprive,
All mindless of the golden fleece, which made them strive.

And eke of private persons many mo,
  That were too long a work to count them all;
Some of sworn friends, that did their faith forgo;
  Some of born brethren, proved unnatural;
  Some of dear lovers, foes perpetual:
Witness their broken bands there to be seen,
  Their garlands rent, their bowers despoiled all;
The monuments whereof there biding been,
As plain as at the first, when they were fresh and green.

The Faerie Queene, IV. i. 19–24, 1596

169 *The Happy Isle*

THUS having passed all peril, I was come
  Within the compass of that island's space;
The which did seem unto my simple doom
  The only pleasant and delightful place,
  That ever trodden was of footing's trace.
For all that nature by her mother wit
  Could frame in earth, and form of substance base,
Was there, and all that nature did omit,
Art, playing second nature's part, supplied it.

No tree, that is of count, in greenwood grows,
  From lowest juniper to cedar tall,
No flower in field, that dainty odour throws,
  And decks his branch with blossoms over all,
  But there was planted, or grew natural:
Nor sense of man so coy and curious nice,
  But there mote find to please itself withal;
Nor heart could wish for any quaint device,
But there it present was, and did frail sense entice.

In such luxurious plenty of all pleasure,
  It seemed a second paradise to guess,
So lavishly enriched with nature's treasure,
  That if the happy souls, which do possess
  Th'Elysian fields, and live in lasting bliss,
Should happen this with living eye to see,
  They soon would loathe their lesser happiness,
And wish to life returned again to be,
That in this joyous place they mote have joyance free.

Fresh shadows, fit to shroud from sunny ray;
  Fair lawns, to take the sun in season due;
Sweet springs, in which a thousand nymphs did play;
  Soft rumbling brooks, that gentle slumber drew;
  High reared mounts, the lands about to view;
Low looking dales, disloigned from common gaze;
  Delightful bowers, to solace lovers true;
False labyrinths, fond runners' eyes to daze;
All which by nature made did nature self amaze.

And all without were walks and alleys dight
  With divers trees, enranged in even ranks;
And here and there were pleasant arbours pight,
  And shady seats, and sundry flowering banks,
  To sit and rest the walkers' weary shanks,
And therein thousand pairs of lovers walked,
  Praising their god, and yielding him great thanks,
Ne ever aught but of their true loves talked,
Ne ever for rebuke or blame of any balked.

disloigned] separated   balked] faltered

All these together by themselves did sport
  Their spotless pleasures, and sweet loves' content.
But far away from these, another sort
  Of lovers linked in true heart's consent;
  Which loved not as these, for like intent,
But on chaste virtue grounded their desire,
  Far from all fraud, or feigned blandishment;
Which in their spirits kindling zealous fire,
Brave thoughts and noble deeds did evermore aspire.

Such were great Hercules, and Hylas dear;
  True Jonathan, and David trusty tried;
Stout Theseus, and Pirithous his fere;
  Pylades and Orestes by his side;
  Mild Titus and Gesippus without pride;
Damon and Pythias whom death could not sever:
  All these, and all that ever had been tied
In bands of friendship, there did live for ever,
Whose lives although decayed, yet loves decayed never.

The Faerie Queene, IV. x. 21–7, 1596

170 *Artegall and Radigund*

SO soon as day, forth dawning from the East,
  Night's humid curtain from the heavens withdrew,
And early calling forth both man and beast,
  Commanded them their daily works renew,
  These noble warriors, mindful to pursue
The last day's purpose of their vowed fight,
  Themselves thereto prepared in order due;
The knight, as best was seeming for a knight,
And th' Amazon, as best it liked herself to dight.

fere] comrade

All in a camis light of purple silk
  Woven upon with silver, subtly wrought,
And quilted upon satin white as milk,
  Trailed with ribbands diversely distraught,
  Like as the workman had their courses taught;
Which was short tucked for light motion
  Up to her ham, but when she list, it raught
Down to her lowest heel, and thereupon
She wore for her defence a mailed habergeon.

And on her legs she painted buskins wore,
  Basted with bends of gold on every side,
And mails between, and laced close afore:
  Upon her thigh her scimitar was tied,
  With an embroidered belt of mickle pride;
And on her shoulder hung her shield, bedecked
  Upon the boss with stones, that shined wide,
As the fair moon in her most full aspect,
That to the moon it mote be like in each respect.

So forth she came out of the city gate,
  With stately port and proud magnificence,
Guarded with many damsels, that did wait
  Upon her person for her sure defence,
  Playing on shawms and trumpets, that from hence
Their sound did reach unto the heaven's height.
  So forth into the field she marched thence,
Where was a rich pavilion ready pight,
Her to receive, till time they should begin the fight.

camis] robe   habergeon] body-armour
basted] sewn   bends] bands

Then forth came Artegall out of his tent,
  All armed to point, and first the lists did enter:
Soon after eke came she, with fell intent,
  And countenance fierce, as having fully bent her,
  That battle's utmost trial to adventure.
The lists were closed fast, to bar the rout
  From rudely pressing to the middle centre;
Which in great heaps them circled all about,
Waiting, how Fortune would resolve that dangerous doubt.

The trumpets sounded, and the field began;
  With bitter strokes it both began, and ended.
She at the first encounter on him ran
  With furious rage, as if she had intended
  Out of his breast the very heart have rended:
But he, that had like tempests often tried,
  From that first flaw himself right well defended.
The more she raged, the more he did abide;
She hewed, she foined, she lashed, she laid on every side.

Yet still her blows he bore, and her forbore,
  Weening at last to win advantage new;
Yet still her cruelty increased more,
  And though power failed, her courage did accrue,
  Which failing he 'gan fiercely her pursue.
Like as a smith that to his cunning feat
  The stubborn metal seeketh to subdue,
Soon as he feels it mollified with heat,
With his great iron sledge doth strongly on it beat.

to point] exactly foined] thrust

So did Sir Artegall upon her lay,
   As if she had an iron anvil been,
That flakes of fire, bright as the sunny ray,
   Out of her steely arms were flashing seen,
   That all on fire ye would her surely ween.
But with her shield so well herself she warded,
   From the dread danger of his weapon keen,
That all that while her life she safely guarded:
But he that help from her against her will discarded.

For with his trenchant blade at the next blow
   Half of her shield he shared quite away,
That half her side itself did naked show,
   And thenceforth unto danger opened way.
   Much was she moved with the mighty sway
Of that sad stroke, that half enraged she grew,
   And like a greedy bear unto her prey,
With her sharp scimitar at him she flew,
That glancing down his thigh, the purple blood forth drew.

Thereat she 'gan to triumph with great boast,
   And to upbraid that chance, which him misfell,
As if the prize she gotten had almost,
   With spiteful speeches, fitting with her well;
   That his great heart 'gan inwardly to swell
With indignation, at her vaunting vain,
   And at her struck with puissance fearful fell:
Yet with her shield she warded it again,
That shattered all to pieces round about the plain.

Having her thus disarmed of her shield,
  Upon her helmet he again her struck,
That down she fell upon the grassy field,
  In senseless swoon, as if her life forsook,
  And pangs of death her spirit overtook.
Whom when he saw before his foot prostrated,
  He to her lept with deadly dreadful look,
And her sunshiny helmet soon unlaced,
Thinking at once both head and helmet to have razed.

But when as he discovered had her face,
  He saw his senses' strange astonishment,
A miracle of nature's goodly grace,
  In her fair visage void of ornament,
  But bathed in blood and sweat together ment;
Which in the rudeness of that evil plight
  Bewrayed the signs of feature excellent;
Like as the moon, in foggy winter's night,
Doth seem to be herself, though darkened be her light.

The Faerie Queene, V. v. 1–12, 1596

171 *A Pastoral*

FROM thence into the open fields he fled,
  Whereas the herds were keeping of their neat,
And shepherds singing to their flocks, that fed,
  Lays of sweet love and youth's delightful heat:
  Him thither eke for all his fearful threat
He followed fast, and chased him so nigh,
  That to the folds, where sheep at night do seat,
And to the little cots, where shepherds lie
In winter's wrathful time, he forced him to fly.

ment] mixed   neat] cattle

There on a day as he pursued the chase,
  He chanced to spy a sort of shepherd grooms,
Playing on pipes, and carolling apace,
  The whiles their beasts there in the budded brooms
  Beside them fed, and nipped the tender blooms;
For other worldly wealth they cared nought.
  To whom Sir Calidore yet sweating comes,
And them to tell him courteously besought,
If such a beast they saw, which he had thither brought.

They answered him, that no such beast they saw,
  Nor any wicked fiend, that mote offend
Their happy flocks, nor danger to them draw:
  But if that such there were (as none they kenned)
  They prayed high God him far from them to send.
Then one of them him seeing so to sweat,
  After his rustic wise, that well he weened,
Offered him drink, to quench his thirsty heat,
And if he hungry were, him offered eke to eat.

The knight was nothing nice, where was no need,
  And took their gentle offer; so adown
They prayed him sit, and gave him for to feed
  Such homely what, as serves the simple clown,
  That doth despise the dainties of the town.
Tho having fed his fill, he there beside
  Saw a fair damsel, which did wear a crown
Of sundry flowers, with silken ribbands tied,
Yclad in home-made green that her own hands had dyed.

sort] company   tho] then

Upon a little hillock she was placed
  Higher than all the rest, and round about
Environed with a garland, goodly graced,
  Of lovely lasses, and them all without
  The lusty shepherd swains sat in a rout,
The which did pipe and sing her praises due,
  And oft rejoice, and oft for wonder shout,
As if some miracle of heavenly hue
Were down to them descended in that earthly view.

And soothly sure she was full fair of face,
  And perfectly well shaped in every limb,
Which she did more augment with modest grace,
  And comely carriage of her countenance trim,
  That all the rest like lesser lamps did dim;
Who her admiring as some heavenly wight,
  Did for their sovereign goddess her esteem,
And carolling her name both day and night,
The fairest Pastorella her by name did hight.

Ne was there herd, ne was there shepherd's swain,
  But her did honour, and eke many a one
Burnt in her love, and with sweet pleasing pain
  Full many a night for her did sigh and groan.
  But most of all the shepherd Coridon
For her did languish, and his dear life spend;
  Yet neither she for him, nor other none
Did care a whit, ne any liking lend:
Though mean her lot, yet higher did her mind ascend.

rout] throng

Her whiles Sir Calidore there viewed well,
   And marked her rare demeanour, which him seemed
So far the mean of shepherds to excel,
   As that he in his mind her worthy deemed,
   To be a prince's paragon esteemed,
He was unwares surprised in subtle bands
   Of the blind boy, ne thence could be redeemed
By any skill out of his cruel hands,
Caught like the bird, which gazing still on others stands.

So stood he still long gazing thereupon,
   Ne any will had thence to move away,
Although his quest were far afore him gone:
   But after he had fed, yet did he stay,
   And sat there still, until the flying day
Was far forth spent, discoursing diversely
   Of sundry things, as fell, to work delay;
And evermore his speech he did apply
To th' herds, but meant them to the damsel's fantasy.

By this the moisty night approaching fast
   Her dewy humour 'gan on th' earth to shed,
That warned the shepherds to their homes to haste
   Their tender flocks, now being fully fed,
   For fear of wetting them before their bed;
Then came to them a good old aged sire,
   Whose silver locks bedecked his beard and head,
With shepherd's hook in hand, and fit attire,
That willed the damsel rise; the day did now expire.

He was to wit by common voice esteemed
  The father of the fairest Pastorell,
And of herself in very deed so deemed;
  Yet was not so, but as old stories tell
  Found her by fortune, which to him befell,
In th' open fields an infant left alone,
  And taking up brought home, and nursed well
As his own child; for other he had none,
That she in tract of time accompted was his own.

She at his bidding meekly did arise,
  And straight unto her little flock did fare:
Then all the rest about her rose likewise,
  And each his sundry sheep with several care
  Gathered together, and them homeward bare;
Whilst every one with helping hands did strive
  Amongst themselves, and did their labours share,
To help fair Pastorella, home to drive
Her fleecy flock; but Coridon most help did give.

But Melibœe (so hight that good old man)
  Now seeing Calidore left all alone,
And night arrived hard at hand, began
  Him to invite unto his simple home;
  Which though it were a cottage clad with loam,
And all things therein mean, yet better so
  To lodge, than in the savage fields to roam.
The knight full gladly soon agreed thereto,
Being his heart's own wish, and home with him did go.

There he was welcomed of that honest sire,
   And of his aged beldame homely well;
Who him besought himself to disattire,
   And rest himself, till supper time befell.
   By which home came the fairest Pastorell,
After her flock she in their fold had tied,
   And supper ready dight, they to it fell
With small ado, and nature satisfied,
The which doth little crave contented to abide.

Tho when they had their hunger slaked well,
   And the fair maid the table ta'en away,
The gentle knight, as he that did excel
   In courtesy, and well could do and say,
   For so great kindness as he found that day,
'Gan greatly thank his host and his good wife;
   And drawing thence his speech another way,
'Gan highly to commend the happy life,
Which shepherds lead, without debate or bitter strife.

'How much' (said he) 'more happy is the state,
   In which ye, father, here do dwell at ease,
Leading a life so free and fortunate,
   From all the tempests of these worldly seas,
   Which toss the rest in dangerous disease;
Where wars, and wrecks, and wicked enmity
   Do them afflict, which no man can appease,
That certės I your happiness envy,
And wish my lot were placed in such felicity.'

'Surely my son' (then answered he again)
   'If happy, then it is in this intent,
That having small, yet do I not complain
   Of want, ne wish for more it to augment,
   But do myself, with that I have, content;
So taught of nature, which doth little need
   Of foreign helps to life's due nourishment:
The fields my food, my flock my raiment breed;
No better do I wear, no better do I feed.

'Therefore I do not any one envy,
   Nor am envied of any one therefore;
They, that have much, fear much to lose thereby,
   And store of cares doth follow riches' store.
   The little that I have grows daily more
Without my care, but only to attend it;
   My lambs do every year increase their score,
And my flock's father daily doth amend it.
What have I, but to praise th' Almighty, that doth send it?

'To them that list the world's gay shows I leave,
   And to great ones such follies do forgive,
Which oft through pride do their own peril weave,
   And through ambition down themselves do drive
   To sad decay, that might contented live.
Me no such cares nor cumbrous thoughts offend,
   Ne once my mind's unmoved quiet grieve,
But all the night in silver sleep I spend,
And all the day, to what I list, I do attend.

'Sometimes I hunt the fox, the vowed foe
  Unto my lambs, and him dislodge away;
Sometimes the fawn I practise from the doe,
  Or from the goat her kid how to convey;
  Another while I baits and nets display,
The birds to catch, or fishes to beguile:
  And when I weary am, I down do lay
My limbs in every shade, to rest from toil,
And drink of every brook, when thirst my throat doth boil.

'The time was once, in my first prime of years,
  When pride of youth forth pricked my desire,
That I disdained amongst mine equal peers
  To follow sheep, and shepherds' base attire:
  For further fortune then I would inquire.
And leaving home, to royal court I sought;
  Where I did sell myself for yearly hire,
And in the Prince's garden daily wrought:
There I beheld such vainness, as I never thought.

With sight whereof soon cloyed, and long deluded
  With idle hopes, which them do entertain,
After I had ten years myself excluded
  From native home, and spent my youth in vain,
  I 'gan my follies to myself to plain,
And this sweet peace, whose lack did then appear.
  Tho back returning to my sheep again
I from thenceforth have learned to love more dear
This lowly quiet life, which I inherit here.'

The Faerie Queene, VI. ix. 4–25, 1596

172 *The Dance of the Graces*

IT was an hill placed in an open plain,
  That round about was bordered with a wood
Of matchless height, that seemed th'earth to disdain,
  In which all trees of honour stately stood,
  And did all winter as in summer bud,
Spreading pavilions for the birds to bower,
  Which in their lower branches sung aloud;
And in their tops the soaring hawk did tower,
Sitting like king of fowls in majesty and power.

And at the foot thereof, a gentle flood
  His silver waves did softly tumble down,
Unmarred with ragged moss or filthy mud,
  Ne mote wild beasts, ne mote the ruder clown
  Thereto approach, ne filth mote therein drown:
But nymphs and fairies by the banks did sit,
  In the wood's shade, which did the waters crown,
Keeping all noisome things away from it,
And to the water's fall tuning their accents fit.

And on the top thereof a spacious plain
  Did spread itself, to serve to all delight,
Either to dance, when they to dance would fain,
  Or else to course about their bases light;
  Ne aught there wanted, which for pleasure might
Desired be, or thence to banish bale:
  So pleasantly the hill with equal height
Did seem to overlook the lowly vale;
Therefore it rightly cleped was mount Acidale.

bases] lines in a game		cleped] named

They say that Venus, when she did dispose
  Herself to pleasance, used to resort
Unto this place, and therein to repose
  And rest herself, as in a gladsome port,
  Or with the Graces there to play and sport;
That even her own Citheron, though in it
  She used most to keep her royal court,
And in her sovereign majesty to sit,
She in regard hereof refused and thought unfit.

Unto this place when as the Elfin Knight
  Approached, him seemed that the merry sound
Of a shrill pipe he playing heard on height,
  And many feet fast thumping th' hollow ground,
  That through the woods their echo did rebound.
He nigher drew, to wit what mote it be;
  There he a troop of ladies dancing found
Full merrily, and making gladful glee,
And in the midst a shepherd piping he did see.

He durst not enter into th' open green,
  For dread of them unwares to be descried,
For breaking of their dance, if he were seen;
  But in the covert of the wood did bide,
  Beholding all, yet of them unespied.
There he did see, that pleased much his sight,
  That even he himself his eyes envied,
An hundred naked maidens lily white,
All ranged in a ring, and dancing in delight.

All they without were ranged in a ring,
  And danced round; but in the midst of them
Three other ladies did both dance and sing,
  The whilst the rest them round about did hem,
  And like a garland did in compass stem:
And in the midst of those same three was placed
  Another damsel, as a precious gem,
Amidst a ring most richly well enchased,
That with her goodly presence all the rest much graced.

Look how the crown, which Ariadne wore
  Upon her ivory forehead that same day,
That Theseus her unto his bridal bore,
  When the bold Centaurs made that bloody fray,
  With the fierce Lapithes, which did them dismay,
Being now placed in the firmament,
  Through the bright heaven doth her beams display,
And is unto the stars an ornament,
Which round about her move in order excellent:

Such was the beauty of this goodly band,
  Whose sundry parts were here too long to tell:
But she, that in the midst of them did stand,
  Seemed all the rest in beauty to excel,
  Crowned with a rosy garland, that right well
Did her beseem. And ever, as the crew
  About her danced, sweet flowers, that far did smell,
And fragrant odours they upon her threw;
But most of all, those three did her with gifts endue.

stem] surround

Those were the Graces, daughters of delight,
  Handmaids of Venus, which are wont to haunt
Upon this hill, and dance there day and night:
  Those three to men all gifts of grace do grant,
  And all, that Venus in herself doth vaunt,
Is borrowed of them. But that fair one,
  That in the midst was placed paravaunt,
Was she to whom that shepherd piped alone,
That made him pipe so merrily, as never none.

She was to wit that jolly shepherd's lass,
  Which piped there unto that merry rout;
That jolly shepherd, which there piped, was
  Poor Colin Clout (who knows not Colin Clout?);
  He piped apace, whilst they him danced about.
Pipe jolly shepherd, pipe thou now apace
  Unto thy love, that made thee low to lout:
Thy love is present there with thee in place,
Thy love is there advanced to be another Grace.

The Faerie Queene, VI. x. 6–16, 1596

173 *The Mask of Mutability*

SO, forth issued the Seasons of the year;
  First, lusty Spring, all dight in leaves of flowers
That freshly budded and new blooms did bear
  (In which a thousand birds had built their bowers
  That sweetly sung, to call forth paramours);
And in his hand a javelin he did bear,
  And on his head (as fit for warlike stours)
A gilt engraven morion he did wear;
That as some did him love, so others did him fear.

paravaunt] foremost stours] tumults morion] helmet

Then came the jolly Summer, being dight
  In a thin silken cassock coloured green,
That was unlined all, to be more light;
  And on his head a garland well beseen
  He wore, from which, as he had chafed been,
The sweat did drop; and in his hand he bore
  A bow and shafts, as he in forest green
Had hunted late the libbard or the boar,
And now would bathe his limbs, with labour heated sore.

Then came the Autumn all in yellow clad,
  As though he joyed in his plenteous store,
Laden with fruits that made him laugh, full glad
  That he had banished hunger, which to-fore
  Had by the belly oft him pinched sore.
Upon his head a wreath that was enrolled
  With ears of corn of every sort he bore;
And in his hand a sickle he did hold,
To reap the ripened fruits the which the earth had yold.

Lastly, came Winter clothed all in frieze,
  Chattering his teeth for cold that did him chill,
Whilst on his hoary beard his breath did freeze;
  And the dull drops that from his purpled bill
  As from a limbec did adown distil.
In his right hand a tipped staff he held,
  With which his feeble steps he stayed still;
For he was faint with cold, and weak with eld,
That scarce his loosed limbs he able was to weld.

libbard] leopard   yold] yielded   limbec] retort   weld] wield

These, marching softly, thus in order went,
  And after them, the Months all riding came;
First, sturdy March with brows full sternly bent,
  And armed strongly, rode upon a ram,
  The same which over Hellespontus swam:
Yet in his hand a spade he also hent,
  And in a bag all sorts of seeds ysame,
Which on the earth he strewed as he went,
And filled her womb with fruitful hope of nourishment.

Next came fresh April full of lustihead,
  And wanton as a kid whose horn new buds;
Upon a bull he rode, the same which led
  Europa floating through th'Argolic floods;
  His horns were gilden all with golden studs
And garnished with garlands goodly dight
  Of all the fairest flowers and freshest buds
Which th'earth brings forth, and wet he seemed in sight
With waves, through which he waded for his love's delight.

Then came fair May, the fairest maid on ground,
  Decked all with dainties of her season's pride,
And throwing flowers out of her lap around:
  Upon two brethren's shoulders she did ride,
  The twins of Leda; which on either side
Supported her like to their sovereign queen.
  Lord! how all creatures laughed, when her they spied,
And leaped and danced as they had ravished been!
And Cupid self about her fluttered all in green.

hent] took ysame] together

And after her, came jolly June arrayed
   All in green leaves, as he a player were;
Yet in his time, he wrought as well as played,
   That by his plough-irons mote right well appear:
   Upon a crab he rode, that him did bear
With crooked crawling steps an uncouth pace,
   And backwards yode, as bargemen wont to fare,
Bending their force contrary to their face,
Like that ungracious crew which feigns demurest grace.

Then came hot July boiling like to fire,
   That all his garments he had cast away;
Upon a lion raging yet with ire
   He boldly rode and made him to obey:
   It was the beast that whilom did foray
The Nemaean forest, till th'Amphytrionide
   Him slew, and with his hide did him array;
Behind his back a scythe, and by his side
Under his belt he bore a sickle circling wide.

The sixth was August, being rich arrayed
   In garment all of gold down to the ground:
Yet rode he not, but led a lovely maid
   Forth by the lily hand, the which was crowned
   With ears of corn, and full her hand was found;
That was the righteous virgin, which of old
   Lived here on earth, and plenty made abound;
But, after wrong was loved and justice sold,
She left th'unrighteous world and was to heaven extolled.

yode] went

Next him, September marched eke on foot;
  Yet was he heavy laden with the spoil
Of harvest's riches, which he made his boot,
  And him enriched with bounty of the soil:
  In his one hand, as fit for harvest's toil,
He held a knife-hook; and in th'other hand
  A pair of weights, with which he did assoil
Both more and less, where it in doubt did stand,
And equal gave to each as justice duly scanned.

Then came October full of merry glee;
  For yet his noll was totty of the must,
Which he was treading in the wine-fats sea,
  And of the joyous oil, whose gentle gust
  Made him so frolic and so full of lust:
Upon a dreadful scorpion he did ride,
  The same which by Diana's doom unjust
Slew great Orion; and eke by his side
He had his ploughing share and coulter ready tied.

Next was November, he full gross and fat,
  As fed with lard, and that right well might seem;
For he had been a-fatting hogs of late,
  That yet his brows with sweat did reek and steam,
  And yet the season was full sharp and breem;
In planting eke he took no small delight:
  Whereon he rode, not easy was to deem;
For it a dreadful Centaur was in sight,
The seed of Saturn and faire Nais, Chiron hight.

noll] head   breem] severe

And after him, came next the chill December:
  Yet he through merry feasting which he made,
And great bonfires, did not the cold remember;
  His Saviour's birth his mind so much did glad:
  Upon a shaggy-bearded goat he rode,
The same wherewith Dan Jove in tender years,
  They say, was nourished by th' Idaean maid;
And in his hand a broad deep bowl he bears;
Of which he freely drinks an health to all his peers.

Then came old January, wrapped well
  In many weeds to keep the cold away;
Yet did he quake and quiver like to quell,
  And blow his nails to warm them if he may;
  For they were numbed with holding all the day
An hatchet keen, with which he felled wood,
  And from the trees did lop the needless spray:
Upon an huge great earth-pot steane he stood;
From whose wide mouth there flowed forth the Roman flood.

And lastly, came cold February, sitting
  In an old waggon, for he could not ride;
Drawn of two fishes for the season fitting,
  Which through the flood before did softly slide
  And swim away: yet had he by his side
His plough and harness fit to till the ground,
  And tools to prune the trees, before the pride
Of hasting prime did make them burgeon round.
So past the twelve Months forth, and their due places found.

steane] vessel

And after these, there came the Day, and Night,
  Riding together both with equal pace,
Th' one on a palfrey black, the other white;
  But Night had covered her uncomely face
  With a black veil, and held in hand a mace,
On top whereof the moon and stars were pight,
  And sleep and darkness round about did trace:
But Day did bear, upon his sceptre's height,
The goodly sun, encompassed all with beamės bright.

Then came the Hours, fair daughters of high Jove
  And timely Night, the which were all endued
With wondrous beauty fit to kindle love;
  But they were virgins all, and love eschewed,
  That might forslack the charge to them foreshewed
By mighty Jove; who did them porters make
  Of heaven's gate (whence all the gods issued)
Which they did daily watch, and nightly wake
By even turns, ne ever did their charge forsake.

And after all came Life, and lastly Death;
  Death with most grim and grisly visage seen,
Yet is he nought but parting of the breath;
  Ne ought to see, but like a shade to ween,
  Unbodied, unsouled, unheard, unseen.
But Life was like a fair young lusty boy,
  Such as they feign Dan Cupid to have been,
Full of delightful health and lively joy,
Decked all with flowers, and wings of gold fit to employ.

The Faerie Queene, VII. vii. 28–46, 1609

174 *Colin Clout at Court*

SO having said, Aglaura him bespake:
'Colin, well worthy were those goodly favours
Bestowed on thee, that so of them dost make,
And them requitest with thy thankful labours.
But of great Cynthia's goodness and high grace
Finish the story which thou hast begun.'
'More eath' (quoth he) 'it is in such a case
How to begin, than know how to have done.
For every gift and every goodly meed,
Which she on me bestowed, demands a day;
And every day, in which she did a deed,
Demands a year it duly to display.
Her words were like a stream of honey fleeting,
The which doth softly trickle from the hive,
Able to melt the hearer's heart unwitting,
And eke to make the dead again alive.
Her deeds were like great clusters of ripe grapes,
Which load the branches of the fruitful vine,
Offering to fall into each mouth that gapes,
And fill the same with store of timely wine.
Her looks were like beams of the morning sun,
Forth looking through the windows of the east,
When first the fleecy cattle have begun
Upon the pearled grass to make their feast.
Her thoughts are like the fume of frankincense,
Which from a golden censer forth doth rise;
And throwing forth sweet odours mounts fro thence
In rolling globes up to the vaulted skies.
There she beholds with high aspiring thought

eath] easy

The cradle of her own creation,
Amongst the seats of Angels heavenly wrought,
Much like an angel in all form and fashion.'
  'Colin' (said Cuddy then) 'thou hast forgot
Thyself, meseems, too much, to mount so high:
Such lofty flight base shepherd seemeth not,
From flocks and fields, to angels and to sky.'
  'True' (answered he), 'but her great excellence
Lifts me above the measure of my might;
That being filled with furious insolence,
I feel myself like one yrapt in spright.
For when I think of her, as oft I ought,
Then want I words to speak it fitly forth;
And when I speak of her what I have thought,
I cannot think according to her worth.
Yet will I think of her, yet will I speak,
So long as life my limbs doth hold together,
And when as death these vital bands shall break,
Her name recorded I will leave for ever.
Her name in every tree I will endoss,
That as the trees do grow, her name may grow;
And in the ground each where will it engross,
And fill with stones, that all men may it know.
The speaking woods and murmuring waters' fall
Her name I'll teach in knowen terms to frame;
And eke my lambs, when for their dams they call,
I'll teach to call for Cynthia by name.
And long while after I am dead and rotten,
Amongst the shepherds' daughters dancing round,
My lays made of her shall not be forgotten,
But sung by them with flowery garlands crowned.

endoss] endorse

And ye, who so ye be, that shall survive,
When as ye hear her memory renewed,
Be witness of her bounty here alive,
Which she to Colin her poor shepherd shewed.'
  Much was the whole assembly of those herds
Moved at his speech, so feelingly he spake;
And stood awhile astonished at his words,
Till Thestylis at last their silence brake,
Saying, 'Why Colin, since thou found'st such grace
With Cynthia and all her noble crew,
Why didst thou ever leave that happy place,
In which such wealth might unto thee accrue,
And back returned'st to this barren soil,
Where cold and care and penury do dwell,
Here to keep sheep, with hunger and with toil?
Most wretched he, that is and cannot tell.'
  'Happy indeed' (said Colin) 'I him hold,
That may that blessed presence still enjoy,
Of fortune and of envy uncomptrolled,
Which still are wont most happy states t'annoy:
But I, by that which little while I proved,
Some part of those enormities did see,
The which in court continually hoved,
And followed those which happy seemed to be.
Therefore I silly man, whose former days
Had in rude fields been altogether spent,
Durst not adventure such unknowen ways,
Nor trust the guile of fortune's blandishment,
But rather chose back to my sheep to turn,
Whose utmost hardness I before had tried,
Than, having learned repentance late, to mourn
Amongst those wretches which I there descried.'

'Shepherd' (said Thestylis), 'it seems of spite
Thou speakest thus 'gainst their felicity,
Which thou enviest, rather than of right,
That aught in them blameworthy thou dost spy.'
'Cause have I none' (quoth he) 'of cankered will
To quite them ill, that me demeaned so well:
But self-regard of private good or ill
Moves me of each, so as I found, to tell,
And eke to warn young shepherds' wandering wit,
Which, through report of that life's painted bliss,
Abandon quiet home, to seek for it,
And leave their lambs to loss, misled amiss.
For sooth to say, it is no sort of life,
For shepherd fit to lead in that same place,
Where each one seeks with malice and with strife,
To thrust down other into foul disgrace,
Himself to raise: and he doth soonest rise
That best can handle his deceitful wit,
In subtle shifts, and finest sleights devise,
Either by slandering his well-deemed name,
Through leasings lewd, and feigned forgery:
Or else by breeding him some blot of blame,
By creeping close into his secrecy;
To which him needs a guileful hollow heart,
Masked with fair dissembling courtesy,
A filed tongue furnished with terms of art,
No art of school, but courtiers' schoolery.
For arts of school have there small countenance,
Counted but toys to busy idle brains,
And there professors find small maintenance,
But to be instruments of others' gains.
Ne is there place for any gentle wit,

Unless to please itself it can apply:
But shouldered is, or out of door quite shit,
As base, or blunt, unmeet for melody.
For each man's worth is measured by his weed,
As harts by horns, or asses by their ears:
Yet asses been not all whose ears exceed,
Nor yet all harts, that horns the highest bears.
For highest looks have not the highest mind,
Nor haughty words most full of highest thoughts:
But are like bladders blowen up with wind,
That being pricked do vanish into noughts.
Even such is all their vaunted vanity,
Nought else but smoke, that fumeth soon away;
Such is their glory that in simple eye
Seem greatest, when their garments are most gay.
So they themselves for praise of fools do sell,
And all their wealth for painting on a wall;
With price whereof, they buy a golden bell,
And purchase highest rooms in bower and hall:
Whiles single truth and simple honesty·
Do wander up and down despised of all;
Their plain attire such glorious gallantry
Disdains so much, that none them in doth call.

Colin Clout's Come Home Again, 584–730, 1595

shit] shut

175

Amoretti

(*i*)

THE merry cuckoo, messenger of spring,
His trumpet shrill hath thrice already sounded;
That warns all lovers wait upon their king,
Who now is coming forth with garland crowned:
With noise whereof the quire of birds resounded
Their anthems sweet devised of love's praise,
That all the woods their echoes back rebounded,
As if they knew the meaning of their lays.
But 'mongst them all, which did love's honour raise,
No word was heard of her that most it ought,
But she his precept proudly disobeys,
And doth his idle message set at nought.
Therefore O love, unless she turn to thee
Ere cuckoo end, let her a rebel be.

(*ii*)

LIKE as a ship that through the ocean wide
By conduct of some star doth make her way,
Whenas a storm hath dimmed her trusty guide,
Out of her course doth wander far astray:
So I whose star, that wont with her bright ray
Me to direct, with clouds is overcast,
Do wander now in darkness and dismay,
Through hidden perils round about me placed.
Yet hope I well, that when this storm is past,
My Helice, the lodestar of my life,
Will shine again, and look on me at last,
With lovely light to clear my cloudy grief.
Till then I wander careful, comfortless,
In secret sorrow and sad pensiveness.

(iii)

WHAT guile is this, that those her golden tresses
  She doth attire under a net of gold;
And with sly skill so cunningly them dresses,
  That which is gold or hair, may scarce be told?
  Is it that men's frail eyes, which gaze too bold,
She may entangle in that golden snare;
  And being caught may craftily enfold
Their weaker hearts, which are not well aware?
Take heed therefore, mine eyes, how ye do stare
  Henceforth too rashly on that guileful net,
In which if ever ye entrapped are,
  Out of her bands ye by no means shall get.
    Fondness it were for any being free,
    To covet fetters, though they golden be.

(iv)

MARK when she smiles with amiable cheer,
  And tell me whereto can ye liken it;
When on each eyelid sweetly do appear
  An hundred Graces as in shade to sit.
  Likest it seemeth in my simple wit
Unto the fair sunshine in summer's day;
  That when a dreadful storm away is flit,
Through the broad world doth spread his goodly ray:
At sight whereof each bird that sits on spray,
  And every beast that to his den was fled,
Comes forth afresh out of their late dismay,
  And to the light lift up their drooping head.
    So my storm-beaten heart likewise is cheered,
    With that sunshine when cloudy looks are cleared.

(*v*)

THE weary year his race now having run,
The new begins his compassed course anew:
With shew of morning mild he hath begun,
Betokening peace and plenty to ensue.
So let us, which this change of weather view,
Change eke our minds and former lives amend;
The old year's sins forepast let us eschew,
And fly the faults with which we did offend.
Then shall the new year's joy forth freshly send
Into the glooming world his gladsome ray;
And all these storms, which now his beauty blend,
Shall turn to calms and timely clear away.
So likewise, love, cheer you your heavy spright,
And change old year's annoy to new delight.

(*vi*)

AFTER long storms and tempests' sad assay,
Which hardly I endured heretofore,
In dread of death and dangerous dismay,
With which my silly bark was tossed sore,
I do at length descry the happy shore,
In which I hope ere long for to arrive;
Fair soil it seems from far and fraught with store
Of all that dear and dainty is alive.
Most happy he that can at last achieve
The joyous safety of so sweet a rest;
Whose least delight sufficeth to deprive
Remembrance of all pains which him oppressed.
All pains are nothing in respect of this,
All sorrows short that gain eternal bliss.

blend] blind

(vii)

FRESH Spring, the herald of love's mighty king,
  In whose coat armour richly are displayed
All sorts of flowers the which on earth do spring
  In goodly colours gloriously arrayed;
  Go to my love, where she is careless laid,
Yet in her winter's bower not well awake;
  Tell her the joyous time will not be stayed
Unless she do him by the forelock take.
Bid her therefore herself soon ready make,
  To wait on Love amongst his lovely crew;
Where every one that misseth then her make
  Shall be by him amerced with penance due.
    Make haste therefore, sweet love, whilst it is prime,
    For none can call again the passed time.

(viii)

OFT when my spirit doth spread her bolder wings,
  In mind to mount up to the purest sky,
It down is weighed with thought of earthly things
  And clogged with burden of mortality,
  Where when that sovereign beauty it doth spy,
Resembling heaven's glory in her light,
  Drawn with sweet pleasure's bait, it back doth fly,
And unto heaven forgets her former flight.
There my frail fancy, fed with full delight,
  Doth bathe in bliss and mantleth most at ease:
Ne thinks of other heaven, but how it might
  Her heart's desire with most contentment please.
    Heart need not with none other happiness,
    But here on earth to have such heaven's bliss.

Amoretti and Epithalamion, 1595

make] mate

176

Epithalamion

YE learned sisters which have oftentimes
Been to me aiding, others to adorn,
Whom ye thought worthy of your graceful rimes,
That even the greatest did not greatly scorn
To hear their names sung in your simple lays,
But joyed in their praise;
And when ye list your own mishaps to mourn,
Which death, or love, or fortune's wreck did raise,
Your string could soon to sadder tenour turn,
And teach the woods and waters to lament
Your doleful dreariment;
Now lay those sorrowful complaints aside,
And having all your heads with garland crowned,
Help me mine own love's praises to resound,
Ne let the same of any be envied:
So Orpheus did for his own bride,
So I unto myself alone will sing;
The woods shall to me answer and my echo ring.

Early before the world's light-giving lamp
His golden beam upon the hills doth spread,
Having dispersed the night's uncheerful damp,
Do ye awake, and with fresh lustihead
Go to the bower of my beloved love,
My truest turtle dove;
Bid her awake; for Hymen is awake,
And long since ready forth his mask to move,
With his bright tead that flames with many a flake,
And many a bachelor to wait on him,
In their fresh garments trim.

tead] torch

Bid her awake therefore and soon her dight,
For lo! the wished day is come at last,
That shall for all the pains and sorrows past
Pay to her usury of long delight;
And whilst she doth her dight,
Do ye to her of joy and solace sing,
That all the woods may answer and your echo ring.

Bring with you all the nymphs that you can hear
Both of the rivers and the forests green,
And of the sea that neighbours to her near,
All with gay garlands goodly well beseen.
And let them also with them bring in hand
Another gay garland
For my fair love of lilies and of roses,
Bound true-love-wise with a blue silk ribband.
And let them make great store of bridal posies,
And let them eke bring store of other flowers
To deck the bridal bowers.
And let the ground whereas her foot shall tread,
For fear the stones her tender foot should wrong,
Be strewed with fragrant flowers all along,
And diapered like the discoloured mead.
Which done, do at her chamber door await,
For she will waken straight,
The whiles do ye this song unto her sing;
The woods shall to you answer and your echo ring.

Ye nymphs of Mulla, which with careful heed
The silver scaly trouts do tend full well,
And greedy pikes which use therein to feed,
(Those trouts and pikes all others do excel)

And ye likewise which keep the rushy lake,
Where none do fishes take,
Bind up the locks the which hang scattered light,
And in his waters, which your mirror make,
Behold your faces as the crystal bright,
That when you come whereas my love doth lie,
No blemish she may spy.
And eke ye lightfoot maids which keep the deer,
That on the hoary mountain use to tower,
And the wild wolves, which seek them to devour,
With your steel darts do chase from coming near,
Be also present here,
To help to deck her and to help to sing,
That all the woods may answer and your echo ring.

Wake now, my love, awake; for it is time.
The rosy morn long since left Tithonės bed,
All ready to her silver coach to climb,
And Phoebus 'gins to shew his glorious head.
Hark how the cheerful birds do chant their lays
And carol of love's praise.
The merry lark her matins sings aloft,
The thrush replies, the mavis descant plays,
The ouzel shrills, the ruddock warbles soft,
So goodly all agree with sweet consent,
To this day's merriment.
Ah! my dear love, why do ye sleep thus long,
When meeter were that ye should now awake,
T' await the coming of your joyous make,
And harken to the birds' love-learned song,
The dewy leaves among?

For they of joy and pleasance to you sing,
That all the woods them answer and their echo ring.

My love is now awake out of her dream,
And her fair eyes, like stars that dimmed were
With darksome cloud, now shew their goodly beams
More bright than Hesperus his head doth rear.
Come now ye damsels, daughters of delight,
Help quickly her to dight,
But first come ye, fair hours, which were begot
In love's sweet paradise, of day and night,
Which do the seasons of the year allot,
And all that ever in this world is fair
Do make and still repair.
And ye three handmaids of the Cyprian queen,
The which do still adorn her beauty's pride,
Help to adorn my beautifullest bride;
And as ye her array, still throw between
Some graces to be seen,
And as ye use to Venus, to her sing,
The whiles the woods shall answer and your echo ring.

Now is my love all ready forth to come;
Let all the virgins therefore well await,
And ye fresh boys that tend upon her groom
Prepare yourselves; for he is coming straight.
Set all your things in seemly good array
Fit for so joyful day,
The joyful'st day that ever sun did see.
Fair sun, shew forth thy favourable ray,
And let thy lifeful heat not fervent be,

For fear of burning her sunshiny face,
Her beauty to disgrace.
O fairest Phoebus, father of the Muse,
If ever I did honour thee aright,
Or sing the thing, that mote thy mind delight,
Do not thy servant's simple boon refuse,
But let this day, let this one day, be mine,
Let all the rest be thine.
Then I thy sovereign praises loud will sing,
That all the woods shall answer and their echo ring.

Hark how the minstrels 'gin to shrill aloud
Their merry music that resounds from far,
The pipe, the tabor, and the trembling crowd,
That well agree withouten breach or jar.
But most of all the damsels do delight,
When they their timbrels smite,
And thereunto do dance and carol sweet,
That all the senses they do ravish quite,
The whiles the boys run up and down the street,
Crying aloud with strong confused noise,
As if it were one voice.
Hymen, Io Hymen, Hymen, they do shout,
That even to the heavens their shouting shrill
Doth reach, and all the firmament doth fill,
To which the people standing all about,
As in approvance do thereto applaud
And loud advance her laud,
And evermore they Hymen, Hymen, sing,
That all the woods them answer and their echo ring.

crowd] fiddle

Lo! where she comes along with portly pace
Like Phoebe from her chamber of the east,
Arising forth to run her mighty race,
Clad all in white, that seems a virgin best.
So well it her beseems that ye would ween
Some angel she had been.
Her long loose yellow locks like golden wire,
Sprinkled with pearl, and pearling flowers a-tween,
Do like a golden mantle her attire,
And being crowned with a garland green,
Seem like some maiden queen.
Her modest eyes abashed to behold
So many gazers, as on her do stare,
Upon the lowly ground affixed are.
Ne dare lift up her countenance too bold,
But blush to hear her praises sung so loud,
So far from being proud.
Nathless do ye still loud her praises sing,
That all the woods may answer and your echo ring.

Tell me, ye merchants' daughters, did ye see
So fair a creature in your town before,
So sweet, so lovely, and so mild as she,
Adorned with beauty's grace and virtue's store?
Her goodly eyes like sapphires shining bright,
Her forehead ivory white,
Her cheeks like apples which the sun hath rudded,
Her lips like cherries charming men to bite,
Her breast like to a bowl of cream uncrudded,
Her paps like lilies budded,
Her snowy neck like to a marble tower,
And all her body like a palace fair,

Ascending up with many a stately stair,
To honour's seat and chastity's sweet bower.
Why stand ye still, ye virgins, in amaze,
Upon her so to gaze,
Whiles ye forget your former lay to sing,
To which the woods did answer and your echo ring?

But if ye saw that which no eyes can see,
The inward beauty of her lively spright,
Garnished with heavenly gifts of high degree,
Much more then would ye wonder at that sight,
And stand astonished like to those which read
Medusa's mazeful head.
There dwells sweet love and constant chastity,
Unspotted faith and comely womanhood,
Regard of honour and mild modesty;
There virtue reigns as queen in royal throne,
And giveth laws alone,
The which the base affections do obey,
And yield their services unto her will;
Ne thought of thing uncomely ever may
Thereto approach to tempt her mind to ill.
Had ye once seen these her celestial treasures,
And unrevealed pleasures,
Then would ye wonder and her praises sing,
That all the woods should answer and your echo ring.

Open the temple gates unto my love,
Open them wide that she may enter in,
And all the posts adorn as doth behove,
And all the pillars deck with garlands trim,

mazeful] amazing

For to receive this saint with honour due,
That cometh in to you.
With trembling steps and humble reverence,
She cometh in, before th' Almighty's view.
Of her ye virgins learn obedience,
When so ye come into those holy places,
To humble your proud faces:
Bring her up to th' high altar, that she may
The sacred ceremonies there partake,
The which do endless matrimony make,
And let the roaring organs loudly play
The praises of the Lord in lively notes,
The whiles with hollow throats
The choristers the joyous anthem sing,
That all the woods may answer and their echo ring.

Behold whiles she before the altar stands,
Hearing the holy priest that to her speaks
And blesseth her with his two happy hands,
How the red roses flush up in her cheeks,
And the pure snow with goodly vermeil stain,
Like crimson dyed in grain,
That even th' angels which continually
About the sacred altar do remain,
Forget their service and about her fly,
Oft peeping in her face that seems more fair,
The more they on it stare.
But her sad eyes, still fastened on the ground,
Are governed with goodly modesty,
That suffers not one look to glance awry,
Which may let in a little thought unsound.

Why blush ye, love, to give to me your hand,
The pledge of all our band?
Sing, ye sweet angels, Alleluia sing,
That all the woods may answer and your echo ring.

Now all is done; bring home the bride again,
Bring home the triumph of our victory,
Bring home with you the glory of her gain,
With joyance bring her and with jollity.
Never had man more joyful day than this,
Whom heaven would heap with bliss.
Make feast therefore now all this live-long day,
This day for ever to me holy is;
Pour out the wine without restraint or stay,
Pour not by cups, but by the bellyful,
Pour out to all that wull,
And sprinkle all the posts and walls with wine,
That they may sweat, and drunken be withal.
Crown ye god Bacchus with a coronal,
And Hymen also crown with wreaths of vine,
And let the Graces dance unto the rest;
For they can do it best:
The whiles the maidens do their carol sing,
To which the woods shall answer and their echo ring.

Ring ye the bells, ye young men of the town,
And leave your wonted labours for this day:
This day is holy; do ye write it down,
That ye for ever it remember may.
This day the sun is in his chiefest height,
With Barnaby the bright,
From whence declining daily by degrees,
He somewhat loseth of his heat and light,

When once the Crab behind his back he sees.
But for this time it ill ordained was,
To choose the longest day in all the year,
And shortest night, when longest fitter were:
Yet never day so long, but late would pass.
Ring ye the bells, to make it wear away,
And bonfires make all day,
And dance about them, and about them sing,
That all the woods may answer, and your echo ring.

Ah! when will this long weary day have end,
And lend me leave to come unto my love?
How slowly do the hours their numbers spend!
How slowly does sad Time his feathers move!
Haste thee, O fairest planet, to thy home
Within the western foam;
Thy tired steeds long since have need of rest.
Long though it be, at last I see it gloom,
And the bright evening star with golden crest
Appear out of the east.
Fair child of beauty, glorious lamp of love,
That all the host of heaven in ranks dost lead,
And guidest lovers through the nightës dread,
How cheerfully thou lookest from above,
And seem'st to laugh atween thy twinkling light,
As joying in the sight
Of these glad many which for joy do sing,
That all the woods them answer and their echo ring.

Now cease, ye damsels, your delights forepast;
Enough is it, that all the day was yours.
Now day is done, and night is nighing fast;
Now bring the bride into the bridal bowers.

Now night is come, now soon her disarray,
And in her bed her lay;
Lay her in lilies and in violets,
And silken curtains over her display,
And odoured sheets, and Arras coverlets.
Behold how goodly my fair love does lie
In proud humility;
Like unto Maia, when as Jove her took,
In Tempe, lying on the flowery grass,
'Twixt sleep and wake, after she weary was,
With bathing in the Acidalian brook.
Now it is night, ye damsels may be gone,
And leave my love alone,
And leave likewise your former lay to sing;
The woods no more shall answer, nor your echo ring.

Now welcome, night, thou night so long expected,
That long day's labour dost at last defray,
And all my cares, which cruel love collected,
Hast summed in one, and cancelled for aye:
Spread thy broad wing over my love and me,
That no man may us see,
And in thy sable mantle us enwrap,
From fear of peril and foul horror free.
Let no false treason seek us to entrap,
Nor any dread disquiet once annoy
The safety of our joy:
But let the night be calm and quietsome,
Without tempestuous storms or sad affray;
Like as when Jove with fair Alcmena lay,
When he begot the great Tirynthian groom;

Or like as when he with thyself did lie,
And begot majesty.
And let the maids and young men cease to sing;
Ne let the woods them answer, nor their echo ring.

Let no lamenting cries, nor doleful tears,
Be heard all night within nor yet without;
Ne let false whispers, breeding hidden fears,
Break gentle sleep with misconceived doubt.
Let no deluding dreams nor dreadful sights
Make sudden sad affrights;
Ne let housefires, nor lightning's helpless harms,
Ne let the Puck, nor other evil sprights,
Ne let mischievous witches with their charms,
Ne let hobgoblins, names whose sense we see not,
Fray us with things that be not.
Let not the screech owl, nor the stork be heard;
Nor the night raven that still deadly yells,
Nor damned ghosts called up with mighty spells,
Nor grisly vultures make us once affeared:
Ne let th' unpleasant quire of frogs still croaking
Make us to wish their choking.
Let none of these their dreary accents sing;
Ne let the woods them answer, nor their echo ring.

But let still silence true night watches keep,
That sacred peace may in assurance reign,
And timely sleep, when it is time to sleep,
May pour his limbs forth on your pleasant plain,
The whiles an hundred little winged loves,
Like divers feathered doves,
Shall fly and flutter round about your bed,

And in the secret dark, that none reproves,
Their pretty stealths shall work, and snares shall spread
To filch away sweet snatches of delight,
Concealed through covert night.
Ye sons of Venus, play your sports at will,
For greedy pleasure, careless of your toys,
Thinks more upon her paradise of joys,
Than what ye do, albeit good or ill.
All night therefore attend your merry play,
For it will soon be day:
Now none doth hinder you, that say or sing;
Ne will the woods now answer, nor your echo ring.

Who is the same, which at my window peeps,
Or whose is that fair face, that shines so bright?
Is it not Cynthia, she that never sleeps,
But walks about high heaven all the night?
O fairest goddess, do thou not envy
My love with me to spy;
For thou likewise didst love, though now unthought,
And for a fleece of wool, which privily
The Latmian shepherd once unto thee brought,
His pleasures with thee wrought.
Therefore to us be favourable now;
And sith of women's labours thou hast charge,
And generation goodly dost enlarge,
Incline thy will t'effect our wishful vow,
And the chaste womb inform with timely seed,
That may our comfort breed:
Till which we cease our hopeful hap to sing;
Ne let the woods us answer, nor our echo ring.

And thou great Juno, which with awful might
The laws of wedlock still dost patronize,
And the religion of the faith first plight
With sacred rites hast taught to solemnize,
And eke for comfort often called art
Of women in their smart,
Eternally bind thou this lovely band,
And all thy blessings unto us impart.
And thou glad Genius, in whose gentle hand
The bridal bower and genial bed remain,
Without blemish or stain,
And the sweet pleasures of their love's delight
With secret aid dost succour and supply,
Till they bring forth the fruitful progeny,
Send us the timely fruit of this same night.
And thou fair Hebe, and thou Hymen free,
Grant that it may so be.
Till which we cease your further praise to sing;
Ne any woods shall answer, nor your echo ring.

And ye high heavens, the temple of the gods,
In which a thousand torches flaming bright
Do burn, that to us wretched earthly clods
In dreadful darkness lend desired light;
And all ye powers which in the same remain,
More than we men can feign,
Pour out your blessing on us plenteously,
And happy influence upon us rain,
That we may raise a large posterity,
Which from the earth, which they may long possess,
With lasting happiness,

Up to your haughty palaces may mount,
And for the guerdon of their glorious merit
May heavenly tabernacles there inherit,
Of blessed saints for to increase the count.
So let us rest, sweet love, in hope of this,
And cease till then our timely joys to sing;
The woods no more us answer, nor our echo ring.

Song, made in lieu of many ornaments,
With which my love should duly have been decked,
Which cutting off through hasty accidents,
Ye would not stay your due time to expect,
But promised both to recompense,
Be unto her a goodly ornament,
And for short time an endless monument.

Amoretti and Epithalamion, 1595

177

Prothalamion

CALM was the day, and through the trembling air
Sweet breathing Zephyrus did softly play,
A gentle spirit, that lightly did delay
Hot Titan's beams, which then did glister fair;
When I whose sullen care,
Through discontent of my long fruitless stay
In prince's court, and expectation vain
Of idle hopes, which still do fly away
Like empty shadows, did afflict my brain,
Walked forth to ease my pain
Along the shore of silver streaming Thames,
Whose rutty bank, the which his river hems,
Was painted all with variable flowers,
And all the meads adorned with dainty gems,

Fit to deck maidens' bowers,
And crown their paramours,
Against the bridal day, which is not long:
  Sweet Thames, run softly, till I end my song.

There, in a meadow, by the river's side,
A flock of nymphs I chanced to espy,
All lovely daughters of the flood thereby,
With goodly greenish locks all loose untied,
As each had been a bride;
And each one had a little wicker basket,
Made of fine twigs entrailed curiously,
In which they gathered flowers to fill their flasket,
And with fine fingers cropped full featously
The tender stalks on high.
Of every sort, which in that meadow grew,
They gathered some; the violet pallid blue,
The little daisy, that at evening closes,
The virgin lily, and the primrose true,
With store of vermeil roses,
To deck their bridegrooms' posies,
Against the bridal day, which was not long:
  Sweet Thames, run softly, till I end my song.

With that, I saw two swans of goodly hue
Come softly swimming down along the Lee;
Two fairer birds I yet did never see.
The snow, which doth the top of Pindus strew,
Did never whiter shew,
Nor Jove himself, when he a swan would be
For love of Leda, whiter did appear:

Yet Leda was they say as white as he,
Yet not so white as these, nor nothing near.
So purely white they were,
That even the gentle stream, the which them bare,
Seemed foul to them, and bade his billows spare
To wet their silken feathers, lest they might
Soil their fair plumes with water not so fair,
And mar their beauties bright,
That shone as heaven's light,
Against their bridal day, which was not long:
  Sweet Thames, run softly, till I end my song.

Eftsoons the nymphs, which now had flowers their fill,
Ran all in haste, to see that silver brood,
As they came floating on the crystal flood.
Whom when they saw, they stood amazed still,
Their wondering eyes to fill.
Them seemed they never saw a sight so fair,
Of fowls so lovely, that they sure did deem
Them heavenly born, or to be that same pair
Which through the sky draw Venus' silver team;
For sure they did not seem
To be begot of any earthly seed,
But rather angels or of angels' breed:
Yet were they bred of Somers-heat they say,
In sweetest season, when each flower and weed
The earth did fresh array,
So fresh they seemed as day,
Even as their bridal day, which was not long:
  Sweet Thames, run softly, till I end my song.

Somers-heat] summer's heat = Somerset

Then forth they all out of their baskets drew
Great store of flowers, the honour of the field,
That to the sense did fragrant odours yield,
All which upon those goodly birds they threw,
And all the waves did strew,
That like old Peneus' waters they did seem,
When down along by pleasant Tempe's shore,
Scattered with flowers, through Thessaly they stream,
That they appear through lilies' plenteous store,
Like a bride's chamber floor.
Two of those nymphs, meanwhile, two garlands bound,
Of freshest flowers which in that mead they found,
The which presenting all in trim array,
Their snowy foreheads therewithal they crowned,
Whilst one did sing this lay,
Prepared against that day,
Against their bridal day, which was not long:
Sweet Thames, run softly, till I end my song.

'Ye gentle birds, the world's fair ornament,
And heaven's glory, whom this happy hour
Doth lead unto your lovers' blissful bower,
Joy may you have and gentle heart's content
Of your love's couplement:
And let fair Venus, that is queen of love,
With her heart-quelling son upon you smile,
Whose smile, they say, hath virtue to remove
All love's dislike, and friendship's faulty guile
For ever to assoil.
Let endless peace your steadfast hearts accord,
And blessed plenty wait upon your board,

And let your bed with pleasures chaste abound,
That fruitful issue may to you afford,
Which may your foes confound,
And make your joys redound,
Upon your bridal day, which is not long:
   Sweet Thames, run softly, till I end my song.'

So ended she; and all the rest around
To her redoubled that her undersong,
Which said, their bridal day should not be long.
And gentle echo from the neighbour ground
Their accents did resound.
So forth those joyous birds did pass along,
Adown the Lee, that to them murmured low,
As he would speak, but that he lacked a tongue,
Yet did by signs his glad affection show,
Making his stream run slow.
And all the fowl which in his flood did dwell
'Gan flock about these twain, that did excel
The rest so far as Cynthia doth shend
The lesser stars. So they, enranged well,
Did on those two attend,
And their best service lend,
Against their wedding day, which was not long:
   Sweet Thames, run softly, till I end my song.

At length they all to merry London came,
To merry London, my most kindly nurse,
That to me gave this life's first native source;
Though from another place I take my name,
An house of ancient fame.

shend] shame

There when they came, whereas those bricky towers,
The which on Thames' broad aged back do ride,
Where now the studious lawyers have their bowers
There whilom wont the Templar Knights to bide,
Till they decayed through pride:
Next whereunto there stands a stately place,
Where oft I gained gifts and goodly grace
Of that great lord, which therein wont to dwell,
Whose want too well now feels my friendless case.
But ah! here fits not well
Old woes but joys to tell
Against the bridal day, which is not long:
  Sweet Thames, run softly, till I end my song.

Yet therein now doth lodge a noble peer,
Great England's glory and the world's wide wonder,
Whose dreadful name late through all Spain did thunder,
And Hercules' two pillars standing near
Did make to quake and fear.
Fair branch of honour, flower of chivalry,
That fillest England with thy triumph's fame,
Joy have thou of thy noble victory,
And endless happiness of thine own name
That promiseth the same:
That through thy prowess and victorious arms,
Thy country may be freed from foreign harms;
And great Elisa's glorious name may ring
Through all the world, filled with thy wide alarms,
Which some brave Muse may sing
To ages following,
Upon the bridal day, which is not long:
  Sweet Thames, run softly, till I end my song.

From those high towers this noble lord issuing,
Like radiant Hesper when his golden hair
In th' Ocean billows he hath bathed fair,
Descended to the river's open viewing,
With a great train ensuing.
Above the rest were goodly to be seen
Two gentle knights of lovely face and feature
Beseeming well the bower of any queen,
With gifts of wit and ornaments of nature,
Fit for so goodly stature;
That like the twins of Jove they seemed in sight,
Which deck the baldric of the heavens bright.
They two forth pacing to the river's side,
Received those two fair birds, their love's delight,
Which at th'appointed tide
Each one did make his bride,
Against their bridal day, which is not long:
 Sweet Thames, run softly, till I end my song.

Prothalamion, or, A Spousal Verse, 1596

MARY HERBERT, COUNTESS OF PEMBROKE

1561–1621

178 *Psalm* 139

O LORD, in me there lieth nought
But to thy search revealed lies;
  For when I sit
  Thou markest it;
No less thou notest when I rise;
Yea, closest closet of my thought
 Hath open windows to thine eyes.

Thou walkest with me when I walk;
  When to my bed for rest I go,
    I find thee there
    And everywhere;
  Not youngest thought in me doth grow,
No, not one word I cast to talk,
  But, yet unuttered, thou dost know.

If forth I march, thou goest before;
  If back I turn, thou comest behind;
    So forth nor back
    Thy guard I lack;
  Nay, on me too thy hand I find.
Well I thy wisdom may adore,
  But never reach with earthy mind.

To shun thy notice, leave thine eye,
  O! whither might I take my way?
    To starry sphere?
    Thy throne is there.
  To dead men's undelightsome stay?
There is thy walk, and there to lie
  Unknown in vain I should assay.

O sun, whom light nor flight can match,
  Suppose thy lightful flightful wings
    Thou lend to me,
    And I could flee
  So far as thee the evening brings,
Even led to west he would me catch,
  Nor should I lurk with western things.

Do thou thy best, O secret night,
In sable veil to cover me,
Thy sable veil
Shall vainly fail;
With day unmasked my night shall be;
For night is day, and darkness light,
O Father of all lights, to thee.

Addl. MS. 12048

ANTHONY MUNDAY

c. 1553–1633

179

Love

AS Love is cause of joy,
So Love procureth care;
As Love doth end annoy,
So Love doth cause despair;
But yet I oft heard say,
And wise men like did give,
That no one at this day
Without a love can live.
And think you I will Love defy?
No, no! I love until I die.

Love knits the sacred knot,
Love heart and hand doth bind;
Love will not shrink one jot,
But Love doth keep his kind;

Love maketh friends of foes,
  Love stays the commonwealth;
Love doth exile all woes
  That would impair our health:
Since Love doth men and monsters move,
What man so fond will love disprove?

Love keeps the happy peace,
  Love doth all strife allay,
Love sendeth rich increase,
  Love keepeth wars away;
Love of itself is all,
  Love hath no fellow-mate;
Love causeth me and shall,
  Love those that love my state.
Then love will I until I die;
And all fond love I will defy.

Zelanto, the Fountain of Fame, 1580

180 *Fedele's Song*

I SERVE a mistress whiter than the snow,
  Straighter than cedar, brighter than the glass,
Finer in trip and swifter than the roe,
  More pleasant than the field of flowering grass;
More gladsome to my withering joys that fade,
Than winter's sun or summer's cooling shade.

Sweeter than swelling grape of ripest wine,
  Softer than feathers of the fairest swan,
Smoother than jet, more stately than the pine,
  Fresher than poplar, smaller than my span,
Clearer than beauty's fiery pointed beam,
Or icy crust of crystal's frozen stream.

Yet is she curster than the bear by kind,
  And harder-hearted than the aged oak,
More glib than oil, more fickle than the wind,
  Stiffer than steel, no sooner bent but broke.
Lo! thus my service is a lasting sore;
Yet will I serve, although I die therefore.

Fedele and Fortunio, 1585

181 *To Colin Clout*

BEAUTY sat bathing by a spring
  Where fairest shades did hide her;
The winds blew calm, the birds did sing,
  The cool streams ran beside her.
My wanton thoughts enticed mine eye
  To see what was forbidden:
But better memory said, fie!
  So vain desire was chidden.
      Hey nonny, nonny, &c.

Into a slumber then I fell,
  When fond imagination
Seemed to see, but could not tell
  Her feature or her fashion.
But even as babes in dreams do smile,
  And sometime fall a-weeping,
So I awaked, as wise this while,
  As when I fell a-sleeping.
      Hey nonny, nonny, &c.

England's Helicon, 1600

ANTHONY MUNDAY

182 *Dirge*

WEEP, weep, ye woodmen, wail;
  Your hands with sorrow wring!
Your master Robin Hood lies dead,
  Therefore sigh as you sing.

Here lies his primer and his beads,
  His bent bow and his arrows keen,
His good sword and his holy cross.
  Now cast on flowers fresh and green;

And, as they fall, shed tears and say
  Well-a, well-a-day! well-a, well-a-day!
Thus cast ye flowers, and sing,
  And on to Wakefield take your way.

Death of Robert, Earl of Huntingdon, 1601

ROBERT WILSON

? 1600

183 *Simplicity's Song*

SIMPLICITY sings it and 'sperience doth prove,
No biding in London for Conscience and Love.
    The country hath no peer,
    Where Conscience comes not once a year;
    And Love so welcome to every town,
    As wind that blows the houses down.
        Sing down, adown, down, down, down.
Simplicity sings it and 'sperience doth prove,
No dwelling in London, no biding in London, for Conscience and Love.

Three Ladies of London, 1584

184 *Conscience's Song*

New brooms, green brooms, will you buy any?
Come, maidens, come quickly, let me take a penny.

MY brooms are not steeped,
  But very well bound:
My brooms be not crooked,
  But smooth-cut and round.
I wish it should please you
  To buy of my broom,
Then would it well ease me
  If market were done.

Have you any old boots,
  Or any old shoon,
Pouch-rings, or buskins,
  To cope for new broom?
If so you have, maidens,
  I pray you bring hither,
That you and I friendly
  May bargain together.

New brooms, green brooms, will you buy any?
Come, maidens, come quickly, let me take a penny.

Ibid.

cope] barter

THOMAS WATSON

c. 1557–1592

185 *Love's Grave*

RESOLVED to dust, entombed here lieth Love,
  Through fault of her who here herself should lie;
He struck her breast, but all in vain did prove
  To fire the ice; and doubting by and by
    His brand had lost his force, he 'gan to try
    Upon himself; which trial made him die.

In sooth no force; let those lament who lust;
  I'll sing a carol-song for obsequy;
For towards me his dealings were unjust,
  And cause of all my passed misery:
    The Fates, I think, seeing what I had passed,
    In my behalf wrought this revenge at last.

But somewhat more to pacify my mind,
  By illing him, through whom I lived a slave,
I'll cast his ashes to the open wind,
  Or write this epitaph upon his grave:
    'Here lieth Love, of Mars the bastard son,
    Whose foolish fault to death himself hath done.'

Hekatompathia, 1582

186 *Time*

TIME wasteth years, and months, and hours,
  Time doth consume fame, honour, wit, and strength,
Time kills the greenest herbs and sweetest flowers,
  Time wears out youth and beauty's looks at length,
    Time doth convey to ground both foe and friend,
    And each thing else but love, which hath no end.

no force] no matter

Time maketh every tree to die and rot,
  Time turneth oft our pleasures into pain,
Time causeth wars and wrongs to be forgot,
  Time clears the sky, which first hung full of rain,
    Time makes an end of all humane desire,
    But only this, which sets my heart on fire.

Time turneth into nought each princely state,
  Time brings a flood from new resolved snow,
Time calms the sea where tempest was of late,
  Time eats whate'er the moon can see below;
    And yet no time prevails in my behove,
    Nor any time can make me cease to love.

Ibid.

187 *The Ditty of the Six Virgins*

WITH fragrant flowers we strew the way,
And make this our chief holiday;
For though this clime were blessed of yore,
Yet was it never proud before.
  O beauteous Queen of second Troy,
  Accept of our unfeigned joy!

Now th'air is sweeter than sweet balm,
And satyrs dance about the palm;
Now earth, with verdure newly dight,
Gives perfect sign of her delight.
  O beauteous Queen of second Troy,
  Accept of our unfeigned joy!

THOMAS WATSON

Now birds record new harmony,
And trees do whistle melody;
Now everything that nature breeds
Doth clad itself in pleasant weeds.
  O beauteous Queen of second Troy,
  Accept of our unfeigned joy!

The Honourable Entertainment at Elvetham, 1591

JOHN LYLY

c. 1554–1606

188 *A Serving Men's Song*

Granichus. O! FOR a bowl of fat Canary,
Rich Palermo, sparkling Sherry,
Some nectar else, from Juno's dairy;
O! these draughts would make us merry.

Psyllus. O! for a wench (I deal in faces,
And in other daintier things);
Tickled am I with her embraces,
Fine dancing in such fairy rings.

Manes. O! for a plump fat leg of mutton,
Veal, lamb, capon, pig, and coney;
None is happy but a glutton,
None an ass but who wants money.

Chorus. Wines (indeed) and girls are good,
But brave victuals feast the blood;
For wenches, wine, and lusty cheer,
Jove would leap down to surfeit here.

Campaspe, 1584

189

Song of Apelles

CUPID and my Campaspe played
At cards for kisses, Cupid paid;
He stakes his quiver, bow, and arrows,
His mother's doves, and team of sparrows;
Loses them too; then, down he throws
The coral of his lip, the rose
Growing on 's cheek (but none knows how);
With these, the crystal of his brow,
And then the dimple of his chin:
All these did my Campaspe win.
At last, he set her both his eyes;
She won, and Cupid blind did rise.
O Love! has she done this to thee?
What shall (alas!) become of me?

Ibid.

190

Trico's Song

WHAT bird so sings, yet so does wail?
O! 'tis the ravished nightingale.
Jug, Jug, Jug, Jug, Tereu, she cries,
And still her woes at midnight rise.
Brave prick song! who is 't now we hear?
None but the lark so shrill and clear;
How at heaven's gates she claps her wings,
The morn not waking till she sings.
Hark, hark, with what a pretty throat
Poor Robin Redbreast tunes his note;
Hark how the jolly cuckoos sing
Cuckoo, to welcome in the spring,
Cuckoo, to welcome in the spring.

Ibid.

191

Sapho's Song

Sapho. O CRUEL Love! on thee I lay
My curse, which shall strike blind the day:
Never may sleep with velvet hand
Charm thine eyes with sacred wand;
Thy jailors shall be hopes and fears,
Thy prison-mates, groans, sighs, and tears;
Thy play to wear out weary times,
Fantastic passions, vows, and rimes;
Thy bread be frowns, thy drink be gall,
Such as when I on Phao call;
The bed thou liest on be despair;
Thy sleep fond dreams; thy dreams long care;
Hope (like thy fool) at thy bed's head
Mock thee, till madness strike thee dead,
As Phao, thou dost me with thy proud eyes;
In thee poor Sapho lives, for thee she dies.

Sapho and Phao, 1584

192

The Song in Making of the Arrows

MY shag-hair Cyclops, come, lets ply
Our Lemnian hammers lustily;
By my wife's sparrows,
I swear these arrows
Shall singing fly
Through many a wanton's eye.
These headed are with golden blisses,
These silver ones feathered with kisses,
But this of lead
Strikes a clown dead,
When in a dance
He falls in a trance,

To see his black-brow lass not buss him,
And then whines out for death t'untruss him.
So, so, our work being done let 's play,
Holiday (boys), cry Holiday!

Ibid.

193 *A Song of Diana's Nymphs*

Telusa. O YES, O yes, if any maid,
Whom leering Cupid has betrayed
To frowns of spite, to eyes of scorn,
And would in madness now see torn
The boy in pieces,
All 3. Let her come
Hither, and lay on him her doom.

Eurota. O yes, O yes, has any lost
A heart, which many a sigh hath cost;
Is any cozened of a tear,
Which (as a pearl) disdain does wear?
All 3. Here stands the thief, let her but come
Hither, and lay on him her doom.

Larissa. Is any one undone by fire,
And turned to ashes through desire?
Did ever any lady weep,
Being cheated of her golden sleep,
Stolen by sick thoughts?
All 3. The pirate 's found,
And in her tears he shall be drowned.
Read his indictment, let him hear
What he 's to trust to: Boy, give ear!

Gallathea, 1592

194 *A Fairy Song*

Omnes. PINCH him, pinch him, black and blue;
Saucy mortals must not view
What the queen of stars is doing,
Nor pry into our fairy wooing.
1 *Fairy.* Pinch him blue.
2 *Fairy.* And pinch him black.
3 *Fairy.* Let him not lack
Sharp nails to pinch him blue and red,
Till sleep has rocked his addle head.

4 *Fairy.* For the trespass he hath done,
Spots o'er all his flesh shall run.
Kiss Endimion, kiss his eyes,
Then to our midnight heidegyes.

Endimion, 1591

195 *A Song of Daphne to the Lute*

MY Daphne's hair is twisted gold,
Bright stars a-piece her eyes do hold,
My Daphne's brow inthrones the Graces,
My Daphne's beauty stains all faces,
On Daphne's cheek grow rose and cherry,
On Daphne's lip a sweeter berry;
Daphne's snowy hand but touched does melt,
And then no heavenlier warmth is felt;
My Daphne's voice tunes all the spheres,
My Daphne's music charms all ears.
Fond am I thus to sing her praise;
These glories now are turned to bays.

Midas, 1592

heidegyes] dances

196 *Pan's Song*

PAN'S Syrinx was a girl indeed,
Though now she 's turned into a reed;
From that dear reed Pan's pipe does come,
A pipe that strikes Apollo dumb;
Nor flute, nor lute, nor gittern can
So chant it, as the pipe of Pan;
Cross-gartered swains, and dairy girls,
With faces smug, and round as pearls,
When Pan's shrill pipe begins to play,
With dancing wear out night and day;
The bagpipe's drone his hum lays by,
When Pan sounds up his minstrelsy;
His minstrelsy! O base! This quill,
Which at my mouth with wind I fill,
Puts me in mind, though her I miss,
That still my Syrinx' lips I kiss.

Ibid.

197 *Song to Apollo*

SING to Apollo, God of Day,
Whose golden beams with morning play,
And make her eyes so brightly shine,
Aurora's face is called divine.
Sing to Phoebus, and that throne
Of diamonds which he sits upon;
Iô, paeans let us sing,
To physic's, and to poesy's king.

Crown all his altars with bright fire,
Laurels bind about his lyre,
A Daphnean coronet for his head,
The Muses dance about his bed,
When on his ravishing lute he plays;
Strew his temple round with bays.
    Iô, paeans let us sing,
    To the glittering Delian king.

Midas, 1592

198 *Song of Accius and Silena*

Silena. O CUPID! monarch over kings,
Wherefore hast thou feet and wings?
It is to show how swift thou art,
When thou wound'st a tender heart.
Thy wings being clipped, and feet held still,
Thy bow so many could not kill.

Accius. It is all one in Venus' wanton school,
Who highest sits, the wise man or the fool.
    Fools in Love's college
    Have far more knowledge,
    To read a woman over,
    Than a neat prating lover.
        Nay, 'tis confessed
        That fools please women best.

Mother Bombie, 1594

GEORGE PEELE

c. 1557–1596

199 *Song of Oenone and Paris*

Oenone. FAIR and fair, and twice so fair,
As fair as any may be;
The fairest shepherd on our green,
A Love for any lady.
Paris. Fair and fair, and twice so fair,
As fair as any may be;
Thy Love is fair for thee alone,
And for no other lady.
Oenone. My Love is fair, my Love is gay,
As fresh as bin the flowers in May;
And of my Love my roundelay,
My merry, merry, merry, roundelay,
Concludes with Cupid's curse:
They that do change old love for new,
Pray gods they change for worse.
Together. They that do change old love for new,
Pray gods they change for worse.

Oenone. Fair and fair, and twice so fair,
As fair as any may be;
The fairest shepherd on our green,
A Love for any lady.
Paris. Fair and fair, and twice so fair,
As fair as any may be;
Thy Love is fair for thee alone,
And for no other lady.

Oenone. My Love can pipe, my Love can sing,
My Love can many a pretty thing,
And of his lovely praises ring
My merry, merry, merry roundelays.
Amen to Cupid's curse:
They that do change old love for new,
Pray gods they change for worse.
Together. They that do change old love for new,
Pray gods they change for worse.

The Arraignment of Paris, 1584

200 *The Shepherd's Dirge*

WELLADAY, welladay, poor Colin, thou art going to the ground,
The love whom Thestylis hath slain,
Hard heart, fair face, fraught with disdain,
Disdain in love a deadly wound.
Wound her, sweet Love, so deep again,
That she may feel the dying pain
Of this unhappy shepherd's swain,
And die for love as Colin died, as Colin died.

Ibid.

201 *Colin's Passion of Love*

O GENTLE Love, ungentle for thy deed,
Thou makest my heart
A bloody mark
With piercing shot to bleed.

Shoot soft, sweet Love, for fear thou shoot amiss,
For fear too keen
Thy arrows been,
And hit the heart where my beloved is.

Too fair that fortune were, nor never I
Shall be so blessed,
Among the rest,
That Love shall seize on her by sympathy.

Then since with Love my prayėrs bear no boot,
This doth remain
To cease my pain,
I take the wound, and die at Venus' foot.

Ibid.

202 *Oenone's Complaint*

MELPOMENE, the Muse of tragic songs,
With mournful tunes, in stole of dismal hue,
Assist a silly nymph to wail her woe,
And leave thy lusty company behind.

Thou luckless wreath! becomes not me to wear
The poplar tree for triumph of my love:
Then as my joy, my pride of love, is left,
Be thou unclothed of thy lovely green;

And in thy leaves my fortune written be,
And them some gentle wind let blow abroad,
That all the world may see how false of love
False Paris hath to his Oenone been.

Ibid.

203 *A Farewell to Sir John Norris and Sir Francis Drake*

HAVE done with care, my hearts! aboard amain,
With stretching sails to plough the swelling waves.
Bid England's shore and Albion's chalky cliffs
Farewell; bid stately Troynovant adieu,
Where pleasant Thames from Isis' silver head
Begins her quiet glide, and runs along
To that brave bridge, the bar that thwarts her course,
Near neighbour to the ancient stony Tower,
The glorious hold that Julius Caesar built.
Change love for arms; girt to your blades, my boys!
Your rests and muskets take, take helm and targe,
And let God Mars his consort make you mirth,
The roaring cannon, and the brazen trump,
The angry sounding drum, the whistling fife,
The shrieks of men, the princely courser's neigh.
Now vail your bonnets to your friends at home,
Bid all the lovely British dames adieu,
That under many a standard well advanced
Have bid the sweet alarms and braves of love.
Bid theatres and proud tragedians,
Bid Mahomet's Poo, and mighty Tamburlaine,
King Charlemagne, Tom Stukeley and the rest,
Adieu. To arms, to arms, to glorious arms!
With noble Norris, and victorious Drake,
Under the sanguine cross, brave England's badge,
To propagate religious piety,
And hew a passage with your conquering swords
By land and sea, wherever Phoebus' eye,

consort] concert   vail] lower

Th' eternal lamp of heaven, lends us light;
By golden Tagus, or the western Ind,
Or through the spacious bay of Portugal,
The wealthy Ocean main, the Tyrrhene sea,
From great Alcides' pillars branching forth
Even to the gulf that leads to lofty Rome;
There to deface the pride of Antichrist,
And pull his paper walls and popery down:
A famous enterprise for England's strength,
To steel your swords on Avarice' triple crown,
And cleanse Augeas' stalls in Italy.
To arms my fellow soldiers! Sea and land
Lie open to the voyage you intend.
And sea or land, bold Britons, far or near,
Whatever course your matchless virtue shapes,
Whether to Europe's bounds, or Asian plains,
To Afric's shore, or rich America,
Down to the shades of deep Avernus crags,
Sail on, pursue your honours to your graves.
Heaven is a sacred covering for your heads,
And every climate virtue's tabernacle.
To arms, to arms, to honourable arms!
Hoise sails, weigh anchors up, plough up the seas
With flying keels, plough up the land with swords.
In God's name venture on, and let me say
To you, my mates, as Caesar said to his,
Striving with Neptune's hills; 'You bear', quoth he,
'Caesar and Caesar's fortune in your ships.'
You follow them, whose swords successful are.
You follow Drake by sea, the scourge of Spain,
The dreadful dragon, terror to your foes,
Victorious in his return from Ind,

In all his high attempts unvanquished;
You follow noble Norris, whose renown,
Won in the fertile fields of Belgia,
Spreads by the gates of Europe to the courts
Of Christian kings and heathen potentates.
You fight for Christ, and England's peerless queen,
Elizabeth, the wonder of the world,
Over whose throne the enemies of God
Have thunder'd erst their vain successless braves.
O, ten times treble happy men, that fight
Under the cross of Christ and England's queen,
And follow such as Drake and Norris are!
All honours do this cause accompany.
All glory on these endless honours waits.
These honours and this glory shall He send,
Whose honour and whose glory you defend.

A Farewell, 1589

204 *The Old Knight*

HIS golden locks time hath to silver turned;
  O time too swift, O swiftness never ceasing!
His youth 'gainst time and age hath ever spurned,
  But spurned in vain; youth waneth by increasing:
Beauty, strength, youth, are flowers but fading seen;
Duty, faith, love, are roots, and ever green.

His helmet now shall make a hive for bees;
  And, lovers' sonnets turned to holy psalms,
A man-at-arms must now serve on his knees,
  And feed on prayers, which are age's alms:
But though from court to cottage he depart,
His saint is sure of his unspotted heart.

And when he saddest sits in homely cell,
  He'll teach his swains this carol for a song:
'Blest be the hearts that wish my sovereign well,
  Curst be the souls that think her any wrong.'
Goddess, allow this aged man his right,
To be your beadsman now, that was your knight.

Polyhymnia, 1590

205 *Song of Coridon and Melampus*

Coridon. MELAMPUS, when will love be void of fears?
Melampus. When jealousy hath neither eyes nor ears.
Coridon. Melampus, when will love be thoroughly shrived?
Melampus. When it is hard to speak, and not believed.
Coridon. Melampus, when is love most malcontent?
Melampus. When lovers range, and bear their bows unbent.
Coridon. Melampus, tell me when love takes least harm?
Melampus. When swains' sweet pipes are puffed, and trulls are warm.
Coridon. Melampus, tell me, when is love best fed?
Melampus. When it hath sucked the sweet that ease hath bred.
Coridon. Melampus, when is time in love ill-spent?
Melampus. When it earns meed, and yet receives no rent.
Coridon. Melampus, when is time well spent in love?
Melampus. When deeds win meeds, and words love's works do prove.

The Hunting of Cupid, 1591;
England's Helicon, 1600

206

Love

WHAT thing is love? for sure love is a thing.
It is a prick, it is a sting,
It is a pretty, pretty thing;
It is a fire, it is a coal,
Whose flame creeps in at every hole;
And as my wit doth best devise,
Love's dwelling is in ladies' eyes,
From whence do glance love's piercing darts,
That make such holes into our hearts;
And all the world herein accord,
Love is a great and mighty lord;
And when he list to mount so high,
With Venus he in heaven doth lie,
And evermore hath been a god,
Since Mars and she played even and odd.

The Hunting of Cupid, 1591; *Drummond MS.*

207

Bethsabe's Song

HOT sun, cool fire, tempered with sweet air,
Black shade, fair nurse, shadow my white hair:
Shine, sun; burn, fire; breathe, air, and ease me;
Black shade, fair nurse, shroud me and please me:
Shadow, my sweet nurse, keep me from burning,
Make not my glad cause cause of mourning.
Let not my beauty's fire
Inflame unstaid desire,
Nor pierce any bright eye
That wandereth lightly.

David and Bethsabe, 1599

208 *Songs from The Old Wife's Tale*

(i)

WHEN as the rye reach to the chin,
And chopcherry, chopcherry ripe within,
Strawberries swimming in the cream,
And school-boys playing in the stream;
Then O, then O, then O my true love said,
Till that time come again,
She could not live a maid.

(ii)

LO! here we come a-reaping, a-reaping,
To reap our harvest fruit,
And thus we pass the years so long,
And never be we mute.

(iii)

A Voice Speaks from the Well

FAIR maiden, white and red,
Comb me smooth, and stroke my head;
And thou shalt have some cockle bread.
Gently dip, but not too deep,
For fear thou make the golden beard to weep.
Fair maid, white and red,
Comb me smooth, and stroke my head;
And every hair a sheave shall be,
And every sheave a golden tree.

The Old Wife's Tale, 1595

ROBERT GREENE

1558–1592

209 *Doralicia's Song*

IN time we see that silver drops
  The craggy stones make soft;
The slowest snail in time, we see,
  Doth creep and climb aloft.

With feeble puffs the tallest pine
  In tract of time doth fall;
The hardest heart in time doth yield
  To Venus' luring call.

Where chilling frost alate did nip,
  There flasheth now a fire;
Where deep disdain bred noisome hate,
  There kindleth now desire.

Time causeth hope to have his hap;
  What care in time not eased?
In time I loathed that now I love,
  In both content and pleased.

Arbasto, 1584

210 *Coridon and Phillis*

PHILLIS kept sheep along the western plains,
  And Coridon did feed his flocks hard by:
This shepherd was the flower of all the swains,
  That traced the downs of fruitful Thessaly,
    And Phillis, that did far her flocks surpass
    In silver hue, was thought a bonny lass.

A bonny lass, quaint in her country 'tire,
  Was lovely Phillis, Coridon swore so;
Her locks, her looks, did set the swain on fire.
  He left his lambs, and he began to woo,
    He looked, he sithed, he courted with a kiss:
    No better could the silly swad than this.

He little knew to paint a tale of love;
  Shepherds can fancy, but they cannot say:
Phillis 'gan smile, and wily thought to prove,
  What uncouth grief poor Coridon did pay;
    She asked him how his flocks or he did fare,
    Yet pensive thus his sighs did tell his care.

The shepherd blushed when Phillis questioned so,
  And swore by Pan it was not for his flocks:
''Tis love, fair Phillis, breedeth all this woe:
  My thoughts are trapped within thy lovely locks,
    Thine eye hath pierced, thy face hath set on fire.
    Fair Phillis kindleth Coridon's desire'

sithed] sighed   swad] clown

'Can shepherds love?', said Phillis to the swain.
  'Such saints as Phillis,' Coridon replied.
'Men, when they lust, can many fancies feign,'
  Said Phillis. This not Coridon denied,
    That lust had lies. 'But love,' quoth he, 'says truth.
    Thy shepherd loves; then, Phillis, what ensueth?'

Phillis was won, she blushed and hung the head;
  The swain stepped to, and cheered her with a kiss:
With faith, with troth, they struck the matter dead;
  So used they when men thought not amiss:
    This love begun and ended both in one;
    Phillis was loved, and she liked Coridon.

Perimedes, 1588

211 *Fawnia*

AH! were she pitiful as she is fair,
  Or but as mild as she is seeming so,
Then were my hopes greater than my despair;
  Then all the world were heaven, nothing woe.
Ah! were her heart relenting as her hand,
  That seems to melt even with the mildest touch,
Then knew I where to seat me in a land
  Under the wide heavens, but yet not such:
So as she shews, so seems the budding rose,
  Yet sweeter far than is an earthly flower;
Sovereign of beauty! like the spray she grows,
  Compassed she is with thorns and cankered bower;
Yet were she willing to be plucked and worn,
She would be gathered, though she grew on thorn.

Ah! when she sings, all music else be still,
  For none must be compared to her note;
Ne'er breathed such glee from Philomela's bill,
  Nor from the morning singer's swelling throat.
Ah! when she riseth from her blissful bed,
  She comforts all the world, as doth the sun;
And at her sight the night's foul vapour 's fled;
  When she is set, the gladsome day is done.
O glorious sun! imagine me the west,
Shine in my arms, and set thou in my breast.

Pandosto, 1588, 1677

212 *Menaphon's Song*

SOME say love,
Foolish love,
    Doth rule and govern all the gods:
I say love,
Inconstant love,
    Sets men's senses far at odds.
Some swear love,
Smooth-face love,
    Is sweetest sweet that men can have:
I say love,
Sour love,
    Makes virtue yield as beauty's slave.
A bitter sweet, a folly worst of all
That forceth wisdom to be folly's thrall.

Love is sweet.
Wherein sweet;
    In fading pleasures that do pain.
Beauty sweet.
Is that sweet,
    That yieldeth sorrow for a gain?
If love's sweet,
Herein sweet,
    That minute's joys are monthly woes.
'Tis not sweet,
That is sweet
    Nowhere, but where repentance grows.
Then love who list, if beauty be so sour:
Labour for me; love rest in prince's bower.

Menaphon, 1589

213 *Sephestia's Song*

WEEP not, my wanton, smile upon my knee;
When thou art old there 's grief enough for thee.
  Mother's wag, pretty boy,
  Father's sorrow, father's joy.
  When thy father first did see
  Such a boy by him and me,
  He was glad, I was woe:
  Fortune changed made him so,
  When he left his pretty boy,
  Last his sorrow, first his joy.

Weep not, my wanton, smile upon my knee;
When thou art old there 's grief enough for thee.
  Streaming tears that never stint,
  Like pearl drops from a flint,

Fell by course from his eyes,
That one another's place supplies:
Thus he grieved in every part,
Tears of blood fell from his heart,
When he left his pretty boy,
Father's sorrow, father's joy.

Weep not, my wanton, smile upon my knee;
When thou art old there 's grief enough for thee.
The wanton smiled, father wept;
Mother cried, baby lept;
More he crowed, more we cried;
Nature could not sorrow hide.
He must go, he must kiss
Child and mother, baby bliss;
For he left his pretty boy,
Father's sorrow, father's joy.

Weep not, my wanton, smile upon my knee;
When thou art old there 's grief enough for thee.

Ibid.

214

Samela

LIKE to Diana in her summer weed,
Girt with a crimson robe of brightest dye,
Goes fair Samela.
Whiter than be the flocks that straggling feed,
When washed by Arethusa's fount they lie,
Is fair Samela.
As fair Aurora in her morning gray,
Decked with the ruddy glister of her love,
Is fair Samela.

Like lovely Thetis on a calmed day,
When as her brightness Neptune's fancy move,
Shines fair Samela.
Her tresses gold, her eyes like glassy streams,
Her teeth are pearl, the breasts are ivory
Of fair Samela.
Her cheeks like rose and lily yield forth gleams,
Her brows bright arches framed of ebony:
Thus fair Samela.
Passeth fair Venus in her bravest hue,
And Juno in the show of majesty,
For she 's Samela.
Pallas in wit, all three, if you will view,
For beauty, wit, and matchless dignity,
Yield to Samela.

Menaphon, 1589

215 *Menaphon's Ditty*

FAIR fields, proud Flora's vaunt, why is 't you smile,
when as I languish?
You golden meads, why strive you to beguile
my weeping anguish?
I live to sorrow, you to pleasure spring:
why do you spring thus?
What? will not Boreas, tempest's wrathful king,
take some pity on us,
And send forth winter in her rusty weed,
to wait my bemoanings;
Whiles I distressed do tune my country reed
unto my groanings?

But heaven, and earth, time, place, and every power
have with her conspired
To turn my blissful sweets to baleful sour,
since fond I desired
The heaven whereto my thoughts may not aspire:
ay me unhappy!
It was my fault t' embrace my bane the fire,
that forceth me to die.
Mine be the pain, but hers the cruel cause
of this strange torment:
Wherefore no time my banning prayers shall pause,
till proud she repent.

Ibid.

216 *Mars and Venus*

MARS in a fury 'gainst love's brightest queen
Put on his helm and took him to his lance;
On Erycinus mount was Mavors seen,
And there his ensigns did the god advance;
And by heaven's greatest gates he stoutly swore,
Venus should die, for she had wronged him sore.

Cupid heard this and he began to cry,
And wished his mother's absence for a while:
'Peace, fool,' quoth Venus, 'is it I must die?
Must it be Mars?' With that she coined a smile:
She trimmed her tresses and did curl her hair,
And made her face with beauty passing fair.

A fan of silver feathers in her hand,
    And in a coach of ebony she went:
She passed the place where furious Mars did stand,
    And out her looks a lovely smile she sent;
        Then from her brows leaped out so sharp a frown,
        That Mars for fear threw all his armour down.

He vowed repentance for his rash misdeed,
    Blaming his choler that had caused his woe:
Venus grew gracious, and with him agreed,
    But charged him not to threaten beauty so,
        For women's looks are such enchanting charms,
        As can subdue the greatest god in arms.

Tullie's Love, 1589

217 *The Shepherd's Ode*

WALKING in a valley green,
Pied with Flora, summer queen,
Where she heaping all her graces,
Niggard seemed in other places,
Spring it was and here did spring
All that nature forth can bring.
Groves of pleasant trees there grow,
Which fruit and shadow could bestow.
Thick-leaved boughs small birds cover,
Till sweet notes themselves discover;
Tunes for number seemed confounded,
Whilst their mixtures music sounded,
'Greeing well, yet not agreed,
That one the other should exceed.
A sweet stream here silent glides,
Whose clear water no fish hides.

Slow it runs, which well bewrayed,
The pleasant shore the current stayed;
In this stream a rock was planted,
Where no art nor nature wanted.
Each thing so did other grace,
As all places may give place;
Only this the place of pleasure,
Where is heaped nature's treasure.
Here mine eyes with wonder stayed;
Eyes amazed and mind afraid,
Ravished with what was beheld,
From departing were withheld.
Musing then with sound advice
On this earthly paradise,
Sitting by the river side
Lovely Phillis was descried.
Gold her hair, bright her eyne,
Like to Phoebus in his shine.
White her brow, her face was fair;
Amber breath perfumed the air;
Rose and lily both did seek,
To shew their glories on her cheek.
Love did nestle in her looks,
Baiting there his sharpest hooks.
Such a Phillis ne'er was seen,
More beautiful than lovės queen.
Doubt it was whose greater grace,
Phillis' beauty or the place.
Her coat was of scarlet red,
All in pleats a mantle spread,
Fringed with gold, a wreath of boughs,
To check the sun from her brows.

In her hand a shepherd's hook,
In her face Diana's look.
Her sheep grazed on the plains;
She had stolen from the swains;
Under a cool silent shade,
By the streams she garlands made.
Thus sat Phillis all alone,
Missed she was by Coridon;
Chiefest swain of all the rest,
Lovely Phillis liked him best.
His face was like Phoebus' love,
His neck white as Venus' dove,
A ruddy cheek filled with smiles,
Such love hath when he beguiles.
His looks brown, his eyes were gray,
Like Titan in a summer day.
A russet jacket, sleevès red,
A blue bonnet on his head;
A cloak of gray fenced the rain;
Thus 'tired was this lovely swain.
A shepherd's hook, his dog tied,
Bag and bottle by his side.
Such was Paris, shepherds say,
When with Oenone he did play.
From his flock strayed Coridon,
Spying Phillis all alone;
By the stream he Phillis spied,
Braver than was Flora's pride,
Down the valley 'gan he track,
Stole behind his true love's back.
The sun shone and shadow made;
Phillis rose and was afraid.

When she saw her lover there,
Smile she did and left her fear.
Cupid that disdain doth loathe,
With desire strake them both.
The swain did woo, she was nice,
Following fashion nayed him twice.
Much ado he kissed her then.
Maidens blush when they kiss men;
So did Phillis at that stour,
Her face was like the rose flower.
Last they 'greed, for love would so,
'Faith' and 'troth' they would no mo;
For shepherds ever held it sin,
To false the love they lived in.
The swain gave a girdle red,
She set garlands on his head.
Gifts were given, they kiss again,
Both did smile for both were fain.
Thus was love 'mongst shepherds sold,
When fancy knew not what was gold.
They wooed and vowed, and that they keep,
And go contented to their sheep. *Tullie's Love*, 1589

218 *The Shepherd's Wife's Song*

AH! what is love? It is a pretty thing,
As sweet unto a shepherd as a king,
And sweeter too;
For kings have cares that wait upon a crown,
And cares can make the sweetest love to frown.
Ah then, ah then,
If country loves such sweet desires gain,
What lady would not love a shepherd swain?

stour] disturbance

His flocks are folded, he comes home at night,
As merry as a king in his delight,
And merrier too;
For kings bethink them what the state require,
Where shepherds careless carol by the fire.
Ah then, ah then,
If country loves such sweet desires gain,
What lady would not love a shepherd swain?

He kisseth first, then sits as blithe to eat
His cream and curds, as doth the king his meat,
And blither too;
For kings have often fears when they do sup,
Where shepherds dread no poison in their cup.
Ah then, ah then,
If country loves such sweet desires gain,
What lady would not love a shepherd swain?

To bed he goes, as wanton then I ween,
As is a king in dalliance with a queen,
More wanton too;
For kings have many griefs affects to move,
Where shepherds have no greater grief than love.
Ah then, ah then,
If country loves such sweet desires gain,
What lady would not love a shepherd swain?

Upon his couch of straw he sleeps as sound,
As doth the king upon his bed of down,
More sounder too;
For cares cause kings full oft their sleep to spill,
Where weary shepherds lie and snort their fill.

Ah then, ah then,
If country loves such sweet desires gain,
What lady would not love a shepherd swain?

Thus with his wife he spends the year as blithe,
As doth the king at every tide or sithe,
And blither too;
For kings have war and broils to take in hand,
Where shepherds laugh, and love upon the land.
Ah then, ah then,
If country loves such sweet desires gain,
What lady would not love a shepherd swain?

Greene's Mourning Garment, 1590

219 *The Palmer's Ode*

OLD Menalcas on a day,
As in field this shepherd lay,
Tuning of his oaten pipe,
Which he hit with many a stripe,
Said to Coridon that he
Once was young and full of glee:
'Blithe and wanton was I then;
Such desires follow men.
As I lay and kept my sheep,
Came the God that hateth sleep,
Clad in armour all of fire,
Hand in hand with Queen Desire;
And with a dart that wounded nigh,
Pierced my heart as I did lie;
That when I woke I 'gan swear,
Phillis' beauty palm did bear.

sithe] time

Up I start, forth went I,
With her face to feed mine eye:
There I saw Desire sit,
That my heart with love had hit,
Laying forth bright beauty's hooks
To entrap my gazing looks.
Love I did and 'gan to woo,
Pray and sigh; all would not do:
Women, when they take the toy,
Covet to be counted coy.
Coy she was, and I 'gan court,
She thought love was but a sport.
Profound hell was in my thought,
Such a pain Desire had wrought,
That I sued with sighs and tears.
Still ingrate she stopped her ears,
Till my youth I had spent.
Last a passion of Repent
Told me flat that Desire
Was a brand of lovės fire,
Which consumeth men in thrall,
Virtue, youth, wit, and all.
At this saw back I start,
Beat Desire from my heart,
Shook off love and made an oath,
To be enemy to both.
Old I was when thus I fled
Such fond toys as cloyed my head.
But this I learned at Virtue's gate,
The way to good is never late.'

Never Too Late, 1590

220 *Infida's Song*

SWEET Adon, darest not glance thine eye
N'oserez vous, mon bel ami?
Upon thy Venus that must die?
Je vous en prie, pity me:
N'oserez vous, mon bel, mon bel,
N'oserez vous, mon bel ami?

See how sad thy Venus lies,
N'oserez vous, mon bel ami?
Love in heart and tears in eyes,
Je vous en prie, pity me:
N'oserez vous, mon bel, mon bel,
N'oserez vous, mon bel ami?

Thy face as fair as Paphos brooks,
N'oserez vous, mon bel ami?
Wherein fancy baits her hooks,
Je vous en prie, pity me:
N'oserez vous, mon bel, mon bel,
N'oserez vous, mon bel ami?

Thy cheeks like cherries that do grow
N'oserez vous, mon bel ami?
Amongst the western mounts of snow,
Je vous en prie, pity me:
N'oserez vous, mon bel, mon bel,
N'oserez vous, mon bel ami?

Thy lips vermilion, full of love,
   N'oserez vous, mon bel ami?
Thy neck as silver-white as dove,
   Je vous en prie, pity me:
N'oserez vous, mon bel, mon bel,
   N'oserez vous, mon bel ami?

Thine eyes, like flames of holy fires,
   N'oserez vous, mon bel ami?
Burn all my thoughts with sweet desires,
   Je vous en prie, pity me:
N'oserez vous, mon bel, mon bel,
   N'oserez vous, mon bel ami?

All thy beauties sting my heart,
   N'oserez vous, mon bel ami?
I must die through Cupid's dart,
   Je vous en prie, pity me:
N'oserez vous, mon bel, mon bel,
   N'oserez vous, mon bel ami?

Wilt thou let thy Venus die?
   N'oserez vous, mon bel ami?
Adon were unkind, say I,
   Je vous en prie, pity me:
N'oserez vous, mon bel, mon bel,
   N'oserez vous, mon bel ami?

To let fair Venus die for woe,
   N'oserez vous, mon bel ami?
That doth love sweet Adon so;
   Je vous en prie, pity me:
N'oserez vous, mon bel, mon bel,
   N'oserez vous, mon bel ami?

Never Too Late, 1590

221 *Eurymachus's Fancy*

WHEN lordly Saturn in a sable robe
Sat full of frowns and mourning in the west,
The evening star scarce peeped from out her lodge,
And Phoebus newly galloped to his rest;
Even then
Did I
Within my boat sit in the silent streams,
All void of cares as he that lies and dreams.

As Phao so a ferryman I was;
The country lasses said I was too fair;
With easy toil I laboured at mine oar,
To pass from side to side who did repair;
And then
Did I
For pains take pence, and Charon-like transport
As soon the swain as men of high import.

When want of work did give me leave to rest,
My sport was catching of the wanton fish;
So did I wear the tedious time away,
And with my labour mended oft my dish;
For why
I thought
That idle hours were calendars of ruth,
And time ill-spent was prejudice to youth.

I scorned to love, for were the nymph as fair,
As she that loved the beauteous Latmian swain,
Her face, her eyes, her tresses, nor her brows
Like ivory, could my affection gain;

For why
I said
With high disdain, 'Love is a base desire,
And Cupid's flames, why they're but watery fire.'

As thus I sat disdaining of proud love,
'Have over, ferryman!', there cried a boy,
And with him was a paragon for hue,
A lovely damsel beauteous and coy,
And there
With her
A maiden, covered with a tawny veil,
Her face unseen, for breeding lovers' bale.

I stirred my boat, and when I came to shore,
The boy was winged, methought it was a wonder;
The dame had eyes like lightning, or the flash
That runs before the hot report of thunder;
Her smiles
Were sweet,
Lovely her face; was ne'er so fair a creature,
For earthly carcase had a heavenly feature.

'My friend,' quoth she, 'sweet ferryman, behold,
We three must pass, but not a farthing fare;
But I will give, for I am queen of love,
The brightest lass thou likest unto thy share;
Choose where
Thou lovest;
Be she as fair as Love's sweet lady is,
She shall be thine, if that will be thy bliss.'

With that she smiled with such a pleasing face,
  As might have made the marble rock relent;
But I, that triumphed in disdain of love,
  Bade fie on him that to fond love was bent,
      And then
      Said thus:
'So light the ferryman for love doth care,
As Venus pass not, if she pay no fare.'

At this a frown sat on her angry brow,
  She winks upon her wanton son hard by:
He from his quiver drew a bolt of fire,
  And aimed so right as that he pierced mine eye:
      And then
      Did she
Draw down the veil that hid the virgin's face,
Whose heavenly beauty lightened all the place.

Straight then I leaned mine arm upon mine ear,
  And looked upon the nymph, that so was fair:
Her eyes were stars, and like Apollo's locks
  Methought appeared the trammels of her hair.
      Thus did
      I gaze,
And sucked in beauty till that sweet desire
Cast fuel on and set my thought on fire.

When I was lodged within the net of love,
  And that they saw my heart was all on flame,
The nymph away, and with her trips along
The winged boy, and with her goes his dame.

O! then
I cried:
'Stay, ladies, stay, and take not any care;
You all shall pass and pay no penny fare.'

Away they fling, and looking coyly back
They laugh at me; oh! with a loud disdain.
I send out sighs to overtake the nymphs,
And tears as lures to call them back again:
But they
Fly thence,
But I sit in my boat, with hand on oar,
And feel a pain, but know not what 's the sore.

At last I feel it is the flame of love.
I strive, but bootless, to express the pain;
It cools, it fires, it hopes, it fears, it frets,
And stirreth passions throughout every vein;
That down
I sat,
And sighing did fair Venus' laws approve,
And swore no thing so sweet and sour as love.

Francesco's Fortunes, 1590

222 *The Penitent Palmer's Ode*

WHILOM in the winter's rage
A palmer old and full of age
Sat and thought upon his youth,
With eyes, tears, and heart's ruth,
Being all with cares yblent,
When he thought on years mis-spent.

When his follies came to mind,
How fond love had made him blind,
And wrapped him in a field of woes,
Shadowed with pleasure's shows,
Then he sighed and said: 'Alas!
Man is sin, and flesh is grass.
I thought my mistress' hairs were gold,
And in her locks my heart I fold;
Her amber tresses were the sight
That wrapped me in vain delight;
Her ivory front, her pretty chin,
Were stales that drew me on to sin;
Her starry looks, her crystal eyes,
Brighter than the sun's arise,
Sparkling pleasing flames of fire,
Yoked my thoughts and my desire,
That I 'gan cry ere I blin,
O! her eyes are paths to sin.
Her face was fair, her breath was sweet,
All her looks for love was meet:
But love is folly, this I know,
And beauty fadeth like to snow.
O! why should man delight in pride,
Whose blossom like a dew doth glide?
When these supposes touched my thought,
That world was vain, and beauty nought,
I 'gan sigh and say, alas!
Man is sin, and flesh is grass.'

Ibid.

stales] snares blin] cease

223 *Maesia's Song*

SWEET are the thoughts that savour of content,
The quiet mind is richer than a crown;
Sweet are the nights in careless slumber spent,
The poor estate scorns Fortune's angry frown.
Such sweet content, such minds, such sleep, such bliss,
Beggars enjoy, when princes oft do miss.

The homely house that harbours quiet rest,
The cottage that affords no pride nor care,
The mean that 'grees with country music best,
The sweet consort of mirth and music's fare,
Obscured life sets down a type of bliss;
A mind content both crown and kingdom is.

Farewell to Follie, 1590

224 *Philomela's Ode in her Arbour*

SITTING by a river's side,
Where a silent stream did glide,
Muse I did of many things,
That the mind in quiet brings.
I 'gan think how some men deem
Gold their god, and some esteem
Honour is the chief content,
That to man in life is lent;
And some others do contend,
Quiet none, like to a friend;
Others hold, there is no wealth
Compared to a perfect health;
Some man's mind in quiet stands,
When he is lord of many lands.

But I did sigh, and said all this
Was but a shade of perfect bliss;
And in my thoughts I did approve,
Nought so sweet as is true love.
Love 'twixt lovers passeth these,
When mouth kisseth and heart 'grees,
With folded arms and lips meeting,
Each soul another sweetly greeting;
For by the breath the soul fleeteth,
And soul with soul in kissing meeteth.
If love be so sweet a thing,
That such happy bliss doth bring,
Happy is love's sugared thrall,
But unhappy maidens all,
Who esteem your virgin blisses
Sweeter than a wife's sweet kisses.
No such quiet to the mind,
As true love with kisses kind;
But if a kiss prove unchaste,
Then is true love quite disgraced.
Though love be sweet, learn this of me
No love sweet but honesty.

Philomela, 1592

225 *Philomela's Second Ode*

IT was frosty winter season,
And fair Flora's wealth was geason.
Meads that erst with green were spread,

geason] scanty

With choice flowers diapered,
Had tawny veils; cold had scanted
What the spring and nature planted.
Leafless boughs there might you see,
All except fair Daphne's tree;
On their twigs no birds perched,
Warmer coverts now they searched;
And by nature's secret reason,
Trained their voices to the season,
With their feeble tunes bewraying,
How they grieved the spring's decaying.
Frosty winter thus had gloomed
Each fair thing that summer bloomed;
Fields were bare, and trees unclad,
Flowers withered, birds were sad;
When I saw a shepherd fold
Sheep in cote to shun the cold.
Himself sitting on the grass,
That with frost withered was,
Sighing deeply, thus 'gan say:
'Love is folly when astray.
Like to love no passion such,
For 'tis madness, if too much;
If too little, then despair.
If too high, he beats the air
With bootless cries; if too low,
An eagle matcheth with a crow.
Thence grows jars. Thus I nnd,
Love is folly, if unkind;
Yet do men most desire
To be heated with this fire,
Whose flame is so pleasing not,

That they burn, yet feel it not.
Yet hath love another kind,
Worse than these unto the mind:
That is, when a wanton's eye
Leads desire clean awry,
And with the bee doth rejoice,
Every minute to change choice,
Counting he were then in bliss,
If that each fair fere were his.
Highly thus is love disgraced,
When the lover is unchaste,
And would taste of fruit forbidden,
'Cause the scape is easily hidden.
Though such love be sweet in brewing,
Bitter is the end ensuing;
For the honour of love he shameth,
And himself with lust defameth,
For a minute's pleasure gaining,
Fame and honour ever staining.
Gazing thus so far awry,
Last the chip falls in his eye;
Then it burns that erst but heat him,
And his own rod 'gins to beat him;
His choicest sweets turn to gall,
He finds lust his sin's thrall;
That wanton women in their eyes
Men's deceivings do comprise;
That homage done to fair faces
Doth dishonour other graces.
If lawless love be such a sin,
Curst is he that lives therein,

fere] companion

For the gain of Venus game
Is the downfall unto shame.'
Here he paused and did stay,
Sighed, and rose, and went away.

Philomela, 1592

226 *Lamilia's Song*

FIE, fie on blind fancy,
It hinders youth's joy:
Fair virgins, learn by me,
To count love a toy.

When Love learned first the A B C of delight,
And knew no figures, nor conceited phrase,
He simply gave to due desert her right,
He led not lovers in dark winding ways,
He plainly willed to love, or flatly answered no;
But now who lists to prove, shall find it nothing so.
Fie, fie then on fancy,
It hinders youth's joy:
Fair virgins, learn by me,
To count love a toy.

For since he learned to use the poet's pen,
He learned likewise with smoothing words to feign,
Witching chaste ears with trothless tongues of men,
And wronged faith with falsehood and disdain.
He gives a promise now, anon he sweareth no;
Who listeth for to prove, shall find his changings so.
Fie, fie then on fancy,
It hinders youth's joy:
Fair virgins, learn by me,
To count love a toy.

Greene's Groatsworth of Wit, 1592

227 *A Palinode*

DECEIVING world, that with alluring toys
Hast made my life the subject of thy scorn,
And scornest now to lend thy fading joys,
To length my life, whom friends have left forlorn.
How well are they that die ere they be born;
And never see thy sleights, which few men shun
Till unawares they helpless are undone.

Oft have I sung of Love and of his fire,
But now I find that poet was advised
Which made full feasts increasers of desire,
And proves weak love was with the poor despised;
For when the life with food is not sufficed,
What thought of love, what motion of delight,
What pleasance can proceed from such a wight?

Witness my want, the murderer of my wit.
My ravished sense, of wonted fury reft,
Wants such conceit, as should in poems fit
Set down the sorrow wherein I am left.
But therefore have high heavens their gifts bereft,
Because so long they lent them me to use,
And I so long their bounty did abuse.

O! that a year were granted me to live,
And for that year my former wits restored,
What rules of life, what counsel would I give!
How should my sin with sorrow be deplored!
But I must die of every man abhorred.
Time loosely spent will not again be won;
My time is loosely spent, and I undone.

Ibid.

ROBERT GREENE

228 *The Description of Sir Geoffrey Chaucer*

HIS stature was not very tall,
Lean he was, his legs were small,
Hosed within a stock of red,
A buttoned bonnet on his head,
From under which did hang, I ween,
Silver hairs both bright and sheen.
His beard was white, trimmed round,
His countenance blithe and merry found.
A sleeveless jacket large and wide,
With many plights and skirts side,
Of water camlet did he wear;
A whittle by his belt he bare,
His shoes were corned, broad before,
His inkhorn at his side he wore,
And in his hand he bore a book.
Thus did this ancient poet look.

Greene's Vision, 1592

THOMAS LODGE

c. 1557–1625

229 *Melancholy*

THE earth, late choked with showers,
  Is now arrayed in green;
Her bosom springs with flowers,
  The air dissolves her teen:
The heavens laugh at her glory,
Yet bide I sad and sorry.

side] long   camlet] material made of hair
whittle] knife   corned] peaked

The woods are decked with leaves,
And trees are clothed gay;
And Flora, crowned with sheaves,
With oaken boughs doth play:
Where I am clad in black,
The token of my wrack.

The birds upon the trees
Do sing with pleasant voices,
And chant in their degrees
Their loves and lucky choices:
When I, whilst they are singing,
With sighs mine arms am wringing.

The thrushes seek the shade,
And I my fatal grave;
Their flight to heaven is made,
My walk on earth I have:
They free, I thrall; they jolly,
I sad and pensive wholly.

Scilla's Metamorphosis, 1589

230

A Fancy

FIRST shall the heavens want starry light,
The seas be robbed of their waves;
The day want sun, and sun want bright,
The night want shade, the dead men graves;
The April flowers and leaf and tree,
Before I false my faith to thee.

First shall the tops of highest hills
  By humble plains be overpried;
And poets scorn the Muses' quills,
  And fish forsake the water-glide,
    And Iris lose her coloured weed,
    Before I fail thee at thy need.

First direful hate shall turn to peace,
  And love relent in deep disdain;
And death his fatal stroke shall cease,
  And envy pity every pain,
    And pleasure mourn, and sorrow smile,
    Before I talk of any guile.

First time shall stay his stayless race,
  And winter bless his brows with corn,
And snow bemoisten July's face,
  And winter spring, and summer mourn,
    Before my pen by help of fame
    Cease to recite thy sacred name.

Rosalynde, 1590

231 *Rosalind's Description*

LIKE to the clear in highest sphere,
  Where all imperial glory shines,
Of selfsame colour is her hair,
  Whether unfolded, or in twines:
    Heigh ho, fair Rosalind!
Her eyes are sapphires set in snow,
  Refining heaven by every wink;
The gods do fear whenas they glow,
  And I do tremble when I think,
    Heigh ho, would she were mine!

Her cheeks are like the blushing cloud,
  That beautifies Aurora's face,
Or like the silver crimson shroud,
  That Phoebus' smiling looks doth grace:
    Heigh ho, fair Rosalind!
Her lips are like two budded roses
  Whom ranks of lilies neighbour nigh,
Within which bounds she balm encloses,
  Apt to entice a deity:
    Heigh ho, would she were mine!

Her neck like to a stately tower,
  Where Love himself imprisoned lies,
To watch for glances every hour
  From her divine and sacred eyes:
    Heigh ho, fair Rosalind!
Her paps are centres of delight,
  Her breasts are orbs of heavenly frame,
Where nature moulds the dew of light
  To feed perfection with the same:
    Heigh ho, would she were mine!

With orient pearl, with ruby red,
  With marble white, with sapphire blue,
Her body every way is fed,
  Yet soft in touch and sweet in view:
    Heigh ho, fair Rosalind!
Nature herself her shape admires;
  The gods are wounded in her sight;
And Love forsakes his heavenly fires,
  And at her eyes his brand doth light:
    Heigh ho, would she were mine!

Then muse not, Nymphs, though I bemoan
The absence of fair Rosalind,
Since for her fair there is fairer none,
Nor for her virtues so divine:
Heigh ho, fair Rosalind;
Heigh ho, my heart! would God that she were mine!

Rosalynde, 1590

232 *Rosalind's Madrigal*

LOVE in my bosom like a bee
Doth suck his sweet;
Now with his wings he plays with me,
Now with his feet.
Within mine eyes he makes his nest,
His bed amidst my tender breast;
My kisses are his daily feast,
And yet he robs me of my rest.
Ah, wanton, will ye?

And if I sleep, then percheth he
With pretty flight,
And makes his pillow of my knee
The livelong night.
Strike I my lute, he tunes the string;
He music plays if so I sing;
He lends me every lovely thing;
Yet cruel he my heart doth sting.
Whist, wanton, still ye!

Else I with roses every day
Will whip you hence,
And bind you, when you long to play,
For your offence.
I'll shut mine eyes to keep you in,
I'll make you fast it for your sin,
I'll count your power not worth a pin.
Alas! what hereby shall I win
If he gainsay me?

What if I beat the wanton boy
With many a rod?
He will repay me with annoy,
Because a god.
Then sit thou safely on my knee,
And let thy bower my bosom be;
Lurk in mine eyes, I like of thee.
O Cupid, so thou pity me,
Spare not, but play thee!

Ibid.

233 *Rosader's Sonnet*

TURN I my looks unto the skies,
Love with his arrows wounds mine eyes;
If so I gaze upon the ground,
Love then in every flower is found;
Search I the shade, to fly my pain,
He meets me in the shade again;
Wend I to walk in secret grove,
Even there I meet with sacred Love;

If so I bain me in the spring,
Even on the brink I hear him sing;
If so I meditate alone,
He will be partner of my moan;
If so I mourn, he weeps with me,
And where I am there will he be.
Whenas I talk of Rosalind,
The god from coyness waxeth kind,
And seems in self-same flames to fry,
Because he loves as well as I.
Sweet Rosalind, for pity rue!
For why than Love I am more true.
He, if he speed, will quickly fly,
But in thy love I live and die.

Rosalynde, 1590

234 *Carpe Diem*

PLUCK the fruit and taste the pleasure,
  Youthful lordings, of delight;
Whilst occasion gives you seizure,
  Feed your fancies and your sight:
    After death, when you are gone,
    Joy and pleasure is there none.

Here on earth nothing is stable,
  Fortune's changes well are known;
Whilst as youth doth then enable,
  Let your seeds of joy be sown:
    After death, when you are gone,
    Joy and pleasure is there none.

for why] because

Feast it freely with your lovers,
  Blithe and wanton sweets do fade;
Whilst that lovely Cupid hovers
  Round about this lovely shade,
    Sport it freely one to one;
    After death is pleasure none.

Now the pleasant spring allureth,
  And both place and time invites:
Out, alas! what heart endureth
  To disclaim his sweet delights?
    After death, when we are gone,
    Joy and pleasure is there none.

Robert, Second Duke of Normandy, 1591

235

Phillis

MY Phillis hath the morning sun
  At first to look upon her;
And Phillis hath morn-waking birds
  Her risings for to honour.
My Phillis hath prime-feathered flowers
  That smile when she treads on them;
And Phillis hath a gallant flock
  That leaps since she doth own them.
But Phillis hath so hard a heart—
  Alas that she should have it!—
As yields no mercy to desert,
  Nor grace to those that crave it.
  Sweet sun, when thou lookest on,
  Pray her regard my moan;
  Sweet birds, when you sing to her,
  To yield some pity, woo her;

Sweet flowers, whenas she treads on,
Tell her, her beauty deads one:
And if in life her love she nill agree me,
Pray her, before I die she will come see me.

Phillis, 1593

236

Fidelity

LOVE guards the roses of thy lips
And flies about them like a bee;
If I approach he forward skips,
And if I kiss he stingeth me.

Love in thine eyes doth build his bower,
And sleeps within their pretty shine;
And if I look the boy will lour,
And from their orbs shoots shafts divine.

Love works thy heart within his fire,
And in my tears doth firm the same;
And if I tempt it will retire,
And of my plaints doth make a game.

Love, let me cull her choicest flowers;
And pity me, and calm her eye;
Make soft her heart, dissolve her lours;
Then will I praise thy deity.

But if thou do not, Love, I'll truly serve her,
In spite of thee, and by firm faith deserve her,

Ibid.

237

Ode

NOW I find thy looks were feigned,
Quickly lost and quickly gained;
Soft thy skin like wool of wethers,
Heart unstable, light as feathers,
Tongue untrusty, subtle sighted,
Wanton will with change delighted.
Siren pleasant, foe to reason,
Cupid plague thee for this treason!

Of thine eyes I made my mirror,
From thy beauty came mine error,
All thy words I counted witty,
All thy smiles I deemed pity,
Thy false tears that me aggrieved
First of all my trust deceived.
Siren pleasant, foe to reason,
Cupid plague thee for this treason!

Feigned acceptance when I asked,
Lovely words with cunning masked,
Holy vows but heart unholy,
Wretched man! my trust was folly.
Lily-white and pretty winking,
Solemn vows but sorry thinking.
Siren pleasant, foe to reason,
Cupid plague thee for this treason!

Now I see, O seemly cruel,
Others warm them at my fuel.
Wit shall guide me in this durance,
Since in love is no assurance.

Change thy pasture, take thy pleasure,
Beauty is a fading treasure.
  Siren pleasant, foe to reason,
  Cupid plague thee for this treason!

Prime youth lasts not, age will follow
And make white these tresses yellow;
Wrinkled face for looks delightful
Shall acquaint the dame despiteful;
And when time shall date thy glory
Then too late thou wilt be sorry.
  Siren pleasant, foe to reason,
  Cupid plague thee for thy treason!

Phillis, 1593

238

Her Rambling

MY mistress when she goes
To pull the pink and rose
Along the river bounds,
And trippeth on the grounds,
And runs from rocks to rocks
With lovely scattered locks,
Whilst amorous wind doth play
With hairs so golden gay,
The water waxeth clear,
The fishes draw her near,
The sirens sing her praise,
Sweet flowers perfume her ways,
And Neptune, glad and fain,
Yields up to her his reign.

William Longbeard, 1593

239 *The Rose*

WHEN I admire the rose,
That nature makes repose
In you the best of many,
More fair and blest than any,
And see how curious art
Hath decked every part,
I think with doubtful view
Whether you be the rose, or the rose is you.

Ibid.

240 *Armistice*

FOR pity, pretty eyes, surcease
To give me war, and grant me peace!
Triumphant eyes, why bear you arms
Against a heart that thinks no harms,
A heart already quite appalled,
A heart that yields, and is enthralled?
Kill rebels, proudly that resist,
Not those that in true faith persist,
And conquered serve your deity.
Will you, alas! command me die?
Then die I yours, and death my cross,
But unto you pertains the loss.

Phoenix Nest, 1593

241 *Sonnet*

O SHADY vales, O fair enriched meads,
  O sacred woods, sweet fields, and rising mountains,
O painted flowers, green herbs, where Flora treads,
  Refreshed by wanton winds and watery fountains;
O all you winged choristers of wood,
  That, perched aloft, your former pains report,
And straight again recount with pleasant mood
  Your present joys in sweet and seemly sort;
O all you creatures whosoever thrive
  On mother earth, in seas, by air or fire,
    More blessed are you than I here under sun.
Love dies in me whenas he doth revive
  In you; I perish under Beauty's ire,
    Where after storms, winds, frosts, your life is won.

Margarite of America, 1596

242 *Old Damon's Pastoral*

FROM Fortune's frowns and change removed,
  Wend silly flocks in blessed feeding;
None of Damon more beloved,
  Feed, gentle lambs, while I sit reading.

Careless worldlings, outrage quelleth
  All the pride and pomp of city;
But true peace with shepherds dwelleth
  (Shepherds who delight in pity).
Whether grace of heaven betideth
  On our humble minds such pleasure,
Perfect peace with swains abideth,
  Love and faith is shepherds' treasure.

On the lower plains the thunder
  Little thrives, and nought prevaileth,
Yet in cities breedeth wonder,
  And the highest hills assaileth.

Envy of a foreign tyrant
  Threateneth kings, not shepherds humble;
Age makes silly swains delirant,
  Thirst of rule gars great men stumble.
What to other seemeth sorry,
  Abject state and humble biding,
Is our joy and country glory;
  Highest states have worse betiding.
Golden cups do harbour poison,
  And the greatest pomp dissembling;
Court of seasoned words hath foison;
  Treason haunts in most assembling.

Homely breasts do harbour quiet,
  Little fear, and mickle solace;
States suspect their bed and diet,
  Fear and craft do haunt the palace.
Little would I, little want I;
  Where the mind and store agreeth,
Smallest comfort is not scanty;
  Least he longs that little seeth.
Time hath been that I have longed,
  (Foolish I, to like of folly)
To converse where honour thronged,
  To my pleasures linked wholly.

delirant] foolish   gars] makes
foison] plentiful crop

Now I see, and seeing sorrow,
  That the day, consumed, returns not.
Who dare trust upon to-morrow,
  When nor time nor life sojourns not?

England's Helicon, 1600

NICHOLAS BRETON

1545?–1626?

243 ### *The Ploughman's Song*

IN the merry month of May,
In a morn by break of day,
Forth I walked by the wood side,
Whereas May was in his pride.
There I spied all alone
Phyllida and Corydon.
Much ado there was, God wot,
He would love and she would not.
She said, never man was true;
He said, none was false to you.
He said, he had loved her long;
She said, love should have no wrong.
Corydon would kiss her then;
She said, maids must kiss no men,
Till they did for good and all.
Then she made the shepherd call
All the heavens to witness truth,
Never loved a truer youth.
Thus with many a pretty oath,
Yea and nay, and faith and troth,
Such as silly shepherds use,
When they will not love abuse,

Love, which had been long deluded,
Was with kisses sweet concluded:
And Phyllida with garlands gay
Was made the Lady of the May.

The Honourable Entertainment at Elvetham, 1591

244 *Phyllis*

SWEET birds! that sit and sing amid the shady valleys,
And see how sweetly Phyllis walks amid her garden alleys,
Go round about her bower, and sing as ye are bidden:
To her is only known his faith that from the world is hidden.
And she among you all that hath the sweetest voice,
Go chirp of him that never told, yet never changed, his choice;

And not forget his faith that lived for ever loved,
Yet never made his fancy known, nor ever favour moved;
And ever let your ground of all your grace be this:
'To you, to you, to you the due of love and honour is,
On you, on you, on you our music all attendeth,
For as on you our Muse begun, in you all music endeth!'

Bower of Delights, 1591?, 1597

245 *To his Muse*

GOOD Muse, rock me asleep
With some sweet harmony;
This weary eye is not to keep
Thy wary company.

NICHOLAS BRETON

Sweet Love, be gone awhile,
  Thou knowest my heaviness;
Beauty is born but to beguile
  My heart of happiness.

See how my little flock,
  That loved to feed on high,
Do headlong tumble down the rock
  And in the valley die.

The bushes and the trees,
  That were so fresh and green,
Do all their dainty colour leese,
  And not a leaf is seen.

The blackbird and the thrush,
  That made the woods to ring,
With all the rest are now at hush,
  And not a note they sing.

Sweet Philomel, the bird
  That hath the heavenly throat,
Doth now, alas! not once afford
  Recording of a note.

The flowers have had a frost,
  Each herb hath lost her savour,
And Phillida the Fair hath lost
  The comfort of her favour.

leese] lose

Now all these careful sights
  So kill me in conceit,
That how to hope upon delights
  It is but mere deceit.

And, therefore, my sweet Muse,
  Thou knowest what help is best;
Do now thy heavenly cunning use
  To set my heart at rest.

And in a dream bewray,
  What Fate shall be my friend;
Whether my life shall still decay,
  Or when my sorrow end.

Bower of Delights, 1591?, 1597

246 *A Supplication*

SWEET Phillis, if a silly swain
  May sue to thee for grace,
See not thy loving shepherd slain,
  With looking on thy face.

But think what power thou hast got
  Upon my flock and me;
Thou seest they now regard me not,
  But all do follow thee.

And if I have so far presumed
  With prying in thine eyes,
Yet let not comfort be consumed,
  That in thy pity lies.

But as thou art that Phillis fair,
  That Fortune favour gives,
So let not Love die in despair,
  That in thy favour lives.

The deer do browse upon the briar,
  The birds do pick the cherries,
And will not Beauty grant Desire
  One handful of her berries?

If it be so that thou hast sworn
  That none shall look on thee,
Yet let me know thou dost not scorn
  To cast a look on me.

But if thy beauty make thee proud,
  Think then what is ordained;
The heavens have never yet allowed,
  That Love should be disdained.

Then lest the Fates that favour Love
  Should curse thee for unkind,
Let me report for thy behove
  The honour of thy mind.

Let Coridon with full consent
  Set down what he hath seen,
That Phillida with Love's content
  Is sworn the shepherds' queen.

Bower of Delights, 1591?, 1597

247

Ipsa Quae

ON a hill there grows a flower,
  Fair befall the dainty sweet!
By that flower there is a bower,
  Where the heavenly Muses meet.

In that bower there is a chair,
  Fringed all about with gold,
Where doth sit the fairest fair
  That did ever eye behold.

It is Phyllis fair and bright,
  She that is the shepherds' joy;
She that Venus did despite,
  And did blind her little boy.

This is she, the wise, the rich,
  That the world desires to see;
This is *ipsa quae* the which
  There is none but only she.

Who would not this face admire?
  Who would not this saint adore?
Who would not this sight desire,
  Though he thought to see no more?

O fair eyes! yet let me see
  One good look, and I am gone;
Look on me, for I am he,
  Thy poor silly Corydon.

Thou that art the shepherds' queen,
   Look upon thy silly swain;
By thy comfort have been seen
   Dead men brought to life again.

Make him live that, dying long,
   Never durst for comfort seek;
Thou shalt hear so sweet a song
   Never shepherd sung the like.

Arbor of Amorous Devices, 1597

248 *A Sweet Lullaby*

COME, little babe, come, silly soul,
   Thy father's shame, thy mother's grief,
Born as I doubt to all our dole,
And to thyself unhappy chief:
      Sing lullaby and lap it warm,
      Poor soul that thinks no creature harm.

Thou little think'st and less dost know
The cause of this thy mother's moan;
Thou want'st the wit to wail her woe,
And I myself am all alone;
      Why dost thou weep? why dost thou wail,
      And knowest not yet what thou dost ail?

Come, little wretch! Ah, silly heart!
Mine only joy, what can I more?
If there be any wrong thy smart,
That may the destinies implore,
      'Twas I, I say, against my will:
      I wail the time, but be thou still.

And dost thou smile? O! thy sweet face!
Would God himself he might thee see!
No doubt thou wouldst soon purchase grace,
I know right well, for thee and me:
  But come to mother, babe, and play,
  For father false is fled away.

Sweet boy, if it by fortune chance
Thy father home again to send,
If death do strike me with his lance,
Yet mayst thou me to him commend;
  If any ask thy mother's name,
  Tell how by love she purchased blame.

Then will his gentle heart soon yield;
I know him of a noble mind;
Although a lion in the field,
A lamb in town thou shalt him find:
  Ask blessing, babe, be not afraid!
  His sugared words hath me betrayed.

Then mayst thou joy and be right glad,
Although in woe I seem to moan;
Thy father is no rascal lad,
A noble youth of blood and bone;
  His glancing looks, if he once smile,
  Right honest women may beguile.

Come, little boy, and rock asleep!
Sing lullaby, and be thou still!
I, that can do nought else but weep,
Will sit by thee and wail my fill:
    God bless my babe, and lullaby,
    From this thy father's quality.

Arbor of Amorous Devices, 1597

249 *An Assurance*

SAY that I should say I love ye,
  Would you say 'tis but a saying?
But if love in prayers move ye,
  Will you not be moved with praying?

Think I think that love should know ye,
  Will you think 'tis but a thinking?
But if love the thought do show ye,
  Will ye lose your eyes with winking?

Write that I do write you blessed,
  Will you write 'tis but a writing?
But if truth and love confess it,
  Will ye doubt the true inditing?

No, I say, and think, and write it,
  Write, and think, and say your pleasure;
Love, and truth, and I indite it,
  You are blessed out of measure.

England's Helicon, 1600

250 *A Report Song*

SHALL we go dance the hay, the hay?
Never pipe could ever play
Better shepherd's roundelay.

Shall we go sing the song, the song?
Never Love did ever wrong.
Fair maids, hold hands all along.

Shall we go learn to woo, to woo?
Never thought came ever to,
Better deed could better do.

Shall we go learn to kiss, to kiss?
Never heart could ever miss
Comfort, where true meaning is.

Thus at base they run, they run,
When the sport was scarce begun.
But I waked, and all was done.

Ibid.

251 *An Odd Conceit*

LOVELY kind, and kindly loving,
Such a mind were worth the moving;
Truly fair, and fairly true,
Where are all these but in you?

Wisely kind, and kindly wise,
Blessed life, where such love lies!
Wise, and kind, and fair, and true,
Lovely live all these in you.

Sweetly dear, and dearly sweet,
Blessed, where these blessings meet!
Sweet, fair, wise, kind, blessed, true,
Blessed be all these in you!

Melancholic Humours, 1600

252 *His Wisdom*

I WOULD thou wert not fair, or I were wise;
I would thou hadst no face, or I no eyes;
I would thou wert not wise, or I not fond;
Or thou not free, or I not so in bond.

But thou art fair, and I can not be wise;
Thy sun-like face hath blinded both mine eyes;
Thou canst not but be wise, nor I but fond;
Nor thou but free, nor I but still in bond.

Yet am I wise to think that thou art fair;
Mine eyes their pureness in thy face repair;
Nor am I fond, that do thy wisdom see;
Nor yet in bond, because that thou art free.

Then in thy beauty only make me wise;
And in thy face the Graces guide mine eyes;
And in thy wisdom only see me fond;
And in thy freedom keep me still in bond

So shalt thou still be fair, and I be wise;
Thy face shine still upon my cleared eyes;
Thy wisdom only see how I am fond;
Thy freedom only keep me still in bond.

So would I thou wert fair, and I were wise;
So would thou hadst thy face, and I mine eyes;
So would I thou wert wise, and I were fond,
And thou wert free and I were still in bond.

The Strange Fortunes of Two Excellent Princes, 1600

253

Aglaia

SYLVAN Muses, can ye sing
Of the beauty of the spring?
Have ye seen on earth that sun,
That a heavenly course hath run?
Have ye lived to see those eyes,
Where the pride of beauty lies?
Have ye heard that heavenly voice,
That may make Love's heart rejoice?
Have ye seen Aglaia, she
Whom the world may joy to see?
If ye have not seen all these,
Then ye do but labour leese,
While ye tune your pipes to play
But an idle roundelay.
And in sad Discomfort's den
Every one go bite her pen,
That she cannot reach the skill,
How to climb that blessed hill,
Where Aglaia's fancies dwell,

Where exceedings do excel;
And in simple truth confess
She is that fair shepherdess,
To whom fairest flocks a-field
Do their service duly yield;
On whom never Muse hath gazed,
But in musing is amazed,
Where the honour is too much
For their highest thoughts to touch.
Thus confess, and get ye gone
To your places every one,
And in silence only speak,
When ye find your speech too weak.
Blessed be Aglaia yet,
Though the Muses die for it.
  Come abroad, ye blessed Muses,
Ye that Pallas chiefly chooses,
When she would commend a creature
In the honour of Love's nature;
For the sweet Aglaia fair,
All to sweeten all the air,
Is abroad this blessed day:
Haste, ye, therefore, come away,
And to kill Love's maladies,
Meet her with your melodies.
Flora hath been all about
And hath brought her wardrobe out,
With her fairest, sweetest flowers,
All to trim up all your bowers.
Bid the shepherds and their swains
See the beauty of their plains,
And command them, with their flocks,

To do reverence on the rocks,
Where they may so happy be
As her shadow but to see.
Bid the birds in every bush
Not a bird to be at hush,
But to sit, chirp, and sing
To the beauty of the spring.
Call the sylvan nymphs together,
Bid them bring their music hither;
Trees their barky silence break,
Crack, yet though they cannot speak.
Bid the purest, whitest swan
Of her feathers make her fan.
Let the hound the hare go chase,
Lambs and rabbits run at base,
Flies be dancing in the sun,
While the silk-worm's webs are spun;
Hang a fish on every hook
As she goes along the brook.
So with all your sweetest powers
Entertain her in your bowers,
Where her ear may joy to hear
How ye make your sweetest choir;
And in all your sweetest vein,
Still, 'Aglaia!' strike the strain.
But when she her walk doth turn,
Then begin as fast to mourn,
All your flowers and garlands wither,
Put up all your pipes together;
Never strike a pleasing strain
Till she come abroad again!

The Passionate Shepherd, 1604

254 *Shepherd and Shepherdess*

WHO can live in heart so glad
As the merry country lad?
Who upon a fair green balk
May at pleasure sit and walk.
And amid the azure skies
See the morning sun arise;
While he hears in every spring
How the birds do chirp and sing;
Or before the hounds in cry
See the hare go stealing by;
Or along the shallow brook
Angling with a baited hook,
See the fishes leap and play
In a blessed sunny day;
Or to hear the partridge call
Till she have her covey all;
Or to see the subtle fox,
How the villain plies the box,
After feeding on his prey
How he closely sneaks away
Through the hedge and down the furrow,
Till he gets into his burrow;
Then the bee to gather honey,
And the little black-haired coney
On a bank for sunny place
With her forefeet wash her face:
Are not these, with thousands mo
Than the courts of kings do know,
The true pleasing spirit's sights
That may breed true love's delights?

plies the box] dodges

But with all this happiness
To behold that shepherdess
To whose eyes all shepherds yield,
All the fairest of the field,
Fair Aglaia, in whose face
Lives the shepherds' highest grace,
In whose worthy-wonder praise
See what her true shepherd says.
She is neither proud nor fine,
But in spirit more divine;
She can neither lour nor leer,
But a sweeter smiling cheer;
She had never painted face,
But a sweeter smiling grace;
She can never love dissemble,
Truth doth so her thoughts assemble
That, where wisdom guides her will,
She is kind and constant still.
All in sum, she is that creature
Of that truest comfort's nature,
That doth show (but in exceedings)
How their praises had their breedings.
Let, then, poets feign their pleasure
In their fictions of love's treasure,
Proud high spirits seek their graces
In their idol-painted faces;
My love's spirit's lowliness,
In affection's humbleness,
Under heaven no happiness
Seeks but in this shepherdess.
For whose sake I say and swear
By the passions that I bear,

Had I got a kingly grace,
I would leave my kingly place
And in heart be truly glad
To become a country lad,
Hard to lie, and go full bare,
And to feed on hungry fare;
So I might but live to be
Where I might but sit to see
Once a day, or all day long,
The sweet subject of my song;
In Aglaia's only eyes
All my worldly paradise.

The Passionate Shepherd, 1604

255 *Olden Love-Making*

IN time of yore when shepherds dwelt
  Upon the mountain rocks;
And simple people never felt
  The pain of lovers' mocks:
But little birds would carry tales
  'Twixt Susan and her sweeting,
And all the dainty nightingales
  Did sing at lovers' meeting:
Then might you see what looks did pass
  Where shepherds did assemble,
And where the life of true love was
  When hearts could not dissemble.

Then 'yea' and 'nay' was thought an oath
  That was not to be doubted,
And when it came to 'faith' and 'troth',
  We were not to be flouted.

Then did they talk of curds and cream,
  Of butter, cheese, and milk;
There was no speech of sunny beam
  Nor of the golden silk.
Then for a gift a row of pins,
  A purse, a pair of knives,
Was all the way that love begins;
  And so the shepherd wives.

But now we have so much ado,
  And are so sore aggrieved,
That when we go about to woo
  We cannot be believed;
Such choice of jewels, rings, and chains,
  That may but favour move,
And such intolerable pains
  Ere one can hit on love;
That if I still shall bide this life
  'Twixt love and deadly hate,
I will go learn the country life
  Or leave the lover's state.

Addl. MS. 34064

THOMAS NASHE

1567–c. 1601

256 *Waning Summer*

FAIR summer droops, droop men and beasts therefore;
So fair a summer look for never more.
All good things vanish, less than in a day,
Peace, plenty, pleasure, suddenly decay.
  Go not yet away, bright soul of the sad year;
  The earth is hell when thou leavest to appear.

What, shall those flowers, that decked thy garland erst,
Upon thy grave be wastefully dispersed?
O trees, consume your sap in sorrow's source;
Streams, turn to tears your tributary course.
  Go not yet hence, bright soul of the sad year;
  The earth is hell when thou leavest to appear.

Written 1592; *Summer's Last Will and Testament*, 1600

257 *Spring*

SPRING, the sweet spring, is the year's pleasant king;
Then blooms each thing, then maids dance in a ring,
Cold doth not sting, the pretty birds do sing:
  Cuckoo, jug-jug, pu-we, to-witta-woo!

The palm and may make country houses gay,
Lambs frisk and play, the shepherds pipe all day,
And we hear aye birds tune this merry lay:
  Cuckoo, jug-jug, pu-we, to-witta-woo!

The fields breathe sweet, the daisies kiss our feet,
Young lovers meet, old wives a-sunning sit;
In every street these tunes our ears do greet:
  Cuckoo, jug-jug, pu-we, to-witta-woo!
    Spring, the sweet spring!

Ibid.

258 *A Clownish Song*

TRIP and go, heave and ho!
Up and down, to and fro,
From the town to the grove,
Two and two let us rove,
A-maying, a-playing;
Love hath no gainsaying.
So merrily trip and go.

Ibid.

259 *Harvest*

MERRY, merry, merry, cheery, cheery, cheery!
Trowl the black bowl to me;
Hey derry, derry, with a poop and a leery,
I'll trowl it again to thee.

Hooky, hooky, we have shorn,
And we have bound,
And we have brought Harvest
Home to town.

Ibid.

260 *In Plague Time*

ADIEU, farewell earth's bliss,
This world uncertain is;
Fond are life's lustful joys,
Death proves them all but toys,
None from his darts can fly.
I am sick, I must die.
Lord, have mercy on us!

THOMAS NASHE

Rich men, trust not in wealth,
Gold cannot buy you health;
Physic himself must fade,
All things to end are made.
The plague full swift goes by.
I am sick, I must die.
        Lord, have mercy on us!

Beauty is but a flower
Which wrinkles will devour;
Brightness falls from the air,
Queens have died young and fair,
Dust hath closed Helen's eye.
I am sick, I must die.
        Lord, have mercy on us!

Strength stoops unto the grave,
Worms feed on Hector brave,
Swords may not fight with fate,
Earth still holds ope her gate.
Come! come! the bells do cry.
I am sick, I must die.
        Lord, have mercy on us!

Wit with his wantonness
Tasteth death's bitterness;
Hell's executioner
Hath no ears for to hear
What vain art can reply.
I am sick, I must die.
        Lord, have mercy on us!

Haste, therefore, each degree,
To welcome destiny.
Heaven is our heritage,
Earth but a player's stage;
Mount we unto the sky.
I am sick, I must die.
Lord, have mercy on us!

Summer's Last Will and Testament, 1600

261 *Autumn*

AUTUMN hath all the summer's fruitful treasure;
Gone is our sport, fled is poor Croydon's pleasure.
Short days, sharp days, long nights come on apace,
Ah! who shall hide us from the winter's face?
Cold doth increase, the sickness will not cease,
And here we lie, God knows, with little ease.
From winter, plague, and pestilence, good Lord, deliver us!

London doth mourn, Lambeth is quite forlorn;
Trades cry, woe worth that ever they were born.
The want of term is town and city's harm;
Close chambers we do want, to keep us warm.
Long banished must we live from our friends;
This low-built house will bring us to our ends.
From winter, plague, and pestilence, good Lord, deliver us!

Ibid.

CHRISTOPHER MARLOWE

1564–1593

262 *Hero and Leander*

First Sestiad

ON Hellespont, guilty of true love's blood,
In view, and opposite, two cities stood,
Sea borderers, disjoined by Neptune's might;
The one Abydos, the other Sestos hight.
At Sestos, Hero dwelt; Hero the fair,
Whom young Apollo courted for her hair,
And offered as a dower his burning throne,
Where she should sit for men to gaze upon.
The outside of her garments were of lawn,
The lining purple silk, with gilt stars drawn;
Her wide sleeves green, and bordered with a grove,
Where Venus in her naked glory strove
To please the careless and disdainful eyes
Of proud Adonis, that before her lies;
Her kirtle blue, whereon was many a stain,
Made with the blood of wretched lovers slain.
Upon her head she ware a myrtle wreath,
From whence her veil reached to the ground beneath.
Her veil was artificial flowers and leaves,
Whose workmanship both man and beast deceives.
Many would praise the sweet smell as she passed,
When 'twas the odour which her breath forth cast;
And there for honey bees have sought in vain,
And, beat from thence, have lighted there again.
About her neck hung chains of pebble-stone,
Which, lightened by her neck, like diamonds shone.

She ware no gloves, for neither sun nor wind
Would burn or parch her hands, but to her mind
Or warm or cool them, for they took delight
To play upon those hands, they were so white.
Buskins of shells all silvered used she,
And branched with blushing coral to the knee,
Where sparrows perched, of hollow pearl and gold,
Such as the world would wonder to behold:
Those with sweet water oft her handmaid fills,
Which, as she went, would chirrup through the bills.
Some say, for her the fairest Cupid pined,
And, looking in her face, was strooken blind.
But this is true, so like was one the other,
As he imagined Hero was his mother;
And oftentimes into her bosom flew,
About her naked neck his bare arms threw,
And laid his childish head upon her breast,
And with still panting rocked, there took his rest.
So lovely fair was Hero, Venus' nun,
As Nature wept, thinking she was undone,
Because she took more from her than she left,
And of such wondrous beauty her bereft;
Therefore, in sign her treasure suffered wrack,
Since Hero's time hath half the world been black.
Amorous Leander, beautiful and young,
(Whose tragedy divine Musaeus sung)
Dwelt at Abydos; since him dwelt there none
For whom succeeding times make greater moan.
His dangling tresses that were never shorn,
Had they been cut and unto Colchos borne,
Would have allured the venturous youth of Greece
To hazard more than for the Golden Fleece.

Fair Cynthia wished his arms might be her sphere;
Grief makes her pale, because she moves not there.
His body was as straight as Circe's wand;
Jove might have sipped out nectar from his hand.
Even as delicious meat is to the taste,
So was his neck in touching, and surpassed
The white of Pelops' shoulder. I could tell ye
How smooth his breast was, and how white his belly,
And whose immortal fingers did imprint
That heavenly path, with many a curious dint,
That runs along his back; but my rude pen
Can hardly blazon forth the loves of men,
Much less of powerful gods; let it suffice
That my slack muse sings of Leander's eyes,
Those orient cheeks and lips, exceeding his
That leapt into the water for a kiss
Of his own shadow, and despising many,
Died ere he could enjoy the love of any.
Had wild Hippolytus Leander seen,
Enamoured of his beauty had he been;
His presence made the rudest peasant melt,
That in the vast uplandish country dwelt;
The barbarous Thracian soldier, moved with nought,
Was moved with him, and for his favour sought.
Some swore he was a maid in man's attire,
For in his looks were all that men desire,
A pleasant smiling cheek, a speaking eye,
A brow for love to banquet royally;
And such as knew he was a man, would say,
'Leander, thou art made for amorous play;
Why art thou not in love, and loved of all?
Though thou be fair, yet be not thine own thrall.'

CHRISTOPHER MARLOWE

The men of wealthy Sestos, every year,
For his sake whom their goddess held so dear,
Rose-cheeked Adonis, kept a solemn feast.
Thither resorted many a wandering guest
To meet their loves; such as had none at all,
Came lovers home from this great festival.
For every street, like to a firmament,
Glistered with breathing stars, who, where they went,
Frighted the melancholy earth, which deemed
Eternal heaven to burn, for so it seemed
As if another Phaeton had got
The guidance of the sun's rich chariot.
But, far above the loveliest, Hero shined,
And stole away th'enchanted gazer's mind;
For like sea-nymphs' inveigling harmony,
So was her beauty to the standers by.
Nor that night-wandering pale and watery star
(When yawning dragons draw her thirling car
From Latmos' mount up to the gloomy sky,
Where, crowned with blazing light and majesty,
She proudly sits) more over-rules the flood,
Than she the hearts of those that near her stood.
Even as, when gaudy nymphs pursue the chase,
Wretched Ixion's shaggy-footed race,
Incensed with savage heat, gallop amain
From steep pine-bearing mountains to the plain;
So ran the people forth to gaze upon her,
And all that viewed her were enamoured on her.
And as in fury of a dreadful fight,
Their fellows being slain or put to flight,
Poor soldiers stand with fear of death dead strooken,

thirling] shooting through the air

So at her presence all, surprised and tooken,
Await the sentence of her scornful eyes;
He whom she favours lives, the other dies.
There might you see one sigh, another rage,
And some, their violent passions to assuage,
Compile sharp satires; but alas! too late,
For faithful love will never turn to hate.
And many, seeing great princes were denied,
Pined as they went, and thinking on her, died.
On this feast day, oh, cursed day and hour!
Went Hero thorough Sestos, from her tower
To Venus' temple, where unhappily,
As after chanced, they did each other spy.
So fair a church as this had Venus none;
The walls were of discoloured jasper stone,
Wherein was Proteus carved, and o'erhead
A lively vine of green sea-agate spread,
Where by one hand light-headed Bacchus hung,
And with the other wine from grapes out-wrung.
Of crystal shining fair the pavement was;
The town of Sestos called it Venus' glass.
There might you see the gods in sundry shapes,
Committing heady riots, incest, rapes:
For know that underneath this radiant floor
Was Danae's statue in a brazen tower;
Jove slyly stealing from his sister's bed
To dally with Idalian Ganymede,
And for his love Europa bellowing loud,
And tumbling with the rainbow in a cloud;
Blood-quaffing Mars heaving the iron net
Which limping Vulcan and his Cyclops set;
Love kindling fire to burn such towns as Troy;

Silvanus weeping for the lovely boy
That now is turned into a cypress tree,
Under whose shade the wood-gods love to be.
And in the midst a silver altar stood;
There Hero sacrificing turtles' blood,
Vailed to the ground, veiling her eyelids close,
And modestly they opened as she rose:
Thence flew love's arrow with the golden head,
And thus Leander was enamoured.
Stone-still he stood, and evermore he gazed,
Till with the fire that from his countenance blazed
Relenting Hero's gentle heart was strook;
Such force and virtue hath an amorous look.
  It lies not in our power to love or hate,
For will in us is over-ruled by fate.
When two are stripped, long ere the course begin,
We wish that one should lose, the other win;
And one especially do we affect
Of two gold ingots, like in each respect.
The reason no man knows; let it suffice,
What we behold is censured by our eyes.
Where both deliberate, the love is slight;
Who ever loved, that loved not at first sight?
  He kneeled, but unto her devoutly prayed;
Chaste Hero to herself thus softly said:
'Were I the saint he worships, I would hear him';
And as she spake these words, came somewhat near him.
He started up; she blushed as one ashamed;
Wherewith Leander much more was inflamed.
He touched her hand; in touching it she trembled;
Love deeply grounded hardly is dissembled.

vailed] sank

These lovers parlied by the touch of hands;
True love is mute, and oft amazed stands.
Thus while dumb signs their yielding hearts entangled,
Their air with sparks of living fire was spangled,
And night, deep drenched in misty Acheron,
Heaved up her head, and half the world upon
Breathed darkness forth (dark night is Cupid's day).
And now begins Leander to display
Love's holy fire with words, with sighs and tears,
Which like sweet music entered Hero's ears;
And yet at every word she turned aside,
And always cut him off as he replied.
At last, like to a bold sharp sophister,
With cheerful hope thus he accosted her:
'Fair creature, let me speak without offence;
I would my rude words had the influence
To lead thy thoughts as thy fair looks do mine;
Then shouldst thou be his prisoner who is thine.
Be not unkind and fair; misshapen stuff
Are of behaviour boisterous and rough.
O! shun me not, but hear me ere you go;
God knows I cannot force love, as you do.
My words shall be as spotless as my youth,
Full of simplicity and naked truth.
This sacrifice, whose sweet perfume descending
From Venus' altar to your footsteps bending
Doth testify that you exceed her far,
To whom you offer, and whose nun you are.
Why should you worship her? her you surpass
As much as sparkling diamonds flaring glass.
A diamond set in lead his worth retains;

sophister] arguer

A heavenly nymph, beloved of human swains,
Receives no blemish, but ofttimes more grace;
Which makes me hope, although I am but base,
Base in respect of thee, divine and pure,
Dutiful service may thy love procure;
And I in duty will excel all other,
As thou in beauty dost exceed Love's mother.
Nor heaven, nor thou, were made to gaze upon;
As heaven preserves all things, so save thou one.
A stately builded ship, well rigged and tall,
The ocean maketh more majestical:
Why vowest thou then to live in Sestos here,
Who on Love's seas more glorious would appear?
Like untuned golden strings all women are,
Which, long time lie untouched, will harshly jar.
Vessels of brass, oft handled, brightly shine;
What difference betwixt the richest mine
And basest mould, but use? for both, not used,
Are of like worth. Then treasure is abused,
When misers keep it; being put to loan,
In time it will return us two for one.
Rich robes themselves and others do adorn;
Neither themselves nor others, if not worn.
Who builds a palace, and rams up the gate,
Shall see it ruinous and desolate.
Ah, simple Hero, learn thyself to cherish;
Lone women, like to empty houses, perish.
Less sins the poor rich man that starves himself
In heaping up a mass of drossy pelf,
Than such as you; his golden earth remains,
Which after his decease some other gains;
But this fair gem, sweet in the loss alone,

When you fleet hence, can be bequeathed to none.
Or if it could, down from th'enamelled sky
All heaven would come to claim this legacy,
And with intestine broils the world destroy,
And quite confound Nature's sweet harmony.
Well therefore by the gods decreed it is
We human creatures should enjoy that bliss.
One is no number; maids are nothing, then,
Without the sweet society of men.
Wilt thou live single still? One shalt thou be
Though never-singling Hymen couple thee.
Wild savages, that drink of running springs,
Think water far excels all earthly things,
But they that daily taste neat wine, despise it.
Virginity, albeit some highly prize it,
Compared with marriage, had you tried them both,
Differs as much as wine and water doth.
Base bullion for the stamp's sake we allow;
Even so for men's impression do we you,
By which alone, our reverend fathers say,
Women receive perfection every way.
This idol which you term virginity
Is neither essence subject to the eye,
No, nor to any one exterior sense;
Nor hath it any place of residence,
Nor is 't of earth or mould celestial,
Or capable of any form at all.
Of that which hath no being do not boast;
Things that are not at all, are never lost.
Men foolishly do call it virtuous;
What virtue is it, that is born with us?
Much less can honour be ascribed thereto;

Honour is purchased by the deeds we do.
Believe me, Hero, honour is not won,
Until some honourable deed be done.
Seek you, for chastity, immortal fame,
And know that some have wronged Diana's name?
Whose name is it, if she be false or not,
So she be fair, but some vile tongues will blot?
But you are fair, ay me! so wondrous fair,
So young, so gentle, and so debonair,
As Greece will think, if thus you live alone,
Some one or other keeps you as his own.
Then, Hero, hate me not, nor from me fly,
To follow swiftly blasting infamy.
Perhaps thy sacred priesthood makes thee loth;
Tell me, to whom madest thou that heedless oath?'
  'To Venus', answered she, and as she spake,
Forth from those two tralucent cisterns brake
A stream of liquid pearl, which down her face
Made milk-white paths, whereon the gods might trace
To Jove's high court. He thus replied: 'The rites
In which love's beauteous empress most delights
Are banquets, Doric music, midnight revel,
Plays, masks, and all that stern age counteth evil.
Thee as a holy idiot doth she scorn,
For thou, in vowing chastity, hast sworn
To rob her name and honour, and thereby
Commit'st a sin far worse than perjury,
Even sacrilege against her deity,
Through regular and formal purity.
To expiate which sin, kiss and shake hands;
Such sacrifice as this Venus demands.'
  Thereat she smiled, and did deny him so

As, put thereby, yet might he hope for mo.
Which makes him quickly reinforce his speech,
And her in humble manner thus beseech:
'Though neither gods nor men may thee deserve,
Yet for her sake whom you have vowed to serve,
Abandon fruitless cold virginity,
The gentle queen of love's sole enemy.
Then shall you most resemble Venus' nun,
When Venus' sweet rites are performed and done.
Flint-breasted Pallas joys in single life,
But Pallas and your mistress are at strife.
Love, Hero, then, and be not tyrannous,
But heal the heart, that thou hast wounded thus;
Nor stain thy youthful years with avarice;
Fair fools delight to be accounted nice.
The richest corn dies, if it be not reaped;
Beauty alone is lost, too warily kept.'
These arguments he used, and many more,
Wherewith she yielded, that was won before.
Hero's looks yielded, but her words made war;
Women are won when they begin to jar.
Thus having swallowed Cupid's golden hook,
The more she strived, the deeper was she strook;
Yet, evilly feigning anger, strove she still,
And would be thought to grant against her will.
So having paused a while, at last she said:
'Who taught thee rhetoric to deceive a maid?
Ay me! such words as these should I abhor,
And yet I like them for the orator.'
  With that Leander stooped to have embraced her,
But from his spreading arms away she cast her,
And thus bespake him: 'Gentle youth, forbear

To touch the sacred garments which I wear.
Upon a rock, and underneath a hill,
Far from the town, where all is whist and still,
Save that the sea, playing on yellow sand,
Sends forth a rattling murmur to the land,
Whose sound allures the golden Morpheus
In silence of the night to visit us,
My turret stands; and there, God knows, I play
With Venus' swans and sparrows all the day.
A dwarfish beldame bears me company,
That hops about the chamber where I lie,
And spends the night, that might be better spent,
In vain discourse and apish merriment.
Come thither.' As she spake this, her tongue tripped.
For unawares 'Come thither' from her slipped;
And suddenly her former colour changed,
And here and there her eyes through anger ranged.
And like a planet moving several ways
At one self instant, she, poor soul, assays,
Loving, not to love at all, and every part
Strove to resist the motions of her heart:
And hands so pure, so innocent, nay such
As might have made heaven stoop to have a touch,
Did she uphold to Venus, and again
Vowed spotless chastity, but all in vain.
Cupid beats down her prayers with his wings;
Her vows above the empty air he flings;
All deep enraged, his sinewy bow he bent,
And shot a shaft that burning from him went;
Wherewith she strooken looked so dolefully,
As made Love sigh to see his tyranny.
And as she wept, her tears to pearl he turned,

And wound them on his arm, and for her mourned.
Then towards the palace of the Destinies,
Laden with languishment and grief, he flies,
And to those stern nymphs humbly made request,
Both might enjoy each other, and be blest.
But with a ghastly dreadful countenance,
Threatening a thousand deaths at every glance,
They answered Love, nor would vouchsafe so much
As one poor word, their hate to him was such.
Hearken awhile, and I will tell you why:
Heaven's winged herald, Jove-born Mercury,
The self-same day that he asleep had laid
Enchanted Argus, spied a country maid,
Whose careless hair, instead of pearl t' adorn it,
Glistered with dew, as one that seemed to scorn it:
Her breath as fragrant as the morning rose,
Her mind pure, and her tongue untaught to gloze;
Yet proud she was, for lofty pride that dwells
In towered courts is oft in shepherds' cells,
And too too well the fair vermilion knew,
And silver tincture of her cheeks, that drew
The love of every swain. On her this god
Enamoured was, and with his snaky rod
Did charm her nimble feet, and made her stay,
The while upon a hillock down he lay,
And sweetly on his pipe began to play,
And with smooth speech her fancy to assay;
Till in his twining arms he locked her fast,
And then he wooed with kisses, and at last,
As shepherds do, her on the ground he laid,
And tumbling in the grass, he often strayed

gloze] prevaricate

Beyond the bounds of shame, in being bold
To eye those parts which no eye should behold;
And like an insolent commanding lover,
Boasting his parentage, would needs discover
The way to new Elysium: but she,
Whose only dower was her chastity,
Having striven in vain, was now about to cry,
And crave the help of shepherds that were nigh.
Herewith he stayed his fury, and began
To give her leave to rise; away she ran;
After went Mercury, who used such cunning,
As she, to hear his tale, left off her running.
Maids are not won by brutish force and might,
But speeches full of pleasure and delight.
And knowing Hermes courted her, was glad
That she such loveliness and beauty had
As could provoke his liking, yet was mute,
And neither would deny nor grant his suit.
Still vowed he love; she wanting no excuse
To feed him with delays, as women use,
Or thirsting after immortality—
All women are ambitious naturally—
Imposed upon her lover such a task
As he ought not perform, nor yet she ask.
A draught of flowing nectar she requested,
Wherewith the king of gods and men is feasted.
He, ready to accomplish what she willed,
Stole some from Hebe (Hebe Jove's cup filled)
And gave it to his simple rustic love;
Which being known (as what is hid from Jove?)
He inly stormed, and waxed more furious
Than for the fire filched by Prometheus,

And thrusts him down from heaven: he wandering here,
In mournful terms, with sad and heavy cheer,
Complained to Cupid. Cupid, for his sake,
To be revenged on Jove did undertake;
And those on whom heaven, earth, and hell relies,
I mean the adamantine Destinies,
He wounds with love, and forced them equally
To dote upon deceitful Mercury.
They offered him the deadly fatal knife,
That shears the slender threads of human life;
At his fair feathered feet the engines laid
Which th'earth from ugly Chaos' den upweighed:
These he regarded not, but did entreat
That Jove, usurper of his father's seat,
Might presently be banished into hell,
And aged Saturn in Olympus dwell.
They granted what he craved, and once again
Saturn and Ops began their golden reign.
Murder, rape, war, lust, and treachery
Were with Jove closed in Stygian empery.
But long this blessed time continued not;
As soon as he his wished purpose got,
He, reckless of his promise, did despise
The love of th'everlasting Destinies.
They seeing it, both Love and him abhorred,
And Jupiter unto his place restored.
And but that Learning, in despite of Fate,
Will mount aloft, and enter heaven gate,
And to the seat of Jove itself advance,
Hermes had slept in hell with Ignorance;
Yet as a punishment they added this,
That he and Poverty should always kiss.

And to this day is every scholar poor;
Gross gold from them runs headlong to the boor.
Likewise, the angry sisters, thus deluded,
To venge themselves on Hermes, have concluded
That Midas' brood shall sit in Honour's chair,
To which the Muses' sons are only heir;
And fruitful wits that in aspiring are,
Shall, discontent, run into regions far;
And few great lords in virtuous deeds shall joy,
But be surprised with every garish toy;
And still enrich the lofty servile clown,
Who with encroaching guile keeps learning down.
Then muse not Cupid's suit no better sped,
Seeing in their loves the Fates were injured.

Second Sestiad

By this, sad Hero, with love unacquainted,
Viewing Leander's face, fell down and fainted.
He kissed her and breathed life into her lips,
Wherewith as one displeased, away she trips.
Yet as she went, full often looked behind,
And many poor excuses did she find
To linger by the way, and once she stayed
And would have turned again, but was afraid,
In offering parley, to be counted light.
So on she goes, and in her idle flight,
Her painted fan of curled plumes let fall,
Thinking to train Leander therewithal.
He, being a novice, knew not what she meant,
But stayed, and after her a letter sent,
Which joyful Hero answered in such sort,
As he had hope to scale the beauteous fort,

Wherein the liberal graces locked their wealth,
And therefore to her tower he got by stealth.
Wide open stood the door, he need not climb;
And she herself before the 'pointed time
Had spread the board, with roses strewed the room,
And oft looked out, and mused he did not come.
At last he came; O! who can tell the greeting
These greedy lovers had at their first meeting.
He asked, she gave, and nothing was denied;
Both to each other quickly were affied.
Look how their hands, so were their hearts united,
And what he did she willingly requited.
Sweet are the kisses, the embracements sweet,
When like desires and affections meet;
For from the earth to heaven is Cupid raised,
Where fancy is in equal balance paised.
Yet she this rashness suddenly repented,
And turned aside, and to herself lamented,
As if her name and honour had been wronged
By being possessed of him for whom she longed;
Ay, and she wished, albeit not from her heart,
That he would leave her turret and depart.
The mirthful god of amorous pleasure smiled
To see how he this captive nymph beguiled;
For hitherto he did but fan the fire,
And kept it down that it might mount the higher.
Now waxed she jealous lest his love abated,
Fearing her own thoughts made her to be hated.
Therefore unto him hastily she goes,
And like light Salmacis, her body throws
Upon his bosom, where with yielding eyes

paised] poised

She offers up herself a sacrifice,
To slake his anger if he were displeased.
O! what god would not therewith be appeased?
Like Aesop's cock, this jewel he enjoyed,
And as a brother with his sister toyed,
Supposing nothing else was to be done,
Now he her favour and good will had won.
But know you not that creatures wanting sense
By nature have a mutual appetence,
And wanting organs to advance a step,
Moved by love's force, unto each other leap?
Much more in subjects having intellect
Some hidden influence breeds like effect.
Albeit Leander, rude in love and raw,
Long dallying with Hero, nothing saw
That might delight him more, yet he suspected
Some amorous rites or other were neglected.
Therefore unto his body hers he clung;
She, fearing on the rushes to be flung,
Strived with redoubled strength; the more she strived,
The more a gentle pleasing heat revived,
Which taught him all that elder lovers know;
And now the same 'gan so to scorch and glow,
As in plain terms, yet cunningly, he craved it;
Love always makes those eloquent that have it.
She, with a kind of granting, put him by it,
And ever as he thought himself most nigh it,
Like to the tree of Tantalus she fled,
And, seeming lavish, saved her maidenhead.
Ne'er king more sought to keep his diadem,
Than Hero this inestimable gem.
Above our life we love a steadfast friend,

Yet when a token of great worth we send,
We often kiss it, often look thereon,
And stay the messenger that would be gone;
No marvel then though Hero would not yield
So soon to part from that she dearly held.
Jewels being lost are found again, this never;
'Tis lost but once, and once lost, lost forever.
  Now had the morn espied her lover's steeds,
Whereat she starts, puts on her purple weeds,
And, red for anger that he stayed so long,
All headlong throws herself the clouds among.
And now Leander, fearing to be missed,
Embraced her suddenly, took leave, and kissed.
Long was he taking leave, and loth to go,
And kissed again, as lovers use to do.
Sad Hero wrung him by the hand and wept,
Saying, 'Let your vows and promises be kept.'
Then, standing at the door, she turned about,
As loth to see Leander going out.
And now the sun that through th' horizon peeps,
As pitying these lovers, downward creeps,
So that in silence of the cloudy night,
Though it was morning, did he take his flight.
But what the secret trusty night concealed,
Leander's amorous habit soon revealed;
With Cupid's myrtle was his bonnet crowned,
About his arms the purple riband wound,
Wherewith she wreathed her largely spreading hair;
Nor could the youth abstain, but he must wear
The sacred ring wherewith she was endowed,
When first religious chastity she vowed;
Which made his love through Sestos to be known,

And thence unto Abydos sooner blown
Than he could sail, for incorporeal Fame,
Whose weight consists in nothing but her name,
Is swifter than the wind, whose tardy plumes
Are reeking water and dull earthly fumes.
Home when he came, he seemed not to be there,
But like exiled air thrust from his sphere,
Set in a foreign place; and straight from thence,
Alcides like, by mighty violence
He would have chased away the swelling main,
That him from her unjustly did detain.
Like as the sun in a diameter
Fires and inflames objects removed far,
And heateth kindly, shining laterally,
So beauty sweetly quickens when 'tis nigh,
But being separated and removed,
Burns where it cherished, murders where it loved.
Therefore even as an index to a book,
So to his mind was young Leander's look.
O! none but gods have power their love to hide;
Affection by the countenance is descried.
The light of hidden fire itself discovers,
And love that is concealed betrays poor lovers.
His secret flame apparently was seen;
Leander's father knew where he had been,
And for the same mildly rebuked his son,
Thinking to quench the sparkles new begun.
But love, resisted once, grows passionate,
And nothing more than counsel lovers hate;
For as a hot proud horse highly disdains
To have his head controlled, but breaks the reins,
Spits forth the ringled bit, and with his hooves

Checks the submissive ground, so he that loves,
The more he is restrained, the worse he fares.
What is it now but mad Leander dares?
'O Hero, Hero!' thus he cried full oft,
And then he got him to a rock aloft,
Where having spied her tower, long stared he on 't,
And prayed the narrow toiling Hellespont
To part in twain, that he might come and go;
But still the rising billows answered 'No.'
With that he stripped him to the ivory skin,
And crying, 'Love, I come', leaped lively in.
Whereat the sapphire-visaged god grew proud,
And made his capering Triton sound aloud,
Imagining that Ganymede, displeased,
Had left the heavens; therefore on him he seized.
Leander strived; the waves about him wound,
And pulled him to the bottom, where the ground
Was strewed with pearl, and in low coral groves
Sweet singing mermaids sported with their loves
On heaps of heavy gold, and took great pleasure
To spurn in careless sort the shipwreck treasure:
For here the stately azure palace stood,
Where kingly Neptune and his train abode.
The lusty god embraced him, called him love,
And swore he never should return to Jove.
But when he knew it was not Ganymede,
For under water he was almost dead,
He heaved him up, and looking on his face,
Beat down the bold waves with his triple mace,
Which mounted up, intending to have kissed him,
And fell in drops like tears, because they missed him.
Leander, being up, began to swim,

And looking back, saw Neptune follow him;
Whereat aghast, the poor soul 'gan to cry:
'O! let me visit Hero ere I die!'
The god put Helle's bracelet on his arm,
And swore the sea should never do him harm.
He clapped his plump cheeks, with his tresses played.
And smiling wantonly, his love bewrayed.
He watched his arms, and as they opened wide,
At every stroke betwixt them would he slide,
And steal a kiss, and then run out and dance,
And as he turned, cast many a lustful glance,
And throw him gaudy toys to please his eye,
And dive into the water, and there pry
Upon his breast, his thighs, and every limb,
And up again, and close behind him swim,
And talk of love. Leander made reply:
'You are deceived, I am no woman, I.'
Thereat smiled Neptune, and then told a tale,
How that a shepherd, sitting in a vale,
Played with a boy so lovely fair and kind,
As for his love both earth and heaven pined;
That of the cooling river durst not drink
Lest water-nymphs should pull him from the brink;
And when he sported in the fragrant lawns,
Goat-footed satyrs and up-staring fauns
Would steal him thence. Ere half this tale was done,
'Ay me!' Leander cried, 'th' enamoured sun,
That now should shine on Thetis' glassy bower,
Descends upon my radiant Hero's tower.
O! that these tardy arms of mine were wings!'
And as he spake, upon the waves he springs.
Neptune was angry that he gave no ear.

And in his heart revenging malice bare;
He flung at him his mace, but as it went
He called it in, for love made him repent.
The mace returning back his own hand hit,
As meaning to be venged for darting it.
When this fresh bleeding wound Leander viewed,
His colour went and came, as if he rued
The grief which Neptune felt. In gentle breasts
Relenting thoughts, remorse, and pity rests;
And who have hard hearts and obdurate minds
But vicious, hare-brained, and illiterate hinds?
The god, seeing him with pity to be moved,
Thereon concluded that he was beloved.
(Love is too full of faith, too credulous,
With folly and false hope deluding us.)
Wherefore, Leander's fancy to surprise,
To the rich Ocean for gifts he flies.
'Tis wisdom to give much; a gift prevails
When deep persuading oratory fails.
By this Leander being near the land
Cast down his weary feet, and felt the sand.
Breathless albeit he were, he rested not
Till to the solitary tower he got,
And knocked and called, at which celestial noise
The longing heart of Hero much more joys
Than nymphs or shepherds when the timbrel rings,
Or crooked dolphin when the sailor sings.
She stayed not for her robes, but straight arose,
And drunk with gladness, to the door she goes;
Where seeing a naked man, she screeched for fear,
(Such sights as this to tender maids are rare)
And ran into the dark herself to hide.

Rich jewels in the dark are soonest spied.
Unto her was he led, or rather drawn
By those white limbs which sparkled through the lawn.
The nearer that he came, the more she fled,
And seeking refuge, slipped into her bed.
Whereon Leander sitting, thus began,
Through numbing cold all feeble, faint, and wan:
'If not for love, yet, love, for pity sake,
Me in thy bed and maiden bosom take;
At least vouchsafe these arms some little room,
Who, hoping to embrace thee, cheerly swum;
This head was beat with many a churlish billow,
And therefore let it rest upon thy pillow.'
Herewith affrighted Hero shrunk away,
And in her lukewarm place Leander lay,
Whose lively heat, like fire from heaven fet,
Would animate gross clay, and higher set
The drooping thoughts of base declining souls,
Than dreary Mars carousing nectar bowls.
His hands he cast upon her like a snare:
She, overcome with shame and sallow fear,
Like chaste Diana, when Actaeon spied her,
Being suddenly betrayed, dived down to hide her;
And as her silver body downward went,
With both her hands she made the bed a tent,
And in her own mind thought herself secure,
O'ercast with dim and darksome coverture.
And now she lets him whisper in her ear,
Flatter, entreat, promise, protest, and swear;
Yet ever as he greedily assayed

fet] fetched
dreary] drear

To touch those dainties, she the harpy played,
And every limb did, as a soldier stout,
Defend the fort and keep the foeman out.
For though the rising ivory mount he scaled,
Which is with azure circling lines empaled,
Much like a globe (a globe may I term this,
By which love sails to regions full of bliss)
Yet there with Sisyphus he toiled in vain,
Till gentle parley did the truce obtain.
Wherein Leander on her quivering breast
Breathless spoke something, and sighed out the rest;
Which so prevailed, as he with small ado
Enclosed her in his arms and kissed her too.
And every kiss to her was as a charm,
And to Leander as a fresh alarm,
So that the truce was broke, and she, alas!
Poor silly maiden, at his mercy was.
Love is not full of pity, as men say,
But deaf and cruel where he means to prey.
Even as a bird, which in our hands we wring,
Forth plungeth and oft flutters with her wing,
She trembling strove; this strife of hers, like that
Which made the world, another world begat
Of unknown joy. Treason was in her thought,
And cunningly to yield herself she sought.
Seeming not won, yet won she was at length;
In such wars women use but half their strength.
Leander now, like Theban Hercules,
Entered the orchard of th'Hesperides,
Whose fruit none rightly can describe but he
That pulls or shakes it from the golden tree.

empaled] encircled

And now she wished this night were never done,
And sighed to think upon th'approaching sun;
For much it grieved her that the bright daylight
Should know the pleasure of this blessed night,
And them like Mars and Erycine display,
Both in each other's arms chained as they lay.
Again she knew not how to frame her look,
Or speak to him who in a moment took
That which so long so charily she kept;
And fain by stealth away she would have crept,
And to some corner secretly have gone,
Leaving Leander in the bed alone.
But as her naked feet were whipping out,
He on the sudden clinged her so about,
That mermaid-like unto the floor she slid,
One half appeared, the other half was hid.
Thus near the bed she blushing stood upright,
And from her countenance behold ye might
A kind of twilight break, which through the hair,
As from an orient cloud, glims here and there;
And round about the chamber this false morn
Brought forth the day before the day was born.
So Hero's ruddy cheek Hero betrayed,
And her all naked to his sight displayed;
Whence his admiring eyes more pleasure took
Than Dis on heaps of gold fixing his look.
By this, Apollo's golden harp began
To sound forth music to the Ocean;
Which watchful Hesperus no sooner heard,
But he the day-bright bearing car prepared,
And ran before, as harbinger of light,

glims] gleams

And with his flaring beams mocked ugly Night
Till she, o'ercome with anguish, shame, and rage,
Danged down to hell her loathsome carriage.
Desunt nonnulla.

Written by 1593; *Hero and Leander*, 1598

263 *The Portents*

NOW evermore, lest some one hope might ease
The Commons' jangling minds, apparent signs arose;
Strange sights appeared; the angry threatening gods
Filled both the earth and seas with prodigies;
Great store of strange and unknown stars were seen
Wandering about the north, and rings of fire
Fly in the air, and dreadful bearded stars,
And comets that presage the fall of kingdoms.
The flattering sky glittered in often flames,
And sundry fiery meteors blazed in heaven,
Now spear-like, long, now like a spreading torch;
Lightning in silence stole forth without clouds,
And from the northern climate, snatching fire
Blasted the Capitol. The lesser stars,
Which wont to run their course through empty night,
At noon-day mustered; Phoebe, having filled
Her meeting horns to match her brother's light,
Strook with th' earth's sudden shadow, waxed pale;
Titan himself, throned in the midst of heaven,
His burning chariot plunged in sable clouds,
And whelmed the world in darkness, making men
Despair of day, as did Thyestes' town,
Mycenae, Phoebus flying through the east.

CHRISTOPHER MARLOWE

Fierce Mulciber unbarred Aetna's gate,
Which flamed not on high, but headlong pitched
Her burning head on bending Hespery.
Coal-black Charybdis whirled a sea of blood;
Fierce mastiffs howled; the vestal fires went out;
The flame in Alba, consecrate to Jove,
Parted in twain, and with a double point
Rose like the Theban brothers' funeral fire;
The earth went off her hinges; and the Alps
Shook the old snow from off their trembling laps.
The ocean swelled as high as Spanish Calpe,
Or Atlas' head; their saints and household gods
Sweat tears, to show the travails of their city.
Crowns fell from holy statues; ominous birds
Defiled the day; at night wild beasts were seen,
Leaving the woods, lodge in the streets of Rome.
Cattle were seen that muttered human speech.
Prodigious births with more and ugly joints
Than nature gives, whose sight appals the mother,
And dismal prophecies were spread abroad.
And they, whom fierce Bellona's fury moves
To wound their arms, sing vengeance; Sibyl's priests,
Curling their bloody locks, howl dreadful things;
Souls quiet and appeased sighed from their graves;
Clashing of arms was heard in untrod woods,
Shrill voices shright, and ghosts encounter men.
Those that inhabited the suburb fields
Fled; foul Erinnys stalked about the walls,
Shaking her snaky hair and crooked pine
With flaming top, much like that hellish fiend
Which made the stern Lycurgus wound his thigh,
Or fierce Agave mad; or like Megaera

That scared Alcides, when by Juno's task
He had before looked Pluto in the face.
Trumpets were heard to sound; and with what noise
An armed battle joins, such and more strange
Black night brought forth in secret. Sulla's ghost
Was seen to walk, singing sad oracles,
And Marius' head above cold Tav'ron peering,
His grave broke open, did affright the boors.

Lucan's First Book, 520–82, 1600

264 *A Fragment*

I WALKED along a stream for pureness rare,
Brighter than sunshine, for it did acquaint
The dullest sight with all the glorious prey,
That in the pebble-paved channel lay.

No molten crystal, but a richer mine,
Even Nature's rarest alchemy ran there,
Diamonds resolved, and substance more divine,
Through whose bright gliding current might appear
A thousand naked nymphs, whose ivory shine,
Enamelling the banks, made them more dear
Then ever was that glorious palace gate,
Where the day-shining sun in triumph sat.

Upon this brim the eglantine and rose,
The tamarisk, olive, and the almond tree,
As kind companions in one union grows,
Folding their twining arms, as oft we see
Turtle-taught lovers either other close,
Lending to dullness feeling sympathy.
And as a costly valance o'er a bed,
So did their garland tops the brook o'erspread.

Their leaves that differed both in shape and show,
(Though all were green) yet difference such in green,
Like to the checkered bent of Iris' bow,
Prided the running main as it had been—

England's Parnassus, 1600

265 *The Passionate Shepherd to his Love*

COME live with me and be my love,
And we will all the pleasures prove,
That hills and valleys, dales and fields,
And all the craggy mountains yields.

There we will sit upon the rocks,
And see the shepherds feed their flocks,
By shallow rivers to whose falls
Melodious birds sing madrigals.

And I will make thee beds of roses
With a thousand fragrant posies,
A cap of flowers, and a kirtle
Embroidered all with leaves of myrtle;

A gown made of the finest wool
Which from our pretty lambs we pull;
Fair lined slippers for the cold,
With buckles of the purest gold;

A belt of straw and ivy buds,
With coral clasps and amber studs:
And if these pleasures may thee move,
Come live with me and be my love.

The shepherds' swains shall dance and sing
For thy delight each May morning:
If these delights thy mind may move,
Then live with me and be my love.

The Passionate Pilgrim, 1599;
England's Helicon, 1600

SIR WALTER RALEGH

c. 1552–1618

266 *Answer to Marlowe*

IF all the world and love were young,
And truth in every shepherd's tongue,
These pretty pleasures might me move
To live with thee and be thy love.

Time drives the flocks from field to fold,
When rivers rage and rocks grow cold,
And Philomel becometh dumb;
The rest complain of cares to come.

The flowers do fade, and wanton fields
To wayward winter reckoning yields;
A honey tongue, a heart of gall,
Is fancy's spring, but sorrow's fall.

Thy gowns, thy shoes, thy beds of roses,
Thy cap, thy kirtle, and thy posies
Soon break, soon wither, soon forgotten,
In folly ripe, in reason rotten.

Thy belt of straw and ivy buds,
Thy coral clasps and amber studs,
All these in me no means can move
To come to thee and be thy love.

But could youth last and love still breed,
Had joys no date nor age no need,
Then these delights my mind might move
To live with thee and be thy love.

England's Helicon, 1600

267 *False Love*

FAREWELL false love, the oracle of lies,
A mortal foe and enemy to rest,
An envious boy, from whom all cares arise,
A bastard vile, a beast with rage possessed,
A way of error, a temple full of treason,
In all effects contrary unto reason.

A poisoned serpent covered all with flowers,
Mother of sighs, and murderer of repose,
A sea of sorrows from whence are drawn such showers,
As moisture lend to every grief that grows,
A school of guile, a net of deep deceit,
A gilded hook, that holds a poisoned bait.

A fortress foiled, which reason did defend,
A Syren song, a fever of the mind,
A maze wherein affection finds no end,
A ranging cloud that runs before the wind,
A substance like the shadow of the sun,
A goal of grief for which the wisest run.

A quenchless fire, a nurse of trembling fear,
  A path that leads to peril and mishap,
A true retreat of sorrow and despair,
  An idle boy that sleeps in pleasure's lap,
    A deep mistrust of that which certain seems,
    A hope of that which reason doubtful deems.

Sith then thy trains my younger years betrayed
  And for my faith ingratitude I find.
And sith repentance hath my wrongs bewrayed
  Whose course was ever contrary to kind.
    False love, desire, and beauty frail adieu!
    Dead is the root whence all these fancies grew.

W. Byrd, *Psalms, Sonnets and Songs*, 1588

268 *A Vision upon this Conceit of the Faerie Queene*

METHOUGHT I saw the grave, where Laura lay,
  Within that temple, where the vestal flame
Was wont to burn, and passing by that way,
  To see that buried dust of living fame,
Whose tomb fair Love and fairer Virtue kept,
  All suddenly I saw the Faerie Queene;
At whose approach the soul of Petrarch wept,
  And from thenceforth those graces were not seen,
For they this Queen attended, in whose stead
  Oblivion laid him down on Laura's hearse.
Hereat the hardest stones were seen to bleed,
  And groans of buried ghosts the heavens did pierce;
    Where Homer's spright did tremble all for grief,
    And cursed th' access of that celestial thief.

Spenser, *Faerie Queene*, 1590

269

The Hermit

LIKE to a hermit poor in place obscure
  I mean to spend my days of endless doubt,
To wail such woes as time cannot recure,
  Where none but death shall ever find me out.

My food shall be of care and sorrow made,
  My drink nought else but tears fallen from mine eyes;
And for my light in such obscured shade
  The flames shall serve that from my heart arise.

A gown of grief my body shall attire,
  My staff of broken hope whereon I'll stay;
Of late repentance linked with long desire
  The couch is framed whereon my limbs I'll lay;

And at my gate despair shall linger still
To let in death when love and fortune will.

Bower of Delights, 1591

270

Diana

PRAISED be Diana's fair and harmless light,
  Praised be the dews, wherewith she moists the ground,
Praised be her beams, the glory of the night,
  Praised be her power, by which all powers abound.

Praised be her nymphs, with whom she decks the woods,
  Praised be her knights, in whom true honour lives,
Praised be that force, by which she moves the floods;
  Let that Diana shine, which all these gives.

In heaven Queen she is among the spheres,
  In earth she Mistress-like makes all things pure,
Eternity in her oft change she bears,
  She beauty is, by her the fair endure.

Time wears her not, she doth his chariot guide,
  Mortality below her orb is placed,
By her the virtue of the stars down slide,
  In her is virtue's perfect image cast.

A knowledge pure it is her worth to know,
With Circes let them dwell that think not so.

The Phoenix Nest, 1593

271 *A Description of Love*

NOW what is love? I pray thee, tell.
  It is that fountain and that well,
Where pleasure and repentance dwell.
It is perhaps that sauncing bell,
That tolls all in to heaven or hell:
And this is love, as I hear tell.

Yet what is love? I pray thee say.
It is a work on holy-day;
It is December matched with May;
When lusty bloods, in fresh array,
Hear ten months after of the play:
And this is love, as I hear say.

sauncing] sacring, at mass

Yet what is love? I pray thee sayn.
It is a sunshine mixed with rain;
It is a tooth-ache, or like pain;
It is a game where none doth gain;
The lass saith no, and would full fain:
And this is love, as I hear sayn.

Yet what is love? I pray thee say.
It is a yea, it is a nay,
A pretty kind of sporting fray;
It is a thing will soon away;
Then take the vantage while you may:
And this is love, as I hear say.

Yet what is love? I pray thee show.
A thing that creeps, it cannot go;
A prize that passeth to and fro;
A thing for one, a thing for mo;
And he that proves must find it so:
And this is love, sweet friend, I trow.

Ibid.

272

Farewell to the Court

LIKE truthless dreams, so are my joys expired,
  And past return are all my dandled days;
My love misled, and fancy quite retired,
  Of all which past, the sorrow only stays.

My lost delights, now clean from sight of land,
  Have left me all alone in unknown ways;
My mind to woe, my life in fortune's hand,
  Of all which past, the sorrow only stays.

As in a country strange without companion,
I only wail the wrong of death's delays,
Whose sweet spring spent, whose summer well nigh done,
Of all which past, the sorrow only stays;

Whom care forewarns, ere age and winter cold,
To haste me hence, to find my fortune's fold.

The Phoenix Nest, 1593

273 *Walsinghame*

'As you came from the holy land
Of Walsinghame,
Met you not with my true love
By the way as you came?'

'How shall I know your true love,
That have met many one
As I went to the holy land,
That have come, that have gone?'

'She is neither white nor brown,
But as the heavens fair,
There is none hath a form so divine
In the earth or the air.'

'Such an one did I meet, good Sir,
Such an angelic face,
Who like a queen, like a nymph did appear
By her gait, by her grace.'

SIR WALTER RALEGH

'She hath left me here all alone,
All alone as unknown,
Who sometimes did me lead with herself,
And me loved as her own.'

'What 's the cause that she leaves you alone
And a new way doth take,
Who loved you once as her own
And her joy did you make?'

'I have loved her all my youth,
But now old as you see,
Love likes not the falling fruit
From the withered tree.

'Know that Love is a careless child,
And forgets promise past;
He is blind, he is deaf when he list
And in faith never fast.

'His desire is a dureless content
And a trustless joy;
He is won with a world of despair
And is lost with a toy.

'Of womenkind such indeed is the love
Or the word love abused,
Under which many childish desires
And conceits are excused.

'But love is a durable fire
In the mind ever burning;
Never sick, never old, never dead,
From itself never turning.'

Rawlinson Poet. MS. 85

274 *To the Queen*

OUR passions are most like to floods and streams;
The shallow murmur, but the deep are dumb.
So when affections yield discourse, it seems
The bottom is but shallow whence they come.
They that are rich in words must needs discover
That they are poor in that which makes a lover.

Wrong not, dear empress of my heart,
The merit of true passion,
With thinking that he feels no smart,
That sues for no compassion;
Since, if my plaints serve not to prove
The conquest of your beauty,
It comes not from defect of love,
But from excess of duty.

For knowing that I sue to serve
A saint of such perfection,
As all desire, but none deserve,
A place in her affection,
I rather choose to want relief
Than venture the revealing;
When glory recommends the grief,
Despair distrusts the healing.

Thus those desires that aim too high,
For any mortal lover,
When reason cannot make them die,
Discretion will them cover.

Yet when discretion doth bereave
  The plaints that they should utter,
Then your discretion may perceive,
  That silence is a suitor.

Silence in love bewrays more woe,
  Than words, though ne'er so witty;
A beggar that is dumb, ye know,
  Deserveth double pity.
Then misconceive not (dearest heart)
  My true, though secret passion,
He smarteth most that hides his smart,
  And sues for no compassion.

Addl. MS. 22602

275 *Affection and Desire*

CONCEIT begotten by the eyes
  Is quickly born, and quickly dies,
For while it seeks our hearts to have,
Meanwhile there reason makes his grave;
For many things the eyes approve,
Which yet the heart doth seldom love.

For as the seeds in springtime sown
Die in the ground ere they be grown,
Such is conceit, whose rooting fails,
As child that in the cradle quails,
Or else within the mother's womb
Hath his beginning, and his tomb.

SIR WALTER RALEGH

Affection follows Fortune's wheels,
And soon is shaken from her heels;
For following beauty or estate,
Her liking still is turned to hate;
For all affections have their change,
And fancy only loves to range.

Desire himself runs out of breath,
And getting, doth but gain his death;
Desire, nor reason hath, nor rest,
And blind doth seldom choose the best;
Desire attained is not desire,
But as the cinders of the fire.

As ships in ports desired are drowned,
As fruit, once ripe, then falls to ground,
As flies that seek for flames are brought
To cinders by the flames they sought;
So fond desire when it attains,
The life expires, the woe remains.

And yet some poets fain would prove
Affection to be perfect love,
And that desire is of that kind,
No less a passion of the mind.
As if wild beasts and men did seek
To like, to love, to choose alike.

Poetical Rhapsody, 1602

276

The Lie

GO, soul, the body's guest,
  Upon a thankless arrant;
Fear not to touch the best;
  The truth shall be thy warrant.
    Go, since I needs must die,
    And give the world the lie.

Say to the court, it glows
  And shines like rotten wood;
Say to the church, it shows
  What 's good, and doth no good:
    If church and court reply,
    Then give them both the lie.

Tell potentates, they live
  Acting by others' action,
Not loved unless they give,
  Not strong but by their faction:
    If potentates reply,
    Give potentates the lie.

Tell men of high condition
  That manage the estate,
Their purpose is ambition,
  Their practice only hate:
    And if they once reply,
    Then give them all the lie.

Tell them that brave it most,
They beg for more by spending,
Who, in their greatest cost,
Seek nothing but commending:
And if they make reply,
Then give them all the lie.

Tell zeal it wants devotion;
Tell love it is but lust;
Tell time it is but motion;
Tell flesh it is but dust:
And wish them not reply,
For thou must give the lie.

Tell age it daily wasteth;
Tell honour how it alters;
Tell beauty how she blasteth;
Tell favour how it falters:
And as they shall reply,
Give every one the lie.

Tell wit how much it wrangles
In tickle points of niceness;
Tell wisdom she entangles
Herself in over-wiseness:
And when they do reply,
Straight give them both the lie.

Tell physic of her boldness;
Tell skill it is prevention;
Tell charity of coldness;
Tell law it is contention:
And as they do reply,
So give them still the lie.

SIR WALTER RALEGH

Tell fortune of her blindness;
  Tell nature of decay;
Tell friendship of unkindness;
  Tell justice of delay:
    And if they will reply,
    Then give them all the lie.

Tell arts they have no soundness,
  But vary by esteeming;
Tell schools they want profoundness,
  And stand too much on seeming:
    If arts and schools reply,
    Give arts and schools the lie.

Tell faith it 's fled the city;
  Tell how the country erreth;
Tell, manhood shakes off pity;
  Tell, virtue least preferreth:
    And if they do reply,
    Spare not to give the lie.

So when thou hast, as I
  Commanded thee, done blabbing,
Although to give the lie
  Deserves no less than stabbing,
    Stab at thee he that will,
    No stab the soul can kill.

Poetical Rhapsody, 1608

277 *The Ocean to Cynthia*

SUFFICETH it to you, my joys interred,
  In simple words that I my woes complain,
You that then died when first my fancy erred,
  Joys under dust that never live again.

If to the living were my Muse addressed,
  Or did my mind her own spirit still inhold,
Were not my living passion so repressed
  As to the dead the dead did these unfold,

Some sweeter words, some more becoming verse,
  Should witness my mishap in higher kind;
But my love's wounds, my fancy in the hearse,
  The idea but resting of a wasted mind,

The blossoms fallen, the sap gone from the tree,
  The broken monuments of my great desires;
From these so lost what may th' affections be?
  What heat in cinders of extinguished fires?

Lost in the mud of those high-flowing streams,
  Which through more fairer fields their courses bend,
Slain with self-thoughts, amazed in fearful dreams,
  Woes without date, discomforts without end,

From fruitful trees I gather withered leaves,
  And glean the broken ears with miser's hand,
Who sometime did enjoy the weighty sheaves;
  I seek fair flowers amid the brinish sand.

resting] remaining

All in the shade, even in the fair sun days,
  Under those healthless trees I sit alone,
Where joyful birds sing neither lovely lays,
  Nor Philomen recounts her direful moan.

No feeding flocks, no shepherds' company,
  That might renew my dolorous conceit,
While happy then, while love and fantasy
  Confined my thoughts on that fair flock to wait;

No pleasing streams fast to the ocean wending,
  The messengers sometimes of my great woe;
But all on earth, as from the cold storms bending,
  Shrink from my thoughts in high heavens and below.

O! hopeful love, my object, and invention,
  O! true desire, the spur of my conceit,
O! worthiest spirit, my mind's impulsion,
  O! eyes transpersant, my affection's bait;

O! princely form, my fancy's adamant,
  Divine conceit, my painės acceptance,
O! all in one! oh, heaven on earth transparent!
  The seat of joys and lovės abundance!

Out of that mass of miracles my Muse
  Gathered those flowers, to her pure senses pleasing;
Out of her eyes (the store of joys) did choose
  Equal delights, my sorrows counterpeising.

Her regal looks my rigorous sighs suppressed;
  Small drops of joys sweetened great worlds of woes;
One gladsome day a thousand cares redressed.
  Whom Love defends, what fortune overthrows?

When she did well, what did there else amiss?
  When she did ill, what empires could have pleased?
No other power effecting woe or bliss,
  She gave, she took, she wounded, she appeased.

. . . . . .

The honour of her love, love still devising,
  Wounding my mind with contrary conceit,
Transferred itself sometime to her aspiring,
  Sometime the trumpet of her thought's retreat.

To seek new worlds for gold, for praise, for glory,
  To try desire, to try love severed far,
When I was gone, she sent her memory,
  More strong than were ten thousand ships of war,

To call me back, to leave great honour's thought,
  To leave my friends, my fortune, my attempt,
To leave the purpose I so long had sought,
  And hold both cares and comforts in contempt.

Such heat in ice, such fire in frost remained,
  Such trust in doubt, such comfort in despair;
Much like the gentle lamb, though lately weaned,
  Plays with the dug, though finds no comfort there.

But as a body, violently slain,
  Retaineth warmth although the spirit be gone,
And by a power in nature moves again,
  Till it be laid below the fatal stone;

Or as the earth, even in cold winter days,
  Left for a time by her life-giving sun,
Doth by the power remaining of his rays
  Produce some green, though not as it hath done;

Or as a wheel, forced by the falling stream,
  Although the course be turned some other way,
Doth for a time go round upon the beam,
  Till, wanting strength to move, it stands at stay;

So my forsaken heart, my withered mind,
  Widow of all the joys it once possessed,
My hopes clean out of sight with forced wind,
  To kingdoms strange, to lands far-off, addressed,

Alone, forsaken, friendless, on the shore,
  With many wounds, with death's cold pangs embraced,
Writes in the dust, as one that could no more,
  Whom love, and time, and fortune, had defaced,

Of things so great, so long, so manifold,
  With means so weak, the soul even then depicting
The weal, the woe, the passages of old,
  And worlds of thoughts described by one last sithing.

sithing] sighing

As if, when after Phoebus is descended,
  And leaves a light much like the past day's dawning,
And, every toil and labour wholly ended,
  Each living creature draweth to his resting,

We should begin by such a parting light
  To write the story of all ages past,
And end the same before th'approaching night.

Such is again the labour of my mind,
  Whose shroud, by sorrow woven now to end,
Hath seen that ever shining sun declined,
  So many years that so could not descend,

But that the eyes of my mind held her beams
  In every part transferred by love's swift thought;
Far off or near, in waking or in dreams,
  Imagination strong their lustre brought.

Such force her angelic appearance had
  To master distance, time, or cruelty;
Such art to grieve, and after to make glad;
  Such fear in love, such love in majesty.

My weary limbs her memory embalmed;
  My darkest ways her eyes made clear as day.
What storms so great but Cynthia's beams appeased?
  What rage so fierce, that love could not allay?

SIR WALTER RALEGH

Twelve years entire I wasted in this war,
  Twelve years of my most happy younger days;
But I in them, and they now wasted are,
  'Of all which past the sorrow only stays'.

So wrote I once, and my mishap foretold,
  My mind still feeling sorrowful success,
Even as before a storm the marble cold
  Doth by moist tears tempestuous times express.

So felt my heavy mind my harms at hand,
  Which my vain thought in vain sought to recure;
At middle day my sun seemed under land,
  When any little cloud did it obscure.

And as the icicles in a winter's day,
  Whenas the sun shines with unwonted warm,

So did my joys melt into secret tears,
  So did my heart dissolve in wasting drops;
And as the season of the year outwears,
  And heaps of snow from off the mountain tops

With sudden streams the valleys overflow,
  So did the time draw on my more despair;
Then floods of sorrow and whole seas of woe
  The banks of all my hope did overbear,

And drowned my mind in depths of misery.
  Sometime I died, sometime I was distract,
My soul the stage of fancy's tragedy;
  Then furious madness, where true reason lacked,

success] sequel

Wrote what it would, and scourged mine own conceit.
  O! heavy heart, who can thee witness bear?
What tongue, what pen, could thy tormenting treat,
  But thine own mourning thoughts which present were?

What stranger mind believe the meanest part?
  What altered sense conceive the weakest woe,
That tare, that rent, that pierced thy sad heart?
  And as a man distract, with treble might,

Bound in strong chains doth strive and rage in vain,
  Till, tired and breathless, he is forced to rest,
Finds by contention but increase of pain,
  And fiery heat inflamed in swollen breast;

So did my mind in change of passion
  From woe to wrath, from wrath return to woe,
Struggling in vain from love's subjection.

Therefore, all lifeless and all helpless bound,
  My fainting spirits sunk, and heart appaled,
My joys and hopes lay bleeding on the ground,
  That not long since the highest heaven scaled.

I hated life and cursed destiny;
  The thoughts of passed times, like flames of hell,
Kindled afresh within my memory
  The many dear achievements that befell

appaled] grew pale

SIR WALTER RALEGH

In those prime years and infancy of love,
  Which to describe were but to die in writing;
Ah! those I sought, but vainly, to remove,
  And vainly shall, by which I perish living.

And though strong reason hold before mine eyes
  The images and forms of worlds past,
Teaching the cause why all those flames that rise
  From forms external can no longer last,

Than that those seeming beauties hold in prime
  Love's ground, his essence, and his empery,
All slaves to age, and vassals unto time,
  Of which repentance writes the tragedy,

But this my heart's desire could not conceive,
  Whose love outflew the fastest flying time,
A beauty that can easily deceive
  Th'arrest of years, and creeping age outclimb,

A spring of beauties which time ripeth not,
  Time that but works on frail mortality,
A sweetness which woe's wrongs outwipeth not,
  Whom love hath chose for his divinity,

A vestal fire that burns but never wasteth,
  That loseth nought by giving light to all,
That endless shines each where, and endless lasteth,
  Blossoms of pride that can nor vade nor fall.

remove] move again   vade] fade

These were those marvellous perfections,
The parents of my sorrow and my envy,
Most deathful and most violent infections;
These be the tyrants that in fetters tie

Their wounded vassals, yet nor kill nor cure,
But glory in their lasting misery,
That, as her beauties would, our woes should dure;
These be the effects of powerful empery.

. . . . . .

Yet have these wonders want, which want compassion;
Yet hath her mind some marks of human race;
Yet will she be a woman for a fashion,
So doth she please her virtues to deface.

And like as that immortal power doth seat
An element of waters, to allay
The fiery sunbeams that on earth do beat,
And temper by cold night the heat of day,

So hath perfection, which begat her mind,
Added thereto a change of fantasy,
And left her the affections of her kind,
Yet free from every evil but cruelty.

. . . . . .

But leave her praise; speak thou of nought but woe;
Write on the tale that Sorrow bids thee tell;
Strive to forget, and care no more to know
Thy cares are known, by knowing those too well.

Describe her now as she appears to thee,
  Not as she did appear in days fordone;
In love, those things that were no more may be,
  For fancy seldom ends where it begun.

. . . . . .

And as a stream by strong hand bounded in
  From nature's course where it did sometime run,
By some small rent or loose part doth begin
  To find escape, till it a way hath won;

Doth then all unawares in sunder tear
  The forced bounds, and, raging, run at large
In th'ancient channels as they wonted were;
  Such is of women's love the careful charge,

Held and maintained with multitude of woes;
  Of long erections such the sudden fall.
One hour diverts, one instant overthrows,
  For which our life 's, for which our fortune 's, thrall,

So many years those joys have dearly bought,
  Of which when our fond hopes do most assure,
All is dissolved; our labours come to nought,
  Nor any mark thereof there doth endure;

No more than, when small drops of rain do fall
  Upon the parched ground by heat updried,
No cooling moisture is perceived at all,
  Nor any show or sign of wet doth bide.

But as the fields, clothed with leaves and flowers,
  The banks of roses smelling precious sweet,
Have but their beauty's date and timely hours,
  And then defaced by winter's cold and sleet,

So far as neither fruit nor form of flower
  Stays for a witness what such branches bare,
But as time gave, time did again devour,
  And change our rising joy to falling care;

So of affection which our youth presented.
  When she that from the sun reaves power and light,
Did but decline her beams as discontented,
  Converting sweetest days to saddest night,

All droops, all dies, all trodden under dust,
  The person, place, and passages forgotten,
The hardest steel eaten with softest rust,
  The firm and solid tree both rent and rotten.

Those thoughts, so full of pleasure and content,
  That in our absence were affection's food,
Are razed out and from the fancy rent,
  In highest grace and heart's dear care that stood;

Are cast for prey to hatred and to scorn;
  Our dearest treasures and our heart's true joys,
The tokens hung on breast and kindly worn,
  Are now elsewhere disposed or held for toys,

And those which then our jealousy removed,
  And others for our sakes then valued dear,
The one forgot, the rest are dear beloved,
  When all of ours doth strange or vild appear.

Those streams seem standing puddles, which before
  We saw our beauties in, so were they clear;
Belphebe's course is now observed no more;

That fair resemblance weareth out of date;
  Our ocean seas are but tempestuous waves,
And all things base, that blessed were of late.

And as a field, wherein the stubble stands
  Of harvest past the ploughman's eye offends,
He tills again, or tears them up with hands,
  And throws to fire as foiled and fruitless ends,

And takes delight another seed to sow;
  So doth the mind root up all wonted thought,
And scorns the care of our remaining woe;
  The sorrows, which themselves for us have wrought,

Are burnt to cinders by new kindled fires;
  The ashes are dispersed into the air;
The sithes, the groans of all our past desires
  Are clean outworn, as things that never were.

. . . . . .

With youth is dead the hope of Love's return,
  Who looks not back to hear our after cries;
Where he is not, he laughs at those that mourn;
  Whence he is gone, he scorns the mind that dies;

removed] moved stands] stalks

When he is absent, he believes no words;
  When reason speaks, he, careless, stops his ears;
Whom he hath left, he never grace affords,
  But bathes his wings in our lamenting tears.

. . . . . .

Unlasting passion, soon outworn conceit,
  Whereon I built, and on so dureless trust!
My mind had wounds, I dare not say deceit,
  Where I resolved her promise was not just.

Sorrow was my revenge and woe my hate;
  I powerless was to alter my desire;
My love is not of time or bound to date;
  My heart's internal heat and living fire

Would not, or could, be quenched with sudden showers;
  My bound respect was not confined to days,
My vowed faith not set to ended hours;
  I love the bearing and not bearing sprays

Which now to others do their sweetness send,
  Th' incarnate, snow-driven white, and purest azure,
Who from high heaven doth on their fields descend,
  Filling their barns with grain, and towers with treasure.

Erring or never erring, such is Love
  As, while it lasteth, scorns th' accompt of those
Seeking but self contentment to improve,
  And hides, if any be, his inward woes,

incarnate] flesh-pink　　　　who] which

And will not know, while he knows his own passion,
  The often and unjust perseverance
In deeds of love and state, and every action
  From that first day and year of their joy's entrance.

. . . . . .

But I, unblessed and ill born creature,
  That did embrace the dust her body bearing,
That loved her both by fancy and by nature,
  That drew, even with the milk in my first sucking,

Affection from the parent's breast that bare me,
  Have found her as a stranger so severe,
Improving my mishap in each degree.
  But love was gone; so would I my life were!

A queen she was to me, no more Belphebe,
  A lion then, no more a milk-white dove;
A prisoner in her breast I could not be;
  She did untie the gentle chains of love.

Love was no more the love of hiding . . .

All trespass and mischance for her own glory.
  It had been such; it was still for the elect;
But I must be th' example in love's story;
  This was of all forepast the sad effect.

But thou, my weary soul and heavy thought,
  Made by her love a burthen to my being,
Dost know my error never was forethought,
  Or ever could proceed from sense of loving.

Of other cause if then it had proceeding,
  I leave the excuse, sith judgement hath been given;
The limbs divided, sundered, and a-bleeding,
  Cannot complain the sentence was uneven.

. . . . . .

This did that nature's wonder, virtue's choice,
  The only paragon of time's begetting,
Divine in words, angelical in voice,
  That spring of joys, that flower of love's own setting,

The Idea remaining of those golden ages,
  That beauty, braving heaven's and earth embalming,
Which after worthless worlds but play on stages;
  Such didst thou her long since describe, yet sithing

That thy unable spirit could not find aught
  In heaven's beauties or in earth's delight,
For likeness fit to satisfy thy thought.
  But what hath it availed thee so to write?

She cares not for thy praise, who knows not theirs;
  It 's now an idle labour, and a tale
Told out of time, that dulls the hearer's ears,
  A merchandise whereof there is no sale.

Leave them, or lay them up with thy despairs!
  She hath resolved, and judged thee long ago.
Thy lines are now a murmuring to her ears,
  Like to a falling stream, which, passing slow,

Is wont to nourish sleep and quietness.

braving] challenging

So shall thy painful labours be perused,
  And draw on rest, which sometime had regard;
But those her cares thy errors have excused;
  Thy days fordone have had their day's reward.

So her hard heart, so her estranged mind,
  In which above the heavens I once reposed;
So to thy error have her ears inclined,

And have forgotten all thy past deserving,
  Holding in mind but only thine offence;
And only now affecteth thy depraving,
  And thinks all vain that pleadeth thy defence.

Yet greater fancy beauty never bred;
  A more desire the heart-blood never nourished;
Her sweetness an affection never fed,
  Which more in any age hath ever flourished.

The mind and virtue never have begotten
  A firmer love, since love on earth had power,
A love obscured, but cannot be forgotten,
  Too great and strong for time's jaws to devour,

Containing such a faith as ages wound not,
  Care, wakeful ever of her good estate,
Fear, dreading loss, which sithes and joys not,
  A memory of the joys her grace begat,

A lasting gratefulness for those comforts past,
  Of which the cordial sweetness cannot die.
These thoughts, knit up by faith, shall ever last,
  These time assays, but never can untie,

Whose life once lived in her pearl-like breast,
  Whose joys were drawn but from her happiness,
Whose heart's high pleasure, and whose mind's true rest,
  Proceeded from her fortune's blessedness;

Who was intentive, wakeful, and dismayed
  In fears, in dreams, in feverous jealousy;
Who long in silence served, and obeyed
  With secret heart and hidden loyalty,

Which never change to sad adversity,
  Which never age, or nature's overthrow,
Which never sickness or deformity,
  Which never wasting care or wearing woe,

If subject unto these she could have been. . . . .

Which never words or wits malicious,
  Which never honour's bait, or world's fame,
Achieved by attempts adventurous,
  Or aught beneath the sun or heaven's frame,

Can so dissolve, dissever, or destroy,
  The essential love of no frail parts compounded,
Though of the same now buried be the joy,
  The hope, the comfort, and the sweetness ended,

But that the thoughts and memories of these
  Work a relapse of passion, and remain
Of my sad heart the sorrow-sucking bees;
  The wrongs received, the scorns, persuade in vain.

And though these medicines work desire to end,
  And are in others the true cure of liking,
The salves that heal love's wounds, and do amend
  Consuming woe, and slake our hearty sithing,

They work not so in thy mind's long disease;
  External fancy time alone recureth,
All whose effects do wear away with ease
  Love of delight, while such delight endureth;

Stays by the pleasure, but no longer stays.

But in my mind so is her love inclosed,
  And is thereof not only the best part,
But into it the essence is disposed.
  O love! (the more my woe) to it thou art

Even as the moisture in each plant that grows;
  Even as the sun unto the frozen ground;
Even as the sweetness to th' incarnate rose;
  Even as the centre in each perfect round;

As water to the fish, to men as air,
  As heat to fire, as light unto the sun;
O love! it is but vain to say thou were;
  Ages and times cannot thy power outrun.

Thou art the soul of that unhappy mind
  Which, being by nature made an idle thought,
Begun even then to take immortal kind,
  When first her virtues in thy spirits wrought.

From thee therefore that mover cannot move,
  Because it is become thy cause of being;
Whatever error may obscure that love,
  Whatever frail effect of mortal living,

Whatever passion from distempered heart,
  What absence, time, or injuries effect,
What faithless friends or deep dissembled art
  Present to feed her most unkind suspect.

Yet as the air in deep caves underground
  Is strongly drawn when violent heat hath rent
Great clefts therein, till moisture do abound,
  And then the same, imprisoned and up-pent,

Breaks out in earthquakes tearing all asunder;
  So, in the centre of my cloven heart,
My heart, to whom her beauties were such wonder,
  Lies the sharp poisoned head of that love's dart,

Which, till all break and all dissolve to dust,
  Thence drawn it cannot be, or therein known.
There, mixed with my heart-blood, the fretting rust
  The better part hath eaten and outgrown.

But what of those or these, or what of aught
  Of that which was, or that which is, to treat?
What I possess is but the same I sought;
  My love was false, my labours were deceit.

Nor less than such they are esteemed to be;
  A fraud bought at the price of many woes;
A guile, whereof the profits unto me—
  Could it be thought premeditate for those?

Witness those withered leaves left on the tree,
  The sorrow-worn face, the pensive mind.
The external shows what may the internal be;
  Cold care hath bitten both the root and vind.

. . . . . .

But stay, my thoughts, make end, give fortune way.
  Harsh is the voice of woe and sorrow's sound;
Complaints cure not, and tears do but allay
  Griefs for a time, which after more abound.

To seek for moisture in the Arabian sands
  Is but a loss of labour and of rest.
The links which time did break of hearty bands

Words cannot knit, or wailings make anew.
  Seek not the sun in clouds when it is set.
On highest mountains, where those cedars grew,
  Against whose banks the troubled ocean beat,

And were the marks to find thy hoped port,
  Into a soil far off themselves remove.
On Sestus' shore, Leander's late resort,
  Hero hath left no lamp to guide her love.

Thou lookest for light in vain, and storms arise;
  She sleeps thy death, that erst thy danger sithed,
Strive then no more; bow down thy weary eyes,
  Eyes which to all these woes thy heart have guided.

vind] vine

She is gone, she is lost, she is found, she is ever fair.
  Sorrow draws weakly, where love draws not too;
Woe's cries sound nothing, but only in love's ear;
  Do then by dying what life cannot do.

Unfold thy flocks and leave them to the fields,
  To feed on hills, or dales, where likes them best,
Of what the summer or the spring time yields,
  For love and time hath given thee leave to rest.

Thy heart which was their fold, now in decay,
  By often storms and winter's many blasts,
All torn and rent becomes misfortune's prey;
  False hope, my shepherd's staff, now age hath brast.

My pipe, which love's own hand gave my desire
  To sing her praises and my woe upon,
Despair hath often threatened to the fire,
  As vain to keep now all the rest are gone.

Thus home I draw, as death's long night draws on;
  Yet, every foot, old thoughts turn back mine eyes.
Constraint me guides, as old age draws a stone
  Against the hill, which over-weighty lies

For feeble arms or wasted strength to move;
  My steps are backward, gazing on my loss,
My mind's affection and my soul's sole love,
  Not mixed with fancy's chaff or fortune's dross.

brast] broken

To God I leave it, who first gave it me,
  And I her gave, and she returned again,
As it was hers; so let his mercies be
  Of my last comforts the essential mean.

But be it so or not, th' effects are past;
Her love hath end; my woe must ever last.

Cecil MS. 144

278 *The Passionate Man's Pilgrimage*

GIVE me my scallop-shell of quiet,
  My staff of faith to walk upon,
My scrip of joy, immortal diet,
My bottle of salvation,
My gown of glory, hope's true gage,
And thus I'll take my pilgrimage.

Blood must be my body's balmer,
No other balm will there be given,
Whilst my soul like a white palmer
Travels to the land of heaven,
Over the silver mountains,
Where spring the nectar fountains;
And there I'll kiss
The bowl of bliss,
And drink my everlasting fill
On every milken hill.
My soul will be a-dry before,
But after it will thirst no more.

And by the happy blissful way
More peaceful pilgrims I shall see,
That have shook off their gowns of clay
And go apparelled fresh like me.
I'll bring them first
To slake their thirst,
And then to taste those nectar suckets,
At the clear wells
Where sweetness dwells,
Drawn up by saints in crystal buckets.

And when our bottles and all we
Are filled with immortality,
Then the holy paths we'll travel,
Strewed with rubies thick as gravel,
Ceilings of diamonds, sapphire floors,
High walls of coral and pearl bowers.

From thence to heaven's bribeless hall
Where no corrupted voices brawl,
No conscience molten into gold,
Nor forged accusers bought and sold,
No cause deferred, nor vain-spent journey,
For there Christ is the King's Attorney,
Who pleads for all without degrees,
And he hath angels, but no fees.

When the grand twelve million jury
Of our sins and direful fury
'Gainst our souls black verdicts give,
Christ pleads his death, and then we live.

Be thou my speaker, taintless pleader,
Unblotted lawyer, true proceeder;
Thou movest salvation even for alms,
Not with a bribed lawyer's palms.

And this is my eternal plea
To him that made heaven, earth, and sea:
Seeing my flesh must die so soon,
And want a head to dine next noon,
Just at the stroke when my veins start and spread,
Set on my soul an everlasting head.
Then am I ready, like a palmer fit,
To tread those blest paths which before I writ.

A. Scoloker, *Daiphantus*, 1604

279 *All the World's a Stage*

WHAT is our life? A play of passion,
Our mirth the music of division.
Our mothers' wombs the tiring-houses be,
Where we are dressed for this short comedy.
Heaven the judicious sharp spectator is,
That sits and marks still who doth act amiss.
Our graves that hide us from the searching sun
Are like drawn curtains when the play is done.
Thus march we, playing, to our latest rest,
Only we die in earnest, that 's no jest.

O. Gibbons, *Madrigals and Mottets*, 1612

SIR WALTER RALEGH

280 *Epitaph*

EVEN such is Time, which takes in trust
Our youth, our joys, and all we have,
And pays us but with age and dust;
Who in the dark and silent grave,
When we have wandered all our ways,
Shuts up the story of our days:
And from which earth, and grave, and dust,
The Lord shall raise me up, I trust.

The Prerogative of Parliaments in England, 1628

ANONYMOUS

281 *His Lady's Might*

THOSE eyes which set my fancy on a fire,
Those crisped hairs which hold my heart in chains,
Those dainty hands which conquered my desire,
That wit which of my thoughts doth hold the reins!
Those eyes, for clearness do the stars surpass,
Those hairs, obscure the brightness of the sun,
Those hands more white than ever ivory was,
That wit, even to the skies hath glory won!
O eyes that pierce our hearts without remorse,
O hairs of right that wear a royal crown,
O hands that conquer more than Caesar's force,
O wit that turns huge kingdoms upside down!
Then Love be judge, what heart may thee withstand,
Such eyes, such hair, such wit, and such a hand.

The Phoenix Nest, 1593

282 *Love's Ending*

SOUGHT by the world, and hath the world disdained,
  Is she, my heart, for whom thou dost endure;
Unto whose grace sith kings have not obtained,
  Sweet is thy choice, though loss of life be sour;
    Yet to the man, whose youth such pains must prove,
    No better end than that which comes by love.

Steer then thy course unto the port of death,
  (Sith thy hard hap no better hap may find,)
Where, when thou shalt unlade thy latest breath,
  Envy herself shall swim, to save thy mind;
    Whose body sunk in search to gain that shore
    Where many a prince had perished before.

And yet, my heart, it might have been foreseen,
  Sith skilful medicines mend each kind of grief;
Then in my breast full safely hadst thou been.
  But thou, my heart, wouldst never me believe,
    Who told thee true when first thou didst aspire,
    Death was the end of every such desire.

Ibid.

283 *The Last Trial*

SET me where Phoebus' heat the flowers slayeth,
  Or where continual snow withstands his forces;
Set me where he his temperate rays displayeth,
  Or where he comes, or where he never courses.
Set me in Fortune's grace, or else discharged,
  In sweet and pleasant air, or dark and glooming,
Where days and nights are lesser, or enlarged,
  In years of strength, in failing age, or blooming.
Set me in heaven, or earth, or in the centre,
  Low in a vale, or on a mountain placed;
Set me to danger, peril, and adventure,
  Graced by fame, or infamy disgraced.
    Set me to these, or any other trial,
    Except my Mistress' anger and denial.

The Phoenix Nest, 1593

284 *Resignation*

THE firmament, with golden stars adorned,
  The sailor's watchful eyes full well contenteth,
And afterward, with tempest overspread,
  The absent lights of heaven he sore lamenteth.
Your face, the firmament of my repose,
  Long time has kept my waking thoughts delighted,
But now the cloud of sorrow overgoes
  Your glorious skies, wherewith I am affrighted.
For I that have my life and fortunes placed
  Within the ship, that by those planets saileth,
By envious chance am overmuch disgraced,
  Seeing the lodestar of my courses faileth:
    And yet content to drown, without repining,
    To have my stars afford the world their shining.

Ibid.

285 *A Night-Piece*

O NIGHT, O jealous night, repugnant to my pleasures,
O night so long desired, yet cross to my content,
There 's none but only thou that can perform my pleasures,
Yet none but only thou that hindereth my intent.

Thy beams, thy spiteful beams, thy lamps that burn too brightly,
Discover all my trains, and naked lay my drifts;
That night by night I hope, yet fail my purpose nightly,
Thy envious glaring gleam defeateth so my shifts.

Sweet night, withhold thy beams, withhold them till to-morrow,
Whose joys, in lack so long, a hell of torments breeds;
Sweet night, sweet gentle night, do not prolong my sorrow;
Desire is guide to me, and love no lodestar needs.

Let sailors gaze on stars and moon so freshly shining,
Let them that miss the way be guided by the light;
I know my lady's bower, there needs no more divining;
Affection sees in dark, and love hath eyes by night.

Dame Cynthia, couch awhile, hold in thy horns for shining,
And glad not louring night with thy too glorious rays;
But be she dim and dark, tempestuous and repining,
That in her spite my sport may work thy endless praise.

And when my will is wrought, then, Cynthia, shine, good lady,
All other nights and days in honour of that night,
That happy, heavenly night, that night so dark and shady,
Wherein my love had eyes that lighted my delight.

Ibid.

286 *Violets and Roses*

SWEET violets, Love's paradise, that spread
Your gracious odours, which you couched bear
Within your paly faces,
Upon the gentle wing of some calm breathing wind,
That plays amidst the plain,
If by the favour of propitious stars you gain
Such grace as in my lady's bosom place to find,
Be proud to touch those places;
And when her warmth your moisture forth doth wear,
Whereby her dainty parts are sweetly fed,
Your honours of the flowery meads, I pray,
You pretty daughters of the earth and sun,
With mild and seemly breathing straight display
My bitter sighs that have my heart undone.

Vermilion roses, that with new day's rise
Display your crimson folds fresh looking fair,
Whose radiant bright disgraces
The rich adorned rays of roseate rising morn,
Ah! if her virgin's hand
Do pluck your pure, ere Phoebus view the land
And vail your gracious pomp in lovely nature's scorn,
If chance my mistress traces
Fast by your flowers to take the summer's air,
Then, woeful blushing, tempt her glorious eyes
To spread their tears, Adonis' death reporting,
And tell Love's torments, sorrowing for her friend,

vail] bring down

Whose drops of blood within your leaves consorting
Report fair Venus' moans withouten end.
Then may remorse, in pitying of my smart,
Dry up my tears, and dwell within her heart.

The Phoenix Nest, 1593

287 *Epigram*

BEAUTY, a silver dew that falls in May;
Love is an egg-shell, with that humour filled;
Desire, a winged boy, coming that way,
Delights and dallies with it in the field.
The fiery sun draws up the shell on high;
Beauty decays, Love dies, Desire doth fly.

Ibid.

288 *Songs set by Thomas Morley*

(*i*)

APRIL is in my mistress' face,
And July in her eyes hath place,
Within her bosom is September,
But in her heart a cold December.

(*ii*)

SHOOT, false Love, I care not.
Spend thy shafts and spare not.
I fear not, I, thy might,
And less I weigh thy spite.
If thou canst, now shoot and harm me.
So lightly I esteem thee,
As now a child I deem thee.

Long thy bow did fear me,
While thy pomp did blear me.
But now I do perceive
Thy art is to deceive;
And every simple lover
All thy falsehood can discover.
Then weep, Love, and be sorry,
For thou hast lost thy glory.

(*iii*)

NOW is the month of maying,
When merry lads are playing
Each with his bonny lass
Upon the greeny grass.

The Spring, clad all in gladness,
Doth laugh at Winter's sadness,
And to the bag-pipe's sound
The nymphs tread out their ground.

Fie then! why sit we musing,
Youth's sweet delight refusing?
Say, dainty nymphs, and speak,
Shall we play barley-break?

(*iv*)

SING we and chant it,
While love doth grant it.
Not long youth lasteth,
And old age hasteth.
Now is best leisure
To take our pleasure.

barley-break] prisoner's base

ANONYMOUS

All things invite us
Now to delight us.
Hence, care, be packing,
No mirth be lacking.
Let spare no treasure
To live in pleasure.

Madrigals, 1594; *Ballets*, 1595

SIR JOHN HARINGTON

1561–1612

289 *Angelica and the Ork*

NOW while Rogero learns the arms and name
Of every British lord, behold a rout
Of citizens and folk of all sorts came,
Some with delight, and some with dread and doubt,
To see a beast so strange, so strong, so tame,
And wondering much they compassed him about.
They thought it was a strange and monstrous thing,
To see a horse that had a griffon's wing.

Wherefore, to make the people marvel more,
And, as it were, to sport himself and play,
He spurred his beast, who straight aloft did soar,
And bare his master westward quite away;
And straight he was beyond our English shore,
Meaning to pass the Irish seas that day;
Saint George his Channel in a little while
He passed, and after saw the Irish isle.

Where men do tell strange tales, that long ago
  Saint Patrick built a solitary cave,
Into the which they that devoutly go,
  By purging of their sins their souls may save;
Now whether this report be true or no,
  I not affirm, and yet I not deprave.
    Crossing from hence to islandward he found
    Angelica unto the rock fast bound;

Naked and bound at this same Isle of Woe,
  For Isle of Woe it may be justly called,
Where peerless pieces are abused so,
  By monster vile to be devoured and thralled;
Where pirates still by land and sea do go,
  Assaulting forts that are but weakly walled;
    And whom they take by flattery or by force,
    They give a monster quite without remorse.

I did declare, not many books before,
  If you the same in memory do keep,
How certain pirates took her at a shore,
  Where the chaste hermit lay by her asleep;
And how at last, for want of other store,
  Although their hearts did melt and eyes did weep,
    Moved with a helpless and a vain compassion,
    Perforce they bound her on this woeful fashion.

And thus the caitiffs left her all forlorn,
  With nothing but the rocks and seas in sight,
As naked as of nature she was born,
  Void of all succour and all comfort quite.

No veil of lawn as then by her was worn,
  To shade the damask rose and lilies white,
    Whose colours were so mixed in every member,
    Fragrant alike in July and December.

Rogero at the first had surely thought,
  She was some image made of alablaster,
Or of white marble, curiously wrought,
  To show the skilful hand of some great master.
But viewing nearer he was quickly taught,
  She had some parts that were not made of plaster;
    Both that her eyes did shed such woeful tears,
    And that the wind did wave her golden hairs.

To see her bound, to hear her mourn and plain,
  Not only made that he his journey stayed,
But caused that he from tears could scant abstain,
  Pity and love his heart so sore assayed.
At last, with words to mitigate her pain,
  Thus much to her in loving sort he said:
    'O lady, worthy only of those bands,
    Wherewith love binds the hearts and not the hands,

'And far unfit for these or any such,
  What wight was found so cruel and unkind,
Quite to expel humanity so much,
  Those polished ivory hands in chains to bind;
About that corps, whom none can worthily touch,
  With hurtful hands unworthy bands to wind?'
    This said, she blushed, seeing those parts were spied,
    The which, though fair, yet nature strives to hide.

Fain would she with her hand have hid her eyes,
  But that her hands were bound unto the stone;
Which made her oft to break to woeful cries,
  Sole remedy where remedy is none.
At last with sobbing voice she doth devise
  To tell the knight the cause of all her moan;
    But from the sea a sudden noise was heard,
    That this her speech and all the matter marred.

Behold, there now appeared the monster great,
  Half underneath and half above the wave,
As when a ship, with wind and weather beat,
  Doth hasten to the haven, itself to save.
So doth the monster haste, in hope to eat
  The dainty morsel he was wont to have;
    Which sight so sore the damsel did appal,
    Rogero could not comfort her at all.

Yet with his spear in hand, though not in rest,
  The ugly Ork upon the brow he strake.
(I call him Ork, because I know no beast,
  Nor fish, from whence comparison to take).
His head and teeth were like a boar, the rest
  A mass, of which I know not what to make.
    He gave him on the brow a mighty knock,
    But pierced no more, than if it were a rock.

And, finding that his blow so small hurt brings,
  He turns again, on fresh him to assay:
The Ork, that saw the shadow of great wings
  Upon the water up and down to play,

With fury great and rage away he flings,
  And on the shore doth leave the certain prey;
    The shadow vain he up and down doth chase,
    The while Rogero layeth him on apace.

Even as an eagle, that espies from high
  Among the herbs a parti-coloured snake,
Or on a bank sunning herself to lie,
  Casting the elder skin, a new to make,
Lies hovering warily, till she may spy
  A vantage sure, the venomed worm to take;
    Then takes him by the back, and beats her wings,
    Maugre the poison of his forked stings:

So doth Rogero, both with sword and spear,
  The cruel monster warily assail,
Not where he fenced is with grisly hair,
  So hard as that no weapon could prevail;
But sometime pricks him near unto his ear,
  Sometime his sides, sometimes his ugly tail.
    But nature had with such strong senses armed him,
    As all his blows but small or nothing harmed him.

So have I seen, ere this, a silly fly
  With mastiff dog in summer's heat to play,
Sometime to sting him in his nose or eye,
  Sometime about his grisly jaws to stay,
And buzzing round about his ears to fly:
  He snaps in vain, for still she whips away,
    And oft so long she dallies in this sort,
    Till one snap comes, and marreth all her sport.

But now Rogero doth this sleight devise:
   Sith that by force he cannot make him yield,
He means to dazzle both the monster's eyes,
   By hidden force of his enchanted shield;
And, being thus resolved, to land he flies,
   And, from all harm the lady fair to shield,
      He puts the precious ring upon her hand,
      Whose virtue was enchantments to withstand.

That ring that worthy Bradamant him sent,
   When she from false Brunello had it ta'en,
With which Melissa into India went,
   And wrought his freedom and Alcina's bane;
That ring he lends the damsel, with intent
   To save her eyes by virtue of the same:
      Then takes he forth the shield, whose light so dazed
      The lookers-on, they fall down all amazed.

The monster, now approaching to the shore,
   Amazed at this, resistance none did make:
Rogero hews upon him more and more,
   But his hard scales no harm thereby did take.
'O Sir,' said she, 'unloosen me, before
   Out of this maze the monster do awake,
      And let your sword slay me this present hour,
      So as this monster may not me devour.'

These woeful words moved so Rogero's mind,
   That straight he did unloose the lady fair,
And caused her by and by to get behind
   Upon his horse; then mounting in the air,

He leaves his Spanish journey first assigned,
And unto Little Britain doth repair;
But by the way be sure he did not miss
To give her many a sweet and friendly kiss.

Orlando Furioso, in English Heroical Verse, x. 76–95, 1591

SAMUEL DANIEL

c. 1563–1619

290 *Sonnets to Delia*

(*i*)

UNTO the boundless ocean of thy beauty
Runs this poor river, charged with streams of zeal,
Returning thee the tribute of my duty,
Which here my love, my youth, my plaints reveal.
Here I unclasp the book of my charged soul,
Where I have cast th'accounts of all my care;
Here have I summed my sighs, here I enroll
How they were spent for thee; look what they are.
Look on the dear expenses of my youth,
And see how just I reckon with thine eyes;
Examine well thy beauty with my truth,
And cross my cares, ere greater sums arise.
Read it, sweet maid, though it be done but slightly;
Who can show all his love, doth love but lightly.

(ii)

THESE plaintive verse, the posts of my desire,
  Which haste for succour to her slow regard,
Bear not report of any slender fire,
  Forging a grief to win a fame's reward.
Nor are my passions limned for outward hue,
  For that no colours can depaint my sorrows;
Delia herself, and all the world, may view
  Best in my face where cares have till'd deep furrows.
No bays I seek to deck my mourning brow,
  O clear-eyed Rector of the holy hill!
My humble accents bear the olive bough
  Of intercession, but to move her will.
    These lines I use to unburden mine own heart;
    My love affects no fame, nor 'steems of art.

(iii)

FAIR is my Love, and cruel as she 's fair
  Her brow shades frowns, although her eyes are sunny;
Her smiles are lightning, though her pride despair;
  And her disdains are gall, her favours honey.
A modest maid, decked with a blush of honour,
  Whose feet do tread green paths of youth and love,
The wonder of all eyes that look upon her,
  Sacred on earth, designed a saint above!
Chastity and Beauty, which were deadly foes,
  Live reconciled friends within her brow;
And had she Pity to conjoin with those,
  Then who had heard the plaints I utter now?
    For had she not been fair, and thus unkind,
    My Muse had slept, and none had known my mind.

(*iv*)

IF this be love, to draw a weary breath,
  To paint on floods till the shore cry to th'air;
With downward looks, still reading on the earth
  The sad memorials of my love's despair:
If this be love, to war against my soul,
  Lie down to wail, rise up to sigh and grieve,
The never-resting stone of care to roll,
  Still to complain my griefs whilst none relieve:
If this be love, to clothe me with dark thoughts,
  Haunting untrodden paths to wail apart;
My pleasures horror, music tragic notes,
  Tears in mine eyes and sorrow at my heart.
    If this be love, to live a living death,
    Then do I love and draw this weary breath.

(*v*)

MY spotless love hovers with purest wings
  About the temple of the proudest frame;
Where blaze those lights, fairest of earthly things,
  Which clear our clouded world with brightest flame.
My ambitious thoughts, confined in her face,
  Affect no honour, but what she can give;
My hopes do rest in limits of her grace;
  I weigh no comfort unless she relieve.
For she that can my heart imparadise
  Holds in her fairest hand what dearest is;
My fortune's wheel's the circle of her eyes,
  Whose rolling grace deign once a turn of bliss!
    All my life's sweet consists in her alone,
    So much I love the most unloving one.

(*vi*)

TIME, cruel Time, come and subdue that brow,
  Which conquers all but thee; and thee too stays,
As if she were exempt from scythe or bow,
  From love or years, unsubject to decays.
Or art thou grown in league with those fair eyes,
  That they may help thee to consume our days?
Or dost thou spare her for her cruelties,
  Being merciless like thee, that no man weighs?
And yet thou see'st thy power she disobeys;
  Cares not for thee, but lets thee waste in vain;
And prodigal of hours and years betrays
  Beauty and Youth to Opinion and Disdain.
    Yet spare her, Time, let her exempted be;
    She may become more kind to thee or me.

(*vii*)

THE star of my mishap imposed this pain,
  To spend the April of my years in grief,
Finding my fortune ever in the wane,
  With still fresh cares, supplied with no relief.
Yet thee I blame not, though for thee 'tis done,
  But these weak wings presuming to aspire,
Which now are melted by thine eyes' bright sun,
  That makes me fall off from my high desire;
And in my fall I cry for help with speed,
  No pitying eye looks back upon my fears,
No succour find I now when most I need,
  My heats must drown in th' ocean of my tears;
    Which still must bear the title of my wrong,
    Caused by those cruel beams that were so strong.

(viii)

LOOK, Delia, how we esteem the half-blown rose,
  The image of thy blush, and summer's honour!
Whilst yet her tender bud doth undisclose
  That full of beauty Time bestows upon her.
No sooner spreads her glory in the air
  But straight her wide-blown pomp comes to decline;
She then is scorn'd that late adorned the fair;
  So fade the roses of those cheeks of thine.
No April can revive thy withered flowers,
  Whose springing grace adorns thy glory now;
Swift, speedy Time, feathered with flying hours,
  Dissolves the beauty of the fairest brow.
    Then do not thou such treasure waste in vain,
    But love now, whilst thou mayst be loved again.

(ix)

BUT love whilst that thou mayst be loved again,
  Now whilst thy May hath filled thy lap with flowers,
Now whilst thy beauty bears without a stain;
  Now use the summer smiles ere winter lours.
And whilst thou spread'st unto the rising sun
  The fairest flower that ever saw the light,
Now joy thy time before thy sweet be done:
  And, Delia, think thy morning must have night,
And that thy brightness sets at length to west,
  When thou wilt close up that which now thou show'st;
And think the same becomes thy fading best,
  Which then shall most enveil and shadow most.
    Men do not weigh the stalk for that it was,
    When once they find her flower, her glory, pass.

(*x*)

WHEN men shall find thy flower, thy glory, pass,
  And thou with careful brow sitting alone
Received hast this message from thy glass,
  That tells the truth and says that all is gone,
Fresh shalt thou see in me the wounds thou madest,
  Though spent thy flame, in me the heat remaining;
I that have loved thee thus before thou fadest,
  My faith shall wax, when thou art in thy waning.
The world shall find this miracle in me,
  That fire can burn when all the matter 's spent;
Then what my faith hath been thyself shalt see,
  And that thou wast unkind thou mayst repent.
    Thou mayst repent that thou hast scorned my tears,
    When winter snows upon thy sable hairs.

(*xi*)

WHEN winter snows upon thy sable hairs,
  And frost of age hath nipped thy beauties near;
When dark shall seem thy day that never clears,
  And all lies withered that was held so dear;
Then take this picture which I here present thee,
  Limned with a pencil not all unworthy;
Here see the gifts that God and Nature lent thee;
  Here read thyself, and what I suffered for thee.
This may remain thy lasting monument,
  Which happily posterity may cherish;
These colours with thy fading are not spent;
  These may remain when thou and I shall perish.
    If they remain, then thou shalt live thereby;
    They will remain, and so thou canst not die.

(xii)

THOU canst not die whilst any zeal abound
  In feeling hearts that can conceive these lines;
Though thou, a Laura, hast no Petrarch found,
  In base attire yet clearly beauty shines.
And I, though born within a colder clime,
  Do feel mine inward heat as great (I know it);
He never had more faith, although more rhyme;
  I love as well, though he could better show it.
But I may add one feather to thy fame,
  To help her flight throughout the fairest isle,
And if my pen could more enlarge thy name,
  Then shouldst thou live in an immortal style.
    For though that Laura better limned be,
    Suffice, thou shalt be loved as well as she.

(xiii)

BEAUTY, sweet Love, is like the morning dew,
  Whose short refresh upon the tender green
Cheers for a time, but till the sun doth shew,
  And straight 'tis gone as it had never been.
Soon doth it fade that makes the fairest flourish;
  Short is the glory of the blushing rose,
The hue which thou so carefully dost nourish,
  Yet which at length thou must be forced to lose.
When thou, surcharged with burden of thy years,
  Shalt bend thy wrinkles homeward to the earth,
And that in beauty's lease expired appears
  The date of age, the calends of our death—
    But ah! no more; this must not be foretold,
    For women grieve to think they must be old.

(*xiv*)

CARE-charmer Sleep, son of the sable Night,
  Brother to Death, in silent darkness born,
Relieve my languish, and restore the light,
  With dark forgetting of my cares return.
And let the day be time enough to mourn
  The shipwreck of my ill-adventured youth;
Let waking eyes suffice to wail their scorn,
  Without the torment of the night's untruth.
Cease, dreams, the images of day-desires,
  To model forth the passions of the morrow;
Never let rising sun approve you liars,
  To add more grief to aggravate my sorrow.
    Still let me sleep, embracing clouds in vain;
    And never wake to feel the day's disdain.

(*xv*)

LET others sing of knights and paladins
  In aged accents and untimely words;
Paint shadows in imaginary lines,
  Which well the reach of their high wits records:
But I must sing of thee, and those fair eyes
  Authentic shall my verse in time to come;
When yet th'unborn shall say, 'Lo where she lies,
  Whose beauty made him speak that else was dumb.'
These are the arks, the trophies I erect,
  That fortify thy name against old age;
And these thy sacred virtues must protect
  Against the dark, and Time's consuming rage.
    Though th'error of my youth in them appear,
    Suffice they shew I lived and loved thee dear.

(*xvi*)

MY cares draw on mine everlasting night,
  In horror's sable clouds sets my life's sun;
My life's sweet sun, my dearest comfort's light,
  Will rise no more to me whose day is done.
I go before unto the myrtle shades,
  To attend the presence of my world's dear;
And there prepare her flowers that never fades,
  And all things fit against her coming there.
If any ask me why so soon I came,
  I'll hide her sin and say it was my lot;
In life and death I'll tender her good name;
  My life nor death shall never be her blot.
    Although this world may seem her deed to blame,
    The Elysian ghosts shall never know the same.

Delia, 1592, 1594

291 *Ode*

NOW each creature joys the other,
  Passing happy days and hours;
One bird reports unto another
  In the fall of silver showers;
Whilst the earth, our common mother,
  Hath her bosom decked with flowers.

Whilst the greatest torch of heaven
  With bright rays warms Flora's lap,
Making nights and days both even,
  Cheering plants with fresher sap;
My field, of flowers quite bereaven,
  Wants refresh of better hap.

Echo, daughter of the Air,
   Babbling guest of rocks and hills,
Knows the name of my fierce Fair,
   And sounds the accents of my ills.
Each thing pities my despair,
   Whilst that she her lover kills.

Whilst that she, O cruel maid,
   Doth me and my love despise,
My life's flourish is decayed
   That depended on her eyes:
But her will must be obeyed,
   And well he ends for love who dies.

Delia, 1592

292 *Rosamond's Appeal*

'OUT from the horror of infernal deeps
   My poor afflicted ghost comes here to plain it,
Attended with my shame that never sleeps,
The spot wherewith my kind and youth did stain it;
My body found a grave where to contain it:
   A sheet could hide my face, but not my sin,
   For fame finds never tomb t' inclose it in.

'And which is worse, my soul is now denied
Her transport to the sweet Elysian rest,
The joyful bliss for ghosts repurified,
The ever-springing gardens of the blest:
Charon denies me waftage with the rest,
   And says my soul can never pass the river,
   Till lovers' sighs on earth shall it deliver.

'So shall I never pass; for how should I
Procure this sacrifice amongst the living?
Time hath long since worn out the memory
Both of my life and life's unjust depriving;
Sorrow for me is dead, for aye reviving.
  Rosamond hath little left her but her name,
  And that disgraced, for time hath wronged the same.

'No Muse suggests the pity of my case;
Each pen doth overpass my just complaint,
Whilst others are preferred, though far more base;
Shore's wife is graced, and passes for a saint;
Her legend justifies her foul attaint;
  Her well-told tale did such compassion find,
  That she is passed, and I am left behind.

'Which seen with grief, my miserable ghost
(Whilom invested in so fair a veil,
Which whilst it lived was honoured of the most,
And being dead, gives matter to bewail)
Comes to solicit thee, since others fail,
  To take this task and in thy woeful song
  To form my case and register my wrong.

'Although I know thy just lamenting Muse,
Toiled in th' affliction of thine own distress,
In others' cares hath little time to use,
And therefore mayst esteem of mine the less;
Yet as thy hopes attend happy redress,
  The joys depending on a woman's grace,
  So move thy mind a woeful woman's case.

'Delia may hap to deign to read our story,
And offer up her sigh among the rest,
Whose merit would suffice for both our glory,
Whereby thou mightst be graced and I be blest;
That indulgence would profit me the best.
  Such power she hath, by whom thy youth is led,
  To joy the living and to bless the dead.

'So I, through beauty made the woeful'st wight,
By beauty might have comfort after death;
That dying fairest by the fairest might
Find life above on earth, and rest beneath.
She that can bless us with one happy breath
  Give comfort to thy Muse to do her best,
  That thereby thou mayst joy and I might rest.'

Thus said: forthwith moved with a tender care
And pity, which myself could never find,
What she desired my Muse deigned to declare,
And therefore willed her boldly tell her mind.
And I more willing took this charge assigned,
  Because her griefs were worthy to be known,
  And telling hers, might hap forget mine own.

Complaint of Rosamond, 1592

293 *Lonely Beauty*

WHAT greater torment ever could have been,
  Than to enforce the fair to live retired?
For what is beauty if it be not seen?
Or what is 't to be seen, unless admired,
And though admired, unless in love desired?
  Never were cheeks of roses, locks of amber,
  Ordained to live imprisoned in a chamber.

SAMUEL DANIEL

Nature created beauty for the view,
Like as the fire for heat, the sun for light;
The fair do hold this privilege as due
By ancient charter, to live most in sight,
And she, that is debarred it, hath not right.
  In vain our friends from this do us dehort,
  For beauty will be where is most resort.

Witness the fairest streets that Thames doth visit,
The wondrous concourse of the glittering fair;
For what rare woman decked with beauty is it,
That thither covets not to make repair?
The solitary country may not stay her;
  Here is the centre of all beauty's best,
  Excepting Delia, left to adorn the west.

Here doth the curious with judicial eyes
Contemplate beauty gloriously attired;
And herein all our chiefest glory lies,
To live where we are praised and most desired.
O! how we joy to see ourselves admired,
  Whilst niggardly our favours we discover;
  We love to be beloved, yet scorn the lover.

Yet would to God my foot had never moved
From country safety, from the fields of rest,
To know the danger to be highly loved,
And live in pomp to brave among the best;
Happy for me, better had I been blest,
  If I unluckily had never strayed,
  But lived at home a happy country maid:

Whose unaffected innocency thinks
No guileful fraud, as doth the courtly liver;
She 's decked with truth; the river where she drinks
Doth serve her for her glass, her counsel-giver;
She loves sincerely, and is loved ever.
  Her days are peace, and so she ends her breath;
  True life, that knows not what 's to die till death!

So should I never have been registered
In the black book of the unfortunate;
Nor had my name enrolled with maids misled,
Which bought their pleasures at so high a rate;
Nor had I taught, through my unhappy fate,
  This lesson, which myself learnt with expense,
  How most it hurts that most delights the sense.

The Complaint of Rosamond, 1592

294 *Henry's Lament*

PITIFUL mouth, saith he, that living gavest
  The sweetest comfort that my soul could wish,
O! be it lawful now, that dead thou havest
This sorrowing farewell of a dying kiss;
And you, fair eyes, containers of my bliss,
  Motives of love, born to be matched never,
  Entombed in your sweet circles, sleep for ever.

SAMUEL DANIEL

Ah, how methinks I see death dallying seeks
To entertain itself in love's sweet place;
Decayed roses of discoloured cheeks
Do yet retain dear notes of former grace;
And ugly death sits fair within her face,
  Sweet remnants resting of vermilion red,
  That death itself doubts whether she be dead.

Wonder of beauty, O! receive these plaints,
These obsequies, the last that I shall make thee;
For lo! my soul that now already faints
(That loved thee living, dead will not forsake thee)
Hastens her speedy course to overtake thee.
  I'll meet my death, and free myself thereby,
  For, ah! what can he do that cannot die?

Yet ere I die, this much my soul doth vow,
Revenge shall sweeten death with ease of mind;
And I will cause posterity shall know
How fair thou wert above all women-kind,
And after ages monuments shall find
  Showing thy beauty's title, not thy name,
  Rose of the world, that sweetened so the same.

The Complaint of Rosamond, 1592

295

Chorus

THEN thus we have beheld
Th' accomplishment of woes,
The full of ruin and
The worst of worst of ills;
And seen all hope expelled,
That ever sweet repose
Shall repossess the land
That Desolation fills,
And where Ambition spills
With uncontrolled hand
All th' issue of all those
That so long rule have held;
To make us no more us,
But clean confound us thus.

And canst, O Nilus, thou,
Father of floods, endure
That yellow Tiber should
With sandy streams rule thee?
Wilt thou be pleased to bow
To him those feet so pure,
Whose unknown head we hold
A power divine to be?
Thou that didst ever see
Thy free banks uncontrolled,
Live under thine own cure;
Ah! wilt thou bear it now?
And now wilt yield thy streams
A prey to other realms?

Draw back thy waters' flow
To thy concealed head;
Rocks strangle up thy waves,
Stop cataracts thy fall,
And turn thy courses so
That sandy deserts dead
(The world of dust that craves
To swallow thee up all)
May drink so much as shall
Revive from vasty graves
A living green, which spread
Far flourishing may grow
On that wide face of death,
Where nothing now draws breath.

Fatten some people there,
Even as thou us hast done,
With plenty's wanton store,
And feeble luxury;
And them as us prepare
Fit for the day of moan,
Respected not before.
Leave levelled Egypt dry,
A barren prey to lie,
Wasted for evermore;
Of plenties yielding none
To recompense the care
Of victors' greedy lust,
And bring forth nought but dust.

And so, O! leave to be,
Sith thou art what thou art;
Let not our race possess
Th' inheritance of shame,
The fee of sin, that we
Have left them for their part;
The yoke of whose distress
Must still upbraid our blame,
Telling from whom it came.
Our weight of wantonness
Lies heavy on their heart,
Who nevermore shall see
The glory of that worth
They left, who brought us forth.

O! then, all-seeing Light,
High president of heaven,
You magistrates, the Stars,
Of that eternal court
Of Providence and Right,
Are these the bounds ye have given,
Th' untranspassable bars
That limit pride so short?
Is greatness of this sort,
That greatness greatness mars,
And wracks itself, self-driven
On rocks of her own might?
Doth Order order so
Disorder's overthrow?

Cleopatra, 1594

296 *Poet and Critic*

Philocosmus.

FOND man, Musophilus, that thus dost spend
In an ungainful art thy dearest days,
Tiring thy wits and toiling to no end,
But to attain that idle smoke of praise;
Now when this busy world cannot attend
Th' untimely music of neglected lays.
Other delights than these, other desires,
This wiser profit-seeking age requires.

Musophilus.

Friend Philocosmus, I confess indeed
I love this sacred art thou set'st so light,
And though it never stand my life in stead,
It is enough it gives myself delight,
The whiles my unafflicted mind doth feed
On no unholy thoughts for benefit.

Be it that my unseasonable song
Come out of time, that fault is in the time,
And I must not do virtue so much wrong
As love her aught the worse for others' crime;
And yet I find some blessed spirits among
That cherish me, and like and grace my rhyme.

A gain, that I do more in soul esteem,
Than all the gain of dust the world doth crave;
And if I may attain but to redeem
My name from dissolution and the grave,
I shall have done enough, and better deem
T' have lived to be, than to have died to have.

Short-breathed mortality would yet extend
  That span of life so far forth as it may,
And rob her fate, seek to beguile her end
  Of some few lingering days of after stay,
That all this little all might not descend
  Into the dark a universal prey.

And give our labours yet this poor delight,
  That when our days do end they are not done;
And though we die, we shall not perish quite,
  But live two lives, where others have but one.

Philocosmus.

Silly desires of self-abusing man,
  Striving to gain th'inheritance of air,
That, having done the uttermost he can,
  Leaves yet, perhaps, but beggary to his heir.
All that great purchase of the breath he wan
  Feeds not his race or makes his house more fair.

And what art thou the better, thus to leave
  A multitude of words to small effect,
Which other times may scorn, and so deceive
  Thy promised name of what thou dost expect?
Besides, some viperous critic may bereave
  Th'opinion of thy worth for some defect,

And get more reputation of his wit,
  By but controlling of some word or sense,
Than thou shalt honour for contriving it,
  With all thy travail, care, and diligence;
Being learned now enough to contradict
  And censure others with bold insolence.

Besides, so many so confusedly sing,
  As diverse discords have the music marred,
And in contempt that mystery doth bring,
  That he must sing aloud that will be heard;
And the received opinion of the thing,
  For some unhallowed strings that vildly jarred,

Hath so unseasoned now the ears of men,
  That who doth touch the tenour of that vein
Is held but vain, and his unreckoned pen
  The title but of levity doth gain.
A poor, light gain, to recompense their toil,
  That thought to get eternity the while.

And therefore, leave the left and outworn course
  Of unregarded ways, and labour how
To fit the times with what is most in force;
  Be new with men's affections that are now;
Strive not to run an idle counter-course
  Out from the scent of humours men allow.

For not discreetly to compose our parts
  Unto the frame of men, which we must be,
Is to put off ourselves, and make our arts
  Rebels to times and to society;
Whereby we come to bury our deserts
  In th' obscure grave of singularity.

Musophilus: Poetical Essays, 1599

297 *English Poetry*

POWER above powers, O heavenly Eloquence,
  That with the strong rein of commanding words
Dost manage, guide, and master th' eminence
  Of men's affections, more than all their swords,
Shall we not offer to thy excellence
  The richest treasure that our wit affords?

Thou that canst do much more with one poor pen,
  Than all the powers of princes can effect;
And draw, divert, dispose and fashion men,
  Better than force or rigour can direct!
Should we this ornament of glory then,
  As th' unmaterial fruits of shades, neglect?

Or should we careless come behind the rest
  In power of words, that go before in worth;
When as our accent's equal to the best,
  Is able greater wonders to bring forth?
When all that ever hotter spirits expressed
  Comes better'd by the patience of the north.

And who, in time, knows whither we may vent
  The treasure of our tongue, to what strange shores
This gain of our best glory shall be sent,
  T' enrich unknowing nations with our stores?
What worlds in th' yet unformed Occident
  May come refined with th' accents that are ours?

Or who can tell for what great work in hand
  The greatness of our style is now ordained?
What powers it shall bring in, what spirits command?
  What thoughts let out, what humours keep restrained?
What mischief it may powerfully withstand;
  And what fair ends may thereby be attained?

And as for Poesy, mother of this force,
  That breeds, brings forth, and nourishes this might,
Teaching it in a loose, yet measured course,
  With comely motions how to go upright;
And fostering it with bountiful discourse,
  Adorns it thus in fashions of delight:

What should I say? since it is well approved
  The speech of Heaven, with whom they have commerce,
That only seem out of themselves removed,
  And do with more than human skills converse:
Those numbers, wherewith Heaven and Earth are moved,
  Show weakness speaks in prose, but power in verse.

Musophilus, 1599

298 *A Pastoral of Tasso*

O HAPPY, golden age!
Not for that rivers ran
With streams of milk, and honey dropped from trees;
Not that the earth did gage
Unto the husbandman
Her voluntary fruits, free without fees;
Not for no cold did freeze,
Nor any cloud beguile
Th' eternal flowering spring,

Wherein lived every thing,
And whereon th' heavens perpetually did smile;
Not for no ship had brought
From foreign shores or wars or wares ill sought.

But only for that name,
That idle name of wind,
That idol of deceit, that empty sound,
Called Honour, which became
The tyrant of the mind,
And so torments our nature without ground,
Was not yet vainly found;
Nor yet sad griefs imparts
Amidst the sweet delights
Of joyful, amorous wights;
Nor were his hard laws known to free-born hearts;
But golden laws like these
Which Nature wrote: 'That's lawful, which doth please.'

Then amongst flowers and springs,
Making delightful sport,
Sat lovers without conflict, without flame;
And nymphs and shepherds sings,
Mixing in wanton sort
Whisperings with songs, then kisses with the same,
Which from affection came.
The naked virgin then
Her roses fresh reveals,
Which now her veil conceals,
The tender apples in her bosom seen;
And oft in rivers clear
The lovers with their loves consorting were.

SAMUEL DANIEL

Honour, thou first didst close
The spring of all delight,
Denying water to the amorous thirst;
Thou taught'st fair eyes to lose
The glory of their light,
Restrained from men, and on themselves reversed.
Thou in a lawn didst first
Those golden hairs incase,
Late spread unto the wind;
Thou madest loose grace unkind;
Gavest bridle to their words, art to their pace.
O Honour, it is thou
That makest that stealth, which Love doth free allow.

It is thy work that brings
Our griefs and torments thus.
But thou, fierce lord of Nature and of Love,
The qualifier of kings;
What dost thou here with us,
That are below thy power, shut from above?
Go, and from us remove;
Trouble the mighty's sleep;
Let us neglected, base,
Live still without thy grace,
And th' use of th' ancient happy ages keep.
Let's love; this life of ours
Can make no truce with Time that all devours.
Let's love; the sun doth set, and rise again;
But when as our short light
Comes once to set, it makes eternal night.

Works, 1601

299 *To Sir Thomas Egerton*

WELL hath the powerful hand of majesty,
  Thy worthiness, and England's hap beside,
Set thee in th' aidfullest room of dignity;
  As th' isthmus these two oceans to divide,
Of rigour and confused uncertainty,
  To keep out th' intercourse of wrong and pride,
    That they engulf not up unsuccoured right,
    By th' extreme current of licentious might.

Now when we see the most combining band,
  The strongest fastening of society,
Law, whereon all this frame of men doth stand,
  Remain concussed with uncertainty,
And seem to foster, rather than withstand
  Contention, and embrace obscurity,
    Only t' afflict, and not to fashion us,
    Making her cure far worse than the disease.

As if she had made covenant with wrong,
  To part the prey made on our weaknesses,
And suffered falsehood to be armed as strong
  Unto the combat, as is righteousness,
Or suited her, as if she did belong
  Unto our passions, and did even profess
    Contention, as her only mystery,
    Which she restrains not, but doth multiply.

Was she the same she's now, in ages past?
  Or was she less, when she was used less;
And grows as malice grows, and so comes cast
  Just to the form of our unquietness?

Or made more slow, the more that strife runs fast,
  Staying t'undo us, ere she will redress?
    That th'ill she checks seems suffered to be ill,
    When it yields greater gain than goodness will.

Must there be still some discord mixed among
  The harmony of men, whose mood accords
Best with contention, tuned t'a note of wrong?
  That when war fails, peace must make war with words,
And be armed unto destruction even as strong,
  As were in ages past our civil swords;
    Making as deep, although unbleeding wounds,
    That, when as fury fails, wisdom confounds.

If it be wisdom, and not cunning, this
  Which so embroils the state of truth with brawls,
And wraps it up in strange confusedness,
  As if it lived immured within the walls
Of hideous terms, framed out of barbarousness
  And foreign customs, the memorials
    Of our subjection, and could never be
    Delivered but by wrangling subtlety.

Whereas it dwells free in the open plain,
  Uncurious, gentle, easy of access;
Certain unto itself, of equal vein,
  One face, one colour, one assuredness.
It's falsehood that is intricate and vain,
  And needs these labyrinths of subtleness.
    For where the cunning'st coverings most appear,
    It argues still that all is not sincere.

Which thy clear-eyed experience well descries,
  Great Keeper of the state of Equity,
Refuge of mercy, upon whom relies
  The succour of oppressed misery;
Altar of safeguard, whereto affliction flies,
  From th'eager pursuit of severity;
    Haven of peace, that labour'st to withdraw
    Justice from out the tempests of the Law.

And set her in a calm and even way,
  Plain, and directly leading to redress,
Barring these counter-courses of delay,
  These wasting, dilatory processes;
Ranging into their right and proper ray
  Errors, demurs, essoins, and traverses,
    The heads of Hydra, springing out of death,
    That gives this monster, malice, still new breath.

That what was made for the utility
  And good of man, might not be turned t' his hurt,
To make him worser by his remedy,
  And cast him down with what should him support;
Nor that the state of Law might lose thereby
  The due respect and reverence of her port,
    And seem a trap to catch our ignorance,
    And to entangle our intemperance.

Since her interpretations and our deeds
  Unto a like infinity arise,
As being a science that by nature breeds
  Contention, strife, and ambiguities;

For altercation controversy feeds,
  And in her agitation multiplies:
    The field of cavil lying all like wide
    Yields like advantage unto either side.

Which made the grave Castilian king devise
  A prohibition, that no advocate
Should be conveyed to th' Indian colonies,
  Lest their new setting, shaken with debate,
Might take but slender root, and so not rise
  To any perfect growth of firm estate,
    For having not this skill how to contend,
    Th' unnourished strife would quickly make an end.

So likewise did the Hungarian, when he saw
  These great Italian Bartolists, who were
Called in of purpose to explain the Law,
  T' embroil it more, and make it much less clear,
Cause them from out his kingdom to withdraw,
  With this infestious skill, some otherwhere;
    Whose learning rather let men farther out,
    And opened wider passages of doubt.

Seeing even injustice may be regular;
  And no proportion can there be betwixt
Our actions, which in endless motion are,
  And th' ordinances, which are always fixed.
Ten thousand laws more cannot reach so far,
  But malice goes beyond, or lives immixed
    So close with goodness, as it ever will
    Corrupt, disguise, or counterfeit it still.

And therefore did those glorious monarchs (who
  Divide with God the style of majesty,
For being good, and had a care to do
  The world right, and to succour honesty)
Ordain this sanctuary, whereunto
  Th' oppressed might fly, this seat of Equity,
    Whereon thy virtues sit with fair renown,
    The greatest grace and glory of the gown.

Which Equity, being the soul of Law,
  The life of justice, and the spirit of right,
Dwells not in written lines, or lives in awe
  Of books, deaf powers, that have nor ears nor sight:
But out of well-weighed circumstance doth draw
  The essence of a judgement requisite;
    And is that Lesbian square, that building fit,
    Plies to the work, not forceth the work to it.

Maintaining still an equal parallel
  Just with th' occasions of humanity,
Making her judgement ever liable
  To the respect of peace and amity;
When surly Law, stern and unaffable,
  Cares only but itself to satisfy;
    And often innocencies scarce defends,
    As that which on no circumstance depends.

But Equity, that bears an even rein
  Upon the present courses, holds in awe
By giving hand a little, and doth gain,
  By a gentle relaxation of the Law:

And yet inviolable doth maintain
The end whereto all constitutions draw;
Which is the welfare of society,
Consisting of an upright policy.

Which first being by necessity composed,
Is by necessity maintained in best estate,
Where, when as justice shall be ill disposed,
It sickens the whole body of the state:
For if there be a passage once disclosed,
That Wrong may enter at the self-same gate
Which serves for Right, clad in a coat of Law,
What violent distempers may it draw?

And therefore dost thou stand to keep the way,
And stop the course that malice seeks to run,
And by thy provident injunctions stay
This never-ending altercation;
Sending contention home, to th' end men may
There make their peace, whereas their strife begun;
And free these pestered streets they vainly wear,
Whom both the state, and theirs, do need elsewhere.

Lest th' humour, which doth thus predominate,
Convert unto itself all that it takes;
And that the Law grow larger than debate,
And come t' exceed th' affairs it undertakes:
As if the only science of the state,
That took up all our wits, for gain it makes;
Not for the good that thereby may be wrought,
Which is not good if it be dearly bought.

What shall we think, whenas ill causes shall
  Enrich men more, and shall be more desired
Than good, as far more beneficial?
  Who then defends the good? Who will be hired
To entertain a right, whose gain is small?
  Unless the advocate, that hath conspired
    To plead a wrong, be likewise made to run
    His client's chance, and with him be undone.

So did the wisest nations ever strive
  To bind the hands of justice up so hard,
That lest she falling to prove lucrative
  Might basely reach them out to take reward;
Ordaining her provisions fit to live
  Out of the public, as a public guard,
    That all preserves, and all doth entertain,
    Whose end is only glory, and not gain.

That even the Sceptre, which might all command,
  Seeing her so unpartial, equal, regular,
Was pleased to put itself into her hand;
  Whereby they both grew more admired far.
And this is that great blessing for this land,
  That both the Prince and people use one bar.
    The Prince, whose cause (as not to be withstood)
    Is never bad, but where himself is good.

This is that balance which committed is
  To thy most even and religious hand,
Great Minister of Justice, who by this
  Shalt have thy name still gracious in this land.

This is that seal of power which doth impress
  Thy acts of right, which shall for ever stand;
    This is that train of state, that pompously
    Attends upon thy reverent dignity.

All glory else besides ends with our breath;
  And men's respects scarce brings us to our grave:
But this of doing good must outlive death,
  And have a right out of the right it gave.
Though th'act but few, th'example profiteth
  Thousands, that shall thereby a blessing have.
    The world's respect grows not but on deserts;
    Power may have knees, but Justice hath our hearts.

Epistles, 1603

300 *To the Lady Margaret, Countess of Cumberland*

HE that of such a height hath built his mind,
  And reared the dwelling of his thoughts so strong,
    As neither fear nor hope can shake the frame
Of his resolved powers, nor all the wind
  Of vanity or malice pierce to wrong
    His settled peace, or to disturb the same:
      What a fair seat hath he, from whence he may
      The boundless wastes and wilds of man survey!

And with how free an eye doth he look down
  Upon these lower regions of turmoil,
    Where all the storms of passions mainly beat
On flesh and blood; where honour, power, renown,

Are only gay afflictions, golden toil;
Where greatness stands upon as feeble feet,
As frailty doth, and only great doth seem
To little minds, who do it so esteem.

He looks upon the mightiest monarch's wars
But only as on stately robberies,
Where evermore the fortune that prevails
Must be the right; the ill-succeeding mars
The fairest and the best faced enterprise.
Great pirate Pompey lesser pirates quails:
Justice he sees, as if seduced, still
Conspires with power, whose cause must not be ill.

He sees the face of right t'appear as manifold,
As are the passions of uncertain man,
Who puts it in all colours, all attires,
To serve his ends, and make his courses hold.
He sees, that let deceit work what it can,
Plot and contrive base ways to high desires,
That the all-guiding Providence doth yet
All disappoint, and mocks this smoke of wit.

Nor is he moved with all the thunder-cracks
Of tyrants' threats, or with the surly brow
Of power, that proudly sits on others' crimes,
Charged with more crying sins than those he checks.
The storms of sad confusion, that may grow
Up in the present for the coming times,
Appal not him, that hath no side at all,
But of himself, and knows the worst can fall.

Although his heart, so near allied to earth,
Cannot but pity the perplexed state
Of troublous and distressed mortality,
That thus make way unto the ugly birth
Of their own sorrows, and do still beget
Affliction upon imbecility:
Yet seeing thus the course of things must run,
He looks thereon not strange, but as foredone.

And whilst distraught ambition compasses,
And is encompassed, whilst as craft deceives.
And is deceived, whilst man doth ransack man,
And builds on blood, and rises by distress,
And th'inheritance of desolation leaves
To great expecting hopes, he looks thereon,
As from the shore of peace, with unwet eye,
And bears no venture in impiety.

Thus, Madame, fares that man, that hath prepared
A rest for his desires, and sees all things
Beneath him, and hath learnt this book of man,
Full of the notes of frailty, and compared
The best of glory with her sufferings;
By whom, I see, you labour all you can
To plant your heart, and set your thoughts as near
His glorious mansion, as your powers can bear.

Which, Madame, are so soundly fashioned
By that clear judgement, that hath carried you
Beyond the feeble limits of your kind,
As they can stand against the strongest head

Passion can make, inured to any hue
  The world can cast; that cannot cast that mind
    Out of her form of goodness, that doth see
    Both what the best and worst of earth can be.

Which makes that, whatsoever here befalls,
  You in the region of yourself remain,
    Where no vain breath of th'impudent molests,
That hath secured within the brazen walls
  Of a clear conscience, that without all stain
    Rises in peace, in innocency rests;
      Whilst all what malice from without procures,
      Shows her own ugly heart, but hurts not yours.

And whereas none rejoice more in revenge,
  Than women use to do, yet you well know,
    That wrong is better checked by being contemned,
Than being pursued, leaving to him t'avenge,
  To whom it appertains, wherein you show
    How worthily your clearness hath condemned
      Base malediction, living in the dark,
      That at the rays of goodness still doth bark.

Knowing the heart of man is set to be
  The centre of this world, about the which
    These revolutions of disturbances
Still roll, where all th'aspects of misery
  Predominate, whose strong effects are such,
    As he must bear, being powerless to redress;
      And that unless above himself he can
      Erect himself, how poor a thing is man.

And how turmoiled they are that level lie
With earth, and cannot lift themselves from thence;
That never are at peace with their desires,
But work beyond their years, and even deny
Dotage her rest, and hardly will dispense
With death; that when ability expires,
Desire lives still, so much delight they have,
To carry toil and travel to the grave.

Whose ends you see, and what can be the best
They reach unto, when they have cast the sum
And reckonings of their glory, and you know,
This floating life hath but this port of rest,
A heart prepared, that fears no ill to come;
And that man's greatness rests but in his show,
The best of all whose days consumed are,
Either in war, or peace conceiving war.

This concord, Madame, of a well-tuned mind
Hath been so set by that all-working hand
Of Heaven, that though the world hath done his worst
To put it out by discords most unkind,
Yet doth it still in perfect union stand
With God and man, nor ever will be forced
From that most sweet accord, but still agree,
Equal in Fortune's inequality.

And this note, Madame, of your worthiness
Remains recorded in so many hearts,
As time nor malice cannot wrong your right
In th'inheritance of fame you must possess,

You that have built you by your great deserts,
  Out of small means, a far more exquisite
    And glorious dwelling for your honoured name,
    Than all the gold that leaden minds can frame.

Epistles, 1603

301 *To the Lady Lucy, Countess of Bedford*

THOUGH Virtue be the same when low she stands
  In th' humble shadows of obscurity,
As when she either sweats in martial bands,

Or sits in court clad with authority;
  Yet, Madame, doth the strictness of her room
Greatly detract from her ability.

For, as in-walled within a living tomb,
  Her hands and arms of action labour not;
Her thoughts, as if abortive from the womb,

Come never born, though happily begot.
  But where she hath, mounted in open sight,
An eminent and spacious dwelling got;

Where she may stir at will, and use her might,
  There is she more herself, and more her own;
There in the fair attire of honour dight,

She sits at ease, and makes her glory known.
  Applause attends her hands; her deeds have grace;
Her worth, new-born, is straight as if full grown.

With such a godly and respected face
  Doth Virtue look, that 's set to look from high;
And such a fair advantage by her place

Hath state and greatness to do worthily.
  And therefore well did your high fortunes meet
With her, that gracing you comes graced thereby;

And well was let into a house so sweet,
  So good, so fair; so fair, so good a guest,
Who now remains as blessed in her seat,

As you are with her residency blessed.
  And this fair course of knowledge, whereunto
Your studies, learned lady, are addressed,

Is th' only certain way that you can go
  Unto true glory, to true happiness:
All passages on earth besides, are so

Encumbered with such vain disturbances,
  As still we lose our rest in seeking it,
Being but deluded with appearances.

And no key had you else that was so fit
  T' unlock that prison of your sex as this,
To let you out of weakness, and admit

Your powers into the freedom of that bliss,
  That sets you there where you may over-see
This rolling world, and view it as it is;

And apprehend how th' outsides do agree
  With th' inward, being of the things we deem
And hold in our ill-cast accounts, to be

Of highest value, and of best esteem.
  Since all the good we have rests in the mind,
By whose proportions only we redeem

Our thoughts from out confusion, and do find
  The measure of ourselves, and of our powers.
And that all happiness remains confined

Within the kingdom of this breast of ours;
  Without whose bounds, all that we look on lies
In others' jurisdictions, others' powers,

Out of the circuit of our liberties.
  All glory, honour, fame, applause, renown,
Are not belonging to our royalties,

But t' others' wills, wherein they are only grown.
  And that unless we find us all within,
We never can without us be our own;

Nor call it right our life that we live in;
  But a possession held for others' use,
That seem to have most interest therein;

Which we do so dissever, part, traduce,
  Let out to custom, fashion and to show,
As we enjoy but only the abuse,

And have no other deed at all to show.
  How oft are we constrained to appear
With other countenance than that we owe;

And be ourselves far off, when we are near!
  How oft are we forced on a cloudy heart
To set a shining face, and make it clear;

Seeming content to put ourselves apart,
  To bear a part of others' weaknesses!
As if we only were composed by art,

Not nature, and did all our deeds address
  T'opinion, not t'a conscience, what is right;
As framed by example, not advisedness,

Into those forms that entertain our sight.
  And though books, Madame, cannot make this mind,
Which we must bring apt to be set aright,

Yet do they rectify it in that kind,
  And touch it so, as that it turns that way
Where judgement lies. And though we cannot find

The certain place of truth, yet do they stay,
  And entertain us near about the same;
And give the soul the best delight, that may

Encheer it most, and most our spirits inflame
  To thoughts of glory, and to worthy ends.
And therefore, in a course that best became

The clearness of your heart, and best commends
  Your worthy powers, you run the rightest way
    That is on earth, that can true glory give,
    By which, when all consumes, your fame shall live.

Epistles, 1603

302 *Chorus*

HOW dost thou wear and weary out thy days,
  Restless Ambition, never at an end!
Whose travels no Herculean pillar stays,
  But still beyond thy rest thy labours tend;
Above good fortune thou thy hopes dost raise,
  Still climbing, and yet never canst ascend;
    For when thou hast attained unto the top
    Of thy desires, thou hast not yet got up.

That height of fortune either is controlled
  By some more powerful overlooking eye,
That doth the fulness of thy grace withhold,
  Or counterchecked with some concurrency,
That it doth cost far more ado to hold
  The height attained, than was to get so high,
    Where stand thou canst not, but with careful toil,
    Nor loose thy hold without thy utter spoil.

There dost thou struggle with thine own distrust,
  And others' jealousies, their counterplot,
Against some underworking pride, that must
  Supplanted be, or else thou standest not;
There wrong is played with wrong, and he that thrust
  Down others, comes himself to have that lot.
    The same concussion doth afflict his breast
    That others shook; oppression is oppressed:

That either happiness dwells not so high,
  Or else above, whereto pride cannot rise;
And that the highest of man's felicity
  But in the region of affliction lies;
And that we climb but up to misery.
  High fortunes are but high calamities.
    It is not in that sphere, where peace doth move;
    Rest dwells below it, happiness above.

For in this height of fortune are imbred
  Those thundering fragors that affright the earth;
From thence have all distemperatures their head,
  That brings forth desolation, famine, dearth;
There certain order is disordered,
  And there it is confusion hath her birth.
    It is that height of fortune doth undo
    Both her own quietness and others' too.

Philotas, 1605

303 *Ulysses and the Siren*

Siren

COME, worthy Greek! Ulysses, come;
  Possess these shores with me!
The winds and seas are troublesome
  And here we may be free.
Here may we sit and view their toil
  That travail in the deep,
And joy the day in mirth the while
  And spend the night in sleep.

Ulysses

Fair nymph, if fame or honour were
 To be attained with ease,
Then would I come and rest me there,
 And leave such toils as these.
But here it dwells, and here must I
 With danger seek it forth:
To spend the time luxuriously
 Becomes not men of worth.

Siren

Ulysses, O! be not deceived
 With that unreal name;
This honour is a thing conceived
 And rests on others' fame;
Begotten only to molest
 Our peace, and to beguile
The best thing of our life, our rest,
 And give us up to toil.

Ulysses

Delicious nymph, suppose there were
 Nor honour nor report,
Yet manliness would scorn to wear
 The time in idle sport;
For toil doth give a better touch
 To make us feel our joy,
And ease finds tediousness as much
 As labour yields annoy.

SAMUEL DANIEL

Siren

Then pleasure likewise seems the shore,
  Whereto tends all your toil,
Which you forgo to make it more,
  And perish oft the while.
Who may disport them diversely
  Find never tedious day,
And ease may have variety,
  As well as action may.

Ulysses

But natures of the noblest frame
  These toils and dangers please;
And they take comfort in the same
  As much as you in ease;
And with the thought of actions past
  Are recreated still;
When pleasure leaves a touch at last,
  To shew that it was ill.

Siren

That doth opinion only cause,
  That 's out of custom bred,
Which makes us many other laws,
  Than ever nature did.
No widows wail for our delights,
  Our sports are without blood;
The world we see by warlike wights
  Receives more hurt than good.

Ulysses

But yet the state of things require
These motions of unrest;
And these great spirits of high desire
Seem born to turn them best;
To purge the mischiefs that increase
And all good order mar,
For oft we see a wicked peace
To be well changed for war.

Siren

Well, well, Ulysses, then I see
I shall not have thee here;
And therefore I will come to thee
And take my fortunes there.
I must be won that cannot win,
Yet lost were I not won,
For beauty hath created been
T'undo, or be undone.

Certain Small Poems, 1605

304

To his Reader

BEHOLD, once more with serious labour here
Have I refurnished out this little frame,
Repaired some parts defective here and there,
And passages new added to the same,
Some rooms enlarged, made some less than they were;
Like to the curious builder who this year
Pulls down and alters what he did the last,
As if the thing in doing were more dear
Than being done, and nothing likes that's past

For that we ever make the latter day
  The scholar of the former, and we find
Something is still amiss that must delay
  Our business, and leave work for us behind.
  As if there were no sabbath of the mind.
    And howsoever be it well or ill
What I have done, it is mine own, I may
    Do whatsoever therewithal I will.

I may pull down, raise, and re-edify;
  It is the building of my life, the fee
Of Nature, all th' inheritance that I
  Shall leave to those which must come after me;
  And all the care I have is but to see
    These lodgings of my affections neatly dressed,
  Wherein so many noble friends there be,
    Whose memories with mine must therein rest.

And glad I am that I have lived to see
  This edifice renewed, who do but long
To live to amend. For man is a tree
  That hath his fruit late ripe, and it is long
  Before he come t' his taste; there doth belong
    So much t' experience, and so infinite
The faces of things are, as hardly we
    Discern which looks the likest unto right.

Besides, these curious times, stuffed with the store
  Of compositions in this kind, do drive
Me to examine my defects the more,
  And oft would make me not myself believe,

SAMUEL DANIEL

Did I not know the world wherein I live,
Which neither is so wise as that would seem,
Nor certain judgement of those things doth give
That it dislikes, nor that it doth esteem.

I know no work from man yet ever came
But had his mark, and by some error showed
That it was his, and yet what in the same
Was rare, and worthy, evermore allowed
Safe convoy for the rest; the good that's sowed,
Though rarely, pays our cost, and who so looks
T' have all things in perfection and in frame
In men's inventions, never must read books.

And howsoever here detraction may
Disvalue this my labour, yet I know
There will be found therein that which will pay
The reckoning for the errors which I owe,
And likewise will sufficiently allow
T' an undistasted judgement fit delight;
And let presumptuous self-opinion say
The worst it can, I know I shall have right.

I know I shall be read, among the rest,
So long as men speak English, and so long
As verse and virtue shall be in request,
Or grace to honest industry belong:
And England, since I use thy present tongue,
Thy form of speech, thou must be my defence
If to new ears it seems not well expressed,
For, though I hold not accent, I hold sense.

And since the measures of our tongue we see
   Confirmed by no edict of power doth rest,
But only underneath the regency
   Of use and fashion, which may be the best
   Is not for my poor forces to contest,
      But as the Peacock, seeing himself too weak,
Confessed the Eagle fairer far to be,
      And yet not in his feathers, but his beak.

Authority of powerful censure may
   Prejudicate the form wherein we mould
The matter of our spirit, but if it pay
   The ear with substance, we have what we would,
   For that is all which must our credit hold.
      The rest (however gay or seeming rich
It be in fashion, wise men will not weigh)
      The stamp will not allow it, but the touch.

And would to God that nothing faulty were
   But only that poor accent in my verse,
Or that I could all other reckonings clear
   Wherewith my heart stands charged, or might reverse
The errors of my judgement passed here
   Or elsewhere, in my books, and unrehearse
      What I have vainly said, or have addressed
      Unto neglect mistaken in the rest.

Which I do hope to live yet to retract
   And crave that England never will take note
That it was mine. I'll disavow mine act,
   And wish it may for ever be forgot;

touch] test, of coin

I trust the world will not of me exact
  Against my will, that hath all else I wrote;
    I will ask nothing therein for my pain,
    But only to have in mine own again.

Certain Small Works, 1607

305 *Shadows*

ARE they shadows that we see?
  And can shadows pleasure give?
Pleasures only shadows be,
  Cast by bodies we conceive,
    And are made the things we deem
    In those figures which they seem.

But these pleasures vanish fast,
  Which by shadows are expressed;
Pleasures are not, if they last;
  In their passing is their best.
    Glory is most bright and gay
    In a flash and so away.

Feed apace, then, greedy eyes
  On the wonder you behold;
Take it sudden as it flies,
  Though you take it not to hold.
    When your eyes have done their part,
    Thought must length it in the heart.

Tethys' Festival, 1610

306

Sorrow

HAD sorrow ever fitter place
To act his part,
Than is my heart,
Where it takes up all the space?
Where is no vein
To entertain
A thought that wears another face.
Nor will I sorrow ever have,
Therein to be,
But only thee,
To whom I full possession gave:
Thou in my name
Must hold the same,
Until thou bring it to the grave.

Hymen's Triumph, 1615

307

Love

LOVE is a sickness full of woes,
All remedies refusing;
A plant that with most cutting grows,
Most barren with best using.
Why so?
More we enjoy it, more it dies;
If not enjoyed, it sighing cries,
Hey ho.

Love is a torment of the mind,
  A tempest everlasting;
And Jove hath made it of a kind,
  Not well, nor full nor fasting.
            Why so?
More we enjoy it, more it dies;
If not enjoyed, it sighing cries,
            Hey ho.

Hymen's Triumph, 1615

308 *Secrecy*

EYES, hide my love, and do not show
  To any but to her my notes,
Who only doth that cipher know,
  Wherewith we pass our secret thoughts;
Belie your looks in others' sight;
And wrong yourselves to do her right.

Ibid.

309 *Constancy*

WHO ever saw so fair a sight,
  Love and Virtue met aright;
  And that wonder Constancy,
  Like a comet to the eye
Seldom ever seen so bright?
  Sound out aloud so rare a thing,
  That all the hills and vales may ring.

Look, lovers look, with passion see,
If that any such there be,
As there cannot but be such,
Who do feel that noble touch
In this glorious company,
Sound out aloud, &c.

Ibid.

310 *A Description of Beauty, translated out of Marino*

O BEAUTY (beams, nay, flame
Of that great lamp of light)
That shines awhile with fame,
But presently makes night!
Like winter's short-lived bright,
Or summer's sudden gleams;
How much more dear, so much less lasting beams.

Winged love away doth fly,
And with it time doth bear;
And both take suddenly
The sweet, the fain, the dear.
A shining day and clear
Succeeds an obscene night;
And sorrow is the hue of sweet delight.

With what then dost thou swell,
O Youth of new-born day?
Wherein doth thy pride dwell,
O Beauty made of clay?
Not with so swift a way
The headlong current flies,
As do the sparkling rays of two fair eyes.

Do not thyself betray
  With wantonizing years,
O Beauty, traitors gay.
  Thy melting life that wears,
  Appearing, disappears;
    And with thy flying days
    Ends all thy good of price, thy fair of praise.

Trust not, vain creditor,
  Thy apt deceived view,
In thy false counsellor,
  That never tells thee true:
  Thy form and flattered hue,
    Which shall so soon transpass,
    Is far more fair than is thy looking-glass.

Enjoy thy April now,
  Whilst it doth freely shine;
This lightning flash and show,
  With that clear spirit of thine,
  Will suddenly decline:
    And thou, fair murdering eyes,
    Shall be Love's tombs, where now his cradle lies.

Old trembling age will come,
  With wrinkled cheeks and stains,
With motion troublesome;
  With skin and bloodless veins,
  That lively visage reaven,
    And made deformed and old,
    Hate sight of glass it loved so to behold.

Thy gold and scarlet shall
  Pale silver colour be;
Thy row of pearls shall fall
  Like withered leaves from tree;
  And thou shalt shortly see
    Thy face and hair to grow
    All ploughed with furrows, over-sown with snow.

That which on Flora's breast,
  All fresh and flourishing,
Aurora newly dressed
  Saw in her dawning spring;
  Quite dry and languishing,
    Deprived of honour quite,
    Day-closing Hesperus beholds at night.

Fair is the lily; fair
  The rose, of flowers the eye;
Both wither in the air,
  Their beauteous colours die;
  And so at length shall lie,
    Deprived of former grace,
    The lilies of thy breasts, the roses of thy face.

What then will it avail,
  O Youth advised ill,
In lap of Beauty frail
  To nurse a wayward will,
  Like snake in sun-warm hill?
    Pluck, pluck betime thy flower,
    That springs, and perisheth in one short hour.

Whole Works, 1623

HENRY CONSTABLE

1562–1613

311 *Of the Nativity of the Lady Rich's Daughter*

FAIR by inheritance, whom born we see
  Both in the wondrous year and on the day
  Wherein the fairest planet beareth sway,
The heavens to thee this fortune do decree:
Thou of a world of hearts in time shalt be
  A monarch great, and with one beauty's ray
  So many hosts of hearts thy face shall slay,
As all the rest for love shall yield to thee.
But even as Alexander when he knew
  His father's conquests wept, lest he should leave
No kingdom unto him for to subdue,
  So shall thy mother thee of praise bereave.
    So many hearts already she hath slain,
    As few behind to conquer shall remain.

Diana, 1592

HENRY CONSTABLE

312 *Sonnets to Diana*

(i)

GRACE full of grace, though in these verses here
My love complains of others than of thee,
Yet thee alone I loved, and they by me,
Thou yet unknown, only mistaken were.
Like him which feels a heat, now here, now there,
Blames now this cause, now that, until he see
The fire indeed from whence they caused be;
Which fire I now do know is you, my dear!
Thus diverse loves dispersed in my verse
In thee alone for ever I unite.
But folly unto thee more to rehearse!
To him I fly for grace that rules above,
That by my grace I may live in delight,
Or by his grace I never more may love.

(ii)

MY lady's presence makes the roses red,
Because to see her lips they blush with shame.
The lily's leaves for envy pale became,
And her white hands in them this envy bred.
The marigold the leaves abroad did spread,
Because the sun's and her power is the same.
The violet of purple colour came,
Dyed in the blood she made my heart to shed.
In brief, all flowers from her their virtue take;
From her sweet breath their sweet smells do proceed;
The living heat, which her eyebeams do make,
Warmeth the ground and quickeneth the seed.
The rain, wherewith she watereth the flowers,
Falls from mine eyes which she dissolves in showers.

(*iii*)

THE sun, his journey ending in the west,
  Taking his lodging up in Thetis' bed,
  Though from our eyes his beams be banished,
Yet with his light th' Antipodes be blest.
Now when the same time brings my sun to rest,
  Which me too oft of rest hath hindered,
  And whiter skin with white sheet covered,
And softer cheek doth on soft pillow rest,
Then I, O sun of suns and light of lights!
  Wish me with those Antipodes to be,
Which see and feel thy beams and heat by nights.
    Well, though the night both cold and darksome is,
  Yet half the day's delight the night grants me,
    I feel my sun's heat, though his light I miss.

(*iv*)

FAIR sun, if you would have me praise your light,
  When night approacheth, wherefore do you fly?
  Time is so short, beauties so many be,
As I have need to see them day and night,
That by continual view my verses might
  Tell all the beams of your divinity;
  Which praise to you and joy should be to me,
You living by my verse, I by your sight.
I by your sight, and not you by my verse;
Need mortal skill immortal praise rehearse?
  No, no, though eyes were blind, and verse were dumb,
    Your beauty should be seen and your fame known;
  For by the wind which from my sighs doth come,
    Your praises round about the world are blown.

(*v*)

NEEDS must I leave and yet needs must I love;
In vain my wit doth tell in verse my woe;
Despair in me, disdain in thee, doth show
How by my wit I do my folly prove.
All this my heart from love can never move.
Love is not in my heart. No, Lady, no,
My heart is love itself. Till I forgo
My heart I never can my love remove.
How can I then leave love? I do intend
Not to crave grace, but yet to wish it still;
Not to praise thee, but beauty to commend;
And so, by beauty's praise, praise thee I will.
For as my heart is love, love not in me,
So beauty thou, beauty is not in thee.

(*vi*)

READY to seek out death in my disgrace,
My mistress 'gan to smooth her gathered brows,
Whereby I am reprieved for a space.
O hope and fear! who half your torments knows?
It is some mercy in a black-mouthed judge
To haste his prisoner's end, if he must die.
Dear, if all other favour you shall grudge,
Do speedy execution with your eye.
With one sole look you leave in me no soul;
Count it a loss to lose a faithful slave.
Would God, that I might hear my last bell toll,
So in your bosom I might dig my grave!
Doubtful delay is worse than any fever;
Or help me soon, or cast me off for ever!

(*vii*)

HOPE, like the hyena, coming to be old,
  Alters his shape, is turned into despair.
Pity my hoary hopes, maid of clear mould;
  Think not that frowns can ever make thee fair.
What harm is it to kiss, to laugh, to play?
  Beauty's no blossom, if it be not used.
Sweet dalliance keepeth wrinkles long away;
  Repentance follows them that have refused.
To bring you to the knowledge of your good,
  I seek, I sue. O! try and then believe!
Each image can be chaste that 's carved of wood;
  You show you live, when men you do relieve.
    Iron with wearing shines; rust wasteth treasure;
    On earth but love there is no other pleasure.

(*viii*)

YOU secret vales, you solitary fields,
  You shores forsaken and you sounding rocks!
If ever groaning heart hath made you yield,
  Or words half spoke that sense in prison locks,
Then 'mongst night shadows whisper out my death;
  That when myself hath sealed my lips from speaking,
Each tell-tale echo, with a weeping breath,
  May both record my truth and true love's breaking.
You pretty flowers, that smile for summer's sake,
  Pull in your heads before my watery eyes
Do turn the meadows to a standing lake,
  By whose untimely floods your glory dies.
    For lo! mine heart, resolved to moistening air,
    Feedeth mine eyes which double tear for tear.

(*ix*)

DEAR to my soul, then leave me not forsaken!
  Fly not! My heart within thy bosom sleepeth;
Even from myself and sense I have betaken
  Me unto thee for whom my spirit weepeth;
And on the shore of that salt teary sea,
  Couched in a bed of unseen seeming pleasure,
Where in imaginary thoughts thy fair self lay,
  But being waked, robbed of my life's best treasure,
I call the heavens, air, earth, and seas to hear
  My love, my truth, and black disdained estate;
Beating the rocks with bellowings of despair,
  Which still with plaints my words reverberate;
    Sighing, 'Alas, what shall become of me?'
    Whilst Echo cries, 'What shall become of me?'

(*x*)

WHILST Echo cries, 'What shall become of me?'
  And desolate my desolations pity,
Thou in thy beauty's carack sit'st to see
  My tragic downfall, and my funeral ditty.
No timbrel, but my heart thou play'st upon,
  Whose strings are stretched unto the highest key;
The diapason, love; love is the unison;
  In love my life and labours waste away.
Only regardless to the world thou leavest me,
  Whilst slain hopes, turning from the feast of sorrow,
Unto despair, their king, which ne'er deceives me,
  Captive my heart, whose black night hates the morrow.
    And he in ruth of my distressed cry
    Plants me a weeping star within mine eye.

(*xi*)

TO live in hell, and heaven to behold;
  To welcome life, and die a living death;
To sweat with heat, and yet be freezing cold;
  To grasp at stars, and lie the earth beneath;
To tread a maze that never shall have end;
  To burn in sighs, and starve in daily tears;
To climb a hill, and never to descend;
  Giants to kill, and quake at childish fears;
To pine for food, and watch th' Hesperian tree;
  To thirst for drink, and nectar still to draw;
To live accursed, whom men hold blest to be,
  And weep those wrongs which never creature saw:
    If this be love, if love in these be founded,
    My heart is love, for these in it are grounded.

(*xii*)

MY tears are true, though others be divine,
  And sing of wars and Troy's new rising frame,
Meeting heroic feet in every line,
  That tread high measures on the scene of fame.
And I, though disaccustoming my Muse
  To sing but low songs in an humble vein,
May one day raise my style as others use,
  And turn *Eleison* to a higher strain:
When re-intombing from oblivious ages
  In better stanzas her surviving wonder,
I may oppose against the monster rages,
  That part desert and excellence asunder;
    That she though coy may yet survive to see
    Her beauty's wonder lives again in me.

Eleison] Have mercy!

HENRY CONSTABLE

(*xiii*)

NOT that thy hand is soft, is sweet, is white,
Thy lips sweet roses, breast sweet lily is,
That love esteems these three the chiefest bliss
Which nature ever made for lips' delight;
But when these three, to show their heavenly might,
Such wonders do, devotion then for this
Commandeth us with humble zeal to kiss
Such things as work miracles in our sight.
A lute of senseless wood, by nature dumb,
Touched by thy hand doth speak divinely well;
And from thy lips and breast sweet tunes do come
To my dead heart, the which new life do give.
Of greater wonders heard we never tell,
Than for the dumb to speak, the dead to live.

(*xiv*)

MIRACLE of the world! I never will deny
That former poets praise the beauty of their days;
But all those beauties were but figures of thy praise,
And all those poets did of thee but prophesy.
Thy coming to the world hath taught us to descry
What Petrarch's Laura meant, for truth the lip bewrays.
Lo! why th' Italians, yet which never saw thy rays,
To find out Petrarch's sense such forged glosses try.
The beauties, which he in a veil enclosed beheld,
But revelations were within his secret heart,
By which in parables thy coming he foretold;
His songs were hymns of thee, which only now before
Thy image should be sung; for thou that goddess art,
Which only we without idolatry adore.

Diana, 1592, 1594; *Harleian Miscellany* ix, 1813

313 *On Sir Philip Sidney*

GIVE pardon, blessed soul, to my bold cries,
  If they, importune, interrupt thy song,
  Which now with joyful notes thou sing'st among
The angel-choristers of heavenly skies.
Give pardon eke, sweet soul, to my slow eyes,
  That since I saw thee now it is so long,
  And yet the tears that unto thee belong
To thee as yet they did not sacrifice.
I did not know that thou wert dead before;
  I did not feel the grief I did sustain;
The greater stroke astonisheth the more;
  Astonishment takes from us sense of pain.
    I stood amazed when others' tears begun,
    And now begin to weep when they have done.

Apology for Poetry, 1595

314 *To God the Son*

GREAT Prince of heaven, begotten of that King
  Who rules the kingdom, that himself did make,
  And of that Virgin-Queen man's shape did take,
Which from King David's royal stock did spring!
No marvel, though thy birth made angels sing,
  And angels' ditties shepherds' pipes awake,
  And kings, like shepherds, humbled for thy sake,
Kneel at thy feet, and gifts of homage bring.
For heaven and earth, the high and low estate,
  As partners of thy birth make equal claim;
Angels, because in heaven God thee begat,
  Shepherds and kings, because thy mother came
    From princely race, and yet by poverty
    Made glory shine in her humility.

Harleian MS. 7553

HENRY CONSTABLE

315 *To Our Blessed Lady*

IN that, O Queen of queens, thy birth was free
  From guilt, which others doth of grace bereave,
  When in their mother's womb they life receive,
God as his sole-born daughter loved thee.
To match thee like thy birth's nobility,
  He thee his Spirit for thy spouse did leave,
  Of whom thou didst his only Son conceive,
And so wast linked to all the Trinity.
Cease then, O queens, who earthly crowns do wear,
  To glory in the pomp of worldly things!
If men such high respect unto you bear,
  Which daughters, wives and mothers are of kings,
    What honour should unto that Queen be done,
    Who had your God for father, spouse and son?

Ibid.

MICHAEL DRAYTON

1563–1631

316 *Song to Beta*

O THOU fair silver Thames, O clearest crystal flood!
Beta alone the phoenix is of all thy watery brood,
  The Queen of virgins only she;
  And thou the Queen of floods shalt be:
Let all thy nymphs be joyful then to see this happy day;
Thy Beta now alone shall be the subject of my lay.

With dainty and delightsome strains of sweetest virelays,
Come, lovely shepherds, sit we down and chant our Beta's praise;
And let us sing so rare a verse,
Our Beta's praises to rehearse,
That little birds shall silent be, to hear poor shepherds sing,
And rivers backward bend their course, and flow unto the spring.

Range all thy swans, fair Thames, together on a rank,
And place them duly one by one, upon thy stately bank;
Then set together all a-good,
Recording to the silver flood,
And crave the tuneful nightingale to help you with her lay,
The ousel and the throstlecock, chief music of our May.

O! see what troops of nymphs been sporting on the strands,
And they been blessed nymphs of peace, with olives in their hands.
How merrily the Muses sing,
That all the flowery meadows ring,
And Beta sits upon the bank, in purple and in pall,
And she the Queen of Muses is, and wears the coronal.

Trim up her golden tresses with Apollo's sacred tree.
O happy sight unto all those that love and honour thee,
The blessed angels have prepared
A glorious crown for thy reward,
Not such a golden crown as haughty Caesar wears,
But such a glittering starry crown as Ariadne bears.

Make her a goodly chapelet of azured columbine,
And wreath about her coronet with sweetest eglantine;
    Bedeck our Beta all with lilies,
    And the dainty daffodillies,
With roses damask, white, and red, and fairest flower delice,
With cowslips of Jerusalem, and cloves of Paradise.

O thou fair torch of heaven, the day's most dearest light,
And thou bright shining Cynthia, the glory of the night;
    You stars the eyes of heaven,
    And thou the gliding levin,
And thou, O gorgeous Iris, with all strange colours dyed,
When she streams forth her rays, then dashed is all your pride.

See how the day stands still, admiring of her face,
And Time, lo! stretcheth forth her arms, thy Beta to embrace;
    The Sirens sing sweet lays,
    The Tritons sound her praise.
Go pass on, Thames, and hie thee fast unto the ocean sea,
And let thy billows there proclaim thy Beta's holiday:

And water thou the blessed root of that green olive tree,
With whose sweet shadow all thy banks with peace preserved be,
    Laurel for poets and conquerors,
    And myrtle for love's paramours,
That fame may be thy fruit, the boughs preserved by peace;
And let the mournful cypress die, now storms and tempest cease.

levin] lightning

We'll strew the shore with pearl where Beta walks alone,
And we will pave her princely bower with richest Indian stone.
Perfume the air and make it sweet,
For such a goddess it is meet,
For if her eyes for purity contend with Titan's light,
No marvel then although they so do dazzle human sight.

Sound out your trumpets then, from London's stately towers,
To beat the stormy winds aback and calm the raging showers;
Set too the cornet and the flute,
The orpharion and the lute,
And tune the tabor and the pipe, to the sweet violons,
And move the thunder in the air, with loudest clarions.

Beta, long may thine altars smoke, with yearly sacrifice,
And long thy sacred temples may their sabbaths solemnize,
Thy shepherds watch by day and night,
Thy maids attend the holy light,
And thy large empire stretch her arms from east unto the west;
And thou under thy feet mayst tread that foul seven-headed beast.

The Shepherd's Garland, 1593

317 *Cassamen and Dowsabell*

FAR in the country of Arden,
There wonned a knight, hight Cassamen,
As bold as Isenbras:
Fell was he and eager bent,
In battle and in tournament,
As was the good sir Topas.

He had, as antique stories tell,
A daughter cleped Dowsabell,
  A maiden fair and free;
And for she was her father's heir,
Full well she was yconned the leir
  Of mickle courtesy.

The silk well couth she twist and twine,
And make the fine march-pine,
  And with the needle work;
And she couth help the priest to say
His matins on a holyday,
  And sing a psalm in kirk.

She ware a frock of frolic green,
Might well become a maiden queen,
  Which seemly was to see;
A hood to that so neat and fine,
In colour like the columbine,
  Ywrought full featously.

Her features all as fresh above,
As is the grass that grows by Dove,
  And lithe as lass of Kent;
Her skin as soft as Lemster wool,
As white as snow on Peakish hull,
  Or swan that swims in Trent.

she was yconned the leir] she knew the learning
march-pine] sweet biscuit Lemster] Leominster hull] hill

This maiden, in a morn betime,
Went forth when May was in the prime,
  To get sweet setywall,
The honeysuckle, the charlock,
The lily, and the lady-smock,
  To deck her summer hall.

Thus as she wandered here and there,
And picked of the bloomy brere,
  She chanced to espy
A shepherd sitting on a bank;
Like Chanticleer he crowed crank,
  And piped full merrily.

He learned his sheep, as he him list,
When he would whistle in his fist,
  To feed about him round;
Whilst he full many a carol sang,
Until the fields and meadows rang,
  And that the woods did sound.

In favour this same shepherd swain
Was like the bedlam Tamberlaine,
  Which held proud kings in awe:
But meek as any lamb mought be,
And innocent of ill as he
  Whom his lewd brother slaw.

setywall] valerian
crank] cheerfully

This shepherd ware a sheep-gray cloak,
Which was of the finest lock,
  That could be cut with shear.
His mittens were of bauzon's skin,
His cockers were of cordiwin,
  His hood of miniver.

His awl and lingel in a thong,
His tar-box on his broad belt hung,
  His breech of Cointree blue;
Full crisp and curled were his locks,
His brows as white as Albion rocks,
  So like a lover true.

And piping still he spent the day,
So merry as the popinjay,
  Which liked Dowsabell;
That would she aught, or would she nought,
This lad would never from her thought;
  She in love-longing fell.

At length she tucked up her frock,
White as a lily was her smock,
  She drew the shepherd nigh:
But then the shepherd piped a-good,
That all his sheep forsook their food,
  To hear his melody.

bauzon] badger   cockers] boots   cordiwin] leather
miniver] white fur   lingel] thread   Cointree] Coventry
popinjay] parrot

'Thy sheep,' quoth she, 'cannot be lean,
That have a jolly shepherd's swain,
The which can pipe so well':
'Yea, but,' saith he, 'their shepherd may,
If piping thus he pine away,
In love of Dowsabell.'

'Of love, fond boy, take thou no keep,'
Quoth she, 'look well unto thy sheep,
Lest they should hap to stray.'
Quoth he, 'So had I done full well,
Had I not seen fair Dowsabell
Come forth to gather May.'

With that she 'gan to vail her head,
Her cheeks were like the roses red,
But not a word she said;
With that the shepherd 'gan to frown,
He threw his pretty pipes adown,
And on the ground him laid.

Saith she, 'I may not stay till night,
And leave my summer hall undight,
And all for love of thee.'
'My cote,' saith he, 'nor yet my fold,
Shall neither sheep nor shepherd hold,
Except thou favour me.'

vail] drop

Saith she, 'Yet liever I were dead,
Than I should lose my maidenhead,
  And all for love of men.'
Saith he, 'Yet are you too unkind,
If in your heart you cannot find
  To love us now and then.

And I to thee will be as kind,
As Colin was to Rosalind,
  Of courtesy the flower.'
'Then will I be as true,' quoth she,
'As ever maiden yet might be
  Unto her paramour.'

With that she bent her snow-white knee,
Down by the shepherd kneeled she,
  And him she sweetly kissed.
With that the shepherd whooped for joy:
Quoth he, 'There 's never shepherd's boy
  That ever was so blest.'

The Shepherd's Garland, 1593

318 *Eclogue*

LATE 'twas in June, the fleece when fully grown,
  In the full compass of the passed year,
The season well by skilful shepherds known,
  That them provide immediately to shear.

Their lambs late waxed so lusty and so strong,
  That time did them their mothers' teats forbid,
And in the fields, the common flocks among,
  Eat of the same grass that the greater did.

When not a shepherd any thing that could,
  But greased his start-ups black as autumn's sloe,
And for the better credit of the wold,
  In their fresh russets every one doth go.

Who now a posy pins not in his cap?
  And not a garland baldric-wise doth wear?
Some, of such flowers as to his hand doth hap;
  Others, such as a secret meaning bear.

He from his lass him lavender hath sent,
  Showing her love, and doth requital crave;
Him rosemary his sweet heart, whose intent
  Is that he her should in remembrance have.

Roses his youth and strong desire express;
  Her sage doth show his sovereignty in all;
The July-flower declares his gentleness;
  Thyme, truth; the pansy, heart's-ease maidens call.

In cotes such simples, simply in request,
  Wherewith proud courts in greatness scorn to mell,
For country toys become the country best,
  And please poor shepherds, and become them well.

When the new-washed flock from the river's side
  Come in as white as January's snow,
The ram with nosegays bears his horns in pride,
  And no less brave the bell-wether doth go.

start-ups] high boots   mell] meddle

After their fair flocks in a lusty rout,
  Came the gay swains with bag-pipes strongly blown,
And busied though this solemn sport about,
  Yet had each one an eye unto his own.

And by the ancient statutes of the field,
  He that his flocks the earliest lamb should bring,
(As it fell out then, Rowland's charge to yield)
  Always for that year was the shepherds' king.

And soon preparing for the shepherds' board,
  Upon a green that curiously was squared,
With country cates being plentifully stored,
  And 'gainst their coming handsomely prepared;

New whig, with water from the clearest stream,
  Green plums, and wildings, cherries chief of feast,
Fresh cheese, and doucets, curds, and clouted cream,
  Spiced sillabubs, and cider of the best;

And to the same down solemnly they sit,
  In the fresh shadow of their summer bowers,
With sundry sweets them every way to fit,
  The neighbouring vale despoiled of her flowers.

And whilst together merry thus they make,
  The sun to west a little 'gan to lean,
Which the late fervour soon again did slake,
  When as the nymphs came forth upon the plain.

whig] whey   doucets] sweets

Here might you many a shepherdess have seen,
  Of which no place, as Cotswold, such doth yield;
Some of it native, some for love, I ween,
  Thither were come from many a fertile field.

There was the widow's daughter of the glen,
  Dear Rosalind, that scarcely brooked compare,
The Moorland maiden, so admired of men,
  Bright Goldy-Locks, and Phillida the fair;

Lettice and Parnell, pretty lovely peats,
  Cusse of the fold, the virgin of the well,
Fair Ambry with the alabaster teats,
  And more, whose names were here too long to tell;

Which now came forward following their sheep,
  Their battening flocks on grassy leas to hold,
Thereby from scathe and peril them to keep,
  Till evening come, that it were time to fold.

When now, at last, as liked the shepherds' king,
  (At whose command they all obedient were)
Was 'pointed, who the roundelay should sing,
  And who again the under-song should bear.

The first whereof he Batte doth bequeath,
  A wittier wag on all the wold 's not found;
Gorbo, the man, that him should sing beneath,
  Which his loud bag-pipe skilfully could sound.

peats] girls

When, amongst all the nymphs that were in sight,
  Batte his dainty Daffodil there missed,
Which, to inquire of, doing all his might,
  Him his companion kindly doth assist.

Batte. Gorbo, as thou camest this way,
  By yonder little hill,
Or as thou through the fields didst stray,
  Saw'st thou my Daffodil?

She 's in a frock of Lincoln green,
  Which colour likes her sight,
And never hath her beauty seen,
  But through a veil of white.

Than roses richer to behold,
  That trim up lovers' bowers,
The pansy and the marigold,
  Though Phoebus' paramours.

Gorbo. Thou well describest the daffodil,
  It is not full an hour,
Since by the spring, near yonder hill,
  I saw that lovely flower.

Batte. Yet my fair flower thou didst not meet,
  Nor news of her didst bring,
And yet my Daffodil 's more sweet
  Than that by yonder spring.

Gorbo. I saw a shepherd, that doth keep
  In yonder field of lilies,
Was making (as he fed his sheep)
  A wreath of daffodillies.

Batte. Yet, Gorbo, thou deludest me still,
  My flower thou didst not see;
For, know, my pretty Daffodil
  Is worn of none but me.

To show itself but near her seat
  No lily is so bold,
Except to shade her from the heat,
  Or keep her from the cold.

Gorbo. Through yonder vale as I did pass,
  Descending from the hill,
I met a smirking bonny lass,
  They call her Daffodil;

Whose presence, as along she went,
  The pretty flowers did greet,
As though their heads they downward bent,
  With homage to her feet.

And all the shepherds that were nigh,
  From top of every hill,
Unto the valleys loud did cry,
  'There goes sweet Daffodil.'

Batte. Ay, gentle shepherd, now with joy
Thou all my flocks dost fill,
That's she alone, kind shepherd's boy;
Let us to Daffodil.

The easy turns and quaintness of the song,
And slight occasion whereupon 'twas raised,
Not one this jolly company among,
As most could well judge, highly that not praised.

When Motto next with Perkin pay their debt,
The Moorland maiden Sylvia that espied,
From th' other nymphs a little that was set,
In a near valley by a river's side;

Whose sovereign flowers her sweetness well expressed,
And honoured sight a little not them moved;
To whom their song they reverently addressed,
Both as her loving, both of her beloved.

Motto. Tell me, thou skilful shepherd swain,
Who 's yonder in the valley set?
Perkin. O! it is she, whose sweets do stain
The lily, rose, the violet.

Motto. Why doth the sun against his kind
Stay his bright chariot in the skies?
Perkin. He pauseth, almost strooken blind,
With gazing on her heavenly eyes.

Motto. Why do thy flocks forbear their food,
Which sometime was their chief delight?
Perkin. Because they need no other good,
That live in presence of her sight.

Motto. How come those flowers to flourish still,
Not withering with sharp winter's breath?
Perkin. She hath robbed Nature of her skill,
And comforts all things with her breath.

Motto. Why slide these brooks so slow away,
As swift as the wild roe that were?
Perkin. O! muse not, shepherd, that they stay,
When they her heavenly voice do hear.

Motto. From whence come all these goodly swains,
And lovely girls attired in green?
Perkin. From gathering garlands on the plains,
To crown thy Sylvia shepherds' queen.

Motto. The sun that lights this world below,
Flocks, brooks, and flowers can witness bear.
Perkin. These shepherds, and these nymphs do know,
Thy Sylvia is as chaste as fair.

Lastly, it came unto the clownish king,
Who, to conclude this shepherds' yearly feast,
Bound as the rest, his roundelay to sing,
As all the other him were to assist.

When she (whom then they little did expect,
The fairest nymph that ever kept in field)
Idea did her sober pace direct
Towards them, with joy that every one beheld.

And whereas other drove their careful keep,
Hers did her follow duly at her will,
For through her patience she had learnt her sheep,
Where'er she went, to wait upon her still.

A milk-white dove upon her hand she brought,
So tame, 'twould go, returning at her call,
About whose neck was in a collar wrought,
'Only like me, my mistress hath no gall.'

To whom her swain (unworthy though he were)
Thus unto her his roundelay applies,
To whom the rest the under part did bear,
Casting upon her their still-longing eyes.

Rowland. Of her pure eyes (that now is seen)
Chorus. Come, let us sing, ye faithful swains.
Rowland. O! she alone the shepherds' queen,
Chorus. Her flock that leads,
The goddess of these meads,
These mountains and these plains.

Rowland. Those eyes of hers that are more clear,
Chorus. Than can poor shepherds' songs express,
Rowland. Than be his beams that rules the year.
Chorus. Fie on that praise,
In striving things to raise,
That doth but make them less.

Rowland. That do the flowery spring prolong,
Chorus. So all things in her sight do joy,
Rowland. And keep the plenteous summer young;
Chorus. And do assuage
The wrathful winter's rage,
That would our flocks annoy.

Rowland. Jove saw her breast that naked lay,
Chorus. A sight most fit for Jove to see,
Rowland. And swore it was the Milky Way,
Chorus. Of all most pure,
The path (we us assure)
To his bright court to be.

Rowland. He saw her tresses hanging down,
Chorus. That moved with the gentle air,
Rowland. And said that Ariadne's crown,
Chorus. With those compared,
The gods should not regard,
Nor Berenice's hair.

Rowland. When she hath watched my flocks by night,
Chorus. O happy flocks that she did keep,
Rowland. They never needed Cynthia's light,
Chorus. That soon gave place,
Amazed with her grace,
That did attend thy sheep.

Rowland. Above, where Heaven's high glories are,
Chorus. When she is placed in the skies,
Rowland. She shall be called the shepherds' star,
Chorus. And evermore,
We shepherds will adore
Her setting and her rise.

c. 1600; *The Shepherd's Garland; Poems Lyric and Pastoral,* 1606

MICHAEL DRAYTON

319 *Rowland's Rhyme*

THAN this great universe no less
Can serve her praises to express.
Betwixt her eyes, the poles of love,
The host of heavenly beauties move,
Depainted in their proper stories,
As well the fixed as wandering glories,
Which from their proper orbs not go,
Whether they gyre swift or slow;
Where from their lips, when she doth speak,
The music of those spheres do break,
Which their harmonious motion breedeth;
From whose cheerful breath proceedeth
That balmy sweetness that gives birth
To every offspring of the earth;
The structure of whose general frame,
And state wherein she moves the same,
Is that proportion, heaven's best treasure,
Whereby it doth all poise and measure,
So that alone her happy sight
Contains perfection and delight.

The Shepherd's Garland, Poems, 1605

320

Sonnets to Idea

(i)

READ here (sweet maid) the story of my woe,
The dreary abstracts of my endless cares,
With my life's sorrow interlined so,
Smoked with my sighs, and blotted with my tears;
The sad memorials of my miseries,
Penned in the grief of mine afflicted ghost;
My life's complaint in doleful elegies,
With so pure love as time could never boast.
Receive the incense which I offer here,
By my strong faith ascending to thy fame,
My zeal, my hope, my vows, my praise, my prayer,
My soul's oblation to thy sacred name:
Which name my Muse to highest heaven shall raise
By chaste desire, true love, and virtue's praise.

(ii)

STAY, speedy Time, behold, before thou pass,
From age to age what thou hast sought to see,
One in whom all the excellencies be,
In whom Heaven looks itself as in a glass.
Time, look thou too in this tralucent glass,
And thy youth past in this pure mirror see,
As the world's beauty in his infancy,
What it was then; and thou before it was.
Pass on, and to posterity tell this,
Yet see thou tell but truly what hath been;
Say to our nephews that thou once hast seen
In perfect human shape all heavenly bliss;
And bid them mourn, nay more, despair with thee,
That she is gone, her like again to see.

(*iii*)

MY heart, imprisoned in a hopeless isle,
Peopled with armies of pale jealous eyes,
The shores beset with thousand secret spies,
Must pass by air, or else die in exile.
He framed him wings with feathers of his thought,
Which by their nature learned to mount the sky;
And with the same he practised to fly,
Till he himself this eagle's art had taught.
Thus soaring still, not looking once below,
So near thine eyes' celestial sun aspired,
That with the rays his wafting pinions fired;
Thus was the wanton cause of his own woe.
Down fell he, in thy beauty's ocean drenched;
Yet there he burns in fire that's never quenched.

(*iv*)

THE glorious sun went blushing to his bed,
When my soul's sun from her fair cabinet
Her golden beams had now discovered,
Lightening the world eclipsed by his set.
Some mused to see the earth envy the air,
Which from her lips exhaled refined sweet,
A world to see, yet how he joyed to hear
The dainty grass make music with her feet.
But my most marvel was when from the skies
So comet-like each star advanced her light,
As though the heaven had now awaked her eyes,
And summoned angels to this blessed sight.
No cloud was seen, but crystalline the air,
Laughing for joy upon my lovely Fair.

(*v*)

MY fair, look from those turrets of thine eyes,
  Into the ocean of a troubled mind,
Where my poor soul, the bark of sorrow, lies,
  Left to the mercy of the waves and wind.
See where she floats, laden with purest love,
  Which those fair islands of thy looks afford,
Desiring yet a thousand deaths to prove,
  Than so to cast her ballast overboard.
See how her sails be rent, her tacklings worn,
  Her cable broke, her surest anchor lost:
Her mariners do leave her all forlorn,
  Yet how she bends towards that blessed coast.
    Lo! where she drowns in storms of thy displeasure,
    Whose worthy prize should have enriched thy treasure.

(*vi*)

IF chaste and pure devotion of my youth,
  Or glory of my April-springing years,
Unfeignеd love in naked, simple truth,
  A thousand vows, a thousand sighs and tears;
Or if a world of faithful service done,
  Words, thoughts, and deeds devoted to her honour,
Or eyes that have beheld her as their sun,
  With admiration ever looking on her;
A life that never joyed but in her love,
  A soul that ever hath adored her name,
A faith that time nor fortune could not move,
  A Muse that unto heaven hath raised her fame;
    Though these, nor these, deserve to be embraced,
    Yet, fair unkind, too good to be disgraced.

(*vii*)

BLACK pitchy night, companion of my woe,
  The inn of care, the nurse of dreary sorrow,
Why lengthenest thou thy darkest hours so,
  Still to prolong my long time looked-for morrow?
Thou sable shadow, image of despair,
  Portrait of hell, the air's black mourning weed,
Recorder of revenge, remembrancer of care,
  The shadow and the veil of every sinful deed!
Death like to thee, so live thou still in death,
  The grave of joy, prison of day's delight.
Let heavens withdraw their sweet ambrosian breath,
  Nor moon nor stars lend thee their shining light;
    For thou alone renew'st that old desire,
    Which still torments me in day's burning fire.

(*viii*)

TO nothing fitter can I thee compare
  Than to the son of some rich pennyfather,
Who having now brought on his end with care,
  Leaves to his son all he had heaped together;
This new rich novice, lavish of his chest,
  To one man gives, doth on another spend,
Then here he riots, yet amongst the rest
  Haps to lend some to one true honest friend.
Thy gifts thou in obscurity dost waste,
  False friends thy kindness, born but to deceive thee,
Thy love, that is on the unworthy placed,
  Time hath thy beauty, which with age will leave thee;
    Only that little which to me was lent
    I give thee back, when all the rest is spent.

(ix)

AN evil spirit, your beauty, haunts me still,
  Wherewith, alas! I have been long possessed,
Which ceaseth not to tempt me to each ill,
  Nor gives me once but one poor minute's rest;
In me it speaks, whether I sleep or wake,
  And when by means to drive it out I try,
With greater torments then it me doth take,
  And tortures me in most extremity;
Before my face it lays down my despairs,
  And hastes me on unto a sudden death,
Now tempting me to drown myself in tears,
  And then in sighing to give up my breath.
    Thus am I still provoked to every evil
    By this good wicked spirit, sweet angel devil.

(x)

WHILST thus my pen strives to eternize thee,
  Age rules my lines with wrinkles in my face,
Where in the map of all my misery
  Is modelled out the world of my disgrace.
Whilst in despite of tyrannizing times,
  Medea-like I make thee young again,
Proudly thou scorn'st my world-outwearing rhymes,
  And murder'st virtue with thy coy disdain;
And though in youth my youth untimely perish,
  To keep thee from oblivion and the grave,
Ensuing ages yet my rhymes shall cherish,
  Where I entombed my better part shall save;
    And though this earthly body fade and die,
    My name shall mount upon eternity.

(*xi*)

DEAR, why should you command me to my rest,
  When now the night doth summon all to sleep?
Methinks this time becometh lovers best;
  Night was ordained together friends to keep.
How happy are all other living things,
  Which though the day disjoin by several flight,
The quiet evening yet together brings,
  And each returns unto his love at night.
O thou that art so courteous else to all,
  Why shouldst thou, Night, abuse me only thus,
That every creature to his kind dost call,
  And yet 'tis thou dost only sever us?
    Well could I wish it would be ever day,
    If, when night comes, you bid me go away.

(*xii*)

WHY should your fair eyes with such sovereign grace
  Disperse their rays on every vulgar spirit,
Whilst I in darkness in the self-same place
  Get not one glance to recompense my merit?
So doth the ploughman gaze the wandering star,
  And only rest contented with the light,
That never learned what constellations are,
  Beyond the bent of his unknowing sight.
O! why should beauty, custom to obey,
  To their gross sense apply herself so ill?
Would God I were as ignorant as they,
  When I am made unhappy by my skill;
    Only compelled on this poor good to boast,
    Heavens are not kind to them that know them most.

(*xiii*)

CALLING to mind since first my love begun,
  Th' incertain times oft varying in their course,
How things still unexpectedly have run,
  As please the Fates, by their resistless force,
Lastly, mine eyes amazedly have seen
  Essex great fall, Tyrone his peace to gain,
The quiet end of that long-living Queen,
  This King's fair entrance, and our peace with Spain,
We and the Dutch at length ourselves to sever.
  Thus the world doth, and evermore shall reel,
Yet to my goddess am I constant ever,
  Howe'er blind Fortune turn her giddy wheel.
    Though heaven and earth prove both to me untrue,
    Yet am I still inviolate to you.

(*xiv*)

HOW many paltry, foolish, painted things,
  That now in coaches trouble every street,
Shall be forgotten, whom no poet sings,
  Ere they be well wrapped in their winding-sheet?
Where I to thee eternity shall give,
  When nothing else remaineth of these days,
And Queens hereafter shall be glad to live
  Upon the alms of thy superfluous praise.
Virgins and matrons reading these my rhymes,
  Shall be so much delighted with thy story,
That they shall grieve they lived not in these times,
  To have seen thee, their sex's only glory.
    So shalt thou fly above the vulgar throng,
    Still to survive in my immortal song.

(*xv*)

SINCE there 's no help, come let us kiss and part.
Nay, I have done; you get no more of me,
And I am glad, yea, glad with all my heart,
That thus so cleanly I myself can free;
Shake hands for ever, cancel all our vows,
And when we meet at any time again,
Be it not seen in either of our brows
That we one jot of former love retain.
Now at the last gasp of Love's latest breath,
When, his pulse failing, Passion speechless lies,
When Faith is kneeling by his bed of death,
And Innocence is closing up his eyes,
Now if thou wouldst, when all have given him over,
From death to life thou mightst him yet recover.

Idea, 1593; *Idea's Mirror*, 1594;
Poems, 1599, 1602, 1605, 1619

321 *Phoebe on Latmus*

IN Ionia whence sprang old poets' fame,
From whom that sea did first derive her name,
The blessed bed whereon the Muses lay,
Beauty of Greece, the pride of Asia,
Whence Archelaus, whom times historify,
First unto Athens brought philosophy:
In this fair region on a goodly plain,
Stretching her bounds unto the bordering main,
The mountain Latmus overlooks the sea,
Smiling to see the ocean billows play:
Latmus, where young Endymion used to keep
His fairest flock of silver-fleeced sheep,

To whom Silvanus often would resort,
At barley-brake to see the Satyrs sport;
And when rude Pan his tabret list to sound,
To see the fair nymphs foot it in a round,
Under the trees which on this mountain grew,
As yet the like Arabia never knew;
For all the pleasures Nature could devise
Within this plot she did imparadise;
And great Diana of her special grace
With vestal rites had hallowed all the place.
Upon this mount there stood a stately grove,
Whose reaching arms to clip the welkin strove,
Of tufted cedars, and the branching pine,
Whose bushy tops themselves do so entwine,
As seemed, when Nature first this work begun,
She then conspired against the piercing sun;
Under whose covert (thus divinely made)
Phoebus' green laurel flourished in the shade,
Fair Venus' myrtle, Mars his warlike fir,
Minerva's olive, and the weeping myrrh,
The patient palm, which thrives in spite of hate,
The poplar, to Alcides consecrate;
Which Nature in such order had disposed,
And therewithal these goodly walks inclosed,
As served for hangings and rich tapestry,
To beautify this stately gallery.
Embroidering these in curious trails along,
The clustered grapes, the golden citrons hung,
More glorious than the precious fruit were these,
Kept by the dragon in Hesperides,
Or gorgeous arras in rich colours wrought,

barley-brake] prisoners' base

With silk from Afric, or from Indy brought.
Out of this soil sweet bubbling fountains crept,
As though for joy the senseless stones had wept,
With straying channels dancing sundry ways,
With often turns, like to a curious maze;
Which breaking forth the tender grass bedewed,
Whose silver sand with orient pearl was strewed,
Shadowed with roses and sweet eglantine,
Dipping their sprays into this crystalline;
From which the birds the purple berries pruned,
And to their loves their small recorders tuned,
The nightingale, wood's herald of the spring,
The whistling ouzel, mavis carolling,
Tuning their trebles to the waters' fall,
Which made the music more angelical;
Whilst gentle Zephyr murmuring among
Kept time, and bare the burthen to the song:
About whose brims, refreshed with dainty showers,
Grew amaranthus, and sweet gilliflowers,
The marigold, Phoebus' beloved friend,
The moly, which from sorcery doth defend,
Violet, carnation, balm, and cassia,
Idea's primrose, coronet of may.
Above this grove a gentle fair ascent,
Which by degrees of milk-white marble went:
Upon the top, a paradise was found,
With which Nature this miracle had crowned,
Empaled with rocks of rarest precious stone,
Which like the flames of Aetna brightly shone,
And served as lanthorns furnished with light,
To guide the wandering passengers by night:
For which fair Phoebe, sliding from her sphere,

Used oft times to come and sport her there,
And from the azure starry-painted sky
Embalmed the banks with precious lunary:
That now her Maenalus she quite forsook,
And unto Latmus wholly her betook,
And in this place her pleasure used to take,
And all was for her sweet Endymion's sake;
Endymion, the lovely shepherds' boy,
Endymion, great Phoebe's only joy,
Endymion, in whose pure-shining eyes
The naked fairies danced the heydegies.
The shag-haired Satyrs' mountain-climbing race
Have been made tame by gazing in his face.
For this boy's love, the water-nymphs have wept,
Stealing oft times to kiss him whilst he slept,
And tasting once the nectar of his breath,
Surfeit with sweet, and languish unto death;
And Jove oft-times bent to lascivious sport,
And coming where Endymion did resort,
Hath courted him, inflamed with desire,
Thinking some nymph was clothed in boy's attire.
And often-times the simple rural swains,
Beholding him in crossing o'er the plains,
Imagined, Apollo from above
Put on this shape, to win some maiden's love.
This shepherd Phoebe ever did behold,
Whose love already had her thoughts controlled;
From Latmus top (her stately throne) she rose,
And to Endymion down beneath she goes.
Her brother's beams now had she laid aside,
Her horned crescent, and her full-faced pride:
For had she come adorned with her light,

No mortal eye could have endured the sight;
But like a nymph, crowned with a flowery twine,
And not like Phoebe, as herself divine.
An azured mantle purfled with a veil,
Which in the air puffed like a swelling sail,
Embosted rainbows did appear in silk,
With wavy streams as white as morning's milk;
Which ever as the gentle air did blow,
Still with the motion seemed to ebb and flow;
About her neck a chain twice twenty fold,
Of rubies, set in lozenges of gold;
Trussed up in trammels, and in curious pleats,
With sphery circles falling on her teats.
A dainty smock of cypress, fine and thin,
O'er cast with curls next to her lily skin;
Through which the pureness of the same did show
Like damask-roses strewed with flakes of snow,
Discovering all her stomach to the waist,
With branches of sweet circling veins enchased.
A coronet she ware of myrtle boughs,
Which gave a shadow to her ivory brows.
No smother-beauty mask did beauty smother.
Great lights dim less yet burn not one another,
Nature abhors to borrow from the mart,
Simples fit beauty, fie on drugs and art.
  Thus came she where her love Endymion lay,
Who with sweet carols sang the night away;
And as it is the shepherds' usual trade,
Oft on his pipe a roundelay he played.
As meek he was as any lamb might be,
Nor never lived a fairer youth than he.
His dainty hand the snow itself did stain,

Or her to whom Jove showered in golden rain;
From whose sweet palm the liquid pearl did swell,
Pure as the drops of Aganippe's well,
Clear as the liquor which fair Hebe spilt;
His sheephook silver, damasked all with gilt,
The staff itself, of snowy ivory,
Studded with coral, tipped with ebony;
His tresses, of the raven's shining black,
Straggling in curls along his manly back;
The balls which nature in his eyes had set,
Like diamonds enclosing globes of jet,
Which sparkled from their milky lids out-right,
Like fair Orion's heaven-adorning light,
The stars on which her heavenly eyes were bent,
And fixed still with lovely blandishment;
For whom so oft disguised she was seen,
As she celestial Phoebe had not been;
Her dainty buskins laced unto the knee,
Her pleated frock, tucked up accordingly.
A nymph-like huntress, armed with bow and dart,
About the woods she scours the long-lived hart.
She climbs the mountains with the light-foot Fauns
And with the Satyrs scuds it o'er the lawns.
In music's sweet delight she shews her skill,
Quavering the cittern nimbly with her quill.
Upon each tree she carves Endymion's name
In gordian knots, with Phoebe to the same.
To kill him venison now she pitched her toils,
And to this lovely ranger brings the spoils;
And thus whilst she by chaste desire is led
Unto the downs where he his fair flocks fed,
Near to a grove she had Endymion spied,

Where he was fishing by a river side
Under a poplar, shadowed from the sun,
Where merrily to court him she begun.

Endimion and Phoebe, 1–164, 1595

322 *Endymion's Convoy*

AND now at length the joyful time drew on,
She meant to honour her Endymion,
And glorify him on that stately mount,
Whereof the goddess made so great account.
She sends Jove's winged herald to the woods,
The neighbour fountains, and the bordering floods,
Charging the Nymphs which did inhabit there,
Upon a day appointed to appear,
And to attend her sacred majesty,
In all their pomp and great solemnity.
Having obtained great Phoebus' free consent,
To further her divine and chaste intent,
Which thus imposed as a thing of weight,
In stately troops appear before her straight
The Fauns and Satyrs from the tufted brakes,
Their bristly arms wreathed all about with snakes,
Their sturdy loins with ropes of ivy bound,
Their horned heads with woodbine chaplets crowned,
With cypress javelins, and about their thighs
The flaggy hair disordered loosely flies;
The Oreads, like to the Spartan maid,
In murrey sendal gorgeously arrayed,
With gallant green scarfs girded in the waist,
Their flaxen hair with silken fillets laced,

Wove with flowers in sweet lascivious wreaths,
Moving like feathers as the light air breathes,
With crowns of myrtle, glorious to behold,
Whose leaves are painted with pure drops of gold,
With trains of fine byss chequered all with frets
Of dainty pinks and precious violets,
In branched buskins of fine cordiwin,
With spangled garters down unto the shin,
Fringed with fine silk, of many a sundry kind,
Which like to pennons waved with the wind.
The Hamadryads from their shady bowers,
Decked up in garlands of the rarest flowers,
Upon the backs of milk-white bulls were set,
With horn and hoof as black as any jet,
Whose collars were great massy golden rings,
Led by their swains in twisted silken strings.
Then did the lovely Dryades appear,
On dappled stags which bravely mounted were,
Whose velvet palms, with nosegays rarely dight,
To all the rest bred wonderful delight.
And in this sort, accompanied with these,
In triumph rid the watery Naiades,
Upon sea-horses, trapped with shining fins,
Armed with their mail, impenetrable skins;
Whose scaly crests, like rainbows bended high,
Seem to control proud Iris in the sky.
Upon a chariot was Endymion laid,
In snowy tissue gorgeously arrayed,
Of precious ivory covered o'er with lawn,
Which by four stately unicorns was drawn.
Of ropes of orient pearl their traces were,

byss] linen   cordiwin] leather

Pure as the path which doth in heaven appear,
With rarest flowers enchased and over-spread,
Which served as curtains to this glorious bed,
Whose seat of crystal in the sun-beams shone,
Like thunder-breathing Jove's celestial throne;
Upon his head a coronet installed
Of one entire and mighty emerald,
With richest bracelets on his lily wrists,
Of heliotropium, linked with golden twists;
A bevy of fair swans, which flying over
With their large wings him from the sun do cover,
And easily wafting as he went along,
Do lull him still with their enchanting song,
Whilst all the Nymphs on solemn instruments
Sound dainty music to their sweet laments.

Endimion and Phoebe, 743–812, 1595

323 *Fame and Fortune*

WHAT time soft night had silently begun
To steal by minutes on the long-lived days,
The furious dog-star, following the bright sun,
With noisome heat infests his cheerful rays,
Filling the earth with many a sad disease;
Which then, inflamed with their intemperate fires,
Herself in light habiliments attires.

And the rathe morning, newly but awake,
Was with fresh beauty burnishing her brows,
Herself beholding in the general lake,
To which she pays her never ceasing vows.
With the new day me willingly to rouse,
Down to fair Thames I gently took my way,
With whom the winds continually do play.

Striving to fancy his chaste breast to move,
  Whereas all pleasures plentifully flow,
When him along the wanton tide doth shove,
  And to keep back, they easily do blow,
  Or else force forward, thinking him too slow;
    Who with his waves would check the winds' embrace,
    Whilst they fan air upon his crystal face:

Still forward sallying from his bounteous source,
  Along the shores lasciviously doth strain,
Making such strange meanders in his course,
  As to his fountain he would back again,
  Or turned about to look upon his train;
    Whose sundry soils with coy regard he greets,
    Till with clear Medway happily he meets.

Steering my compass by this wandering stream,
  Whose flight preached to me time's swift-posting hours,
Delighted thus, as with some pretty dream,
  Where pleasure wholly had possessed my powers,
  And looking back on London's stately towers,
    So Troy, thought I, her stately head did rear,
    Whose crazed ribs the furrowing plough doth ear.

Weary, at length a willow tree I found,
  Which on the bank of this brave river stood,
Whose root with rich grass greatly did abound,
  Forced by the fluxure of the swelling flood,
  Ordained (it seemed) to sport his nymphish brood,
    Whose curled top envied the heavens great eye
    Should view the stock it was maintained by.

ear] plough

MICHAEL DRAYTON

The lark, that holds observance to the sun,
  Quavered her clear notes in the quiet air,
And on the river's murmuring bass did run,
  Whilst the pleased heaven her fairest livery ware,
  The place such pleasure gently did prepare;
    The flowers my smell, the flood my taste to steep,
    And the much softness lulled me asleep.

When in a vision as it seemed to me,
  Triumphal music from the flood arose,
As when the sovereign we embarged see,
  And by fair London for her pleasure rows,
  Whose tender welcome the glad city shows;
    The people swarming on the pestered shores,
    And the curled waters over-spread with oars.

A troop of nymphs came suddenly on land,
  In the full end of this triumphal sound,
And me encompassed, taking hand in hand,
  Casting themselves about me in a round,
  And so down set them on the easy ground,
    Bending their clear eyes with a modest grace
    Upon my swart and melancholy face.

Next, 'twixt two ladies, came a goodly knight,
  As newly brought from some distressful place,
To me who seemed some right worthy wight,
  Though his attire were miserably base,
  And time had worn deep furrows in his face;
    Yet, though cold age had frosted his fair hairs,
    It rather seemed with sorrow than with years.

The one a lady of a princely port,
  Leading this sad lord, scarcely that could stand;
The other, fleering in disdainful sort,
  With scornful gestures drew him by the hand,
  Who, lame and blind, yet bound with many a band:
    When I perceived nearer as they came,
    This fool was Fortune, and the braver Fame.

Fame had the right hand in a robe of gold,
  (Whose train old Time obsequiously did bear)
Whereon in rich embroidery was enrolled
  The names of all that worthies ever were,
  Which all might read depainted lively there,
    Set down in lofty well-composed verse,
    Fitt'st the great deeds of heroes to rehearse.

On her fair breast she two broad tablets wore,
  Of crystal one, the other ebony;
On which engraven were all names of yore
  In the clear tomb of living memory,
  Or the black book of endless obloquy;
    The first with poets and with conquerors piled,
    That with base worldlings everywhere defiled.

And in her words appeared (as a wonder)
  Her present force and after-during might,
Which, softly spoke, far off were heard to thunder
  About the world, that quickly took their flight,
  And brought the most obscurest things to light;
    That still the farther off, the greater still
    Did make our good, or manifest our ill.

Fortune, as blind as he whom she did lead,
  Changing her feature often in an hour,
Fantastically carrying her head,
  Soon would she smile, and suddenly would lour,
  And with one breath her words were sweet and sour;
    Upon stark fools she amorously would glance,
    And upon wise men coyly look askance.

About her neck, in manner of a chain,
  Torn diadems and broken sceptres hung;
If any on her steadfastly did lean,
  Them to the ground despitefully she flung;
  And in this posture as she passed along,
    She bags of gold out of her bosom drew,
    Which she to sots and arrant idiots threw.

A dusky veil did hide her sightless eyes,
  Like clouds that cover our uncertain lives,
Whereon were portrayed direful tragedies,
  Fools wearing crowns, and wise men clogged in gyves;
  How all things she preposterously contrives,
    Which, as a map, her regency discovers
    In camps, in courts, and in the way of lovers.

The Legend of Robert, Duke of Normandy, 1–119, 1596.

324 *King Henry to Rosamond*

WHEN first the post arrived at my tent,
And brought the letters Rosamond had sent,
Think from his lips but what dear comfort came,
When in mine ear he softly breathed thy name.

Straight I enjoined him of thy health to tell,
Longing to hear my Rosamond did well;
With new inquiries then I cut him short,
When of the same he gladly would report,
That with the earnest haste my tongue oft trips,
Catching the words half spoke out of his lips:
This told, yet more I urge him to reveal,
To lose no time, whilst I unripped the seal.
The more I read, still do I err the more,
As though mistaking somewhat said before:
Missing the point, the doubtful sense is broken,
Speaking again what I before had spoken.
   Still in a swoon my heart revives and faints
'Twixt hopes, despairs, 'twixt smiles and deep complaints,
As these sad accents sort in my desires,
Smooth calms, rough storms, sharp frost, and raging fires,
Put on with boldness, and put back with fears,
For oft thy troubles do extort my tears.
O! how my heart at that black line did tremble,
That blotted paper should thyself resemble.
O! were there paper but near half so white,
The gods thereon their sacred laws would write
With pens of angels' wings; and for their ink,
That heavenly nectar, their immortal drink!
Majestic courage strives to have suppressed
This fearful passion, stirred up in my breast;
But still in vain the same I go about,
My heart must break within, or woes break out.
Am I at home pursued with private hate,
And war comes raging to my palace gate?
Is meagre Envy stabbing at my throne,
Treason attending when I walk alone?

And am I branded with the curse of Rome,
And stand condemned by a council's doom?
And by the pride of my rebellious son,
Rich Normandy with armies over-run?
Fatal my birth, unfortunate my life,
Unkind my children, most unkind my wife.
Grief, cares, old age, suspicion to torment me,
Nothing on earth to quiet or content me;
So many woes, so many plagues, to find,
Sickness of body, discontent of mind;
Hopes left, helps reft, life wronged, joy interdicted,
Banished, distressed, forsaken, and afflicted.
Of all relief hath Fortune quite bereft me,
Only my love yet to my comfort left me?
And is one beauty thought so great a thing,
To mitigate the sorrows of a king?
Barred of that choice the vulgar often prove,
Have we, than they, less privilege in love?
Is it a king the woeful widow hears?
Is it a king dries up the orphans' tears?
Is it a king regards the client's cry?
Gives life to him, by law condemned to die?
Is it his care the commonwealth that keeps,
As doth the nurse her baby whilst it sleeps?
And that poor king of all those hopes prevented,
Unheard, unhelped, unpitied, unlamented?
  Yet let me be with poverty oppressed,
Of earthly blessings robbed and dispossessed;
Let me be scorned, rejected, and reviled,
And from my kingdom let me live exiled;
Let the world's curse upon me still remain,
And let the last bring on the first again;

All miseries that wretched man may wound,
Leave for my comfort only Rosamond.
For thee swift Time his speedy course doth stay,
At thy command the Destinies obey;
Pity is dead, that comes not from thine eyes,
And at thy feet even Mercy prostrate lies.
  If I were feeble, rheumatic, or cold,
These were true signs that I were waxed old;
But I can march all day in massy steel,
Nor yet my arms' unwieldy weight do feel;
Nor waked by night with bruise or bloody wound,
The tent my bed, no pillow but the ground.
For very age had I lain bed-rid long,
One smile of thine again could make me young.
Were there in art a power but so divine,
As is in that sweet angel-tongue of thine,
That great enchantress, which once took such pains
To put young blood into old Aeson's veins,
And in groves, mountains, and the moorish fen,
Sought out more herbs than had been known to men,
And in the powerful potion that she makes,
Put blood of men, of birds, of beasts, and snakes,
Never had needed to have gone so far,
To seek the soils where all those simples are;
One accent from thy lips the blood more warms,
Than all her philtres, exorcisms, and charms.
Thy presence hath repaired, in one day,
What many years with sorrows did decay,
And made fresh beauty in her flower to spring
Out of the wrinkles of time's ruining.
Even as the hungry winter-starved earth,
When she by nature labours towards her birth,

Still as the day upon the dark world creeps,
One blossom forth after another peeps,
Till the small flower, whose root at last unbound
Gets from the frosty prison of the ground,
Spreading the leaves unto the powerful noon,
Decked in fresh colours smiles upon the sun.
  Never unquiet care lodged in that breast,
Where but one thought of Rosamond did rest;
Nor thirst nor travail, which on war attend,
Ere brought the long day to desired end;
Nor yet did pale fear or lean famine live,
Where hope of thee did any comfort give.
Ah! what injustice then is this of thee,
That thus the guiltless dost condemn for me?
When only she (by means of my offence)
Redeems thy pureness and thy innocence.
When to our wills perforce obey they must,
That 's just in them, whate'er in us unjust;
Of what we do, not them, account we make,
The fault craves pardon for th' offender's sake;
And what to work a prince's will may merit,
Hath deep'st impression in the gentlest spirit.
  If 't be my name that doth thee so offend,
No more myself shall be mine own name's friend;
If it be that which thou dost only hate,
That name in my name lastly has his date.
Say, 'tis accurst and fatal, and dispraise it;
If written, blot it; if engraven, raze it;
Say, that of all names 'tis a name of woe,
Once a king's name, but now it is not so:
And when all this is done, I know 'twill grieve thee,
And therefore (Sweet) why should I now believe thee?

Nor shouldst thou think those eyes with envy lour,
Which, passing by thee, gaze up to thy tower;
But rather praise thine own, which be so clear,
Which from the turret like two stars appear.
Above, the sun doth shine; beneath, thine eye,
Mocking the heaven, to make another sky.
The little stream which by thy tower doth glide,
Where oft thou spend'st the weary evening-tide,
To view thee well, his course would gladly stay,
As loth from thee to part so soon away,
And with salutes thyself would gladly greet,
And offer up some small drops at thy feet;
But finding that the envious banks restrain it,
T'excuse itself, doth in this sort complain it,
And therefore this sad bubbling murmur keeps,
And for thy want within the channel weeps.
And as thou dost into the water look,
The fish, which see thy shadow in the brook,
Forget to feed, and all amazed lie,
So daunted with the lustre of thine eye.
And that sweet name, which thou so much dost wrong,
In time shall be some famous poet's song;
And with the very sweetness of that name
Lions and tigers men shall learn to tame.
The careful mother, at her pensive breast,
With Rosamond shall bring her babe to rest;
The little birds (by men's continual sound)
Shall learn to speak and prattle Rosamond;
And when in April they begin to sing,
With Rosamond shall welcome in the spring;
And she in whom all rarities are found,
Shall still be said to be a Rosamond.

The little flowers dropping their honeyed dew,
Which (as thou writest) do weep upon thy shoe,
Not for thy fault (sweet Rosamond) do moan,
Only lament, that thou so soon art gone;
For if thy foot touch hemlock as it goes,
That hemlock 's made more sweeter than the rose.
Of Jove or Neptune, how they did betray,
Speak not, of Io or Amymone;
When she, for whom Jove once became a bull,
Compared with thee, had been a tawny trull;
He a white bull, and she a whiter cow,
Yet he nor she near half so white as thou.
Long since (thou know'st) my care provided for
To lodge thee safe from jealous Ellinor;
The labyrinth's conveyance guides thee so,
(Which only Vaughan, thou, and I, do know)
If she do guard thee with an hundred eyes,
I have an hundred subtle Mercuries,
To watch that Argus which my love doth keep,
Until eye after eye fall all to sleep.
And those stars which look in, but look to see
(Wondering) what star here on the earth should be;
As oft the moon, amidst the silent night,
Hath come to joy us with her friendly light,
And by the curtain helped mine eye to see,
What envious night and darkness hid from me;
When I have wished that she might ever stay,
And other worlds might still enjoy the day.
What should I say? Words, tears, and sighs be spent,
And want of time doth further help prevent.
My camp resounds with fearful shocks of war,
Yet in my breast more dangerous conflicts are;

Yet is my signal to the battle's sound
The blessed name of beauteous Rosamond.
Accursed be that heart, that tongue, that breath,
Should think, should speak, or whisper of thy death;
For in one smile or lour from thy sweet eye
Consists my life, my hope, my victory.
Sweet Woodstock, where my Rosamond doth rest,
Be blest in her, in whom thy king is blest:
For though in France awhile my body be,
My heart remains (dear Paradise) in thee.

England's Heroical Epistles, 1597

325 *The Earl of Surrey to Geraldine*

THE Earl of Surrey, that renowned lord,
Th' old English glory bravely that restored,
That prince and poet (a name more divine),
Falling in love with beauteous Geraldine
Of the Geraldi, which derive their name
From Florence, whither, to advance her fame,
He travels, and in public jousts maintained
Her beauty peerless, which by arms he gained;
But staying long, fair Italy to see,
To let her know him constant still to be,
From Tuscany this letter to her writes,
Which her rescription instantly invites.

From learned Florence, long time rich in fame,
From whence thy race, thy noble grandsires, came,
To famous England, that kind nurse of mine,
Thy Surrey sends to heavenly Geraldine;

Yet let not Tuscan think I do it wrong,
That I from thence write in my native tongue,
That in these harsh-tuned cadences I sing,
Sitting so near the Muses' sacred spring;
But rather think itself adorned thereby,
That England reads the praise of Italy.
Though to the Tuscans I the smoothness grant,
Our dialect no majesty doth want
To set thy praises in as high a key,
As France, or Spain, or Germany, or they.
What day I quit the Foreland of fair Kent,
And that my ship her course for Flanders bent,
Yet think I with how many a heavy look
My leave of England and of thee I took,
And did entreat the tide, if it might be,
But to convey me one sigh back to thee.
Up to the deck a billow lightly skips,
Taking my sigh, and down again it slips;
Into the gulf itself it headlong throws,
And as a post to England-ward it goes.
As I sat wondering how the rough seas stirred,
I might far off perceive a little bird,
Which, as she fain from shore to shore would fly,
Had lost herself in the broad vasty sky,
Her feeble wing beginning to deceive her,
The seas of life still gaping to bereave her;
Unto the ship she makes, which she discovers,
And there, poor fool, a while for refuge hovers;
And when at length her flagging pinion fails,
Panting she hangs upon the rattling sails,
And being forced to loose her hold with pain,
Yet beaten off she straight lights on again,

And tossed with flaws, with storms, with wind, with weather,
Yet still departing thence, still turneth thither;
Now with the poop, now with the prow doth bear,
Now on this side, now that, now here, now there.
Methinks these storms should be my sad depart,
The silly helpless bird is my poor heart,
The ship to which for succour it repairs,
That is yourself, regardless of my cares.
Of every surge doth fall, or wave doth rise,
To some one thing I sit and moralize.
  When for thy love I left the Belgic shore,
Divine Erasmus and our famous More,
Whose happy presence gave me such delight
As made a minute of a winter's night,
With whom a while I stayed at Rotterdam,
Now so renowned by Erasmus' name,
Yet every hour did seem a world of time,
Till I had seen that soul-reviving clime,
And thought the foggy Netherlands unfit,
A watery soil to clog a fiery wit.
And as that wealthy Germany I passed,
Coming unto the Emperor's court at last,
Great learned Agrippa, so profound in art,
Who the infernal secrets doth impart,
When of thy health I did desire to know,
Me in a glass my Geraldine did show,
Sick in thy bed and, for thou couldst not sleep,
By a wax taper set the light to keep.
I do remember thou didst read that ode
Sent back whilst I in Thanet made abode,
Where when thou camest unto that word of love,
Even in thine eyes I saw how passion strove.

That snowy lawn which covered thy bed,
Methought looked white, to see thy cheek so red;
Thy rosy cheek, oft changing in my sight,
Yet still was red, to see the lawn so white;
The little taper, which should give thee light,
Methought waxed dim, to see thine eye so bright;
Thine eye again supplied the taper's turn,
And with his beams more brightly made it burn;
The shrugging air about thy temples hurls,
And wrapped thy breath in little clouded curls,
And as it did ascend, it straight did seize it,
And as it sunk, it presently did raise it.
Canst thou by sickness banish beauty so?
Which if put from thee knows not where to go,
To make her shift and for her succour seek
To every rivelled face, each bankrupt cheek.
If health preserved, thou beauty still dost cherish,
If that neglected, beauty soon doth perish.
Care draws on care, woe comforts woe again,
Sorrow breeds sorrow, one grief brings forth twain;
If live or die, as thou dost so do I,
If live, I live, and if thou die, I die;
One heart, one love, one joy, one grief, one troth,
One good, one ill, one life, one death to both.
  If Howard's blood thou hold'st as but too vile,
Or not esteem'st of Norfolk's princely style;
If Scotland's coat no mark of fame can lend,
That lion placed in our bright silver bend,
(Which as a trophy beautifies our shield
Since Scottish blood discoloured Flodden field,
When the proud Cheviot our brave ensign bare

rivelled] wrinkled

As a rich jewel in a lady's hair,
And did fair Bramston's neighbouring valleys choke
With clouds of cannons, fire-disgorged smoke),
Or Surrey's earldom insufficient be
And not a dower so well contenting thee:
Yet am I one of great Apollo's heirs,
The sacred Muses challenge me for theirs.
By princes my immortal lines are sung,
My flowing verses graced with every tongue;
The little children, when they learn to go,
By painful mothers daded to and fro,
Are taught my sugared numbers to rehearse,
And have their sweet lips seasoned with my verse.
  When heaven would strive to do the best it can,
And put an angel's spirit into a man,
The utmost power it hath it then doth spend,
When to the world a poet it doth intend;
That little difference 'twixt the gods and us,
By them confirmed, distinguished only thus:
Whom they, in birth, ordain to happy days,
The gods commit their glory to our praise;
T' eternal life when they dissolve their breath,
We likewise share a second power by death.
  When time shall turn those amber locks to gray,
My verse again shall gild and make them gay,
And trick them up in knotted curls anew,
And to thy autumn give a summer's hue;
That sacred power that in my ink remains
Shall put fresh blood into thy withered veins,
And on thy red decayed, thy whiteness dead,
Shall set a white more white, a red more red.

daded] led tottering

When thy dim sight thy glass cannot descry,
Nor thy crazed mirror can discern thine eye,
My verse, to tell th' one what the other was,
Shall represent them both, thine eye and glass;
Where both thy mirror and thine eye shall see
What once thou saw'st in that, that saw in thee;
And to them both shall tell the simple truth,
What that in pureness was, what thou in youth.
  If Florence once should lose her old renown,
As famous Athens, now a fisher town,
My lines for thee a Florence shall erect,
Which great Apollo ever shall protect,
And with the numbers from my pen that falls
Bring marble mines to re-erect those walls.
Nor beauteous Stanhope, whom all tongues report
To be the glory of the English court,
Shall by our nation be so much admired,
If ever Surrey truly were inspired.
And famous Wyatt, who in numbers sings
To that enchanting Thracian harper's strings,
To whom Phoebus, the poets' god, did drink
A bowl of nectar filled up to the brink,
And sweet-tongued Bryan, whom the Muses kept
And in his cradle rocked him whilst he slept,
In sacred verses most divinely penned,
Upon thy praises ever shall attend.
  What time I came into this famous town
And made the cause of my arrival known,
Great Medices a list for triumphs built;
Within the which, upon a tree of gilt,
Which was with sundry rare devices set,
I did erect thy lovely counterfeit

To answer those Italian dames' desire,
Which daily came thy beauty to admire;
By which my lion, in his gaping jaws,
Held up my lance, and in his dreadful paws
Reacheth my gauntlet unto him that dare
A beauty with my Geraldine's compare.
Which when each manly valiant arm assays,
After so many brave triumphant days
The glorious prize upon my lance I bare,
By herald's voice proclaimed to be thy share.
The shivered staves, here for thy beauty broke,
With fierce encounters passed at every shock,
When stormy courses answered cuff for cuff,
Denting proud beavers with the counter-buff,
Upon an altar, burnt with holy flame,
I sacrificed as incense to thy fame;
Where, as the phoenix from her spiced fume
Renews herself in that she doth consume,
So from these sacred ashes live we both,
Even as that one Arabian wonder doth.
When to my chamber I myself retire,
Burnt with the sparks that kindled all this fire,
Thinking of England, which my hope contains,
The happy isle where Geraldine remains,
Of Hunsdon, where those sweet celestial eyne
At first did pierce this tender breast of mine,
Of Hampton Court and Windsor, where abound
All pleasures that in paradise were found:
Near that fair castle is a little grove,
With hanging rocks all covered from above,
Which on the bank of goodly Thames doth stand,
Clipped by the water from the other land;

Whose bushy top doth bid the sun forbear
And checks his proud beams that would enter there;
Whose leaves, still muttering as the air doth breathe,
With the sweet bubbling of the stream beneath,
Doth rock the senses, whilst the small birds sing,
Lulled asleep with gentle murmuring;
Where light-foot fairies sport at prison-base
(No doubt there is some power frequents the place):
There the soft poplar and smooth beech do bear
Our names together carved everywhere,
And gordian knots do curiously entwine
The names of Henry and of Geraldine.
O! let this grove in happy times to come
Be called the lovers' blest Elysium;
Whither my mistress wonted to resort,
In summer's heat in those sweet shades to sport.
A thousand sundry names I have it given,
And called it Wonder-hider, Cover-heaven,
The roof where beauty her rich court doth keep,
Under whose compass all the stars do sleep.
There is one tree which now I call to mind,
Doth bear these verses carved in his rind:
When Geraldine shall sit in thy fair shade,
Fan her sweet tresses with perfumed air,
Let thy large boughs a canopy be made
To keep the sun from gazing on my fair;
And when thy spreading branched arms be sunk,
And thou no sap nor pith shalt more retain,
Even from the dust of thy unwieldy trunk
I will renew thee, phoenix-like, again,
And from thy dry decayed root will bring
A new-born stem, another Aeson's spring.

I find no cause, nor judge I reason why
My country should give place to Lombardy;
As goodly flowers on Thamesis do grow
As beautify the banks of wanton Po;
As many nymphs as haunt rich Arno's strand,
By silver Severn tripping hand in hand;
Our shade 's as sweet, though not to us so dear,
Because the sun hath greater power there;
This distant place doth give me greater woe,
Far off, my sighs the farther have to go.
Ah absence! why thus shouldst thou seem so long?
Or wherefore shouldst thou offer time such wrong,
Summer so soon to steal on winter's cold,
Or winter's blasts so soon make summer old?
Love did us both with one self-arrow strike,
Our wounds both one, our cure should be the like,
Except thou hast found out some mean by art,
Some powerful medicine to withdraw the dart;
But mine is fixed, and absence being proved,
It sticks too fast, it cannot be removed.
Adieu, adieu! from Florence when I go
By my next letters Geraldine shall know,
Which if good fortune shall by course direct,
From Venice by some messenger expect;
Till when, I leave thee to thy heart's desire—
By him that lives thy virtues to admire.

England's Heroical Epistles, 1597

BARNABE BARNES

c. 1569–1609

326

Content

AH, sweet Content! where is thy mild abode?
  Is it with shepherds and light-hearted swains,
Which sing upon the downs, and pipe abroad,
  Tending their flocks and cattle on the plains?
Ah, sweet Content! where dost thou safely rest?
  In heaven with angels which the praises sing
Of him that made, and rules at his behest,
  The minds and hearts of every living thing?
Ah, sweet Content! where doth thine harbour hold?
  Is it in churches, with religious men,
Which please the gods with prayers manifold,
  And in their studies meditate it then?
    Whether thou dost in heaven or earth appear,
    Be where thou wilt, thou wilt not harbour here.

Parthenophil and Parthenophe, 1593

327

Ode

WHY doth heaven bear a sun
  To give the world a heat?
  Why, there, have stars a seat?
On earth, when all is done,
Parthenophe's bright sun
  Doth give a greater heat;

And in her heaven there be
  Such fair bright blazing stars,
  Which still make open wars
With those in heaven's degree.
These stars far brighter be
  Than brightest of heaven's stars.

Why doth earth bring forth roses,
  Violets, or lilies,
  Or bright daffodillies?
In her clear cheeks she closes
Sweet damask roses;
  In her neck white lilies;

Violets in her veins.
  Why do men sacrifice
  Incense to deities?
Her breath more favour gains,
And please the heavenly veins,
  More than rich sacrifice.

Parthenophil and Parthenophe, 1593

328 *God's Virtue*

THE world's bright comforter, whose beamsome light
  Poor creatures cheereth, mounting from the deep,
  His course doth in prefixed compass keep;
And, as courageous giant, takes delight
To run his race and exercise his might,
  Till him, down galloping the mountain's steep,
  Clear Hesperus, smooth messenger of sleep,
Views; and the silver ornament of night
Forth brings, with stars past number in her train,
  All which with sun's long borrowed splendour shine.
The seas, with full tide swelling, ebb again;
  All years to their old quarters new resign;
    The winds forsake their mountain-chambers wild,
    And all in all things with God's virtue filled.

Spiritual Sonnets, 1595

BARNABE BARNES

329 *The Life of Man*

A BLAST of wind, a momentary breath,
  A watery bubble symbolized with air,
  A sun-blown rose, but for a season fair,
A ghostly glance, a skeleton of death;
A morning dew, pearling the grass beneath,
  Whose moisture sun's appearance doth impair;
  A lightning glimpse, a muse of thought and care,
A planet's shot, a shade which followeth,
A voice which vanisheth so soon as heard,
  The thriftless heir of time, a rolling wave,
A show, no more in action than regard,
  A mass of dust, world's momentary slave,
    Is man, in state of our old Adam made,
    Soon born to die, soon flourishing to fade.

Ibid.

GILES FLETCHER c. 1549–1611

330 *Time*

IN time the strong and stately turrets fall,
  In time the rose and silver lilies die,
In time the monarchs captive are, and thrall,
  In time the sea and rivers are made dry;
The hardest flint in time doth melt asunder;
  Still living fame in time doth fade away;
The mountains proud we see in time come under;
  And earth, for age, we see in time decay.
The sun in time forgets for to retire
  From out the east where he was wont to rise;
The basest thoughts we see in time aspire,
  And greedy minds in time do wealth despise.
    Thus all, sweet Fair, in time must have an end,
    Except thy beauty, virtues, and thy friend.

Licia, 1593

BARTHOLOMEW GRIFFIN ob. 1602

331 *Sleep*

CARE-CHARMER sleep, sweet ease in restless misery,
  The captive's liberty, and his freedom's song,
Balm of the bruised heart, man's chief felicity,
  Brother of quiet death, when life is too, too long!
A comedy it is, and now an history.
  What is not sleep unto the feeble mind?
It easeth him that toils and him that 's sorry,
  It makes the deaf to hear, to see the blind.
Ungentle sleep, thou helpest all but me,
  For when I sleep my soul is vexed most.
It is Fidessa that doth master thee;
  If she approach, alas, thy power is lost.
    But here she is. See, how he runs amain!
    I fear at night he will not come again.

Fidessa, more Chaste than Kind, 1596

332 *Youth*

I HAVE not spent the April of my time,
  The sweet of youth, in plotting in the air,
But do at first adventure seek to climb,
  Whilst flowers of blooming years are green and fair.
I am no leaving of all-withering age,
  I have not suffered many winter lours;
I feel no storm unless my Love do rage,
  And then in grief I spend both days and hours.
This yet doth comfort, that my flower lasted,
  Until it did approach my sun too near,
And then, alas! untimely was it blasted,
  So soon as once thy beauty did appear.
    But after all, my comfort rests in this,
    That for thy sake my youth decayed is.

Ibid.

WILLIAM SHAKESPEARE

1564–1616

333

The Courser

BUT, lo! from forth a copse that neighbours by,
  A breeding jennet, lusty, young, and proud,
Adonis' trampling courser doth espy,
  And forth she rushes, snorts and neighs aloud:
    The strong-necked steed, being tied unto a tree,
    Breaketh his rein, and to her straight goes he.

Imperiously he leaps, he neighs, he bounds,
  And now his woven girths he breaks asunder;
The bearing earth with his hard hoof he wounds,
  Whose hollow womb resounds like heaven's thunder;
    The iron bit he crusheth 'tween his teeth,
    Controlling what he was controlled with.

His ears up-pricked, his braided hanging mane,
  Upon his compassed crest now stand on end;
His nostrils drink the air, and forth again,
  As from a furnace, vapours doth he send:
    His eye, which scornfully glisters like fire,
    Shows his hot courage and his high desire.

Sometime he trots, as if he told the steps,
  With gentle majesty and modest pride;
Anon he rears upright, curvets and leaps,
  As who should say, 'Lo! thus my strength is tried;
    And this I do to captivate the eye
    Of the fair breeder that is standing by.'

jennet] Spanish mare

What recketh he his rider's angry stir,
His flattering 'Holla', or his 'Stand, I say'?
What cares he now for curb or pricking spur,
For rich caparisons or trappings gay?
He sees his love, and nothing else he sees,
For nothing else with his proud sight agrees.

Look, when a painter would surpass the life,
In limning out a well-proportioned steed,
His art with nature's workmanship at strife,
As if the dead the living should exceed;
So did this horse excel a common one,
In shape, in courage, colour, pace and bone.

Round-hoofed, short-jointed, fetlocks shag and long,
Broad breast, full eye, small head, and nostril wide,
High crest, short ears, straight legs and passing strong,
Thin mane, thick tail, broad buttock, tender hide:
Look, what a horse should have he did not lack,
Save a proud rider on so proud a back.

Sometime he scuds far off, and there he stares;
Anon he starts at stirring of a feather;
To bid the wind a base he now prepares,
And whether he run or fly they know not whether;
For through his mane and tail the high wind sings,
Fanning the hairs, who wave like feathered wings.

He looks upon his love, and neighs unto her;
She answers him as if she knew his mind;
Being proud, as females are, to see him woo her,
She puts on outward strangeness, seems unkind,
Spurns at his love and scorns the heat he feels,
Beating his kind embracements with her heels.

Then, like a melancholy malcontent,
He vails his tail that, like a falling plume,
Cool shadow to his melting buttock lent:
He stamps, and bites the poor flies in his fume.
His love, perceiving how he was enraged,
Grew kinder, and his fury was assuaged.

His testy master goeth about to take him;
When lo! the unbacked breeder, full of fear,
Jealous of catching, swiftly doth forsake him,
With her the horse, and left Adonis there.
As they were mad, unto the wood they hie them,
Out-stripping crows that strive to over-fly them.

Venus and Adonis, 259–324, 1593

334

Poor Wat

AND when thou hast on foot the purblind hare,
Mark the poor wretch, to overshoot his troubles
How he outruns the wind, and with what care
He cranks and crosses with a thousand doubles:
The many musits through the which he goes
Are like a labyrinth to amaze his foes.

Sometime he runs among a flock of sheep,
To make the cunning hounds mistake their smell,
And sometime where earth-delving conies keep,
To stop the loud pursuers in their yell,
And sometime sorteth with a herd of deer;
Danger deviseth shifts; wit waits on fear:

musits] hedge-gaps

For there his smell with others being mingled,
The hot scent-snuffing hounds are driven to doubt,
Ceasing their clamorous cry till they have singled
With much ado the cold fault cleanly out;
Then do they spend their mouths: Echo replies,
As if another chase were in the skies.

By this, poor Wat, far off upon a hill,
Stands on his hinder legs with listening ear,
To hearken if his foes pursue him still:
Anon their loud alarums he doth hear;
And now his grief may be compared well
To one sore sick that hears the passing-bell.

Then shalt thou see the dew-bedabbled wretch
Turn, and return, indenting with the way;
Each envious briar his weary legs doth scratch,
Each shadow makes him stop, each murmur stay:
For misery is trodden on by many,
And being low never relieved by any.

Venus and Adonis, 679–708, 1593

335 *Venus Abandoned*

'NAY then,' quoth Adon, 'you will fall again
Into your idle over-handled theme;
The kiss I gave you is bestowed in vain,
And all in vain you strive against the stream;
For by this black-faced night, desire's foul nurse,
Your treatise makes me like you worse and worse.

'If love have lent you twenty thousand tongues,
And every tongue more moving than your own,
Bewitching like the wanton mermaid's songs,
Yet from mine ear the tempting tune is blown;
For know, my heart stands armed in mine ear,
And will not let a false sound enter there;

'Lest the deceiving harmony should run
Into the quiet closure of my breast;
And then my little heart were quite undone,
In his bedchamber to be barred of rest.
No, lady, no; my heart longs not to groan,
But soundly sleeps, while now it sleeps alone.

'What have you urged that I cannot reprove?
The path is smooth that leadeth on to danger;
I hate not love, but your device in love,
That lends embracements unto every stranger.
You do it for increase: O strange excuse!
When reason is the bawd to lust's abuse.

'Call it not love, for Love to heaven is fled,
Since sweating Lust on earth usurped his name;
Under whose simple semblance he hath fed
Upon fresh beauty, blotting it with blame;
Which the hot tyrant stains and soon bereaves,
As caterpillars do the tender leaves.

'Love comforteth like sunshine after rain,
But Lust's effect is tempest after sun;
Love's gentle spring doth always fresh remain,
Lust's winter comes ere summer half be done.
Love surfeits not, Lust like a glutton dies;
Love is all truth, Lust full of forged lies.

'More I could tell, but more I dare not say;
  The text is old, the orator too green.
Therefore, in sadness, now I will away;
  My face is full of shame, my heart of teen:
    Mine ears, that to your wanton talk attended,
    Do burn themselves for having so offended.'

With this he breaketh from the sweet embrace
  Of those fair arms which bound him to her breast,
And homeward through the dark laund runs apace;
  Leaves Love upon her back deeply distressed.
    Look, how a bright star shooteth from the sky,
    So glides he in the night from Venus' eye;

Which after him she darts, as one on shore
  Gazing upon a late-embarked friend,
Till the wild waves will have him seen no more,
  Whose ridges with the meeting clouds contend:
    So did the merciless and pitchy night
    Fold in the object that did feed her sight.

Whereat amazed, as one that unaware
  Hath dropped a precious jewel in the flood,
Or 'stonished as night-wanderers often are,
  Their light blown out in some mistrustful wood;
    Even so confounded in the dark she lay,
    Having lost the fair discovery of her way.

And now she beats her heart, whereat it groans,
  That all the neighbour caves, as seeming troubled,
Make verbal repetition of her moans;
  Passion on passion deeply is redoubled:
    'Ay me!' she cries, and twenty times, 'Woe, woe!'
    And twenty echoes twenty times cry so.

She, marking them, begins a wailing note,
  And sings extemporally a woeful ditty;
How love makes young men thrall and old men dote;
  How love is wise in folly, foolish-witty:
    Her heavy anthem still concludes in woe,
    And still the choir of echoes answer so.

Her song was tedious, and outwore the night,
  For lovers' hours are long, though seeming short:
If pleased themselves, others, they think, delight
  In such like circumstance, with such like sport:
    Their copious stories, oftentimes begun,
    End without audience, and are never done.

For who hath she to spend the night withal,
  But idle sounds resembling parasites;
Like shrill-tongued tapsters answering every call,
  Soothing the humour of fantastic wits?
    She says, ''Tis so': they answer all, ' 'Tis so';
    And would say after her, if she said 'No'.

Lo! here the gentle lark, weary of rest,
  From his moist cabinet mounts up on high,
And wakes the morning, from whose silver breast
  The sun ariseth in his majesty;
    Who doth the world so gloriously behold,
    That cedar-tops and hills seem burnished gold.

Venus and Adonis, 769–858, 1593

336 *Midnight*

THE locks between her chamber and his will,
Each one by him enforced, retires his ward;
But as they open they all rate his ill,
Which drives the creeping thief to some regard:
The threshold grates the door to have him heard;
Night-wandering weasels shriek to see him there;
They fright him, yet he still pursues his fear.

As each unwilling portal yields him way,
Through little vents and crannies of the place
The wind wars with his torch to make him stay,
And blows the smoke of it into his face,
Extinguishing his conduct in this case:
But his hot heart, which fond desire doth scorch,
Puffs forth another wind that fires the torch.

And being lighted, by the light he spies
Lucretia's glove, wherein her needle sticks:
He takes it from the rushes where it lies,
And gripping it, the needle his finger pricks;
As who should say, 'This glove to wanton tricks
Is not inured; return again in haste;
Thou seest our mistress' ornaments are chaste.'

But all these poor forbiddings could not stay him;
He in the worst sense construes their denial:
The door, the wind, the glove, that did delay him,
He takes for accidental things of trial;
Or as those bars which stop the hourly dial,
Who with a lingering stay his course doth let,
Till every minute pays the hour his debt.

'So, so,' quoth he, 'these lets attend the time,
  Like little frosts that sometime threat the spring,
To add a more rejoicing to the prime,
  And give the sneaped birds more cause to sing.
  Pain pays the income of each precious thing;
    Huge rocks, high winds, strong pirates, shelves and
      sands,
    The merchant fears, ere rich at home he lands.'

Now he is come unto the chamber door,
  That shuts him from the heaven of his thought,
Which with a yielding latch, and with no more,
  Hath barred him from the blessed thing he sought.
  So from himself impiety hath wrought,
    That for his prey to pray he doth begin,
    As if the heavens should countenance his sin.

But in the midst of his unfruitful prayer,
  Having solicited th' eternal power
That his foul thoughts might compass his fair fair,
  And they would stand auspicious to the hour,
  Even there he starts: quoth he, 'I must deflower;
    The powers to whom I pray abhor this fact,
    How can they then assist me in the act?

'Then Love and Fortune be my gods, my guide!
  My will is backed with resolution:
Thoughts are but dreams till their effects be tried;
  The blackest sin is cleared with absolution.
  Against love's fire fear's frost hath dissolution.
    The eye of heaven is out, and misty night
    Covers the shame that follows sweet delight.'

sneaped] nipped fact] crime

This said, his guilty hand plucked up the latch,
  And with his knee the door he opens wide.
The dove sleeps fast that this night-owl will catch:
  Thus treason works ere traitors be espied.
  Who sees the lurking serpent steps aside;
    But she, sound sleeping, fearing no such thing,
    Lies at the mercy of his mortal sting.

Into the chamber wickedly he stalks,
  And gazeth on her yet unstained bed.
The curtains being close, about he walks,
  Rolling his greedy eyeballs in his head:
  By their high treason is his heart misled;
    Which gives the watchword to his hand full soon,
    To draw the cloud that hides the silver moon.

Look, as the fair and fiery-pointed sun,
  Rushing from forth a cloud, bereaves our sight;
Even so, the curtain drawn, his eyes begun
  To wink, being blinded with a greater light:
  Whether it is that she reflects so bright,
    That dazzleth them, or else some shame supposed,
    But blind they are, and keep themselves enclosed.

O! had they in that darksome prison died,
  Then had they seen the period of their ill;
Then Collatine again, by Lucrece' side,
  In his clear bed might have reposed still:
  But they must ope, this blessed league to kill,
    And holy-thoughted Lucrece to their sight
    Must sell her joy, her life, her world's delight.

Her lily hand her rosy cheek lies under,
  Cozening the pillow of a lawful kiss;
Who, therefore angry, seems to part in sunder,
  Swelling on either side to want his bliss;
  Between whose hills her head entombed is:
    Where like a virtuous monument she lies,
    To be admired of lewd unhallowed eyes.

Without the bed her other fair hand was,
  On the green coverlet, whose perfect white
Showed like an April daisy on the grass,
  With pearly sweat, resembling dew of night.
  Her eyes, like marigolds, had sheathed their light,
    And canopied in darkness sweetly lay,
    Till they might open to adorn the day.

Her hair, like golden threads, played with her breath;
  O modest wantons! wanton modesty!
Showing life's triumph in the map of death,
  And death's dim look in life's mortality.
  Each in her sleep themselves so beautify,
    As if between them twain there were no strife,
    But that life lived in death, and death in life.

Her breasts, like ivory globes circled with blue,
  A pair of maiden worlds unconquered,
Save of their lord no bearing yoke they knew,
  And him by oath they truly honoured.
  These worlds in Tarquin new ambition bred;
    Who, like a foul usurper, went about
    From this fair throne to heave the owner out.

What could he see but mightily he noted?
What did he note but strongly he desired?
What he beheld, on that he firmly doted,
And in his will his wilful eye he tired.
With more than admiration he admired
Her azure veins, her alablaster skin,
Her coral lips, her snow-white dimpled chin.

The Rape of Lucrece, 302–420, 1594

337 *Opportunity*

'O OPPORTUNITY! thy guilt is great,
'Tis thou that executest the traitor's treason;
Thou set'st the wolf where he the lamb may get;
Whoever plots the sin, thou point'st the season;
'Tis thou that spurn'st at right, at law, at reason;
And in thy shady cell, where none may spy him,
Sits Sin to seize the souls that wander by him.

'Thou makest the vestal violate her oath;
Thou blow'st the fire when temperance is thaw'd;
Thou smother'st honesty, thou murder'st troth;
Thou foul abettor! thou notorious bawd!
Thou plantest scandal and displacest laud:
Thou ravisher, thou traitor, thou false thief,
Thy honey turns to gall, thy joy to grief!

'Thy secret pleasure turns to open shame,
Thy private feasting to a public fast,
Thy smoothing titles to a ragged name,
Thy sugared tongue to bitter wormwood taste:
Thy violent vanities can never last.
How comes it, then, vile Opportunity,
Being so bad, such numbers seek for thee?

'When wilt thou be the humble suppliant's friend,
  And bring him where his suit may be obtained?
When wilt thou sort an hour great strifes to end?
  Or free that soul which wretchedness hath chained?
  Give physic to the sick, ease to the pained?
    The poor, lame, blind, halt, creep, cry out for thee;
    But they ne'er meet with Opportunity.

'The patient dies while the physician sleeps;
  The orphan pines while the oppressor feeds;
Justice is feasting while the widow weeps;
  Advice is sporting while infection breeds:
  Thou grant'st no time for charitable deeds:
    Wrath, envy, treason, rape, and murder's rages,
    Thy heinous hours wait on them as their pages.

'When Truth and Virtue have to do with thee,
  A thousand crosses keep them from thy aid:
They buy thy help; but Sin ne'er gives a fee;
  He gratis comes; and thou art well appaid,
  As well to hear as grant what he hath said.
    My Collatine would else have come to me
    When Tarquin did, but he was stayed by thee.

'Guilty thou art of murder and of theft,
  Guilty of perjury and subornation,
Guilty of treason, forgery, and shift,
  Guilty of incest, that abomination;
  An accessary by thine inclination
    To all sins past, and all that are to come,
    From the creation to the general doom.

sort] choose   appaid] contented

'Mis-shapen Time, copesmate of ugly Night,
  Swift subtle post, carrier of grisly care,
Eater of youth, false slave to false delight,
  Base watch of woes, sin's pack-horse, virtue's snare;
  Thou nursest all, and murderest all that are.
    O! hear me, then, injurious, shifting Time,
    Be guilty of my death, since of my crime.

'Why hath thy servant, Opportunity,
  Betrayed the hours thou gavest me to repose?
Cancelled my fortunes, and enchained me
  To endless date of never-ending woes?
  Time's office is to fine the hate of foes,
    To eat up errors by opinion bred,
    Not spend the dowry of a lawful bed.

'Time's glory is to calm contending kings,
  To unmask falsehood and bring truth to light,
To stamp the seal of time in aged things,
  To wake the morn and sentinel the night,
  To wrong the wronger till he render right,
    To ruinate proud buildings with thy hours,
    And smear with dust their glittering golden towers;

'To fill with worm-holes stately monuments,
  To feed oblivion with decay of things,
To blot old books and alter their contents,
  To pluck the quills from ancient ravens' wings,
  To dry the old oak's sap and cherish springs,
    To spoil antiquities of hammered steel,
    And turn the giddy round of Fortune's wheel;

copesmate] companion fine] end

'To show the beldam daughters of her daughter,
  To make the child a man, the man a child,
To slay the tiger that doth live by slaughter,
  To tame the unicorn and lion wild,
  To mock the subtle, in themselves beguiled,
    To cheer the ploughman with increaseful crops,
    And waste huge stones with little water-drops.

'Why work'st thou mischief in thy pilgrimage,
  Unless thou couldst return to make amends?
One poor retiring minute in an age
  Would purchase thee a thousand thousand friends,
  Lending him wit that to bad debtors lends:
    O! this dread night, wouldst thou one hour come back,
    I could prevent this storm and shun thy wrack.

'Thou ceaseless lackey to eternity,
  With some mischance cross Tarquin in his flight:
Devise extremes beyond extremity,
  To make him curse this cursed crimeful night:
  Let ghastly shadows his lewd eyes affright,
    And the dire thought of his committed evil
    Shape every bush a hideous shapeless devil.

'Disturb his hours of rest with restless trances;
  Afflict him in his bed with bedrid groans;
Let there bechance him pitiful mischances
  To make him moan, but pity not his moans;
  Stone him with harden'd hearts, harder than stones;
    And let mild women to him lose their mildness,
    Wilder to him than tigers in their wildness.

'Let him have time to tear his curled hair,
  Let him have time against himself to rave,
Let him have time of time's help to despair,
  Let him have time to live a loathed slave,
  Let him have time a beggar's orts to crave,
    And time to see one, that by alms doth live,
    Disdain to him disdained scraps to give.

'Let him have time to see his friends his foes,
  And merry fools to mock at him resort;
Let him have time to mark how slow time goes
  In time of sorrow, and how swift and short
  His time of folly and his time of sport;
    And ever let his unrecalling crime
    Have time to wail th' abusing of his time.

'O Time! thou tutor both to good and bad,
  Teach me to curse him that thou taught'st this ill;
At his own shadow let the thief run mad,
  Himself himself seek every hour to kill:
  Such wretched hands such wretched blood should spill;
    For who so base would such an office have
    As slanderous deathsman to so base a slave?

'The baser is he, coming from a king,
  To shame his hope with deeds degenerate:
The mightier man, the mightier is the thing
  That makes him honoured, or begets him hate;
  For greatest scandal waits on greatest state.
    The moon being clouded presently is missed,
    But little stars may hide them when they list.

orts] fragments

'The crow may bathe his coal-black wings in mire,
  And unperceived fly with the filth away;
But if the like the snow-white swan desire,
  The stain upon his silver down will stay.
  Poor grooms are sightless night, kings glorious day;
    Gnats are unnoted whereso'er they fly,
    But eagles gazed upon with every eye.

'Out, idle words! servants to shallow fools,
  Unprofitable sounds, weak arbitrators!
Busy yourselves in skill-contending schools;
  Debate where leisure serves with dull debaters;
  To trembling clients be you mediators:
    For me, I force not argument a straw,
    Since that my case is past the help of law.'

The Rape of Lucrece, 876–1022, 1594

338 *Troy Depicted*

AT last she calls to mind where hangs a piece
  Of skilful painting, made for Priam's Troy;
Before the which is drawn the power of Greece,
  For Helen's rape the city to destroy,
  Threatening cloud-kissing Ilion with annoy;
    Which the conceited painter drew so proud,
    As heaven, it seemed, to kiss the turrets bowed.

A thousand lamentable objects there,
  In scorn of nature, art gave lifeless life;
Many a dry drop seemed a weeping tear,
  Shed for the slaughtered husband by the wife.
  The red blood reeked, to show the painter's strife;
    And dying eyes gleamed forth their ashy lights,
    Like dying coals burnt out in tedious nights.

force] care for

There might you see the labouring pioneer,
  Begrimed with sweat, and smeared all with dust;
And from the towers of Troy there would appear
  The very eyes of men through loop-holes thrust,
  Gazing upon the Greeks with little lust:
    Such sweet observance in this work was had,
    That one might see those far-off eyes look sad.

In great commanders grace and majesty
  You might behold, triumphing in their faces;
In youth quick bearing and dexterity;
  And here and there the painter interlaces
  Pale cowards, marching on with trembling paces;
    Which heartless peasants did so well resemble,
    That one would swear he saw them quake and tremble.

In Ajax and Ulysses, O! what art
  Of physiognomy might one behold;
The face of either ciphered either's heart;
  Their face their manners most expressly told:
  In Ajax' eyes blunt rage and rigour rolled;
    But the mild glance that sly Ulysses lent
    Showed deep regard and smiling government.

There pleading might you see grave Nestor stand,
  As 'twere encouraging the Greeks to fight,
Making such sober action with his hand,
  That it beguiled attention, charmed the sight;
  In speech, it seemed, his beard, all silver white,
    Wagged up and down, and from his lips did fly
    Thin winding breath, which purled up to the sky.

About him were a press of gaping faces,
  Which seemed to swallow up his sound advice;
All jointly listening, but with several graces,
  As if some mermaid did their ears entice,
  Some high, some low, the painter was so nice.
    The scalps of many, almost hid behind,
    To jump up higher seemed, to mock the mind.

Here one man's hand leaned on another's head,
  His nose being shadowed by his neighbour's ear;
Here one being thronged bears back, all bollen and red;
  Another, smothered, seems to pelt and swear;
  And in their rage such signs of rage they bear,
    As, but for loss of Nestor's golden words,
    It seemed they would debate with angry swords.

For much imaginary work was there;
  Conceit deceitful, so compact, so kind,
That for Achilles' image stood his spear,
  Gripped in an armed hand; himself behind
  Was left unseen, save to the eye of mind:
    A hand, a foot, a face, a leg, a head,
    Stood for the whole to be imagined.

And from the walls of strong-besieged Troy,
  When their brave hope, bold Hector, marched to field,
Stood many Trojan mothers, sharing joy
  To see their youthful sons bright weapons wield;
  And to their hope they such odd action yield,
    That through their light joy seemed to appear,
    Like bright things stained, a kind of heavy fear.

bollen] swollen   pelt] rage

And from the strand of Dardan, where they fought,
  To Simois' reedy banks the red blood ran,
Whose waves to imitate the battle sought
  With swelling ridges; and their ranks began
  To break upon the galled shore, and than
    Retire again, till meeting greater ranks
    They join, and shoot their foam at Simois' banks.

The Rape of Lucrece, 1366–1442, 1594

339

Song to Silvia

WHO is Silvia? what is she,
  That all our swains commend her?
Holy, fair, and wise is she;
  The heaven such grace did lend her,
That she might admired be.

Is she kind as she is fair?
  For beauty lives with kindness.
Love doth to her eyes repair,
  To help him of his blindness;
And, being helped, inhabits there.

Then to Silvia let us sing,
  That Silvia is excelling;
She excels each mortal thing
  Upon the dull earth dwelling;
To her let us garlands bring.

Two Gentlemen of Verona, 1594–1595?

340

Dumain's Rhymes

ON a day, alack the day!
Love, whose month is ever May,
Spied a blossom passing fair
Playing in the wanton air:
Through the velvet leaves the wind,
All unseen, can passage find;
That the lover, sick to death,
Wished himself the heaven's breath.
'Air', quoth he, 'thy cheeks may blow;
Air, would I might triumph so!
But alack! my hand is sworn
Ne'er to pluck thee from thy thorn:
Vow, alack! for youth unmeet,
Youth so apt to pluck a sweet.
Do not call it sin in me,
That I am forsworn for thee;
Thou for whom Jove would swear
Juno but an Ethiop were;
And deny himself for Jove,
Turning mortal for thy love.'

Love's Labour's Lost, 1594–1595?

341

Ver and Hiems

Ver

WHEN daisies pied and violets blue
And lady-smocks all silver-white
And cuckoo-buds of yellow hue
Do paint the meadows with delight,

can] could

The cuckoo then, on every tree,
Mocks married men; for thus sings he,
Cuckoo!
Cuckoo, cuckoo! O, word of fear,
Unpleasing to a married ear!

When shepherds pipe on oaten straws,
And merry larks are ploughmen's clocks,
When turtles tread, and rooks, and daws,
And maidens bleach their summer smocks,
The cuckoo then, on every tree,
Mocks married men; for thus sings he,
Cuckoo!
Cuckoo, cuckoo! O, word of fear,
Unpleasing to a married ear!

Hiems

When icicles hang by the wall,
And Dick the shepherd blows his nail,
And Tom bears logs into the hall,
And milk comes frozen home in pail;
When blood is nipped, and ways be foul,
Then nightly sings the staring owl,
Tu-whit, tu-who! a merry note,
While greasy Joan doth keel the pot.

When all aloud the wind doth blow,
And coughing drowns the parson's saw,
And birds sit brooding in the snow,
And Marian's nose looks red and raw,

When roasted crabs hiss in the bowl,
Then nightly sings the staring owl,
Tu-whit, tu-who! a merry note,
While greasy Joan doth keel the pot.

Love's Labour's Lost, 1594–1595?

342 *Fairy Songs*

(*i*)

OVER hill, over dale,
  Thorough bush, thorough brier,
Over park, over pale,
  Thorough flood, thorough fire:
I do wander everywhere,
Swifter than the moonės sphere;
And I serve the fairy queen,
To dew her orbs upon the green.
The cowslips tall her pensioners be;
In their gold coats spots you see;
Those be rubies, fairy favours,
In those freckles live their savours.

(*ii*)

YOU spotted snakes with double tongue,
  Thorny hedgehogs, be not seen;
Newts and blind-worms, do no wrong;
  Come not near our fairy queen.

keel] cool

Philomel, with melody,
Sing in our sweet lullaby;
Lulla, lulla, lullaby; lulla, lulla, lullaby!
Never harm,
Nor spell nor charm,
Come our lovely lady nigh.
So, good night, with lullaby.

Weaving spiders, come not here;
Hence, you long-legged spinners, hence!
Beetles black, approach not near;
Worm nor snail, do no offence.

Philomel, with melody,
Sing in our sweet lullaby;
Lulla, lulla, lullaby; lulla, lulla, lullaby!
Never harm,
Nor spell nor charm,
Come our lovely lady nigh.
So, good night, with lullaby.

Midsummer Night's Dream, 1595–1596?

343 *Two Epilogues*

(*i*)

Puck. NOW the hungry lion roars,
And the wolf behowls the moon;
Whilst the heavy ploughman snores,
All with weary task fordone.
Now the wasted brands do glow,
Whilst the screech-owl, screeching loud,
Puts the wretch that lies in woe
In remembrance of a shroud.

Now it is the time of night
  That the graves, all gaping wide,
Every one lets forth his sprite,
  In the church-way paths to glide:
And we fairies, that do run
  By the triple Hecate's team,
From the presence of the sun,
  Following darkness like a dream,
Now are frolic; not a mouse
Shall disturb this hallow'd house.
I am sent with broom before,
To sweep the dust behind the door.

Enter OBERON *and* TITANIA, *with their Train.*

Oberon. Through the house give glimmering light
  By the dead and drowsy fire;
Every elf and fairy sprite
  Hop as light as bird from briar;
And this ditty after me
Sing, and dance it trippingly.

Titania. First, rehearse your song by rote.
To each word a warbling note.
Hand in hand, with fairy grace,
Will we sing, and bless this place.
[*Song and dance.*

Oberon. Now, until the break of day,
Through this house each fairy stray.
To the best bride-bed will we,
Which by us shall blessed be;
And the issue there create
Ever shall be fortunate.

So shall all the couples three
Ever true in loving be;
And the blots of Nature's hand
Shall not in their issue stand.
Never mole, hare-lip, nor scar,
Nor mark prodigious, such as are
Despised in nativity,
Shall upon their children be.
With this field-dew consecrate,
Every fairy take his gait,
And each several chamber bless,
Through this palace, with sweet peace;
And the owner of it blest
Ever shall in safety rest.
        Trip away;
        Make no stay;
Meet me all by break of day.

(*ii*)

Puck. IF we shadows have offended,
Think but this, and all is mended,
That you have but slumbered here,
While these visions did appear.
And this weak and idle theme,
No more yielding but a dream,
Gentles, do not reprehend.
If you pardon, we will mend.
And, as I am an honest Puck,
If we have unearned luck
Now to 'scape the serpent's tongue,
We will make amends ere long;

Else the Puck a liar call.
So, good night unto you all.
Give me your hands, if we be friends,
And Robin shall restore amends.

Midsummer Night's Dream, 1595–1596?

344

A Casket Song

TELL me where is fancy bred,
Or in the heart or in the head?
How begot, how nourished?
Reply, reply.

It is engendered in the eyes,
With gazing fed; and fancy dies
In the cradle where it lies.
Let us all ring fancy's knell.
I'll begin it. Ding, dong, bell.
Chorus. Ding, dong, bell.

Merchant of Venice, 1596–1597?

345

Balthasar's Song

SIGH no more, ladies, sigh no more,
Men were deceivers ever;
One foot in sea, and one on shore,
To one thing constant never.
Then sigh not so,
But let them go,
And be you blithe and bonny,
Converting all your sounds of woe
Into Hey nonny, nonny.

Sing no more ditties, sing no mo
  Of dumps so dull and heavy;
The fraud of men was ever so,
  Since summer first was leavy.
    Then sigh not so,
    But let them go,
  And be you blithe and bonny,
Converting all your sounds of woe
  Into Hey nonny, nonny.

Much Ado About Nothing, 1598–1599?

346 *Claudio's Laments*

(*i*)

DONE to death by slanderous tongues
  Was the Hero that here lies:
Death, in guerdon of her wrongs,
  Gives her fame which never dies.
So the life that died with shame
Lives in death with glorious fame.
Hang thou there upon the tomb,
Praising her when I am dumb.

(*ii*)

PARDON, goddess of the night,
  Those that slew thy virgin knight,
For the which, with songs of woe,
Round about her tomb they go.
    Midnight, assist our moan;
    Help us to sigh and groan,
      Heavily, heavily.

Graves, yawn and yield your dead,
Till death be uttered,
Heavily, heavily.
Now unto thy bones good night!
Yearly will I do this rite.

Ibid.

347 *Orlando's Rhymes*

WHY should this a desert be?
For it is unpeopled? No;
Tongues I'll hang on every tree,
That shall civil sayings show.
Some, how brief the life of man
Runs his erring pilgrimage,
That the stretching of a span
Buckles in his sum of age;
Some, of violated vows
'Twixt the souls of friend and friend.
But upon the fairest boughs,
Or at every sentence end,
Will I Rosalinda write,
Teaching all that read to know
The quintessence of every spright
Heaven would in little show.
Therefore Heaven Nature charged
That one body should be filled
With all graces wide enlarged:
Nature presently distilled
Helen's cheek, but not her heart,
Cleopatra's majesty,
Atalanta's better part,
Sad Lucretia's modesty.

Thus Rosalind of many parts
   By heavenly synod was devised,
Of many faces, eyes, and hearts,
   To have the touches dearest prized.
Heaven would that she these gifts should have,
And I to live and die her slave.

As You Like It, 1599–1600?

348 *Amiens's Songs*

(*i*)

UNDER the greenwood tree
   Who loves to lie with me,
And turn his merry note
   Unto the sweet bird's throat,
Come hither, come hither, come hither:
      Here shall he see
      No enemy
But winter and rough weather.

Who doth ambition shun,
   And loves to live i' the sun,
Seeking the food he eats,
   And pleased with what he gets,
Come hither, come hither, come hither:
      Here shall he see
      No enemy
But winter and rough weather.

(*ii*)

BLOW, blow, thou winter wind,
Thou art not so unkind
As man's ingratitude;
Thy tooth is not so keen,
Because thou art not seen,
Although thy breath be rude.
Heigh-ho! sing, heigh-ho! unto the green holly:
Most friendship is feigning, most loving mere folly.
Then heigh-ho! the holly!
This life is most jolly.

Freeze, freeze, thou bitter sky,
That dost not bite so nigh
As benefits forgot:
Though thou the waters warp,
Thy sting is not so sharp
As friend remembered not.
Heigh-ho! sing, heigh-ho! unto the green holly:
Most friendship is feigning, most loving mere folly.
Then heigh-ho! the holly!
This life is most jolly.

(*iii*)

WHAT shall he have that killed the deer?
His leather skin and horns to wear.
Then sing him home.
Take thou no scorn to wear the horn;
It was a crest ere thou wast born:
Thy father's father wore it,
And thy father bore it:
The horn, the horn, the lusty horn
Is not a thing to laugh to scorn.

Ibid.

349

The Pages' Song

IT was a lover and his lass,
  With a hey, and a ho, and a hey nonino,
That o'er the green corn-field did pass,
  In spring time, the only pretty ring time,
When birds do sing, hey ding a ding, ding;
Sweet lovers love the spring.

Between the acres of the rye,
  With a hey, and a ho, and a hey nonino,
Those pretty country folks would lie,
  In spring time, the only pretty ring time,
When birds do sing, hey ding a ding, ding;
Sweet lovers love the spring.

This carol they began that hour,
  With a hey, and a ho, and a hey nonino,
How that a life was but a flower
  In spring time, the only pretty ring time,
When birds do sing, hey ding a ding, ding;
Sweet lovers love the spring.

And therefore take the present time,
  With a hey, and a ho, and a hey nonino;
For love is crowned with the prime
  In spring time, the only pretty ring time,
When birds do sing, hey ding a ding, ding;
Sweet lovers love the spring.

As You Like It, 1599–1600?

350

Feste's Songs

(i)

O MISTRESS mine, where are you roaming?
O! stay and hear; your true love 's coming,
That can sing both high and low.
Trip no further, pretty sweeting;
Journeys end in lovers meeting,
Every wise man's son doth know.

What is love? 'Tis not hereafter;
Present mirth hath present laughter;
What 's to come is still unsure.
In delay there lies no plenty;
Then come kiss me, sweet and twenty;
Youth 's a stuff will not endure.

(ii)

COME away, come away, death,
And in sad cypress let me be laid.
Fly away, fly away, breath;
I am slain by a fair cruel maid.
My shroud of white, stuck all with yew,
O! prepare it.
My part of death, no one so true
Did share it.

Not a flower, not a flower sweet,
On my black coffin let there be strown;
Not a friend, not a friend greet
My poor corpse, where my bones shall be thrown.

A thousand thousand sighs to save,
        Lay me, O! where
Sad true lover never find my grave,
        To weep there.

(*iii*)

WHEN that I was and a little tiny boy,
  With hey, ho, the wind and the rain;
A foolish thing was but a toy,
  For the rain it raineth every day.

But when I came to man's estate,
  With hey, ho, the wind and the rain;
'Gainst knaves and thieves men shut their gate,
  For the rain it raineth every day.

But when I came, alas! to wive,
  With hey, ho, the wind and the rain;
By swaggering could I never thrive,
  For the rain it raineth every day.

But when I came unto my beds,
  With hey, ho, the wind and the rain;
With toss-pots still had drunken heads,
  For the rain it raineth every day.

A great while ago the world begun,
  With hey, ho, the wind and the rain;
But that 's all one, our play is done,
  And we'll strive to please you every day.

Twelfth Night, 1599–1600?

351 *Ophelia's Song*

HOW should I your true love know
  From another one?
By his cockle hat and staff,
  And his sandal shoon.

He is dead and gone, lady,
  He is dead and gone;
At his head a grass-green turf,
  At his heels a stone.

White his shroud as the mountain snow,
  Larded with sweet flowers;
Which bewept to the grave did not go
  With true-love showers.

Hamlet, 1600–1601?

352 *A Song at the Moated Grange*

TAKE, O! take those lips away,
  That so sweetly were forsworn,
And those eyes, the break of day,
  Lights that do mislead the morn;
But my kisses bring again,
        Bring again,
Seals of love, but sealed in vain,
        Sealed in vain.

Measure for Measure, 1604–1605?

353

A Drinking Song

COME, thou monarch of the vine,
 Plumpy Bacchus, with pink eyne!
In thy fats our cares be drowned,
With thy grapes our hairs be crowned.
 Cup us, till the world go round,
 Cup us, till the world go round!

Antony and Cleopatra, 1606–1607?

354

Song to Imogen

HARK! hark! the lark at heaven's gate sings,
 And Phoebus 'gins arise,
His steeds to water at those springs
 On chaliced flowers that lies;
And winking Mary-buds begin
 To ope their golden eyes;
With every thing that pretty is,
 My lady sweet, arise!
  Arise, arise!

Cymbeline, 1609–1610?

355

Fidele's Dirge

FEAR no more the heat o' the sun,
 Nor the furious winter's rages;
Thou thy worldly task hast done,
 Home art gone, and ta'en thy wages.
Golden lads and girls all must,
As chimney-sweepers, come to dust.

fats] vats

Fear no more the frown o' the great,
  Thou art past the tyrant's stroke;
Care no more to clothe and eat,
  To thee the reed is as the oak.
The sceptre, learning, physic, must
All follow this, and come to dust.

Fear no more the lightning-flash,
  Nor the all-dreaded thunder-stone;
Fear not slander, censure rash;
  Thou hast finished joy and moan.
All lovers young, all lovers must
Consign to thee, and come to dust.

No exorciser harm thee!
Nor no witchcraft charm thee!
Ghost unlaid forbear thee!
Nothing ill come near thee!
Quiet consummation have,
And renowned be thy grave!

Ibid.

356 *Autolycus's Songs*

(*i*)

WHEN daffodils begin to peer,
  With heigh! the doxy, over the dale,
Why, then comes in the sweet o' the year;
  For the red blood reigns in the winter's pale.

The white sheet bleaching on the hedge,
  With heigh! the sweet birds, O, how they sing!
Doth set my pugging tooth on edge,
  For a quart of ale is a dish for a king.

The lark, that tirra-lirra chants,
  With heigh! with heigh! the thrush and the jay,
Are summer songs for me and my aunts,
  While we lie tumbling in the hay.

(ii)

JOG on, jog on, the footpath way,
  And merrily hent the stile-a;
A merry heart goes all the day,
  Your sad tires in a mile-a.

(iii)

LAWN as white as driven snow;
Cyprus black as e'er was crow;
Gloves as sweet as damask roses;
Masks for faces and for noses;
Bugle-bracelet, necklace amber,
Perfume for a lady's chamber;
Golden coifs and stomachers,
For my lads to give their dears;
Pins and poking-sticks of steel;
What maids lack from head to heel:
Come buy of me, come; come buy, come buy;
Buy, lads, or else your lasses cry:
Come buy.

(*iv*)

WILL you buy any tape,
Or lace for your cape,
My dainty duck, my dear-a?
Any silk, any thread,
Any toys for your head,
Of the new'st and finest, finest wear-a?
Come to the pedlar;
Money 's a meddler,
That doth utter all men's ware-a.

Winter's Tale, 1610–1611?

357 *Ariel's Songs*

(*i*)

COME unto these yellow sands,
And then take hands:
Curtsied when you have, and kissed
The wild waves whist,
Foot it featly here and there;
And, sweet sprites, the burden bear.
Hark, hark!
Bow, wow
The watch-dogs bark,
Bow, wow,
Hark, hark! I hear
The strain of strutting Chanticleer
Cry, Cock-a-diddle-dow.

(ii)

FULL fathom five thy father lies;
  Of his bones are coral made;
Those are pearls that were his eyes:
  Nothing of him that doth fade,
But doth suffer a sea-change
Into something rich and strange:
Sea nymphs hourly ring his knell.
                    Ding-dong!
  Hark! now I hear them,
                    Ding-dong, bell!

(iii)

WHERE the bee sucks, there suck I,
  In a cowslip's bell I lie,
There I couch when owls do cry,
On the bat's back I do fly
After summer merrily.
  Merrily, merrily, shall I live now
  Under the blossom that hangs on the bough.

Tempest, 1611–1612?

358 *A Bridal Song*

ROSES, their sharp spines being gone,
  Not royal in their smells alone,
  But in their hue;
Maiden pinks, of odour faint,
Daisies smell-less, yet most quaint,
  And sweet thyme true;

WILLIAM SHAKESPEARE

Primrose, firstborn child of Ver,
Merry springtime's harbinger,
   With her bells dim;
Oxlips in their cradles growing,
Marigolds on death-beds blowing,
   Larks'-heels trim:

All dear Nature's children sweet
Lie 'fore bride and bridegroom's feet,
   Blessing their sense.
Not an angel of the air,
Bird melodious or bird fair,
   Be absent hence.

The crow, the slanderous cuckoo, nor
The boding raven, nor chough hoar,
   Nor chattering pie,
May on our bride-house perch or sing,
Or with them any discord bring,
   But from it fly.

Two Noble Kinsmen, 1612–1613?

359 *Fifty Sonnets*

(i)

FROM fairest creatures we desire increase,
That thereby beauty's rose might never die,
But as the riper should by time decease,
His tender heir might bear his memory:
But thou, contracted to thine own bright eyes,
Feed'st thy light's flame with self-substantial fuel,
Making a famine where abundance lies,
Thyself thy foe, to thy sweet self too cruel.
Thou that art now the world's fresh ornament
And only herald to the gaudy spring,
Within thine own bud buriest thy content
And, tender churl, makest waste in niggarding.
Pity the world, or else this glutton be,
To eat the world's due, by the grave and thee.

(ii)

WHEN forty winters shall besiege thy brow,
And dig deep trenches in thy beauty's field,
Thy youth's proud livery, so gazed on now,
Will be a tattered weed, of small worth held:
Then being asked where all thy beauty lies,
Where all the treasure of thy lusty days,
To say, within thine own deep-sunken eyes,
Were an all-eating shame and thriftless praise.
How much more praise deserved thy beauty's use,
If thou couldst answer, 'This fair child of mine
Shall sum my count, and make my old excuse',
Proving his beauty by succession thine.
This were to be new made when thou art old,
And see thy blood warm when thou feel'st it cold.

(*iii*)

LOOK in thy glass, and tell the face thou viewest
Now is the time that face should form another;
Whose fresh repair if now thou not renewest,
Thou dost beguile the world, unbless some mother.
For where is she so fair whose uneared womb
Disdains the tillage of thy husbandry?
Or who is he so fond will be the tomb
Of his self-love, to stop posterity?
Thou art thy mother's glass, and she in thee
Calls back the lovely April of her prime;
So thou through windows of thine age shalt see,
Despite of wrinkles, this thy golden time.
But if thou live, remembered not to be,
Die single, and thine image dies with thee.

(*iv*)

WHEN I do count the clock that tells the time,
And see the brave day sunk in hideous night;
When I behold the violet past prime,
And sable curls, all silvered o'er with white;
When lofty trees I see barren of leaves,
Which erst from heat did canopy the herd,
And summer's green all girded up in sheaves,
Borne on the bier with white and bristly beard,
Then of thy beauty do I question make,
That thou among the wastes of time must go,
Since sweets and beauties do themselves forsake
And die as fast as they see others grow;
And nothing 'gainst Time's scythe can make defence
Save breed, to brave him when he takes thee hence.

(*v*)

WHEN I consider every thing that grows
  Holds in perfection but a little moment,
That this huge stage presenteth nought but shows
  Whereon the stars in secret influence comment;
When I perceive that men as plants increase,
  Cheered and checked even by the self-same sky,
Vaunt in their youthful sap, at height decrease,
  And wear their brave state out of memory;
Then the conceit of this inconstant stay
  Sets you most rich in youth before my sight,
Where wasteful Time debateth with Decay,
  To change your day of youth to sullied night;
    And, all in war with Time for love of you,
    As he takes from you, I engraft you new.

(*vi*)

WHO will believe my verse in time to come,
  If it were filled with your most high deserts?
Though yet, heaven knows, it is but as a tomb
  Which hides your life and shows not half your parts.
If I could write the beauty of your eyes
  And in fresh numbers number all your graces,
The age to come would say, 'This poet lies;
  Such heavenly touches ne'er touched earthly faces.'
So should my papers, yellowed with their age,
  Be scorned, like old men of less truth than tongue.
And your true rights be termed a poet's rage
  And stretched metre of an antique song:
    But were some child of yours alive that time,
    You should live twice—in it and in my rhyme.

(vii)

SHALL I compare thee to a summer's day?
  Thou art more lovely and more temperate:
Rough winds do shake the darling buds of May,
  And summer's lease hath all too short a date:
Sometime too hot the eye of heaven shines,
  And often is his gold complexion dimmed;
And every fair from fair sometime declines,
  By chance, or nature's changing course untrimmed;
But thy eternal summer shall not fade,
  Nor lose possession of that fair thou owest,
Nor shall death brag thou wander'st in his shade,
  When in eternal lines to time thou growest;
    So long as men can breathe, or eyes can see,
    So long lives this, and this gives life to thee.

(viii)

DEVOURING Time, blunt thou the lion's paws,
  And make the earth devour her own sweet brood;
Pluck the keen teeth from the fierce tiger's jaws,
  And burn the long-lived phoenix in her blood;
Make glad and sorry seasons as thou fleets,
  And do whate'er thou wilt, swift-footed Time,
To the wide world and all her fading sweets;
  But I forbid thee one most heinous crime:
O! carve not with thy hours my Love's fair brow,
  Nor draw no lines there with thine antique pen;
Him in thy course untainted do allow
  For beauty's pattern to succeeding men.
    Yet, do thy worst, old Time: despite thy wrong,
    My Love shall in my verse ever live young.

(*ix*)

SO is it not with me as with that Muse,
Stirred by a painted beauty to his verse,
Who heaven itself for ornament doth use
And every fair with his fair doth rehearse,
Making a couplement of proud compare,
With sun and moon, with earth and sea's rich gems,
With April's first-born flowers, and all things rare
That heaven's air in this huge rondure hems.
O! let me, true in love, but truly write,
And then believe me, my love is as fair
As any mother's child, though not so bright
As those gold candles fixed in heaven's air:
Let them say more that like of hear-say well;
I will not praise that purpose not to sell.

(*x*)

MY glass shall not persuade me I am old,
So long as youth and thou are of one date;
But when in thee time's furrows I behold,
Then look I death my days should expiate.
For all that beauty that doth cover thee
Is but the seemly raiment of my heart,
Which in thy breast doth live, as thine in me:
How can I then be elder than thou art?
O! therefore, Love, be of thyself so wary,
As I, not for myself, but for thee will;
Bearing thy heart, which I will keep so chary,
As tender nurse her babe from faring ill.
Presume not on thy heart when mine is slain;
Thou gavest me thine, not to give back again.

(*xi*)

LET those who are in favour with their stars
  Of public honour and proud titles boast,
Whilst I, whom fortune of such triumph bars,
  Unlooked-for joy in that I honour most.
Great princes' favourites their fair leaves spread
  But as the marigold at the sun's eye,
And in themselves their pride lies buried,
  For at a frown they in their glory die.
The painful warrior famoused for fight,
  After a thousand victories once foiled,
Is from the book of honour razed quite,
  And all the rest forgot for which he toiled:
    Then happy I, that love and am beloved,
    Where I may not remove nor be removed.

(*xii*)

WEARY with toil, I haste me to my bed,
  The dear repose for limbs with travel tired;
But then begins a journey in my head
  To work my mind, when body's work 's expired:
For then my thoughts, from far where I abide,
  Intend a zealous pilgrimage to thee,
And keep my drooping eyelids open wide,
  Looking on darkness which the blind do see:
Save that my soul's imaginary sight
  Presents thy shadow to my sightless view,
Which, like a jewel hung in ghastly night,
  Makes black night beauteous and her old face new.
    Lo! thus, by day my limbs, by night my mind,
    For thee and for myself no quiet find.

(*xiii*)

HOW can I then return in happy plight,
That am debarred the benefit of rest?
When day's oppression is not eased by night,
But day by night and night by day oppressed,
And each, though enemies to either's reign,
Do in consent shake hands to torture me,
The one by toil, the other to complain
How far I toil, still farther off from thee.
I tell the day, to please him thou art bright
And dost him grace when clouds do blot the heaven:
So flatter I the swart-complexioned night,
When sparkling stars twire not thou gild'st the even.
But day doth daily draw my sorrows longer,
And night doth nightly make grief's strength seem stronger.

(*xiv*)

WHEN in disgrace with fortune and men's eyes
I all alone beweep my outcast state,
And trouble deaf heaven with my bootless cries,
And look upon myself, and curse my fate,
Wishing me like to one more rich in hope,
Featured like him, like him with friends possessed,
Desiring this man's art, and that man's scope,
With what I most enjoy contented least;
Yet in these thoughts myself almost despising,
Haply I think on thee, and then my state,
Like to the lark at break of day arising
From sullen earth, sings hymns at heaven's gate;
For thy sweet love remembered such wealth brings
That then I scorn to change my state with kings.

twire] twinkle

(*xv*)

WHEN to the sessions of sweet silent thought
  I summon up remembrance of things past,
I sigh the lack of many a thing I sought,
  And with old woes new wail my dear time's waste:
Then can I drown an eye, unused to flow,
  For precious friends hid in death's dateless night,
And weep afresh love's long since cancelled woe,
  And moan the expense of many a vanished sight:
Then can I grieve at grievances foregone,
  And heavily from woe to woe tell o'er
The sad account of fore-bemoaned moan,
  Which I new pay as if not paid before.
    But if the while I think on thee, dear friend,
    All losses are restored and sorrows end.

(*xvi*)

THY bosom is endeared with all hearts,
  Which I by lacking have supposed dead;
And there reigns love, and all love's loving parts,
  And all those friends which I thought buried.
How many a holy and obsequious tear
  Hath dear religious love stolen from mine eye,
As interest of the dead, which now appear
  But things removed that hidden in thee lie!
Thou art the grave where buried love doth live,
  Hung with the trophies of my lovers gone,
Who all their parts of me to thee did give,
  That due of many now is thine alone.
    Their images I loved I view in thee,
    And thou, all they, hast all the all of me.

(*xvii*)

IF thou survive my well-contented day,
  When that churl Death my bones with dust shall cover,
And shalt by fortune once more re-survey
  These poor rude lines of thy deceased lover,
Compare them with the bettering of the time,
  And though they be outstripped by every pen,
Reserve them for my love, not for their rhyme,
  Exceeded by the height of happier men.
O! then vouchsafe me but this loving thought:
  'Had my friend's Muse grown with this growing age,
A dearer birth than this his love had brought,
  To march in ranks of better equipage:
    But since he died and poets better prove,
    Theirs for their style I'll read, his for his love.'

(*xviii*)

FULL many a glorious morning have I seen
  Flatter the mountain-tops with sovereign eye,
Kissing with golden face the meadows green,
  Gilding pale streams with heavenly alchemy;
Anon permit the basest clouds to ride
  With ugly rack on his celestial face,
And from the forlorn world his visage hide,
  Stealing unseen to west with this disgrace:
Even so my sun one early morn did shine,
  With all-triumphant splendour on my brow;
But, out! alack! he was but one hour mine,
  The region cloud hath masked him from me now.
    Yet him for this my love no whit disdaineth;
    Suns of the world may stain when heaven's sun staineth.

region] upper air

(*xix*)

WHY didst thou promise such a beauteous day,
And make me travel forth without my cloak,
To let base clouds o'ertake me in my way,
Hiding thy bravery in their rotten smoke?
'Tis not enough that through the cloud thou break,
To dry the rain on my storm-beaten face,
For no man well of such a salve can speak
That heals the wound and cures not the disgrace:
Nor can thy shame give physic to my grief;
Though thou repent, yet I have still the loss;
The offender's sorrow lends but weak relief
To him that bears the strong offence's cross.
Ah! but those tears are pearl which thy love sheds,
And they are rich and ransom all ill deeds.

(*xx*)

TAKE all my loves, my Love, yea, take them all;
What hast thou then more than thou hadst before?
No love, my Love, that thou mayst true love call;
All mine was thine before thou hadst this more.
Then, if for my love thou my love receivest,
I cannot blame thee for my love thou usest;
But yet be blamed, if thou thyself deceivest
By wilful taste of what thyself refusest.
I do forgive thy robbery, gentle thief,
Although thou steal thee all my poverty;
And yet love knows it is a greater grief
To bear love's wrong than hate's known injury.
Lascivious grace, in whom all ill well shows,
Kill me with spites; yet we must not be foes.

(*xxi*)

SO am I as the rich, whose blessed key
Can bring him to his sweet up-locked treasure,
The which he will not every hour survey,
For blunting the fine point of seldom pleasure.
Therefore are feasts so solemn and so rare,
Since, seldom coming, in the long year set,
Like stones of worth they thinly placed are,
Or captain jewels in the carcanet.
So is the time that keeps you as my chest,
Or as the wardrobe which the robe doth hide,
To make some special instant special blest
By new unfolding his imprisoned pride.
Blessed are you, whose worthiness gives scope,
Being had, to triumph; being lacked, to hope.

(*xxii*)

WHAT is your substance, whereof are you made,
That millions of strange shadows on you tend?
Since every one hath, every one, one shade,
And you, but one, can every shadow lend.
Describe Adonis, and the counterfeit
Is poorly imitated after you;
On Helen's cheek all art of beauty set,
And you in Grecian tires are painted new:
Speak of the spring and foison of the year,
The one doth shadow of your beauty show,
The other as your bounty doth appear;
And you in every blessed shape we know.
In all external grace you have some part,
But you like none, none you, for constant heart.

carcanet] collar   foison] abundance

(xxiii)

O! HOW much more doth beauty beauteous seem
By that sweet ornament which truth doth give!
The rose looks fair, but fairer we it deem
For that sweet odour which doth in it live.
The canker-blooms have full as deep a dye
As the perfumed tincture of the roses,
Hang on such thorns, and play as wantonly,
When summer's breath their masked buds discloses:
But, for their virtue only is their show,
They live unwooed, and unrespected fade;
Die to themselves. Sweet roses do not so;
Of their sweet deaths are sweetest odours made;
And so of you, beauteous and lovely youth,
When that shall vade, by verse distils your truth.

(xxiv)

NOT marble, nor the gilded monuments
Of princes, shall outlive this powerful rhyme;
But you shall shine more bright in these contents
Than unswept stone, besmeared with sluttish time.
When wasteful war shall statues overturn,
And broils root out the work of masonry,
Nor Mars his sword nor war's quick fire shall burn
The living record of your memory.
'Gainst death and all oblivious enmity
Shall you pace forth; your praise shall still find room
Even in the eyes of all posterity
That wear this world out to the ending doom.
So, till the judgment that yourself arise,
You live in this, and dwell in lovers' eyes.

vade] fade

(*xxv*)

LIKE as the waves make towards the pebbled shore,
  So do our minutes hasten to their end;
Each changing place with that which goes before,
  In sequent toil all forwards do contend.
Nativity, once in the main of light,
  Crawls to maturity, wherewith being crowned,
Crooked eclipses 'gainst his glory fight,
  And Time that gave doth now his gift confound.
Time doth transfix the flourish set on youth
  And delves the parallels in beauty's brow,
Feeds on the rarities of nature's truth,
  And nothing stands but for his scythe to mow.
    And yet to times in hope my verse shall stand,
    Praising thy worth, despite his cruel hand.

(*xxvi*)

AGAINST my Love shall be, as I am now,
  With Time's injurious hand crushed and o'erworn;
When hours have drained his blood and filled his brow
  With lines and wrinkles; when his youthful morn
Hath travelled on to age's steepy night,
  And all those beauties whereof now he 's king
Are vanishing or vanished out of sight,
  Stealing away the treasure of his spring;
For such a time do I now fortify
  Against confounding age's cruel knife,
That he shall never cut from memory
  My sweet Love's beauty, though my lover's life.
    His beauty shall in these black lines be seen,
    And they shall live, and he in them still green.

(xxvii)

WHEN I have seen by Time's fell hand defaced
The rich proud cost of outworn buried age;
When sometime lofty towers I see down razed,
And brass eternal slave to mortal rage;
When I have seen the hungry ocean gain
Advantage on the kingdom of the shore,
And the firm soil win of the watery main,
Increasing store with loss, and loss with store;
When I have seen such interchange of state,
Or state itself confounded to decay,
Ruin hath taught me thus to ruminate,
That Time will come and take my Love away.
This thought is as a death, which cannot choose
But weep to have that which it fears to lose.

(xxviii)

TIRED with all these, for restful death I cry;
As to behold desert a beggar born,
And needy nothing trimmed in jollity,
And purest faith unhappily forsworn,
And gilded honour shamefully misplaced,
And maiden virtue rudely strumpeted,
And right perfection wrongfully disgraced,
And strength by limping sway disabled,
And art made tongue-tied by authority,
And folly, doctor-like, controlling skill,
And simple truth miscalled simplicity,
And captive good attending captain ill.
Tired with all these, from these would I be gone,
Save that, to die, I leave my Love alone.

(*xxix*)

THUS is his cheek the map of days outworn,
  When beauty lived and died as flowers do now,
Before these bastard signs of fair were born,
  Or durst inhabit on a living brow;
Before the golden tresses of the dead,
  The right of sepulchres, were shorn away,
To live a second life on second head;
  Ere beauty's dead fleece made another gay:
In him those holy antique hours are seen,
  Without all ornament, itself and true,
Making no summer of another's green,
  Robbing no old to dress his beauty new;
    And him as for a map doth Nature store,
    To show false Art what beauty was of yore.

(*xxx*)

NO longer mourn for me when I am dead,
  Than you shall hear the surly sullen bell
Give warning to the world that I am fled
  From this vile world, with vilest worms to dwell:
Nay, if you read this line, remember not
  The hand that writ it; for I love you so,
That I in your sweet thoughts would be forgot,
  If thinking on me then should make you woe.
O! if, I say, you look upon this verse,
  When I perhaps compounded am with clay,
Do not so much as my poor name rehearse,
  But let your love even with my life decay;
    Lest the wise world should look into your moan,
    And mock you with me after I am gone.

(*xxxi*)

THAT time of year thou mayst in me behold
  When yellow leaves, or none, or few, do hang
Upon those boughs which shake against the cold,
  Bare ruined choirs, where late the sweet birds sang.
In me thou see'st the twilight of such day
  As after sunset fadeth in the west;
Which by and by black night doth take away,
  Death's second self, that seals up all in rest.
In me thou see'st the glowing of such fire,
  That on the ashes of his youth doth lie,
As the death-bed whereon it must expire,
  Consumed with that which it was nourished by.
    This thou perceivest, which makes thy love more strong,
    To love that well which thou must leave ere long.

(*xxxii*)

BUT be contented: when that fell arrest
  Without all bail shall carry me away,
My life hath in this line some interest,
  Which for memorial still with thee shall stay.
When thou reviewest this, thou dost review
  The very part was consecrate to thee:
The earth can have but earth, which is his due;
  My spirit is thine, the better part of me:
So then thou hast but lost the dregs of life,
  The prey of worms, my body being dead,
The coward conquest of a wretch's knife,
  Too base of thee to be remembered.
    The worth of that is that which it contains,
    And that is this, and this with thee remains.

(xxxiii)

OR I shall live your epitaph to make,
  Or you survive when I in earth am rotten;
From hence your memory death cannot take,
  Although in me each part will be forgotten.
Your name from hence immortal life shall have,
  Though I, once gone, to all the world must die:
The earth can yield me but a common grave,
  When you entombed in men's eyes shall lie.
Your monument shall be my gentle verse,
  Which eyes not yet created shall o'er-read;
And tongues to be your being shall rehearse,
  When all the breathers of this world are dead:
    You still shall live—such virtue hath my pen—
    Where breath most breathes, even in the mouths of men.

(xxxiv)

FAREWELL! thou art too dear for my possessing,
  And like enough thou know'st thy estimate:
The charter of thy worth gives thee releasing;
  My bonds in thee are all determinate.
For how do I hold thee but by thy granting?
  And for that riches where is my deserving?
The cause of this fair gift in me is wanting,
  And so my patent back again is swerving.
Thyself thou gavest, thy own worth then not knowing,
  Or me, to whom thou gavest it, else mistaking;
So thy great gift, upon misprision growing,
  Comes home again, on better judgement making.
    Thus have I had thee, as a dream doth flatter,
    In sleep a king, but, waking, no such matter.

(xxxv)

THEN hate me when thou wilt; if ever, now;
  Now, while the world is bent my deeds to cross,
Join with the spite of fortune, make me bow,
  And do not drop in for an after-loss:
Ah! do not, when my heart hath 'scaped this sorrow,
  Come in the rearward of a conquered woe;
Give not a windy night a rainy morrow,
  To linger out a purposed overthrow.
If thou wilt leave me, do not leave me last,
  When other petty griefs have done their spite,
But in the onset come; so shall I taste
  At first the very worst of fortune's might.
    And other strains of woe, which now seem woe,
    Compared with loss of thee will not seem so.

(xxxvi)

HOW like a winter hath my absence been
  From thee, the pleasure of the fleeting year!
What freezings have I felt, what dark days seen!
  What old December's bareness everywhere!
And yet this time removed was summer's time,
  The teeming autumn, big with rich increase,
Bearing the wanton burden of the prime,
  Like widowed wombs after their lords' decease:
Yet this abundant issue seemed to me
  But hope of orphans and unfathered fruit;
For summer and his pleasures wait on thee,
  And, thou away, the very birds are mute.
    Or, if they sing, 'tis with so dull a cheer,
    That leaves look pale, dreading the winter's near.

(*xxxvii*)

FROM you have I been absent in the spring,
When proud pied April, dressed in all his trim,
Hath put a spirit of youth in every thing,
That heavy Saturn laughed and leaped with him.
Yet nor the lays of birds, nor the sweet smell
Of different flowers in odour and in hue,
Could make me any summer's story tell,
Or from their proud lap pluck them where they grew:
Nor did I wonder at the lily's white,
Nor praise the deep vermilion in the rose;
They were but sweet, but figures of delight,
Drawn after you, you pattern of all those.
Yet seemed it winter still, and, you away,
As with your shadow I with these did play.

(*xxxviii*)

THE forward violet thus did I chide:
'Sweet thief, whence didst thou steal thy sweet that smells,
If not from my Love's breath? The purple pride
Which on thy soft cheek for complexion dwells
In my Love's veins thou hast too grossly dyed.'
The lily I condemned for thy hand,
And buds of marjoram had stolen thy hair;
The roses fearfully on thorns did stand,
One blushing shame, another white despair;
A third, nor red nor white, had stolen of both,
And to his robbery had annexed thy breath;
But, for his theft, in pride of all his growth
A vengeful canker eat him up to death.
More flowers I noted, yet I none could see
But sweet or colour it had stolen from thee.

(*xxxix*)

WHERE art thou, Muse, that thou forget'st so long
  To speak of that which gives thee all thy might?
Spend'st thou thy fury on some worthless song,
  Darkening thy power, to lend base subjects light?
Return, forgetful Muse, and straight redeem
  In gentle numbers time so idly spent;
Sing to the ear that doth thy lays esteem
  And gives thy pen both skill and argument.
Rise, resty Muse, my Love's sweet face survey,
  If Time have any wrinkle graven there;
If any, be a satire to decay,
  And make Time's spoils despised every where.
    Give my Love fame faster than Time wastes life;
    So thou prevent'st his scythe and crooked knife.

(*xl*)

MY love is strengthened, though more weak in seeming;
  I love not less, though less the show appear:
That love is merchandized whose rich esteeming
  The owner's tongue doth publish everywhere.
Our love was new, and then but in the spring,
  When I was wont to greet it with my lays,
As Philomel in summer's front doth sing,
  And stops her pipe in growth of riper days:
Not that the summer is less pleasant now
  Than when her mournful hymns did hush the night,
But that wild music burthens every bough,
  And sweets grown common lose their dear delight.
    Therefore, like her, I sometime hold my tongue,
    Because I would not dull you with my song.

resty] inert

(*xli*)

TO me, fair friend, you never can be old,
For as you were when first your eye I eyed,
Such seems your beauty still. Three winters cold
Have from the forests shook three summers' pride;
Three beauteous springs to yellow autumn turned
In process of the seasons have I seen,
Three April perfumes in three hot Junes burned,
Since first I saw you fresh, which yet are green.
Ah! yet doth beauty, like a dial-hand,
Steal from his figure, and no pace perceived;
So your sweet hue, which methinks still doth stand,
Hath motion, and mine eye may be deceived.
For fear of which, hear this, thou age unbred;
Ere you were born was beauty's summer dead.

(*xlii*)

WHEN in the chronicle of wasted time
I see descriptions of the fairest wights,
And beauty making beautiful old rhyme,
In praise of ladies dead and lovely knights,
Then, in the blazon of sweet beauty's best,
Of hand, of foot, of lip, of eye, of brow,
I see their antique pen would have expressed
Even such a beauty as you master now.
So all their praises are but prophecies
Of this our time, all you prefiguring;
And, for they looked but with divining eyes,
They had not skill enough your worth to sing:
For we, which now behold these present days,
Have eyes to wonder, but lack tongues to praise.

(xliii)

NOT mine own fears, nor the prophetic soul
  Of the wide world dreaming on things to come,
Can yet the lease of my true love control,
  Supposed as forfeit to a confined doom.
The mortal moon hath her eclipse endured,
  And the sad augurs mock their own presage;
Incertainties now crown themselves assured,
  And peace proclaims olives of endless age.
Now with the drops of this most balmy time
  My love looks fresh, and Death to me subscribes,
Since, spite of him, I'll live in this poor rhyme,
  While he insults o'er dull and speechless tribes.
    And thou in this shalt find thy monument,
    When tyrants' crests and tombs of brass are spent.

(xliv)

O! NEVER say that I was false of heart,
  Though absence seemed my flame to qualify.
As easy might I from myself depart
  As from my soul, which in thy breast doth lie:
That is my home of love; if I have ranged,
  Like him that travels, I return again,
Just to the time, not with the time exchanged,
  So that myself bring water for my stain.
Never believe, though in my nature reigned
  All frailties that besiege all kinds of blood,
That it could so preposterously be stained,
  To leave for nothing all thy sum of good;
    For nothing this wide universe I call,
    Save thou, my rose; in it thou art my all.

(xlv)

ALAS! 'tis true I have gone here and there,
  And made myself a motley to the view,
Gored mine own thoughts, sold cheap what is most dear,
  Made old offences of affections new.
Most true it is that I have looked on truth
  Askance and strangely; but, by all above,
These blenches gave my heart another youth,
  And worse essays proved thee my best of love.
Now all is done, have what shall have no end:
  Mine appetite I never more will grind
On newer proof, to try an older friend,
  A god in love, to whom I am confined.
    Then give me welcome, next my heaven the best,
    Even to thy pure and most most loving breast.

(xlvi)

LET me not to the marriage of true minds
  Admit impediments. Love is not love
Which alters when it alteration finds,
  Or bends with the remover to remove.
O, no! it is an ever-fixed mark,
  That looks on tempests and is never shaken;
It is the star to every wandering bark,
  Whose worth 's unknown, although his height be taken.
Love 's not Time's fool, though rosy lips and cheeks
  Within his bending sickle's compass come;
Love alters not with his brief hours and weeks,
  But bears it out even to the edge of doom.
    If this be error, and upon me proved,
    I never writ, nor no man ever loved.

(xlvii)

NO, Time, thou shalt not boast that I do change:
  Thy pyramids built up with newer might
To me are nothing novel, nothing strange;
  They are but dressings of a former sight.
Our dates are brief, and therefore we admire
  What thou dost foist upon us that is old;
And rather make them born to our desire,
  Than think that we before have heard them told.
Thy registers and thee I both defy,
  Not wondering at the present nor the past,
For thy records and what we see doth lie,
  Made more or less by thy continual haste.
    This I do vow, and this shall ever be;
    I will be true, despite thy scythe and thee.

(xlviii)

THE expense of spirit in a waste of shame
  Is lust in action; and till action, lust
Is perjured, murderous, bloody, full of blame,
  Savage, extreme, rude, cruel, not to trust;
Enjoyed, no sooner but despised straight;
  Past reason hunted; and no sooner had,
Past reason hated, as a swallowed bait,
  On purpose laid to make the taker mad:
Mad in pursuit, and in possession so;
  Had, having, and in quest to have, extreme;
A bliss in proof, and proved, a very woe;
  Before, a joy proposed; behind, a dream.
    All this the world well knows; yet none knows well
    To shun the heaven that leads men to this hell.

(*xlix*)

THINE eyes I love, and they, as pitying me,
Knowing thy heart torment me with disdain,
Have put on black and loving mourners be,
Looking with pretty ruth upon my pain.
And truly not the morning sun of heaven
Better becomes the grey cheeks of the east,
Nor that full star that ushers in the even,
Doth half that glory to the sober west,
As those two mourning eyes become thy face:
O! let it then as well beseem thy heart
To mourn for me, since mourning doth thee grace,
And suit thy pity like in every part.
Then will I swear beauty herself is black,
And all they foul that thy complexion lack.

(*l*)

POOR soul, the centre of my sinful earth,
Feeding these rebel powers that thee array,
Why dost thou pine within and suffer dearth,
Painting thy outward walls so costly gay?
Why so large cost, having so short a lease,
Dost thou upon thy fading mansion spend?
Shall worms, inheritors of this excess,
Eat up thy charge? Is this thy body's end?
Then, soul, live thou upon thy servant's loss,
And let that pine to aggravate thy store;
Buy terms divine in selling hours of dross;
Within be fed, without be rich no more:
So shalt thou feed on Death, that feeds on men,
And Death once dead, there 's no more dying then.

Sonnets, 1609

360

Youth and Age

CRABBED age and youth cannot live together:
  Youth is full of pleasance, age is full of care;
Youth like summer morn, age like winter weather;
  Youth like summer brave, age like winter bare.
Youth is full of sport, age's breath is short;
  Youth is nimble, age is lame;
Youth is hot and bold, age is weak and cold;
  Youth is wild, and age is tame.
Age, I do abhor thee, youth, I do adore thee;
  O! my love, my love is young:
Age, I do defy thee. O! sweet shepherd, hie thee,
  For methinks thou stays too long.

The Passionate Pilgrim, 1599

361

The Phoenix and the Turtle

LET the bird of loudest lay,
  On the sole Arabian tree,
  Herald sad and trumpet be,
To whose sound chaste wings obey.

But thou shrieking harbinger,
  Foul precurrer of the fiend,
  Augur of the fever's end,
To this troop come thou not near.

From this cession interdict
  Every fowl of tyrant wing,
  Save the eagle, feathered king;
Keep the obsequy so strict.

WILLIAM SHAKESPEARE

Let the priest in surplice white
   That defunctive music can,
   Be the death-divining swan,
Lest the requiem lack his right.

And thou treble-dated crow,
   That thy sable gender makest
   With the breath thou givest and takest,
'Mongst our mourners shalt thou go.

Here the anthem doth commence:
   Love and constancy is dead;
   Phoenix and the turtle fled
In a mutual flame from hence.

So they loved, as love in twain
   Had the essence but in one;
   Two distincts, division none;
Number there in love was slain.

Hearts remote, yet not asunder;
   Distance, and no space was seen
   'Twixt the turtle and his queen;
But in them it were a wonder.

So between them love did shine,
   That the turtle saw his right
   Flaming in the phoenix' sight;
Either was the other's mine.

can] knows

Property was thus appalled,
  That the self was not the same;
  Single nature's double name
Neither two nor one was called.

Reason, in itself confounded,
  Saw division grow together,
  To themselves yet either neither,
Simple were so well compounded:

That it cried, 'How true a twain
  Seemeth this concordant one!
  Love hath reason, reason none,
If what parts can so remain.'

Whereupon it made this threne
  To the phoenix and the dove,
  Co-supremes and stars of love,
As chorus to their tragic scene.

THRENOS

Beauty, truth, and rarity,
Grace in all simplicity,
Here enclosed in cinders lie.

Death is now the phoenix' nest;
And the turtle's loyal breast
To eternity doth rest,

Leaving no posterity:
'Twas not their infirmity,
It was married chastity.

property] individuality threne] lament

Truth may seem, but cannot be;
Beauty brag, but 'tis not she;
Truth and beauty buried be.

To this urn let those repair
That are either true or fair;
For these dead birds sigh a prayer.

R. Chester, *Love's Martyr*, 1601

GEORGE CHAPMAN

1559?–1634

362 *Night*

KNEEL then with me, fall worm-like on the ground,
And from th' infectious dunghill of this round,
From men's brass wits and golden foolery,
Weep, weep your souls, into felicity.
Come to this house of mourning, serve the Night,
To whom pale Day (with whoredom soaked quite)
Is but a drudge, selling her beauty's use
To rapes, adulteries, and to all abuse.
Her labours feast imperial Night with sports,
Where loves are Christmass'd, with all pleasure's sorts;
And whom her fugitive and far-shot rays
Disjoin, and drive into ten thousand ways,
Night's glorious mantle wraps in safe abodes,
And frees their necks from servile labour's loads.
Her trusty shadows succour men dismayed,
Whom Day's deceitful malice hath betrayed.
From the silk vapours of her ivory port,
Sweet Protean dreams she sends of every sort;

Some taking forms of princes, to persuade
Of men deject, we are their equals made;
Some clad in habit of deceased friends,
For whom we mourned, and now have wished amends;
And some (dear favour) lady-like attired,
With pride of beauty's full meridian fired,
Who pity our contempts, revive our hearts;
For wisest ladies love the inward parts.
  If these be dreams, even so are all things else,
That walk this round by heavenly sentinels:
But from Night's port of horn she greets our eyes
With graver dreams inspired with prophecies,
Which oft presage to us succeeding chances,
We proving that awake, they show in trances.
If these seem likewise vain, or nothing are,
Vain things, or nothing, come to virtue's share;
For nothing more than dreams with us she finds.
Then since all pleasures vanish like the winds,
And that most serious actions, not respecting
The second light, are worth but the neglecting;
Since day, or light, in any quality,
For earthly uses do but serve the eye;
And since the eye's most quick and dangerous use
Enflames the heart, and learns the soul abuse;
Since mournings are preferred to banquetings,
And they reach heaven, bred under sorrow's wings;
Since Night brings terror to our frailties still,
And shameless Day doth marble us in ill:
  All you possessed with indepressed spirits,
Endued with nimble, and aspiring wits,
Come consecrate with me to sacred Night
Your whole endeavours, and detest the light.

Sweet Peace's richest crown is made of stars,
Most certain guides of honoured mariners;
No pen can anything eternal write,
That is not steeped in humour of the Night.
  Hence beasts and birds to caves and bushes then,
And welcome Night, ye noblest heirs of men;
Hence Phoebus to thy glassy strumpet's bed,
And never more let Themis' daughters spread
Thy golden harness on thy rosy horse,
But in close thickets run thy oblique course.
  See now ascends the glorious bride of brides,
Nuptials, and triumphs, glittering by her sides;
Juno and Hymen do her train adorn,
Ten thousand torches round about them borne;
Dumb silence, mounted on the Cyprian star,
With becks rebukes the winds before his car,
Where she advanced; beats down with cloudy mace
The feeble light to black Saturn's palace.
Behind her, with a brace of silver hinds,
In ivory chariot, swifter than the winds,
Is great Hyperion's horned daughter drawn,
Enchantress-like decked in disparent lawn,
Circled with charms and incantations,
That ride huge spirits, and outrageous passions.
Music, and mood, she loves, but love she hates,
As curious ladies do their public cates.
This train, with meteors, comets, lightnings,
The dreadful presence of our empress sings:
Which grant for ever (O eternal Night)
Till virtue flourish in the light of light.

The Shadow of Night, 1594

363 *Corinna Bathes*

IN a loose robe of tinsel forth she came,
  Nothing but it betwixt her nakedness
And envious light. The downward-burning flame
  Of her rich hair did threaten new access
Of venturous Phaeton to scorch the fields;
  And thus to bathing came our poet's goddess,
Her handmaids bearing all things pleasure yields
    To such a service; odours most delighted,
    And purest linen which her looks had whited.

Then cast she off her robe and stood upright,
  As lightning breaks out of a labouring cloud;
Or as the morning heaven casts off the night;
  Or as that heaven cast off itself, and showed
Heaven's upper light, to which the brightest day
  Is but a black and melancholy shroud;
Or as when Venus strived for sovereign sway
    Of charmful beauty in young Troy's desire,
    So stood Corinna, vanishing her tire.

A soft enflowered bank embraced the fount;
  Of Chloris' ensigns, an abstracted field,
Where grew melanthy, great in bees' account,
  Amareus, that precious balm doth yield,
Enamelled pansies, used at nuptials still,
  Diana's arrow, Cupid's crimson shield,
Ope-morn, night-shade, and Venus's navel,
    Solemn violets, hanging head as shamed,
    And verdant calaminth, for odour famed;

Sacred nepenthe, purgative of care,
  And sovereign rumex, that doth rancour kill,
Sya and hyacinth, that Furies wear,
  White and red jessamines, merry, meliphill,
Fair crown-imperial, emperor of flowers,
  Immortal amaranth, white aphrodill,
And cup-like twillpants, strewed in Bacchus' bowers.
    These cling about this nature's naked gem,
    To taste her sweets, as bees do swarm on them.

And now she used the fount where Niobe,
  Tombed in herself, poured her lost soul in tears
Upon the bosom of this Roman Phoebe;
  Who, bathed and odoured, her bright limbs she rears,
And drying her on that disparent round,
  Her lute she takes to enamour heavenly ears,
And try if, with her voice's vital sound,
    She could warm life through those cold statues spread,
    And cheer the dame that wept when she was dead.

And thus she sung, all naked as she sat,
  Laying the happy lute upon her thigh,
    Not thinking any near to wonder at
    The bliss of her sweet breast's divinity.

The Song of Corinna

'Tis better to contemn than love,
  And to be fair than wise,
  For souls are ruled by eyes:
And Jove's *bird seized by* Cypris' *dove*

It is our grace and sport to see,
Our beauty's sorcery,
That makes, like destiny,
Men follow us the more we flee;
That sets wise glosses on the fool,
And turns her cheeks to books,
Where wisdom sees in looks
Derision, laughing at his school,
Who, loving, proves profaneness holy,
Nature our fate, our wisdom folly.

Ovid's Banquet of Sense, 1595

364 *Love and Philosophy*

MUSES that sing Love's sensual empery,
And lovers kindling your enraged fires
At Cupid's bonfires burning in the eye,
Blown with the empty breath of vain desires;
You that prefer the painted cabinet
Before the wealthy jewels it doth store ye,
That all your joys in dying figures set,
And stain the living substance of your glory:
Abjure those joys, abhor their memory,
And let my love the honoured subject be
Of love, and honour's complete history;
Your eyes were never yet let in to see
The majesty and riches of the mind,
But dwell in darkness; for your God is blind.

A Coronet for his Mistress Philosophy, 1595

365 *De Guiana, Carmen Epicum*

WHAT work of honour and eternal name
For all the world t' envy, and us t' achieve,
Fills me with fury, and gives armed hands
To my heart's peace, that else would gladly turn
My limbs and every sense into my thoughts
Rapt with the thirsted action of my mind?
O Clio, Honour's Muse, sing in my voice;
Tell the attempt, and prophesy th' exploit
Of his Eliza-consecrated sword,
That in this peaceful charm of England's sleep
Opens most tenderly her aged throat,
Offering to pour fresh youth through all her veins,
That flesh of brass and ribs of steel retains.
  Riches, and conquest, and renown I sing,
Riches with honour, conquest without blood,
Enough to seat the monarchy of earth,
Like to Jove's eagle, on Eliza's hand.
Guiana, whose rich feet are mines of gold,
Whose forehead knocks against the roof of stars,
Stands on her tip-toes at fair England looking,
Kissing her hand, bowing her mighty breast,
And every sign of all submission making,
To be her sister, and the daughter both
Of our most sacred Maid; whose barrenness
Is the true fruit of virtue, that may get,
Bear and bring forth anew in all perfection,
What heretofore savage corruption held
In barbarous Chaos; and in this affair
Become her father, mother, and her heir.
Then most admired sovereign, let your breath

Go forth upon the waters, and create
A golden world in this our iron age,
And be the prosperous forewind to a fleet,
That, seconding your last, may go before it,
In all success of profit and renown.
Doubt not but your election was divine,
As well by fate as your high judgement order'd,
To raise him with choice bounties, that could add
Height to his height; and like a liberal vine,
Not only bear his virtuous fruit aloft,
Free from the press of squint-eyed Envy's feet,
But deck his gracious prop with golden bunches,
And shroud it with broad leaves of rule o'er-grown
From all black tempests of invasion.
  Those conquests that like general earthquakes shook
The solid world, and made it fall before them,
Built all their brave attempts on weaker grounds
And less persuasive likelihoods than this;
Nor was there ever princely fount so long
Pour'd forth a sea of rule with so free course,
And such ascending majesty as you.
Then be not like a rough and violent wind,
That in the morning rends the forests down,
Shoves up the seas to heaven, makes earth to tremble,
And tombs his wasteful bravery in the even.
But as a river from a mountain running,
The further he extends, the greater grows,
And by his thrifty race strengthens his stream,
Even to join battle with th' imperious sea,
Disdaining his repulse, and in despight
Of his proud fury, mixeth with his main,
Taking on him his title and commands:

So let thy sovereign Empire be increased,
And with Iberian Neptune part the stake,
Whose trident he the triple world would make.
  You then that would be wise in wisdom's spite,
Directing with discredit of direction,
And hunt for honour, hunting him to death,
With whom before you will inherit gold,
You will lose gold, for which you lose your souls;
You that choose nought for right, but certainty,
And fear that valour will get only blows,
Placing your faith in Incredulity;
Sit till you see a wonder, Virtue rich;
Till Honour, having gold, rob gold of honour;
Till, as men hate desert that getteth nought,
They loathe all getting that deserveth nought,
And use you gold-made men as dregs of men;
And till your poison'd souls, like spiders lurking
In sluttish chinks, in mists of cobwebs hide
Your foggy bodies, and your dunghill pride.
  O Incredulity! the wit of fools,
That slovenly will spit on all things fair,
The coward's castle, and the sluggard's cradle,
How easy 'tis to be an infidel!
  But you patrician spirits that refine
Your flesh to fire, and issue like a flame
On brave endeavours, knowing that in them
The tract of heaven in morn-like glory opens;
That know you cannot be the kings of earth,
Claiming the rights of your creation,
And let the mines of earth be kings of you;
That are so far from doubting likely drifts,
That in things hardest y' are most confident;

You that know death lives where power lives unused,
Joying to shine in waves that bury you,
And so make way for life even through your graves;
That will not be content like horse to hold
A thread-bare beaten way to home affairs,
But where the sea, in envy of your reign,
Closeth her womb as fast as 'tis disclosed,
That she like Avarice might swallow all,
And let none find right passage through her rage,
There your wise souls, as swift as Eurus, lead
Your bodies through, to profit and renown,
And scorn to let your bodies choke your souls
In the rude breath and prison'd life of beasts;
You that herein renounce the course of earth,
And lift your eyes for guidance to the stars;
That live not for yourselves, but to possess
Your honour'd country of a general store,
In pity of the spoil rude self-love makes
Of them whose lives and yours one air doth feed,
One soil doth nourish, and one strength combine;
You that are blest with sense of all things noble:—
In this attempt your complete worths redouble.
   But how is Nature at her heart corrupted,
(I mean even in her most ennobled birth)
How in excess of sense is sense bereft her!
That her most lightning-like effects of lust
Wound through her flesh, her soul, her flesh unwounded,
And she must need incitements to her good,
Even from that part she hurts. O! how most like
Art thou, heroic author of this act,
To this wrong'd soul of nature; that sustain'st
Pain, charge, and peril for thy country's good,

And she, much like a body numb'd with surfeits,
Feels not thy gentle applications
For the health, use, and honour of her powers.
Yet shall my verse through all her ease-lock'd ears
Trumpet the noblesse of thy high intent,
And if it cannot into act proceed,
The fault and bitter penance of the fault
Make red some other's eyes with penitence,
For thine are clear; and what more nimble spirits,
Apter to bite at such unhooked baits,
Gain by our loss, that must we needs confess
Thy princely valour would have purchased us,
Which shall be fame eternal to thy name,
Though thy contentment, in thy grave desires
Of our advancement, fail deserved effect.
O! how I fear thy glory which I love,
Lest it should dearly grow by our decrease.
Natures, that stick in golden-gravell'd springs,
In muck-pits cannot 'scape their swallowings.
  But we shall forth, I know; gold is our fate,
Which all our acts doth fashion and create.
  Then in the Thespiad's bright prophetic fount,
Methinks I see our Liege rise from her throne,
Her ears and thoughts in steep amaze erected
At the most rare endeavour of her power.
And now she blesseth with her wonted graces
Th' industrious knight, the soul of this exploit,
Dismissing him to convoy of his stars.
And now for love and honour of his worth,
Our twice-born nobles bring him, bridegroom-like,
That is espoused for virtue to his love,
With feasts and music, ravishing the air,

GEORGE CHAPMAN

To his Argolian fleet, where round about
His bating colours English valour swarms,
In haste, as if Guianian Orenoque
With his fell waters fell upon our shore.
And now a wind, as forward as their spirits,
Sets their glad feet on smooth Guiana's breast,
Where, as if each man were an Orpheus,
A world of savages fall tame before them,
Storing their theft-free treasuries with gold;
And there doth plenty crown their wealthy fields,
There learning eats no more his thriftless books,
Nor valour, estridge-like, his iron arms.
There beauty is no strumpet for her wants,
Nor Gallic humours putrefy her blood;
But all our youth take Hymen's lights in hand,
And fill each roof with honour'd progeny.
There makes society adamantine chains,
And joins their hearts with wealth whom wealth disjoin'd.
There healthful recreations strew their meads,
And make their mansions dance with neighbourhood,
That here were drown'd in churlish avarice.
And there do palaces and temples rise
Out of the earth, and kiss the enamour'd skies,
Where new Britannia humbly kneels to heaven,
The world to her, and both at her blest feet,
In whom the circles of all Empire meet.

L. Keymis, *Relation of the Second Voyage to Guiana*, 1596

estridge] ostrich

366 *Repentance*

HIS most kind sister all his secrets knew,
And to her singing like a shower he flew,
Sprinkling the earth, that to their tombs took in
Streams dead for love to leave his ivory skin,
Which yet a snowy foam did leave above,
As soul to the dead water that did love;
And from thence did the first white roses spring
(For love is sweet and fair in every thing)
And all the sweetened shore, as he did go,
Was crowned with odorous roses, white as snow.
Love-blest Leander was with love so filled,
That love to all that touched him he instilled.
And as the colours of all things we see
To our sight's powers communicated be;
So to all objects that in compass came
Of any sense he had, his sense's flame
Flowed from his parts with force so virtual,
It fired with sense things mere insensual.
  Now, with warm baths and odours comforted,
When he lay down he kindly kissed his bed,
As consecrating it to Hero's right,
And vowed thereafter that whatever sight
Put him in mind of Hero, or her bliss,
Should be her altar to prefer a kiss.
  Then laid he forth his late enriched arms,
In whose white circle Love writ all his charms,
And made his characters sweet Hero's limbs,
When on his breast's warm sea she sideling swims.
And as those arms, held up in circle, met,
He said: 'See, sister, Hero's carcanet,

Which she had rather wear about her neck,
Than all the jewels that doth Juno deck.'
  But, as he shook with passionate desire
To put in flame his other secret fire,
A music so divine did pierce his ear,
As never yet his ravished sense did hear:
When suddenly a light of twenty hues
Brake through the roof, and like the rainbow views
Amazed Leander; in whose beams came down
The goddess Ceremony, with a crown
Of all the stars, and heaven with her descended.
Her flaming hair to her bright feet extended,
By which hung all the bench of deities;
And in a chain, compact of ears and eyes,
She led Religion; all her body was
Clear and transparent as the purest glass:
For she was all presented to the sense;
Devotion, Order, State, and Reverence
Her shadows were; Society, Memory;
All which her sight made live, her absence die.
A rich disparent pentacle she wears,
Drawn full of circles and strange characters;
Her face was changeable to every eye;
One way looked ill, another graciously;
Which while men viewed, they cheerful were and holy;
But looking off, vicious and melancholy.
The snaky paths to each observed law
Did Policy in her broad bosom draw:
One hand a mathematic crystal sways,
Which gathering in one line a thousand rays

disparent] diverse
pentacle] five-pointed star

From her bright eyes, Confusion burns to death,
And all estates of men distinguisheth.
By it Morality and Comeliness
Themselves in all their sightly figures dress.
Her other hand a laurel rod applies,
To beat back Barbarism and Avarice,
That followed, eating earth and excrement
And human limbs; and would make proud ascent
To seats of gods, were Ceremony slain;
The Hours and Graces bore her glorious train,
And all the sweets of our society
Were sphered and treasured in her bounteous eye.
Thus she appeared, and sharply did reprove
Leander's bluntness in his violent love;
Told him how poor was substance without rites,
Like bills unsigned, desires without delights;
Like meats unseasoned; like rank corn that grows
On cottages, that none or reaps or sows:
Not being with civil forms confirmed and bounded,
For human dignities and comforts founded,
But loose and secret, all their glories hide;
Fear fills the chamber, darkness decks the bride.
  She vanished, leaving pierced Leander's heart
With sense of his unceremonious part,
In which, with plain neglect of nuptial rites,
He close and flatly fell to his delights:
And instantly he vowed to celebrate
All rites pertaining to his married state.
So up he gets, and to his father goes,
To whose glad ears he doth his vows disclose:
The nuptials are resolved with utmost power,
And he at night would swim to Hero's tower.

From whence he meant to Sestos' forked bay
To bring her covertly, where ships must stay,
Sent by his father, throughly rigged and manned,
To waft her safely to Abydos' strand.
There leave we him, and with fresh wing pursue
Astonished Hero, whose most wished view
I thus long have forborne, because I left her
So out of countenance, and her spirits bereft her.
To look of one abashed is impudence,
When of slight faults he hath too deep a sense.
Her blushing het her chamber: she looked out,
And all the air she purpled round about,
And after it a foul black day befell,
Which ever since a red morn doth foretell,
And still renews our woes for Hero's woe,
And foul it proved, because it figured so
The next night's horror, which prepare to hear;
I fail, if it profane your daintiest ear.
Then thou most strangely-intellectual fire,
That proper to my soul hast power t' inspire
Her burning faculties, and with the wings
Of thy unsphered flame visit'st the springs
Of spirits immortal; now (as swift as Time
Doth follow Motion) find th' eternal clime
Of his free soul, whose living subject stood
Up to the chin in the Pierian flood,
And drunk to me half this Musaean story,
Inscribing it to deathless memory:
Confer with it, and make my pledge as deep,
That neither's draught be consecrate to sleep.

of] on het] heated

Tell it how much his late desires I tender
(If yet it know not) and to light surrender
My soul's dark offspring, willing it should die
To loves, to passions, and society.

Hero and Leander, iii. 73–198, 1598

367 *The Wedding of Alcmane and Mya*

THIS told, strange Teras touched her lute, and sung
This ditty, that the torchy evening sprung.

Epithalamion Teratos.

Come, come, dear Night, Love's mart of kisses,
Sweet close of his ambitious line,
The fruitful summer of his blisses;
Love's glory doth in darkness shine.

O! come, soft rest of cares, come, Night,
Come, naked Virtue's only tire,
The reaped harvest of the light,
Bound up in sheaves of sacred fire.
Love calls to war;
Sighs his alarms,
Lips his swords are,
The field his arms.

Come, Night, and lay thy velvet hand
On glorious Day's outfacing face;
And all thy crowned flames command,
For torches to our nuptial grace.
Love calls to war;
Sighs his alarms,
Lips his swords are,
The field his arms.

No need have we of factious Day,
  To cast, in envy of thy peace,
Her balls of discord in thy way:
  Here Beauty's day doth never cease;
Day is abstracted here,
And varied in a triple sphere.
Hero, Alcmane, Mya, so outshine thee,
Ere thou come here, let Thetis thrice refine thee.
      Love calls to war;
        Sighs his alarms,
      Lips his swords are,
        The field his arms.

      The evening star I see:
        Rise, youths, the evening star
        Helps Love to summon war;
      Both now embracing be.

Rise, youths, Love's rite claims more than banquets, rise:
Now the bright marigolds, that deck the skies,
Phoebus' celestial flowers, that, contrary
To his flowers here, ope when he shuts his eye,
And shut when he doth open, crown your sports.
Now Love in Night and Night in Love exhorts
Courtship and dances; all your parts employ,
And suit Night's rich expansure with your joy.
Love paints his longings in sweet virgins' eyes:
Rise, youths, Love's rite claims more than banquets, rise.
  Rise, virgins, let fair nuptial loves enfold
Your fruitless breasts; the maidenheads ye hold
Are not your own alone, but parted are;
Part in disposing them your parents share,

And that a third part is; so must ye save
Your loves a third, and you your thirds must have.
Love paints his longings in sweet virgins' eyes:
Rise, youths, Love's rite claims more than banquets, rise.

Herewith the amorous spirit, that was so kind
To Teras' hair, and combed it down with wind,
Still as it, comet-like, brake from her brain,
Would needs have Teras gone, and did refrain
To blow it down; which, staring up, dismayed
The timorous feast; and she no longer stayed;
But, bowing to the bridegroom and the bride,
Did, like a shooting exhalation, glide
Out of their sights: the turning of her back
Made them all shriek, it looked so ghastly black.

Hero and Leander, v. 425–490, 1598

HENRY CHETTLE

c. 1560–c. 1607

368 *Aeliana's Ditty*

TRUST not his wanton tears,
  Lest they beguile ye;
Trust not his childish sight,
  He breatheth slily.
Trust not his touch,
  His feeling may defile ye;
Trust nothing that he doth,
  The wag is wily.
If you suffer him to prate,
You will rue it over late;

Beware of him, for he is witty.
Quickly strive the boy to bind,
Fear him not, for he is blind;
If he gets loose, he shows no pity.

Piers Plainness' Seven Years' Prenticeship, 1595

369 *Damelus' Song to His Diaphenia*

DIAPHENIA, like the daffodowndilly,
White as the sun, fair as the lily,
Heigh ho, how I do love thee!
I do love thee as my lambs
Are beloved of their dams;
How blest were I if thou wouldst prove me!

Diaphenia, like the spreading roses,
That in thy sweets all sweets encloses,
Fair sweet, how I do love thee!
I do love thee as each flower
Loves the sun's life-giving power,
For, dead, thy breath to life might move me.

Diaphenia, like to all things blessed,
When all thy praises are expressed,
Dear joy, how I do love thee!
As the birds do love the spring,
Or the bees their careful king:
Then in requite, sweet virgin, love me!

England's Helicon, 1600

RICHARD BARNFIELD

1574–1627

370 *A Shepherd's Complaint*

MY flocks feed not,
   My ewes breed not,
My rams speed not,
   All is amiss.
Love is dying,
Faith's defying,
Heart's denying,
   Causer of this.

All our merry jigs are quite forgot;
All my lady's love is lost, God wot;
Where our faith was firmly fixed in love,
There annoy is placed without remove.

One silly cross
Wrought all my loss,
O frowning Fortune, cursed fickle dame!
For now I see
Inconstancy
More in women than in many men to be.

In black mourn I,
All fear scorn I,
Love hath forlorn me,
   Living in thrall.
Heart is bleeding,
All help needing,
O cruel speeding
   Fraught with gall!

RICHARD BARNFIELD

My shepherd's pipe will sound no deal;
My wether's bell rings doleful knell;
My curtall dog, that wont to have played,
Plays not at all, but seems afraid.

My sighs so deep
Procures to weep
With howling noise to see my doleful plight.
How sighs resound
Through harkless ground,
Like a thousand vanquished men in bloody fight.

Clear wells spring not,
Sweet birds sing not,
Loud bells ring not
Cheerfully.
Herds stand weeping,
Flocks all sleeping,
Nymphs back creeping
Fearfully.

All our pleasures known to us poor swains,
All our merry meetings on the plains,
All our evening sports from us are fled,
All our loves are lost, for Love is dead.

Farewell, sweet lass,
The like ne'er was
For a sweet content, the cause of all my woe.
Poor Corydon
Must live alone,
Other help for him I know there 's none.

T. Weelkes, *Madrigals*, 1597

371

Ode

AS it fell upon a day
In the merry month of May,
Sitting in a pleasant shade
Which a grove of myrtles made,
Beasts did leap and birds did sing,
Trees did grow and plants did spring;
Every thing did banish moan
Save the nightingale alone.
She, poor bird, as all forlorn,
Leaned her breast up-till a thorn,
And there sung the dolefull'st ditty,
That to hear it was great pity.
Fie, fie, fie, now would she cry,
Teru, teru, by and by,
That to hear her so complain
Scarce I could from tears refrain;
For her griefs so lively shown
Made me think upon mine own.
Ah! thought I, thou mourn'st in vain,
None takes pity on thy pain;
Senseless trees, they cannot hear thee,
Ruthless beasts, they will not cheer thee;
King Pandion, he is dead,
All thy friends are lapped in lead;
All thy fellow birds do sing
Careless of thy sorrowing.
Whilst as fickle Fortune smiled,
Thou and I were both beguiled.
Every one that flatters thee
Is no friend in misery;

RICHARD BARNFIELD

Words are easy, like the wind;
Faithful friends are hard to find;
Every man will be thy friend,
Whilst thou hast wherewith to spend;
But, if store of crowns be scant,
No man will supply thy want.
If that one be prodigal,
Bountiful, they will him call;
And with such-like flattering,
Pity but he were a king.
If he be addict to vice,
Quickly him they will entice.
If to women he be bent,
They have at commandèment.
But if Fortune once do frown,
Then farewell his great renown;
They that fawned on him before
Use his company no more.
He, that is thy friend indeed,
He will help thee in thy need;
If thou sorrow, he will weep;
If thou wake, he cannot sleep;
Thus of every grief, in heart,
He with thee doth bear a part.
These are certain signs to know
Faithful friend from flattering foe.

Poems in Divers Humors, 1598

RICHARD BARNFIELD

372 *A Comparison of the Life of Man*

MAN'S life is well compared to a feast,
  Furnished with choice of all variety;
To it comes Time; and as a bidden guest
  He sets him down, in pomp and majesty;
The three-fold Age of man the waiters be.
    Then with an earthen voider (made of clay)
  Comes Death, and takes the table clean away.

Poems in Divers Humors, 1598

JOSEPH HALL

1574–1656

373 *The Olden Days*

TIME was, and that was termed the time of gold,
When world and time were young, that now are old,
When quiet Saturn swayed the mace of lead,
And pride was yet unborn, and yet unbred.
Time was, that while the autumn fall did last,
Our hungry sires gaped for the falling mast.
Could no unhusked acorn leave the tree,
But there was challenge made whose it might be.
And if some nice and lickerous appetite
Desired more dainty dish of rare delight,
They scaled the stored crab with clasped knee,
Till they had sated their delicious eye;
Or searched the hopeful thicks of hedgy-rows,
For briary berries, or haws, or sourer sloes;
Or when they meant to fare the finest of all,
They licked oak-leaves besprent with honey fall.
As for the thrice three-angled beech-nut shell,
Or chestnut's armed husk, and hid kernel,

No squire durst touch; the law would not afford,
Kept for the court, and for the king's own board.
Their royal plate was clay, or wood, or stone;
The vulgar, save his hand, else had he none.
Their only cellar was the neighbour brook;
None did for better care, for better look.
Was then no plaining of the brewer's scape,
Nor greedy vintner mixed the strained grape.
The king's pavilion was the grassy green,
Under safe shelter of the shady treen.
Under each bank men laid their limbs along,
Not wishing any ease, not fearing wrong;
Clad with their own, as they were made of old,
Not fearing shame, not feeling any cold.
But when, by Ceres' housewifery and pain,
Men learned to bury the reviving grain,
And father Janus taught the new-found vine
Rise on the elm, with many a friendly twine,
And base desire bade men to delven low,
For needless metals, then 'gan mischief grow.
Then farewell, fairest age, the world's best days,
Thriving in ill as it in age decays.
Then crept in pride, and peevish covetise,
And men grew greedy, discordous, and nice.
Now man, that erst hail-fellow was with beast,
Wox on to ween himself a god at least.
No airy fowl can take so high a flight,
Though she her daring wings in clouds have dight;
Nor fish can dive so deep in yielding sea,
Though Thetis' self should swear her safety;
Nor fearful beast can dig his cave so low,
All could he further than Earth's centre go;

As that the air, the earth, or ocean,
Should shield them from the gorge of greedy man.
Hath utmost Ind aught better than his own?
Then utmost Ind is near, and rife to gon.
O Nature! was the world ordained for nought,
But fill man's maw, and feed man's idle thought?
Thy grandsire's words savoured of thrifty leeks,
Or manly garlic; but thy furnace reeks
Hot steams of wine; and can aloof descry
The drunken draughts of sweet autumnity.
They naked went, or clad in ruder hide,
Or home-spun russet, void of foreign pride;
But thou canst mask in garish gaudery,
To suite a fool's far-fetched livery.
A French head joined to neck Italian;
Thy thighs from Germany, and breast fro Spain;
An Englishman in none, a fool in all;
Many in one, and one in severall.
Then men were men; but now the greater part
Beasts are in life, and women are in heart.
Good Saturn self, that homely emperor,
In proudest pomp was not so clad of yore,
As is the under-groom of the ostlery,
Husbanding it in work-day yeomanry.
Lo! the long date of those expired days,
Which the inspired Merlin's word foresays:
'When dunghill peasants shall be dight as kings,
Then one confusion another brings.'
Then farewell, fairest age, the world's best days,
Thriving in ill, as it in age decays.

Virgidemiarum, 1597

rife to gon] easy to go

JOHN MARSTON

c. 1575–1634

374

To Detraction

FOUL canker of fair virtuous action,
  Vile blaster of the freshest blooms on earth,
Envy's abhorred child, Detraction,
  I here expose to thy all-tainting breath
    The issue of my brain; snarl, rail, bark, bite,
    Know that my spirit scorns Detraction's spite.

Know that the genius which attendeth on
  And guides my powers intellectual,
Holds in all vile repute Detraction;
  My soul, an essence metaphysical,
    That in the basest sort scorns critics' rage,
    Because he knows his sacred parentage.

My spirit is not puffed up with fat fume
  Of slimy ale, nor Bacchus' heating grape.
My mind disdains the dungy muddy scum
  Of abject thoughts, and envy's raging hate.
    True judgement slight regards opinion;
    A sprightly wit disdains Detraction.

A partial praise shall never elevate
  My settled censure of mine own esteem.
A cankered verdict of malignant hate
  Shall ne'er provoke me worse myself to deem.
    Spite of despite and rancour's villainy,
    I am myself, so is my poesy.

The Scourge of Villainy, 1598

JOHN MARSTON

375 *To Everlasting Oblivion*

THOU mighty gulf, insatiate cormorant,
Deride me not, though I seem petulant
To fall into thy chops. Let others pray
Forever their fair poems flourish may.
But as for me, hungry Oblivion,
Devour me quick, accept my orison,
My earnest prayers, which do importune thee,
With gloomy shade of thy still empery
To veil both me and my rude poesy.

Far worthier lines in silence of thy state
Do sleep securely, free from love or hate,
From which this living ne'er can be exempt,
But whilst it breathes will hate and fury tempt.
Then close his eyes with thy all-dimming hand,
Which not right glorious actions can withstand.
Peace, hateful tongues, I now in silence pace;
Unless some hound do wake me from my place,
I with this sharp, yet well-meant poesy,
Will sleep secure, right free from injury
Of cankered hate or rankest villainy.

The Scourge of Villainy, 1598

THOMAS DEKKER

c. 1570–c. 1632

376 *May*

O! THE month of May, the merry month of May,
So frolic, so gay, and so green, so green, so green!
O! and then did I unto my true Love say,
Sweet Peg, thou shalt be my Summer's Queen.

Now the nightingale, the pretty nightingale,
  The sweetest singer in all the forest's choir,
Entreats thee, sweet Peggy, to hear thy true Love's tale:
  Lo! yonder she sitteth, her breast against a briar.

But O! I spy the cuckoo, the cuckoo, the cuckoo;
  See where she sitteth; come away, my joy:
Come away, I prithee, I do not like the cuckoo
  Should sing where my Peggy and I kiss and toy.

O! the month of May, the merry month of May,
  So frolic, so gay, and so green, so green, so green!
And then did I unto my true Love say,
  Sweet Peg, thou shalt be my Summer's Queen.

The Shoemaker's Holiday, 1600

377 *Saint Hugh*

COLD 's the wind, and wet 's the rain,
  Saint Hugh be our good speed!
Ill is the weather that bringeth no gain,
  Nor helps good hearts in need.

Troll the bowl, the jolly nut-brown bowl,
  And here, kind mate, to thee!
Let 's sing a dirge for Saint Hugh's soul,
  And down it merrily.

Down-a-down, hey, down-a-down,
  Hey derry derry down-a-down!
Ho! well done, to me let come,
  Ring compass, gentle joy!

Ibid.

378

Fortune

FORTUNE smiles, cry holy day!
  Dimples on her cheeks do dwell.
Fortune frowns, cry well-a-day!
  Her love is heaven, her hate is hell.
Since heaven and hell obey her power,
Tremble when her eyes do lour;
  Since heaven and hell her power obey,
  When she smiles cry holy day!
    Holy day with joy we cry,
    And bend, and bend, and merrily
    Sing hymns to Fortune's deity,
    Sing hymns to Fortune's deity.

Let us sing merrily, merrily, merrily!
  With our song let heaven resound,
  Fortune's hands our heads have crowned;
Let us sing merrily, merrily, merrily!

Old Fortunatus, 1600

379

A Priest's Song

VIRTUE'S branches wither, virtue pines,
  O pity, pity, and alack the time!
Vice doth flourish, vice in glory shines,
  Her gilded boughs above the cedar climb.

Vice hath golden cheeks, O pity, pity!
  She in every land doth monarchize.
Virtue is exiled from every city,
  Virtue is a fool, vice only wise.

O pity, pity! virtue weeping dies.
  Vice laughs to see her faint, alack the time!
This sinks; with painted wings the other flies.
  Alack, that best should fall, and bad should climb!

O pity, pity, pity! mourn, not sing!
Vice is a saint, virtue an underling.
Vice doth flourish, vice in glory shines,
Virtue's branches wither, virtue pines.

Ibid.

380 *The Basket-Maker's Song*

ART thou poor, yet hast thou golden slumbers?
    O sweet content!
Art thou rich, yet is thy mind perplexed?
    O punishment!
Dost thou laugh to see how fools are vexed
To add to golden numbers, golden numbers?
O sweet content! O sweet content!
    Work apace, apace, apace, apace;
    Honest labour bears a lovely face;
  Then hey nonny nonny, hey nonny nonny!

Canst drink the waters of the crisped spring?
    O sweet content!
Swim'st thou in wealth, yet sink'st in thine own tears?
    O punishment!
Then he that patiently want's burden bears
No burden bears, but is a king, a king!
O sweet content! O sweet content!
    Work apace, apace, apace, apace;
    Honest labour bears a lovely face;
  Then hey nonny nonny, hey nonny nonny!

Patient Grissill, 1603

381

A Cradle Song

GOLDEN slumbers kiss your eyes,
Smiles awake you when you rise.
Sleep, pretty wantons, do not cry,
And I will sing a lullaby:
Rock them, rock them, lullaby.

Care is heavy, therefore sleep you;
You are care, and care must keep you.
Sleep, pretty wantons, do not cry,
And I will sing a lullaby:
Rock them, rock them, lullaby.

Patient Grissill, 1603

382

A Bridal Song

BEAUTY, arise, show forth thy glorious shining!
Thine eyes feed love, for them he standeth pining;
Honour and youth attend to do their duty
To thee, their only sovereign, Beauty.
Beauty, arise, whilst we, thy servants, sing
Io to Hymen, wedlock's jocund king.
Io to Hymen, Io, Io, sing,
Of wedlock, love, and youth is Hymen king.

Beauty, arise, thy glorious lights display,
Whilst we sing Io, glad to see this day.
Io to Hymen, Io, Io, sing,
Of wedlock, love, and youth is Hymen king.

Ibid.

383

Troynovant

TROYNOVANT is now no more a city.
O great pity! is 't not pity?
And yet her towers on tip-toe stand,
Like pageants built in fairy land,
And her marble arms,
Like to magic charms,
Bind thousands fast unto her,
That for her wealth and beauty daily woo her.
Yet for all this, is 't not pity,
Troynovant is now no more a city?

Troynovant is now a summer arbour,
Or the nest wherein doth harbour
The eagle, of all birds that fly
The sovereign, for his piercing eye.
If you wisely mark,
'Tis besides a park,
Where runs, being newly born,
With the fierce lion the fair unicorn,
Or else it is a wedding hall,
Where four great Kingdoms hold a festival.

Troynovant is now a bridal chamber,
Whose roof is gold, floor is of amber,
By virtue of that holy light,
That burns in Hymen's hand, more bright
Than the silver moon,
Or the torch at noon.

Hark what the echoes say!
Britain till now ne'er kept a holiday.
For Jove dwells here. And 'tis no pity,
If Troynovant be now no more a city.

Entertainment to James, 1604

384 *Country Glee*

HAYMAKERS, rakers, reapers and mowers,
Wait on your Summer Queen;
Dress up with musk-rose her eglantine bowers,
Daffodils strew the green.
Sing, dance and play,
'Tis holiday;
The sun does bravely shine
On our ears of corn.
Rich as a pearl
Comes every girl;
This is mine, this is mine, this is mine;
Let us die, ere away they be borne.

Bow to the Sun, to our Queen, and that fair one
Come to behold our sports.
Each bonny lass here is counted a rare one,
As those in princes' courts.
These and we
With country glee
Will teach the woods to resound,
And the hills with Echo's hollow.
Skipping lambs
Their bleating dams
'Mongst kids shall trip it round;
For joy thus our wenches we follow.

Wind, jolly huntsmen, your neat bugles shrilly,
Hounds make a lusty cry;
Spring up, you falconers, the partridges freely,
Then let your brave hawks fly.
Horses amain,
Over ridge, over plain;
The dogs have the stag in chase.
'Tis a sport to content a king.
So ho ho! through the skies
How the proud bird flies,
And sousing kills with a grace!
Now the deer falls. Hark, how they ring!

Written by 1624; *The Sun's Darling*, 1656

SIR JOHN DAVIES

1569–1626

385

Orchestra

WHERE lives the man that never yet did hear
Of chaste Penelope, Ulysses' queen?
Who kept her faith unspotted twenty year,
Till he returned, that far away had been,
And many men and many towns had seen;
Ten year at siege of Troy he lingering lay,
And ten year in the midland sea did stray.

Homer, to whom the Muses did carouse
A great deep cup with heavenly nectar filled:
The greatest deepest cup in Jove's great house,
(For Jove himself had so expressly willed,)
He drank off all, ne let one drop be spilled;
Since when his brain, that had before been dry,
Became the wellspring of all poetry.

sousing] swooping down

SIR JOHN DAVIES

Homer doth tell, in his abundant verse,
The long laborious travails of the man,
And of his lady too he doth rehearse,
How she illudes, with all the art she can,
Th' ungrateful love which other lords began;
For of her lord false fame long since had sworn,
That Neptune's monsters had his carcass torn.

All this he tells, but one thing he forgot,
One thing most worthy his eternal song;
But he was old and blind and saw it not,
Or else he thought he should Ulysses wrong,
To mingle it his tragic acts among;
Yet was there not, in all the world of things,
A sweeter burden for his Muse's wings.

The courtly love Antinous did make,
Antinous, that fresh and jolly knight,
Which of the gallants, that did undertake
To win the widow, had most wealth and might,
Wit to persuade, and beauty to delight:
The courtly love he made unto the queen,
Homer forgot, as if it had not been.

Sing then, Terpsichore, my light Muse, sing
His gentle art and cunning courtesy!
You, lady, can remember everything,
For you are daughter of queen Memory;
But sing a plain and easy melody,
For the soft mean that warbleth but the ground
To my rude ear doth yield the sweetest sound.

Only one night's discourse I can report:
When the great torchbearer of heaven was gone
Down, in a mask, unto the Ocean's court,
To revel it with Tethys, all alone
Antinous, disguised and unknown,
Like to the spring in gaudy ornament,
Unto the castle of the princess went.

The sovereign castle of the rocky isle,
Wherein Penelope the princess lay,
Shone with a thousand lamps, which did exile
The shadows dark, and turned the night to day.
Not Jove's blue tent, what time the sunny ray
Behind the bulwark of the earth retires,
Is seen to sparkle with more twinkling fires.

That night the queen came forth from far within,
And in the presence of her court was seen;
For the sweet singer Phemius did begin
To praise the worthies that at Troy had been;
Somewhat of her Ulysses she did ween
In his grave hymn the heavenly man would sing,
Or of his wars, or of his wandering.

Pallas that hour, with her sweet breath divine,
Inspired immortal beauty in her eyes,
That with celestial glory she did shine
Brighter than Venus, when she doth arise
Out of the waters to adorn the skies.
The wooers, all amazed, do admire
And check their own presumptuous desire.

Only Antinous, when at first he viewed
Her star-bright eyes that with new honour shined,
Was not dismayed; but therewithal renewed
The noblesse and the splendour of his mind;
And as he did fit circumstances find,
Unto the throne he boldly 'gan advance,
And with fair manners wooed the queen to dance:

'Goddess of women! sith your heavenliness
Hath now vouchsafed itself to represent
To our dim eyes, which though they see the less,
Yet are they blest in their astonishment,
Imitate heaven, whose beauties excellent
Are in continual motion day and night,
And move thereby more wonder and delight.

'Let me the mover be, to turn about
Those glorious ornaments that youth and love
Have fixed in you, every part throughout;
Which if you will in timely measure move,
Not all those precious gems in heaven above
Shall yield a sight more pleasing to behold,
With all their turns and tracings manifold.'

With this the modest princess blushed and smiled,
Like to a clear and rosy eventide,
And softly did return this answer mild:
'Fair sir! you needs must fairly be denied,
Where your demand cannot be satisfied.
My feet, which only nature taught to go,
Did never yet the art of footing know.

'But why persuade you me to this new rage?
For all disorder and misrule is new,
For such misgovernment in former age
Our old divine forefathers never knew;
Who if they lived, and did the follies view,
Which their fond nephews make their chief affairs,
Would hate themselves, that had begot such heirs.'

'Sole heir of virtue, and of beauty both!
Whence cometh it', Antinous replies,
'That your imperious virtue is so loth
To grant your beauty her chief exercise?
Or from what spring doth your opinion rise,
That dancing is a frenzy and a rage,
First known and used in this new-fangled age?

'Dancing, bright lady, then began to be,
When the first seeds whereof the world did spring,
The fire, air, earth, and water, did agree
By Love's persuasion, nature's mighty king,
To leave their first discorded combating,
And in a dance such measure to observe,
As all the world their motion should preserve.

'Since when they still are carried in a round,
And changing come one in another's place;
Yet do they neither mingle nor confound,
But every one doth keep the bounded space
Wherein the dance doth bid it turn or trace.
This wondrous miracle did Love devise,
For dancing is love's proper exercise.

'Like this he framed the gods' eternal bower,
 And of a shapeless and confused mass,
By his through-piercing and digesting power,
 The turning vault of heaven formed was,
 Whose starry wheels he hath so made to pass,
  As that their movings do a music frame,
  And they themselves still dance unto the same.

'Or if this all, which round about we see,
 As idle Morpheus some sick brains hath taught,
Of undivided motes compacted be,
 How was this goodly architecture wrought?
 Or by what means were they together brought?
  They err that say they did concur by chance;
  Love made them meet in a well-ordered dance!

'As when Amphion with his charming lyre
 Begot so sweet a siren of the air,
That, with her rhetoric, made the stones conspire
 The ruins of a city to repair,
 A work of wit and reason's wise affair;
  So Love's smooth tongue the motes such measure taught,
  That they joined hands, and so the world was wrought.

'How justly then is dancing termed new,
 Which with the world in point of time began?
Yea, Time itself, whose birth Jove never knew,
 And which is far more ancient than the sun,
 Had not one moment of his age outrun,
  When out leaped Dancing from the heap of things
  And lightly rode upon his nimble wings.

'Reason hath both their pictures in her treasure;
Where Time the measure of all moving is,
And Dancing is a moving all in measure.
Now, if you do resemble that to this,
And think both one, I think you think amiss;
But if you judge them twins, together got,
And Time first born, your judgement erreth not.

'Thus doth it equal age with Age enjoy,
And yet in lusty youth forever flowers;
Like Love, his sire, whom painters make a boy,
Yet is he eldest of the heavenly powers;
Or like his brother Time, whose winged hours,
Going and coming, will not let him die,
But still preserve him in his infancy.'

This said, the queen, with her sweet lips divine,
Gently began to move the subtle air,
Which gladly yielding, did itself incline
To take a shape between those rubies fair;
And being formed, softly did repair,
With twenty doublings in the empty way,
Unto Antinous' ears, and thus did say:

'What eye doth see the heaven, but doth admire
When it the movings of the heavens doth see?
Myself, if I to heaven may once aspire,
If that be dancing, will a dancer be;
But as for this, your frantic jollity,
How it began, or whence you did it learn,
I never could with reason's eye discern.'

Antinous answered: 'Jewel of the earth!
 Worthy you are that heavenly dance to lead;
But for you think our Dancing base of birth,
 And newly born but of a brain-sick head,
 I will forthwith his antique gentry read,
  And, for I love him, will his herald be,
  And blaze his arms, and draw his pedigree.

'When Love had shaped this world, this great fair wight,
 That all wights else in this wide womb contains,
And had instructed it to dance aright
 A thousand measures, with a thousand strains,
 Which it should practise with delightful pains,
  Until that fatal instant should revolve,
  When all to nothing should again resolve;

'The comely order and proportion fair
 On every side did please his wandering eye;
Till, glancing through the thin transparent air,
 A rude disordered rout he did espy
 Of men and women, that most spitefully
  Did one another throng and crowd so sore,
  That his kind eye, in pity, wept therefore.

'And swifter than the lightning down he came,
 Another shapeless chaos to digest;
He will begin another world to frame,
 For Love, till all be well, will never rest.
 Then with such words as cannot be expressed
  He cuts the troops, that all asunder fling,
  And ere they wist he casts them in a ring.

'Then did he rarefy the element,
   And in the centre of the ring appear;
The beams that from his forehead spreading went
   Begot a horror and religious fear
   In all the souls that round about him were,
      Which in their ears attentiveness procures,
      While he, with such like sounds, their minds allures:

'How doth Confusion's mother, headlong Chance,
   Put Reason's noble squadron to the rout?
Or how should you, that have the governance
   Of Nature's children, heaven and earth throughout,
   Prescribe them rules, and live yourselves without?
      Why should your fellowship a trouble be,
      Since man's chief pleasure is society?

'If sense hath not yet taught you, learn of me
   A comely moderation and discreet,
That your assemblies may well ordered be;
   When my uniting power shall make you meet,
   With heavenly tunes it shall be tempered sweet,
      And be the model of the world's great frame,
      And you, earth's children, Dancing shall it name.

'Behold the world, how it is whirled round!
   And for it is so whirled, is named so;
In whose large volume many rules are found
   Of this new art, which it doth fairly show.
   For your quick eyes in wandering to and fro,
      From east to west, on no one thing can glance,
      But, if you mark it well, it seems to dance.

'First you see fixed in this huge mirror blue
Of trembling lights a number numberless;
Fixed, they are named, but with a name untrue;
For they all move and in a dance express
The great long year that doth contain no less
Than threescore hundreds of those years in all,
Which the sun makes with his course natural.

'What if to you these sparks disordered seem,
As if by chance they had been scattered there?
The gods a solemn measure do it deem
And see a just proportion everywhere,
And know the points whence first their movings were,
To which first points when all return again,
The axletree of heaven shall break in twain.

'Under that spangled sky five wandering flames,
Besides the king of day and queen of night,
Are wheeled around, all in their sundry frames,
And all in sundry measures do delight;
Yet altogether keep no measure right;
For by itself each doth itself advance,
And by itself each doth a galliard dance.

'Venus, the mother of that bastard Love,
Which doth usurp the world's great marshal's name,
Just with the sun her dainty feet doth move,
And unto him doth all her gestures frame;
Now after, now afore, the flattering dame
With divers cunning passages doth err,
Still him respecting that respects not her.

'For that brave sun, the father of the day,
Doth love this earth, the mother of the night;
And, like a reveller in rich array,
Doth dance his galliard in his leman's sight,
Both back and forth and sideways passing light.
His gallant grace doth so the gods amaze,
That all stand still and at his beauty gaze.

'But see the earth when she approacheth near,
How she for joy doth spring and sweetly smile;
But see again her sad and heavy cheer,
When changing places he retires a while;
But those black clouds he shortly will exile,
And make them all before his presence fly,
As mists consumed before his cheerful eye.

'Who doth not see the measure of the moon?
Which thirteen times she danceth every year,
And ends her pavan thirteen times as soon
As doth her brother, of whose golden hair
She borroweth part, and proudly doth it wear.
Then doth she coyly turn her face aside,
That half her cheek is scarce sometimes descried.

'Next her, the pure, subtle, and cleansing fire
Is swiftly carried in a circle even,
Though Vulcan be pronounced by many a liar
The only halting god that dwells in heaven;
But that foul name may be more fitly given
To your false fire, that far from heaven is fall,
And doth consume, waste, spoil, disorder all.

'And now behold your tender nurse, the air,
And common neighbour that aye runs around;
How many pictures and impressions fair
Within her empty regions are there found,
Which to your senses dancing do propound?
For what are breath, speech, echoes, music, winds,
But dancings of the air, in sundry kinds?

'For, when you breathe, the air in order moves,
Now in, now out, in time and measure true,
And when you speak, so well she dancing loves,
That doubling oft and oft redoubling new
With thousand forms she doth herself endue;
For all the words that from your lips repair
Are nought but tricks and turnings of the air.

'Hence is her prattling daughter, Echo, born,
That dances to all voices she can hear.
There is no sound so harsh that she doth scorn,
Nor any time wherein she will forbear
The airy pavement with her feet to wear;
And yet her hearing sense is nothing quick,
For after time she endeth every trick.

'And thou, sweet music, dancing's only life,
The ear's sole happiness, the air's best speech,
Lodestone of fellowship, charming rod of strife,
The soft mind's paradise, the sick mind's leech,
With thine own tongue thou trees and stones canst teach,
That when the air doth dance her finest measure,
Then art thou born, the gods' and men's sweet pleasure.

'Lastly, where keep the winds their revelry,
  Their violent turnings and wild whirling hays,
But in the air's tralucent gallery?
  Where she herself is turned a hundred ways,
  While with those maskers wantonly she plays.
    Yet in this misrule they such rule embrace
    As two, at once, encumber not the place.

'If then fire, air, wandering and fixed lights,
  In every province of th' imperial sky,
Yield perfect forms of dancing to your sights,
  In vain I teach the ear that which the eye,
  With certain view, already doth descry;
    But for your eyes perceive not all they see,
    In this I will your senses' master be.

'For lo! the sea that fleets about the land,
  And like a girdle clips her solid waist,
Music and measure both doth understand;
  For his great crystal eye is always cast
  Up to the moon, and on her fixed fast;
    And as she danceth in her pallid sphere,
    So danceth he about the centre here.

'Sometimes his proud green waves in order set,
  One after other, flow unto the shore;
Which when they have with many kisses wet,
  They ebb away in order, as before;
  And to make known his courtly love the more,
    He oft doth lay aside his three-forked mace,
    And with his arms the timorous earth embrace.

hays] country dances

'Only the earth doth stand forever still:
Her rocks remove not, nor her mountains meet,
Although some wits enriched with learning's skill
Say heaven stands firm and that the earth doth fleet,
And swiftly turneth underneath their feet;
Yet, though the earth is ever steadfast seen,
On her broad breast hath dancing ever been.

'For those blue veins that through her body spread,
Those sapphire streams which from great hills do spring,
The earth's great dugs, for every wight is fed
With sweet fresh moisture from them issuing,
Observe a dance in their wild wandering;
And still their dance begets a murmur sweet,
And still the murmur with the dance doth meet.

'Of all their ways, I love Meander's path,
Which, to the tunes of dying swans, doth dance
Such winding sleights. Such turns and tricks he hath,
Such creeks, such wrenches, and such dalliance,
That, whether it be hap or heedless chance,
In his indented course and wriggling play,
He seems to dance a perfect cunning hay.

'But wherefore do these streams forever run?
To keep themselves forever sweet and clear;
For let their everlasting course be done,
They straight corrupt and foul with mud appear.
O ye sweet nymphs, that beauty's loss do fear,
Contemn the drugs that physic doth devise,
And learn of Love this dainty exercise.

'See how those flowers, that have sweet beauty too,
The only jewels that the earth doth wear,
When the young sun in bravery her doth woo,
As oft as they the whistling wind do hear,
Do wave their tender bodies here and there;
And though their dance no perfect measure is,
Yet oftentimes their music makes them kiss.

'What makes the vine about the elm to dance
With turnings, windings, and embracements round?
What makes the lodestone to the north advance
His subtle point, as if from thence he found
His chief attractive virtue to redound?
Kind nature first doth cause all things to love;
Love makes them dance, and in just order move.

'Hark how the birds do sing, and mark then how,
Jump with the modulation of their lays,
They lightly leap and skip from bough to bough;
Yet do the cranes deserve a greater praise,
Which keep such measure in their airy ways,
As when they all in order ranked are,
They make a perfect form triangular.

'In the chief angle flies the watchful guide;
And all the followers their heads do lay
On their foregoers' backs, on either side;
But, for the captain hath no rest to stay
His head, forwearied with the windy way,
He back retires; and then the next behind,
As his lieutenant, leads them through the wind.

'But why relate I every singular?
  Since all the world's great fortunes and affairs
Forward and backward rapt and whirled are,
  According to the music of the spheres;
  And Change herself her nimble feet upbears
    On a round slippery wheel, that rolleth aye,
    And turns all states with her imperious sway;

'Learn then to dance, you that are princes born,
  And lawful lords of earthly creatures all;
Imitate them, and thereof take no scorn,
  For this new art to them is natural.
  And imitate the stars celestial;
    For when pale death your vital twist shall sever,
    Your better parts must dance with them forever.

'Thus Love persuades, and all the crowd of men,
  That stands around, doth make a murmuring,
As when the wind, loosed from his hollow den,
  Among the trees a gentle bass doth sing,
  Or as a brook, through pebbles wandering;
    But in their looks they uttered this plain speech:
    That they would learn to dance, if Love would teach.

'Then, first of all, he doth demonstrate plain
  The motions seven that are in nature found;
Upward and downward, forth and back again,
  To this side and to that, and turning round;
  Whereof a thousand brawls he doth compound,
    Which he doth teach unto the multitude,
    And ever with a turn they must conclude.

brawls] court dances

'As, when a nymph, arising from the land,
Leadeth a dance with her long watery train,
Down to the sea she wries to every hand,
And every way doth cross the fertile plain;
But when, at last, she falls into the main,
Then all her traverses concluded are,
And with the sea her course is circular.

'Thus when at first Love had them marshalled,
As erst he did the shapeless mass of things,
He taught them rounds and winding hays to tread,
And about trees to cast themselves in rings;
As the two Bears, whom the first mover flings
With a short turn about heaven's axletree,
In a round dance for ever wheeling be.

'But after these, as men more civil grew,
He did more grave and solemn measures frame;
With such fair order and proportion true,
And correspondence every way the same,
That no fault-finding eye did ever blame;
For every eye was moved at the sight
With sober wondering and with sweet delight.

'Not those young students of the heavenly book,
Atlas the great, Prometheus the wise,
Which on the stars did all their lifetime look,
Could ever find such measures in the skies,
So full of change and rare varieties;
Yet all the feet whereon these measures go
Are only spondees, solemn, grave, and slow.

'But for more divers and more pleasing show,
  A swift and wandering dance he did invent,
With passages uncertain, to and fro,
  Yet with a certain answer and consent
  To the quick music of the instrument.
    Five was the number of the music's feet,
    Which still the dance did with five paces meet.

'A gallant dance! that lively doth bewray
  A spirit and a virtue masculine;
Impatient that her house on earth should stay,
  Since she herself is fiery and divine.
  Oft doth she make her body upward flyne
    With lofty turns and caprioles in the air,
    Which with the lusty tunes accordeth fair.

'What shall I name those current traverses,
  That on a triple dactyl foot do run,
Close by the ground, with sliding passages?
  Wherein that dancer greatest praise hath won,
  Which with best order can all orders shun;
    For everywhere he wantonly must range,
    And turn, and wind, with unexpected change.

'Yet is there one, the most delightful kind,
  A lofty jumping, or a leaping round,
When, arm in arm, two dancers are entwined,
  And whirl themselves with strict embracements bound,
  And still their feet an anapest do sound;
    An anapest is all their music's song,
    Whose first two feet are short, and third is long;

flyne] fly

'As the victorious twins of Leda and Jove,
  That taught the Spartans dancing on the sands
Of swift Eurotas, dance in heaven above,
  Knit and united with eternal bands;
  Among the stars their double image stands,
    Where both are carried with an equal pace,
    Together jumping in their turning race.

'This is the net wherein the sun's bright eye
  Venus and Mars entangled did behold;
For in this dance their arms they so imply,
  As each doth seem the other to enfold.
  What if lewd wits another tale have told,
    Of jealous Vulcan, and of iron chains?
    Yet this true sense that forged lie contains.

'These various forms of dancing Love did frame,
  And besides these, a hundred million mo;
And as he did invent, he taught the same,
  With goodly gesture and with comely show,
  Now keeping state, now humbly honouring low.
    And ever for the persons and the place,
    He taught most fit and best according grace.

'For Love, within his fertile working brain,
  Did then conceive those gracious virgins three,
Whose civil moderation did maintain
  All decent order and conveniency,
  And fair respect, and seemly modesty;
    And then he thought it fit they should be born,
    That their sweet presence dancing might adorn.

honouring] bowing

'Hence is it that these Graces painted are
With hand in hand, dancing an endless round,
And with regarding eyes, that still beware
That there be no disgrace amongst them found;
With equal foot they beat the flowery ground,
Laughing or singing, as their passions will;
Yet nothing that they do becomes them ill.

'Thus Love taught men, and men thus learned of Love
Sweet music's sound with feet to counterfeit;
Which was long time before high-thundering Jove
Was lifted up to heaven's imperial seat;
For though by birth he were the prince of Crete,
Nor Crete nor heaven should that young prince have seen,
If dancers with their timbrels had not been.

'Since when all ceremonious mysteries,
All sacred orgies and religious rites,
All pomps and triumphs and solemnities,
All funerals, nuptials, and like public sights,
All parliaments of peace, and warlike fights,
All learned arts, and every great affair,
A lively shape of dancing seems to bear.

'For what did he, who with his ten-tongued lute
Gave beasts and blocks an understanding ear,
Or rather into bestial minds and brutes
Shed and infused the beams of reason clear?
Doubtless, for men that rude and savage were,
A civil form of dancing he devised,
Wherewith unto their gods they sacrificed.

'So did Musaeus, so Amphion did,
And Linus with his sweet enchanting song,
And he whose hand the earth of monsters rid,
And had men's ears fast chained to his tongue,
And Theseus to his wood-born slaves among
Used dancing as the finest policy
To plant religion and society.

'And therefore, now, the Thracian Orpheus' lyre
And Hercules himself are stellified,
And in high heaven, amidst the starry choir,
Dancing their parts, continually do slide;
So, on the zodiac, Ganymede doth ride,
And so is Hebe with the Muses nine,
For pleasing Jove with dancing, made divine.

'Wherefore was Proteus said himself to change
Into a stream, a lion, and a tree,
And many other forms fantastic strange,
As in his fickle thought he wished to be?
But that he danced with such facility,
As like a lion he could pace with pride,
Ply like a plant, and like a river slide.

'And how was Caeneus made at first a man,
And then a woman, then a man again,
But in a dance? which when he first began,
He the man's part in measure did sustain;
But when he changed into a second strain,
He danced the woman's part another space,
And then returned unto his former place.

'Hence sprang the fable of Tiresias,
  That he the pleasure of both sexes tried;
For in a dance he man and woman was,
  By often change of place, from side to side;
  But for the woman easily did slide,
    And smoothly swim with cunning hidden art,
    He took more pleasure in a woman's part.

'So to a fish Venus herself did change,
  And swimming through the soft and yielding wave,
With gentle motions did so smoothly range,
  As none might see where she the water drave;
  But this plain truth that falsed fable gave,
    That she did dance with sliding easiness,
    Pliant and quick in wandering passages.

'And merry Bacchus practised dancing too,
  And to the Lydian numbers rounds did make;
The like he did in th' eastern India do,
  And taught them all, when Phoebus did awake,
  And when at night he did his coach forsake,
    To honour heaven, and heaven's great rolling eye,
    With turning dances and with melody.

'Thus they who first did found a commonweal,
  And they who first religion did ordain,
By dancing first the people's hearts did steal;
  Of whom we now a thousand tales do feign.
  Yet do we now their perfect rules retain,
    And use them still in such devices new,
    As in the world, long since their withering, grew.

'For after towns and kingdoms founded were,
Between great states arose well-ordered war,
Wherein most perfect measure doth appear;
Whether their well-set ranks respected are
In quadrant forms or semicircular,
Or else the march, when all the troops advance
And to the drum in gallant order dance.

'And after wars, when white-winged victory
Is with a glorious triumph beautified,
And every one doth Io, Io! cry,
While all in gold the conqueror doth ride,
The solemn pomp that fills the city wide
Observes such rank and measure everywhere,
As if they all together dancing were.

'The like just order mourners do observe,
But with unlike affection and attire,
When some great man that nobly did deserve,
And whom his friends impatiently desire,
Is brought with honour to his latest fire.
The dead corpse too in that sad dance is moved,
As if both dead and living dancing loved.

'A diverse cause, but like solemnity,
Unto the temple leads the bashful bride,
Which blusheth like the Indian ivory
Which is with dip of Tyrian purple dyed;
A golden troop doth pass on every side
Of flourishing young men and virgins gay,
Which keep fair measure all the flowery way.

'And not alone the general multitude,
But those choice Nestors, which in council grave
Of cities and of kingdoms do conclude,
Most comely order in their sessions have;
Wherefore the wise Thessalians ever gave
The name of leader of their country's dance
To him that had their country's governance.

'And those great masters of the liberal arts
In all their several schools do dancing teach;
For humble grammar first doth set the parts
Of congruent and well-according speech,
Which rhetoric, whose state the clouds doth reach,
And heavenly poetry do forward lead,
And divers measures diversely do tread.

'For rhetoric, clothing speech in rich array,
In looser numbers teacheth her to range
With twenty tropes, and turnings every way,
And various figures, and licentious change;
But poetry, with rule and order strange,
So curiously doth move each single pace,
As all is marred if she one foot misplace.

'These arts of speech the guides and marshals are,
But logic leadeth reason in a dance,
Reason, the cynosure and bright lodestar
In this world's sea, t'avoid the rocks of chance;
For with close following and continuance,
One reason doth another so ensue
As, in conclusion, still the dance is true.

'So music to her own sweet tunes doth trip,
With tricks of 3, 5, 8, 15, and more;
So doth the art of numbering seem to skip
From even to odd, in her proportioned score;
So do those skills, whose quick eyes do explore
The just dimension both of earth and heaven,
In all their rules observe a measure even.

'Lo! this is Dancing's true nobility,
Dancing, the child of Music and of Love;
Dancing itself, both love and harmony,
Where all agree and all in order move;
Dancing, the art that all arts do approve;
The fair character of the world's consent,
The heaven's true figure, and th' earth's ornament.'

The queen, whose dainty ears had borne too long
The tedious praise of that she did despise,
Adding once more the music of the tongue
To the sweet speech of her alluring eyes,
Began to answer in such winning wise
As that forthwith Antinous' tongue was tied,
His eyes fast fixed, his ears were open wide.

'Forsooth,' quoth she, 'great glory you have won
To your trim minion, Dancing, all this while,
By blazing him Love's first begotten son,
Of every ill the hateful father vile,
That doth the world with sorceries beguile,
Cunningly mad, religiously profane,
Wit's monster, reason's canker, sense's bane.

'Love taught the mother that unkind desire
To wash her hands in her own infant's blood;
Love taught the daughter to betray her sire
Into most base unworthy servitude;
Love taught the brother to prepare such food
To feast his brothers that the all-seeing sun,
Wrapped in a cloud, the wicked sight did shun.

'And even this self-same Love hath dancing taught,
An art that showeth th'idea of his mind
With vainness, frenzy, and misorder fraught;
Sometimes with blood and cruelties unkind,
For in a dance Tereus' mad wife did find
Fit time and place, by murdering her son,
T'avenge the wrong his traitorous sire had done.

'What mean the mermaids when they dance and sing,
But certain death unto the mariner?
What tidings do the dancing dolphins bring,
But that some dangerous storm approacheth near?
Then sith both Love and Dancing liveries bear
Of such ill hap, unhappy may they prove
That, sitting free, will either dance or love!'

Yet once again Antinous did reply:
'Great Queen! condemn not Love the innocent,
For this mischievous Lust, which traitorously
Usurps his name and steals his ornament;
For that true Love, which dancing did invent,
Is he that tuned the world's whole harmony,
And linked all men in sweet society.

'He first extracted from th' earth-mingled mind
That heavenly fire, or quintessence divine,
Which doth such sympathy in beauty find
As is between the elm and fruitful vine,
And so to beauty ever doth incline;
Life's life it is, and cordial to the heart,
And of our better part the better part.

'This is true Love, by that true Cupid got,
Which danceth galliards in your amorous eyes,
But to your frozen heart approacheth not;
Only your heart he dares not enterprise,
And yet through every other part he flies,
And everywhere he nimbly danceth now,
That in yourself yourself perceive not how.

'For your sweet beauty daintily transfused
With due proportion throughout every part,
What is it but a dance where Love hath used
His finer cunning and more curious art?
Where all the elements themselves impart,
And turn, and wind, and mingle with such measure,
That th' eye that sees it surfeits with the pleasure.

'Love in the twinkling of your eyelids danceth,
Love danceth in your pulses and your veins,
Love, when you sew, your needle's point advanceth,
And makes it dance a thousand curious strains
Of winding rounds, whereof the form remains,
To show that your fair hands can dance the hay,
Which your fine feet would learn as well as they.

'And when your ivory fingers touch the strings
Of any silver-sounding instrument,
Loves makes them dance to those sweet murmurings
With busy skill and cunning excellent.
O! that your feet those tunes would represent
With artificial motions to and fro,
That Love this art in every part might show!

'Yet your fair soul, which came from heaven above
To rule this house (another heaven below),
With divers powers in harmony doth move;
And all the virtues that from her do flow
In a round measure, hand in hand do go;
Could I now see, as I conceive, this dance,
Wonder and love would cast me in a trance.

'The richest jewel in all the heavenly treasure,
That ever yet unto the earth was shown,
Is perfect concord, th' only perfect pleasure
That wretched earth-born men have ever known;
For many hearts it doth compound in one,
That whatso one doth will, or speak, or do,
With one consent they all agree thereto.

'Concord's true picture shineth in this art,
Where divers men and women ranked be,
And every one doth dance a several part,
Yet all as one in measure do agree,
Observing perfect uniformity;
All turn together, all together trace,
And all together honour and embrace.

'If they whom sacred Love hath linked in one
Do as they dance, in all their course of life,
Never shall burning grief nor bitter moan
Nor factious difference nor unkind strife
Arise between the husband and the wife;
For whether forth, or back, or round he go,
As doth the man, so must the woman do.

'What if by often interchange of place
Sometime the woman gets the upper hand?
That is but done for more delightful grace,
For on that part she doth not ever stand;
But as the measure's law doth her command,
She wheels about, and ere the dance doth end,
Into her former place she doth transcend.

'But not alone this correspondence meet
And uniform consent doth dancing praise;
For comeliness, the child of order sweet,
Enamels it with her eye-pleasing rays;
Fair comeliness ten hundred thousand ways
Through dancing sheds itself, and makes it shine
With glorious beauty and with grace divine.

'For comeliness is a disposing fair
Of things and actions in fit time and place,
Which doth in dancing show itself most clear
When troops confused, which here and there do trace
Without distinguishment or bounded space,
By dancing rule into such ranks are brought,
As glads the eye and ravisheth the thought.

'Then why should reason judge that reasonless,
Which is wit's offspring, and the work of art,
Image of concord and of comeliness?
Who sees a clock moving in every part,
A sailing pinnace, or a wheeling cart,
But thinks that reason, ere it came to pass,
The first impulsive cause and mover was?

'Who sees an army all in rank advance,
But deems a wise commander is in place,
Which leadeth on that brave victorious dance?
Much more in dancing's art, in dancing's grace,
Blindness itself may reason's footsteps trace;
For of love's maze it is the curious plot,
And of man's fellowship the true-love knot.

'But if these eyes of yours, lodestars of love,
Showing the world's great dance to your mind's eye,
Cannot, with all their demonstrations, move
Kind apprehension in your fantasy
Of dancing's virtue and nobility,
How can my barbarous tongue win you thereto,
Which heaven and earth's fair speech could never do?

'O Love, my king! if all my wit and power
Have done you all the service that they can,
O! be you present in this present hour
And help your servant and your true liegeman!
End that persuasion which I erst began!
For who in praise of dancing can persuade
With such sweet force as Love, which dancing made?'

Love heard his prayer, and swifter than the wind,
  Like to a page in habit, face, and speech,
He came, and stood Antinous behind,
  And many secrets of his thoughts did teach.
  At last a crystal mirror he did reach
    Unto his hands, that he with one rash view
    All forms therein by Love's revealing knew.

And humbly honouring, gave it to the queen
  With this fair speech: 'See, fairest queen,' quoth he,
'The fairest sight that ever shall be seen,
  And th' only wonder of posterity,
  The richest work in nature's treasury;
    Which she disdains to show on this world's stage,
    And thinks it far too good for our rude age.

'But in another world, divided far
  In the great fortunate triangled isle,
Thrice twelve degrees removed from the north star,
  She will this glorious workmanship compile,
  Which she hath been conceiving all this while
    Since the world's birth; and will bring forth at last,
    When six and twenty hundred years are past.'

Penelope the queen, when she had viewed
  The strange eye-dazzling admirable sight,
Fain would have praised the state and pulchritude;
  But she was stroken dumb with wonder quite.
  Yet her sweet mind retained her thinking might;
    Her ravished mind in heavenly thoughts did dwell;
    But what she thought no mortal tongue can tell.

You, lady Muse, whom Jove the counsellor
  Begot of Memory, Wisdom's treasuress,
To your divining tongue is given a power
  Of uttering secrets, large and limitless;
  You can Penelope's strange thoughts express,
    Which she conceived, and then would fain have told,
    When she the wondrous crystal did behold.

Her winged thoughts bore up her mind so high
  As that she weened she saw the glorious throne,
Where the bright moon doth sit in majesty;
  A thousand sparkling stars about her shone,
  But she herself did sparkle more alone,
    Than all those thousand beauties would have done,
    If they had been confounded all in one.

And yet she thought those stars moved in such measure
  To do their sovereign honour and delight,
As soothed her mind with sweet enchanting pleasure,
  Although the various change amazed her sight,
  And her weak judgement did entangle quite;
    Beside, their moving made them shine more clear,
    As diamonds moved more sparkling do appear.

This was the picture of her wondrous thought.
  But who can wonder that her thought was so,
Sith Vulcan, king of fire, that mirror wrought,
  Which things to come, present, and past doth know,
  And there did represent in lively show
    Our glorious English court's divine image,
    As it should be in this our golden age?

SIR JOHN DAVIES

Away, Terpsichore, light Muse, away!
  And come, Urania, prophetess divine!
Come, Muse of heaven, my burning thirst allay!
  Even now for want of sacred drink I tine;
  In heavenly moisture dip this pen of mine,
    And let my mouth with nectar overflow,
    For I must more than mortal glory show!

O! that I had Homer's abundant vein,
  I would hereof another *Ilias* make!
Or else the man of Mantua's charmed brain,
  In whose large throat great Jove the thunder spake!
  O! that I could old Geoffrey's muse awake,
    Or borrow Colin's fair heroic style,
    Or smooth my rhymes with Delia's servant's file!

O! could I, sweet companion, sing like you,
  Which of a shadow, under a shadow sing!
Or like fair Salue's sad lover true!
  Or like the bay, the marigold's darling,
  Whose sudden verse Love covers with his wing!
    O! that your brains were mingled all with mine,
    T' enlarge my wit for this great work divine!

Yet Astrophel might one for all suffice,
  Whose supple Muse chameleon-like doth change
Into all forms of excellent device;
  So might the swallow, whose swift muse doth range
  Through rare Ideas and inventions strange,
    And ever doth enjoy her joyful spring,
    And sweeter than the nightingale doth sing.

tine] perish

O! that I might that singing swallow hear,
To whom I owe my service and my love!
His sugared tunes would so enchant mine ear,
And in my mind such sacred fury move,
As I should knock at heaven's great gate above
With my proud rhymes; while of this heavenly state
I do aspire the shadow to relate.

Orchestra, or A Poem of Dancing, 1596

386 *To Queen Elizabeth*

TO that clear Majesty which in the north
Doth, like another sun, in glory rise;
Which standeth fixed, yet spreads her heavenly worth,
Lodestone to hearts, and lodestar to all eyes;

Like heaven in all; like th' earth in this alone,
That though great states by her support do stand,
Yet she herself supported is of none,
But by the finger of the Almighty's hand;

To the divinest and the richest mind,
Both by art's purchase and by nature's dower,
That ever was from heaven to earth confined,
To show the utmost of a creature's power;

To that great Spirit, which doth great kingdoms move,
The sacred spring, whence right and honour streams,
Distilling virtue, shedding peace and love,
In every place, as Cynthia sheds her beams;

I offer up some sparkles of that fire,
  Whereby we reason, live, and move, and be;
These sparks by nature evermore aspire,
  Which makes them to so high an Highness flee.

Fair Soul, since, to the fairest body knit,
  You give such lively life, such quickening power,
Such sweet celestial influence to it,
  As keeps it still in youth's immortal flower;

(As, where the sun is present all the year,
  And never doth retire his golden ray,
Needs must the spring be everlasting there,
  And every season like the month of May,)

O! many, many years may you remain,
  A happy Angel to this happy land;
Long, long may you on earth our Empress reign,
  Ere you in heaven a glorious Angel stand.

Stay long (sweet Spirit) ere thou to heaven depart,
Which makest each place a heaven wherein thou art.

Nosce Teipsum, Dedication, 1599

387 *Knowledge and Reason*

WHAT is this knowledge but the sky-stolen fire,
  For which the thief still chained in ice doth sit,
And which the poor rude Satyr did admire,
  And needs would kiss, but burnt his lips with it?

What is it but the cloud of empty rain,
  Which when Jove's guest embraced, he monsters got,
Or the false pails, which oft being filled with pain
  Received the water, but retained it not?

Shortly, what is it but the fiery coach,
  Which the youth sought, and sought his death withal,
Or the boy's wings, which when he did approach
  The sun's hot beams, did melt and let him fall?

And yet, alas! when all our lamps are burned,
  Our bodies wasted, and our spirits spent;
When we have all the learned volumes turned,
  Which yield men's wits both help and ornament:

What can we know, or what can we discern,
  When error chokes the windows of the mind?
The divers forms of things how can we learn,
  That have been ever from our birthday blind?

When Reason's lamp, which, like the sun in sky,
  Throughout man's little world her beams did spread,
Is now become a sparkle, which doth lie
  Under the ashes, half extinct, and dead:

How can we hope, that through the eye and ear,
  This dying sparkle, in this cloudy place,
Can recollect these beams of knowledge clear,
  Which were infused in the first minds by grace?

So might the heir, whose father hath in play
  Wasted a thousand pounds of ancient rent,
By painful earning of a groat a day
  Hope to restore the patrimony spent.

The wits, that dived most deep and soared most high,
  Seeking man's powers, have found his weakness such.
Skill comes so slow, and life so fast doth fly;
  We learn so little, and forget so much.

For this the wisest of all moral men
  Said, he knew nought, but that he nought did know;
And the great mocking master mocked not then,
  When he said, truth was buried deep below.

For how may we to others' things attain,
  When none of us his own soul understands?
For which the devil mocks our curious brain,
  When 'Know thyself' his oracle commands.

For why should we the busy soul believe,
  When boldly she concludes of that, and this,
When of herself she can no judgement give,
  Nor how, nor whence, nor where, nor what she is?

All things without, which round about we see,
  We seek to know, and how therewith to do;
But that whereby we reason, live, and be,
  Within ourselves, we strangers are thereto.

We seek to know the moving of each sphere,
And the strange cause of th' ebbs and floods of Nile;
But of that clock within our breasts we bear
The subtle motions we forget the while.

We that acquaint ourselves with every zone
And pass both tropics, and behold the poles,
When we come home, are to ourselves unknown,
And unacquainted still with our own souls.

We study speech, but others we persuade;
We leechcraft learn, but others cure with it;
We interpret laws, which other men have made,
But read not those which in our hearts are writ.

Nosce Teipsum, stt. xi–xxvi, 1599

388 *Affliction*

IF aught can teach us aught, Affliction's looks,
Making us look into ourselves so near,
Teach us to know ourselves beyond all books,
Or all the learned schools that ever were.

This mistress lately plucked me by the ear,
And many a golden lesson hath me taught;
Hath made my senses quick, and reason clear,
Reformed my will, and rectified my thought.

So do the winds and thunders cleanse the air;
So working seas settle and purge the wine;
So lopped and pruned trees do flourish fair;
So doth the fire the drossy gold refine.

Neither Minerva nor the learned Muse,
  Nor rules of art, nor precepts of the wise,
Could in my brain those beams of skill infuse,
  As but the glance of this dame's angry eyes.

She within lists my ranging mind hath brought,
  That now beyond myself I list not go;
Myself am centre of my circling thought,
  Only myself I study, learn, and know.

I know my body 's of so frail a kind
  As force without, fevers within, can kill;
I know the heavenly nature of my mind,
  But 'tis corrupted both in wit and will;

I know my soul hath power to know all things,
  Yet is she blind and ignorant in all;
I know I am one of nature's little kings,
  Yet to the least and vilest things am thrall.

I know my life 's a pain and but a span,
  I know my sense is mocked with everything;
And to conclude, I know myself a man,
  Which is a proud, and yet a wretched thing.

Ibid., stt. xxxviii–xlv, 1599

389 *The Soul and the Body*

BUT how shall we this union well express?
  Nought ties the soul; her subtlety is such,
She moves the body, which she doth possess,
  Yet no part toucheth, but by virtue's touch.

Then dwells she not therein as in a tent;
  Nor as a pilot in his ship doth sit;
Nor as the spider in his web is pent;
  Nor as the wax retains the print in it;

Nor as a vessel water doth contain;
  Nor as one liquor in another shed;
Nor as the heat doth in the fire remain;
  Nor as a voice throughout the air is spread.

But as the fair and cheerful morning light
  Doth here and there her silver beams impart,
And in an instant doth herself unite
  To the transparent air, in all and part;

Still resting whole, when blows the air divide,
  Abiding pure, when th' air is most corrupted,
Throughout the air her beams dispersing wide,
  And when the air is tossed, not interrupted:

So doth the piercing soul the body fill,
  Being all in all, and all in part diffused,
Indivisible, incorruptible still,
  Not forced, encountered, troubled or confused.

And as the sun above the light doth bring,
  Though we behold it in the air below,
So from th' eternal Light the soul doth spring,
  Though in the body she her powers do show.

Nosce Teipsum, stt. ccxxv–ccxxxi, 1599

390 *To the Nightingale*

EVERY night from even till morn,
Love's chorister amid the thorn
Is now so sweet a singer;
So sweet, as for her song I scorn
Apollo's voice and finger.

But nightingale, sith you delight
Ever to watch the starry night,
Tell all the stars of heaven,
Heaven never had a star so bright,
As now to earth is given.

Royal Astraea makes our day
Eternal with her beams, nor may
Gross darkness overcome her.
I now perceive why some do write,
No country hath so short a night,
As England hath in summer.

Hymns of Astraea, 1599

391 *To the Rose*

EYE of the garden, queen of flowers,
Love's cup wherein he nectar pours,
Ingendered first of nectar;
Sweet nurse-child of the spring's young hours,
And beauty's fair character.

Best jewel that the earth doth wear,
Even when the brave young sun draws near,
To her hot love pretending;
Himself likewise like form doth bear
At rising and descending.

Rose of the queen of love beloved;
England's great kings, divinely moved,
Gave roses in their banner;
It showed that beauty's rose indeed
Now in this age should them succeed,
And reign in more sweet manner.

Hymns of Astraea, 1599

392 *A Contention betwixt a Wife, a Widow, and a Maid*

Wife. WIDOW, well met; whither go you to-day,
Will you not to this solemn offering go?
You know it is Astraea's holy day,
The Saint to whom all hearts devotion owe.

Widow. Marry, what else? I purposed so to do;
Do you not mark how all the wives are fine,
And how they have sent presents ready too
To make their offering at Astraea's shrine.

See then the shrine and tapers burning bright.
Come, friend, and let us first ourselves advance;
We know our place and if we have our right,
To all the parish we must lead the dance.

But soft, what means this bold presumptuous maid
To go before without respect of us?
Your forwardness (proud girl) must now be stayed;
Where learned you to neglect your betters thus?

Maid. Elder you are, but not my betters here,
This place to maids a privilege must give;
The Goddess being a maid holds maidens dear,
And grants to them her own prerogative.

Besides, on all true virgins at their birth
Nature hath set a crown of excellence,
That all the wives and widows of the earth
Should give them place and do them reverence.

Wife. If to be born a maid be such a grace,
So was I born and graced by nature too,
But seeking more perfection to embrace
I did become a wife as others do.

Widow. And if the maid and wife such honour have,
I have been both, and hold a third degree;
Most maids are wards, and every wife a slave,
I have my livery sued and I am free.

Maid. That is the fault that you have maidens been
And were not constant to continue so:
The fall of angels did increase their sin,
In that they did so pure a state forgo.

But wife and widow, if your wits can make
Your state and persons of more worth than mine,
Advantage to this place I will not take,
I will both place and privilege resign.

Wife. Why, marriage is an honourable state,
Widow. And widowhood is a reverend degree,
Maid. But maidenhead that will admit no mate
Like majesty itself must sacred be.

Wife. The wife is mistress of her family,
Widow. Much more the widow for she rules alone:
Maid. But mistress of mine own desires am I,
When you rule others' wills and not your own.

Wife. Only the wife enjoys the virtuous pleasure.
Widow. The widow can abstain from pleasures known.
Maid. But th'uncorrupted maid observes such measure
As being by pleasures wooed she cares for none.

Wife. The wife is like a fair supported vine.
Widow. So was the widow but now stands alone,
For being grown strong, she needs not to incline.
Maid. Maids, like the earth, supported are of none.

Wife. The wife is as a diamond richly set.
Maid. The maid unset doth yet more rich appear,
Widow. The widow a jewel in the cabinet,
Which though not worn is still esteemed as dear.

Wife. The wife doth love, and is beloved again.
Widow. The widow is awaked out of that dream.
Maid. The maid's white mind had never such a stain.
No passion troubles her clear virtue's stream.

Yet if I would be loved, loved would I be,
Like her, whose virtue in the bay is seen:
Love to wife fadeth with satiety,
Where love never enjoyed is ever green.

Widow. Then what 's a virgin but a fruitless bay?
Maid. And what 's a widow but a roseless briar?
And what are wives but woodbines which decay
The stately oaks by which themselves aspire,

And what is marriage but a tedious yoke?
Widow. And what virginity, but sweet self love?
Wife. And what 's a widow but an axle broke,
Whose one part failing, neither part can move?

Widow. Wives are as birds in golden cages kept:
Wife. Yet in those cages cheerfully they sing.
Widow. Widows are birds out of those cages lept,
Whose joyful notes make all the forest ring.

Maid. But maids are birds amidst the woods secure,
Which never hand could touch, nor net could take,
Nor whistle could deceive nor bait allure,
But free unto themselves do music make.

Wife. The wife is as the turtle with her mate,
Widow. The widow as the widow dove alone,
Whose truth shines most in her forsaken state,
Maid. The maid a Phoenix, and is still but one.

Wife. The wife 's a soul unto her body tied,
Widow. The widow a soul departed into bliss,
Maid. The maid an angel which was stellified,
And now t' as fair a house descended is.

Wife. Wives are fair houses kept and furnished well,
Widow. Widows old castles void, but full of state,
Maid. But maids are temples where the gods do dwell,
To whom alone themselves they dedicate.

But marriage is a prison during life,
Where one way out but many entries be.
Wife. The nun is kept in cloister, not the wife:
Wedlock alone doth make the virgin free.

Maid. The maid is ever fresh like morn in May.
Wife. The wife with all her beams is beautified,
Like to high noon, the glory of the day.
Widow. The widow like a mild sweet eventide.

Wife. An office well supplied is like the wife.
Widow. The widow like a gainful office void.
Maid. But maids are like contentment in this life,
Which all the world have sought, but none enjoyed.

Go, wife, to Dunmow, and demand your flitch.
Widow. Go, gentle maid, go lead the apes in hell.
Wife. Go, widow, make some younger brother rich,
And then take thought and die, and all is well.

Alas! poor maid, that hast no help nor stay.
Widow. Alas! poor wife, that nothing dost possess.
Maid. Alas! poor widow, charity doth say,
Pity the widow and the fatherless.

Widow. But happy widows have the world at will.
Wife. But happier wives, whose joys are ever double.
Maid. But happiest maids, whose hearts are calm and still,
Whom fear, nor hope, nor love, nor hate doth trouble.

Wife. Every true wife hath an indented heart,
Wherein the covenants of love are writ,
Whereof her husband keeps the counterpart,
And reads his comforts and his joys in it.

Widow. But every widow's heart is like a book,
Where her joys past imprinted do remain;
But when her judgement's eye therein doth look,
She doth not wish they were to come again.

Maid. But the maid's heart a fair white table is,
Spotless and pure where no impressions be,
But the immortal characters of bliss,
Which only God doth write and angels see.

Wife. But wives have children; what a joy is this!
Widow. Widows have children too, but maids have none.
Maid. No more have angels, yet they have more bliss,
Then ever yet to mortal man was known.

Wife. The wife is like a fair manured field.
Widow. The widow once was such, but now doth rest.
Maid. The maid, like Paradise, undressed, untilled,
Bears crops of native virtue in her breast.

Wife. Who would not die a wife, as Lucrece died?
Widow. Or live a widow, as Penelope?
Maid. Or be a maid, and so be stellified,
As all the Virtues, and the Graces be.

Wife. Wives are warm climates well inhabited:
But maids are frozen zones where none may dwell.
Maid. But fairest people in the north are bred,
Where Africa breeds monsters black as hell.

Wife. I have my husband's honour and his place.
Widow. My husband's fortunes all survive to me.
Maid. The moon doth borrow light, you borrow grace,
When maids by their own virtues graced be.

White is my colour, and no hue but this
It will receive, no tincture can it stain.
Wife. My white hath took one colour, but it is
An honourable purple dyed in grain.

Widow. But it hath been my fortune to renew
My colour twice from that it was before,
But now my black will take no other hue,
And therefore now I mean to change no more.

Wife. Wives are fair apples served in golden dishes,
Widow. Widows good wine, which time makes better much.
Maid. But maids are grapes desired by many wishes,
But that they grow so high as none can touch.

Wife. I have a daughter equals you, my girl.
Maid. The daughter doth excel the mother then,
As pearls are better than the mother of pearl;
Maids loose their value, when they match with men.

Widow. The man with whom I matched, his worth was such,
As now I scorn a maid should be my peer.
Maid. But I will scorn the man you praise so much,
For maids are matchless, and no mate can bear.

Hence is it that the virgin never loves,
Because her like she finds not anywhere:
For likeness evermore affection moves,
Therefore the maid hath neither love nor peer.

Wife. Yet many virgins married wives would be,
Widow. And many a wife would be a widow fain.
Maid. There is no widow but desires to see,
If so she might, her maiden days again.

Wife. There never was a wife that liked her lot:
Widow. Nor widow but was clad in mourning weeds.
Maid. Do what you will, marry, or marry not,
Both this estate and that repentance breeds.

Wife. But she, that this estate and that hath seen,
Doth find great odds between the wife and girl.
Maid. Indeed she doth, as much as is between
The melting hailstone and the solid pearl.

Wife. If I were widow, my merry days were past,
Widow. Nay, then you first become sweet pleasure's guest.
For maidenhead is a continual fast,
And marriage is a continual feast.

Maid. Wedlock indeed hath oft compared been
To public feasts, where meet a public rout;
Where they that are without would fain go in,
And they that are within would fain go out.

Or to the jewel, which this virtue had,
That men were mad till they might it obtain,
But when they had it they were twice as mad,
Till they were dispossessed of it again.

Wife. Maids cannot judge, because they cannot tell,
What comforts and what joys in marriage be.
Maid. Yes, yes, though blessed saints in heaven do dwell
They do the souls in purgatory see.

Widow. If every wife do live in purgatory,
Then sure it is that widows live in bliss,
And are translated to a state of glory,
But maids as yet have not attained to this.

Maid. Not maids? To spotless maids this gift is given
To live in incorruption from their birth:
And what is that, but to inherit heaven,
Even while they dwell upon the spotted earth.

The perfectest of all created things;
The purest gold that suffers no allay;
The sweetest flower that on th' earth's bosom springs;
The pearl unbored, whose prize no price can pay.

The crystal glass that will no venom hold;
The mirror wherein angels love to look;
Diana's bathing fountain, clear and cold;
Beauty's fresh rose, and virtue's living book.

Of love and fortune both the mistress born;
The sovereign spirit that will be thrall to none;
The spotless garment that was never worn;
The princely eagle that still flies alone.

She sees the world, yet her clear thought doth take
No such deep print as to be changed thereby;
As when we see the burning fire doth make
No such impression as doth burn the eye.

Wife. No more (sweet maid), our strife is at an end;
Cease now, I fear we shall transformed be
To chattering pies, as they that did contend
To match the Muses in their harmony.

Widow. Then let us yield the honour and the place,
And let us both be suitors to the maid,
That since the Goddess gives her special grace,
By her clear hands the Offering be conveyed.

Maid. Your speech, I doubt, hath some displeasure moved,
Yet let me have the Offering, I will see:
I know she hath both wives and widows loved,
Though she would neither wife nor widow be.

Written 1602; *Poetical Rhapsody*, 1608

393 *The Mariner's Song*

CYNTHIA, Queen of seas and lands,
That fortune everywhere commands,
Sent forth Fortune to the sea
To try her fortune every way.
There did I Fortune meet, which makes me now to sing,
There is no fishing to the sea, nor service to the king.

All the nymphs of Thetis' train
Did Cynthia's fortune entertain.
Many a jewel, many a gem,
Was to her fortune brought by them.
Her fortune sped so well, as makes me now to sing,
There is no fishing to the sea, nor service to the king.

Fortune, that it might be seen,
That she did serve a royal queen,
A frank and royal hand did bear,
And cast her favours everywhere.
Some toys fell to my share, which makes me now to sing,
There is no fishing to the sea, nor service to the king.

Written 1602; *Ibid.*

GEORGE CLIFFORD, EARL OF CUMBERLAND

1558–1605

394 *To Cynthia*

MY thoughts are winged with hopes, my hopes with love.
  Mount, Love, unto the moon in clearest light,
And say, as she doth in the heavens move,
  In earth so wanes and waxeth my delight.
And whisper this but softly in her ears:
'Hope oft doth hang the head, and Trust shed tears.'

And you, my thoughts, that some mistrust do carry,
  If for mistrust my mistress do you blame,
Say, though you alter, yet you do not vary,
  As she doth change and yet remain the same.
Distrust doth enter hearts, but not infect,
And love is sweetest seasoned with suspect.

If she for this with clouds do mask her eyes,
  And make the heavens dark with her disdain,
With windy sighs disperse them in the skies,
  Or with thy tears dissolve them into rain.
Thoughts, hopes, and love, return to me no more,
Till Cynthia shine as she hath done before.

J. Dowland, *First Book of Songs or Ayres*, 1597

ROBERT DEVEREUX, EARL OF ESSEX

1566–1601

395 *Change*

CHANGE thy mind since she doth change,
  Let not fancy still abuse thee.
Thy untruth cannot seem strange,
  When her falsehood doth excuse thee.
Love is dead, and thou art free.
She doth live, but dead to thee.

Whilst she loved thee best awhile,
  See how she hath still delayed thee,
Using shows for to beguile
  Those vain hopes that have betrayed thee.
Now thou seest, although too late,
Love loves truth, which women hate.

Love no more since she is gone;
  She is gone and loves another.
Being once deceived by one,
  Leave her love, but love none other.
She was false, bid her adieu.
She was best, but yet untrue.

Love, farewell, more dear to me,
  Than my life which thou preservest.
Life, all joys are gone from thee,
  Others have what thou deservest.
O! my death doth spring from hence,
I must die for her offence.

Die, but yet before thou die,
  Make her know what she hath gotten.
She in whom my hopes did lie
  Now is changed, I quite forgotten.
She is changed, but changed base,
Baser in so vild a place.

R. Dowland, *A Musical Banquet*, 1610

396

Content

HAPPY were he could finish forth his fate
  In some unhaunted desert, most obscure
From all societies, from love and hate
  Of worldly folk; then might he sleep secure;
Then wake again, and give God ever praise,
  Content with hips and haws and bramble-berry;
In contemplation spending all his days,
  And change of holy thoughts to make him merry;
Where, when he dies, his tomb may be a bush,
Where harmless robin dwells with gentle thrush.

Chetham MS. 8012

SIR FRANCIS BACON

1561–1626

397

The Life of Man

THE world 's a bubble, and the life of man
  Less than a span,
In his conception wretched, from the womb,
    So to the tomb;
Curst from the cradle, and brought up to years,
    With cares and fears.
Who then to frail mortality shall trust,
But limns on water, or but writes in dust.

Yet since with sorrow here we live oppressed,
    What life is best?
Courts are but only superficial schools
    To dandle fools.
The rural parts are turned into a den
    Of savage men.
And where 's a city from all vice so free,
But may be termed the worst of all the three?

Domestic cares afflict the husband's bed,
    Or pains his head.
Those that live single take it for a curse,
    Or do things worse.
Some would have children; those that have them none,
    Or wish them gone.
What is it then to have or have no wife,
But single thraldom, or a double strife?

Our own affections still at home to please
    Is a disease;
To cross the sea to any foreign soil,
    Perils and toil.
Wars with their noise affright us; when they cease,
    W' are worse in peace.
What then remains, but that we still should cry,
Not to be born, or being born to die?

T. Farnaby, *Florilegium Epigrammatum Graecorum*, 1629

398

Beauty

BEAUTY is but a vain and doubtful good;
A shining gloss that vadeth suddenly;
A flower that dies when first it 'gins to bud;
A brittle glass that 's broken presently:
A doubtful good, a gloss, a glass, a flower,
Lost, vaded, broken, dead within an hour.

And as goods lost are seld or never found,
As vaded gloss no rubbing will refresh,
As flowers dead lie withered on the ground,
As broken glass no cement can redress,
So beauty blemished once for ever lost,
In spite of physic, painting, pain, and cost.

The Passionate Pilgrim, 1599

399

A Night Watch

GOOD night, good rest. Ah! neither be my share:
She bade good night that kept my rest away;
And daffed me to a cabin hanged with care,
To descant on the doubts of my decay.
'Farewell,' quoth she, 'and come again to-morrow.'
Fare well I could not, for I supped with sorrow.

Yet at my parting sweetly did she smile,
In scorn of friendship, nill I construe whether:
'T may be, she joyed to jest at my exile,
'T may be, again to make me wander thither.
'Wander,' a word for shadows like myself,
As take the pain, but cannot pluck the pelf.

Lord! how mine eyes throw gazes to the east;
My heart doth charge the watch; the morning rise
Doth cite each moving sense from idle rest.
Not daring trust the office of mine eyes,
While Philomela sits and sings, I sit and mark,
And wish her lays were tuned like the lark;

For she doth welcome daylight with her ditty,
And drives away dark, dismal, dreaming night:
The night so packed, I post unto my pretty;
Heart hath his hope, and eyes their wished sight;
Sorrow changed to solace, and solace mixed with sorrow;
For why, she sighed and bade me come to-morrow.

Were I with her, the night would post too soon;
But now are minutes added to the hours;
To spite me now, each minute seems a moon;
Yet not for me, shine sun to succour flowers!
Pack night, peep day; good day, of night now borrow:
Short, night, to-night, and length thyself to-morrow.

The Passionate Pilgrim, 1599

EDMUND BOLTON

1575?–1633?

400 *A Palinode*

AS withereth the primrose by the river,
As fadeth summer's sun from gliding fountains,
As vanisheth the light-blown bubble ever,
As melteth snow upon the mossy mountains:
So melts, so vanisheth, so fades, so withers
The rose, the shine, the bubble, and the snow
Of praise, pomp, glory, joy (which short life gathers),
Fair praise, vain pomp, sweet glory, brittle joy.

The withered primrose by the mourning river,
  The faded summer's sun from weeping fountains,
The light-blown bubble vanished for ever,
  The molten snow upon the naked mountains,
Are emblems that the treasures we up-lay
Soon wither, vanish, fade, and melt away.

For as the snow, whose lawn did overspread
  Th' ambitious hills, which giant-like did threat
To pierce the heaven with their aspiring head,
  Naked and bare doth leave their craggy seat;
Whenas the bubble, which did empty fly
  The dalliance of the undiscerned wind,
On whose calm rolling waves it did rely,
  Hath shipwreck made, where it did dalliance find;
And when the sunshine which dissolved the snow,
  Coloured the bubble with a pleasant vary,
And made the rathe and timely primrose grow,
  Swarth clouds withdraw, which longer time do tarry:
O! what is praise, pomp, glory, joy, but so
As shine by fountains, bubbles, flowers, or snow?

England's Helicon, 1600

401 *To Favonius*

As to the blooming prime,
  Bleak winter being fled
From compass of the clime,
  When nature lay as dead,
The rivers dulled with time,
  The green leaves withered,
Fresh Zephiri (the western brethren) be;
So th' honour of your favour is to me.

For as the plains revive,
And put on youthful green;
As plants begin to thrive,
That disattired had been,
And arbours now alive
In former pomp are seen;
So if my spring had any flowers before,
Your breaths, Favonius, hath increased the store.

England's Helicon, 1600

ANONYMOUS

402 ## *Phyllida's Love Call*

Phyl. CORYDON, arise, my Corydon!
Titan shineth clear.
Cor. Who is it that calleth Corydon?
Who is it that I hear?
Phyl. Phyllida, thy true Love, calleth thee,
Arise then, arise then,
Arise and keep thy flock with me!
Cor. Phyllida, my true Love, is it she?
I come then, I come then,
I come and keep my flock with thee.

Phyl. Here are cherries ripe, my Corydon;
Eat them for my sake.
Cor. Here 's my oaten pipe, my lovely one,
Sport for thee to make.

Phyl. Here are threads, my true Love, fine as silk,
To knit thee, to knit thee
A pair of stockings white as milk.
Cor. Here are reeds, my true Love, fine and neat,
To make thee, to make thee
A bonnet to withstand the heat.

Phyl. I will gather flowers, my Corydon,
To set in thy cap.
Cor. I will gather pears, my lovely one,
To put in thy lap.
Phyl. I will buy my true Love garters gay
For Sundays, for Sundays,
To wear about his legs so tall.
Cor. I will buy my true Love yellow say
For Sundays, for Sundays,
To wear about her middle small.

Phyl. When my Corydon sits on a hill
Making melody—
Cor. When my lovely one goes to her wheel
Singing cheerily—
Phyl. Sure methinks my true Love doth excel
For sweetness, for sweetness,
Sir Pan, that old Arcadian knight.
Cor. And methinks my true Love bears the bell
For clearness, for clearness,
Beyond the nymphs that be so bright.

Phyl. Had my Corydon, my Corydon,
Been, alack! her swain—
Cor. Had my lovely one, my lovely one,
Been in Ida plain—

say] silk

Phyl. Cynthia Endymion had refused,
Preferring, preferring,
My Corydon to play withal.
Cor. The queen of love had been excused,
Bequeathing, bequeathing,
My Phyllida the golden ball.

Phyl. Yonder comes my mother, Corydon,
Whither shall I fly?
Cor. Under yonder beech, my lovely one,
While she passeth by.
Phyl. Say to her thy true Love was not here;
Remember, remember,
To-morrow is another day.
Cor. Doubt me not, my true Love, do not fear;
Farewell then, farewell then,
Heaven keep our loves alway.

England's Helicon, 1600

EDWARD FAIRFAX

ob. 1635

403 *Pluto's Council*

ABOUT their prince each took his wonted seat
On thrones red-hot, ybuilt of burning brass:
Pluto in middest heaved his trident great,
Of rusty iron huge that forged was;
The rocks on which the salt sea billows beat,
And Atlas' tops, the clouds in height that pass,
Compared to his huge person mole-hills be,
So his rough front, his horns so lifted he.

The tyrant proud frowned from his lofty cell,
And with his looks made all his monsters tremble;
His eyes, that full of rage and venom swell,
Two beacons seem, that men to arms assemble;
His feltered locks, that on his bosom fell,
On rugged mountains briars and thorns resemble;
His yawning mouth, that foamed clotted blood,
Gaped like a whirlpool wide in Stygian flood.

And as Mount Etna vomits sulphur out,
With clifts of burning crags, and fire and smoke,
So from his mouth flew kindled coals about,
Hot sparks and smells, that man and beast would choke.
The gnarring porter durst not whine for dout;
Still were the Furies, while their sovereign spoke;
And swift Cocytus stayed his murmur shrill,
While thus the murderer thundered out his will.

'Ye powers infernal, worthier far to sit
Above the sun, whence you your offspring take,
With me that whilom, through the welkin flit,
Down tumbled headlong to this empty lake,
Our former glory still remember it,
Our bold attempts and war we once did make
'Gainst him, that rules above the starry sphere,
For which like traitors we lie damned here.

'And now instead of clear and gladsome sky,
Of Titan's brightness that so glorious is,
In this deep darkness lo! we helpless lie,
Hopeless again to joy our former bliss;

feltered] matted clifts] clefts gnarring] snarling
dout] fear flit] airy

And more, which makes my griefs to multiply,
  That sinful creature, man, elected is;
    And in our place the heavens possess he must,
    Vile man, begot of clay, and born of dust.

'Nor this sufficed, but that he also gave
  His only son, his darling, to be slain,
To conquer so hell, death, sin and the grave,
  And man condemned to restore again.
He brake our prisons and would algates save
  The souls that here should dwell in woe and pain,
    And now in heaven with him they live always,
    With endless glory crowned and lasting praise.

'But why recount I thus our passed harms?
  Remembrance fresh makes weakened sorrows strong:
Expulsed were we with injurious arms
  From those due honours, us of right belong.
But let us leave to speak of these alarms,
  And bend our forces 'gainst our present wrong:
    Ah! see you not how he attempted hath
    To bring all lands, all nations to his faith?

'Then, let us careless spend the day and night,
  Without regard what haps, what comes or goes;
Let Asia subject be to Christians' might,
  A prey be Sion to her conquering foes;
Let her adore again her Christ aright,
  Who her before all nations whilom chose;
    In brazen tables be his lore ywrit,
    And let all tongues and lands acknowledge it.

algates] all ways

'So shall our sacred altars all be his,
Our holy idols tumbled in the mould;
To him the wretched man that sinful is
Shall pray, and offer incense, myrrh and gold;
Our temples shall their costly deckings miss,
With naked walls and pillars freezing cold;
Tribute of souls shall end and our estate,
Or Pluto reign in kingdoms desolate.

'O! be not then the courage perished clean,
That whilom dwelt within your haughty thought,
When, armed with shining fire and weapons keen,
Against the angels of proud heaven we fought.
I grant we fell on the Phlegrean green,
Yet good our cause was, though our fortune nought,
For chance assisteth oft th' ignobler part;
We lost the field, yet lost we not our heart.

'Go then, my strength, my hope, my spirits, go;
These western rebels with your power withstand;
Pluck up these weeds, before they overgrow
The gentle garden of the Hebrews' land;
Quench out this spark, before it kindle so,
That Asia burn, consumed with the brand.
Use open force, or secret guile unspied;
For craft is virtue 'gainst a foe defied.

'Among the knights and worthies of their train,
Let some like outlaws wander uncouth ways;
Let some be slain in field; let some again
Make oracles of women's yeas and nays,

And pine in foolish love; let some complain
 On Godfrey's rule, and mutines 'gainst him raise:
  Turn each one's sword against his fellow's heart;
  Thus kill them all or spoil the greatest part.'

Before his words the tyrant ended had,
 The lesser devils arose with ghastly roar,
And thronged forth about the world to gad;
 Each land they filled, river, stream and shore,
The Goblins, Fairies, Fiends and Furies mad,
 Ranged in flowery dales and mountains hoar;
  And under every trembling leaf they sit,
  Between the solid earth and welkin flit.

Tasso's Godfrey of Bulloigne, iv. 6–18, 1600

404 *A Prayer Brings Rain*

AT these high words great heaven began to shake,
 The fixed stars, the planets wandering still;
Trembled the air, the earth and ocean quake,
 Spring, fountain, river, forest, dale and hill;
From north to east a lightning flash outbrake,
 And coming drops presaged with thunders shrill:
  With joyful shouts the soldiers on the plain
  These tokens bless of long-desired rain.

A sudden cloud, as when Helias prayed,
 Not from dry earth exhaled by Phoebus' beams,
Arose; moist heaven his windows open laid,
 Whence clouds by heaps outrush, and watery streams;
The world o'erspread was with a gloomy shade,
 That like a dark and mirksome even it seems;
  The dashing rain from molten skies down fell,
  And o'er their banks the brooks and fountains swell.

Thy walls are made of precious stones,
  Thy bulwarks diamonds square;
Thy gates are of right orient pearl,
  Exceeding rich and rare.

Thy turrets and thy pinnacles
  With carbuncles do shine;
Thy very streets are paved with gold,
  Surpassing clear and fine.

Ah, my sweet home, Hierusalem,
  Would God I were in thee!
Would God my woes were at an end,
  Thy joys that I might see!

Thy gardens and thy gallant walks
  Continually are green;
There grows such sweet and pleasant flowers
  As nowhere else are seen.

Quite through the streets, with silver sound,
  The flood of life doth flow;
Upon whose banks on every side
  The wood of life doth grow.

There trees for evermore bear fruit,
  And evermore do spring;
There evermore the angels sit,
  And evermore do sing.

ANONYMOUS

Our Lady sings *Magnificat*
  With tune surpassing sweet;
And all the virgins bear their part,
  Sitting about her feet.

Hierusalem, my happy home,
  Would God I were in thee!
Would God my woes were at an end,
  Thy joys that I might see!

Addl. MS. 15225

FRANCIS DAVISON

c. 1575–c. 1619

406 *To Cupid*

LOVE, if a God thou art,
  Then evermore thou must
  Be merciful and just.
If thou be just, O! wherefore doth thy dart
Wound mine alone, and not my lady's heart?

  If merciful, then why
  Am I to pain reserved,
  Who have thee truly served;
While she, that by thy power sets not a fly,
Laughs thee to scorn, and lives in liberty?

Then, if a God thou wouldst accounted be,
Heal me like her, or else wound her like me.

Poetical Rhapsody, 1602

407 *His Farewell to his Unkind and Unconstant Mistress*

SWEET, if you like and love me still,
And yield me love for my goodwill,
And do not from your promise start,
When your fair hand gave me your heart;
    If dear to you I be,
    As you are dear to me:
Then yours I am, and will be ever,
Nor time nor place my love shall sever,
But faithful will I still persever,
    Like constant marble stone,
    Loving but you alone.

But if you favour mo than me,
Who love thee still, and none but thee;
If others do the harvest gain
That 's due to me for all my pain;
    If that you love to range,
    And oft to chop and change:
Then get you some new-fangled mate;
My doting love shall turn to hate,
Esteeming you, though too too late,
    Not worth a pebble stone,
    Loving not me alone.

Ibid.

408 *Her Commendation*

SOME there are as fair to see to;
  But by Art and not by Nature.
Some as tall and goodly be too;
  But want Beauty to their stature.

Some have gracious kind behaviour,
  But are foul, or simple creatures;
Some have wit, but want sweet favour,
  Or are proud of their good features.
    Only you in court or city,
    Are both fair, tall, kind, and witty.

Poetical Rhapsody, 1602

409 *Three Epitaphs*

(*i*)

WIT'S perfection, Beauty's wonder,
  Nature's pride, the Graces' treasure,
Virtue's hope, his friends' sole pleasure,
This small marble stone lies under;
  Which is often moist with tears,
  For such loss in such young years.

(*ii*)

Lovely boy, thou art not dead,
But from earth to heaven fled,
For base earth was far unfit
For thy beauty, grace, and wit.

(*iii*)

Thou alive on earth, sweet boy,
Hadst an angel's wit, and face;
And now dead, thou dost enjoy
In high heaven an angel's place.

Ibid.

WALTER DAVISON

1581–c. 1608

410 ### *Ode*

AT her fair hands how have I grace entreated,
With prayers oft repeated,
Yet still my love is thwarted:
Heart, let her go, for she'll not be converted.
Say, shall she go?
O! no, no, no, no, no.
She is most fair, though she be marble hearted.

How often have my sighs declared mine anguish,
Wherein I daily languish,
Yet doth she still procure it:
Heart, let her go, for I cannot endure it.
Say, shall she go?
O! no, no, no, no, no.
She gave the wound, and she alone must cure it.

WALTER DAVISON

The trickling tears, that down my cheeks have flowed,
My love have often showed;
Yet still unkind I prove her:
Heart, let her go, for nought I do can move her.
    Say, shall she go?
    O! no, no, no, no, no.
Though me she hate, I cannot choose but love her.

But shall I still a true affection owe her,
Which prayers, sighs, tears do shew her;
And shall she still disdain me?
Heart, let her go, if they no grace can gain me.
    Say, shall she go?
    O! no, no, no, no, no.
She made me hers, and hers she will retain me.

But if the love that hath, and still doth burn me,
No love at length return me,
Out of my thoughts I'll set her:
Heart, let her go, oh heart, I pray thee let her.
    Say, shall she go?
    O! no, no, no, no, no.
Fixed in the heart, how can the heart forget her?

But if I weep and sigh, and often wail me,
Till tears, sighs, prayers fail me,
Shall yet my love persever?
Heart, let her go, if she will right thee never.
    Say, shall she go?
    O! no, no, no, no, no.
Tears, sighs, prayers fail, but true love lasteth ever.

Poetical Rhapsody, 1602

WALTER DAVISON

411 *To his Lady, who had Vowed Virginity*

EVEN as my hand my pen on paper lays,
My trembling hand my pen from paper stays,
Lest that thine eyes, which shining made me love you,
Should, frowning on my suit, bid cease to move you,
So that I fare like one at his wit's end,
Hoping to gain, and fearing to offend.
What pleaseth Hope, the same Despair mislikes,
What Hope sets down, those lines Despair outstrikes,
So that my nursing-murthering pen affords
A grave and cradle to my new-born words.
But whilst, like clouds tossed up and down the air,
I racked hang 'twixt Hope and sad Despair,
Despair is beaten vanquished from the field,
And unto conquering Hope my heart doth yield.

For when mine eyes unpartially are fixed
On thy rose cheeks with lilies intermixed,
And on thy forehead like a cloud of snow,
From under which thine eyes like suns do show,
And all those parts which curiously do meet,
'Twixt thy large-spreading hair and pretty feet,
Yet looking on them all, discern no one,
That owes not homage unto Cupid's throne;
Then Chastity (methinks) no claim should lay
To this fair realm, under Love's sceptre's sway.
For only to the queen of amorous pleasure
Belongs thy Beauty's tributary treasure,
(Treasure, which doth more than those riches please,
For which men plough long furrows in the seas).

WALTER DAVISON

If you were wrinkled old, or Nature's scorn,
Or time your Beauty's colours had outworn;
Or were you mewed up from gazing eyes,
Like to a cloistered nun, which living dies:
Then might you wait on Chastity's pale queen,
Not being fair, or being fair, not seen.
But you are fair, so passing passing fair,
That love I must, though loving I despair,
For when I saw your eyes (O cursed bliss!)
Whose light I would not have, nor yet would miss,
(For 'tis their light alone by which I live,
And yet their sight alone my death's wound give)
Looking upon your heart-entangling look,
I like a heedless bird was snared and took.
It lies not in our will to hate or love,
For Nature's influence our will doth move,
And love of Beauty Nature hath innated,
In hearts of men when first they were created.
For even as rivers to the ocean run,
Returning back, from whence they first begun;
Or as the sky about the earth doth wheel,
Or giddy air like to a drunkard reel:
So with the course of Nature doth agree,
That eyes, which Beauty's adamant do see,
Should on affection's line trembling remain,
True-subject-like eyeing their sovereign.

If of mine eyes you also could bereave me,
As you already of my heart deceive me,
Or could shut up my ravished ears, through which
You likewise did my enchanted heart bewitch,
Or had in absence both these ills combined,

(For by your absence I am deaf and blind,
And, neither ears nor eyes in aught delight,
But in your charming speech, and gracious sight)
To root out love all means you can invent
Were all but labour lost, and time ill spent,
For as the sparks being spent, which fire procure,
The fire doth brightly-burning still endure,
Though absence so your sparkling eyes remove,
My heart still burns in endless flames of love.

Then strive not 'gainst the stream, to none effect,
But let due love yield love a due respect;
Nor seek to ruin what yourself begun,
Or loose a knot that cannot be undone.
But unto Cupid's bent conform your will,
For will you, nill you, I must love you still.
But if your will did swim with Reason's tide,
Or followed Nature's never-erring guide,
It cannot choose but bring you unto this,
To tender that which by you gotten is.
Why were you fair to be besought of many,
If you live chaste, not to be won of any?
For if that Nature love to Beauty offers,
And Beauty shun the love that Nature proffers,
Then, either unjust Beauty is to blame,
With scorn to quench a lawful kindled flame,
Or else, unlawfully if love we must,
And be unloved, then Nature is unjust.
Unjustly then Nature hath hearts created,
There to love most, where most their love is hated,
And flattering them with a fair-seeming ill,
To poison them with Beauty's sugared pill.

WALTER DAVISON

Think you that Beauty's admirable worth
Was to no end, or idle end brought forth?
No, no; from Nature never deed did pass,
But it by wisdom's hand subscribed was.
But you in vain are fair, if fair not viewed,
Or being seen, men's hearts be not subdued,
Or making each man's heart your Beauty's thrall,
You be enjoyed of no one at all.
For as the lion's strength to seize his prey,
And fearful hare's light foot to run away,
Are as an idle talent but abused,
And fruitless had, if, had, they be not used,
So you in vain have Beauty's bonds to show,
By which men's eyes engaged hearts do owe,
If Time shall cancel them before you gain
Th' indebted tribute to your Beauty's reign.

But if (these reasons being vainly spent)
You fight it out to the last argument;
Tell me but how one body can enclose,
As loving friends, two deadly hating foes.
But when as contraries are mixed together,
The colour made doth differ much from either,
Whilst mutually at strife they do impeach
The gloss and lustre proper unto each.
So, where one body jointly doth invest
An angel's face and cruel tiger's breast,
There dieth both allegiance and command,
For self-divided kingdoms cannot stand.
But as a child, that knows not what is what,
Now craveth this, and now affecteth that,
And having, weighs not that which he requires,

But is unpleased, even in his pleased desires:
Chaste Beauty so, both will and will not have
The self-same thing it childishly doth crave;
And wanton-like, now love, now hate affecteth,
And love, or hate obtained as fast neglecteth.
So (like the web Penelope did weave,
Which made by day, she did at night unreave)
Fruitless affection's endless thread is spun,
At one self instant twisted, and undone.
Nor yet is this chaste Beauty's greatest ill,
For where it speaketh fair, it there doth kill.
A marble heart under an amorous look
Is of a flattering bait the murdering hook;
For from a lady's shining-frowning eyes
Death's sable dart and Cupid's arrow flies.

Since then from Chastity and Beauty spring
Such muddy streams, where each doth reign as king,
Let tyrant Chastity's usurped throne
Be made the seat of Beauty's grace alone;
And let your Beauty be with this sufficed,
That my heart's city is by it surprised.
Raze not my heart, nor to your Beauty raise
Blood-gilded trophies of your Beauty's praise;
For wisest conquerors do towns desire,
On honourable terms and not with fire.

Poetical Rhapsody, 1602

I. S.

412 *Sonnet*

WERE I as base as is the lowly plain,
And you (my Love) as high as heaven above,
Yet should the thoughts of me, your humble swain,
Ascend to heaven, in honour of my love.
Were I as high as heaven above the plain,
And you (my Love) as humble and as low
As are the deepest bottoms of the main,
Wheresoe'er you were, with you my love should go.
Were you the earth (dear Love) and I the skies,
My love should shine on you like to the sun,
And look upon you with ten thousand eyes,
Till heaven waxed blind, and till the world were done.
Wheresoe'er I am, below, or else above you.
Wheresoe'er you are, my heart shall truly love you.

Poetical Rhapsody, 1602

CHARLES BEST c. 1570–1627

413 *The Moon*

LOOK how the pale queen of the silent night
Doth cause the ocean to attend upon her,
And he, as long as she is in his sight,
With her full tide is ready her to honour;
But when the silver waggon of the moon
Is mounted up so high he cannot follow,
The sea calls home his crystal waves to moan,
And with low ebb doth manifest his sorrow:
So you, that are the sovereign of my heart,
Have all my joys attending on your will,
My joys, low ebbing when you do depart,
When you return, their tide my heart doth fill.
So as you come, and as you do depart,
Joys ebb and flow within my tender heart. *Ib.* 1608

414 *Madrigal*

MY Love in her attire doth show her wit,
  It doth so well become her:
For every season she hath dressings fit,
  For winter, spring, and summer.
No beauty she doth miss,
  When all her robes are on:
But Beauty's self she is,
  When all her robes are gone.

Ibid., 1602

415 *Of Cynthia*

TH' ancient readers of heaven's book,
  Which with curious eye did look
    Into Nature's story,
All things under Cynthia took
    To be transitory.

This the learned only knew,
But now all men find it true,
    Cynthia is descended,
With bright beams, and heavenly hue,
    And lesser stars attended.

Lands and seas she rules below,
Where things change, and ebb, and flow,
    Spring, wax old, and perish;
Only Time, which all doth mow,
    Her alone doth cherish.

Time's young hours attend her still,
And her eyes and cheeks do fill,
    With fresh youth and beauty:
All her lovers old do grow,
But their hearts, they do not so
    In their love and duty.

Poetical Rhapsody, 1602

JOHN LILLIAT

c. 1550–c. 1599

416 *False Love*

WHEN love on time and measure makes his ground,
  Time that must end, though love can never die,
'Tis love betwixt a shadow and a sound,
  A love not in the heart but in the eye;
A love that ebbs and flows, now up, now down,
A morning's favour and an evening's frown.

Sweet looks show love, yet they are but as beams;
  Fair words seem true, yet they are but as wind;
Eyes shed their tears, yet are but outward streams;
  Sighs paint a sadness in the falsest mind.
Looks, words, tears, sighs, show love when love they leave;
False hearts can weep, sigh, swear, and yet deceive.

R. Jones, *First Book of Airs*, 1600

THOMAS CAMPION

1567–1620

417

Proserpina

HARK, all you ladies that do sleep,
The fairy queen Proserpina
Bids you awake, and pity them that weep.
You may do in the dark
What the day doth forbid.
Fear not the dogs that bark;
Night will have all hid.

But if you let your lovers moan,
The fairy queen Proserpina
Will send abroad her fairies every one,
That shall pinch black and blue
Your white hands and fair arms,
That did not kindly rue
Your paramours' harms.

In myrtle arbours on the downs,
The fairy queen Proserpina,
This night by moonshine, leading merry rounds,
Holds a watch with sweet Love,
Down the dale, up the hill;
No plaints or groans may move
Their holy vigil.

All you that will hold watch with Love,
The fairy queen Proserpina
Will make you fairer than Dione's dove.
Roses red, lilies white,
And the clear damask hue,
Shall on your cheeks alight.
Love will adorn you.

All you that love or loved before,
The fairy queen Proserpina
Bids you increase that loving humour more.
They that have not yet fed
On delight amorous,
She vows that they shall lead
Apes in Avernus.

Astrophel and Stella, 1591

418 *Love's Pilgrims*

WHAT fair pomp have I spied of glittering ladies,
With locks sparkled abroad, and rosy coronet
On their ivory brows, tracked to the dainty thighs
With robes like Amazons, blue as violet,
With gold aglets adorned, some in a changeable
Pale, with spangs wavering taught to be moveable?

Then those knights, that afar off with dolorous viewing
Cast their eyes hitherward, lo! in an agony,
All unbraced, cry aloud, their heavy state rueing:
Moist cheeks with blubbering, painted as ebony
Black; their feltered hair torn with wrathful hand;
And whiles astonied stark in a maze they stand.

But hark! what merry sound, what sudden harmony.
Look, look near the grove, where the ladies do tread
With their knights the measures wayed by the melody.
Wantons! whose traversing make men enamoured;
Now they feign an honour, now by the slender waist
He must lift her aloft, and seal a kiss in haste.

sparkled] spread spangs] spangles feltered] matted traversing] crossing honour] bow

Straight down under a shadow for weariness they lie
  With pleasant dalliance, hand knit with arm in arm;
Now close, now set aloof, they gaze with an equal eye,
  Changing kisses alike; straight with a false alarm,
    Mocking kisses alike, pout with a lovely lip.
    Thus drowned with jollities their merry days do slip.

But stay! now I discern they go on a pilgrimage
  Towards Love's holy land, fair Paphos or Cyprus.
Such devotion is meet for a blithesome age;
  With sweet youth it agrees well to be amorous.
    Let old angry fathers lurk in an hermitage;
    Come! we'll associate this jolly pilgrimage.

Ibid.

419 *Kisses*

MY Love bound me with a kiss
  That I should no longer stay.
When I felt so sweet a bliss,
  I had less power to pass away.
Alas! that women do not know
Kisses make men loth to go.

Yes, she knows it but too well,
  For I heard when Venus' dove
In her ear did softly tell
  That kisses were the seals of love.
O! muse not then though it be so,
Kisses make men loth to go.

Wherefore did she thus inflame
  My desires, heat my blood,
Instantly to quench the same,
  And starve whom she had given food?
I the common sense can show;
Kisses make men loth to go.

Had she bid me go at first,
  It would ne'er have grieved my heart;
Hope delayed had been the worst.
  But ah! to kiss and then to part!
How deep it struck, speak, gods, you know.
Kisses make men loth to go.

Astrophel and Stella, 1591; R. Jones,
Second Book of Songs and Airs, 1601

420 *Content*

A DAY, a night, an hour of sweet content
  Is worth a world consumed in fretful care.
Unequal Gods! in your arbitrament
  To sort us days whose sorrows endless are!
    And yet what were it, as a fading flower,
    To swim in bliss a day, a night, an hour?

What plague is greater than the grief of mind?
  The grief of mind that eats in every vein,
In every vein that leaves such clods behind,
  Such clods behind as breed such bitter pain,
    So bitter pain that none shall ever find,
    What plague is greater than the grief of mind.

Doth sorrow fret thy soul? O direful spirit!
  Doth pleasure feed thy heart? O blessed man!
Hast thou been happy once? O heavy plight!
  Are thy mishaps forepassed? O happy then!
    Or hast thou bliss in eld? O bliss too late!
    But hast thou bliss in youth? O sweet estate!

Astrophel and Stella, 1591

421

Neptune

OF Neptune's empire let us sing,
  At whose command the waves obey,
To whom the rivers tribute pay,
  Down the high mountains sliding;
To whom the scaly nation yields
Homage for the crystal fields
      Wherein they dwell;
And every sea-god pays a gem,
Yearly out of his watery cell,
To deck great Neptune's diadem.

The Tritons dancing in a ring,
Before his palace gates, do make
The water with their echoes quake,
  Like the great thunder sounding:
The sea-nymphs chant their accents shrill;
  And the Sirens, taught to kill
      With their sweet voice,
Make every echoing rock reply,
Unto their gentle murmuring noise,
The praise of Neptune's empery.

Written in 1594 for *Gesta Grayorum:*
Poetical Rhapsody, 1602

422

Laura

ROSE-CHEEKED Laura, come;
Sing thou smoothly with thy beauty's
Silent music, either other
Sweetly gracing.

Lovely forms do flow
From concent divinely framed;
Heaven is music, and thy beauty's
Birth is heavenly.

These dull notes we sing
Discords need for helps to grace them;
Only beauty purely loving
Knows no discord;

But still moves delight,
Like clear springs renewed by flowing,
Ever perfect, ever in them-
selves eternal.

Observations in the Art of English Poesy, 1602

423

Roses

NOW hath Flora robbed her bowers
To befriend this place with flowers.
Strew about, strew about!
The sky rained never kindlier showers.
Flowers with bridals well agree,
Fresh as brides and bridegrooms be.
Strew about, strew about!

And mix them with fit melody.
Earth hath no princelier flowers
Than roses white and roses red,
But they must still be mingled;
And as a rose new plucked from Venus' thorn,
So doth a bride her bridegroom's bed adorn.

Divers divers flowers affect
For some private dear respect.
    Strew about, strew about!
Let every one his own protect;
But he 's none of Flora's friend,
That will not the rose commend.
    Strew about, strew about!
Let princes princely flowers defend.
Roses, the garden's pride,
Are flowers for love and flowers for kings,
In courts desired and weddings;
And as a rose in Venus' bosom worn,
So doth a bridegroom his bride's bed adorn.

Lord Hay's Mask, 1607

424 *The Stars Dance*

ADVANCE your choral motions now,
  You music-loving lights.
This night concludes the nuptial vow,
  Make this the best of nights;
So bravely crown it with your beams,
  That it may live in fame,
As long as Rhenus or the Thames
  Are known by either name.

Once more again, yet nearer move
  Your forms at willing view;
Such fair effects of joy and love
  None can express but you.
Then revel midst your airy bowers,
  Till all the clouds do sweat,
That pleasure may be poured in showers
  On this triumphant seat.

Long since hath lovely Flora thrown
  Her flowers and garlands here;
Rich Ceres all her wealth hath shown,
  Proud of her dainty cheer.
Changed then to human shape, descend,
  Clad in familiar weed,
That every eye may here commend
  The kind delights you breed.

The Lords' Mask, 1613

425 *Dismissal*

THE hours of sleepy night decay apace,
  And now warm beds are fitter than this place.
All time is long that is unwilling spent,
But hours are minutes when they yield content.
The gathered flowers we love that breathe sweet scent,
But leave them, their sweet odour being spent.
    It is a life is never ill,
    To lie and sleep in roses still.

The rarer pleasure is, it is more sweet,
And friends are kindest when they seldom meet.
Who would not hear the nightingale still sing,
Or who grew ever weary of the spring?
The day must have her night, the spring her fall;
All is divided, none is lord of all.
    It were a most delightful thing
    To live in a perpetual spring.

The Mountebank's Mask, 1618; *Ashmolean MS*. 36–37

426 *Songs from Lute Books*

(*i*)

MY sweetest Lesbia, let us live and love;
  And, though the sager sort our deeds reprove,
Let us not weigh them. Heaven's great lamps do dive
Into their west, and straight again revive.
But soon as once set is our little light,
Then must we sleep one ever-during night.

If all would lead their lives in love like me,
Then bloody swords and armour should not be;
No drum nor trumpet peaceful sleeps should move,
Unless alarm came from the camp of Love.
But fools do live and waste their little light,
And seek with pain their ever-during night.

When timely death my life and fortune ends,
Let not my hearse be vexed with mourning friends
But let all lovers, rich in triumph, come
And with sweet pastimes grace my happy tomb.
And, Lesbia, close up thou my little light,
And crown with love my ever-during night.

(ii)

THOUGH you are young and I am old,
Though your veins hot and my blood cold,
Though youth is moist and age is dry,
Yet embers live when flames do die.

The tender graft is easily broke,
But who shall shake the sturdy oak?
You are more fresh and fair than I,
Yet stubs do live when flowers do die.

Thou, that thy youth dost vainly boast,
Know, buds are soonest nipped with frost.
Think that thy fortune still doth cry:
'Thou fool, to-morrow thou must die.'

(iii)

I CARE not for these ladies that must be wooed and prayed:
Give me kind Amaryllis, the wanton country maid.
Nature Art disdaineth; her beauty is her own.
Her when we court and kiss, she cries: 'Forsooth, let go!'
But when we come where comfort is, she never will say no.

If I love Amaryllis, she gives me fruit and flowers;
But if we love these ladies, we must give golden showers.
Give them gold that sell love, give me the nut-brown lass,
Who when we court and kiss, she cries: 'Forsooth, let go!'
But when we come where comfort is, she never will say no.

These ladies must have pillows and beds by strangers wrought.
Give me a bower of willows, of moss and leaves unbought,
And fresh Amaryllis with milk and honey fed,
Who when we court and kiss, she cries: 'Forsooth, let go!'
But when we come where comfort is, she never will say no.

(iv)

FOLLOW thy fair sun, unhappy shadow.
Though thou be black as night,
And she made all of light,
Yet follow thy fair sun, unhappy shadow.

Follow her whose light thy light depriveth.
Though here thou livest disgraced,
And she in heaven is placed,
Yet follow her whose light the world reviveth.

Follow those pure beams whose beauty burneth,
That so have scorched thee,
As thou still black must be,
Till her kind beams thy black to brightness turneth.

Follow her, while yet her glory shineth.
There comes a luckless night,
That will dim all her light;
And this the black unhappy shade divineth.

Follow still, since so thy fates ordained.
The sun must have his shade,
Till both at once do fade,
The sun still proved, the shadow still disdained.

(*v*)

WHEN to her lute Corinna sings,
Her voice revives the leaden strings,
And doth in highest notes appear,
As any challenged echo clear.
But when she doth of mourning speak,
E'en with her sighs the strings do break.

And as her lute doth live or die,
Led by her passion, so must I.
For when of pleasure she doth sing,
My thoughts enjoy a sudden spring;
But if she doth of sorrow speak,
E'en from my heart the strings do break.

(*vi*)

FOLLOW your saint, follow with accents sweet;
Haste you, sad notes, fall at her flying feet.
There, wrapped in cloud of sorrow, pity move,
And tell the ravisher of my soul I perish for her love.
But if she scorns my never-ceasing pain,
Then burst with sighing in her sight, and ne'er return again.

All that I sung still to her praise did tend.
Still she was first, still she my songs did end.
Yet she my love and music both doth fly,
The music that her echo is, and beauty's sympathy.
Then let my notes pursue her scornful flight;
It shall suffice that they were breathed, and died for her delight.

(*vii*)

THOU art not fair, for all thy red and white,
   For all those rosy ornaments in thee.
Thou art not sweet, though made of mere delight,
   Nor fair nor sweet, unless thou pity me.
I will not soothe thy fancies. Thou shalt prove
That beauty is no beauty without love.

Yet love not me, nor seek thou to allure
   My thoughts with beauty, were it more divine
Thy smiles and kisses I cannot endure,
   I'll not be wrapped up in those arms of thine.
Now show it, if thou be a woman right,
Embrace and kiss and love me in despite.

(*viii*)

THE man of life upright,
   Whose guiltless heart is free
From all dishonest deeds
   Or thought of vanity:

The man whose silent days
   In harmless joys are spent,
Whom hopes cannot delude,
   Nor sorrow discontent:

That man needs neither towers
   Nor armour for defence,
Nor secret vaults to fly
   From thunder's violence.

He only can behold
   With unaffrighted eyes
The horrors of the deep
   And terrors of the skies.

Thus scorning all the cares
   That fate or fortune brings,
He makes the heaven his book,
   His wisdom heavenly things,

Good thoughts his only friends,
   His wealth a well-spent age,
The earth his sober inn
   And quiet pilgrimage.

(*ix*)

WHEN thou must home to shades of underground,
   And there arrived, a new admired guest,
The beauteous spirits do engirt thee round,
   White Iope, blithe Helen and the rest,
To hear the stories of thy finished love
From that smooth tongue, whose music hell can move:

Then wilt thou speak of banqueting delights,
   Of masks and revels which sweet youth did make,
Of tourneys and great challenges of knights,
   And all these triumphs for thy beauty's sake.
When thou hast told these honours done to thee,
Then tell, O! tell, how thou didst murder me.

(*x*)

WHERE are all thy beauties now, all hearts enchaining?
Whither are thy flatterers gone with all their feigning?
All fled; and thou alone still here remaining.

Thy rich state of twisted gold to bays is turned.
Cold as thou art are thy loves that so much burned.
Who die in flatterers' arms are seldom mourned.

Yet in spite of envy this be still proclaimed,
That none worthier than thyself thy worth hath blamed;
When their poor names are lost, thou shalt live famed.

When thy story long time hence shall be perused,
Let the blemish of thy rule be thus excused:
'None ever lived more just, none more abused.'

(*xi*)

NEVER weather-beaten sail more willing bent to shore,
Never tired pilgrim's limbs affected slumber more,
Than my weary spright now longs to fly out of my troubled breast.
O! come quickly, sweetest Lord, and take my soul to rest.

Ever blooming are the joys of Heaven's high Paradise.
Cold age deafs not there our ears, nor vapour dims our eyes;
Glory there the sun outshines, whose beams the blessed only see.
O! come quickly, glorious Lord, and raise my spright to thee.

(xii)

JACK and Joan they think no ill,
But loving live, and merry still;
Do their week-days' work, and pray
Devoutly on the holy day;
Skip and trip it on the green,
And help to choose the Summer Queen;
Lash out at a country feast
Their silver penny with the best.

Well can they judge of nappy ale,
And tell at large a winter tale;
Climb up to the apple loft,
And turn the crabs till they be soft.
Tib is all the father's joy,
And little Tom the mother's boy.
All their pleasure is content,
And care to pay their yearly rent.

Joan can call by name her cows,
And deck her windows with green boughs;
She can wreaths and tutties make,
And trim with plums a bridal cake.
Jack knows what brings gain or loss,
And his long flail can stoutly toss;
Make the hedge which others break,
And ever thinks what he doth speak.

Now you courtly dames and knights,
That study only strange delights,
Though you scorn the home-spun gray
And revel in your rich array;

Though your tongues dissemble deep
And can your heads from danger keep:
Yet for all your pomp and train,
Securer lives the silly swain.

(xiii)

GIVE beauty all her right;
She 's not to one form tied.
Each shape yields fair delight,
Where her perfections bide.
Helen I grant might pleasing be,
And Rosamond was as sweet as she.

Some the quick eye commends,
Some swelling lips and red;
Pale looks have many friends,
Through sacred sweetness bred.
Meadows have flowers that pleasure move,
Though roses are the flowers of love.

Free beauty is not bound
To one unmoved clime.
She visits every ground,
And favours every time.
Let the old loves with mine compare,
My sovereign is as sweet and fair.

(xiv)

THERE is none, O! none but you,
That from me estrange your sight,
Whom mine eyes affect to view,
Or chained ears hear with delight.

Other beauties others move,
  In you I all graces find.
Such is the effect of love
  To make them happy that are kind.

Women in frail beauty trust.
  Only seem you fair to me;
Yet prove truly kind and just,
  For that may not dissembled be.

Sweet, afford me then your sight;
  That, surveying all your looks,
Endless volumes I may write,
  And fill the world with envied books.

Which when after ages view,
  All shall wonder and despair;
Woman to find man so true,
  Or man a woman half so fair.

(*xv*)

COME, you pretty false-eyed wanton,
  Leave your crafty smiling.
Think you to escape me now
  With slippery words beguiling?
No, you mocked me th' other day,
When you got loose, you fled away.
But since I have caught you now,
  I'll clip your wings for flying;
Smothering kisses fast I'll heap,
  And keep you so from crying.

Sooner may you count the stars,
  And number hail down-pouring,
Tell the osiers of the Thames,
  Or Goodwin Sands devouring,
Than the thick-showered kisses here,
Which now thy tired lips must bear.
Such a harvest never was,
  So rich and full of pleasure;
But 'tis spent as soon as reaped,
  So trustless is love's treasure.

Would it were dumb midnight now,
  When all the world lies sleeping.
Would this place some desert were,
  Which no man hath in keeping.
My desires should then be safe,
And when you cried, then would I laugh.
But if aught might breed offence,
  Love only should be blamed.
I would live your servant still,
  And you my saint unnamed.

(*xvi*)

KIND are her answers,
  But her performance keeps no day;
    Breaks time, as dancers
From their own music when they stray.
    All her free favours
And smooth words wing my hopes in vain.
O! did ever voice so sweet but only feign?
Can true love yield such delay,
    Converting joy to pain?

Lost is our freedom
When we submit to women so.
Why do we need them
When in their best they work our woe?
There is no wisdom
Can alter ends by Fate prefixed.
O! why is the good of man with evil mixed?
Never were days yet called two,
But one night went betwixt.

(*xvii*)

NOW winter nights enlarge
The number of their hours,
And clouds their storms discharge
Upon the airy towers.
Let now the chimneys blaze,
And cups o'erflow with wine;
Let well-tuned words amaze
With harmony divine.
Now yellow waxen lights
Shall wait on honey Love,
While youthful revels, masks, and courtly sights
Sleep's leaden spells remove.

This time doth well dispense
With lovers' long discourse.
Much speech hath some defence
Though beauty no remorse.
All do not all things well:
Some measures comely tread,
Some knotted riddles tell,
Some poems smoothly read.

The Summer hath his joys,
And Winter his delights.
Though Love and all his pleasures are but toys,
They shorten tedious nights.

(*xviii*)

SHALL I come, sweet Love, to thee,
When the evening beams are set?
Shall I not excluded be?
Will you find no feigned let?
Let me not, for pity, more
Tell the long hours at your door.

Who can tell what thief or foe
In the covert of the night
For his prey will work my woe,
Or through wicked foul despite?
So may I die unredressed,
Ere my long love be possessed.

But to let such dangers pass,
Which a lover's thoughts disdain,
'Tis enough in such a place
To attend love's joys in vain.
Do not mock me in thy bed,
While these cold nights freeze me dead.

(*xix*)

THRICE toss these oaken ashes in the air;
Thrice sit thou mute in this enchanted chair;
Then thrice three times tie up this true love's knot,
And murmur soft: 'She will, or she will not.'

Go burn these poisonous weeds in yon blue fire,
These screech-owl's feathers and this prickling briar,
This cypress gathered at a dead man's grave,
That all thy fears and cares an end may have.

Then come, you fairies, dance with me a round;
Melt her hard heart with your melodious sound.
In vain are all the charms I can devise;
She hath an art to break them with her eyes.

(*xx*)

COME, O! come, my life's delight,
   Let me not in languor pine.
Love loves no delay; thy sight
   The more enjoyed the more divine.
O! come, and take from me
The pain of being deprived of thee.

Thou all sweetness dost enclose,
   Like a little world of bliss.
Beauty guards thy looks. The rose
   In them pure and eternal is.
Come then and make thy flight
As swift to me as heavenly light.

(*xxi*)

THERE is a garden in her face,
   Where roses and white lilies grow;
A heavenly paradise is that place,
   Wherein all pleasant fruits do flow.
There cherries grow which none may buy,
Till 'Cherry-ripe' themselves do cry.

Those cherries fairly do enclose
  Of orient pearl a double row,
Which when her lovely laughter shows,
  They look like rosebuds filled with snow.
Yet them nor peer nor prince can buy,
Till 'Cherry-ripe' themselves do cry.

Her eyes like angels watch them still;
  Her brows like bended bows do stand,
Threatening with piercing frowns to kill
  All that attempt with eye or hand
Those sacred cherries to come nigh,
Till 'Cherry-ripe' themselves do cry.

A Book of Airs, 1601; *Two Books of Airs*, n.d.; *Third Book of Airs*, n.d.; *Fourth Book of Airs*, n.d.

ANONYMOUS

427 *Songs set by Philip Rosseter*

(*i*)

AND would you see my mistress' face?
  It is a flowery garden place,
Where knots of beauties have such grace
That all is work and nowhere space.

It is a sweet delicious morn,
Where day is breeding, never born;
It is a meadow yet unshorn
Which thousand flowers do adorn.

It is the heaven's bright reflex,
Weak eyes to dazzle and to vex;
It is th' Idea of her sex,
Envy of whom doth world perplex.

It is a face of death that smiles,
Pleasing though it kills the whiles,
Where death and love in pretty wiles
Each other mutually beguiles.

It is fair beauty's freshest youth,
It is the feigned Elysium's truth,
The spring that wintered hearts reneweth;
And this is that my soul pursueth.

(ii)

WHAT is a day, what is a year of vain delight and pleasure?
Like to a dream it endless dies,
And from us like a vapour flies;
And this is all the fruit that we find, which glory in worldly treasure.

He that will hope for true delight, with virtue must be graced.
Sweet folly yields a bitter taste
Which ever will appear at last;
But if we still in virtue delight, our souls are in heaven placed.

(*iii*)

WHETHER men do laugh or weep,
Whether they do wake or sleep,
Whether they die young or old,
Whether they feel heat or cold;
There is underneath the sun
Nothing in true earnest done.

All our pride is but a jest;
None are worst and none are best.
Grief and joy and hope and fear
Play their pageants everywhere;
Vain opinion all doth sway,
And the world is but a play.

Powers above in clouds do sit
Mocking our poor apish wit,
That so lamely with such state
Their high glory imitate.
No ill can be felt but pain,
And that happy men disdain.

A Book of Airs, 1601

428 *Song set by Nicholas Yonge*

BROWN is my Love, but graceful;
And each renowned whiteness
Matched with thy lovely brown loseth its brightness.

Fair is my Love, but scornful;
Yet have I seen despised
Dainty white lilies, and sad flowers well prized.

Musica Transalpina, 1597

429 *Song set by Michael Cavendish*

FAUSTINA hath the fairer face,
And Phillida the feater grace;
Both have mine eye enriched.
This sings full sweetly with her voice,
Her fingers make as sweet a noise;
Both have mine ear bewitched.
Ay me! sith Fates have so provided,
My heart, alas! must be divided.

Airs and Madrigals, 1598

430 *Songs set by Thomas Weelkes*

(*i*)

IN pride of May
The fields are gay,
The birds do sweetly sing.
So Nature would
That all things should
With joy begin the Spring.

Then, Lady dear,
Do you appear
In beauty like the Spring.
I well dare say
The birds that day
More cheerfully will sing.

(ii)

NOW is my Chloris fresh as May,
All clad in green and flowers gay.
O! might I think August were near,
That harvest joy might soon appear!
But she keeps May throughout the year,
And August never comes the near.
Yet I will hope, though she be May,
August will come another day.

(iii)

LIKE two proud armies marching in the field,
Joining a thundering fight, each scorns to yield;
So in my heart your Beauty and my Reason,
The one claims the crown, the other says 'tis treason.
But O! your Beauty shineth as the sun,
And dazzled Reason yields as quite undone.

(iv)

THREE times a day my prayer is,
To gaze my fill on Thoralis.
And three times thrice I daily pray
Not to offend that sacred may.
But all the year my suit must be
That I may please, and she love me.

Ballets and Madrigals, 1598; *Madrigals*, 1600

431 *Song set by John Farmer*

TAKE Time while Time doth last,
Mark how Fair fadeth fast,
Beware if Envy reign,
Take heed of proud Disdain.
Hold fast now in thy youth,
Regard thy vowed Truth,
Lest when thou waxeth old
Friends fail and Love grow cold.

Madrigals, 1599

432 *Song set by John Bennet*

THYRSIS, sleepest thou? Holla! Let not sorrow stay us.
Hold up thy head, man, said the gentle Meliboeus.
See Summer comes again, the country's pride adorning,
Hark how the cuckoo singeth this fair April morning.
O! said the shepherd, and sighed as one all undone,
Let me alone, alas, and drive him back to London.

Madrigals, 1599

433 *Songs set by John Dowland*

(i)

DEAR, if you change, I'll never choose again;
Sweet, if you shrink, I'll never think of love;
Fair, if you fail, I'll judge all beauty vain;
Wise, if too weak, mo wits I'll never prove.
Dear, Sweet, Fair, Wise, change, shrink, nor be not weak;
And, on my faith, my faith shall never break.

Earth with her flowers shall sooner heaven adorn;
  Heaven her bright stars through earth's dim globe shall move;
Fire heat shall lose, and frosts of flames be born;
  Air, made to shine, as black as hell shall prove.
Earth, Heaven, Fire, Air, the world transformed shall view,
Ere I prove false to faith, or strange to you.

(ii)

COME away, come, sweet Love! The golden morning breaks;
All the earth, all the air, of love and pleasure speaks.
  Teach thine arms then to embrace,
        And sweet
        Rosy
      Lips to kiss,
  And mix our souls in mutual bliss.
  Eyes were made for beauty's grace,
        Viewing,
        Rueing
      Love's long pain,
  Procured by beauty's rude disdain.

Come away, come, sweet Love! The golden morning wastes,
While the sun from his sphere his fiery arrows casts,
  Making all the shadows fly,
        Playing,
        Staying
      In the grove,
  To entertain the stealth of love.
  Thither, sweet Love, let us hie,
        Flying,
        Dying
      In desire,
  Winged with sweet hopes and heavenly fire.

Come away, come, sweet Love! Do not in vain adorn
Beauty's grace, that should rise like to the naked morn.
  Lilies on the riverside
          And fair
          Cyprian
        Flowers new-blown
  Desire no beauties but their own.
  Ornament is nurse of pride;
          Pleasure,
          Measure,
        Love's delight.
  Haste then, sweet Love, our wished flight.

(iii)

I SAW my lady weep,
  And Sorrow proud to be advanced so
In those fair eyes where all perfections keep.
  Her face was full of woe;
But such a woe, believe me, as wins more hearts,
Than Mirth can do with her enticing parts.

  Sorrow was there made fair,
  And Passion wise, tears a delightful thing;
Silence beyond all speech a wisdom rare.
  She made her sighs to sing,
And all things with so sweet a sadness move,
As made my heart at once both grieve and love.

  O fairer than aught else
The world can show, leave off in time to grieve.
Enough, enough your joyful looks excels;
  Tears kills the heart, believe.
  O! strive not to be excellent in woe,
Which only breeds your beauty's overthrow.

(*iv*)

FINE knacks for ladies, cheap, choice, brave and new!
  Good pennyworths! but money cannot move.
I keep a fair but for the Fair to view;
  A beggar may be liberal of love.
Though all my wares be trash, the heart is true.

Great gifts are guiles and look for gifts again;
  My trifles come as treasures from my mind.
It is a precious jewel to be plain;
  Sometimes in shell the orient'st pearls we find.
  Of others take a sheaf, of me a grain.

Within this pack pins, points, laces, and gloves,
  And divers toys fitting a country fair,
But in my heart, where duty serves and loves,
  Turtles and twins, court's brood, a heavenly pair.
Happy the heart that thinks of no removes!

(*v*)

COME, ye heavy states of night,
  Do my father's spirit right.
Soundings baleful let me borrow,
Burdening my song with sorrow.
Come, sorrow, come, her eyes that sings
By thee are turned into springs.

Come, you virgins of the night,
That in dirges sad delight,
Choir my anthems. I do borrow
Gold nor pearl, but sounds of sorrow.
Come, sorrow, come, her eyes that sings
By thee are turned into springs.

(*vi*)

CLEAR or cloudy, sweet as April showering,
  Smooth or frowning, so is her face to me,
Pleased or smiling, like mild May all flowering,
  When skies blue silk, and meadows carpets be;
Her speeches, notes of that night bird that singeth,
Who, thought all sweet, yet jarring notes out-ringeth.

Her grace like June, when earth and trees be trimmed
  In best attire of complete beauty's height;
Her love again like summer's days be-dimmed
  With little clouds of doubtful constant faith;
Her trust, her doubt, like rain and heat in skies
Gently thundering, she lightning to mine eyes.

Sweet summer-spring that breatheth life and growing
  In weeds as well as into herbs and flowers,
And seeds of service, divers sorts in sowing,
  Some haply seeming, and some being, yours;
Rain on your herbs and flowers that truly serve,
And let your weeds lack dew, and duly starve.

(*vii*)

BEHOLD a wonder here,
  Love hath received his sight,
Which many hundred year
  Hath not beheld the light.

Such beams infused be
  By Cynthia in his eyes,
As first have made him see
  And then have made him wise.

Love now no more will weep
   For them that laugh the while;
Nor wake for them that sleep,
   Nor sigh for them that smile.

So powerful is the beauty
   That Love doth now behold,
As Love is turned to duty
   That 's neither blind nor bold.

This Beauty shows her might
   To be of double kind,
In giving Love his sight
   And striking Folly blind.

(*viii*)

WEEP you no more, sad fountains;
   What need you flow so fast?
Look how the snowy mountains
   Heaven's sun doth gently waste.
      But my sun's heavenly eyes
         View not your weeping,
         That now lies sleeping
      Softly, now softly lies
            Sleeping.

Sleep is a reconciling,
   A rest that peace begets.
Doth not the sun rise smiling
   When fair at even he sets?

Rest you then, rest, sad eyes,
Melt not in weeping,
While she lies sleeping
Softly, now softly lies
Sleeping.

(*ix*)

WHAT poor astronomers are they
Take women's eyes for stars,
And set their thoughts in battle 'ray
To fight such idle wars;
When in the end they shall approve
'Tis but a jest drawn out of love.

And love itself is but a jest
Devised by idle heads,
To catch young fancies in the nest
And lay them in fools' beds;
That being hatched in beauty's eyes
They may be flidge ere they be wise.

But yet it is a sport to see
How wit will run on wheels,
While will cannot persuaded be
With that which reason feels;
That women's eyes and stars are odd,
And Love is but a feigned god.

flidge] fledglings

But such as will run mad with will,
  I cannot clear their sight,
But leave them to their study still
  To look where is no light;
Till time too late we make them try
They study false astronomy.

First, Second and Third Books of Songs or Airs, 1597, 1600, 1603

434 *Songs set by Robert Jones*

(*i*)

A WOMAN'S looks
  Are barbed hooks,
That catch by art
The strongest heart,
When yet they spend no breath.
  But let them speak,
  And sighing break
  Forth into tears,
  Their words are spears
That wound our souls to death.

  The rarest wit
  Is made forget,
  And like a child
  Is oft beguiled
With Love's sweet-seeming bait.
  Love with his rod
  So like a god
  Commands the mind
  We cannot find,
Fair shows hide foul deceit.

Time, that all things
In order brings,
Hath taught me now
To be more slow
In giving faith to speech:
Since women's words
No truth affords,
And when they kiss
They think by this
Us men to overreach.

(*ii*)

SHE whose matchless beauty staineth
What best judgement fair'st maintaineth,
She, O she, my love disdaineth.

Can a creature so excelling
Harbour scorn in beauty's dwelling,
All kind pity thence expelling?

Pity beauty much commendeth,
And the embracer oft befriendeth,
When all eye-contentment endeth.

Time proves beauty transitory.
Scorn, the stain of beauty's glory,
In time makes the scorner sorry.

None adores the sun declining,
Love all love falls to resigning,
When the sun of love leaves shining

So when flower of beauty fails thee,
And age stealing on assails thee,
Then mark what this scorn avails thee.

Then those hearts, which now complaining
Feel the wounds of thy disdaining,
Shall contemn thy beauty waning.

Yea, thine own heart, now dear-prized,
Shall, with spite and grief surprised,
Burst to find itself despised.

When like harms have them requited,
Who in others' harms delighted,
Pleasingly the wronged are righted.

Such revenge my wrongs attending,
Hope still lives on time depending,
By thy plagues my torments ending.

(iii)

ONCE did I love, and yet I live
  Though love and truth be now forgotten.
Then did I joy, now do I grieve
  That holy vows must needs be broken.

Hers be the blame that caused it so;
  Mine be the grief though it be mickle.
She shall have shame; I cause to know
  What 'tis to love a dame so fickle.

Love her that list! I am content,
  For that chameleon-like she changeth,
Yielding such mists as may prevent
  My sight to view her when she rangeth.

Let him not vaunt that gains my loss,
  For when that he and time hath proved her,
She may him bring to weeping cross.
  I say no more, because I loved her.

(*iv*)

FAREWELL, dear Love, since thou wilt needs be gone.
Mine eyes do show my life is almost done.
    Nay, I will never die,
    So long as I can spy.
    There be many mo,
    Though that she do go.
  There be many mo, I fear not.
  Why then, let her go, I care not.

Farewell, farewell, since this I find is true,
I will not spend more time in wooing you.
    But I will seek elsewhere
    If I may find her there.
    Shall I bid her go?
    What and if I do?
  Shall I bid her go, and spare not?
  O! no, no, no, no, I dare not.

Ten thousand times farewell! Yet stay awhile!
Sweet, kiss me once; sweet kisses time beguile.
I have no power to move.
How now, am I in love?
Wilt thou needs be gone?
Go then, all is one.
Wilt thou needs be gone? O hie thee!
Nay, stay, and do no more deny me.

Once more farewell! I see 'Loth to depart'
Bids oft adieu to her that holds my heart.
But seeing I must lose
Thy love which I did choose,
Go thy ways for me,
Since it may not be.
Go thy ways for me. But whither?
Go, O! but where I may come thither.

What shall I do? My Love is now departed.
She is as fair as she is cruel-hearted.
She would not be entreated
With prayers oft repeated.
If she come no more
Shall I die therefore?
If she come no more, what care I?
Faith! let her go, or come, or tarry.

(*v*)

LIFE is a poet's fable,
And all her days are lies
Stolen from Death's reckoning table;
For I die, for I die; as I speak,
Death times the notes that I do break.

Childhood doth die in youth,
And youth in old age dies.
I thought I lived in truth,
But I die, but I die, now I see,
Each age of Death makes one degree.

Farewell the doting score
Of world's arithmetic.
Life, I'll trust thee no more;
Till I die, till I die, for thy sake
I'll go by Death's new almanac.

This instant of my song
A thousand men lie sick,
A thousand knells are rung;
And I die, and I die as they sing;
They are but dead and I dying.

Death is but Life's decay,
Lifetime Time wastes away.
Then reason bids me say
That I die, that I die, though my breath
Prolongs this space of lingering death.

(vi)

LOVE winged my hopes and taught me how to fly
Far from base earth, but not to mount too high.
For true pleasure
Lives in measure,
Which, if men forsake,
Blinded they into folly run, and grief for pleasure take.

But my vain hopes, proud of their new-taught flight,
Enamoured, sought to woo the sun's fair light,
Whose rich brightness
Moved their lightness
To aspire so high,
That, all scorched and consumed with fire, now drowned in woe they lie.

And none but Love their woeful hap did rue;
For Love did know that their desires were true.
Though Fate frowned,
And now drowned
They in sorrow dwell,
It was the purest light of heaven for whose fair love they fell.

(vii)

O! HOW my thoughts do beat me,
Which by deep sighs entreat thee.
Hey ho, fie, what a thing is this,
Thus to lie still when we might kiss,
And play and fool
Here in the cool
Of the stillest, clearest, sweetest evening
Philomel did ever choose for singing.

See how my lips complain them;
Thy lips should just detain them.
Ay me! hark how the nightingales
In the dark each to other calls;
Whilst thou, O! thou
Darest not avow
The enjoying of the truest pleasure
Love did ever hoard up in his treasure.

(*viii*)

MY Love is neither young nor old,
Not fiery hot, nor frozen cold;
But fresh and fair as springing briar,
Blooming the fruit of love's desire.

Not snowy white nor rosy red,
But fair enough for shepherd's bed;
And such a Love was never seen
On hill or dale or country green.

(*ix*)

DO not, O do not prize thy beauty at too high a rate;
Love to be loved whilst thou art lovely, lest thou love too late.
Frowns print wrinkles in thy brows,
At which spiteful age doth smile,
Women in their froward vows
Glorying to beguile.

Wert thou the only world's-admired, thou canst love but one;
And many have before been loved, thou art not loved alone.
Couldst thou speak with heavenly grace,
Sappho might with thee compare;
Blush the roses in thy face,
Rosamund was as fair.

Pride is the canker that consumeth beauty in her prime.
They that delight in long debating feel the curse of time.
All things with the time do change,
That will not the time obey.
Some e'en to themselves seem strange
Thorough their own delay.

(*x*)

IN Sherwood lived stout Robin Hood,
An archer great, none greater;
His bow and shafts were sure and good,
Yet Cupid's were much better.
Robin could shoot at many a hart and miss,
Cupid at first could hit a heart of his.
Hey! jolly Robin,
Ho! jolly Robin,
Hey! jolly Robin Hood.
Love finds out me,
As well as thee,
To follow me to the green wood.

A noble thief was Robin Hood,
Wise was he could deceive him;
Yet Marian in his bravest mood
Could of his heart bereave him.
No greater thief lies hidden under skies,
Than Beauty closely lodged in women's eyes.
Hey! jolly Robin, &c.

An outlaw was this Robin Hood,
His life free and unruly;
Yet to fair Marian bound he stood,
And love's debt paid her duly.
Whom curb of strictest law could not hold in,
Love with obeyedness and a wink could win.
Hey! jolly Robin, &c.

Now wend we home, stout Robin Hood,
  Leave we the woods behind us;
Love-passions must not be withstood,
  Love everywhere will find us.
I lived in field and town, and so did he;
I got me to the woods; Love followed me.
    Hey! jolly Robin, &c.

(*xi*)

THE sea hath many thousand sands,
  The sun hath motes as many,
The sky is full of stars, and love
  As full of woes as any.
Believe me, that do know the elf,
And make no trial by thyself.

It is in truth a pretty toy
  For babes to play withal.
But O! the honeys of our youth
  Are oft our age's gall.
Self-proof in time will make thee know
He was a prophet told thee so.

A prophet that Cassandra-like
  Tells truth without belief,
For headstrong youth will run his race
  Although his goal be grief.
Love's martyr, when his heat is past,
Proves Care's confessor at the last.

First and Second Books of Songs and Airs, 1600, 1601; *Ultimum Vale*, 1608; *A Musical Dream*, 1609; *Muses' Garden for Delights*, 1610

435

Song set by John Daniel

LET not Chloris think, because
  She hath envassalled me,
That her beauty can give laws
  To others that are free.
I was made to be the prey
  And booty of her eyes;
In my bosom, she may say,
  Her greatest kingdom lies.

Though others may her brow adore,
Yet more must I, that therein see far more,
Than any other's eyes have power to see;
She is to me
More than to any others she can be.
I can discern more secret notes,
That in the margin of her cheeks Love quotes,
Than any else besides have art to read;
No looks proceed
From those fair eyes but to me wonder breed.

O! then why
Should she fly
From him to whom her sight
Doth add so much above her might?
Why should not she
Still joy to reign in me?

Songs for the Lute, Viol and Voice, 1606

436 *Song set by Richard Carlton*

E'EN as the flowers do wither
That maidens fair do gather,
So doth their beauty blazing,
Whereon there is such gazing.

As day is dimmed with the night,
So age doth vade the red and white,
And death consumes e'en in an hour
The virgin's weed, that dainty flower.

And unto them it may be told,
Who clothe most rich in silk and gold,
Ye dames, for all your pride and mirth,
Your beauty shall be turned to earth.

Madrigals, 1601

437 *Songs set by Thomas Ford*

(*i*)

UNTO the temple of thy Beauty,
And to the tomb where Pity lies,
I, pilgrim-clad with zeal and duty,
Do offer up my heart, mine eyes.
My heart, lo! in the quenchless fire
On Love's burning altar lies,
Conducted thither by Desire
To be Beauty's sacrifice.

But Pity, on thy sable hearse
   Mine eyes the tears of sorrow shed;
What though tears cannot fate reverse,
   Yet are they duties to the dead.
O mistress, in thy sanctuary
   Why wouldst thou suffer cold Disdain
To use his frozen cruelty,
   And gentle Pity to be slain.

Pity that to thy Beauty fled,
   And with thy Beauty should have lived,
Ah! in thy heart lies buried,
   And never more may be revived.
Yet this last favour, dear, extend,
   To accept these vows, these tears I shed,
Duties which I thy pilgrim send
   To Beauty living, Pity dead.

(ii)

SINCE first I saw your face, I resolved to honour and renown ye;
If now I be disdained, I wish my heart had never known ye.
What? I that loved and you that liked, shall we begin to wrangle?
No, no, no, my heart is fast, and cannot disentangle.

If I admire or praise you too much, that fault you may forgive me,
Or if my hands had strayed but a touch, then justly might you leave me.
I asked you leave, you bade me love; is 't now a time to chide me?
No, no, no, I'll love you still, what fortune e'er betide me.

The sun, whose beams most glorious are, rejecteth no beholder,
And your sweet beauty past compare made my poor eyes the
bolder.
Where beauty moves, and wit delights, and signs of kindness
bind me,
There, O there! where'er I go, I'll leave my heart behind me.

Music of Sundry Kinds, 1607

438 *Song set by William Corkine*

SWEET Cupid, ripen her desire,
Thy joyful harvest may begin;
If age approach a little nigher,
'Twill be too late to get it in.

Cold winter storms lay standing corn,
Which once too ripe will never rise,
And lovers wish themselves unborn,
When all their joys lie in their eyes.

Then, sweet, let us embrace and kiss.
Shall beauty shale upon the ground?
If age bereave us of this bliss,
Then will no more such sport be found.

Airs, 1610

shale] drop as a husk

439

The Disdainful Shepherdess

O! WHAT a plague is love,
  How shall I bear it?
She will unconstant prove,
  I greatly fear it.
It so torments my mind,
  That my strength faileth.
She wavers with the wind,
  As the ship saileth.
Please her the best you may,
She looks another way.
Alas and well a day!
    Phillida flouts me.

At the fair yesterday,
  She did pass by me;
She looked another way,
  And would not spy me.
I woo'd her for to dine,
  I could not get her.
Dick had her to the wine,
  He might entreat her.
With Daniel she did dance,
On me she would not glance.
O thrice unhappy chance!
    Phillida flouts me.

Fair maid, be not so coy,
  Do not disdain me.
I am my mother's joy,
  Sweet, entertain me.

She'll give me when she dies,
  All things that 's fitting,
Her poultry and her bees
  And her geese sitting;
A pair of mallard's beds,
And barrel full of shreds;
And yet, for all these goods,
    Phillida flouts me.

Thou shalt eat curds and cream,
  All the year lasting;
And drink the crystal stream,
  Pleasant in tasting;
Whig and whey till thou burst
  And bramble berries,
Pie-lid and pasty-crust,
  Pears, plums, and cherries.
Thy raiment shall be thin,
Made of a wether's skin;
All is not worth a pin,
    Phillida flouts me.

Cupid hath shot his dart,
  And hath me wounded;
It pricked my tender heart,
  And ne'er rebounded.
I was a fool to scorn
  His bow and quiver;
I am like one forlorn,
  Sick of a fever.

whig] a drink made of whey

Now I may weep and mourn,
Whilst with Love's flames I burn;
Nothing will serve my turn;
Phillida flouts me.

I am a lively lad,
Howe'er she take me;
I am not half so bad,
As she would make me.
Whether she smile or frown,
She may deceive me.
Ne'er a girl in the town,
But fain would have me.
Since she doth from me fly,
Now I may sigh and die,
And never cease to cry
Phillida flouts me.

In the last month of May
I made her posies;
I heard her often say
That she loved roses.
Cowslips and gilliflowers
And the white lily,
I brought to deck the bowers
For my sweet Philly.
But she did all disdain,
And threw them back again;
Therefore it 's flat and plain
Phillida flouts me.

ANONYMOUS

Fair maiden, have a care,
And in time take me;
I can have those as fair,
If you forsake me.
For Doll the dairy-maid
Laughed at me lately,
And wanton Winifred
Favours me greatly.
One cast milk on my clothes,
T' other played with my nose;
What wanton toys are those?
Phillida flouts me.

I cannot work and sleep
All at a season;
Grief wounds my heart so deep,
Without all reason.
I fade and pine away,
With grief and sorrow;
I fall quite to decay
Like any shadow.
I shall be dead, I fear,
Within a thousand year;
All is for grief and care;
Phillida flouts me.

She hath a clout of mine
Wrought with good Coventry,
Which she keeps for a sign
Of my fidelity.

Coventry] cloth of Coventry blue

But in faith, if she frown,
  She shall not wear it;
I'll give it Doll my maid,
  And she shall tear it.
Since 't will no better be,
I'll bear it patiently;
Yet all the world may see
    Phillida flouts me.

Roxburghe Ballads, vi. 460

440 *The Green Willow*

THE poor soul sat sighing by a sycamore tree;
    Sing willow, willow, willow!
With his hand in his bosom, and his head upon his knee;
      O! willow, willow, willow, willow,
      O! willow, willow, willow, willow,
        Shall be my garland.
  Sing all a green willow, willow, willow, willow!
  Ay me, the green willow must be my garland.

He sight in his singing, and made a great moan,
I am dead to all pleasure, my true love she is gone.

The mute bird sat by him was made tame by his moans;
The true tears fell from him would have melted the stones.

Come all you forsaken, and mourn you with me;
Who speaks of a false love, mine 's falser than she.

Let Love no more boast her, in palace nor bower,
It buds, but it blasteth, ere it be a flower.

sight] sighed

Thou fair and more false, I die with thy wound;
Thou hast lost the truest lover that goes upon the ground.

Let nobody chide her, her scorns I approve;
She was born to be false, and I to die for love.

Take this for my farewell and latest adieu;
Write this on my tomb, that in love I was true.

Addl. MS., 15117

441 *A Testament*

I THAT whilom lived secure,
And spent my days in joy;
I that thought this life most sure,
And death was but a toy;
Ay me, poor soul!
Vain hope did me deceive,
For I this life must leave;
Go, cause the bell to toll!

Hie, good maid, lay down the bed,
And draw the curtains round;
Tell the world that I am dead,
And eke who gave the wound;
Ay me, poor soul!
Alas! for love I die;
Good gentle nephew, hie,
Go, cause the bell to toll!

I am young and I am fair,
And yet I am disdained;
I love him that doth not care
How sore my heart be pained;

ANONYMOUS

Ay me, poor soul!
To think on this disdain,
It cuts my heart in twain;
Go, cause the bell to toll!

Some for me do feel like pain,
And think no grief like theirs;
Thus, I see, Love rules and reigns,
And feeds with hopes and fears;
Ay me, poor soul!
But none more wronged than I;
Come, death, and let me die;
Go, cause the bell to toll!

Ere I die, this will I make,
Which will shall still abide.
God, I hope, will not forsake
My soul, for which he died;
Ay me, poor soul!
My body I bequeath
Unto the earth beneath;
For now the bell doth toll.

I bequeath my turtle dove
Unto the virgins all;
I bequeath to you my love,
Whose love to me is small;
Ay me, poor soul!
My heart, I think, will break,
I may no longer speak;
For now the bell doth toll.

ANONYMOUS

I bequeath to Vesta queen
  My chaste virginity;
I bequeath my gown of green
  To maids of high degree;
    Ay me, poor soul!
  And all my rings and pearls
  Unto the younger girls;
    For now the bell doth toll.

I bequeath my Golden Book
  Unto the Golden Fleece;
I bequeath my cripping hook
  Unto my little niece;
    Ay me, poor soul!
  And all my vellet bonnets,
  With all my songs and sonnets;
    For now the bell doth toll.

I bequeath unto the poor
  My prayers and my tears;
I bequeath the rich no more
  Than bounty, Nestor's years;
    Ay me, poor soul!
  My debtors and my foes
  I do forgive and loose;
    For now the bell doth toll.

Come to me, ye fair young maids,
  And bear these words in mind;
Youth decays and beauty fades,
  And true love is hard to find;

cripping] crimping   vellet] velvet

ANONYMOUS

Ay me, poor soul!
Though beauty make you trim,
Yet death will make you grim,
Even when the bell doth toll.

Now adieu ten thousand times,
False love, false world, and all;
Though not I, yet these my rhymes,
Fair maids, possess you shall,
And nothing else.
My life is not mine own,
My soul away is flown;
Go, ring out all the bells!

Harvard College MS.

NOTES

The *Additional, Egerton, Harleian*, and *Royal MSS*. cited in the references are in the British Museum; the *Ashmolean* and *Rawlinson Poetical MSS*. in the Bodleian. The following notes refer to poems by their numbers in this collection.

3. Elizabeth of York, wife of Henry VII, died on 11 February 1503. Some final stanzas of less interest are here omitted.

5, 6. The Latin scraps are from the Vulgate; those in *5* from the *Psalms* used in the *Officium Defunctorum*.

10–14. The ascriptions in the sources to Henry VIII and Cornish may possibly relate to the musical settings only, and not the words.

15. I cannot trace the Christian name of Heath. Chants by him are in *Mornyng and Evenyng Prayer and Communion* (John Day, 1565). He does not appear to have been of the Chapel Royal.

17. In line 24 I read 'ilka den' for the 'ylke aden' of the MS.

22. Additional verses, probably by William Forrest, in *Harleian MS*. 1703 tell us that Heywood wrote this on Princess Mary (*nat*. 18 February 1516) at the age of 18.

24. The hind has been thought to refer to Anne Boleyn, but the sonnet is partly adapted from Petrarch, *Sonetto* clvii.

38, 41, 43. These are not definitely ascribed to Wyatt in the MS., but his authorship can be accepted.

42. In stanza 7, line 6, 'Am left' is G. F. Nott's emendation for the 'Armeles' of the MS.

51. The authorship may be doubtful, as the only Sir Thomas Gravener or Grosvenor traceable seems to have been knighted some years after Wyatt's death.

52. Possibly one ought to read 'proffer' for 'pleasure' in tercet 11, line 2, to secure a rhyme.

53. The friend lamented was Henry Fitzroy, Duke of Richmond, son of Henry VIII.

64. This has been attributed to Anne Boleyn, and more commonly to her brother George, Viscount Rochford, but only by conjecture. It has also been identified with a 'Soulknill of M. Edwards' (cf. *81*) mentioned in an Epistle to Gascoigne's *Posies* (1575). But it is in several MSS., always anonymously.

67. A shorter version is found in the play of *Gammer Gurton's Needle* (1575) by 'Mr. S.' who is more likely to be William Stevenson than John Still, and he or John Bridges, for whom the play has also been claimed, may be the author.

70. Quoted in *Hamlet*, v. i. 69 sqq.

75. Ascribed to the Earl of Surrey in *England's Helicon* (1600), but perhaps only because Surrey's name is on Tottel's title-page.

77. A Robert Phelipps was a Gentleman of the Chapel under Edward VI, and a Philip van Wilder, lutenist, who died in 1554, seems to appear in court records as 'Philippe' or 'Mr. Phelips'.

78. An acrostic on Somerset, but this hardly justifies an ascription to him.

80. An autograph MS. at St. John's, Cambridge, described by M. Hearsey in *The Review of English Studies* for July 1932, may yield a better text.

91. I do not attach much importance to a theory that the author of this was not Gascoigne, but Sir Christopher Hatton.

94. A shorter version in *The Paradise of Dainty Devices* is ascribed to 'M.B.', probably the otherwise unknown Mr. Bewe, who appears elsewhere in that collection.

95, *96*. Thomas Proctor is known only as the editor of *The Gorgeous Gallery*. The initials T. P. are appended to *95*, and *96* appears with it in a group of poems headed 'Pretie pamphlets by T. Proctor'.

98. The tune of Green Sleeves is referred to in *Merry Wives*, II. i. 64; v. v. 22.

99. Percy's text is late and obviously corrupt. I have emended very freely with the help of his *Reliques* (ed. Wheatley, i. 195), a Scottish version in Allan Ramsay's *Tea-Table Miscellany* (ed. 1733) 114, Sir Arthur Quiller-Couch's reconstruction in *The Oxford Book of English Verse*, and the quotation in *Othello*,

II. iii. 92. There is another allusion to the poem in *Tempest*, IV. i. 221.

119. Ascribed to Dyer in *Rawlinson Poet. MS*. 148, f. 65; elsewhere anonymous.

120. Said to be from a MS. (now unknown) of *c*. 1600, and there ascribed to Dyer.

127. Ascribed in error to E. O. (Vere) in *Astrophel and Stella* (1591), where 'Myra' becomes 'Joan'.

136. The ascription to Greville is due to a conjecture of Charles Lamb, well supported, I think, by internal evidence.

137–44. These and other poems are ascribed to Anomos in *A Poetical Rhapsody*, and the editor, Francis Davison, tells us that Anomos was his dear friend, and that the poems were 'written (as appeareth by divers things to Sir Philip Sidney living, and of him dead) almost twenty years since, when Poetry was far from that perfection, to which it hath now attained'. Most of their first lines, with others, occur in a list of poems by 'A. W.' in Davison's hand (*Harleian MS*. 280, f. 102). 'A. W.' has been interpreted as 'Anonymous Writer'. An author has also been sought in Anthony Wingfield, Arthur Warren, and Andrew Willet. To these I can only add the possibility of Ambrose Willoughby.

146. The authorship of Tilney, who suffered for the Babington plot, must remain doubtful. It rests upon a rather hesitating ascription of *Locrine* to him by Sir George Buck in a manuscript note on a copy of the play.

154. The composers of song-books do not, for the most part—Campion is a notable exception—appear to have written their own verses, or to have troubled to record the authors. This looks to me rather like Dyer, to whom Dr. Fellowes ascribes it. But I know of no authority.

178. I have taken only part of the long *Psalm*.

180. Munday's authorship is not undisputed. The play is anonymous, but has variant epistles signed A. M. and M. A., and these verses also appear in *England's Helicon* as by 'Shep. [herd] Tonie'. The argument in favour of identifying Shepherd

Tonie with Munday is pretty strong. But the play has also been claimed for George Chapman and Stephen Gosson.

181. This is also a Shepherd Tonie poem.

182. The play was by Munday and Chettle (cf. *368*) jointly, and either might have written the poem.

187. The ascription to Watson is in *England's Helicon*.

189–98. These songs are not in the early quartos of the plays, the dates of which are given in the references. They were added in Edward Blount's collection of 1632. Much is to be said for the theory that they were written for Blount by Dekker, Middleton, and perhaps others in the seventeenth century. But the question is still sufficiently open to justify their appearance under Lyly's name here.

191. In line 10 I read 'I on' for the unintelligible 'you' of Blount and Lyly's editors.

204. This is printed as 'A Sonnet', at the end of Peele's *Polyhymnia*, which describes the tilt of 17 November 1590, in which Sir Henry Lee gave up his title of Champion at the Tilt, and is generally regarded as Peele's. But in W. Segar, *Honor Military and Civil* (1602), iii. 54, it is written in the first person, and in *Addl. MS*. 28635, f. 88v, it is ascribed, probably by Sir John Harington, to Lee himself. In *Addl. MS*. 33963, f. 109 and in John Dowland's *First Book of Airs* (1597) it is anonymous. A poem by Lee, in a very similar strain, is in *Rawlinson Poet. MS*. 148, f. 75v and Dowland's *Second Book* (1600), and another in Robert Dowland's *A Musicall Banquet* (1610).

211. This may not be Greene's. It is on the back of the title-page in the 1677 *Dorastus and Fawnia*, but not in the 1607, 1629, and 1632 editions, which still bear the earlier title, *Pandosto*, or in those of 1636 and 1648. Lines 1–4 form part of a song in Martin Peerson's *Private Music* (1620).

244–8. These are not certainly Breton's, since both *The Bower of Delights* and *The Arbor of Amorous Devices*, although issued as 'By N. B. Gent', contain also poems by other men, and confirming ascriptions to him of 245–7 in *England's Helicon* may not rest on independent authority.

265. Marlowe's editors have overlooked a sixteenth-century text, preserved with *Her Answer* (266), by Lilliat (cf. *416*) in *Rawlinson Poet. MS.* 148, f. 96v.

266–76, 278–80. The evidence, often slight or conflicting, as to Ralegh's authorship is set out in Miss A. M. C. Latham's edition of 1929. She remains doubtful as to *269* and *270*, ascriptions of which to him in *England's Helicon* (1600) were removed by cancel-slips substituting 'Ignoto'. This may, however, have been due, not to doubt, but to a desire to preserve anonymity. There are no other claimants, and I share the belief that there is a good deal of Ralegh in *The Phoenix Nest*, which may perhaps include some of the pieces *281–5*, here given as anonymous.

270. In line 10, I read 'In earth' for the 'In ay' of *The Phoenix Nest*. 'In air (ayr)' is nearer, but makes a less good antithesis.

277. This is evidently a rough draft of an afterpiece to the original poem of *Cynthia* known to Spenser in 1589, but now lost. It probably dates from Ralegh's disgrace of 1592. The dots show divisions in the MS., which is in Ralegh's hand, but there are also many cancelled lines, and several stanzas are left incomplete or faulty. The allusion in line 4 of the first stanza on page 481 is to *272*.

280. This appears by itself in many manuscripts, and is sometimes said to have been written on the night before Ralegh's execution. A version also forms the inappropriate last stanza of a longer poem ascribed to him (Latham, 70), the authenticity of which I doubt.

287. A single stanza, salvaged from a poem.

310. In stanza 8, line 7, I read with Grosart 'over-sown' for the 'over-swone' of 1623 and the 'over-swol'n' of some editors.

312. It is not certain that (*v*)–(*xii*) are Constable's. They are found only in the 1594 edition, which was 'augmented with divers Quatorzains of honourable and learned personages'. These included some by Sidney, but authors other than Constable have not been traced for the rest. Most of the sonnets of 1592 are also in *Addl. MS.* 28635, f. 89, a transcript of a MS. belonging to Sir John Harington, and here they are headed 'Mr Henry Conestables sonets to the Lady Ritche, 1589'.

NOTES

312 (*xii*). In line 6, I read 'To' for the 'And' of 1594 and the editors.

315. This is ascribed to Donne in the 1635 edition of his poems and in some MSS., but is not accepted as his by recent editors.

318. In stanza 8, line 2, I read 'Come in' for the 'Comming' of 1606.

323. I have given the text of 1619, which represents revision at more than one date. In 1596, stanza 8, lines 3, 4, ran—

'As when great Beta in her pomp we see,
When she by London on the water goes.'

358. This may be either Shakespeare's or Fletcher's.

359 (*l*). The print reads:

'Poore soule the center of my sinfull earth,
My sinfull earth these rebbell powres that thee array.'

I have accepted one of many emendations.

360. The publisher's ascription to Shakespeare is of very doubtful authority.

368, *369*. Henry Constable has long been credited with *369*, which is one of four poems printed over the initials 'H. C.' in *England's Helicon*. But H. E. Rollins pointed out that one of these had already appeared in *Piers Plainness*, and no doubt all four must stand or fall together. There is no obvious similarity to the style of Constable's sonnets. I ought, however, to add, which Rollins does not, that the attribution of *Piers Plainness* itself to Chettle is only a plausible conjecture. The book only has the initials H. C.

370. The ascription to Barnfield rests on the fact that a version in *England's Helicon* (1600) is followed by *371*, which is certainly his, with the heading 'Another of the same Sheepheards'. Both poems are among the 'Sonnets To sundry notes of Musicke' appended to *The Passionate Pilgrim* (cf. *398*).

380–2. Dekker wrote *Patient Grissill* with Chettle (cf. *368*) and William Haughton. It is a plausible conjecture that he contributed the songs.

384. Again Dekker's authorship of the song is conjectural, since *The Sun's Darling* was printed as by him and John Ford.

385. I cannot resist a note on the poets referred to in the final stanzas, some of whom, obscure to us, must have been familiar to readers of 1596. Chaucer, Spenser, Daniel, and Sidney are there. For the 'shadow' song, Chapman's *Shadow of Night* (1594) and, far from plausibly, Edward Guilpin's *Skialetheia* (1598) have been guessed at. One might add the *Fragmentum Umbrae* in Campion's *Poemata* (1595), and perhaps 'companion' may hint at his name. In the same book Campion has an epigram:

Ad Io. Davisium.

Quod nostros, Davisi, laudas recitasque libellos
 Vultu quo nemo candidiore solet:
Ad me mitte tuos, iam pridem postulo, res est
 In qua persolvi gratia vera potest.

In the next allusion 'Salue's', printed as 'Salues', must be a trisyllable, to scan, but affords no clue. If it is a misprint, which is not very likely, one might think of Greene's Samela, or Drayton's Sylvia, rather than her of *Two Gentlemen of Verona*. But Sylvia first appears in eclogues of 1606, although a bit of one of them, which does not name her, is in *England's Helicon* (1600). One would gladly identify 'the bay, the marigold's darling', who gets such dainty commendation. A sonnet by Charles Best (cf. *413*) in *Poetical Rhapsody* (1608) has been called in aid. Normally in sixteenth-century poetry (e.g. Gilles Durant and Thomas Watson) the lover is the marigold and the lady the sun. Best's marigold appears, rather obscurely, to be both the lover and the lady, whose name was Mary. The sonnet comes late, but Charles Best may be the same who was a contemporary of Davies at the Middle Temple from 1592. There is, however, no 'bay', and we can hardly link the term with the 'ocean' of *413*. In T. Cutwode's *Caltha Poetarum* (1599), of which Mr. Percy Simpson reminds me, there is a 'bee', who is the lover of the marigold. But this, too, is later than *Orchestra*, and although 'bey' is a spelling of 'bee' in 1535, the *O.E.D.* does not give 'bay'. Moreover, an early reader wrote very appropriately on his copy of the *Caltha*, now in the Bodleian:

'the foolishest poet that ever I redd.
put out ye candle I'le to bedd.'

The 'swallow' is not necessarily Drayton because of 'Ideas', which is probably here only an abstract term like 'inventions'. It is true that the form in 1596 is *Idæas*, and that normally, while the print capitalizes freely, it keeps italics for proper names. One of the few exceptions, however, is in the line

'An Art that sheweth th' *Idæa* of his mind.'

Perhaps the best guess has been that the 'swallow' is Richard Martin, a Middle Temple friend, to whom *Orchestra* was dedicated in 1596. Possibly Davies might write 'I owe my service' of a dedicatee, although there was no difference of seniority between the two as lawyers. Soon after 1596 they quarrelled violently. Later they were reconciled, but when reprinting *Orchestra* in 1622, Davies substituted for the original dedication one 'To the Prince'; and omitted the last five stanzas, with the unintelligible note, 'Here are wanting some Stanzas describing Queene Elizabeth', added five others not here reprinted, and noted the poem on the title-page as 'Not Finished'. According to Anthony Wood (*Athenae*, i. 374) Martin was an 'eminent' poet, and left 'Various Poems', which Wood had seen. None are now known, except a jesting sonnet among the *Panegyrick Verses* to T. Coryat's *Crudities* (1611). The setting of the Earl of Essex's poem (*395*) is ascribed by Dowland to a Richard Martin, who may or may not be the same. But for the obvious analogy of 'Swallow' and 'Martin', I should have taken the swallow to be Ralegh, the 'summer's nightingale' of Spenser's dedicatory sonnet. This is an inconclusive note. I can only hope that some more intrepid researcher than myself may succeed in solving its problems.

390, 391. These are acrostics on the name 'Elisabetha Regina'.

394. The ascription is due to a list of poems made by Francis Davison in *Harleian MS.* 280.

398, 399. These are printed as Shakespeare's in *The Passionate Pilgrim* (1599), but the ascriptions of that book carry little or no authority.

402. A copy, with considerable variants and notes of an air, is preserved by Lilliat (cf. *416*) in *Rawlinson Poet. MS.* 148, f. 88v. There are some alterations, which may suggest his authorship.

405. I have followed Sir Arthur Quiller-Couch's selection in *The Oxford Book of English Verse* of eleven stanzas from the twenty-six of the MS., in which the poem is said to be 'made by f: B: p: To the tune of Diana'. Another version of nineteen stanzas is in N. Ault, *Elizabethan Lyrics* from *The Song of Mary, the Mother of Christ* (1601).

412. It has been conjectured, but not plausibly, that I. S. was Joshua Sylvester.

415. This was sung at a show given by the Earl of Cumberland (cf. *394*), and might be by him.

416. Lilliat preserved a considerable collection of his poems, with some by other men, in *Rawlinson Poet. MS.* 148, the dates in which run from 1589 to 1599. He seems to have been a musician in Oxford, and is probably the same John Lilliat who is recorded, apparently in a group of singing men and choristers, in a Christ Church list of 1565 (Clark, *Register* II, 2. 13). In 1590 Magdalen paid 'Liliot' for music-books (Bloxam, ii. 278). The MS. has *416* on f. 112v, with a setting and the heading 'Uni, soli, semper J. L.', not clearly in Lilliat's own hand. The first stanza, differently set, is also on f. 113, with a reference to an earlier leaf, now lost, for the rest.

417–20. These are in a group of songs, probably for an entertainment, printed among 'Poems and Sonnets of Sundry other Noblemen and Gentlemen' after Sidney's in *Astrophel and Stella* (1591). Only the first stanza of *419* is there given. The group is subscribed 'Content', but can be reasonably assigned to Campion, in whose song-book of 1601 *417* reappears. An ascription of *420* to Vere in *England's Parnassus* (1600) is probably due to the fact that 'E. O.' was placed in 1591 at the end of a following poem (127), which is really Greville's.

425. I owe my knowledge of this MS. to N. Ault, *Elizabethan Lyrics* (ed. 2), where it is followed by two lines which seem to me to be the beginning of an independent parting speech by the maskers. A lost MS. of the mask is said, by Collier, to have borne the name of Marston, and much of the dialogue cannot be Campion's. But I agree with Bullen and Vivian that this song, which is not in all the MSS., is more like him than Marston.

426 (viii). This is ascribed to Bacon in *Royal MS.* 17. B. *l*, but

Campion, unlike other lutenists, seems only to have set his own words.

426 (x). The subject appears to be Queen Elizabeth.

427. The *Book of Airs* (1601) contains music by both Campion and Rosseter. It has been conjectured that Campion may have written the words for Rosseter's settings, as well as for his own.

433 (vi). I emend the text by inserting 'well as' in stanza 3, line 2, and reading 'seeds' for 'sees' in line 3.

434 (iv). Snatches from this are sung in *Twelfth Night*, III. iii.

434 (v). I have a feeling that this might be by Nashe.

434 (ix). P. Vivian would assign this to Campion.

435. John Daniel was a brother of Samuel, some of whose verses he sets. This, too, might conceivably be his.

440. Parts of a version of this make Desdemona's song in *Othello*, IV. iii.

441. I am indebted to the Harvard College Library for leave to reprint this. It was sent by William Crowe, Public Orator at Oxford, through Thomas Caldecott, to Bishop Percy in 1792, for a fourth volume of the *Reliques* which never appeared. A note by Crowe to Caldecott says that it was found at Mr. Powell's near Oxford, and another by Caldecott to Percy that he and Crowe found it 'amongst Milton's Papers'. Milton's father-in-law was Richard Powell of Forest Hill, Oxfordshire. The temper of the poem seems to be Elizabethan. It was printed by Leah Dennis, *The Text of the Percy-Warton Letters* (*Publications of the Modern Language Association of America* (December 1931)).

INDEX OF AUTHORS

INDEX OF AUTHORS

The references are to the numbers of the poems.

INDEX OF AUTHORS

INDEX OF FIRST LINES

INDEX OF FIRST LINES

The references are to pages.

INDEX OF FIRST LINES

INDEX OF FIRST LINES

INDEX OF FIRST LINES

INDEX OF FIRST LINES

INDEX OF FIRST LINES

INDEX OF FIRST LINES